CW00815724

CASES AND MATERIALS

LAW OF CONTRACT

CASES AND MATERIALS

LAW OF CONTRACT

Richard Stone LLB, LLM
Professor of Law, Nottingham Law School

and

Neil Lucas LLM, Dip. Ed.
Senior Lecturer in Law, Nottingham Law School

First published in Great Britain 1996 by Blackstone Press Limited,
Aldine Place, London W12 8AA.   Telephone 0181–740 2277

© Nottingham Law School, Nottingham Trent University, 1996

ISBN: 1 85431 526 9

Reprinted with amendments, 1997

British Library Cataloguing in Publication Data
A CIP catalogue record for this book is available from the British Library.

Typeset by Style Photosetting Limited, Mayfield, East Sussex
Printed by Livesey Limited, Shrewsbury, Shropshire

All rights reserved. No part of this book may be reproduced or transmitted in any form
or by any means, electronic or mechanical, including photocopying, recording, or an
information storage or retrieval system without prior permission from the publisher.

FOREWORD

All law students are aware that if they are to succeed in their studies they will need commitment and determination. In addition to this they must be provided with good teaching and good materials, and whilst this is normally the case with the teaching it is not always true of the material.

However, help is at hand. Blackstone Press, in association with Nottingham Law School, have developed a unique series of Study Manuals which it is hoped will assist hard-pressed students to achieve their ultimate goal.

The Study Texts replicate, as far as possible, the experience of being guided through a subject by an expert tutor. These Cases and Materials manuals are intended to provide you with the experience, necessary for all law students, of dealing with primary sources (e.g. cases and statutes) and academic commentaries (e.g. journal articles). The idea is for them to serve as a portable library. You should, of course, take full advantage of any opportunity to explore at first hand the vast range of materials available in a well-stocked library.

Of course, in using this volume you have an advantage over the student using a library. The materials have been extracted and are presented in the same order as they are dealt with in the Study Text. This will enable you to analyse the materials and understand the way in which they complement and expand upon the guidance given by the Study Text.

With the above approach in mind, we have presented the cases, statutes and other material without linking commentary. In addition, the extracts from the cases are often longer than can be found in many casebooks. This will encourage you to become familiar with the need to extract from a judgment the important paragraphs, and to realise that statements of general principle and statutory provisions often become more understandable when considered in context.

Not all cases referred to in the Study Text are reproduced, only those necessary for answering the Self Assessment Questions (SAQs) and working through the Activities. Some chapters include an outline answer to End of Chapter Assessment Questions in the Study Text, but these are only provided for guidance and should not be regarded as the only answer that could be given.

We hope that you will find these volumes useful, and that they will help you develop your legal skills as well as your understanding of the law.

CONTENTS

ACKNOWLEDGMENTS

Nottingham Law School and the publishers would like to thank the following for permission to reproduce copyright material:

Butterworth & Co. (Publishers) Ltd: extracts from the All England Law Reports, Commercial Cases and the Law Times Reports.

Canada Law Book Company: extracts from the Dominion Law Reports.

Eclipse Group Ltd: extracts from the Industrial Relations Law Reports.

Incorporated Council of Law Reporting for England & Wales: extracts from the Law Reports and the Weekly Law Reports.

Law Book Company of Australia: extracts from the Commonwealth Law Reports.

Lloyd's of London Press: extracts from the Lloyd's Law Reports.

Sweet & Maxwell Ltd: extracts from Miller 'Felthouse v Bindley Re-visited' (1972) 35 MLR 489; Treitel, Law of Contract, 8th ed, pp. 8, 24, 27 and 42; and the English Reports.

T & T Clark: extracts from the Times Law Reports.

TABLE OF CASES

Cases reported in full are shown in heavy type. The page at which the report is printed is shown in heavy type.

TABLE OF STATUTES

Statutes, and sections thereof, which are set out in full or in part are shown in heavy type. The page at which the statute or section is printed is shown in heavy type.

CHAPTER ONE

THE PHENOMENA OF AGREEMENT

1.1 The Phenomena of Agreement

1.1.1 THE 'OBJECTIVE' TEST

Treitel, G., *The Law of Contract*, 9th edn, p. 8

The objective test

An offer is an expression of willingness to contract on certain terms, made with the intention that it shall become binding as soon as it is accepted by the person to whom it is addressed. Under the objective test of agreement, an apparent intention to be bound may suffice, *i.e.* the alleged offeror (A) may be bound if his conduct is such as to induce a reasonable person to believe that he intends to be bound, even though in fact he has no such intention. For example, if A offers to sell a book to B for £10 and B accepts the offer, A cannot escape liability merely by showing that his actual intention was to offer the book to B for £20, or that he intended the offer to relate to a book different from that specified in the offer.

1.1.2 THE NEED FOR MATCHING 'OFFER AND ACCEPTANCE'

GIBSON v *MANCHESTER CITY COUNCIL* [1979] 1 All ER 972 (HL)

The plaintiff alleged that an exchange of correspondence had led to a contract for the sale and purchase of his council house.

LORD DIPLOCK: My Lords, this is an action for specific performance of what is claimed to be a contract for the sale of land. The only question in the appeal is of a kind with which the courts are very familiar. It is whether in the correspondence between the parties there can be found a legally enforceable contract for the sale by the Manchester Corporation to Mr Gibson of the dwelling-house of which he was the occupying tenant at the relevant time in 1971. That question is one that, in my view, can be answered by applying to the particular documents relied on by Mr Gibson as constituting the contract, well settled, indeed elementary, principles of English law. This being so, it is not the sort of case in which leave would have been likely to be granted to appeal to your Lordships' House, but for the fact that it is a test case. The two documents principally relied on by Mr Gibson were in standard forms used by the council in dealing with applications from tenants of council houses to purchase the freehold of their homes under a scheme that had been adopted by the council during a period when it was under Conservative Party control. Political control passed to the Labour Party as a result of the local government elections held in May 1971. The scheme was then abandoned. It was decided that no more council houses should be sold to any tenant with whom a legally binding contract of sale had not already been concluded. At the date of this decision there were a considerable number of tenants, running into hundreds, whose applications to purchase the houses which they occupied had reached substantially the same stage as that of Mr Gibson. The two documents in the same standard form as those on which he principally relies had passed between each one of them and the council. So their rights too are likely to depend on the result of this appeal.

My Lords, the contract of which specific performance is sought to be enforced is a contract for the sale of land. It is thus subject to the requirements as to writing laid down in s. 40 of the Law of Property Act 1925; but nothing turns on this since the only contract that is alleged is one made by letters and accompanying documents passing between the parties. The outcome of this appeal depends on their true construction.

In the Manchester County Court where the action started, the case was pleaded in the conventional way. The particulars of claim alleged an offer in writing by the council to sell the freehold interest in the house to Mr Gibson at a price of £2,180 and an acceptance in writing of that offer by Mr Gibson. The judge (his Honour Judge Bailey) followed the same conventional approach to the question that fell to be decided. He looked to see whether there was an offer of sale and an acceptance. He held that, on their true construction, the documents relied on as such in the particulars of claim did amount to an offer and an acceptance respectively and so constituted a legally enforceable contract. He ordered specific performance of an open contract for the sale to Mr Gibson of the freehold interest in the house at the price of £2,180.

The council's appeal against this judgment was dismissed by the majority of the Court of Appeal (Lord Denning MR and Ormrod LJ); Geoffrey Lane LJ dissented. Lord Denning MR rejected what I have described as the conventional approach of looking to see whether on the true construction of the documents relied on there can be discerned an offer and acceptance. One ought, he said, to 'look at the correspondence as a whole and at the conduct of the parties and see therefrom whether the parties have come to an agreement on everything that was material'. This approach, which in referring to the conduct of the parties where there is no allegation of part performance appears to me to overlook the provisions of s. 40 of the Law of Property Act 1925, led him however to the conclusion that there should be imported into the agreement to be specifically performed additional conditions, against use except as a private dwelling-house and againt advertising and a restriction not to sell or lease the property for five years. These are conditions which would not be implied by law in an open contract for the sale of land. The reason for so varying the county court judge's order was that clauses in these terms were included in the standard form of 'Agreement for Sale of a Council House' which, as appears from the earlier case of *Storer* v *Manchester City Council* [1974] 3 All ER 824, was entered into by the council and council tenants whose applications to purchase the freehold of their council house reached the stage at which contracts were exchanged. There was, however, no reference to this standard form of agreement in any of the documents said to constitute the contract relied on in the instant case, nor was there any evidence that Mr Gibson had knowledge of its terms at or before the time that the alleged contract was concluded.

Ormrod LJ, who agreed with Lord Denning MR, adopted a similar approach but he did also deal briefly with the construction of the document relied on by Mr Gibson as an unconditional offer of sale by the council. On this he came to the same conclusion as the county court judge.

Geoffrey Lane LJ in a dissenting judgment, which for my part I find convincing, adopted the conventional approach. He found that on the true construction of the documents relied on as constituting the contract, there never was an offer by the council acceptance of which by Mr Gibson was capable in law of constituting a legally enforceable contract. It was but a step in the negotiations for a contract which, owing to the change in the political complexion of the council, never reached fruition.

My Lords, there may be certain types of contract, though I think they are exceptional, which do not fit easily into the normal analysis of a contract as being constituted by offer and acceptance; but a contract alleged to have been made by an exchange of correspondence between the parties in which the successive communications other than the first are in reply to one another is not one of these. I can see no reason in the instant case for departing from the conventional approach of looking at the handful of documents relied on as constituting the contract sued on and seeing whether on their true construction there is to be found in them a contractual offer by the council to sell the house to Mr Gibson and an acceptance of that offer by Mr Gibson. I venture to think that it was by departing from this conventional approach that the majority of the Court of Appeal was led into error.

The genesis of the relevant negotiations in the instant case is a form filled in by Mr Gibson on 28th November 1970 enquiring what would be the price of buying his council house at 174 Charlestown Road, Blackley, and expressing his interest in obtaining a mortgage from the council. The form was a detachable part of a brochure which had been circulated by the council to tenants who had previously expressed an interest in buying their houses. It contained details of a new scheme for selling council houses that had been recently adopted by the council. The scheme provided for a sale at market value less a discount dependent on the length of time the puchaser had been a council tenant. This, in the case of Mr Gibson, would have amounted to 20%. The scheme also provided for the provision by the council of advances on mortgage which might amount to as much as the whole of the purchase price.

As a result of that enquiry Mr Gibson's house was inspected by the council's valuer and on 10th February 1971 the letter which is relied on by Mr Gibson as the offer by the council to sell the house to him was sent from the city treasurer's department. It was in the following terms:

Dear Sir,

'Purchase of Council House
'Your Reference Number 82463 03

I refer to your request for details of the cost of buying your Council house. *The Corporation may be prepared to sell the house to you at the purchase price of £2,725 less 20% = £2,180 (freehold).*

Maximum mortgage the Corporation may grant:	£2,177 repayable over 20 years.
Annual fire insurance premium:	£2·45
Monthly Repayment charge calculated by:—	
(i) flat rate repayment method:	£19.02

If you wish to pay off some of the purchase price at the start and therefore require a mortgage for less than the amount quoted above, the monthly instalment will change; in these circumstances, I will supply new figures on request. The above repayment figures apply so long as the interest rate charged on home loans is 8½%. The interest rate will be subject to variation by the Corporation after giving not less than three months' written notice, and if it changes, there will be an adjustment to the monthly instalment payable. This letter should not be regarded as firm offer of a mortgage.

If you would like to make formal application to buy your Council house, please complete the enclosed application form and return it to me as soon as possible.

Yours faithfully,
(Sgd) H. R. Page
City Treasurer

Mr Robert Gibson.

My Lords, the words I have italicised seem to me, as they seemed to Geoffrey Lane LJ, to make it quite impossible to construe this letter as a contractual offer capable of being converted into a legally enforceable open contract for the sale of land by Mr Gibson's written acceptance of it. The words 'may be prepared to sell' are fatal to this; so is the invitation, not, be it noted, to accept the offer, but 'to make formal application to buy' on the enclosed application form. It is, to quote Geoffrey Lane LJ, a letter setting out the financial terms on which it may be the council would be prepared to consider a sale and purchase in due course.

Both Ormrod LJ and the county court judge, in reaching the conclusion that this letter was a firm offer to sell the freehold interest in the house for £2,180, attached importance to the fact that the second paragraph, dealing with the financial details of the mortgage of which Mr Gibson had asked for particulars, stated expressly, 'This letter should not be regarded as a firm offer of a mortgage'. The necessary implication from this, it is suggested, is that the first paragraph of the letter *is* to be regarded as a firm offer to sell despite the fact that this is plainly inconsistent with the express language of that paragraph. My Lords, with great respect, this surely must be fallacious. If the final sentence had been omitted the wording of the second paragraph, unlike that of the first, with its use of the indicative mood in such expressions as 'the interest rate *will* change', might have been understood by council tenants to whom it was addressed as indicating a firm offer of a mortgage of the amount and on the terms for repayment stated if the council were prepared to sell the house at the stated price. But, whether or not this be the explanation of the presence of the last sentence in the second paragraph, it cannot possibly affect the plain meaning of the words used in the first paragraph.

Mr Gibson did fill in the application form enclosed with this letter. It was in three sections: section A headed 'Application to buy a council house', section B 'Application for a loan to buy a council house', and section C 'Certificate to be completed by all applicants'. He left blank the space for the purchase price in section A and sent the form to the council on 5th March 1971 with a covering letter in which he requested the council either to undertake at their own expense to carry out repairs to the tarmac path forming part of the premises or to make a deduction from the purchase price to cover the cost of repairs. The letter also intimated that Mr Gibson would like to make a down payment of £500 towards the purchase price instead of borrowing the whole amount on mortgage. In reply to the request made in this letter the council, by letter of 12th March 1971, said that the condition of the property had been taken into consideration in fixing the purchase price and that repairs to the tarmac by the council could not be authorised at this stage. This letter was acknowledged by Mr Gibson by his letter to the council of 18th March 1971 in which he asked the council to 'carry on with the purchase as per my application already in your possession'.

My Lords, the application form and letter of 18th March 1971 were relied on by Mr Gibson as an unconditional acceptance of the council's offer to sell the house; but this cannot be so unless there was a contractual offer by the council available for acceptance, and, for the reason already given I am of opinion that there was none. It is unnecessary to consider whether the application form and Mr Gibson's letters of 5th and 18th March 1971 are capable of amounting to a contractual offer by him to purchase the freehold interest in the house at a price of £2,180 on the terms of an open contract, for there is no suggestion that, even if it were, it was ever accepted by the council. Nor would it ever have been even if there had been no change in the political control of the council, as the policy of the council before the change required the incorporation in all agreements for sale of council houses to tenants of the conditions referred by Lord Denning MR in his judgment and other conditions inconsistent with an open contract.

I therefore feel compelled to allow the appeal. One can sympathise with Mr Gibson's disappointment on finding that his expectations that he would be able to buy his council house at 20% below its market value in the autumn of 1970 cannot be realised. Whether one thinks this makes it a hard case perhaps depends on the political views that one holds about council housing policy. But hard cases offer a strong temptation to let them have their proverbial consequences. It is a temptation that the judicial mind must be vigilant to resist.

Lords Edmund-Davies, Russell, Fraser and Keith concurred.

1.2 Offer

1.2.1 AN OFFER MAY BE MADE TO A SPECIFIC PERSON, A GROUP OF PERSONS OR THE WORLD AT LARGE

CARLILL v CARBOLIC SMOKE BALL CO. [1893] 1 QB 256 (CA)

This case concerned an advertisement for a patent medicine.

LINDLEY LJ: The first observation I will make is that we are not dealing with any inference of fact. We are dealing with an express promise to pay 100*l*. in certain events. Read the advertisement how you will, and twist it about as you will, here is a distinct promise expressed in language which is perfectly unmistakable – '100*l*. reward will be paid by the Carbolic Smoke Ball Company to any person who contracts the influenza after having used the ball three times daily for two weeks according to the printed directions supplied with each ball'.

We must first consider whether this was intended to be a promise at all, or whether it was a mere puff which meant nothing. Was it a mere puff? My answer to that question is No, and I base my answer upon this passage: '1000*l*. is deposited with the Alliance Bank, shewing our sincerity in the matter'. Now, for what was that money deposited or that statement made except to negative the suggestion that this was a mere puff and meant nothing at all? The deposit is called in aid by the advertiser as proof of his sincerity in the matter – that is, the sincerity of his promise to pay this 100*l*. in the event which he has specified. I say this for the purpose of giving point to the observation that we are not inferring a promise; there is the promise, as plain as words can make it.

Then it is contended that it is not binding. In the first place, it is said that it is not made with anybody in particular. Now that point is common to the words of this advertisement and to the words of all other advertisements offering rewards. They are offers to anybody who performs the conditions named in the advertisement, and anybody who does perform the condition accepts the offer. In point of law this advertisement is an offer to pay 100*l*. to anybody who will perform these conditions, and the performance of the conditions is the acceptance of the offer. That rests upon a string of authorities, the earliest of which is *Williams* v *Carwardine* (1833) 4 B & Ad 621, which has been followed by many other decisions upon advertisements offering rewards.

But then it is said, 'Supposing that the performance of the conditions is an acceptance of the offer, that acceptance ought to have been notified'. Unquestionably, as a general proposition, when an offer is made, it is necessary in order to make a binding contract, not only that it should be accepted, but that the acceptance should be notified. But is that so in cases of this kind? I apprehend that they are an exception to that rule, or, if not an exception, they are open to the observation that the notification of the acceptance need not precede the performance. This offer is a continuing offer. It was never revoked, and if notice of acceptance is required – which I doubt very much, for I rather think the true view is that which was expresed and explained by Lord Blackburn in the case of *Brogden* v *Metropolitan Ry. Co.* (1877) 2 App Cas 666 – if notice of acceptance is required, the person who makes the offer gets the notice of acceptance contemporaneously with his notice of the performance of the condition. If he gets notice of the acceptance before his offer is revoked, that in principle is all you want. I, however, think that the true view, in a case of this kind, is that the person who makes the offer shews by his language and from the nature of the transaction that he does not expect and does not require notice of the acceptance apart from notice of the performance.

We, therefore, find here all the elements which are necessary to form a binding contract enforceable in point of law . . .

1.2.2 AN OFFER MUST BE DISTINGUISHED FROM AN INVITATION TO TREAT

1.2.2.1 Shop and self-service situations

PHARMACEUTICAL SOCIETY OF GREAT BRITAIN v *BOOTS CASH CHEMISTS (SOUTHERN) LTD* [1953] 1 QB 401 (CA)

When is a contract made in a self-service shop?

SOMERVELL LJ: This is an appeal from a decision of the Lord Chief Justice on an agreed statement of facts, raising a question under section 18(1)(a)(iii) of the Pharmacy and Poisons Act 1933. The plaintiffs are the Pharmaceutical Society, incorporated by Royal charter. One of their duties is to take all reasonable steps to enforce the provisions of the Act. The provision in question is contained in section 18. [His Lordship read the section and stated the facts, and continued:] It is not disputed that in a chemist's shop where this self-service system does not prevail a customer may go in and ask a young woman assistant, who will not herself be a registered pharmacist, for one of these articles on the list, and the transaction may be completed and the article paid for, although the registered pharmacist, who will no doubt be on the premises, will not know anything himself of the transaction, unless the assistant serving the customer, or the customer, requires to put a question to him. It is right that I should emphasize, as did the Lord Chief Justice, that these are not dangerous drugs. They are substances which contain very small proportions of poison, and I imagine that many of them are the type of drug which has a warning as to what doses are to be taken. They are drugs which can be obtained, under the law, without a doctor's prescription.

The point taken by the plaintiffs is this: it is said that the purchase is complete if and when a customer going round the shelves takes an article and puts it in the receptacle which he or she is carrying, and that therefore, if that is right, when the customer comes to the pay desk, having completed the tour of the premises, the registered pharmacist, if so minded, has no power to say: 'This drug ought not to be sold to this customer'. Whether and in what circumstances he would have that power we need not inquire, but one can, of course, see that there is a difference if supervision can only be exercised at a time when the contract is completed.

I agree with the Lord Chief Justice in everything that he said, but I will put the matter shortly in my own words. Whether the view contended for by the plaintiffs is a right view depends on what are the legal implications of this layout – the invitation to the customer. Is a contract to be regarded as being completed when the article is put into the receptacle, or is this to be regarded as a more organized way of doing what is done already in many types of shops – and a bookseller is perhaps the best example – namely, enabling customers to have free access to what is in the shop, to look at the different articles, and then, ultimately, having got the ones which they wish to buy, to come up to the assistant saying 'I want this'? The assistant in 999 times out of 1,000 says 'That is all right', and the money passes and the transaction is completed. I agree with what the Lord Chief Justice has said, and with the reasons which he has given for his conclusion, that in the case of an ordinary shop, although goods are displayed and it is intended that customers should go and choose what they want, the contract is not completed until the customer having indicated the articles which he needs, the shop-keeper, or someone on his behalf, accepts that offer. Then the contract is completed. I can see no reason at all, that being clearly the normal position, for drawing any different implication as a result of this layout.

The Lord Chief Justice, I think, expressed one of the most formidable difficulties in the way of the plaintiffs' contention when he pointed out that, if the plaintiffs are right, once an article has been placed in the receptacle the customer himself is bound and would have no right, without paying for the first article, to substitute an article which he saw later of a similar kind and which he perhaps preferred. I can see no reason for implying from this self-service arrangement any implication other than that which the Lord Chief Justice found in it, namely, that it is a convenient method of enabling customers to see what there is and choose, and possibly put back and substitute, articles which they wish to have, and then to go up to the cashier and offer to buy what they have so far chosen. On that conclusion the case fails, because it is admitted that there was supervision in the sense required by the Act and at the appropriate moment of time. For these reasons, in my opinion, the appeal should be dismissed.

Birkett and Romer LJJ concurred.

1.2.2.2 Advertisements and circulars

PARTRIDGE v CRITTENDEN [1968] 2 All ER 421 (QB)

An advertisement for wild birds appeared in a newspaper. Was this an 'offer'?

ASHWORTH J: . . . the real point of substance in this case arose from the words 'offer for sale', and it is to be noted in s. 6 of the Act of 1954 that the operative words are 'any person sells, offers for sale or has in his possession for sale'. For some reason which counsel for the respondent has not been able to explain, those responsible for the prosecution in this case chose, out of the trio of possible offences, the one which could not succeed. There was a sale here, in my view, because Mr Thomspon sent his cheque and the bird was sent in reply; and a completed sale. On the evidence there was also a plain case of the appellant having in possession for sale this particular bird; but they chose to prosecute him for offering for sale, and they relied on the advertisement.

A similar point arose before this court in 1960 dealing, it is true, with a different statute but with the same words, that is *Fisher* v *Bell* [1960] 3 All ER 731. The relevant words of the Act in that case were: 'Any person who offers for sale any knife.' Lord Parker CJ in giving judgment said this:

> The sole question is whether the exhibition of that knife in the window with the ticket constituted an offer for sale within the statute. I think that most lay people would be inclined to the view (as, indeed, I was myself when I first read these papers), that if a knife were displayed in a window like that with a price attached to it, it was nonsense to say that that was not offering it for sale. The knife is there inviting people to buy it, and in ordinary language it is for sale; but any statute must be looked at in the light of the general law of the country . . .

The words are the same here 'offer for sale', and in my judgment the law of the country is equally plain as it was in regard to articles in a shop window, namely that the insertion of an advertisement in the form adopted here under the title 'Classified Advertisements' is simply an invitation to treat. That is really sufficient to dispose of this case. I should perhaps in passing observe that the editors of the publication Criminal Law Review had an article dealing with *Fisher* v *Bell* in which a way round that decision was at least contemplated, suggesting that, while there might be one meaning of the phrase 'offer for sale' in the law of contract, a criminal court might take a stricter view, particularly having in mind the purpose of the Act, which in *Fisher* v *Bell* was directed to the stocking of flick knives, and in this case is directed to the selling of wild birds. For my part, however, that is met entirely by the quotation which appears in Lord Parker CJ's judgment in *Fisher* v *Bell*, that: 'It appears to me to be a naked usurpation of the legislative function under the thin disguise of interpretation . . .'. For my part I would allow this appeal and quash the conviction.

LORD PARKER CJ: I agree and with less reluctance than in *Fisher* v *Bell*, to which Ashworth J has referred, and the case of *Mella* v *Monahan* [1961] Crim LR 175. I say 'with less reluctance' because I think that when one is dealing with advertisements and circulars, unless they indeed come from manufacturers, there is business sense in their being construed as invitations to treat and not offers for sale. In a very different context Lord Herschell in *Grainger & Son* v *Gough (Surveyor of Taxes)* [1896] AC 325, said this in dealing with a price-list:

> The transmission of such a price-list does not amount to an offer to supply an unlimited quantity of the wine described at the price named, so that as soon as an order is given there is a binding contract to suppy that quantity. If it were so, the merchant might find himself involved in any number of contractual obligations to supply wine of a particular description which he would be quite unable to carry out, his stock of wine of that description being necessarily limited.

It seems to me accordingly that not only is that the law, but common sense supports it.

1.2.2.3 Negotiations for the sale of land

See *Gibson* v *Manchester City Council*, above, 1.1.

1.2.2.4 Tenders

GREAT NORTHERN RAILWAY CO. v *WITHAM* (1873) LR 9 CP 16
(Court of Common Pleas)

BRETT J: The company advertised for tenders for the supply of stores, such as they might think fit to order, for one year. The defendant made a tender offering to supply them for

that period at certain fixed prices; and the company accepted his tender. If there were
no other objection, the contract between the parties would be found in the tender and
the letter accepting it. This action is brought for the defendant's refusal to deliver the
goods ordered by the company; and the objection to the plaintiffs' right to recover this,
that the contract is unilateral. I do not, however, understand what objection that is to a
contract. Many contracts are obnoxious to the same complaint. If I say to another, 'If you
will go to York, I will give you 100*l*.,' that is in a certain sense a unilateral contract. He
has not promised to go to York. But, if he goes, it cannot be doubted that he will be
entitled to receive the 100*l*. His going to York at my request is a sufficient consideration
for my promise. So, if one says to another, 'If you will give me an order for iron, or other
goods, I will supply it at a given price,' if the order is given, there is a complete contract
which the seller is bound to perform. There is in such a case ample consideration for the
promise. So, here, the company having given the defendant an order at his request, his
acceptance of the order would bind them. If any authority could have been found to
sustain Mr Seymour's contention, I should have considered that a rule ought to be
granted. But none has been cited. *Burton* v *Great Northern Railway Co.* (1854) 9 Ex 507 is
not at all to the purpose. This is a matter of every day's practice; and I think it would
be wrong to countenance the notion that a man who tenders for the supply of goods in
this way is not bound to deliver them when an order is given. I agree that this judgment
does not decide the question whether the defendant might have absolved himself from
the further performance of the contract by giving notice.

Keating and Grove JJ concurred.

1.2.2.5 Auction sales

HARRIS v *NICKERSON* (1873) LR 8 QB 286 (Court of Queen's Bench)

Did the advertisement of an auction sale constitute an 'offer'?

BLACKBURN J: I am of the opinion that the judge was wrong. The facts were that the
defendant advertised bona fide that certain things would be sold by auction on the days
named, and on the third day a certain class of things, viz., office furniture, without any
previous notice of their withdrawal, were not put up. The plaintiff says, inasmuch as I
confided in the defendant's advertisement, and came down to the auction to buy the
furniture (which it is found as a fact he was commissioned to buy) and have had no
opportunity of buying, I am entitled to recover damages from the defendant, on the
ground that the advertisement amounted to a contract by the defendant with anybody
that should act upon it, that all the things advertised would be actually put up for sale,
and that he would have an opportunity of bidding for them and buying. This is certainly
a startling proposition, and would be excessively inconvenient if carried out. It amounts
to saying that anyone who advertises a sale by publishing an advertisement becomes
responsible to everybody who attends the sale for his cab hire or travelling expenses. As
to the cases cited: in the case of *Warlow* v *Harrison* (1859) 29 LJ QB 14, the opinion of the
majority of the judges in the Exchequer Chamber appears to have been that an action
would lie for not knocking down the lot to the highest bona fide bidder when the sale
was advertised as without reserve; in such a case it may be that there is a contract to sell
to the highest bidder, and that if the owner bids there is a breach of the contract; there
is very plausible ground at all events for saying, as the minority of the Court thought,
that the auctioneer warrants that he has power to sell without reserve. In the present
case, unless every declaration of intention to do a thing creates a binding contract with
those who act upon it, and in all cases after advertising a sale the auctioneer must give
notice of any articles that are withdrawn, or be liable to an action, we cannot hold the
defendant liable.

QUAIN J: I am of the same opinion. To uphold the judge's decision it is necessary to go
to the extent of saying that when an auctioneer issues an advertisement of the sale of
goods, if he withdraws any part of them without notice, the persons attending may all
maintain actions against him. In the present case, it is to be observed that the plaintiff

bought some other lots; but it is said he had a commission to buy the furniture, either the whole or in part, and that therefore he has a right of action against the defendant. Such a proposition seems to be destitute of all authority; and it would be introducing an extremely inconvenient rule of law to say that an auctioneer is bound to give notice of the withdrawal or to be held liable to everybody attending the sale. The case is certainly of the first impression. When a sale is advertised as without reserve, and a lot is put up and bid for, there is ground for saying, as was said in *Warlow v Harrison*, that a contract is entered into between the auctioneer and the highest bona fide bidder; but that has no application to the present case; here the lots were never put up and no offer was made by the plaintiff nor promise made by the defendant, except by his advertisement that certain goods would be sold. It is impossible to say that this is a contract with everybody attending the sale, and that the auctioneer is to be liable for their expenses if any single article is withdrawn. *Spencer v Harding* (1870) LR 5 CP 561, which was cited by the plaintiff's counsel, as far as it goes, is a direct authority against his proposition.

ARCHIBALD J: I am of the same opinion. This is an attempt on the part of the plaintiff to make a mere declaration of intention a binding contract. He has utterly failed to show authority or reason for his proposition. If a false and fraudulent representation had been made out, it would have been quite another matter. But to say that a mere advertisement that certain articles will be sold by auction amounts to a contract to indemnify all who attend, if the sale of any part of the articles does not take place, is a proposition without authority or ground for supporting it.

1.3   Termination of Offer

1.3.1   REVOCATION

BYRNE & CO. v *VAN TIENHOVEN & CO.* (1880) 5 CPD 344 (CP)

LINDLEY J: There is no doubt that an offer can be withdrawn before it is accepted, and it is immaterial whether the offer is expressed to be open for acceptance for a given time or not: *Routledge v Grant* (1828) 4 Bing 653. For the decision of the present case, however, it is necessary to consider two other questions, viz.: 1. Whether a withdrawal of an offer has any effect until it is communicated to the person to whom the offer has been sent? Whether posting a letter of withdrawal is a communication to the person to whom the letter is sent?

It is curious that neither of these questions appears to have actually been decided in this country. As regards the first question, I am aware that Pothier and some other writers of celebrity are of opinion that there can be no contract if an offer is withdrawn before it is accepted, although the withdrawal is not communicated to the person to whom the offer has been made. The reason for this opinion is that there is not in fact any such consent by both parties as is essential to constitute a contact between them. Against this view, however, it has been urged that a state of mind not notified cannot be regarded in dealings between man and man; and that an uncommunicated revocation is for all practical purposes and in point of law no revocation at all. This is the view taken in the United States: see *Tayloe v Merchants Fire Insurance Co.* 9 Howard 5 Ct Rep 390 cited in Benjamin on Sales, pp. 56–58, and it is adopted by Mr Benjamin. The same view is taken by Mr Pollock in his excellent work on Principles of Contract, ed. ii., p. 10, and by Mr Leake in his Digest of the Law of Contracts, p. 43. This view, moreover, appears to me much more in accordance with the general principles of English law than the view maintained by Pothier. I pass, therefore, to the next question, viz., whether posting the letter of revocation was a sufficient communication of it to the plaintiff. The offer was posted on the 1st of October, the withdrawal was posted on the 8th, and did not reach the plaintiff until after he had posted his letter of the 11th, accepting the offer. It may be taken as now settled that where an offer is made and accepted by letters sent through the post, the contract is completed the moment the letter accepting the offer is posted:

Harris' Case (1872) LR 7 Ch App 587; *Dunlop* v *Higgins* (1848) 1 HLC 381, even although it never reaches its destination. When, however, these authorities are looked at, it will be seen that they are based upon the principle that the writer of the offer has expressly or impliedly assented to treat an answer to him by a letter duly posted as a sufficient acceptance and notification to himself, or, in other words, he has made the post office his agent to receive the acceptance and notification of it. But this principle appears to me to be inapplicable to the case of the withdrawal of an offer. In this particular case I can find no evidence of any authority in fact given by the plaintiffs to the defendants to notify a withdrawal of their offer by merely posting a letter; and there is no legal principle or decision which compels me to hold, contrary to the fact, that the letter of the 8th of October is to be treated as communicated to the plaintiff on that day or on any day before the 20th, when the letter reached them. But before that letter had reached the plaintiffs they had accepted the offer, both by telegram and by post; and they had themselves resold the tin plates at a profit.

In my opinion the withdrawal by the defendants on the 8th of October of their offer of the 1st was inoperative; and a complete contract binding on both parties was entered into on the 11th of October, when the plaintiffs accepted the offer of the 1st, which they had no reason to suppose had been withdrawn. Before leaving this part of the case it may be as well to point out the extreme injustice and inconvenience which any other conclusion would produce. If the defendants' contention were to prevail no person who had received an offer by post and had accepted it would know his position until he had waited such a time as to be quite sure that a letter withdrawing the offer had not been posted before his acceptance of it. It appears to me that both legal principles, and practical convenience require that a person who has accepted an offer not known to him to have been revoked, shall be in a position safely to act upon the footing that the offer and acceptance constitute a contract binding on both parties.

DICKINSON v DODDS (1876) 2 Ch D 463 (CA)

Notice of the offeror's withdrawal of his offer came via a third party.

MELLISH LJ: The first question is, whether this document of the 10th of June, 1874, which was signed by Dodds, was an agreement to sell, or only an offer to sell, the property therein mentioned to Dickinson; and I am clearly of opinion that it was only an offer, although it is in the first part of it, independently of the postscript, worded as an agreement. I apprehend that, until acceptance, so that both parties are bound, even though an instrument is so worded as to express that both parties agree, it is in point of law only an offer, and, until both parties are bound, neither party is bound. It is not necessary that both parties should be bound within the Statute of Frauds, for, if one party makes an offer in writing, and the other accepts it verbally, that will be sufficient to bind the person who has signed the written document. But, if there be no agreement, either verbally or in writing, then, until acceptance, it is in point of law an offer only, although worded as if it were an agreement. But it is hardly necessary to resort to that doctrine in the present case, because the postscript calls it an offer, and says, 'This offer to be left over until February, 9 o'clock a.m.'. Well, then, this being only an offer, the law says – and it is a perfectly clear rule of law – that, although it is said that the offer is to be left open until Friday morning at 9 o'clock, that did not bind Dodds. He was not in point of law bound to hold the offer over until 9 o'clock on Friday morning. He was not so bound either in law or in equity. Well, that being so, when on the next day he made an agreement with Allan to sell the property to him, I am not aware of any ground on which it can be said that that contract with Allan was not as good and binding a contract as ever was made. Assuming Allan to have known (there is some dispute about it, and Allan does not admit that he knew of it, but I will assume that he did) that Dodds had made the offer to Dickinson, and had given him till Friday morning at 9 o'clock to accept it, still in point of law that could not prevent Allan from making a more favourable offer than Dickinson, and entering at once into a binding agreement with Dodds.

Then Dickinson is informed by Berry that the property has been sold by Dodds to Allan. Berry does not tell us from whom he heard it, but he says that he did hear it, that he knew it, and that he informed Dickinson of it. Now, stopping there, the question which arises is this – If an offer has been made for the sale of property, and before that offer is accepted, the person who has made the offer enters into a binding agreement to sell the property to somebody else, and the person to whom the offer was first made receives notice in some way that the property has been sold to another person, can he after that make a binding contract by the acceptance of the offer? I am of opinion that he cannot. The law may be right or wrong in saying that a person who has given to another a certain time within which to accept an offer is not bound by his promise to give that time; but, if he is not bound by that promise, and may still sell the property to someone else, and if it be the law that, in order to make a contract, the two minds must be in agreement at some one time, that is, at the time of the acceptance, how is it possible that when the person to whom the offer has been made knows that the person who has made the offer has sold the property to someone else, and that, in fact, he has not remained in the same mind to sell it to him, he can be at liberty to accept the offer and thereby make a binding contract? It seems to me that would be simply absurd. If a man makes an offer to sell a particular horse in his stable, and says, 'I will give you until the day after tomorrow to accept the offer', and the next day goes and sells the horse to somebody else, and receives the purchase-money from him, can the person to whom the offer was originally made then come and say, 'I accept', so as to make a binding contract, and so as to be entitled to recover damages for the non-delivery of the horse? If the rule of law is that a mere offer to sell property, which can be withdrawn at any time, and which is made dependent on the acceptance of the person to whom it is made, is a mere *nudum pactum*, how is it possible that the person to whom the offer has been made can by acceptance make a binding contract after he knows that the person who has made the offer has sold the property to some one else? It is admitted law that, if a man who makes an offer dies, the offer cannot be accepted after he is dead, and parting with the property has very much the same effect as the death of the owner, for it makes the performance of the offer impossible. I am clearly of opinion that, just as when a man who has made an offer dies before it is accepted it is impossible that it can then be accepted, so when once the person to whom the offer was made knows that the property has been sold to someone else, it is too late for him to accept the offer, and on that ground I am clearly of opinion that there was no binding contract for the sale of this property by Dodds to Dickinson, and even if there had been, it seems to me that the sale of the property to Allan was first in point of time. However, it is not necessary to consider, if there had been two binding contracts, which of them would be entitled to priority in equity, because there is no binding contract between Dodds and Dickinson.

James LJ and Bagallay JA concurred.

Treitel, G., *Law of Contract*, 9th edn., p. 40

. . . The rule that communication of withdrawal need not come from the offeror can be a regrettable source of uncertainty. It puts on the offeree the possibly difficult task of deciding whether his source of information is reliable, and it may also make it hard for him to tell exactly when the offer was withdrawn. In *Dickinson v Dodds*, for example, it is not clear whether this occurred when the plaintiff realised that the defendant had (a) sold the land to the third party, or (b) begun to negotiate with the third party, or (c) simply decided not to sell to the plaintiff. Certainty would be promoted if the rule were that the withdrawal must be communicated by the offeror, as well as to the offeree.

1.3.2 REVOCATION IN UNILATERAL CONTRACTS

ERRINGTON v *ERRINGTON & WOODS* [1952] 1 All ER 149 (CA)

DENNING LJ: The facts are reasonably clear. In 1936 the father bought the house for his son and daughter-in-law to live in. The father put down £250 in cash and borrowed £500 from a building society on the security of the house, repayable with interest by instalments of 15s. a week. He took the house in his own name and made himself responsible for the instalments. The father told the daughter-in-law that the £250 was a present for them, but he left them to pay the building society instalments of 15s. a week themselves. He handed the building society book to the daughter-in-law and said to her: 'Don't part with this book. The house will be your property when the mortgage is paid.' He said that when he retired he would transfer it into their names. She has, in fact, paid the building society instalments regularly from that day to this with the result that much of the mortgage has been repaid, but there is a good deal yet to be paid. The rates on the house came to 10s. a week. The couple found that they could not pay those as well as the building society instalments so the father said he would pay them and he did so.

It is to be noted that the couple never bound themselves to pay the instalments to the building society, and I see no reason why any such obligation should be implied. It is clear law that the court is not to imply a term unless it is necessary, and I do not see that it is necessary here. Ample content is given to the whole arrangement by holding that the father promised that the house should belong to the couple as soon as they had paid off the mortgage. The parties did not discuss what was to happen if the couple failed to pay the instalments to the building society, but I should have thought it clear that, if they did fail to pay the instalments, the father would not be bound to transfer the house to them. The father's promise was a unilateral contract – a promise of the house in return for their act of paying the instalments. It could not be revoked by him once the couple entered on performance of the act, but it would cease to bind him if they left it incomplete and unperformed, which they have not done. If that was the position during the father's lifetime, so it must be after his death. If the daugter-in-law continues to pay all the building society instalments, the couple will be entitled to have the property transferred to them as soon as the mortgage is paid off, but if she does not do so, then the building society will claim the instalments from the father's estate and the estate will have to pay them. I cannot think that in those circumstances the estate would be bound to transfer the house to them, any more than the father himself would have been.

Somervell and Hodson LJJ concurred.

DAULIA LTD v FOUR MILLBANK NOMINEES [1978] 2 All ER 557 (CA)

GOFF LJ: . . . I therefore turn to the first question. Was there a concluded unilateral contract by the defendants to enter into a contract for sale on the agreed terms?

The concept of a unilateral or 'if' contract is somewhat anomalous, because it is clear that, at all events until the offeree starts to perform the condition, there is no contract at all, but merely an offer which the offeror is free to revoke. Doubts have been expressed whether the offeror becomes bound so soon as the offeree starts to perform or satisfy the condition, or only when he has fully done so. In my judgment, however, we are not concerned in this case with any such problem, because in my view the plaintiffs had fully performed or satisfied the condition when they presented themselves at the time and place appointed with a banker's draft for the deposit and their part of the written contract for sale duly engrossed and signed, and the retendered [sic] the same, which I understand to mean proferred it for exchange. Actual exchange, which never took place, would not in my view have been part of the satisfaction of the condition but something additional which was inherently necessary to be done by the plaintiffs to enable, not to bind, the defendants to perform the unilateral contract.

Accordingly in my judgment, the answer to the first question must be in the affirmative.

Even if my reasoning so far be wrong the conclusion in my view is still the same for the following reasons. Whilst I think the true view of a unilateral contract must in general be that the offeror is entitled to require full performance of the condition which he has imposed and short of that he is not bound, that must be subject to one important qualification, which stems from the fact that there must be an implied obligation on the part of the offeror not to prevent the condition becoming satisfied, which obligation it seems to me must arise as soon as the offeree starts to perform. Until then the offeror can revoke the whole thing, but once the offeree has embarked on performance it is too late for the offeror to revoke his offer.

1.4 Acceptance

1.4.1 THE FACT OF ACCEPTANCE

HYDE v *WRENCH* (1840) 3 Beav 334 (Rolls Court)

LORD LANGDALE MR: Under the circumstances stated in this bill, I think there exists no valid binding contract between the parties for the purchase of the property. The defendant offered to sell it for £1,000, and if that had been at once unconditionally accepted, there would undoubtedly have been a perfect binding contract; instead of that, the plaintiff made an offer of his own, to purchase the property for £950, and he thereby rejected the offer previously made by the defendant. I think that it was not afterwards competent for him to revive the proposal of the defendant, by tendering an acceptance of it; and that, therefore, there exists no obligation of any sort between the parties; the demurrer must be allowed.

STEVENSON v *McLEAN* (1880) 5 QBD 346 (QB)

Did a telegram inquiring about delivery constitute a counter-offer?

LUSH J: This is an action for non-delivery of a quantity of iron which it was alleged the defendant contracted to sell to the plaintiffs at 40s. per ton, nett cash. The trial took place before me at the last assizes at Leeds, when a verdict was given for the plaintiffs for 1900l., subject to further consideration on the question whether, under the circumstances, the correspondence between the parties amounted to a contract, and subject also, if the verdict should stand, to a reference, if required by the defendant, to ascertain the amount of damages. The question of law was argued before me on the 7th of May last.

The plaintiffs are makers of iron and iron merchants at Middlesborough. The defendant being possessed of warrants for iron, which he had originally bought of the plaintiffs, wrote on the 24th of September to the plaintiffs from London, where he carries on his business: 'I see that No. 3 has been sold for immediate delivery at 39s., which means a higher price for warrants. Could you get me an offer for the whole or part of my warrants? I have 3800 tons, and the brands you know.'

On the 26th one of the plaintiffs wrote from Liverpool: 'Your letter has followed me here. The pig iron trade is at present very excited, and it is difficult to decide whether prices will be maintained or fall as suddenly as they have advanced. Sales are being made freely for forward delivery chiefly, but not in warrants. It may, however, be found advisable to sell the warrants as maker's iron. I would recommend you to fix your price, and if you will write me your limit to Middlesborough, I shall probably be able to wire you something definite on Monday.' This letter was crossed by a letter written on the same day by the clerk of one Fossick, the defendant's broker in London, and which was in these terms:

> Referring to R. A. McLean's letter to you re warrants, I have seen him again to-day, and he considers 39s. too low for same. At 40s. he says he would consider an offer. However, I shall be obliged by your kindly wiring me, if possible, your best offer for all or part of the warrants he has to dispose of.

On the 27th (Saturday) the plaintiffs sent to Fossick the following telegram:

> Cannot make an offer today; warrants rather easier. Several sellers think might get 39s. 6d. if you could wire firm offer subject reply Tuesday noon.

In answer to this Fossick wrote on the same day: 'Your telegram duly to hand re warrants. I have seen Mr McLean, but he is not inclined to make a firm offer. I do not think he is likely to sell at 39s. 6d., but will probably prefer to wait. Please let me know immediately you get any likely offer.'

On the same day the defendant, who had then received the Liverpool letter of the 26th, wrote himself to the plaintiffs as follows:

Mr Fossick's clerk shewed me a telegram from him yesterday mentioning 39s. for No. 3 as present price, 40s. for forward delivery. I instructed the clerk to wire you that I would now sell for 40s., nett cash, open till Monday.

No such telegram was sent by Fossick's clerk.

The plaintiffs were thus on the 28th (Sunday) in possession of both letters, the one from Fossick stating that the defendant was not inclined to make a firm offer; and the other from the defendant himself, to the effect that he would sell for 40s., nett cash, and would hold it open all Monday. This it was admitted must have been the meaning of 'open till Monday'.

On the Monday morning, at 9.42, the plaintiffs telegraphed to the defendant: 'Please wire whether you would accept forty for delivery over two months, or if not, longest limit you would give'.

This telegram was received at the office at Moorgate at 10.1 a.m., as an inquiry, expecting an answer for his guidance, and this, I think, is the sense in which the defendant ought to have regarded it.

It is apparent throughout the correspondence, that the plaintiffs did not contemplate buying the iron on speculation, but that their acceptance of the defendant's offer depended on their finding someone to take the warrants off their hands. All parties knew that the market was in an unsettled state, and that no one could predict at the early hour when the telegram was sent how the prices would range during the day. It was reasonable that, under these circumstances, they should desire to know before business began whether they were to be at liberty in case of need to make any and what concession as to the time or times of delivery, which would be the time or times of payment, or whether the defendant was determined to adhere to the terms of his letter; and it was highly unreasonable that the plaintiffs should have intended to close the negotiation while it was uncertain whether they could find a buyer or not, having the whole of the business hours of the day to look for one. Then, again, the form of the telegram is one of inquiry. It is not 'I offer forty for delivery over two months', which would have likened the case to *Hyde* v *Wrench* (1840) 3 Bear 334, where one party offered his estate for 1000l., and the other answered by offering 950l. Lord Langdale, in that case, held that after the 950l. had been refused, the party offering it could not, by then agreeing to the original proposal, claim the estate, for the negotiation was at an end by the refusal of his counter proposal. Here there is no counter proposal. The words are, 'Please wire whether you would accept forty for delivery over two months, or, if not, the longest limit you would give'. There is nothing specific by way of offer or rejection, but a mere inquiry, which should have been answered and not treated as a rejection of the offer. This ground of objection therefore fails.

1.4.2   THE BATTLE OF THE FORMS

BUTLER MACHINE TOOL CO. v *EX-CELL-O CORPORATION*
[1979] 1 All ER 965 (CA)

LORD DENNING MR: This case is a 'battle of forms'. The suppliers of a machine, Butler Machine Tool Co. Ltd ('the sellers'), on 23rd May 1969 quoted a price for a machine tool of £75,535. Delivery was to be given in ten months. On the back of the quotation there were terms and conditions. One of them was a price variation clause. It provided for an increase in the price if there was an increase in the costs and so forth. The machine tool was not delivered until November 1970. By that time costs had increased so much that the sellers claimed an additional sum of £2,892 as due to them under the price variation clause.

The buyers, Ex-Cell-O Corpn, rejected the excess charge. They relied on their own terms and conditions. They said: 'We did not accept the sellers' quotation as it was. We gave an order for the self-same machine at the self-same price, but on the back of our order we had our own terms and conditions. Our terms and conditions did not contain any price variation clause'.

The judge held that the price variation clause in the sellers' form continued through the whole dealing and so the sellers were entitled to rely on it. He was clearly influenced by a passage in the 24th edition of Anson's Law of Contract, of which the editor is Professor Guest; and also by a passage in Treitel's The Law of Contract. The judge said that the sellers did all that was necessary and reasonable to bring the price variation clause to the notice of the buyers. He thought that the buyers would not 'browse over the conditions' of the sellers, and then, by printed words in their (the buyers') document, trap the sellers into a fixed price contract.

I am afraid that I cannot agree with the suggestion that the buyers 'trapped' the sellers in any way. Neither party called any oral evidence before the judge. The case was decided on the documents alone. I propose therefore to go through them.

On 23rd May 1969 the sellers offered to deliver one 'Butler' double column plano-miller for the total price of £75,535, 'Delivery: 10 months (Subject to confirmation at time of ordering) Other terms and conditions are on the reverse of this quotation'. On the back there were 16 conditions in small print starting with this general condition:

All orders are accepted only upon and subject to the terms set out in our quotation and the following conditions. These terms and conditions shall prevail over any terms and conditions in the Buyer's order.

Clause 3 was the price variation clause. It said:

. . . Prices are based on present day costs of manufacture and design and having regard to the delivery quoted and uncertainty as to the cost of labour, materials etc., during the period of manufacture, we regret that we have no alternative but to make it a condition of acceptance of order that goods will be charged at prices ruling upon date of delivery.

The buyers, Ex-Cell-O, replied on 27th May 1969 giving an order in these words: 'Please supply on terms and conditions as below and overleaf'. Below there was a list of the goods ordered, but there were differences from the quotation of the sellers in these respects: (i) there was an additional item for the cost of installation, £3,100; (ii) there was a different delivery date; instead of 10 months, it was 10 to 11 months. Overleaf there were different terms as to the cost of carriage, in that it was to be paid to the delivery address of the buyers; whereas the sellers' terms were ex warehouse. There were different terms as to the right to cancel for late delivery. The buyers in their conditions reserved the right to cancel if delivery was not made by the agreed date, whereas the sellers in their conditions said that cancellation of order due to late delivery would not be accepted.

On the foot of the buyers' order there was a tear-off slip:

Acknowledgement: Please sign and return to Ex-Cell-O Corp. (England) Ltd. We accept your order on the Terms and Conditions stated thereon – and undertake to deliver by . . . Date . . . Signed . . .

In that slip the delivery date and signature were left blank ready to be filled in by the sellers.

On 5th June 1969 the sellers wrote this letter to the buyers:

We have pleasure in acknowledging receipt of your official order dated 27th May covering the supply of one 'Butler' Double Column Plano-Miller . . . This is being entered in accordance with our revised quotation of 23rd May for delivery in 10/11 months, ie March/April, 1970. We return herewith, duly completed, your acknowledgement of order form.

They enclosed the acknowledgment form duly filled in with the delivery date, March/April 1970, and signed by the Butler Machine Tool Co. Ltd.

No doubt a contract was then concluded. But on what terms? The sellers rely on their general conditions and on their last letter which said 'in accordance with our revised quotation of 23rd May' (which had on the back the price variation clause). The buyers rely on the acknowledgment signed by the sellers which accepted the buyers' order 'on the terms and conditions stated thereon' (which did not include a price variation clause).

If those documents are analysed in our traditional method, the result would seem to me to be this: the quotation of 23rd May 1969 was an offer by the sellers to the buyers containing the terms and conditions on the back. The order of 27th May 1969 purported to be an acceptance of that offer in that it was for the same machine at the same price, but it contained such additions as to cost of installation, date of delivery and so forth, that it was in law a rejection of the offer and constituted a counter offer. That is clear from *Hyde* v *Wrench* (1840) 3 Bear 334. As Megaw J said in *Trollope & Colls Ltd* v *Atomic Power Construction Ltd* [1962] 3 All ER 1035: . . . the counter-offer kills the original offer'. The letter of the sellers of 5th June 1969 was an acceptance of that counter-offer, as is shown by the acknowledgment which the sellers signed and returned to the buyers. The reference to the quotation of 23rd May 1969 referred only to the price and identity of the machine.

To go on with the facts of the case. The important thing is that the sellers did not keep the contractual date of delivery which was March/April 1970. The machine was ready about September 1970 but by that time the buyers' production schedule had to be rearranged as they could not accept delivery until November 1970. Meanwhile the sellers had invoked the price increase clause. They sought to charge the buyers an increase due to the rise in costs between 27th May 1969 (when the order was given) and 1st April 1970 (when the machine ought to have been delivered). It came to £2,892. The buyers rejected the claim. The judge held that the sellers were entitled to the sum of £2,892 under the price variation clause. He did not apply the traditional method of analysis by way of offer and counter-offer. He said that in the quotation of 23rd May 1969 'one finds the price variation clause appearing under a most emphatic heading stating that it is a term or condition that is to prevail'. So he held that it did prevail.

I have much sympathy with the judge's approach to this case. In many of these cases our traditional analysis of offer, counter-offer, rejection, acceptance and so forth is out-of-date. This was observed by Lord Wilberforce in *New Zealand Shipping Co. Ltd* v *AM Satterthwaite* [1974] 1 All ER 1015. The better way is to look at all the documents passing between the parties and glean from them, or from the conduct of the parties, whether they have reached agreement on all material points, even though there may be differences between the forms and conditions printed on the back of them. As Lord Cairns LC said in *Brogden* v *Metropolitan Railway* (1877) 2 App Cas 666:

> . . . there may be a *consensus* between the parties far short of a complete mode of expressing it, and that *consensus* may be discovered from letters or from other documents of an imperfect and incomplete description.

Applying this guide, it will be found that in most cases when there is a 'battle of forms' there is a contract as soon as the last of the forms is sent and received without objection being taken to it. That is well observed in Benjamin on Sale. The difficulty is to decide which form, or which part of which form, is a term or condition of the contract. In some cases the battle is won by the man who fires the last shot. He is the man who puts forward the latest term and conditions: and, if they are not objected to by the other party, he may be taken to have agreed to them. Such was *British Road Services Ltd* v *Arthur V Crutchley & Co. Ltd* [1968] 1 All ER 811 per Lord Pearson; and the illustration given by Professor Guest in Anson's Law of Contract where he says that 'the terms of the contract consist of the terms of the offer subject to the modifications contained in the acceptance'. That may however go too far. In some cases, however, the battle is won by the man who gets the blow in first. If he offers to sell at a named price on the terms and conditions stated on the back and the buyer orders the goods purporting to accept the offer on an order form with his own different terms and conditions on the back, then, if the difference is so material that it would affect the price, the buyer ought not to be allowed to take advantage of the difference unless he draws it specifically to the attention of the seller. There are yet other cases where the battle depends on the shots fired on both sides. There is a concluded contract but the forms vary. The terms and conditions of both parties are to be construed together. If they can be reconciled so as to give a harmonious result, all well and good. If differences are irreconcilable, so that they are mutually contradictory, then the conflicting terms may have to be scrapped and replaced by a reasonable implication.

In the present case the judge thought that the sellers in their original quotation got their blow in first; especially by the provision that 'These terms and conditions shall prevail over any terms and conditions in the Buyer's order'. It was so emphatic that the price variation clause continued through all the subsequent dealings and that the buyer must be taken to have agreed to it. I can understand that point of view. But I think that the documents have to be considered as a whole. And, as a matter of construction, I think the acknowledgment of 5th June 1969 is the decisive document. It makes it clear that the contract was on the buyers' terms and not the sellers' terms: and the buyers' terms did not include a price variation clause.

I would therefore allow the appeal and enter judgment for the buyers.

Lawton and Bridge LJJ concurred.

1.4.3   COMMUNICATION OF ACCEPTANCE

1.4.3.1   The postal rule

ADAMS v LINDSELL (1818) 1 B & Ald 681 (KB)

When does an acceptance sent by post take effect?

Action for non-delivery of wool according to agreement. At the trial at the last Lent Assizes for the county of Worcester, before Burrough J it appeared that the defendants, who were dealers in wool, at St. Ives, in the county of Huntingdon, had, on Tuesday the 2nd of September 1817, written the following letter to the plaintiffs, who were woollen manufacturers residing in Bromsgrove, Worcestershire. 'We now offer you eight hundred tods of wether fleeces, of a good fair quality of our country wool, at 35s. 6d. per tod, to be delivered at Leicester, and to be paid for by two months' bill in two months, and to be weighed up by your agent within fourteen days, receiving your answer in course of post.'

This letter was misdirected by the defendants, to Bromsgrove, Leicestershire, in consequence of which it was not received by the plaintiffs in Worcestershire till 7p.m. on Friday, September 5th. On that evening the plaintiffs wrote an answer, agreeing to accept the wool on the terms proposed. The course of the post between St. Ives and Bromsgrove is through London, and consequently this answer was not received by the defendants till Tuesday, September 9th. On the Monday September 8th, the defendants not having, as they expected, received an answer on Sunday September 7th (which in case their letter had not been misdirected, would have been in the usual course of the post), sold the wool in question to another person. Under these circumstances, the learned judge held, that the delay having been occasioned by the neglect of the defendants, the jury must take it, that the answer did come back in due course of post; and that then the defendants were liable for the loss that had been sustained: and the plaintiffs accordingly recovered a verdict.

Jervis having in Easter term obtained a rule nisi for a new trial, on the ground that there was no binding contract between the parties, Dauncey, Puller, and Richardson, shewed cause. They contended, that at the moment of the acceptance of the offer of the defendants by the plaintiffs, the former became bound. And that was on the Friday evening, when there had been no change of circumstances. They were then stopped by the Court, who called upon Jervis and Campbell in support of the rule. They relied on *Payne* v *Cave* (1789) 3 Term Rep 148, and more particularly on *Cooke* v *Oxley* (1790) 3 Term Rep 653. In that case, Oxley who had proposed to sell goods to Cooke, and given him a certain time at his request, to determine whether he would buy them or not, was held not liable to the performance of the contract, even though Cooke, within the specified time, had determined to buy them, and given Oxley notice to that effect. So here the defendants who have proposed by letter to sell this wool, are not to be held liable, even though it be now admitted that the answer did come back in due course of post. Till the plaintiffs' answer was actually received, there could be no binding contract between the parties; and before then, the defendants had retracted their offer, by selling the wool to other persons.

But the court said, that if that were so, no contract could ever be completed by the post. For if the defendants were not bound by their offer when accepted by the plaintiffs till the answer was received, then the plaintiffs ought not to be bound till after they had received the notification that the defendants had received their answer and assented to it. And so it might go on ad infinitum. The defendants must be considered in law as making, during every instant of the time their letter was travelling, the same identical offer to the plaintiffs; and then the contract is completed by the acceptance of it by the latter. Then as to the delay in notifying the acceptance, that arises entirely from the mistake of the defendants, and it therefore must be taken as against them, that the plaintiffs' answer was received in course of post.

Rule discharged.

1.4.3.2   Justification for the postal rule

Treitel, G., *Law of Contract*, 9th edn, p. 24

The rule is in truth an arbitrary one, little better or worse than its competitors. When a contract is made by post, one of the parties may be prejudiced if a posted acceptance is lost or delayed; for the offeree may believe that there is a contract and the offeror that there is none, and each may act in reliance on his belief. The posting rule favours the offeree, and is sometimes justified on the ground that an offeror who chooses to start negotiations by post takes the risk of delay and accidents in the post; or on the ground that the offeror can protect himself by expressly stipulating that he is not bound until actual receipt of the acceptance. Neither justification is wholly satisfactory, for the negotiations may have been started by the offeree, and the offer may be made on a form provided by the offeree, in which case he, and not the offeror, will for practical purposes be in control of its terms. The rule does, however, serve a possibly useful function in limiting the offeror's power to withdraw his offer at will: it makes a posted acceptance binding although that acceptance only reaches the offeror after a previously postal withdrawal reaches the offeree.

1.4.3.3   Exceptions to the postal rule

HOLWELL SECURITIES LTD v *HUGHES* [1974] 1 All ER 161 (ChD)

The offeror had required 'notice in writing'.

TEMPLEMAN J: Mr Macpherson's main submission turns on this: he says if you look at the contract cases, offer and acceptance, right at the beginning of the law of contract, you will find that it is possible to accept an offer by putting the accceptance in the post, and that the time for the contract is the date when the acceptance is put in the post not the date when it is received, and notwithstanding that it may not be received. He says here we have an offer, and the exercise of the option by notice is the acceptance, so that it is pure contract. He cited for that proposition – which I think nobody quarrels with – *Anson's Law of Contract*, 23rd edn (1969), p. 44, which is dealing with the manner of acceptance, and at p. 46:

> To understand the leading authority on this point, it is necessary to know that an offer made to one who is not in immediate communication with the offeror remains open and available for acceptance until the lapse of such a time as is prescribed by the offeror, or is reasonable as regards the nature of the transaction. During this time the offer is a continuing offer and may be turned into contract by acceptance.

The editor says it was undoubtedly necessary for the court to establish some definite rule as to the time of a postal acceptance, and convenience pointed to the time when the letter was posted rather than to the time when it was received by the offeror. Then he goes on, at p. 47:

> Various attempts have been made to justify this rule analytically. One line of reasoning attempts to eliminate any difficulties as to consensus by treating the Post Office as the agent of the offeror not only for delivering the offer, but for receiving the notification of its acceptance; yet there is a certain artificiality in looking at the transaction in this way. Another supposes that the offeror must be considered as making, during every instant of the time his letter is travelling, the same identical offer to the offeree; and then the contact is completed by the acceptance of it by the latter. But this does not explain why posting uniquely constitutes *an acceptance without notification*. The better explanation would seem to be that, if hardship is caused, as it obviously may be, by the delay or loss of a letter of acceptance, some rule is necessary, and the rule at which the courts have arrived, whether or not it can logically be supported, is probably as satisfactory as any other would be.

It is to be observed that the author says that in the case of an offer, when all you have to do is to accept, without being told how to accept or what you have to do, then posting is an *'acceptance without notification'*. But, of course, in all cases in contract it depends on the wording of the contact itself and in the present case the contact requires acceptance by notification. It is quite clear from that passage, and from the other authorities which Mr Macpherson read to me, that if you have merely got an offer which says nothing about the method of acceptance then it can be accepted by post, if that is the usual course of dealing, and the time when the acceptance is posted is the date of the contract.

The cases which Mr Macpherson cited were *Henthorn v Fraser* [1892] 2 Ch 27, where the headnote reads:

> where the circumstances under which an offer is made are such that it must have been within the contemplation of the parties that, according to the ordinary usages of mankind, the post might be used as a means of communicating the acceptance of it, the acceptance is complete as soon as it is posted.

Mr Macpherson says of course it was within the contemplation of the parties in the present case that the notice exercising the option should be sent by post, and so it was. But there is a difference between the case where you have a requirement of notice in writing to be given to the intending vendor and a case such as *Henthorn v Fraser* where you have an open offer with nothing said about how it can be accepted, and then the law, for the reasons given by Anson, does not require notification but requires posting as being sufficient to constitute acceptance.

To the same effect was *Stevenson v McLean* (1880) 5 QBD 346 and the nearest case I think for Mr Macpherson's purpose was *Bruner v Moore* [1904] 1 Ch 305 which did concern an option. In that case there was an option to purchase certain patent rights during the period of six months from the date of the agreement. The option said nothing as to how the option was to be exercised. In the event Farwell J held that on the construction of that option and in the events which had then happened the option was in fact exercised in due time, so, as Mr Whitworth pointed out, what the judge had to say about acceptance is obiter. Nevertheless, of course, it is obiter, to which I should pay very great attention. He said, at p. 316:

> It is now argued that this option, having expired on March 29th, a telegram and letter sent on the 28th, but not reaching the defendant until the 30th, were too late. In my opinion this contention fails also, for the option was duly exercised when the telegram was sent and the letter was posted, and he cites Lord Herschell in *Henthorn v Fraser* [1892] 2 Ch 27, 33

> 'Where the circumstances are such that it must have been within the contemplation of the parties that, according to the ordinary usages of mankind, the post might be used as a means of communicating the acceptance of an offer, the acceptance is complete as soon as it is posted'. In the present case the parties are American citizens staying

temporarily at London hotels when they signed the contract. That contract obviously contemplates the events that in fact happened – that the two parties would separate and would visit various parts of Europe, and would communicate with one another constantly by letter and telegram. If there ever was a case in which the parties contemplated 'the post might be used as a means of communicating' on all subjects connected with the contract, this is that case. I hold, therefore, that the option was duly exercised.

The authorities, particularly *Bruner v Moore*, and two later cases, *Household Fire and Carriage Accident Insurance v Grant* (1879) 4 Ex D 216 and *In re Imperial Land Co. of Marseilles, Harris' case* (1872) 7 Ch App 587 which Mr Macpherson cited, do show that where you have an offer and no mode of acceptance is prescribed but it is to be assumed from the circumstances that post is one of the mediums of acceptance, then you can accept through the post, and the time of acceptance is the time of posting. But that has no relevance where the mode of acceptance is prescribed and in the present case this option prescribes that it shall be exercisable by notice in writing to the intending vendor. If, as I think, this means that notice must be given to the intending vendor, then we are dealing not with the cases which Mr Macpherson cites, which relate to offer and acceptance without more, we are dealing with the question of how you are entitled to give notice to an intending vendor, what you have to do in order to satisfy the requirements, and it seems to me from section 196 of the Law of Property Act 1925 and also as a matter of construction, that the intending vendor must get the notice, and subject only to the exemptions provided by section 196, namely, that you take every possible, reasonable precaution by giving it by registered post, and the notice is not returned undelivered. But it will be noticed that, when you use the registered post procedure, it is not the time when you hand it over to the Post Office which counts but the time when, in the normal course of events, it ought to, and nearly always does, reach the addressee. Accordingly, I do not think the cases which Mr Macpherson cited are relevant here and in my judgment the notice had to be received by the defendant, and it clearly was not received.

Buckley and Lawton LJJ concurred.

1.4.3.4   Acceptance by telex, etc.

ENTORES v MILES FAR EAST CORPORATION [1955] 2 QB 327 (CA)

DENNING LJ: This is an application for leave to serve notice of a writ out of the jurisdiction. The grounds are that the action is brought to recover damages for breach of a contract made within the jurisdiction or by implication to be governed by English law.

The plaintiffs are an English company. The defendants are an American corporation with agents all over the world, including a Dutch company in Amsterdam. The plaintiffs say that the contract was made by Telex between the Dutch company in Amsterdam and the English company in London. Communications by Telex are comparatively new. Each company has a teleprinter machine in its office; and each has a Telex number like a telephone number. When one company wishes to send a message to the other, it gets the Post Office to connect up the machines. Then a clerk at one end taps the message on to his machine just as if it were a typewriter, and it is instantaneously passed to the machine at the other end, which automatically types the message onto paper at that end.

The relevant Telex messages in this case were as follows: September 8, 1954: Dutch company: 'Offer for account our associates Miles Far East Corporation Tokyo up to 400 tons Japanese cathodes sterling 240 longton c.i.f. shipment Mitsui Line September 28 or October 10 payment by letter of credit. Your reply Telex Amsterdam 12174 or phone 81490 before 4 p.m. invited.' English company: 'Accept 100 longtons cathodes Japanese shipment latest October 10 sterling £239 10s. longton c.i.f. London/Rotterdam payment letter of credit stop please confirm latest tomorrow.' Dutch company: 'We received O.K. Thank you.' September 9, 1954: English company: 'Regarding our telephone conversation a few minutes ago we note that there is a query on the acceptance of our bid for 100 tons payment in sterling and you are ascertaining that your Tokyo office will confirm the price to be longton we therefore await to hear from you further.' September 10, 1954: English company: 'Is the price for the sterling cathodes understood to be for longton by Japan as you were going to find this out yesterday?' Dutch company: 'Yes, price £239 10s. for longton.'

At that step there was a completed contract by which the defendants agreed to supply 100 tons of cathodes at a price of £239 10s. a ton. The offer was sent by Telex from England offering to pay £239 10s. a ton for 100 tons, and accepted by Telex from Holland. The question for our determination is where was the contract made?

When a contract is made by post it is clear law throughout the common law countries that the acceptance is complete as soon as the letter is put into the post box, and that is the place where the contract is made. But there is no clear rule about contracts made by telephone or by Telex. Communications by these means are virtually instantaneous and stand on a different footing.

The problem can only be solved by going in stages. Let me first consider a case where two people make a contract by word of mouth in the presence of one another. Suppose, for instance, that I shout an offer to a man across a river or a courtyard but I do not hear his reply because it is drowned by an aircraft flying overhead. There is no contract at that moment. If he wishes to make a contract, he must wait till the aircraft is gone and then shout back his acceptance so that I can hear what he says. Not until I have his answer am I bound. I do not agree with the observations of Hill J in *Newcomb* v *De Roos* (1859) 2 E & E 271.

Now take a case where two people make a contract by telephone. Suppose, for instance, that I make an offer to a man by telephone and, in the middle of his reply, the line goes 'dead' so that I do not hear his words of acceptance. There is no contract at that moment. The other man may not know the precise moment when the line failed. But he will know that the telephone conversation was abruptly broken off: because people usually say something to signify the end of the conversation. If he wishes to make a contract, he must therefore get through again so as to make sure that I heard. Suppose next, that the line does not go dead, but it is nevertheless so indistinct that I do not catch what he says and I ask him to repeat it. He then repeats it and I hear his acceptance. The contract is made, not on the first time when I do not hear, but only the second time when I do hear. If he does not repeat it, there is no contract. The contract is only complete when I have his answer accepting the offer.

Lastly, take the Telex. Suppose a clerk in a London office taps out on the teleprinter an offer which is immediately recorded on a teleprinter in a Manchester office, and a clerk at that end taps out an acceptance. If the line goes dead in the middle of the sentence of acceptance, the teleprinter motor will stop. There is then obviously no contract. The clerk at Manchester must get through again and send his complete sentence. But it may happen that the line does not go dead, yet the message does not get through to London. Thus the clerk at Manchester may tap out his message of acceptance and it will not be recorded in London because the ink at the London end fails, or something of that kind. In that case, the Manchester clerk will not know of the failure but the London clerk will know of it and will immediately send back a message 'not receiving'. Then, when the fault is rectified, the Manchester clerk will repeat his message. Only then is there a contract. If he does not repeat it, there is no contract. It is not until his message is received that the contract is complete.

In all the instances I have taken so far, the man who sends the message of acceptance knows that it has not been received or he has reason to know it. So he must repeat it. But, suppose that he does not know that his message did not get home. He thinks it has. This may happen if the listener on the telephone does not catch the words of acceptance, but nevertheless does not trouble to ask for them to be repeated: or the ink on the teleprinter fails at the receiving end, but the clerk does not ask for the message to be repeated: so that the man who sends an acceptance reasonably believes that his message has been received. The offeror in such circumstances is clearly bound, because he will be estopped from saying that he did not receive the message of acceptance. It is his own fault that he did not get it. But if there should be a case where the offeror without any fault on his part does not receive the message of acceptance – yet the sender of it reasonably believes it has got home when it has not – then I think there is no contract.

My conclusion is, that the rule about instantaneous communications between the parties is different from the rule about the post. The contract is only complete when the acceptance is received by the offeror; and the contract is made at the place where the acceptance is received.

In a matter of this kind, however, it is very important that the countries of the world should have the same rule. I find that most of the European countries have substantially the same rule as that I have stated. Indeed, they apply it to contracts by post as well as instantaneous communications. But in the United States of America it appears as if instantaneous communications are treated in the same way as postal communications. In view of this divergence, I think that we must consider the matter on principle: and so considered, I have come to the view I have stated, and I am glad to see that Professor Winfield in this country (55 Law Quarterly Review, 514), and Professor Williston in the United States of America (Contracts, § 82, p. 239), take the same view.

Applying the principles which I have stated, I think that the contract in this case was made in London where the acceptance was received. It was, therefore, a proper case for service out of the jurisdiction.

Birkett and Parker LJJ concurred.

BRINKIBON LTD v *STAHAG STAHL GMBH* [1982] 1 All ER 293 (HL)

LORD WILBERFORCE: My Lords, the appellants desire to sue in this country the respondents, an Austrian company, for breach of an alleged contract for the supply of steel. In order to do so, they must obtain leave to serve notice of their writ upon the respondents under one or other of the provisions of RSC, Ord. 11, r. 1(1). Those relied upon are paragraphs (f) and (g). To satisfy (f), the appellants must show that the contract was 'made within the jurisdiction'; to come within (g) they must establish that the action is in respect of a breach committed within the jurisdiction. The Court of Appeal has decided against the appellants under both paragraphs.

The question whether a contract was made within the jurisdiction will often admit of a simple answer: if both parties are in England at the time of making it, or if it is contained in a single document signed by both parties in England, there is no difficulty. But in the case of contracts involving negotiations, where one party is abroad, the answer may be difficult to find. Sophisticated analysis may be required to decide when the last counter-offer was made into a contract by acceptance, or at what point a clear consensus was reached and by virtue of what words spoken or of what conduct. In the case of successive telephone conversations it may indeed be most artificial to ask where the contract was made: if one asked the parties, they might say they did not know – or care. The place of making a contract is usually irrelevant as regards validity, or interpretation, or enforcement. Unfortunately it remains in Order 11 as a test for purposes of jurisdiction, and courts have to do their best with it.

In the present case it seems that if there was a contract (a question which can only be decided at the trial), it was preceded by and possibly formed by a number of telephone conversations and telexes between London and Vienna, and there are a number of possible combinations upon which reliance can be placed. At this stage we must take the alternatives which provide evidence of a contract in order to see if the test is satisfied. There are two: (i) A telex dated May 3, 1979, from the respondents in Vienna, said to amount to a counter-offer, followed by a telex from the appellants in London to the respondents in Vienna dated May 4, 1979, said to amount to an acceptance. (ii) The above telex dated May 3, 1979, from the respondents followed by action, by way of opening a letter of credit, said to have amounted to an acceptance by conduct.

The first of these alternatives neatly raises the question whether an acceptance by telex sent from London but received in Vienna causes a contract to be made in London, or in Vienna. If the acceptance had been sent by post, or by telegram, then, on existing authorities, it would have been complete when put into the hands of the post office – in London. If on the other hand it had been telephoned, it would have been complete when heard by the offeror – in Vienna. So in which category is a telex communication to be placed? Existing authority of the Court of Appeal decides in favour of the latter category, i.e. a telex is to be assimilated to other methods of instantaneous communication: see *Entores Ltd* v *Miles Far East Corporation* [1955] 2 QB 327. The appellants ask that this case, which has stood for 30 years, should now be reviewed.

Now such review as is necessary must be made against the background of the law as to the making of contracts. The general rule, it is hardly necessary to state, is that a contract is formed *when* acceptance of an offer is communicated by the offeree to the offeror. And if it is necessary to determine *where* a contract is formed (as to which I have already commented) it appears logical that this should be at the place where acceptance is communicated to the offeror. In the common case of contracts, whether oral or in writing inter praesentes, there is no difficulty; and again logic demands that even where there is not mutual presence at the same place and at the same time, if communication is instantaneous, for example by telephone or radio communciation, the same result should follow.

Then there is the case – very common – of communication at a distance, to meet which the so called 'postal rule' has developed. I need not trace its history: it has firmly been in the law at least since *Adams* v *Lindsell* (1818) 1 B & Ald 681. The rationale for it, if left somewhat obscure by Lord Ellenborough CJ, has since been well explained. Mellish LJ in *In re Imperial Land Co. of Marseilles (Harris' Case)* (1872) LR 7 Ch App 587, 594 ascribed it to the extraordinary and mischievous consequences which would follow if it were held that an offer might be revoked at any time until the letter accepting it had been actually received: and its foundation in convenience was restated by Thesiger LJ in *Household Fire and Carriage Accident Insurance Co. Ltd* v *Grant* (1879) 4 Ex D 216, 223. In these cases too it seems logical to say that the place, as well as the time, of acceptance should be *where* (as *when*) the acceptance is put into the charge of the post office.

In this situation, with a general rule covering instantaneous communication inter praesentes, or at a distance, with an exception applying to non-instantaneous communications at a distance, how should communications by telex be categorised? In *Entores Ltd* v *Miles Far East Corporation* [1955] 2 QB 327 the Court of Appeal classified them with instantaneous communications. Their ruling, which has passed into the textbooks, including *Williston on Contracts*, 3rd edn, 1957, appears not to have caused either adverse comment, or any difficulty to business men. I would accept it as a general rule. Where the condition of simultaneity is met, and where it appears to be within the mutual intention of the parties that contractual exchanges should take place in this way, I think it a sound rule, but not necessarily a universal rule.

Since 1955 the use of telex communication has been greatly expanded, and there are many variants on it. The senders and recipients may not be the principals to the contemplated contract. They may be servants or agents with limited authority. The message may not reach, or be intended to reach, the designated recipient immediately: messages may be sent out of office hours, or at night, with the intention, or upon the assumption, that they will be read at a later time. There may be some error or default at the recipient's end which prevents receipt at the time contemplated and believed in by the sender. The message may have been sent and/or received through machines operated by third persons. And many other variations may occur. No universal rule can cover all such cases: they must be resolved by reference to the intentions of the parties, by sound business practice and in some cases by a judgment where the risks should lie: see *Household Fire and Carriage Accident Insurance Co. Ltd* v *Grant* (1879) 4 Ex D 216, 227 *per* Baggallay LJ and *Henthorn* v *Fraser* [1892] 2 Ch 27 *per* Lord Herschell.

The present case is, as *Entores Ltd* v *Miles Far East Corporation* [1955] 2 QB 327 itself, the simple case of instantaneous communication between principals, and, in accordance with the general rule, involves that the contract (if any) was made when and where the acceptance was received. This was on May 4, 1979, in Vienna.

The alternative argument under this head was that the contract was made by an offer made from Vienna (as above, on May 3, 1979) and an acceptance by conduct in the United Kingdom. The conduct relied upon was the giving of instructions by the appellants to set up a letter of credit, as requested in the respondents' telex of May 3, 1979. The appellants' telex of May 4, 1979, opened with the words 'confirm having opened our irrevocable letter of credit No. 0761/79 on account of Midestrade Est., Chiasso, Switzerland . . .' Midestrade Est. is, it appears, the company behind the appellants – a fact which raises the question whether a letter of credit on their account satisfied the terms of the respondents' request. I need not come to a conclusion on this point because I am satisfied that the letter of credit was not opened in the United Kingdom. Instructions were indeed given by the appellants to their bank in the United

Kingdom to open it, and that bank gave instructions on May 4, 1979, to their correspondent in Vienna, but these steps were between the appellants and their agents only. They could not amount, in my opinion, to an acceptance of the offer of May 3, 1979. This took place, if at all, when the correspondent bank in Vienna notified the respondents: this they did in Vienna. On neither ground, therefore, can it be said that the contract was made within the jurisdiction and the case under subparagraph (f) must fail.

That under subparagraph (g) can be more shortly dealt with. The breach pleaded is that the defendants (respondents) 'have not opened a performance bond and have delivered no steel' (points of claim paragraph 7). Each of these acts should have been performed outside the jurisdiction and failure to do them must be similarly located.

On both points, therefore, I find myself in agreement with the Court of Appeal, and the appeal must be dismissed.

LORD FRASER OF TULLYBELTON: My Lords, I am in full agreement with the reasoning of my noble and learned friends, Lord Wilberforce and Lord Brandon of Oakbrook. I wish only to add a comment on the subject of *where* a contract is made, when it is made by an offer accepted by telex between parties in different countries. The question is whether acceptance by telex falls within the general rule that it requires to be notified to the offeror in order to be binding, or within the exception of the postal rule whereby it becomes binding when (and where) it is handed over to the post office. The posting rule is based on considerations of practical convenience, arising from the delay that is inevitable in delivering a letter. But it has been extended to apply to telegrams sent through the post office, and in strict logic there is much to be said for applying it also to telex messages sent by one business firm directly to another. There is very little, if any, difference in the mechanics of transmission between a private telex from one business office to another, and a telegram sent through the post office – especially one sent from one large city to another. Even the element of delay will not be greatly different in the typical case where the operator of the recipient's telex is a clerk with no authority to conclude contracts, who has to hand it to his principal. In such a case a telex message is not in fact received instantaneously by the responsible principal. I assume that the present case is a case of that sort.

Nevertheless I have reached the opinion that, on balance, an acceptance sent by telex directly from the acceptor's office to the offeror's office should be treated as if it were an instantaneous communication between principals, like a telephone conversation. One reason is that the decision to that effect in *Entores* v *Miles Far East Corporation* [1955] 2 QB 327 seems to have worked without leading to serious difficulty or complaint from the business community. Secondly, once the message has been received on the offeror's telex machine, it is not unreasonable to treat it as delivered to the principal offeror, because it is his responsibility to arrange for prompt handling of messages within his own office. Thirdly, a party (the acceptor) who tries to send a message by telex can generally tell if his message has not been received on the other party's (the offeror's) machine, whereas the offeror, of course, will not know if an unsuccessful attempt has been made to send an acceptance to him. It is therefore convenient that the acceptor, being in the better position, should have the responsibility of ensuring that his message is received. For these reasons I think it is right that in the ordinary simple case, such as I take this to be, the general rule and not the postal rule should apply. But I agree with both my noble and learned friends that the general rule will not cover all the many variations that may occur with telex messages.

1.4.4   REVOCATION OF ACCEPTANCE

Treitel, G., *Law of Contract*, 9th edn, p. 27

Revocation of posted acceptance. An offeree may, after posting an acceptance, attempt to revoke it by a later communication which reaches the offeror before, or at the same time as, the acceptance. There is no English authority on the effectiveness of such a revocation. One view is that the revocation has no effect, since, once a contract has been concluded, it cannot be dissolved by the unilateral act of one party. But this argument has little to commend it if (as has been suggested above) it is undesirable to resolve what are really issues of policy by making 'logical' deductions from some 'general' rule as to the effect of posted acceptances. As a matter of policy, the issue is whether the offeror would be unjustly prejudiced by allowing the offeree to rely on the subsequent revocation. On the one hand, it can be argued that the offeror cannot be prejudiced by such revocation as he had no right to have his offer accepted and as he cannot have relied on its having been accepted before he knew of the acceptance. Against this, it can be argued that, once the acceptance has been posted, the offeror can no longer withdraw his offer, and that reciprocity demands that the offeree should likewise be held to his acceptance. For if the offeree could revoke the acceptance he would be able, without risk to himself, to speculate at the expense of the offeror. He could post his acceptance early in the morning of a working day and could, if the market moved against him, revoke his acceptance the same afternoon, while the offeror had no similar freedom of action. It has been suggested that the offeror should take this risk just as much as he takes the risk of loss or delay; but here again it is submitted that while the offeror may take the risks of accidents in the post, he should not have to take risks due entirely to the conduct of the offeree.

So far, it has been assumed that it is in the offeror's interest to uphold the contract. But to hold the acceptance binding as soon as it was posted, in spite of an overtaking communication purporting to revoke it, might cause hardship to the *offeror*. This is particularly true where he has acted in reliance on the revocation. Suppose that A offers to sell B a car. B posts an acceptance of the offer and then telexes: 'ignore my letter I do not want the car'. A then sells the car to C. Could B change his mind yet again, and claim damages from A? There are several ways of avoiding such an unjust result. The first is to say that there had once been a contract but that it was later rescinded by mutual consent: B's telex was an offer to release A, which A accepted by conduct; communication of such acceptance could be deemed to have been waived. The second is to regard B's telex as a repudiation amounting to a breach of contract; and to say that, by 'accepting' the breach, A has put an end to the contract. This analysis is preferable from A's point of view if the sale to C is for a lower price than that to B, for it would enable A to claim the difference from B as damages.

1.4.5 ACCEPTANCE BY SILENCE

FELTHOUSE v *BINDLEY* (1862) 11 CB (NS) 869 (CP)

WILLES J: I am of opinion that the rule to enter a nonsuit should be made absolute. The horse in question had belonged to the plaintiff's nephew, John Felthouse. In December, 1860, a conversation took place between the plaintiff and his nephew relative to the purchase of the horse by the former. The uncle seems to have thought that he had on that occasion bought the horse for 30*l.*, the nephew that he had sold it for 30 guineas: but there was clearly no complete bargain at that time. On the 1st of January, 1861, the nephew writes, – 'I saw my father on Saturday. He told me that you considered you had bought the horse for 30*l.* If so, you are labouring under a mistake, for 30 guineas was the price I put upon him, and you never heard me say less. When you said you would have him, I considered you were aware of the price'. To this the uncle replies on the following day – 'Your price, I admit, – was 30 guineas. I offered 30*l.*; never offered more: and you said the horse was mine. However, as there may be a mistake about him, I will split the difference. If I hear no more about him, I consider the horse mine at 30*l.* 15*s.*' It is clear that there was no complete bargain on the 2nd of January; and it is also clear that the uncle had no right to impose upon the nephew a sale of his horse for 30*l.* 15*s.* unless he chose to comply with the condition of writing to repudiate the offer. The nephew might, no doubt, have bound his uncle to the bargain by writing to him: the uncle might also have retracted his offer at any time before acceptance. It stood an open offer: and so things remained until the 25th of February, when the nephew was about to sell his farming stock by auction. The horse in question being catalogued with the rest of the stock, the auctioneer (the defendant) was told that it was already sold. It is clear, therefore, that the nephew in his own mind intended his uncle to have the horse at the price which he (the uncle) had named, – 30*l.* 15*s.*: but he had not communicated such his intention to his uncle, or done anything to bind himself. Nothing, therefore, had been done to vest the property in the horse in the plaintiff down to the 25th of February, when the horse was sold by the defendant. It appears to me that, independently of the subsequent letters, there had been no bargain to pass the property in the horse to the plaintiff, and therefore that he had no right to complain of the sale. Then, what is the effect of the subsequent correspondence? The letter of the auctioneer amounts to nothing. The more important letter is that of the nephew, of the 27th of February, which is relied on as shewing that he intended to accept and did accept the terms offered by his uncle's letter of the 2nd of January. That letter, however, may be treated either as an acceptance then for the first time made by him, or as a memorandum of a bargain complete before the 25th of February, sufficient within the statute of frauds. It seems to me that the former is the more likely construction: and, if so, it is clear that the plaintiff cannot recover. But, assuming that there had been a complete parol bargain before the 25th of February, and that the letter of the 27th was a mere expression of the terms of that prior bargain, and not a bargain then for the first time concluded, it would be directly contrary to the decision of the court of Exchequer in *Stockdale* v *Dunlop*, 6 M & W 224, to hold that that acceptance had relation back to the previous offer so as to bind third persons in rspect of a dealing with the property by them in the interim. In that case, Messrs H & Co., being the owners of two ships, called the 'Antelope' and the 'Maria', trading to the coast of Africa, and which were then expected to arrive in Liverpool with cargoes of palm-oil, agreed *verbally* to sell the plaintiffs two hundred tons of oil, – one hundred tons to arrive by the 'Antelope', and one hundred tons by the 'Maria'. The 'Antelope' did afterwards arrive with one hundred tons of oil on board, which were delivered by H & Co. to the plaintiffs. The 'Maria', having fifty tons of oil on board, was lost by perils of the sea. The plaintiffs having insured the oil on board the 'Maria', together with their expected profits thereon, – it was held that they had no insurable interest, as the contract they had entered into with H & Co., being verbal only, was incapable of being enforced.

BYLES J: I am of the same opinion, and have nothing to add to what has fallen from my Brother Willes.

KEATING J: I am of the same opinion. Had the question arisen as between the uncle and the nephew, there would probably have been some difficulty. But, as between the uncle and the auctioneer, the only question we have to consider is whether the horse was the property of the plaintiff at the time of the sale on the 25th of February. It seems to me that nothing had been done at that time to pass the property out of the nephew and vest it in the plaintiff. A proposal had been made, but there had before that day been no acceptance binding the nephew.

WILLES J: *Coats* v *Chaplin*, 3 QB 483, 2 Gale & D 552, is an authority to shew that John Felthouse might have had a remedy against the auctioneer. There, the traveller of Morrisons, tradesmen in London, verbally ordered goods for Morrisons of the plaintiffs, manufacturers at Paisley. No order was given as to sending the goods. The plaintiffs gave them to the defendants, carriers, directed to Morrisons, to be taken to them, and also sent an invoice by post to Morrisons, who received it. The goods having been lost by the defendants' negligence, and not delivered to Morrisons, – it was held that the defendants were liable to the plaintiffs.

Miller CJ, '*Felthouse* v *Bindley* Re-visited' (1972), 35 MLR, p. 489

An interesting and unresolved point which has given rise to a certain amount of academic discussion is that of the extent to which it is open to an offeror effectively to waive the need for any formal communication of acceptance. Here, it appears, an initial distinction must be drawn between unilateral and bilateral contracts. In the potentially unilateral contract the position is reasonably straightforward. The offeror will normally be impliedly taken to have waived the need for communication and it is clear that it is competent to him to do this. Performance by the offeree of the requested act will generally suffice and notification of an intention to perform is unnecessary. Authority for this general proposition is to be found in the well known case of *Carlill* v *Carbolic Smoke*

Ball Co. [1893] 1 QB 256. Here, it may be remembered, the plaintiff successfully claimed that she was entitled to the sum of £100 which had been advertised as being payable to anyone who caught influenza after using the defendant's smoke ball in the prescribed manner and for the prescribed period of time. The Court of Appeal emphatically discounted the need for any communication of acceptance by the offeree and, taking an analogous example of a reward for finding a lost dog, Bowen LJ said,

> The essence of the transaction is that the dog should be found, and it is not necessary under such circumstances, as it seems to me, that in order to make the contract binding there should be any notification of acceptance. It follows from the nature of the thing that the performance of the condition is sufficient acceptance without the notification of it, and a person who makes an offer in an advertisement of that kind makes an offer which must be read in the light of that common-sense reflection. He does, therefore, in his offer impliedly indicate that he does not require notification of the acceptance of the offer.

The position in the potentially bilateral contract is, however, more complicated. Of such cases one can safely say that it is not open to an offer to stipulate as against an unwilling offeree that the latter's silence will be regarded as equivalent to acceptance. He cannot force him to take a positive course of action under penalty of being contractually bound if he does not. Nor, by the same token, can he circumscribe the offeree's freedom of action by providing that a similar significance will be attributed to an ordinary everyday act of an offeree. As Corbin has graphically put it,

> If A offers his land to B for a price, saying that B may signify his acceptance by eating his breakfast or by hanging out his flag on Washington's birthday . . . he does not thereby make such action by B operative as an acceptance against B's will. If B shows that he had no intent to accept, and that he ate his breakfast merely because he was hungry, or hung out his flag because it was his patriotic custom, . . . no contract has been made even though A truly believed that B meant to accept.

Suppose, though, that the offeree is not unwilling and indeed has every intention of agreeing to the terms proposed by the offeror. The question then arises as to whether a contract may be concluded in such circumstances by either conduct which is indicative of this assent or indeed by mere silence. Some authorities certainly suggest that active conduct short of communication will suffice where the offeror has expressly or impliedly waived the need for a communication of acceptance. Thus if A sends unsolicited goods to B it is clear that his offer to supply may be accepted by B's using or consuming the goods without more. This, in effect, occurred in *Weatherby v Banham* (1832) 5 C & P 228 where the plaintiffs recovered the price of periodicals which they had sent unsolicited to the defendant who had received and presumably used them. Similarly if A offers to buy certain goods from B it seems clear that a contract may be concluded by B's dispatching the goods and that they will prima facie be at A's risk from the time of dispatch. An analogous situation was considered in *Taylor v Allon* [1965] 1 All ER 557 where a Divisional Court heard an appeal against a conviction for using a motor cycle on a road without insurance cover against third-party risks. Briefly, the accused's insurance policy had admittedly expired on the relevant day, but he had been issued with a temporary cover note which not having been requested, clearly amounted to no more than an offer to insure. Equally clearly on the facts of the case this offer had not been accepted by the appellant who had intended throughout to insure with another company. Hence no contract was in force and the conviction was upheld. The case is of interest in the present context, however, in that Lord Parker was prepared to envisage that the result might have been different if the appellant *had* taken the car out onto the road in reliance upon the offer. According to his Lordship,

> It may be, although I find it unneccessary to decide in this case, that there can be an acceptance of such an offer by conduct and without communication with the insurance company. It may well be, as it seems to me, that if a man took his motor car out on the road in reliance on this temporary cover note, albeit there had been no communication of that fact to the insurance company, there would be an acceptance.

This, with respect, would appear to be an entirely sensible conclusion which has the added advantage of according with the assumptions of the ordinary driver. It would also lend support to the view that it is open to the offeror to impliedly waive the need for a communication of acceptance in the potentially bilateral contract.

The leading English case of *Felthouse* v *Bindley* (1862) 11 CB (NS) 869 might, however, be thought to point conclusively in the opposite direction. In this case the plaintiff and his nephew had been negotiating about the sale of a horse and had failed to reach agreement over the price. The plaintiff thereupon wrote to the nephew saying, 'If I hear no more about him, I consider the horse is mine at £30 15s'. The nephew did not reply, but he resolved to accept the offer and informed the defendant auctioneer, who was selling off his farming stock, that the horse in question was not to be disposed of as it had already been sold. The auctioneer mistakenly sold the horse and he was sued by the plaintiff in conversion. The Common Pleas held for the auctioneer on the ground that the plaintiff had no title to sue since at the date of the auction the nephew had not effectively accepted the offer. Given that he had admittedly told the auctioneer that the horse was reserved for his uncle and that the latter had equally assumed that this was so, it is not clear why anything further should have been regarded as essential to the formation of a contract. On balance it is submitted that the approach of the Common Pleas was wrong in principle and that the actual result of the case can only be supported because there had been no delivery, part payment or memorandum in writing to satisfy the then requirements of the Statute of Frauds. This was the alternative reason given by the Common Pleas and it was the reason which appears to have been emphasised by the Exchequer Chamber when affirming the decision on appeal.

If one is prepared to concede that positive conduct falling short of communication is sufficient to conclude a bilateral contract, this still leaves open the question of whether silence coupled with mental assent would be equally sufficient where the offeror has purported to waive the need for notification. The additional difficulty here is, of course, that the lack of any outward expression of assent would effectively enable the offeree to deny or assert the fact of acceptance to suit his own convenience. Lord Denning clearly appreciated the point in *Robophone Facilities* v *Blank* [1966] 3 All ER 128 when he discussed the effect of a clause providing that, 'This agreement shall become binding on the [plaintiffs] only upon acceptance thereof by signature . . . on their behalf'. His Lordship was clear that notwithstanding this terminology,

> Signing without notification is not enough. It would be deplorable if it were. The plaintiffs would be able to keep the form in their office unsigned, and then play fast and loose as they pleased. The defendant would not know whether or not there was a contract binding them to supply or him to take. Just as mental acceptance is not enough, nor is internal acceptance within the plaintiff's office.

This statement accords with the views expressed in the House of Lords in the old case of *Brogden* v *Metropolitan Railway* (1876) 2 App Cas 666, and it may well be productive of justice where, as in the *Robophone* case itself, the offer is submitted on a standard form agreement drawn up by the offeree. It is not, however, difficult to envisage other situations where insistence on the need for such notification might well work substantial injustice. Thus suppose that A writes to B offering to buy his car for £100 and adding, 'There is no need to reply. If I do not hear from you within the week, I shall assume you accept.' If B wishes to take up the offer and remains silent it would hardly be satisfactory to permit A to deny the existence of a contract on the ground that acceptance had not been notified when he himself had expressly stated that it was unneccessary. Again it would have been equally unsatisfactory if the uncle in *Felthouse* v *Bindley* could have pointed to the lack of notification if it had been he who was being sued by the nephew for damages for non-acceptance. Presumably if A and the uncle are to be regarded as having entered a contract to purchase then B and the nephew must be regarded as having entered a contract to sell. Notwithstanding the admitted difficulties involved, it is tentatively submitted that in such cases there may be an effective waiver of the need for communication of acceptance, and, moreover, a contract may be concluded without the need for any external manifestation of assent. A similar view is expressed in section 72(1)(b) of the American Restatement on Contracts which reads,

Where an offeree fails to reply to an offer, his silence and inaction operate as an acceptance . . . where the offeror has stated or given the offeree reason to understand that assent may be made by silence and the offeree intends to accept.

1.5   Inchoate Agreements

SCAMMELL & NEPHEW LTD v OUSTON [1941] 1 All ER 14 (HL)

The parties agreed to contract on (unspecified) 'hire purchase terms'.

LORD WRIGHT: . . . It is a necessary requirement that an agreement, in order to be binding, must be sufficiently definite to enable the court to give it a practical meaning. Its terms must be so definite, or capable of being made definite without further agreement of the parties, that the promises and performances to be rendered by each party are reasonably certain. In my opinion, that requirement was not satisfied in this case.

However, I think that the other reason, which is that the parties never in intention, nor even in appearance, reached an agreement, is a still sounder reason against enforcing the claim. In truth, in my opinion, their agreement was inchoate, and never got beyond negotiations. They did, indeed, accept the position that there should be some form of hire-purchase agreement, but they never went on to complete their agreement by settling between them what the terms of the hire-purchase agreement were to be. The furthest point they reached was an understanding or agreement to agree upon hire-purchase terms. However, as Lord Dunedin said in *May & Butcher Ltd v R* (reported in a note to *Foley v Classique Coaches Ltd*), at p. 21:

> To be a good contract there must be a concluded bargain, and a concluded contract is one which settles everything that is necessary to be settled and leaves nothing to be settled by agreement between the parties. Of course it may leave something which still has to be determined, but then that determination must be a determination which does not depend upon the agreement between the parties.

In this case, MacKinnon LJ thought that the agreement of the parties was complete and nothing was left for them to agree. Whatever was lacking in their agreement could and should, he thought, be supplied by the court by invoking the standard of reasonableness, on the principles laid down by this House in *Hillas & Co. Ltd v Arcos Ltd* (1932) 147 LT 503. The view of MacKinnon LJ as I have already indicated, was, if I have understood correctly, that there was a contract for a hire-purchase agreement, and that no further agreement of the parties was necessary, because the court could determine for the parties what was a reasonable hire-purchase agreement, and thus the contract would be complete. I am unable to concur in this conclusion. In the first place, the appellants, at least in their letter of February 10, 1938, expressly stated that the transaction was subject to mutual acceptance of the hire-purchase agreement. This was not demurred to by the respondents. The letter was written before any difficulty had arisen about the condition or description of the Bedford van. It seems to me that this attitude was sensible both from the point of view of business and of law. It is here necessary to remember what a hire-purchase agreement is. It is not a contract of sale, but of bailment. The owner of the chattel lets it out on hire for a periodic rent on the terms that, on completion of the agreed number of payments, and on due compliance with the various terms of the agreement, the hirer is to have the option to buy the chattel on payment of 1s. or some nominal sum. The condition that the hirer is not to become owner automatically on completion of the agreed payments, but merely has an option to purchase, was adopted to avoid difficulties under the Factors Act or the Bills of Sale Act, as explained by this House in *Helby v Matthews* [1895] AC 471 and *McEntire v Crossley Brothers* [1895] AC 457. While the bailment continues, the property remains in the letter. Such a transaction, though not a contract of sale, is used in practice to carry out a sale transaction, with the advantage to the buyer of credit facilities. Though the property in the chattel does not pass while the agreement is current, the hirer gets the use of it. What would be the price if it were a contract of sale has to be increased by whatever sum is necessary for interest and bank charges until the periodic instalments have been discharged. Terms must accordingly be arranged in respect of the period of the bailment as to user, repairs, insurance, rights of retaking possession on the hirer's default, and various other matters. A hire-purchase agreement is, therefore, in practice a complex arrangement. Thus, when, in the letter of December 8, 1937, the condition of hire purchase was introduced into what had seemed, on the letters, to be proceeding as a contract of sale, there was a complete change in the character of the transaction, and a complex arrangement had necessarily to be substituted for a simple agreement to sell. It was not even clear who were to be parties to the hire-purchase agreement, or what their respective roles were to be. The respondents, it is clear, were necessary parties. The appellants also were necessary parties, because it was their chattel which was being dealt with. The finance company was also a necessary party. However, there were at least two possible ways of carrying out the deal. The hire-purchase agreement might be in such terms that the appellants were the letters and the respondents the hirers, and the purchase price was to be discharged by periodic instalments in the form of negotiable instruments, payable to the appellants, thus enabling the appellants to discount the bills with the finance company, who, on the security of the bills drawn by the respondents and indorsed by the appellants, would pay the appellants the purchase price at once, keeping as their eventual profit the extra amount which was added to the price for interest and bank charges. Such an arrangement must obviously involve the making of a special tripartite agreement. Another possible method would be for the appellants to agree with the respondents to sell the van to the finance company on the stipulation that the latter should agree to let the van to the respondents under a hire-purchase agreement. Clearly in that case also a special tripartite agreement would be necessary. There was perhaps a third possible mode under which the appellants sold the van for cash (at least as regards the balance, for the transaction was, in part, barter) to the respondents, who, having become purchasers, then transferred the van to the finance company on a hire-purchase agreement in consideration of the company advancing the price. Even in such a case, the appellants would, I think, in practice be a necessary party, because the finance company would require the undertaking of the appellants to transfer the van direct to them and the respondents' concurrence in that undertaking. Otherwise, the finance company would be paying cash without at once obtaining their security in the form of the van. Thus a tripartite agreement would be necessary. However, I need not consider that case, because it was clearly not contemplated by the parties. The correspondence shows that the terms of the hire-purchase agreement were to be matters of joint concern to the three parties who were to agree upon them. What is clear is that, while a hire-purchase agreement was being demanded, its exact form and its exact terms were left for future agreement. The true view may be that the letter of December 8, 1937, amounts to nothing more than an announcement that the deal is only to proceed upon a hire-purchase basis, the parties anticipating that the terms of such an agreement would be settled between them in due course.

What I have said will sufficiently explain why I do not feel able to agree with MacKinnon LJ that there was a complete and enforceable agreement concluded between the parties. He cited *Hillas & Co. Ltd* v *Arcos Ltd* (1932) 147 LT 503 in support of his view, but that was a quite different case. There was in that case a contract for the supply of Russian timber in 1930, which also gave an option to the buyers to purchase a further supply of 100,000 standards in the ensuing year. The option clause was extremely bare and meagre, but it was held as a matter of construction that the 100,000 standards were to be soft wood goods of fair specification for delivery during 1931. It was decided by this House, reversing the judgment of the Court of Appeal and restoring the judgment of MacKinnon J that no further agreement was necessary or contemplated. The court could not, indeed, make a contract for the parties, or go outside the words they had used, except in so far as there were appropriate implications of law, as, for instance, the implication of what was just and reasonable where the contractual intention was clear but the contract was silent in some detail which the court could thus fill in. Thus the condition of 'fair specification over the season' 1931 enabled the court, with the help of expert evidence, to identify what was a fair and reasonable specification and a fair and reasonable distribution by way of instalment deliveries of the contract quantity. Certain other matters were similarly dealt with. In the same way, the court has, in proper circumstances, found itself able to determine what is a reasonable price when the price is not specified in the contract, as was done in *Foley v Classique Coaches Ltd* [1934] 2 KB 1, rightly, as I think, distinguishing *May & Butcher Ltd v R* [1934] 2 KB 17n or to determine what is a reasonable time, or what are reasonable instalments. Many other examples of this principle might be given. In addition, the court may import terms on the proof of custom or by implication. However, it is, in my opinion, a very different matter to make an entire contract for the parties, as the court would be doing if the course suggested by MacKinnon LJ was adopted. That is simply making a contract for the parties. The analogy he cited of a c.i.f. contract is, in my opinion, no true analogy. These initial letters have a definite and complete meaning under the law merchant, just as much as the meaning of a bill of exchange, or the general effect of a marine insurance contract, is determined by the law merchant. The law has not defined, and cannot of itself define, what are the normal and reasonable terms of a hire-purchase agreement. Though the general character of such an agreement is familiar, it is necessary for the parties in each case to agree upon the particular terms. It may perhaps be that this might be done in particular circumstances by general words of reference. For instance, if it were stipulated that there should be 'a usual' hire-purchase agreement, the court might be able, if supplied with appropriate evidence, to define what are the terms of such an agreement. However, there was nothing of the sort in this case, and I reserve my opinion on any such hypothetical case. I think this appeal should be allowed.

W. N. HILLAS AND CO. LTD v ARCOS LTD (1932) Com Cas 23 (HL)

An option clause failed to specify the goods concerned.

LORD TOMLIN: In the present case one or two preliminary observations fall to be made.

First, the parties were both intimately acquainted with the course of business in the Russian softwood timber trade and had without difficulty carried out the sale and purchase of 22,000 standards under the first part of the document of May 31, 1930.

Secondly, although the question here is whether clause 9 of the document of May 21, 1930, with the letter of December 22, 1930, constitutes a contract, the validity of the whole of the document of May 21, 1930, is really in question so far as the matter depends upon the meaning of the phrase 'of fair specification'; and

Thirdly, it is indisputable, having regard to clause 11, which provides that 'this agreement cancels all previous agreements', that the parties intended by the document of May 21, 1930, to make, and believed that they had made, some concluded bargain.

The case against the appellants is put on two grounds.

First it is said that there is in clause 9 no sufficient description of the goods to be sold; and

Secondly it is said that clause 9 contemplates a future bargain the terms of which remain to be settled.

As to the first point it is plain that something must necessarily be implied in clause 9. The words '100,000 standards' without more do not even indicate that timber is the subject-matter of the clause. The implication at the least of the words 'of softwood goods' is, in my opinion, inevitable, and if this is so I see no reason to separate the words 'of fair specification' from the words 'of softwood goods'. In my opinion there is a necessary implication of the words 'of softwood goods of fair specification' after the words '100,000 standards' in clause 9.

What then is the meaning of '100,000 standards of softwood goods of fair specification for delivery during 1931'?

If the words 'of fair specification' have no meaning which is certain or capable of being made certain then not only can there be no contract under clause 9 but there cannot have been a contract with regard to the 22,000 standards mentioned at the beginning of the document of May 21, 1930. This may be the proper conclusion; but before it is reached it is, I think, necessary to exclude as impossible all reasonable meanings which would give certainty to the words. In my opinion this cannot be done.

The parties undoubtedly attributed to the words in connexion with the 22,000 standards, some meaning which was precise or capable of being made precise. Scrutton

LJ laid stress upon the evidence of Mr Hillas as indicating a different view on the part of the parties. I am unable to think that upon a question of construction such evidence if directed to the intention of the parties was admissible at all. In fact, I think, Mr Hillas' evidence was misunderstood. It really amounted, in my opinion, to nothing more than a statement as to how the parties would in the first instance proceed, just as on a purchase of property at its fair value the parties would no doubt first endeavour to reach agreement as to the fair value.

Reading the document of May 21, 1930, as a whole, and having regard to the admissible evidence as to the course of the trade, I think that upon their true construction the words 'of fair specification over the season, 1930', used in connexion with the 22,000 standards, mean that the 22,000 standards are to be satisfied in goods distributed over kinds, qualities, and sizes in the fair proportions having regard to the output of the season 1930, and the classifications of that output in respect of kinds, qualities, and sizes. That is something which if the parties fail to agree can be ascertained just as much as the fair value of a property.

I have already expressed the view that clause 9 must be read as '100,000 standards of fair specification for delivery during 1931' and these words, I think, have the same meaning, *mutatis mutandis*, as the words relating to the 22,000 standards. Thus, there is a description of the goods which if not immediately yet ultimately is capable of being rendered certain.

The second point upon clause 9 that it contemplates a future agreement remains to be considered.

The form of the phrases 'the option of entering into a contract' and 'such contract to stipulate that' upon which stress has been laid by the respondents seems to me unimportant. These phrases are but an inartificial way of indicating that there is no contract till the option is exercised. The sentence that such contract is to stipulate that whatever the conditions are the buyers are to obtain the goods at a certain reduction is more difficult: The words 'whatever the conditions are' being governed by the word 'that' which follows the words 'to stipulate' must be intended to be part of the contract. If so the word 'conditions' cannot mean terms of the contract, but must connote some extrinsic condition of affairs, and the condition of affairs referred to is, I think, the conditions as to supply and demand which may prevail during 1931.

Upon this view of the matter it cannot, I think, be said that there is nothing more than an agreement to make an agreement.

It was also urged as a minor point that there was no provision as to shipment and that this was an essential of such a contract.

I am not prepared without further consideration to accept the view that in the absence of a provision in relation to shipment there can be no contract in law in such a case as the present.

In my opinion, however, the point does not arise here. Clause 9 is one of the clauses containing the conditions upon which the sale of the 22,000 standards is made. This fact together with the presence of the word 'also' in clause 9 satisfies me that upon the true construction of the document the sale conditions in relation to the 22,000 standards are so far as applicable imported into the option for the sale of the 100,000 standards, and in particular that clause 6 relating to shipping dates and loading instructions is so imported.

Reference was made in the course of the arguments before your Lordships and in the judgments in the Court of Appeal to the unreported case before your Lordships' House of *May and Butcher* v *The King* [1934] 2 KB 17.

In the agreement there under consideration there was an express provision that the price of the goods to be sold should be subsequently fixed between the parties. Your Lordships' House reached the conclusion that there was no contract, rejecting the appellants' contention that the agreement should be construed as an agreement to sell at the fair or reasonable price or alternatively at a price to be fixed under the arbitration clause contained in the agreement.

That case does not, in my opinion, afford any assistance in determining the present case, the result of which must depend upon the meaning placed upon the language employed.

My Lords, it is only after anxious consideration that I recommend to your Lordships a conclusion upon the construction of the relevant documents contrary to that unanimously reached by the Court of Appeal. This is my justification for having stated my reasons at some length.

Lords Warrington, Macmillan, Thankerton and Wright concurred.

FOLEY v CLASSIQUE COACHES [1934] 2 KB 1 (CA)

A contract for the supply of petrol referred to 'a price to be agreed by the parties.'

SCRUTTON LJ: In this appeal I think that the Lord Chief Justice's decision was right, and I am glad to come to that conclusion, because I do not regard the appellants' contention as an honest one.

The nature of the case is this: the respondent, the plaintiff in the action, had some land, part of which was occupied by petrol pumps. Adjoining that land was some vacant land belonging to him which the appellants wanted to use as the headquarters for their char-à-bancs, and they approached the respondent, who was willing to sell on the terms that the appellants obtained all their petrol from him. It is quite clear that unless the appellants had agreed to this they would never have got the land. There was a discussion whether this term about the petrol and the agreement to purchase the land should be put in one document or two, but ultimately it was decided to put them in two documents of even date. One relates specifically to the sale and purchase of the land, and that was to go through on condition that the appellants undertook to enter into the petrol agreement, the terms of which had been already agreed. On the same day the second agreement was signed reciting that it was supplemental to the agreement of even date, that is the agreement for the sale of the land. The petrol agreement includes a clause that if any dispute or difference should arise on the subject-matter or construction 'the same shall be submitted to arbitration in the usual way.' It is quite clear that the parties intended to make an agreement, and for the space of three years no doubt entered the mind of the appellants that they had a business agreement, for they acted on it during that time. The petrol supplied by the respondent was non-combine petrol, but he had also combine petrol pumps. The non-combine petrol was supplied to the appellants at a price lower than that paid by the public, and an account was rendered periodically in writing and paid. In the third year some one acting for the appellants thought he could get better petrol elsewhere, and on September 29, 1933, their solicitor, thinking he saw a way out of the agreement, wrote on behalf of the appellants the letter of September 29, 1933, repudiating the agreement. Possibly the solicitor had heard something about the decision of the House of Lords in *May and Butcher* v *The King* [1934] 2 KB 17 but probably had not heard of *Braithwaite* v *Foreign Hardwood Co.* [1905] 2 KB 543, in which the Court of Appeal decided that the wrongful repudiation of a contract by one party relieves the other party from the performance of any conditions precedent. If the solicitor had known of that decision he would not have written the letter in the terms he did. Thereafter the respondent brought his action claiming damages for breach of the agreement, a declaration that the agreement is binding, and an injunction to restrain the appellants from purchasing petrol from any other person. The Lord Chief Justice decided that the respondent was entitled to judgment, as there was a binding agreement by which the appellants got the land on condition that they should buy their petrol from the respondent. I observe that the appellants' solicitor in his letter made no suggestion that the land would be returned, and I suppose the appellants would have been extremely annoyed if they had been asked to return it when they repudiated the condition.

A good deal of the case turns upon the effect of two decisions of the House of Lords which are not easy to fit in with each other. The first of these cases is *May and Butcher* v *The King*, which related to a claim in respect of a purchase of surplus stores from a Government department. In the Court of Appeal two members of the Court took the view that inasmuch as there was a provision that the price of the stores which were to be offered from time to time was to be agreed there was no binding contract because an agreement to make an agreement does not constitute a contract, and that the language of clause 10 that any dispute as to the construction of the agreement was to be submitted to arbitration was irrelevant, because there was not an agreement, although the parties thought there was. In the second case, *Hillas & Co.* v *Arcos* (1932) 147 LT 503, there was an agreement between Hillas & Co. and the Russian authorities under which Hillas & Co. were to take in one year 22,000 standards of Russian timber, and in the same agreement they had an option to take in the next year 100,000 standards, with no particulars as to the kind of timber or as to the terms of shipment or any of the other matters one expects to find dealt with on a sale of a large quantity of Russian timber over a period. The Court of Appeal, which included Greer LJ and myself, both having a very large experience in these timber cases, came to the conclusion that as the House of Lords in *May and Butcher* v *The King* considered that where a detail had to be agreed upon there was no agreement until that detail was agreed, we were bound to follow the decision in *May and Butcher* v *The King* and hold that there was no effective agreement in respect of the option, because the terms had not been agreed. It was, however, held by the House of Lords in *Hillas & Co.* v *Arcos* that we were wrong in so deciding and that we had misunderstood the decision in *May and Butcher* v *The King*. The House took this line: it is quite true that there seems to be considerable vagueness about the agreement but the parties contrived to get through it on the contract for 22,000 standards, and so the House thought there was an agreement as to the option which the parties would be able to get through also despite the absence of details. It is true that in the first year the parties got through quite satisfactorily; that was because during that year the great bulk of English buyers were boycotting the Russian sellers. In the second year the position was different. The English buyers had changed their view and were buying large quantities of Russian timber, so that different conditions were then prevailing. In *Hillas & Co.* v *Arcos* the House of Lords said that they had not laid down universal principles of construction in *May and Butcher* v *The King*, and that each case must be decided on the construction of the particular document, while in *Hillas & Co.* v *Arcos* they found that the parties believed they had a contract. In the present case the parties obviously believed they had a contract and they acted for three years as if they had; they had an arbitration clause which relates to the subject-matter of the agreement as to the supply of petrol, and it seems to me that this arbitration clause applies to any failure to agree as to the price. By analogy to the case of a tied house there is to be implied in this contract a term that the petrol shall be supplied at a reasonable price and shall be of reasonable quality. For these reasons I think the Lord Chief Justice was right in holding that there was an effective and enforceable contract, although as to the future no definite price had been agreed with regard to the petrol.

Greer and Maughan LJJ concurred.

1.6 Intention to Create Legal Relations

JONES v *VERNON'S POOLS LTD* [1938] 2 All ER 626 (Liverpool Assizes)

ATKINSON J: The defendant company exists for the purpose of running pools on football matches, and anybody who wants to share in one of these pools must apply for and obtain from the defendants a coupon. He then has to fill in his selections, and post the coupon to the company in time for them, I gather, to receive it on the Saturday morning before the games are played . . .

The plaintiff's case is that on October 1 he sent to the defendants two coupons of his own and one of his wife's, entering for pools which were to apply to the matches to be played on October 2. One coupon sent in, which we have called P1, contained a considerable number of selections, and one feature of that coupon at any rate is that the penny points pool was filled in *in extenso* . . .

The plaintiff says that he also prepared and sent in a coupon which we call P2. The original is not produced, but he produces a copy. The feature of that copy is that it refers to the same penny points pool in respect of which there may be a number of selections on P1, and on this coupon there were 81 different selections. Here, however, it is filled in in the short way, occupying a very small part of the form, and in respect of those selections a sum of 6s. 9d. was owing. Just above the figures in P1, there is a little space in which the person sending in the coupons is told this:

If more than one coupon or sheet is submitted the number for Oct. 2, 1937, must be entered here.

In that space on P1 he filled in the figure 2, because, as he says, he was sending two coupons, and in the list of amounts he added the 6s, 9d. which was owing, or would become owing, in respect of P2, making up altogether a sum of 18s. 9d. He in fact owed in respect of previous coupons the sum of 19s. 9d., but for some reason or other he sent with this coupon the sum of £1 0s. 9d. – a postal order for £1, a postal order for 6d., and 3d. in stamps. The same day, the Thursday, his wife had filled in P3, making her selections, in respect of which the sum of 7s. 9d. was owing. They swear that the three coupons were pinned together, and that the two postal orders were pinned to them, with the 3d. in stamps attached to one of the postal orders, and that these documents were put in one envelope.

As it turned out, the selections on P2 would have met with extraordinary success. In respect of one column, he would have been entitled to £1,785 2s. 3d., in respect of two other columns or lines to £249 13s. 4d., in respect of two other lines £44 11s., in respect of eight lines to £43, and another eight lines £2 8s., amounting in all to £2,137 14s. 7d. Indeed, it would have been an amazingly successful coupon. To his surprise, he heard nothing from the defendants. He wired about it and wrote about it and had interviews about it, but the defendants told him that they could find no trace of P2. They received coupon P1, and they received his postal order, but they said that they had never received the other coupon, and that therefore, to their regret, he could not get division of the funds available.

Being quite certain he had posted this coupon, he brings this action, which, of course, at once raises two questions: (i) the question of fact of whether or not he sent it, and (ii) whether or not, if he did send it, he is entitled to maintain this action.

I am not going to decide the question of whether or not he posted it. I do not think that there is any need to do so. I would have to hear a good deal of evidence from the defendants, and there is no use wasting time deciding that question of fact when, even if I decided that the document was received by the defendants, I would still be satisfied that the plaintiff had no claim . . .

When all is said and done, this coupon is sent in on certain terms which are printed on the back of every coupon, and the plaintiff admits that he knew perfectly well what these rules were, and that he read them, and if anybody can understand them he can. He makes no suggestion that there is anything in those rules which misled him in any way, or that he could not understand them, or that there was anything ambiguous about them, or that he thought they meant anything different from what in fact they do. It seems to me that the purpose of these rules is this. The defendants wish it to be made quite clear that they are conducting these pools on certain clear lines, and they intend to say by these conditions: 'Everybody who comes into these pools must understand that there are no legal obligations either way in connection with these pools. We are going to do our best. Every care will be taken, and we employ accountants, but this money must be sent in on the clearest understanding that this is a gentleman's agreement, an agreement which carries with it no legal obligations on either side, and confers no legal rights.'

That there can be agreements of that kind, recognised by law, is perfectly clear from the case of *Rose & Frank Co.* v *J R Crompton & Brothers Ltd* [1925] AC 445, where a complicated arrangement was made between an American firm and certain English companies relating to the method of doing business together, which was expresed to be a gentlemen's agreement, and to confer no legal rights. Disputes arose on that agreement, but it was held that those words governed the whole agreement. There is nothing unlawful or against the law in having a gentlemen's agreement, and the law would recognise to the full an agreement of that kind.

This purports to be an agreement of that kind, an agreement which is merely to confer rights short of legal rights, rights which cannot be enforced at law. The very first condition is this:

This coupon is an entry form containing the conditions on which it may be completed and submitted to us and on which alone we are prepared to receive and, if we think fit, to accept it as an entry.

In other words, it is making quite clear that these conditions which follow govern the whole relationship between the defendants and anybody sending in coupons. Secondly:

> It is a basic condition of the sending in and the acceptance of this coupon that it is intended and agreed that the conduct of the pools and everything done in connection therewith and all arrangements relating thereto (whether mentioned in these rules or to be implied) and this coupon and any agreement or transaction entered into or payment made by or under it shall not be attended by or give rise to any legal relationship, rights, duties or consequences whatsoever or be legally enforceable or the subject of litigation, but all such arrangements, agreements and transactions are binding in honour only.

That is a clause which seems to me to express in the fullest and clearest way that everything that follows in these rules is subject to that basic or overriding condition that everything that is promised, every statement made with relation to what a person sending the coupon may expect, or may be entitled to, is governed by that clause.

If it means what I think that they intend it to mean, and what certainly everybody who sent a coupon and who took the trouble to read it would understand, it means that they all trusted to the defendants' honour, and to the care they took, and that they fully understood that there should be no claim possible in respect of the transactions.

One can see at once the impossibility of any other basis. I am told that there are a million coupons received every week-end. Just imagine what it would mean if half the people in the country could come forward and suddenly claim that they had posted and sent in a coupon which they never had, bring actions against the pool alleging that, and calling evidence to prove that they had sent in a coupon containing the list of winning teams, and if Vernons had to fight case after case to decide whether or not those coupons had been sent in and received. The business could not be carried on for a day on terms of that kind. It could only be carried on on the basis that everybody is trusting them, and taking the risk themselves of things going wrong. It seems to me that, even if the plaintiff established that this coupon was received, it was received on the basis of these rules, and that he has agreed in the clearest way that, if anything does goes wrong, he is to have no legal claim. In other words, he has agreed that the money which *prima facie* became due to him if that coupon reached them is not to be the subject of an action at law. There is to be no legal liability to pay. He has got to trust to them, and, if something goes wrong, as I say, it is his funeral, and not theirs. I am convinced that that is the position here, and, even if the coupon were received, he has failed to establish that he would have a claim which he could come to the courts to enforce. Therefore I give judgment for the defendants.

1.6.1 FAMILY ARRANGEMENTS

BALFOUR v BALFOUR [1919] 2 KB 571 (CA)

ATKIN LJ: The defence to this action on the alleged contract is that the defendant, the husband, entered into no contract with his wife, and for the determination of that it is necesary to remember that there are agreements between parties which do not result in contracts within the meaning of that term in our law. The ordinary example is where two parties agree to take a walk together, or where there is an offer and an acceptance of hospitality. Nobody would suggest in ordinary circumstances that those agreements result in what we know as a contract, and one of the most usual forms of agreement which does not constitute a contract appears to me to be the arrangements which are made between husband and wife. It is quite common, and it is the natural and inevitable result of the relationship of husband and wife, that the two spouses should make arrangements between themselves – agreements such as are in dispute in this action – agreements for allowances, by which the husband agrees that he will pay to his wife a certain sum of money, per week, or per month, or per year, to cover either her own expenses or the necessary expenses of the household and of the children of the marriage, and in which the wife promises either expressly or impliedly to apply the allowance for the purpose for which it is given. To my mind those agreements, or many of them, do not result in contracts at all, and they do not result in contracts even though there may be what as between other parties would constitute consideration for the agreement. The consideration, as we know, may consist either in some right, interest, profit or benefit accruing to one party, or some forbearance, detriment, loss or responsibility given, suffered or undertaken by the other. That is a well-known definition, and it constantly happens, I think, that such arrangements made between husband and wife are arrangements in which there are mutual promises, or in which there is consideration in form within the definition that I have mentioned. Nevertheless they are not contracts, and they are not contracts because the parties did not intend that they should be attended by legal consequences. To my mind it would be of the worst possible example to hold that agreements such as this resulted in legal obligations which could be enforced in the courts. It would mean this, that when the husband makes his wife a promise to give her an allowance of 30s. or 2l. a week, whatever he can afford to give her, for the maintenance of the household and children, and she promises so to apply it, not only could she sue him for his failure in any week to supply the allowance, but he could sue her for non-performance of the obligation, express or implied, which she had undertaken upon her part. All I can say is that the small courts of this country would have to be multiplied one hundredfold if these arrangements were held to result in legal obligations. They are not sued upon, not because the parties are reluctant to enforce their legal rights when the agreement is broken, but because the parties, in the inception of the arrangement, never intended that they should be sued upon. Agreements such as these are outside the realm of contracts altogether. The common law does not regulate the form of agreements between spouses. Their promises are not sealed with seals and sealing wax. The consideration that really obtains for them is that natural love and affection which counts for so little in these cold courts. The terms may be repudiated, varied or renewed as performance proceeds or as disagreements develop, and the principles of the common law as to exoneration and discharge and accord and satisfaction are such as find no place in the domestic code. The parties themselves are advocates, judges, courts, sheriff's officer and reporter. In respect of these promises each house is a domain into which the King's writ does not seek to run, and to which his officers do not seek to be admitted. The only question in this case is whether or not this promise was of such a class or not. For the reasons given by my brethren it appears to me to be plainly established that the promise here was not intended by either party to be attended by legal consequences. I think the onus was upon the plaintiff, and the plaintiff has not established any contract. The parties were living together, the wife intending to return. The suggestion is that the husband bound himself to pay 30l. a month under all circumstances, and she bound herself to be satisfied with that sum under all circumstances, and, although she was in ill-health and alone in the country, that out of that sum she undertook to defray the whole of the medical expenses that might fall upon her, whatever might be the development of her illness, and in whatever expenses it might involve her. To my mind neither party contemplated such a result. I think that the parol evidence upon which the case turns does not establish a contract. I think that the letters do not evidence such a contract, or amplify the oral evidence which was given by the wife, which is not in dispute. For these reasons I think the judgment of the court below was wrong and that this appeal should be allowed.

Warrington and Duke LJJ concurred.

MERRITT v MERRITT [1970] 2 All ER 760 (CA)

LORD DENNING MR: Husband and wife married as long ago as 1941. After the war in 1949 they got a building plot and built a house. It was a freehold house, no. 133, Clayton Road, Hook, Chessington. It was in the husband's name, with a considerable sum on mortgage with a building society. There they lived and brought up their three children, two daughters, aged now 20 and 17, and a boy now 14. The wife went out to work and contributed to the household expenses.

Early in 1966 they came to an agreement whereby the house was to be put in joint names. That was done. It reflected the legal position when a house is acquired by a husband and wife by financial contributions of each.

But, unfortunately, about that time the husband formed an attachment for another woman. He left the house and went to live with her. The wife then pressed the husband for some arrangement to be made for the future. On May 25 they talked it over in the husband's car. The husband said that he would make the wife a monthly payment of £40 and told her that out of it she would have to make the outstanding payments to the building society. There was only £180 outstanding. He handed over the building society's mortgage book to his wife. She was herself going out to work, earning net £7 10s. a week. Before she left the car she insisted that he put down in writing a further agreement. It forms the subject of the present action. He wrote these words on a piece of paper:

> In consideration of the fact that you will pay all charges in connection with the house at 133 Clayton Road, Chessington, Surrey, until such time as the mortgage repayment has been completed, when the mortgage has been completed, I will agree to transfer the property into your sole ownership.

Signed, John Merritt. May 25, 1966.

The wife took that paper away with her. She did, in fact, over the ensuing months pay off the balance of the mortgage, partly, maybe, out of the money the husband gave her, £40 a month, and partly out of her own earnings. When the mortgage had been paid off, he reduced the £40 a month down to £25 a month.

The wife asked the husband to transfer the house into her sole ownership. He refused to do so. She brought an action in the Chancery Division for a declaration that the house should belong to her and for an order that he should make the conveyance. The judge made the order; but the husband now appeals to this court.

The first point taken on his behalf by Mr Thompson is that the agreement was not intended to have legal relations. It was, he says, a family arrangement such as was considered by the court in *Balfour* v *Balfour* [1919] 2 KB 571 and in *Jones* v *Padavatton* [1969] 1 WLR 328. So the wife could not sue upon it.

I do not think those cases have any application here. The parties there were living together in amity. In such cases their domestic arrangements are ordinarily not intended to create legal relations. It is altogether different when the parties are not living in amity but are separated, or about to separate. They then bargain keenly. They do not rely on honourable understandings. They want everything cut and dried. It may safely be presumed that they intend to create legal relations.

Mr Thompson then relied on the recent case of *Gould* v *Gould* [1970] 1 QB 275, when the parties had separated, and the husband agreed to pay the wife £12 a week 'so long as he could manage it'. The majority of the court thought those words introduced such an element of uncertainty that the agreement was not intended to create legal relations. But for that element of uncertainty, I am sure the majority would have held the agreement to be binding. They did not differ from the general proposition which I stated at p. 280 that:

> when husband and wife, at arm's length, decide to separate, and the husband promises to pay a sum as maintenance to the wife during the separation, the court does, as a rule, impute to them an intention to create legal relations.

In all these cases the court does not try to discover the intention by looking into the minds of the parties. It looks at the situation in which they were placed and asks itself: Would reasonable people regard the agreement as intended to be binding?

Mr Thompson sought to say that this agreement was uncertain because of the arrangement for £40 a month maintenance. That is obviously untenable. Next he said that there was no consideration for the agreement. That point is no good. The wife paid the outstanding amount to the building society. That was ample consideration. It is true that the husband paid her £40 a month which she may have used to pay the building society. But still her act in paying was good consideration.

Mr Thompson took a small point about rates. There was nothing in it. The rates were adjusted fairly between the parties afterwards.

Finally, Mr Thompson said that, under section 17 of the Act of 1882, this house would be owned by husband and wife jointly: and that, even if this house were transferred to the wife, she should hold it on trust for them both jointly. There is nothing in this point either. This paper which the husband signed dealt with the beneficial ownership of the house. It was intended to belong entirely to the wife.

I find myself in entire agreement with the judgment of Stamp J. This appeal should be dismissed.

Widgery and Karminski LJJ concurred.

SIMPKINS v *PAYS* [1955] 3 All ER 10 (Chester Assizes)

SELLERS J: Happily this is an unusual type of case to come before a court of law, and it arises out of what seems to be a popular occupation of the public – competing in a competition in a Sunday newspaper. In this particular case there was a contest, No. 397, in the 'Sunday Empire News' of June 27, 1954, a competition whereby readers were invited to place, in order of merit, eight fashions, or articles of attire. The plaintifff and the defendant, along with the defendant's grand-daughter, sent in a coupon with three forecasts on it. The middle line of the second forecast chanced to be successful, as appeared in the publication of the same newspaper on Sunday, July 4, 1954. This coupon won the prize of £750, being apparently the only coupon containing what was said to be the correct forecast, and this action is brought to recover one-third of that amount, £250.

The plaintiff had been living in the defendant's house from some time in 1950, since some six months after the defendant's husband died. The defendant, who gave evidence here, was a lady of some eighty-three years of age. The plaintiff was much younger. They lived together in harmony, the plaintiff paying a weekly sum for her board and lodging to the defendant. I am satisfied that the plaintiff was greatly interested in betting and in competing, where chance was an element, for some fortuitous prize, and she had been competing for some time in newspaper competitions, including those in the 'News of the World' and the 'Sunday Empire News', before she went to these premises. When she became a lodger at the defendant's premises she found that the defendant was competing in the 'News of the World' competitions, and they seem to have joined forces. At the same time, however, until about the beginning of May, 1954, the plaintiff apparently unbeknown to the defendant, was filling up alone, week by week, a similar sort of competition in the 'Sunday Empire News', which she kept in her room. About the beginning of May, 1954, something happened which brought the two parties to this action to take an interest in the 'Sunday Empire News'. They do not give the same version as to how that came about, and it does not matter very much, except that it may assist one in trying to see where the truth lies. The plaintiff says that she left a copy of the 'Sunday Empire News' in the living room of the house occupied by the defendant and that the defendant took it up, took an interest in it and discussed competing in the competition in the paper. The defendant says that it was the plaintiff who brought the paper down and said: 'Why don't you compete in this as well?' It may be that the truth lies somewhere between the two, but on the whole I think that the plaintiff's version is the preferable one, and that, when the defendant did get to know about the paper and they were discussing it, the plaintiff may have said to her: 'Well, why don't you compete?'

The result of it was that each week for the next seven or eight weeks the two parties to this action, together with the defendant's grand-daughter, Miss Esme Pays, sent in a coupon with forecasts on it. As far as the 'Sunday Empire News' is concerned, I am satisfied that the method of doing this was for the defendant to make her forecast, put it on a piece of paper, for the grand-daughter to make hers and put it on the same piece of paper, and then, when the plaintiff came home, perhaps rather late at night, when the defedant was in bed, the plaintiff would pick this piece of paper up and would fill in the coupon in her own room, putting her own line in first, then putting the grand-daughter's line in second, and the defendant's line in third, and the coupon would be dispatched on the Monday. The evidence is a little uncertain as to who actually paid for the necessary stamps for the postage, or for the twopence-halfpenny stamps which had to be sent for each line forecast. On the final week, the winning week, payment was, I think, made by the plaintiff, but it was not a matter between them of much moment. The amount involved was not very great, and I accept the plaintiff's evidence that the payment was made by each of them more or less alternately, and possibly the defendant paid more frequently. It depended a little on who most frequently had the stamps. There was no hard and fast rule. In regard to the winning coupon, the defendant had asked the plaintiff to get the stamps and deduct the amount from her weekly payment for board and lodging, but, apparently, it was not deducted. The weekly payment was 30s., and, as I understand the defendant, the plaintiff paid 30s. that week. There may have been a little confusion there; I do not think it matters. The entrance money is not a vital matter in this sort of transaction. It might well be done informally, one party paying one time, the other party paying another time. It might be the case that, in fact, all the stamps were bought and paid for by the defendant. The substantial matter was, on what basis were these forecasts being made?

On each of the occasions when the plaintiff made out the coupon during those seven or eight weeks, she put down the forecasts in the way which I have indicated, and entered in the appropriate place on the coupon 'Mrs Pays, 11, Trevor Street, Wrexham', that is to say, the defendant's name and address, as if the coupon had been the defendant's. There were, in fact, three forecasts on each coupon, and I accept the plaintiff's evidence that, when the matter first came to be considered, what was said, when they were going to do it in that way, was: 'We will go shares', or words to that effect. Whether that was said by the plaintiff or by the defendant does not really matter. 'Shares' was the word used, and I do not think anything very much more specific was said. I think that that was the basis of the arrangement; and it may well be that the plaintiff was right when she said in her evidence, that the defendant said: 'You're lucky, May, and if we win we will go shares'.

If my conclusion that there was an arrangement to share any prize money is not correct, the alternative position to that of these three persons competing together as a 'syndicate', as counsel for the plaintiff put it, would mean that the plaintiff, despite her propensity for having a gamble, suddenly abandoned all her interest in the competition in the 'Sunday Empire News' when the defendant became interested, and handed the competition over to the defendant. I think that that is most improbable, and I accept the plaintiff's evidence that she did not do that. She combined her efforts with the defendant's in the way which I have indicated, and from then onwards she had shares in the result. In a family circle – and this household had some element of a family circle about it although there was no relationship between the plaintiff and the defendant and her grand-daughter – or even among very close friends, the facts might indicate that, if anyone rendered a service to an old lady in filling up her coupon, that person also intended to render a service by making some forecasts, and, in such a case, all that the other person was doing was to help the old lady to make her forecasts, and to give her the benefit of the other person's skill or capacity to guess, whichever it is, so that the venture would be entirely that of the person in whose name the coupon was sent. On the facts of this case, and on the probabilities as I see them, I do not think that was what happened here, and I prefer the plaintiff's evidence to that given on behalf of the defendant as to how the arrangement came into being, and how it was carried out.

[His Lordship reviewed the evidence, and continued:] Although the coupon sent in the defendant's name was successful, the competition was not, in fact, won by the forecast of either the plaintiff or the defendant, because the middle line was composed, not by either of the parties, but by the defendant's grand-daughter. The defendant's case involves that, whichever forecast won – whether it was the plaintiff's or the defendant's, or the grand-daughter's – the whole prize was to go to the defendant. I think that that is highly improbable.

On the finding of fact that the plaintiff's evidence is right as to what was said about the shares, learned counsel for the defendant not unnaturally said: 'Even if that is so, the court cannot enforce this contract unless the arrangement made at the time was one which was intended to give rise to legal consequences'. It may well be there are many family associations where some sort of rough and ready statement is made which would not, in a proper estimate of the circumstances, establish a contract which was contemplated to have legal consequences, but I do not so find here. I think that in the present case there was a mutuality in the arrangement between the parties. It was not very formal, but certainly it was, in effect, agreed that every week the forecast should go in in the name of the defendant, and that if there was success, no matter who won, all should share equally. It seems to be the implication from, or the interpretation of, what was said that this was in the nature of a very informal syndicate so that they should all get the benefit of success. It would, also, be wrong, I think, to say from what was arranged that, because the grand-daughter's forecast was the one which was successful of those submitted by the defendant, the plaintiff and the defendant should receive nothing. Although the grand-daughter was not a party before the court and I have not had the benefit of her evidence, on this arrangement she would, in my opinion, be as entitled to a third share as the others, because, although she was not, apparently, present when this bargain was made, both the others knew, at any rate soon after the outset, that she was coming in. It is possible, of course, although the plaintiff is not concerned in this, that the grand-daughter's effort was only to assist the defendant. The grand-daughter may accept that, but it makes no difference to the fact that the plaintiff and the defendant entered into an agreement to share, and, accordingly the plaintiff was entitled to one-third. I so find and give judgment for the amount of £250.

1.7   End of Chapter Assessment Question

Bill is the proprietor of an antiques shop. On Thursday, he placed an advert in the *Antiques Gazette*, For Sale, Mahogany Table circa 1780, English £2,500.' Alan read the advert on Friday and telephoned Bill saying, 'I need such a table for a client, but I can only pay £2,000'. Bill replied that he could not accept less than £2,250, but stated that he would not sell that item to anyone else before Wednesday, while Alan considered the matter.

On Monday, Alan rang Bill, but, Bill had closed his shop to go to an auction. Alan therefore sent a fax message which was received on Bill's fax machine. In the message, Alan agreed to buy the table for £2,250. Later that day, Mary, Bill's cleaner, accidentally dropped the fax message into the waste bin, before Bill had read it.

While at the auction, Bill mentioned the table to another dealer, Tom, who immediately agreed to buy it for £2,500. The next day, Tom happened to meet Alan in the local pub and told Alan of his extraordinary luck in acquiring the table for £2,500. Alan went home and immediately posted a letter to Bill in which he agreed to buy the table for £2,250. That same afternoon, Bill had written to Alan stating that he was no longer willing to sell the table for £2,250.

Advise Alan.

There are a number of issues which require consideration in the question, but on one issue in particular it is necessary to read the judgments of Lords Wilberforce and Fraser in *Brinkibon Ltd* v *Stahag Stahl und Stahlwarenhandels GmbH* [1983] 2 AC 34; [1982] 1 All ER 293; [1982] 2 WLR 164.

1.8   End of Chapter Assessment Outline Answer

It would seem unlikely that Bill's advert in the *Antiques Gazette* is anything other than an invitation to treat (*Partridge* v *Crittenden, Spencer* v *Harding*).
   Alan's telephone offer: 'I need such a table for a client, but I can only pay £2,000' is rejected by Bill's statement that he could not accept less than £2,250.
   Is Bill's statement that he could not accept less than £2,250 an offer or an invitation to treat? The objective test applies. Is it an expression of willingness to contract accompanied by a statement of the contractual terms (offer) or a mere statement of the minimum price he would be prepared to consider (an invitation to treat?) *Harvey* v *Facey* – 'Lowest price for Bumper Hall Pen, £900' suggests invitation to treat, but the present case involves a table not land, and a statement by Bill that he would not sell the item to anyone else before Wednesday. *Harvey* v *Facey* might be distinguished, and Bill's statement treated as an offer.
   If Bill's statement were to be an offer Bill is not legally bound by his promise not to sell to anyone else before Wednesday since Alan has given no consideration in return for such promise (*Routledge* v *Grant*). Hence, the offer can be withdrawn at any time before acceptance.
   Alan's fax message would seem to be a reasonable means of purported acceptance, bearing in mind that the telephone has proved to be fruitless. Assuming the fax to be the equivalent of a teleprinter *Brinkibon Ltd* v *Stahag Stahl GmbH* decides that such acceptance is effective *where* it reaches the offeror, but it does not decide precisely when. This issue is considered *obiter* by Lords Wilberforce and Fraser in *Brinkibon*:

LORD WILBERFORCE: The message may not reach, or be intended to reach, the designated recipient immediately: messages may be sent out of office hours, or at night, with the intention, or on the assumption that they will be read at a later time. There may be some error or default at the recipient's end which prevents receipt at the time contemplated and believed in by the sender . . . No universal rule can cover all such cases; they must be resolved by reference to the intentions of the parties, by sound business practice and in some cases by a judgment where the risks should lie.

LORD FRASER: (no doubt assuming the message to have been sent during normal business hours): . . . once the message has been received on the offeror's telex machine, it is not unreasonable to treat it as delivered to the principal offeror, because it is his responsibility to arrange for prompt handling of messages within his own office.

Dependent upon circumstances, and which of the *obiter* were to apply, acceptance might be effective when received on Bill's fax machine or not at all since Bill never read it.

If acceptance is communicated when received on Bill's fax machine, Alan may sue Bill for breach of contract. If not, Bill may revoke his offer at any time before any later purported acceptance by Alan. An offer may be revoked at any time prior to acceptance provided that revocation is communicated to the offeree either by the offeror or by a reliable third party (*Dickinson* v *Dodds*); revocation may be express or implied, as in *Dickinson* v *Dodds*, where the house was sold to a third party. Hence, Bill's sale of the table to Tom for £2,500 constitutes implied revocation which is communicated to Alan in the local pub, provided that Tom is a reliable source. If Tom is not a reliable source the revocation is ineffective.

If so, then if post is a reasonable means of acceptance, which it may or may not be, Alan's letter of acceptance will be effective upon posting under the postal acceptance rule (*Adams* v *Lindsell*). If the postal acceptance rule does not apply Bill's letter of revocation will be effective provided that it reaches Alan before Alan's letter of acceptance reaches Bill.

CHAPTER TWO

CONSIDERATION AND PRIVITY OF CONTRACT

2.1 Consideration

2.1.1 EXECUTORY, EXECUTED AND PAST CONSIDERATION

See *CARLILL* v *CARBOLIC SMOKE BALL CO.* above, 1.2.1

RE McARDLE [1951] Ch 669 (CA)

Payment was sought and promised after work had been completed.

William Edward McArdle by his will dated August 16, 1933, appointed the National Provincial Bank Ltd to be his executor and trustee and directed them to hold his residuary estate, subject to the prior life interest in it of his wife Holly McArdle, upon trust for all his children who should attain twenty-one. The testator died on February 8, 1935. He was survived by four sons and a daughter, who all attained the age of twenty-one years.

In 1943 one of the sons, Montague Terence McArdle, known as Monty McArdle, was livng with his wife Marjorie McArdle in a bungalow called Gravel Hill at Wimborne, which formed part of the testator's residuary estate. Monty McArdle and his wife executed certain works of improvement and repair to this property, the cost of which, amounting to 488*l*, was paid by Mrs Marjorie McArdle. The improvements and repairs were substantially completed by Christmas, 1943, and were finally completed in 1944.

In April, 1945, Monty McArdle presented to each of his three brothers and his sister a document which he and they signed in the following terms: 'To Mrs Marjorie McArdle, Gravel Hill, Wimborne. In consideration of your carrying out certain alterations and improvements to the property known as Gravel Hill Poultry Farm, Wimborne, at present occupied by you, We the beneficiaries under the Will of William Edward McArdle Hereby agree that the Executors, the N. P. Bank Limited of No. 1 Princes Street, London, E.C.2, shall repay to you from the said estate when so distributed the sum of 488*l*. in settlement of the amount spent on such improvements. Dated April 30, 1945.'

Mrs Holly McArdle died in 1948, and in 1950 Mrs Monty McArdle requested the National Provincial Bank Ltd to pay to her the 488*l*. in accordance with the document of 1945. The testator's children, other than Monty McArdle, having refused to agree to the payment, the bank paid 488*l*. into court under s. 63 of the Trustee Act 1925.

By this summons Mrs Marjorie McArdle asked for payment out to herself of the sum of 488*l*., the defendants to the summons being the testator's children, other than Monty McArdle.

JENKINS LJ: . . . The document which is said to operate as an equitable assignment is the document of April 30, 1945, signed by the five children of the testator. That document on the face of it purports to be an agreement for valuable consideration under which, when Mrs Marjorie McArdle has carried out certain alterations and improvements to the property known as Gravel Hill Poultry Farm, in consideraton of her so doing, the five children agree that she is to be paid a sum of 488*l*., representing the cost of the work, out of the testator's estate when distributed. That is what it purports to be; and I think, notwithstandng the argument to the contrary, that it is really perfectly plain, so far as the construction of the document is concerned, that what it contemplates is the doing by Mrs Marjorie McArdle of work yet to be done; and her doing that work is to form the consideraton by virtue of which she is to be entitled to receive 488*l*. out of the estate.

That is what the document is, and if the document had correctly represented the facts, for my part I have no doubt that it would have operated as a valid equitable assignment of 488*l*., subject to Mrs Marjorie McArdle's performing her part of the bargain by providing the consideration she had contracted to provide in the form of doing the work. There might have been room for difficulty, and for argument, whether the work had been properly done or not, but those matters could have been resolved one way or the other, if necessary by an action; and ultimately, if Mrs McArdle showed that she had done the work contracted for, her title to the 488*l*. would have been complete and, the agreement being for valuable consideration, it would not have mattered that further steps had to be taken in order to perfect her title.

But the true position was that, as the work had in fact all been done and nothing remained to be done by Mrs Marjorie McArdle at all, the consideration was a wholly past consideration, and, therefore, the beneficiaries' agreement for the repayment to her of the 488*l*. out of the estate was nudum pactum, a promise with no consideraton to support it. That being so, it is impossible for her to rely upon this document as constituting an equitable assignment for valuable consideraton.

Lord Evershed MR, and Hodson LJ concurred.

RE CASEY'S PATENTS [1892] 1 Ch 104 (CA)

BOWEN LJ: . . . The document is one by which the signatories agree with Mr Casey to give him 'one-third share of the patents above mentioned, the same to take effect from this date'. It cannot be denied that that is an equitable assignment if it is anything. It is not an agreement to take effect at some future date. It is an agreement to give him the share as from the date of the document, and it immediately passes in Equity the right to the third share.

But then it was said by Mr Daniel, 'But there is no consideration, and this document is not under seal'. We will see if there is consideraton. The consideration is stated, such as it is. It is, 'in consideration of your services as the practical manager in working our patents as above for transit by steamer'. Then says Mr Daniel, 'Yes, but that is a future consideration, and a future consideration, if nothing were done under it or nothing was proved to be done, would fail'. The answer to that is that the consideration is not the rendering of the services, as is plain from the fact that the document is to take effect in Equity from the date. The consideraton must be something other than rendering services in the future. It is the promise to render them which those words imply, that constitutes the consideration; and the promise to render future services, if an effectual promise, is certainly good consideration. Then, driven from that, Mr Daniel said, 'Oh! but it is past services that it means, and past services are not a consideraton for anything'. Well, that raises the old question – or might raise it, if there was not an answer to it – of *Lampleigh* v *Braithwait* (1615) Hob 105, a subject of great interest to every scientific lawyer, as to whether a past service will support a promise. I do not propose to discuss that question, or, perhaps, I should not have finished this week. I should have to examine the whole state of the law as to, and the history of the subject of, consideraton, which, I need hardly say, I do not propose to do. But the answer to Mr Daniel's point is clear. Even if it were true, as some scientific students of law believe, that a past service cannot support a future promise, you must look at the document and see if the promise cannot receive a proper effect in some other way. Now, the fact of a past service raises an implicaton that at the time it was rendered it was to be paid for, and, if it was a service which was to be paid for, when you get in the subsequent document a promise to pay, that promise may be treated either as an admission which evidences or as a positive bargain which fixes the amount of that reasonable remuneration on the faith of which the service was originally rendered. So that here for past services there is ample justification for the promise to give the third share. Therefore, this is an equitable assignment which cannot be impeached.

Fry LJ, and Lindley LJ concurred.

2.1.2 SUFFICIENCY OF CONSIDERATION

CHAPPELL & CO. v NESTLÉ CO. LTD [1959] 2 All ER 701 (HL)

The appellants offered a record to members of the public who sent in three chocolate wrappers, plus 1s. 6d.

LORD REID: . . . I can now turn to what appears to me to be the crucial question in this case: was the 1s. 6d. an 'ordinary retail selling price' within the meaning of s. 8? That involves two questions, what was the nature of the contract between the respondents Nestlé and a person who sent 1s. 6d. plus three wrappers in acceptance of their offer, and what is meant by 'ordinary retail selling price' in this context. To determine the nature of the contract, one must find the intention of the parties as shown by what they said and did. The respondents Nestlé's intention can hardly be in any doubt. They were not setting out to trade in gramophone records. They were using these records to increase their sales of chocolate. Their offer was addressed to everyone. It might be accepted by a person who was already a regular buyer of their chocolate; but, much more important to them, it might be accepted by people who might become regular buyers of their chocolate if they could be induced to try it and found they liked it. The inducement was something calculated to look like a bargain, a record at a very cheap price. It is in evidence that the ordinary price for a dance record is 6s. 6d. It is true that the ordinary record gives much longer playing time than Nestlé's records and it may have other advantages. But the reader of the respondents Nestlé's offer was not in a position to know that. It seems to me clear that the main intention of the offer was to induce people interested in this kind of music to buy (or, perhaps, get others to buy) chocolate which otherwise would not have been bought. It is, of course, true that some wrappers might come from chocolate which had already been bought, or from chocolate which would have been bought without the offer, but that does not seem to me to alter the case. Where there is a large number of transactions – the notice mentions 30,000 records – I do not think we should simply consider an isolated case where it would be impossible to say whether there had been a direct benefit from the acquisition of the wrappers or not. The requirement that wrappers should be sent was of great importance to the respondents Nestlé; there would have been no point in their simply offering records for 1s. 6d. each. It seems to me quite unrealistic to divorce the buying of the chocolate from the supplying of the records. It is a perfectly good contract if a person accepts an offer to supply goods if he (a) does something of value to the supplier and (b) pays money; the consideration is both (a) and (b). There may have been cases where the acquisition of the wrappers conferred no direct benefit on the respondents Nestlé but there must have been many cases where it did. I do not see why the possibility that, in some cases, the acquisition of the wrappers did not directly benefit the respondents Nestlé should require us to exclude from consideration the cases where it did; and even where there was no direct benefit from the acquisition of the wrappers there may have been an indirect benefit by way of advertisement.

Lord Tucker and Lord Somervell concurred; Viscount Simonds and Lord Keith dissented.

2.1.2.1 Performance of existing duty imposed by law

GLASBROOK BROS LTD v GLAMORGAN COUNTY COUNCIL [1925] AC 270 (HL)

Could the police authority claim payment for the provision of police services during a strike?

VISCOUNT FINLAY: My Lords, the appellants are the owners of collieries on the Garngoch Common in the county of Glamorgan. In 1921 there was a national coal strike which began on April 1 and lasted till July 4, at which date work was generally resumed. The men at the appellants' collieries were, however, dissatisfied with the terms of settlement and refused to resume work. In these collieries over 1,000 men had been employed, and they remained idle until September 4, 1921. The 'safety men', as they are called, who were engaged in working the pumps on which the preservation of the mine from flooding depended, remained at work. If the working of the pumps had been stopped the mine in the course of a few days would have been most seriously damaged by the accumulation of water. The strikers endeavoured to get these 'safety men' to join in the strike, the effect of which would have been that in three or four days the mine would have been drowned out. Under these circumstances the agent of the owners, Mr Alfred James, went to the Gowerton Police Station to arrange with the superintendent, Colonel Smith, for police protection. He asked that an adequate force of police should be billeted in the houses in the immediate vicinity of the collieries. Colonel Smith thought that protection would be best afforded by a flying column moving from point to point as required, but Mr Alfred James insisted that a 'garrison' near the mines should be provided, and Colonel Smith acquiesced. Mr James in his evidence described what ensued as follows:

Q. Did he then tell you something about a form?
A. Yes.
Q. What did he say exactly about the form?
A. As near as I remember he said: 'You will of course have to sign a form of requisition'. I said: 'Yes – that is the usual procedure in matters of this description' – and he told me it was, so I said: 'All right, I will sign the form'.

The form was accordingly signed. It is headed: 'Form of Requisition for Special Services of Police'. It stated that certain men, seventy in all, were required for special duty at the Garngoch and Cape Collieries on the occasion of a strike from 6 p.m. on July 9. The form concluded 'I hereby guarantee payment on the conditions specified in Clause "C" in the Second Schedule to this form'.

This was signed by Mr James and addressed to the chief constable. The schedule stated the terms as to payment, accommodation and food.

The seventy men arrived on the evening of the same day. The safety men remained at work, and it was admitted at the trial that police protection in some shape or form was required. No pressure was put upon Mr James to sign the requisition; as his evidence shows, he was prepared to sign it and he knew that it was usual in such cases.

The action in this case was brought to recover the amount due on the terms of the requisition.

The colliery owners repudiated liability on the grounds that there was no consideration for the promise to pay for the police protection and that such an agreement was against public policy. The case was tried by Bailhache J and he entered judgment for the plaintiffs saying: 'There is an obligation on the police to afford efficient protection, but if an individual asks for special protection in a particular form, for the special protection so asked for in that particular form, the individual must pay.'

This decision was affirmed by a majority on the appeal (Banks and Scrutton LJJ; Atkin LJ dissenting). The colliery owners now appeal and ask that judgment should be entered for them.

It appears to me that there is nothing in the first point made for the colliery owners that there was no consideraton for the promise. It is clear that there was abundant consideration. The police authorities thought that it would be best to give protection by means of a flying column of police, but the colliery owners wanted the 'garrison' and promised to pay for it if it was sent . . .

VISCOUNT CAVE LC: . . . I conclude, therefore, that the practice of lending constables for special duty in consideraton of payment is not illegal or against public policy; and I pass to the second question – namely, whether in this particular case the lending of the seventy constables to be billeted in the appellants' colliery was a legitimate application of the principle. In this connection I think it important to bear in mind exactly what it was that the learned trial judge had to decide. It was no part of his duty to say – nor did he purport to say – whether in his judgment the billeting of the seventy men at the colliery was necessary for the prevention of violence or the protection of the mines from criminal injury. The duty of determining such questions is cast by law, not upon the courts after the event, but upon the police authorities at the time when the decision has to be taken; and a court which attempted to review such a decision from the point of view of its wisdom or prudence would (I think) be exceedng its proper functions. The question for the court was whether on July 9, 1921, the police authorities, acting reasonably and in good faith, considered a police garrison at the colliery necessary for the protection of life and property from violence, or, in other words, whether the decision of the chief constable in refusing special protection unless paid for was such a decision as a man in his position and with his duties could reasonably take. If in the judgment of the police authorities, formed reasonably and in good faith, the garrison was necessary for the protection of life and property, then they were not entitled to make a charge for it, for that would be to exact payment for the performance of a duty which they clearly owed to the appellants and their servants; but if they thought the garrison a superfluity and only acceded to Mr James' request with a view to meeting his wishes, then in my opinion they were entitled to treat the garrison duty as a special duty and to charge for it. Now, upon this point the Divisional Superintendent Colonel Smith, who was a highly experienced officer, gave specific and detailed evidence; and the learned judge having seen him in the witness box and heard his examination and cross-examination accepted his evidence upon the point, as the following extract from the judgment shows:

> Colonel Smith says that if the matter had been left entirely to him without this requisition, he would have protected this colliery, and he would have protected it amply, but in quite a different way, and I accept his evidence that that is so. He would not have sent his garrison there, and in my judgment, while not desiring for a moment to suggest that it was not the bounden duty of the county council to protect this colliery, and not for one moment suggesting that the performing of a legal duty will support a promise to pay, I have come to the conclusion that when a colliery company or an individual requisitions police protection of a special character for a particular purpose, he must pay for it, and he must pay for it whether he makes a contract to pay or whether he does not – a promise to pay would be implied under those circumstances. In this case, of course, there is an express promise, and in my judgment this promise is not without consideration and must be fulfilled.

Upon this point Sir John Simon in his powerful argument for the appellants contended that the true inference to be drawn from the evidence was that the police authority, having a discretion to elect between protecting the collieries (which admittedly required protection in some form) by means of the 'mobile body' to which Colonel Smith referred or by means of a garrison, chose the latter alternative in consideration of payment, and that they could not so (as he put it) 'sell their discretion'. Upon the evidence, I do not think that they did anything of the kind. Colonel Smith said clearly that the police garrison was no part of his scheme of protection and did not help him in his scheme at all; that he had an ample force by which to protect the collieries from outside and was well able to cope with the situaton. It does not appear that the provision of the garrison, who were brought in from distant parts of the county, relieved the force on the spot from any of their duties, or that the local force was reduced in consequence; and I think that the true inference is that the garrison formed an additional and not a substituted or alternative means of protection.

Lord Shaw concurred; Lord Carson and Lord Blanesburgh dissented.

2.1.2.2 Performance of existing contractual duty

STILK v *MYRICK* (1809) 2 Camp 317 (Campbell's Report)

Sailors had been promised extra payments for working the ship 'short-handed'.

LORD ELLENBOROUGH: I think *Harris v Watson* (1791) Peake 102 was rightly decided; but I doubt whether ground of public policy, upon which Lord Kenyon is stated to have proceeded, be the true principle on which the decision is to be supported. Here, I say, the agreement is void for want of consideration. There was no consideraton for the ulterior pay promised to the mariners who remained with the ship. Before they sailed from London they had undertaken to do all that they could under all the emergencies of the voyage. They had sold all their services till the voyage should be completed. If they had been at liberty to quit the vessel at Cronstadt, the case would have been quite different; or if the captain had capriciously discharged the two men who were wanting, the others might not have been compellable to take the whole duty on themselves, and their agreeing to do so might have been a sufficient consideraton for the promise of an advance of wages. But the desertion of a part of the crew is to be considered an emergency of the voyage as much as their death; and those who remain are bound by the terms of their original contract to exert themselves to the utmost to bring the ship in safety to her destined port. Therefore, without looking to the policy of this agreement, I think it is void for want of consideration, and that the plaintiff can only recover at the rate of £5 a month.

Verdict accordingly.

WILLIAMS v ROFFEY BROS & NICHOLLS (CONTRACTORS) LTD
[1990] 1 All ER 512 (CA)

GLIDEWELL LJ (giving the first judgment at the invitation of Purchas LJ): This is an appeal against the decision of Mr Rupert Jackson QC sitting as an assistant recorder given on 31 January 1989 in the Kingston-upon-Thames County Court, entering judgment for the plaintiff for £3,500 damages with £1,400 interest and costs and dismissing the defendants' counterclaim.

The facts

The plaintiff is a carpenter. The defendants are building contractors who in September 1985 had entered into a contract with Shepherd's Bush Housing Association Ltd to refurbish a block of flats called Twynholm Mansions, Lillie Road, London SW6. The defendants were the main contractors for the works. There are 28 flats in Twynholm Mansions, but the work of refurbishment was to be carried out in 27 of the flats.

The defendants engaged the plaintiff to carry out the carpentry work in the refurbishment of the 27 flats, including work to the structure of the roof. Originally, the plaintiff was engaged on three separate sub-contracts, but these were all superseded by a sub-contract in writing made on 21 January 1986 by which the plaintiff undertook to provide the labour for the carpentry work to the roof of the block and for the first and second fix carpentry work required in each of the 27 flats for a total price of £20,000.

The judge found that, though there was no express term providing for payment to be made in stages, the contract of 21 January 1986 was subject to an implied term that the defendants would make interim payments to the plaintiff, related to the amount of work done, at reasonable intervals.

The plaintiff and his men began work on 10 October 1985. The judge found that by 9 April 1986 the plaintiff had completed the work to the roof, had carried out the first fix to all 27 flats and had substantially completed the second fix to 9 flats. By this date the defendants had made interim payments totalling £16,200.

It is common ground that by the end of March 1986 the plaintiff was in financial difficulty. The judge found that there were two reasons for this, namely: (i) that the agreed price of £20,000 was too low to enable the plaintiff to operate satisfactorily and at a profit. Mr Cottrell, a surveyor employed by the defendants, said in evidence that a reasonable price for the works would have been £23,783; (ii) that the plaintiff failed to supervise his workmen adequately.

The defendants, as they made clear, were concerned lest the plaintiff did not complete the carpentry work on time. The main contract contained a penalty clause. The judge found that on 9 April 1986 the defendants promised to pay the plaintiff the further sum of £10,300, in addition to the £20,000, to be paid at the rate of £575 for each flat in which the carpentry work was completed.

The plaintiff and his men continued work on the flats until the end of May 1986. By that date the defendants, after their promise on 9 April 1986, had made only one further payment of £1,500. At the end of May the plaintiff ceased work on the flats. I will describe later the work which, according to the judge's findings, then remained to be done. Suffice it to say that the defendants engaged other carpenters to complete the work, but in the result incurred one week's time penalty in their contract with the building owners.

The action

The plaintiff commenced this action by specially endorsed writ on 10 March 1987. He originally claimed the sum of £32,708.70. In a reamended statement of claim served on 3 March 1988 his claim was reduced to £10,847.07. It was, I think, at about this time that the matter was transferred to the county court.

. . .

The judge's conclusions

The judge found that the defendants' promise to pay an additional £10,300, at the rate of £575 per completed flat, was part of an oral agreement made between the plaintiff and the defendants on 9 April 1986, by way of variation to the original contract.

The judge also found that before the plaintiff ceased work at the end of May 1986 the carpentry in 17 flats had been substantially (but not totally) completed. This means that between the making of the agreement on 9 April 1986 and the date when the plaintiff ceased work, eight further flats were substantially completed.

The judge calculated that this entitled the plaintiff to receive £4,600 (8 x £575) 'less some small deduction for defective and incomplete items'. He held that the plaintiff was also entitled to a reasonable proportion of the £2,200 which was outstanding from the original contract sum. (I believe this figure should be £2,300, but this makes no practical difference.) Adding these two amounts, he decided that the plaintiff was entitled to further payments totalling £5,000 against which he had only received £1,500, and that the defendants were therefore in breach of contract, entitling the plaintiff to cease work.

The issues

Before us counsel for the defendants advances two arguments. His principal submission is that the defendants' admitted promise to pay an additional £10,300, at the rate of £575 per completed flat, is unenforceable since there was no consideration for it. This issue was not raised in the defence, but we are told that the argument was advanced at the trial without objection, and that there was equally no objection to it being argued before us. . . .

Was there consideration for the defendants' promise made on 9 April 1986 to pay an additional price at the rate of £575 per completed flat?

The judge made the following findings of fact which are relevant on this issue. (i) The sub-contract price agreed was too low to enable the plaintiff to operate satisfactorily and at a profit. Mr Cottrell, the defendants' surveyor, agreed that this was so. (ii) Mr Roffey, the managing director of the defendants, was persuaded by Mr Cottrell that the defendants should pay a bonus to the plaintiff. The figure agreed at the meeting on 9 April 1986 was £10,300.

The judge quoted and accepted the evidence of Mr Cottrell to the effect that a main contractor who agrees too low a price with a sub-contractor is acting contrary to his own interests. He will never get the job finished without paying more money.

The judge therefore concluded:

> In my view where the original sub-contract price is too low, and the parties subsequently agree that the additional moneys shall be paid to the sub-contractor, this agreement is in the interests of both parties. This is what happened in the present case, and in my opinion the agreement of 9 April 1986 does not fail for lack of consideraton.

In his address to us counsel for the defendants outlined the benefits to the defendants which arose from their agreement to pay the additional £10,300 as (i) seeking to ensure that the plaintiff continued work and did not stop in breach of the sub-contract, (ii) avoiding the penalty for delay and (iii) avoiding the trouble and expense of engaging other people to complete the carpentry work.

However, counsel submits that, though the defendants may have derived, or hoped to derive, practical benefits from their agreement to pay the 'bonus', they derived no benefit in law, since the plaintiff was promising to do no more than he was already bound to do by his sub-contract, ie continue with the carpentry work and complete it on time. Thus there was no consideraton for the agreement.

Counsel for the defendants relies on the principle of law which, traditionally, is based on the decision in *Stilk* v *Myrick* (1809) 2 Camp 317, 170 ER 1168. That was a decision at first instance of Lord Ellenborough CJ. On a voyage to the Baltic, two seamen deserted. The captain agreed with the rest of the crew that if they worked the ship back to London without the two seamen being replaced, he would divide between them the pay which would have been due to the two deserters. On arrival at London this extra pay was refused, and the plaintiff's action to recover his extra pay was dismissed. Counsel for the defendant argued that such an agreement was contrary to public policy, but Lord Ellenborough CJ's judgment (as reported in Campbell's Reports) was based on lack of consideration . . .

In *North Ocean Shipping Co. Ltd* v *Hyundai Construction Co. Ltd, The Atlantic Baron* [1978] 3 All ER 1170, [1979] QB 705 Mocatta J regarded the general principle of the decision in *Stilk* v *Myrick* as still being good law. He referred to two earlier decisions of this court, dealing with wholly different subjects, in which Denning LJ sought to escape from the confines of the rule, but was not accompanied in this attempt by the other members of the court.

In *Ward* v *Byham* [1956] 2 All ER 318, [1956] 1 WLR 496 the plaintiff and the defendant lived together unmarried for five years, during which time the plaintiff bore their child. After the parties ended their relationship, the defendant promised to pay the plaintiff £1 per week to maintain the child, provided that she was well looked after and happy. The defendant paid this sum for some months, but ceased to pay when the plaintiff married another man. On her suing for the amount due at £1 per week, he pleaded that there was no consideration for his agreement to pay for the plaintiff to maintain her child, since she was obliged by law to do so: see s. 42 of the National Assistance Act 1948. The county court judge upheld the plaintiff mother's claim, and this court dismissed the defendant's appeal.

Denning LJ said ([1956] 2 All ER 318 at 319, [1956] 1 WLR 496 at 498):

I approach the case, therefore, on the footing that, in looking after the child, the mother is only doing what she is legally bound to do. Even so, I think that there was sufficient consideration to support the promise. I have always thought that a promise to perform an existing duty, or the performance of it, should be regarded as good consideration, because it is a benefit to the person to whom it is given. Take this very case. It is as much a benefit for the father to have the child looked after by the mother as by a neighbour. If he gets the benefit for which he stipulated, he ought to honour his promise, and he ought not to avoid it by saying that the mother was herself under a duty to maintain the child. I regard the father's promise in this case as what is sometimes called a unilateral contract, a promise in return for an act, a promise by the father to pay £1 a week in return for the mother's looking after the child. Once the mother embarked on the task of looking after the child, there was a binding contract. So long as she looked after the child, she would be entitled to £1 a week. The case seems to me to be within the decision of *Hicks* v *Gregory* ((1849) 8 CB 378, 137 ER 556) on which the judge relied. I would dismiss the appeal.

However, Morris LJ put it rather differently. He said ([1956] 2 All ER 318 at 320, [1956] 1 WLR 496 at 498–499):

Counsel for the father submits that there was a duty on the mother to support the child, that no affiliation proceedings were in prospect or were contemplated, and that the effect of the arrangement that followed the letter was that the father was merely agreeing to pay a bounty to the mother. It seems to me that the terms of the letter negative those submissions, for the father says: 'providing you can prove that [the child] will be well looked after and happy and also that she is allowed to decide for herself whether or not she wishes to come and live with you'. The father goes on to say that the child is then well and happy and looking much stronger than ever before. 'If you decide what to do let me know as soon as possible'. It seems to me, therefore, that the father was saying, in effect: Irrespective of what may be the strict legal position, what I am asking is that you shall prove that the child will be well looked after and happy, and also that you must agree that the child is to be allowed to decide for herself whether or not she wishes to come and live with you. If those conditions were fulfilled the father was agreeable to pay. On those terms, which in fact became operative, the father agreed to pay £1 a week. In my judgment, there was ample consideration there to be found for his promise, which I think was binding.

Parker LJ agreed. As I read the judgment of Morris LJ, he and Parker LJ held that, though in maintaining the child the plaintiff was doing no more than she was obliged to do by law, nevertheless her promise that the child would be well looked after and happy was a practical benefit to the father, which amounted to consideration for his promise.

In *Williams* v *Williams* [1957] 1 All ER 305, [1957] 1 WLR 148, a wife left her husband, and he promised to make her a weekly payment for her maintenance. On his failing to honour his promise, the wife claimed the arrears of payment, but her husband pleaded that, since the wife was guilty of desertion she was bound to maintain herself, and thus there was no consideration for his promise. Denning LJ reiterated his view that –

a promise to perform an existing duty is, I think, sufficient consideration to support a promise, so long as there is nothing in the transaction which is contrary to the public interest.

(See [1957] 1 All ER 305 at 307, [1957] 1 WLR 148 at 151.)

However, the other members of the court (Hodson and Morris LJJ) declined to agree with this expression of view, though agreeing with Denning LJ in finding that there was consideration because the wife's desertion might not have been permanent and thus there was a benefit to the husband. . . . There is, however, another legal concept of relatively recent development which is relevant, namely that of economic duress. Clearly, if a sub-contractor has agreed to undertake work at a fixed price, and before he has completed the work declines to continue with it unless the contractor agrees to pay an increased price, the sub-contractor may be held guilty of securing the contractor's promise by taking unfair advantage of the difficulties he will cause if he does not complete the work. In such a case an agreement to pay an increased price may well be voidable because it was entered into under duress. Thus this concept may provide another answer in law to the question of policy which has troubled the courts since before *Stilk* v *Myrick* (1809) 2 Camp 317, 170 ER 1168, and no doubt led at the date of that decision to a rigid adherence to the doctrine of consideration.

This possible application of the concept of economic duress was referred to by Lord Scarman, delivering the judgment of the Judicial Committee of the Privy Council in *Pao On* v *Lau Yiu* [1979] 3 All ER 65 at 76, [1980] AC 614 at 632. He said:

Their Lordships do not doubt that a promise to perform, or the performance of, a pre-existing contractual obligation to a third party can be valid consideration. In *New Zealand Shipping Co. Ltd* v *A M Satterthwaite & Co. Ltd* [1974] 1 All ER 1015 at 1021, [1975] AC 154 at 168 the rule and the reason for the rule were stated as follows: 'An agreement to do an act which the promisor is under an existing obligation to a third party to do, may quite well amount to valid consideration: . . . the promisee obtains the benefit of a direct obligation . . . This proposition is illustrated and supported by *Scotson* v *Pegg* (1861) 6 H & N 295, 158 ER 121 which their Lordships consider to be good law.' Unless, therefore, the guarantee was void as having been made for an illegal consideration or voidable on the ground of economic duress, the extrinsic evidence establishes that it was supported by valid consideration. Counsel for the defendants submits that the consideration is illegal as being against public policy. He submits that to secure a party's promise by a threat of repudiation of a pre-existing contractual obligation owed to another can be, and in the circumstances of this case was, an abuse of a dominant bargaining position and so contrary to public policy . . . This submission found favour with the majority in the Court of Appeal. Their Lordships, however, consider it misconceived.

Lord Scarman then referred to *Stilk* v *Myrick* and its predecessor *Harris* v *Watson* (1791) Peake 102, [1775–1802] All ER Rep 493 and to *Williams* v *Williams*, before turning to the development of this branch of the law in the United States of America. He then said [1979] 3 All ER 65 at 77–78, [1980] AC 614 at 634–635):

Their Lordships' knowledge of this developing branch of American law is necessarily limited. In their judgment it would be carrying audacity to the point of foolhardiness for them to attempt to extract from the American case law a principle to provide an answer to the question now under consideration. That question, their Lordships repeat, is whether, in a case where duress is not established, public policy may nevertheless invalidate the consideration if there has been a threat to repudiate a pre-existing contractual obligation or an unfair use of a dominating bargaining position. Their Lordships' conclusion is that where businessmen are negotiating at arm's length it is unnecessary for the achievement of justice, and unhelpful in the development of the law, to invoke such a rule of public policy. It would also create unacceptable anomaly. It is unnecessary because justice requires that men, who have negotiated at arm's length, be held to their bargains unless it can be shown that their consent was vitiated by fraud, mistake or duress. If a promise is induced by coercion of a man's will, the doctrine of duress suffices to do justice. The party coerced, if he chooses and acts in time, can avoid the contract. If there is no coercion, there can be no reason for avoiding the contract where there is shown to be a real consideration which is otherwise legal. Such a rule of public policy as is now being considered would be unhelpful because it would render the law uncertain. It would become a question of fact and degree to determine in each case whether there had been, short of duress, an unfair use of a strong bargaining position. It would create anomaly because, if public policy invalidates the consideration, the effect is to make the contract void. But unless the facts are such as to support a plea of non est factum, which is not suggested in this case, duress does no more than confer on the victim the opportunity, if taken in time, to avoid the contract. It would be strange if conduct less than duress could render a contract void, whereas duress does no more than render a contract voidable. Indeed, it is the [defendants'] case in this appeal that such an anomaly is the correct result. Their case is that the [plaintiffs], having lost by cancellation the safeguard of the subsidiary agreement are without the safeguard of the guarantee because its consideration is contrary to public policy, and that they are debarred from restoration to their position under the subsidiary agreement because the guarantee is void, not voidable. The logical consequence of counsel's submission for the defendant is that the safeguard which all were at all times agreed the [plaintiffs] should have (the safeguard against fall in value of the shares) has been lost by the application of a rule of public policy. The law is not, in their Lordships' judgment, reduced to countenancing such stark injustice: nor is it necessary, when one bears in mind the protection offered otherwise by the law to one who contracts in ignorance of what he is doing or under duress. Accordingly, the submission that the additional consideration established by the extrinsic evidence is invalid on the ground of public policy is rejected.

It is true that *Pao On* v *Lau Yiu* is a case of a tripartite relationship, ie a promise by A to perform a pre-existing contractual obligation owed to B, in return for a promise of payment by C. But Lord Scarman's words seem to me to be of general application, equally applicable to a promise made by one of the original two parties to a contract.

Accordingly, following the view of the majority in *Ward* v *Byham* and of the whole court in *Williams* v *Williams* and that of the Privy Council in *Pao On* v *Lau Yiu* the present state of the law on this subject can be expressed in the following proposition: (i) if A has entered into a contract with B to do work for, or to supply goods or services to, B in return of payment by B and (ii) at some stage before A has completely performed his obligations under the contract B has reason to doubt whether A will, or will be able to, complete his side of the bargain and (iii) B thereupon promises A an additional payment in return for A's promise to perform his contractual obligations on time and (iv) as a result of giving his promise B obtains in practice a benefit, or obviates a disbenefit, and (v) B's promise is not given as a result of economic duress or fraud on the part of A, then (vi) the benefit to B is capable of being consideration for B's promise, so that the promise will be legally binding.

As I have said, counsel for the defendants accepts that in the present case by promising to pay the extra £10,300 the defendants secured benefits. There is no finding, and no suggestion, that in this case the promise was given as a result of fraud or duress.

If it be objected that the propositions above contravene the principle in *Stilk* v *Myrick*, I answer that in my view they do not: they refine and limit the application of that principle, but they leave the principle unscathed, eg where B secures no benefit by his promise. It is not in my view surprising that a principle enunciated in relation to the rigours of seafaring life during the Napoleonic wars should be subjected during the succeeding 180 years to a process of refinement and limitation in its application in the present day.

It is therefore my opinion that on his findings of fact in the present case, the judge was entitled to hold, as he did, that the defendants' promise to pay the extra £10,300 was supported by valuable consideration, and thus constituted an enforceable agreement.

As a subsidiary argument, counsel for the defendants submits that on the facts of the present case the consideration, even if otherwise good, did not 'move from the promisee.' This submission is based on the principle illustrated in the decision in *Tweddle* v *Atkinson* (1861) 1 B & S 393, [1861–73] All ER Rep 369.

My understanding of the meaning of the requirement that 'consideration must move from the promisee' is that such consideration must be provided by the promisee, or arise out of his contractual relationship with the promisor. It is consideration provided by somebody else, not a party to the contract, which does not 'move from the promisee.' This was the situation in *Tweddle* v *Atkinson*, but it is, of course, not the situation in the present case. Here the benefits to the defendants arose out of their agreement of 9 April 1986 with the plaintiff, the promisee. In this respect I would adopt the following passage from *Chitty on Contracts*, 25th edn, 1983 para. 173, and refer to the authorities there cited:

> The requirement that consideration must move from the promisee is most generally satisfied where some detriment is suffered by him: e.g. where he parts with money or goods, or renders services, in exchange for the promise. But the requirement may equally well be satisfied where the promisee confers a benefit on the promisor without *in fact* suffering any detriment. (*Chitty's* emphasis.)

That is the situation in this case.

I repeat, therefore, my opinion that the judge was, as a matter of law, entitled to hold that there was valid consideration to support the agreement under which the defendants promised to pay an additional £10,300 at the rate of £575 per flat.

For these reasons I would dismiss this appeal.

Russell and Purchas LJJ concurred.

2.1.2.3   Performance of existing duty owed to third party

SHADWELL v *SHADWELL* (1860) 9 CB(NS) 159 (Court of Common Bench)

Was a promise to pay money on the plaintiff's marriage enforceable?

ERLE CJ: The question raised by the demurrer to the replication to the fourth plea is, whether there is a consideration which will support the action on the promise to pay the annuity of 150*l*. per annum. If there be such a consideration, it is a marriage, and therefore the promise is within the Statute of Frauds, and the consideration must appear in the writing containing the promise, that is, in the letter of the 11th of August, 1838, construed with the surrounding circumstances to be gathered therefrom, together with the averments on the record.

The circumstances are, that the plaintiff had made an engagement to marry one Ellen Nicholl, that his uncle had promised to assist him at starting, – by which, as I understand the words, he meant on commencing his married life. Then the letter containing the promise declared on is sent, to specify what that assistance would be, namely, 150*l.* per annum during the uncle's life, and until the plaintiff's professional income should be acknowledged by him to exceed 600 guineas per annum; and the declaration avers, that the plaintiff, relying on this promise, without any revocation on the part of the uncle, did marry Ellen Nicholl.

Now, do these facts shew that the promise was in consideration either of a loss to be sustained by the plaintiff or a benefit to be derived from the plaintiff to the uncle, at his, the uncle's, request? My answer is in the affirmative.

First, do these facts shew a loss sustained by the plaintiff at his uncle's request? When I answer this in the affirmative, I am aware that a man's marriage with the woman of his choice is in one sense a boon, and in that sense the reverse of a loss: yet, as between the plaintiff and the party promising to supply an income to support the marriage, it may well be also a loss. The plaintiff may have made a most material change in his position, and induced the object of his affection to do the same, and may have incurred pecuniary liabilities resulting in embarrassments which would be in every sense a loss if the income which hd been promised should be withheld; and, if the promise was made in order to induce the parties to marry, the promise so made would be in legal effect a request to marry.

Secondly, do these facts shew a benefit derived from the plaintiff to the uncle, at his request? In answering again in the affirmative, I am at liberty to consider the relation in which the parties stood and the interest in the settlement of his nephew which the uncle declares. The marriage primarily affects the parties thereto; but in a secondary degree it may be an object of interest to a near relative, and in that sense a benefit to him. This benefit is also derived from the plaintiff at the uncle's request. If the promise of the annuity was intended as an inducement to the marriage, and the averment that the plaintiff, relying on the promise, married, is an averment that the promise was one inducement to the marriage, this is the consideration averred in the declaration; and it appears to me to be expressed in the letter, construed with the surrounding circumstances.

No case shewing a strong analogy to the present was cited: but the importance of enforcing promises which have been made to induce parties to marry has been often recognized; and the cases cited, of *Montefiori* v *Montefiori*, 1 W B1 363, and *Bold* v *Hutchinson*, 20 Beavan 250, are examples. I do not feel it necessary to advert to the numerous authorities referred to in the learned arguments addressed to us, because the decision turns upon the question of fact, whether the consideration for the promise is proved as pleaded. I think it is; and therefore my judgment on the first demurrer is for the plaintiff.

The second demurrer raises the question whether the plaintiff's continuance at the bar was made a condition precedent to the right of the annuity. I think not. The uncle promises to continue the annuity until the professional income exceeds the sum mentioned. I find no stipulation that the annuity shall cease if professional diligence ceases, – no limitation except a defeasance in case of an amount of income from the other source. If the prospect of success at the bar had failed, a continuance to attend the courts might be an unreasonable expense. My judgment on this demurrer is also for the plaintiff.

The above is the judgment of my Brother Keating and myself.

Byles J dissented.

SCOTSON v *PEGG* (1861) 6 H&N 295 (Court of Exchequer)

The plaintiff delivered coal to the defendant. Was this good consideration, since the plaintiff was contractually bound to a third party to deliver the coal?

MARTIN B: I am of opinion that the plea is bad, both on principle and in law. It is bad in law because the ordinary rule is, that any act done whereby the contracting party receives a benefit is a good consideration for a promise by him. Here the benefit is the delivery of the coals to the defendant. It is consistent with the declaration that there may have been some dispute as to the defendant's right to have the coals, or it may be that the plaintiffs detained them for demurrage; in either case there would be good consideration that the plaintiffs, who were in possession of the coals, would allow the defendant to take them out of the ship. Then is it any answer that the plaintiffs had entered into a prior contract with other persons to deliver the coals to their order upon the same terms, and that the defendant was a stranger to that contract? In my opinion it is not. We must deal with this case as if no prior contract had been entered into. Suppose the plaintiffs had no chance of getting their money from the other persons who might perhaps have become bankrupt. The defendant gets a benefit by the delivery of the coals to him, and it is immaterial that the plaintiffs had previously contracted with third parties to deliver to their order.

WILDE B: I am also of opinion that the plaintiffs are entitled to judgment. The plaintiffs say, that in consideration that they would deliver to the defendant a cargo of coals from their ship, the defendant promised to discharge the cargo in a certain way. The defendant, in answer, says 'You made a previous contract with other persons that thay should discharge the cargo in the same way, and therefore there is no consideration for my promise.' But why is there no consideration? It is said, because the plaintiffs, in delivering the coals are only performing that which they were already bound to do. But to say that there is no consideration is to say that it is not possible for one man to have an interest in the performance of a contract made by another. But if a person chooses to promise to pay a sum of money in order to induce another to perform that which he has already contracted with a third person to do, I confess I cannot see why such a promise should not be binding. Here the defendant, who was a stranger to the original contract, induced the plaintiffs to part with the cargo, which they might not otherwise have been willing to do, and the delivery of it to the defendant was a benefit to him. I accede to the proposition that if a person contracts with another to do a certain thing, he cannot make the performance of it a consideration for a new promise to the same individual. But there is no authority for the proposition that where there has been a promise to one person to do a certain thing, it is not possible to make a valid promise to another to do the same thing. Therefore, deciding this matter on principle, it is plain to my mind that the delivery of the coals to the defendant was a good consideration for his promise, although the plaintiffs had made a previous contract to deliver them to the order of other persons.

NEW ZEALAND SHIPPING CO. LTD v SATTERTHWAITE & CO. LTD
[1975] AC 154 (PC)

LORD WILBERFORCE: The facts of this case are not in dispute. An expensive drilling machine was received on board the ship *Eurymedon* at Liverpool for transhipment to Wellington pursuant to the terms of a bill of lading no. 1262 dated June 5, 1964. The shipper was the maker of the drill, Ajax Machine Tool Co. Ltd ('the consignor'). The bill of lading was issued by agents for the Federal Steam Navigation Co. Ltd ('the carrier'). The consignee was A. M. Satterthwaite & Co. Ltd of Christchurch, New Zealand ('the consignee'). For several years before 1964 the New Zealand Shipping Co. Ltd ('the stevedore') had carried out all stevedoring work in Wellington in respect of the ships owned by the carrier, which was wholly owned subsidiary of the stevedore. In addition to this stevedoring work the stevedore generally acted as agent for the carrier in New Zealand; and in such capacity as general agent (not in the course of their stevedoring functions) the stevedore received the bill of lading at Wellington on July 31, 1964. Clause 1 of the bill of lading, on the construction of which this case turns, was in the same terms as bills of lading usually issued by the stevedore and its associated companies in respect of ordinary cargo carried by their ships from the United Kingdom to New Zealand. The consignee became the holder of the bill of lading and owner of the drill prior to August 14, 1964. On that dae the drill was damaged as a result of the stevedore's negligence during unloading.

At the foot of the first page of the bill of lading the following words were printed in small capitals:

In accepting this bill of lading the shipper, consignee and the owners of the goods, and the holders of this bill of lading agree to be bound by all of its conditions, exceptions and provisions whether written, printed or stamped on the front or back hereof.

... The incorporation in the bill of lading of the rules scheduled to the Carriage of Goods by Sea Act 1924 meant that the carrier and the ship were discharged from all liability in respect of the damage to the drill unless suit was brought against them within one year after delivery. No action was commenced until April 1967, when the consignee sued the stevedore in negligence, claiming £880 the cost of repairing the damaged drill.

The question in the appeal is whether the stevedore can take the benefit of the time limitation provision. . . . It was on this point that the Court of Appeal differed from Beattie J holding that it had not been shown that any consideration for the shipper's promise as to exemption moved from the promisee, i.e., the appellant company.

If the choice, and the antithesis, is between a gratuitous promise, and a promise for consideration, as it must be in the absence of a tertium quid, there can be little doubt which, in commercial reality, this is. The whole contract is of a commercial character, involving service on one side, rates of payment on the other, and qualifying stipulations as to both. The relations of all parties to each other are commercial relations entered into for business reasons of ultimate profit. To describe one set of promises, in this context, as gratuitous, or nudum pactum, seems paradoxical and is prima facie implausible. It is only the precise analysis of this complex of relations into the classical offer and acceptance, with identifiable consideration, that seems to present difficulty, but this same difficulty exists in many situations of daily life, e.g., sales at auction; supermarket purchases; boarding an omnibus; purchasing a train ticket; tenders for the supply of goods; offers of rewards; acceptance by post; warranties of authority by agents; manufacturers' guarantees; gratuitous bailments; bankers' commercial credits. These are all examples which show that English law, having committed itself to a rather technical and schematic doctrine of contract in application takes a practical approach, often at the cost of forcing the facts to fit uneasily into the marked slots of offer, acceptance and consideration.

In their Lordships' opinion the present contract presents much less difficulty than many of those above referred to. It is one of carriage from Liverpool to Wellington. The carrier assumes an obligation to transport the goods and to discharge at the port of arrival. The goods are to be carried and discharged, so the transaction is inherently contractual. It is contemplated that a part of this contract, viz. discharge, may be performed by independent contractors – viz. the appellant. By clause 1 of the bill of lading the shipper agrees to exempt from liability the carrier, his servants and independent contractors in respect of the performance of this contract of carriage. Thus, if the carriage, including the discharge, is wholly carried out by the carrier, he is exempt. If part is carried out by him and part by his servants, he and they are exempt. If part is carried out by him and part by an independent contractor, he and the independent contractor are exempt. The exemption is designed to cover the whole carriage from loading to discharge, by whomsoever it is performed: the performance attracts the exemption or immunity in favour of whoever the performer turns out to be. There is possibly more than one way of analysing this business transaction into the necessary components; that which their Lordships would accept is to say that the bill of lading brought into existence a bargain initially unilateral but capable of becoming mutual, between the shipper and the appellant, made through the carrier as agent. This became a full contract when the appellant performed services by discharging the goods. The performance of these services for the benefit of the shipper was the consideration for the agreement by the shipper that the appellant should have the benefit of the exemptions and limitations contained in the bill of lading. The conception of a 'unilateral' contract of this kind was recognized in *Great Northern Railway Co. v Witham* (1873) LR 9 CP 16 and is well established. This way of regarding the matter is very close to if not identical to that accepted by Beattie J in the Supreme Court: he analysed the transaction as one of an offer open to acceptance by action such as was found in *Carlill v Carbolic Smoke Ball Co.* [1893] 1 QB 256. But whether one describes the shippers' promise to exempt as an offer to be accepted by performance or as a promise in exchange for an act seems in the present context to be a matter of semantics. The words of Bowen LJ in *Carlill v Carbolic Smoke Ball Co.* [1893] 1 QB 256, 268: 'why should not an offer be made to all the world which is to ripen into a contract with anybody who comes forward and performs the condition?' seem to bridge both conceptions: he certainly seems to draw no distinction between an offer which matures into a contract when accepted and a promise which matures into a contract after performance, and, though in some special contexts (such as in connection with the right to withdraw) some further refinement may be needed, either analysis may be equally valid. On the main point in the appeal, their Lordships are in substantial agreement with Beattie J.

The following points require mention. 1. In their Lordships' opinion, consideration may quite well be provided by the appellant, as suggested, even though (or if) it was already under an obligation to discharge to the carrier. (There is no direct evidence of the existence or nature of this obligation, but their Lordships are prepared to assume it.) An agreement to do an act which the promisor is under an existing obligation to a third party to do, may quite well amount to valid consideration and does so in the the present case: the promisee obtains the benefit of a direct obligation which he can enforce. This proposition is illustrated and supported by *Scotson* v *Pegg* (1861) 6 H & N 295 which their Lordships consider to be good law. . . .

Viscount Dilhorne and Lord Simon of Glaisdale dissented from the above majority judgment.

2.1.3 PART PAYMENT OF DEBTS

D & C BUILDERS LTD v *REES* [1966] 2 QB 617 (CA)

LORD DENNING MR: . . . it is a daily occurrence that a merchant or tradesman, who is owed a sum of money, is asked to take less. The debtor says he is in difficulties. He offers a lesser sum in settlement, cash down. He says he cannot pay more. The creditor is considerate. He accepts the proffered sum and forgives him the rest of the debt. The question arises: Is the settlement binding on the creditor? The answer is that, in point of law, the creditor is not bound by the settlement. He can the next day sue the debtor for the balance: and get judgment. The law was so stated in 1602 by Lord Coke in *Pinnel's Case* (1602) 5 Co Rep 117 – and accepted in 1889 by the House of Lords in *Foakes* v *Beer* (1884) 9 App Cas 605.

Now, suppose that the debtor, instead of paying the lesser sum in cash, pays it by cheque. He makes out a cheque for the amount. The creditor accepts the cheque and cashes it. Is the position any different? I think not. No sensible distinction can be taken between payment of a lesser sum by cash and payment of it by cheque. The cheque, when given, is conditional payment. When honoured, it is actual payment. It is then the same as cash. If a creditor is not bound when he receives payment by cash, he should not be bound when he receives payment by cheque. This view is supported by the leading case of *Cumber* v *Wane* (1721) 1 Stra 426, which has suffered many vicissitudes but was, I think, rightly decided in point of law.

Sibree v *Tripp* is easily distinguishable. There the plaintiffs brought an action for £500. It was settled by the defendant giving three promissory notes amounting in all to £250. Those promissory notes were given upon a new contract, in substitution for the debt sued for, and not as conditional payment. The plaintiff's only remedy thenceforward was on the notes and not on the debt.

Goddard v *O'Brien* (1882) 9 QBD 37 is not so easily distinguishable. There a creditor was owed £125 for some slates. He met the debtor and agreed to accept £100 in discharge of it. The debtor gave a cheque for £100. The creditor gave a written receipt 'in settlement on the said cheque being honoured'. The cheque was clearly given by way of conditional payment. It was honoured. The creditor sued the debtor for the balance of £25. He lost because the £100 was paid by cheque and not by cash. The decision was criticised by Fletcher Moulton LJ in *Hirachand Punamchand* v *Temple* [1911] 2 KB 330 and by the editors of Smith's leading Cases, 13th ed, 1929, Vol. 1, p.380. It was, I think, wrongly decided. In point of law payment of a lesser sum, whether by cash or by cheque, is no discharge of a greater sum.

Dankwerts and Winn LJJ concurred in the result.

FOAKES v *BEER* (1884) 9 App Cas 605 (HL)

Mrs Beer had agreed to accept a judgment debt in instalments. Did this preclude her from recovering interest on the debt?

EARL OF SELBORNE LC: My Lords, upon the construction of the agreement of the 21st of December 1876, I cannot differ from the conclusion in which both the courts below were agreed. If the operative part could properly be controlled by the recitals, I think there would be much reason to say that the only thing contemplated by the recitals was giving time for payment, without any relinquishment, on the part of the judgment creditor, of any portion of the amount recoverable (whether for principal or for interest) under the judgment. But the agreement of the judgment creditor, which follows the recitals, is that she 'will not take any proceedings whatever on the judgment,' if a certain condition is fulfilled. What is that condition? Payment of the sum of £150 in every half year, 'until the whole of the said sum of £2090 19s' (the aggregate amount of the principal debt and costs, for which judgment had been entered) 'shall have been fully paid and satisfied.' A particular 'sum' is here mentioned, which does not include the interest then due, or future interest. Whatever was meant to be payable at all, under this agreement, was clearly to be payable by half-yearly instalments of £150 each; any other construction must necessarily make the conditional promise nugatory. But to say that the half-yearly payments were to continue till the whole sum of £2090 19s., 'and interest thereon,' should have been fully paid and satisfied, would be to introduce very important words into the agreement, which are not there, and of which I cannot say that they are necessarily implied. Although, therefore, I may (as indeed I do) very much doubt whether the effect of the agreement, as a conditional waiver of the interest to which she was by law entitled under the judgment, was really present to the mind of the judgment creditor, still I cannot deny that it might have that effect, if capable of being legally enforced.

But the question remains, whether the agreement is capable of being legally enforced. Not being under seal, it cannot be legally enforced against the respondent, unless she received consideration for it from the appellant, or unless, though without consideraton, it operates by way of accord and satisfaction, so as to extinguish the claim for interest. What is the consideration? On the face of the agreement none is expressed, except a present payment of £500, on account and in part of the larger debt then due and payable by law under the judgment. The appellant did not contract to pay the future instalments of £150 each, at the times therein mentioned; much less did he give any new security, in the shape of negotiable paper, or in any other form. The promise de futuro was only that of the respondent, that if the half-yearly payments of £150 each were regularly paid she would 'take no proceedings whatever on the judgment'. No doubt if the appellant had been under no antecedent obligation to pay the whole debt, his fulfilment of the condition might have imported some consideration on his part for that promise. But he was under that antecedent obligation; and payment at those deferred dates, by the forbearance and indulgence of the creditor, of the residue of the principal debt and costs, could not (in my opinion) be a consideraton for the relinquishment of interest and discharge of the judgment, unless the payment of the £500, at the time of signing the agreement, was such a consideration. As to accord and satisfaction, in point of fact there could be no complete satisfaction, so long as any future instalment remained payable; and I do not see how any mere payments on account could operate in law as a satisfaction ad interim, conditionally upon other payments being afterwards duly made, unless there was a consideration sufficient to support the agreement while still unexecuted. Nor was anything, in fact, done by the respondent in this case, on the receipt of the last payment, which could be tantamount to an acquittance, if the agreement did not previously bind her.

The question, therefore, is nakedly raised by this appeal, whether your Lordships are now prepared, not only to overrule, as contrary to the law, the doctrine stated by Sir Edward Coke to have been laid down by all the judges of the Common Pleas in *Pinnel's Case* in 1602, and repeated in his note to Littleton, s. 344(2), but to treat a prospective agreement, not under seal, for satisfaction of a debt, by a series of payments on account to a total amount less than the whole debt, as binding in law, provided those payments are regularly made; the case not being one of a composition with a common debtor, agreed to, inter se, by several creditors. I prefer so to state the question instead of treating it (as it was put at the Bar) as depending on the authority of the case of *Cumber v Wane* (1721) 1 Stra 426, decided in 1718. It may well be that distinctions, which in later cases have been held sufficient to exclude the application of that doctrine, existed and were improperly disregarded in *Cumber v Wane*; and yet that the doctrine itself may be law, rightly recognised in *Cumber v Wane*, and not really contradicted by any later authorities. And this appears to me to be the true state of the case. The doctrine itself, as laid down by Sir Edward Coke, may have been criticised, as questionable in principle, by some persons whose opinions are entitled to respect, but it has never been judicially overruled; on the contrary I think it has always, since the sixteenth century, been accepted as law. If so, I cannot think that your Lordships would do right, if you were now to reverse, as erroneous, a judgment of the Court of Appeal, proceeding upon a doctrine which has been accepted as part of the law of England for 280 years.

The doctrine, as stated in *Pinnel's Case*, is 'that payment of a lesser sum on the day' (it would of course be the same after the day), 'in satisfaction of a greater, cannot be any satisfaction for the whole, because it appears to the judges, that by no possibility a lesser sum can be a satisfaction to the plaintiff for a greater sum'. As stated in Coke Littleton, 212, it is, 'where the condition is for payment of £20, the obligor or feoffor cannot at the time appointed pay a lesser sum in satisfaction of the whole, because it is apparent that a lesser sum of money cannot be a satisfaction of a greater;' adding (what is beyond controversy), that an acquittance under seal, in full satisfaction of the whole, would (under like circumstances) be valid and binding.

The distinction between the effect of a deed under seal, and that of an agreement by parol, or by writing not under seal, may seem arbitrary, but it is established in our law; nor is it really unreasonable or practically inconvenient that the law should require particular solemnities to give a gratuitous contract the force of a binding obligation. If the question be (as, in the actual state of the law, I think it is), whether consideration is, or is not, given in a case of this kind, by the debtor who pays down part of the debt presently due from him, for a promise by the creditor to relinquish, after certain further payments on account, the residue of the debt, I cannot say that I think consideration is given, in the sense in which I have always understood that word as used in our law. It might be (and indeed I think it would be) an improvement in our law, if a release or acquittance of the whole debt, on payment of any sum which the creditor might be content to receive by way of accord and satisfaction (though less than the whole), were held to be, generally, binding, though not under seal; nor should I be unwilling to see equal force given to a prospective agreement, like the present, in writing though not under seal; but I think it impossible, without refinements which practically alter the sense of the word, to treat such a release or acquittance as supported by any new consideration proceeding from the debtor. All the authorities subsequent to *Cumber v Wane*, which were relied upon by the appellant at your Lordships' Bar (such as *Sibree v Tripp* (1846) 15 M & W 23, *Curlewis v Clark* (1849) 3 Ex 375, and *Goddard v O'Brien* (1882) 9 QBD 37) have proceeded upon the distinction, that, by giving negotiable paper or otherwise, there had been some new consideration for a new agreement, distinct from mere money payments in or towards discharge of the original liability. I think it unnecessary to go through those cases, or to examine the particular grounds on which each of them was decided. There are no such facts in the case now before your Lordships. What is called 'any benefit, or even any legal possibility of benefit,' in Mr Smith's notes to *Cumber v Wane*, is not (as I conceive) that sort of benefit which a creditor may derive from getting payment of part of the money due to him from a debtor who might otherwise keep him at arm's length, or possibly become insolvent, but is some independent benefit, actual or contingent, or a kind which might in law be a good and valuable consideraton for any other sort of agreement not under seal.

My conclusion is, that the order appealed from should be affirmed, and the appeal dismissed, with costs, and I so move your Lordships.

RE SELECTMOVE LTD [1995] 2 All ER 531 (CA)

In this case. the company was trying to enforce an alleged promise by the Inland Revenue ('the Crown') to accept the payment of a tax debt by instalments.

PETER GIBSON LJ: There are two elements to the consideration which the company claims was provided by it to the Crown. One is the promise to pay off its existing liability by instalments from 1 February 1992. The other is the promise to pay future PAYE and NIC as they fell due. Mr Nugee suggested that implicit in the latter was the promise to continue trading. But that cannot be spelt out of Mr ffooks' evidence as to what he agreed with Mr Polland. Accordingly, the second element is no more than a promise to pay that which it was bound to pay under the fiscal legislation at the date at which it was bound to make such payment. If the first element is not good consideration, I do not see why the second element should be either.

The judge held that the case fell within the principle of *Foakes* v *Beer* (1884) 9 App Cas 605, [1881–5] All ER Rep 106. In that case a judgment debtor and creditor agreed that in consideration of the debtor paying part of the judgment debt and costs immediately and the remainder by instalments the creditor would not take any proceedings on the judgment. The House of Lords held that the agreement was nudum pactum, being without consideration, and did not prevent the creditor, after payment of the whole debt and costs, from proceeding to enforce payment of the interest on the judgment. Although their Lordships were unanimous in the result, that case is notable for the powerful speech of Lord Blackburn, who made plain his disagreement with the course the law had taken in and since *Pinnel's Case* (1602) 5 Co Rep 117a, [1558–1774] All ER Rep 612 and which the House of Lords in *Foakes* v *Beer* decided should not be reversed. Lord Blackburn expressed his conviction that—

all men of business, whether merchants or tradesmen, do every day recognise and act on the ground that prompt payment of a part of their demand may be more beneficial to them than it would be to insist on their rights and enforce payment of the whole. (See 9 App Cas 605 at 622, [1881–5] All ER Rep 106 at 115.)

Yet it is clear that the House of Lords decided that a practical benefit of that nature is not good consideration in law.

Foakes v *Beer* has been followed and applied in numerous cases subsequently, of which I shall mention two. In *Vanbergen* v *St Edmunds Properties Ltd* [1933] 2 KB 223 at 231, [1933] All ER Rep 488 at 491 Lord Hanworth MR said:

It is a well established principle that a promise to pay a sum which the debtor is already bound by law to pay to the promisee does not afford any consideration to support the contract.

More recently in *D & C Builders Ltd* v *Rees* [1965] 3 All ER 837 at 841, [1966] 2 QB 617 at 626 this court also applied *Foakes* v *Beer*, Danckwerts LJ saying that the case—

settled definitely the rule of law that payment of a lesser sum than the amount of a debt due cannot be a satisfaction of the debt, unless there is some benefit to the creditor added so that there is an accord and satisfaction.

Mr Nugee, however, submitted that an additional benefit to the Crown was conferred by the agreement in that the Crown stood to derive practical benefits therefrom: it was likely to recover more from not enforcing its debt against the company, which was known to be in financial difficulties, than from putting the company into liquidation. He pointed to the fact that the company did in fact pay its further PAYE and NIC liabilities and £7,000 of its arrears. He relied on the decision of this court in *Williams* v *Roffey Bros & Nicholls (Contractors) Ltd* [1990] 1 All ER 512, [1991] 1 QB 1 for the proposition that a promise to perform an existing obligation can amount to good consideration provided that there are practical benefits to the promisee.

In that case the defendant, which had a building contract, sub-contracted work to the plaintiff at a price which left him in financial difficulty and there was a risk that the work would not be completed by the plaintiff. The defendant agreed to make additional payments to the plaintiff in return for his promise to carry out his existing obligations. The plaintiff sued for payment under the original agreement and the further agreement. The defendant argued that its promise to make additional payments was unenforceable and relied on *Stilk* v *Myrick* (1809) 2 Camp 317, 170 ER 1168, in which Lord Ellenborough CJ held to be unenforceable for want of consideration a promise by a ship's captain to seamen, hired to crew the ship to and from the Baltic, of extra pay for working the ship back from the Baltic after two men had deserted. This court rejected that argument without overruling *Stilk* v *Myrick*. Glidewell LJ, with whom Purchas and Russell LJJ agreed, expressed the law to be this:

> '... (i) if A has entered into a contract with B to do work for, or to supply goods or services to, B in return for payment by B and (ii) at some stage before A has completely performed his obligations under the contract B has reason to doubt whether A will, or will be able to, complete his side of the bargain and (iii) B thereupon promises A an additional payment in return for A's promise to perform his contractual obligations on time and (iv) as a result of giving his promise B obtains in practice a benefit, or obviates a disbenefit, and (v) B's promise is not given as a result of economic duress or fraud on the part of A, then (vi) the benefit to B is capable of being consideration for B's promise, so that the promise will be legally binding.' (See [1990] 1 All ER 512 at 521–522, [1991] 1 QB 1 at 15–16.)

Mr Nugee submitted that although Glidewell LJ in terms confined his remarks to a case where B is to do the work for or supply goods or services to A, the same principle must apply where B's obligation is to pay A, and he referred to an article by Adams and Brownsword 'Contract, Consideration and the Critical Path' (1990) 53 MLR 536 at 539–540 which suggests that *Foakes* v *Beer* might need reconsideration. I see the force of the argument, but the difficulty that I feel with it is that if the principle of *Williams'* case is to be extended to an obligation to make payment, it would in effect leave the principle in *Foakes* v *Beer* without any application. When a creditor and a debtor who are at arm's length reach agreement on the payment of the debt by instalments to accommodate the debtor, the creditor will no doubt always see a practical benefit to himself in so doing. In the absence of authority there would be much to be said for the enforceability of such a contract. But that was a matter expressly considered in *Foakes* v *Beer* yet held not to constitute good consideration in law. *Foakes* v *Beer* was not even referred to in *Williams'* case, and it is in my judgment impossible, consistently with the doctrine of precedent, for this court to extend the principle of *Williams'* case to any circumstances governed by the principle of *Foakes* v *Beer*. If that extension is to be made, it must be by the House of Lords or, perhaps even more appropriately, by Parliament after consideration by the Law Commission.

In my judgment, the judge was right to hold that if there was an agreement between the company and the Crown it was unenforceable for want of consideration.

Stuart-Smith and Balcombe LJJ concurred.

2.1.4 PROMISSORY ESTOPPEL

CENTRAL LONDON PROPERTY TRUST LTD v *HIGH TREES HOUSE LTD*
[1947] KB 130 (HC)

DENNING J: By a lease under seal made on September 24, 1937, the plaintiffs, Central London Property Trust Ltd, granted to the defendants, High Trees House Ltd, a subsidiary of the plaintiff company, a tenancy of a block of flats for the term of ninety-nine years from September 29, 1937, at a ground rent of 2,500*l.* a year. The block of flats was a new one and had not been fully occupied at the beginning of the war owing to the absence of people from London. With war conditions prevailing, it was apparent to those responsible that the rent reserved under the lease could not be paid out of the profits of the flats and, accordingly, discussions took place between the directors of the two companies concerned, which were closely associated, and an arrangement was made between them which was put into writing. On January 3, 1940, the plaintiffs wrote to the defendants in these terms, 'we confirm the arrangement made between us by which the ground rent should be reduced as from the commencement of the lease to 1,250*l.* per annum', and on April 2, 1940, a confirmatory resolution to the same effect was passed by the plaintiff company. On March 20, 1941, a receiver was appointed by the debenture holders of the plaintiffs and on his death on February 28, 1944, his place was taken by his partner. The defendants paid the reduced rent from 1941 down to the beginning of 1945 by which time all the flats in the block were fully let, and continued to pay it thereafter. In September, 1945, the then receiver of the plaintiff company looked into the matter of the lease and ascertained that the rent actually reserved by it was 2,500*l*. On September 21, 1945, he wrote to the defendants saying that rent must be paid at the full rate and claiming that arrears amounting to 7,916*l*. were due. Subsequently, he instituted the present friendly proceedings to test the legal position in regard to the rate at which rent was payable. In the action the plaintiffs sought to recover 625*l*, being the amount represented by the difference between rent at the rate of 2,500*l*. and 1,250*l*. per annum for the quarters ending September 29, and December 25, 1945. By their defence the defendants pleaded (I.) that the letter of January 3, 1940, constituted an agreement that the rent reserved should be 1,250*l*. only, and that such agreement related to the whole term of the lease, (2.) they pleaded in the alternative that the plaintiff company were estopped from alleging that the rent exceeded 1,250*l*. per annum and (3.) as a further alternative, that by failing to demand rent in excess of 1,250*l*. before their letter of September 21, 1945 (received by the defendants on September 24), they had waived their rights in respect of any rent, in excess of that at the rate of 1,250*l*. which had accrued up to September 24, 1945.

If I were to consider this matter without regard to recent developments in the law, there is no doubt that had the plaintiffs claimed it, they would have been entitled to recover ground rent at the rate of 2,500*l*. a year from the beginning of the term, since the lease under which it was payable was a lease under seal which, according to the old common law, could not be varied by an agreement by parol (whether in writing or not), but only by deed. Equity, however stepped in, and said that if there has been a variation of a deed by a simple contract (which in the case of a lease required to be in writing would have to be evidenced by writing), the courts may give effect to it as is shown in *Berry* v *Berry* [1929] 2 KB 316. That equitable doctrine, however, could hardly apply in the present case because the variation here might be said to have been made without consideration. With regard to estoppel, the representation made in relation to reducing the rent, was not a representation of an existing fact. It was a representation, in effect, as to the future, namely, that payment of the rent would not be enforced at the full rate but only at the reduced rate. Such a representation would not give rise to an estoppel, because, as was said in *Jorden* v *Money* (1854) 5 HL 185, a representation as to the future must be embodied as a contract or be nothing.

But what is the position in view of developments in the law in recent years? The law has not been standing still since *Jorden* v *Money*. There has been a series of decisions over the last fifty years which, although they are said to be cases of estoppel are not really such. They are cases in which a promise was made which was intended to create legal relations and which, to the knowledge of the person making the promise, was going to be acted on by the person to whom it was made, and which was in fact so acted on. In such cases the courts have said that the promise must be honoured. The cases to which I particularly desire to refer are: *Fenner* v *Blake* [1900] 1 QB 426, *In re Wickham*, [1917] 34 TLR 158, *Re William Porter & Co. Ltd* [1937] 2 All ER 361 and *Buttery* v *Pickard* [1946] WN 25. As I have said they are not cases of estoppel in the strict sense. They are really promises – promises intended to be binding, intended to be acted on, and in fact acted on. *Jorden* v *Money* can be distinguished, because there the promisor made it clear that she did not intend to be legally bound, whereas in the cases to which I refer the proper inference was that the promisor did intend to be bound. In each case the court held the promise to be binding on the party making it, even though under the old common law it might be difficult to find any consideration for it. The courts have not gone so far as to give a cause of action in damages for the breach of such a promise, but they have refused to allow the party making it to act inconsistently with it. It is in that sense, and that sense only, that such a promise gives rise to an estoppel. The decisions are a natural result of the fusion of law and equity: for the cases of *Hughes* v *Metropolitan Ry. Co*, *Birmingham* (1877) 2 App Cas 439 and *District Land Co.* v *London & North Western Ry. Co.* (1888) 40 Ch D 268 and *Salisbury (Marquess)* v *Gilmore* [1942] 2 KB 38, afford a sufficient basis for saying that a party would not be allowed in equity to go back on such a promise. In my opinion, the time has now come for the validity of such a promise to be recognised. The logical consequence, no doubt is that a promise to accept a smaller sum in discharge of a larger sum, if acted upon, is binding notwithstanding the absence of consideration: and if the fusion of law and equity leads to this result, so much the better. That aspect was not considered in *Foakes* v *Beer*. At this time of day however, when law and equity have been joined together for over seventy years, principles must be reconsidered in the light of their combined effect. It is to be noticed that in the Sixth Interim Report of the Law Revision Committee, pars. 35, 40, it is recommended that such a promise as that to which I have referred, should be enforceable in law even though no consideration for it has been given by the promisee. It seems to me that, to the extent I have mentioned, that result has now been achieved by the decisions of the courts.

I am satisfied that a promise such as that to which I have referred is binding and the only question remaining for my consideration is the scope of the promise in the present case. I am satisfied on all the evidence that the promise here was that the ground rent should be reduced to 1,250*l*. a year as a temporary expedient while the block of flats was not fully, or substantially fully let, owing to the conditions prevailing. That means that the reduction in the rent applied throughout the years down to the end of 1944, but early in 1945 it is plain that the flats were fully let, and, indeed the rents received from them (many of them not being affected by the Rent Restrictions Acts), were increased beyond the figure at which it was originally contemplated that they would be let. At all events the rent from them must have been very considerable. I find that the conditions prevailing at the time when the reduction in rent was made, had completely passed away by the early months of 1945. I am satisfied that the promise was understood by all parties only to apply under the conditions prevailing at the time when it was made, namely, when the flats were only partially let, and that it did not extend any further than that. When the flats became fully let, early in 1945, the reduction ceased to apply.

In those circumstances, under the law as I hold it, it seems to me that rent is payable at the full rate for the quarters ending September 29 and December 25, 1945.

If the case had been one of estoppel, it might be said that in any event the estoppel would cease when the conditions to which the representation applied came to an end, or it also might be said that it would only come to an end on notice. In either case it is only a way of ascertaining what is the scope of the representation. I prefer to apply the principle that a promise intended to be binding, intended to be acted on and in fact acted on, is binding so far as its terms properly apply. Here it was binding as covering the period down to the early part of 1945, and as from that time full rent is payable.

I therefore give judgment for the plaintiff company for the amount claimed.

HUGHES v *METROPOLITAN RAILWAY CO.* (1877) 2 App Cas 439 (HL)

Was a notice to repair suspended by intervening negotiations?

LORD CAIRNS LC: My Lords, the decree of the Court of Appeal which is brought before your Lordships in this case is one which has the support of all five Judges who constituted the Court of Appeal at the time. One of the learned Judges, Mr Baron Cleasby, no doubt assented to the decision with some hesitation, but it was a unanimous decision of the court.

My Lords, I own that the able argument which your Lordships have heard has raised no doubt whatever in my mind as to the propriety of that decision. I say the propriety of the decision, although at the same time I am not able, as to one part of the case, to take the view which one, at least, of the learned Judges who pronounced the decision, appears to have taken. Lord Justice James, in the observations which he made, is reported to have said this: 'I am of opinion from all this correspondence, that the lessor (that is the present Appellant) lulled the Defendants to sleep, intentionally lulled them to sleep, until it was too late for them to do the repairs, that he intentionally induced them to wait till the six months were nearly over, and then sought to enforce the forfeiture'. That not merely states a case which would entitle the Court of Equity to give relief, but states a case as against the Appellant which imputes to him a serious offence in point of morals. My Lords, I am bound to say, and I think the Appellant is entitled that I should at once say, that I see no evidence whatever for fixing upon the Appellant the stain which these observations would fix upon him. I am unable to see that there is any evidence in this case, that there was any intention on the part of the Appellant, to lull the Defendants to sleep, in order that he might wait until the six months were nearly over, and then take advantage of a forfeiture. For reasons which I am about to state, I am of opinion that the Appellant cannot take advantage of a forfeiture, but in my opinion there was no intention whatever on his part to practise any wrong upon the Respondents. I think that both parties, almost unintentionally – I have very little doubt, without reflection – placed themselves in a position in which the one, the Appellant, as against the other the Repondents, was not entitled to enforce the forfeiture which he might have enforced at law; but that arose, not from any intention on his part to do a wrong to the Respondents, but merely from circumstances which had occurred, and to which I am now about to refer.

My Lords, the Appellant was the landlord of certan premises in the Euston Road, the lease of which, an old and a long lease, was vested in the Respondents. There were in the lease covenants to repair, and to repair after notice. Notice had been given and served upon the Respondents by the Appellant on the 22nd of October, 1874; it was a notice to repair the premises within six months; that six months would therefore expire on the 22nd of April, 1875. Nothing was done by the Respondents between the 22nd of October and the 28th of November. On the 28th of November the agents of the Respondents wrote to the solicitors of the Appellant a very important letter. There can be no doubt that the letter refers to the premises in question, although it refers also to other premises. It states that the notice to repair had been received, and that the repairs required by the covenants of the lease 'shall be forthwith commenced', but then it adds: 'It occurs to us that the freeholder may be desirous of obtaining possession of the company's interests, which, as you know, is but a short one, and so we propose to defer commencing the repairs until we hear from you as to the probability of an arrangement such as we suggest'. Now, if these two parties, the Appellant and the Respondents, were really minded to treat for the purchase of this lease, of course it was to the interest of both parties that the doing of these repairs should be suspended, and that the property should be bought as it then stood, because it might be desired to apply it to purposes for which the repairs would be useless – and I read this as a definite intimation on the part of the Respondents that they would not proceed to execute the repairs (although they stated their readiness to commence forthwith), if they found that there was a probability of an arrangement to purchase being come to.

The Appellant, when he received that letter, might have said, I have no intention of becoming a purchaser; or he might have said, I may become a purchaser; but if a negotiation is to be commenced you must understand that it is to be without prejudice to my notice to repair; you must go and make the repairs as if there was no negotiation; or he might have said simply, I will adopt what you propose and enter upon a negotiation, saying nothing farther. That third course is the course which he took, and it is a course which, as it seems to me, when taken, carried with it the intimation that he was satisfied with the footing upon which the matter was put by the letter which he was answering. This is what his solicitors say in their letter of the 1st December: 'If the company are the owners of [certain other houses] and are willing to sell them all [that is all the houses], and give immediate possession, our client will, on learning the price, consider whether it is worth while to acquire the company's interest or not. In mentioning the price, please to give us particulars of the tenancies and rents paid to the company.'

Now, that being a letter which, as it appears to me, acceded to the suggestion that the repairs were to be deferred until it was ascertained whether an agreement could be made for the purchase, on the 4th of December that letter of the 1st was replied to, and replied to in this way: 'We are in receipt of yours of the 1st instant. The particulars and terms asked for shall be sent in the course of a few days'. Again, on the 30th of December, the agents of the Respondents write to the solicitors of the Appellant: 'We send you herewith a statement of the company's receipts and payments in respect of the houses in Euston Road as requested by you. The company will agree to surrender the whole of the lease in consideration of a payment of £3,000. We shall be glad to hear from you at your early convenience'. That is followed by the particulars of the Metropolitan Railway Company's interest in the houses in Euston Road, the property of Mr Hughes. There is a somewhat lengthy schedule, and it is obvious that the preparation of that schedule was a work which would easily account for the lapse of time between the 4th and the 30th of December. It was a schedule which was required by the Appellant. Time was required to prepare it, and your Lordships come therefore to the 30th of December with clear proof that no time whatever had been lost between the 28th of November and that day.

The offer, then, standing upon the letter of the 30th of December, that letter is replied to by the solicitors of the Appellant in these words: 'We have duly received your letter of yesterday's date enclosing a statement of the company's receipts and payments in respect of the houses in Euston Road, and at the same time intimating that the company will agree to surrender the whole of the leases in consideration of the payment of £3000. Having regard, however, to the state of repair in which the houses now are, and to the large expenditure which will be required to put them in a proper condition, the whole of which the company are liable to bear under the covenants in the leases, we think the price asked for is out of all reason. We must therefore request you to reconsider the question of price, having regard to the previous observations, and to the fact that the company have already been served with notice to put the premises in repair, and we shall be glad to receive in due course a modified proposal from you'.

My Lords, I think it unnecessary to go beyond that letter. That is a letter which, a price of £3,000 having been proposed, repudiates the price, refuses to give it, and asks for a modified proposal. No modified proposal, in point of fact, was made. But I will put the matter in the most favourable way for the Appellant. I will assume that in place of asking for a modified proposal that had been a letter which had at once terminated the negotiation. No farther proposal having been made in substance the negotiation then determined. I will assume that the letter, upon the face of it, had terminated the negotiation, and now I ask your Lordships to consider what would be the consequence. There had been a notice in October to repair in six months. The effect of the letter of November, as it seems to me, was to propose to the Appellant, and the farther letter of the Appellant had the effect of an assent by the Appellant, to suspend the operation of that notice in order to enter upon a negotiation for the purchase and sale of the lease. That negotiation was entered upon, and, as I have assumed, came to an end on the 31st of December. My Lords, it appears to me that in the eye of a Court of Equity, or in the eye of any court dealing upon principles of Equity, it must be taken that all the time which had elapsed between the giving of the notice in October and the letter of the 28th of November was waived as a part of the six months during which the repairs were to be executed, and that all the time from the 28th of November until the conclusion of the negotiation, which I have assumed to be on the 31st of December, was also waived – that it was impossible that any part of that time should afterwards be counted as against the tenant in a six months' notice to repair. The result would be, that it would be on the 31st of December, as the first time, that time would begin to run, for the purpose of repairs, as against the tenant.

Then occurs the question, what time from the 31st of December would be given? My Lords, what a Court of Equity would have done if it had found that the tenant after the 31st of December had taken no steps to make the repairs, and that a period of six months had run from the 31st of December without any repairs having been made, it is not necessary here to consider. In point of fact the repairs were made within six months, from the 31st of December; and my Lords, I cannot but think that the lease having prescribed a period of six months, as that which in the eyes of the contracting parties was a reasonable period, within which to make such repairs as those, a Court of Equity would hold, and would be bound to hold, that the negotiation having been broken off on the 31st of December, the repairs were in this case executed within that which according to the view of the parties was a reasonable time for the execution of such repairs.

My Lords, it is upon those grounds that I am of opinion that the decision of the court below is correct. It was not argued at your Lordships' Bar, and it could not be argued, that there was any right of a Court of Equity, or any practice of a Court of Equity, to give relief in cases of this kind, by way of mercy, or by way merely of saving property from forfeiture, but it is the first principle upon which all Courts of Equity proceed, that if parties who have entered into definite and distinct terms involving certain legal results

– certain penalties or legal forfeiture – afterwards by their own act or with their own consent enter upon a course of negotiation which has the effect of leading one of the parties to suppose that the strict rights arising under the contract will not be enforced, or will be kept in suspense, or held in abeyance, the person who otherwise might have enforced those rights will not be allowed to enforce them where it would be inequitable having regard to the dealings which have thus taken place between the parties. My Lords, I repeat that I attribute to the Appellant no intention here to take advantage of, to lay a trap for, or to lull into false security those with whom he was dealing; but it appears to me that both parties by entering upon the negotiation which they entered upon, made it an inequitable thing that the exact period of six months dating from the month of October should afterwards be measured out as against the Respondents as the period during which the repairs must be executed.

I therefore propose to your Lordships that the decree which is appealed against should be affirmed, and the present appeal dismissed with costs.

Lords Selborne, Blackburn, O'Hagan and Gordon concurred.

2.1.4.1 Need for reliance

THE POST CHASER [1982] 1 All ER 19 (HC)

ROBERT GOFF J: . . . I turn then to the second question in the case, viz whether the buyers waived their right to reject the sellers' tender of documents. Both counsel for the buyers and counsel for the sellers were in agreement that the applicable principles were those of equitable estoppel.

In considering this question, it was common ground between counsel that I had first to consider whether, on the facts found, there was an unequivocal representation by the buyers that they did not intend to enforce their strict legal right to reject the sellers' tender of documents, though it was recognised, having regard in particular to the speech of Lord Salmon in the *Vanden Avenue* case [1978] 2 Lloyd's Rep 109 at 126–127, that such a representation could be inferred from the buyers' conduct if they behaved or wrote in such a way that reasonable sellers would be led to believe that the buyers were waiving the relevant defect. Counsel for the buyers submitted that, on the facts of the present case, there was no such representation from the buyers. He submitted that the mere fact that the buyers, on receipt of the sellers' declaration of the Post Chaser on 10 January, made no protest or statement that they were accepting under reserve could of itself give rise to no representation by them. Next he submitted that the request by the buyers to Kievit on 20 January, to present the documents to Conti, could likewise give rise to no representation, because this request was made against the background of Conti's message of 17 January to the buyers (who passed it on to the sellers on the same day) that Lewis & Peat had 'declined tender' but that Conti were 'insisting tender be accepted and feel everything should be ok' so that it should reasonably have been understood as no more than a request to Kievit to present the documents to Conti to enable them to see if they could persuade Lewis & Peat to accept them.

Now I accept counsel for the buyers' submission that the mere absence of protest or reserve on the part of the buyers when they received the declaration could not of itself give rise to any unequivocal representation on their part that they waived their rights. Of course, I take into account the board's findings that, having regard to the usual length of strings in the particular trade and the duty on each party to pass on the notice as soon as possible, the buyers should have been on notice that the declaration was late; and I also take account of the board's view that the buyers should have challenged the declaration and reserved their rights. Even so, I do not find it possible to conclude that the *mere* fact of receiving the declaration without protest or reserve constituted an unequivocal representation by the buyers that they waived their rights.

However, the buyers' message of 20 January seems to me to fall into a different category. It was in terms an unqualified request to Kievit to present the documents to the buyers' own sub-buyers, Conti. Furthermore, it was accompanied by the buyers' request to debit them in respect of the difference between their purchase price ($792.50) and their sale price to Conti ($605) which reinforced the impression that this was not intended to be a provisional presentation in the hope that Conti could persuade Lewis & Peat to accept the documents but was a representation by the buyers that they were prepared to accept the documents, thus waiving any defect in the prior declaration of shipment. In my judgment, this was a sufficiently unequivocal representation for the purposes of waiver.

However, there next arises the question whether there was any sufficient reliance by the sellers on this representation to give rise to an equitable estoppel. Here there arose a difference between counsel for the sellers and counsel for the buyers as to the degree of reliance which is required. It is plain, however, from the speech of Lord Cairns LC in *Hughes* v *Metropolitan Rly. Co.* (1877) 2 App Cas 439 at 448, [1874–80] All ER Rep 187 at 191 that the representor will not be allowed to enforce his rights 'where it would be inequitable having regard to the dealings which have taken place between the parties'. Accordingly there must be such action, or inaction, by the representee on the faith of the representation as will render it inequitable to permit the representor to enforce his strict legal rights.

On the findings of fact in the award before the court, there is no finding of any reliance by the sellers on the buyers' representation, save the fact that the documents covering the parcel on the Post Chaser were accordingly presented by Kievit (who in this context must be taken to have acted on behalf of the sellers) to Conti. That was done on 20 January; and by 22 January the sellers were informed by the buyers that NOGA had rejected the documents, following which the documents were passed back up the string to the sellers. The question therefore arises whether such action constituted sufficient reliance by the sellers on the buyers' representation to render it inequitable for the buyers thereafter to enforce their right to reject the documents. . . .

I approach the matter as follows. The fundamental principle is that stated by Lord Cairns LC, viz that the representor will not be allowed to enforce his rights where it would be inequitable having regard to the dealings which have thus taken place between the parties'. To establish such inequity, it is not necessary to show detriment; indeed, the representee may have benefited from the representation, and yet it may be inequitable, at least without reasonable notice, for the representor to enforce his legal rights. Take the facts of *Central London Property Trust Ltd* v *High Trees House Ltd* (1946) [1956] 1 All ER 256, [1947] KB 130, the case in which Denning J breathed new life into the doctrine of equitable estoppel. The representation was by a lessor to the effect that he would be content to accept a reduced rent. In such a case, although the lessee has benefited from the reduction in rent, it may well be inequitable for the lessor to insist on his legal right to the unpaid rent, because the lessee has conducted his affairs on the basis that he would only have to pay rent at the lower rate; and a court might well think it right to conclude that only after reasonable notice could the lessor return to charging rent at the higher rate specified in the lease. Furthermore it would be open to the court, in any particular case, to infer from the circumstances of the case that the representee must have conducted his affairs in such a way that it would be inequitable for the representor to enforce his rights, or to do so without reasonable notice. But it does not follow that in every case in which the representee has acted, or failed to act, in reliance on the representation, it will be inequitable for the representor to enforce his rights for the nature of the action, or inaction, may be insufficient to give rise to the equity, in which event a necessary requirement stated by Lord Cairns LC for the application of the doctrine would not have been fulfilled.

This, in my judgment, is the principle which I have to apply in the present case. Here, all that happened was that the sellers, through Kievit, presented the documents on the same day as the buyers made their representation; and within two days the documents were rejected. Now on these simple facts, although it is plain that the sellers did actively rely on the buyers' representation, and did conduct their affairs in reliance on it, by presenting the documents, I cannot see anything which would render it inequitable for the buyers thereafter to enforce their legal right to reject the documents. In particular, having regard to the very short time which elapsed between the date of the representation and the date of the presentation of the documents on the one hand and the date of rejection on the other hand, I cannot see that, in the absence of any evidence that the sellers' position had been prejudiced by reason of their action in reliance on the representation, it is possible to infer that they suffered any such prejudice. In these circumstances, a necessary element for the application of the doctrine of equitable estoppel is lacking; and I decide this point in favour of the buyers.

2.1.4.2 Suspensory nature of doctrine

TOOL METAL MANUFACTURING CO. LTD v TUNGSTEN ELECTRIC CO. LTD
[1955] 2 All ER 657 (HL)

What constitutes notice of an intention to end a variation of a contract which has been operating as a promissory estoppel?

VISCOUNT SIMONDS: . . . the appellants (hereinafter called 'T.M.M.C.'), by writ issued on September 11, 1950, claimed from the respondents (hereinafter called 'TECO'), as compensation under cl. 5 of the deed as from January 1, 1947, to January 26, 1950, a quantified sum of £84,050, and an account of compensation payable under the same clause from January 26, 1950, to July 27, 1950, when the licence terminated. To this claim TECO put in a number of defences. They pleaded that the provisions of cl. 5 were void on three separate grounds: (a) because they imposed a penalty; (b) because they were an unreasonable restraint of trade; and (c) because they contravened s. 38 of the Patents and Designs Act, 1907. They also pleaded that the delivery of the counterclaim in the first action did not operate as notice to terminate the equitable arrangement which, as was held in that action, existed at any rate until such delivery, and that it was a condition of its termination that the notice determining it (a) should be unequivocal, and (b) should specify the date of termination, and, further, that that date should give them a reasonable time to adjust their business affairs to meet the altered circumstances. To this, in effect, T.M.M.C. replied that the delivery of the counterclaim was a sufficient intimation of their intention to reassert their legal rights and that, that intimation having been given, equity demanded nothing more than that a reasonable time should be allowed before they sought to enforce them. And they further said (nor was this denied by TECO) that, on this footing, a reasonable time was given, since the counterclaim was delivered in March, 1946, and compensation claimed from January, 1947. . . .

My Lords, the decision of the Court of Appeal in the first action was based on nothing else than the principle of equity stated in this House in *Hughes* v *Metropolitan Ry. Co.* (1877) 2 App Cas at p. 448 and interpreted by Bowen LJ in *Birmingham & District Land Co.* v *London & North Western Ry. Co.* (1888) 40 ChD at p. 286 in these terms:

> It seems to me to amount to this, that if persons who have contractual rights against others induce by their conduct those against whom they have such rights to believe that such rights will either not be enforced or will be kept in suspense or abeyance for some particular time, those persons will not be allowed by a court of equity to enforce the rights until such time has elapsed, without at all events placing the parties in the same position as they were before.

These last words are important, for they emphasise that the gist of the equity lies in the fact that one party has by his conduct led the other to alter his position. I lay stress on this, because I would not have it supposed, particularly in commercial transactions, that mere acts of indulgence are apt to create rights, and I do not wish to lend the authority of this House to the statement of the principle which is to be found in *Combe* v *Combe* ([1951] 1 All ER 767 at p. 770) and may well be far too widely stated.

The difficulty in the present case lies in the fact that, in the first action, in which it was held that between these parties the principle applies, neither of them in any pleading or other statement between the delivery of the counterclaim in March, 1946 and judgment in April, 1950, took their stand on its existence. TECO asserted a binding agreement for the complete and final abrogation of any compensation: T.M.M.C., though willing to make some concession in regard to the past, denied any agreement in respect of any period at all. The position of neither of them was compatible with the existence of an equitable arrangement by which the right to receive, and the obligation to pay, compensation were suspended for a period which lasted at least until March, 1946, and for a debatable period thereafter.

My Lords, I think that, at this point, the issue is a very narrow one. On the one hand, it is said that a plea resting on the denial of an agreement cannot be a notice determining that agreement. This is the view taken by Romer LJ, in which the other members of the Court of Appeal concurred. On the other hand, it is urged that, since the suspensory period is due to the gratuitous willingness of the one party to forgo their rights, nothing can be a clearer intimation that they propose no longer to forgo them than a claim which, though it may ask too much, can leave the other party in no doubt that they must not expect further indulgence. The problem may, perhaps, be stated in this way: Did equity require that T.M.M.C. should expressly and unequivocally refer to an equitable arrangement which TECO had not pleaded and they did not recognise? Or was it sufficient for them by a reassertion of their legal rights to proclaim that the period of indulgence was over? In favour of the latter view, it is added that such an attitude on the part of T.M.M.C. could not surprise TECO who had not hesitated to bring against them a serious charge of fraud.

My Lords, it is not clear to me what conclusion the Court of Appeal would have reached but for the authority of *Canadian Pacific Ry. Co. v Regem* [1931] AC 414, to which I must refer later. For my part, I have, after some hesitation, formed the opinion that, as soon as the counterclaim was delivered, TECO must be taken to know that the suspensory period was at an end and were bound to put their house in order. The position is a very artificial one, but it was their own ignorance of a suspensory period, or at least their failure to plead it, which created the difficulty, and I do not think that they can take advantage of their own ignorance or default and say that they were entitled to a further period of grace until a further notice was given. Equity demands that all the circumstances of the case should be regarded, and I think that the fair and reasonable view is that TECO could not, after they had received the counterclaim, regard themselves as entitled to further indulgence.

It was, however, urged on behalf of TECO that, even if the counterclaim could otherwise be regarded as a sufficient notice that the equitable arrangement was at an end, yet it was defective in that it did not name a certain future date at which it was to take effect. To this the reply was made that equity did not require a future date to be named in the notice, but that what it did require was that a reasonable time should be allowed to elapse before it was sought to enforce it. Here, too, the Court of Appeal favoured the view of TECO, again feeling themselves constrained by the decision in the *Canadian Pacific Railway* case. And here, too, I am forced to the opposite conclusion. Equity is not held in a strait-jacket. There is no universal rule that an equitable arrangement must always be determined in one way. It may, in some cases, be right and fair that a dated notice should be given. But in this case, what was the position in January, 1947, which I take to be the critical date? Then for nine months TECO must, in my opinion, be taken to have been aware that T.M.M.C. proposed to stand on their legal rights. It is not denied that those nine months gave them ample time to readjust their position. I cannot regard it as a requirement of equity that, in such circumstances, they should have been expressly notified in March, 1946, that they would have nine months and no more to take such steps as the altered circumstances required. In coming to this conclusion, I do not think I run counter to any authority that was cited to us, unless it be the *Canadian Pacific Railway* case to which I must now refer.

My Lords, in his judgment in the Court of Appeal, Romer LJ introduced that case with these words ([1954] 2 All ER at p. 41):

> In my opinion, although in many cases the equity, to which *Hughes v Metropolitan Ry. Co.* gave recognition and high authority, is satisfied by merely conforming to the terms in which Lord Cairns (and subsequently Bowen LJ) formulated it, there are other cases where justice requires that the resumption of legal rights which have been suspended for a period must be preceded by a notification to the other party concerned specifying a fixed period of grace during which that party can put his house in order, and that in such cases a notificaton such as that will be a condition precedent to the valid re-assumption of the owner's legal rights. Such a case was *Canadian Pacific Ry. Co. v Regem.*

My Lords it is undoubtedly the fact that the *Canadian Pacific Railway* case decided that what I have called a 'dated notice' was required in that case to terminate an existing licence, and that the Crown, the licensor, had in that case the duty and the risk of fixing a reasonable period of notice, but I must observe that, not only was the equitable principle, which was recognised in *Hughes'* case not invoked, but Lord Russell of Killowen, in delivering the opinion of the Board, expressly disclaimed any reference to that or any other equitable principle. The relevant problem that was whether a licence to occupy land by placing telegraph poles thereon had been revoked by the institution of proceedings by the Crown, and the question was what term in regard to revocation should be implied in the licence which the Crown was assumed to have granted. I have no doubt that the question is analogous to that which we have to decide in this case, for the implication of a term as to revocation, on which the licence is silent, must depend on what is fair and reasonable between the parties. The court will be guided by the same principles in the one case and the other. The passage which I cited from Bowen LJ's judgment in the *Birmingham* case ended with these words (40 ChD at p. 286):

> That is the principle to be applied. I will not say it is not a principle that was recognised by courts of law as well as of equity. It is not necessary to consider how far it was always a principle of common law.

Nor, my Lords, is it necessary today, but in the House of Justice it would be difficult to distinguish between the equitable principle recognised in *Hughes'* case and the rule well established at common law long before the fusion of law and equity that a licensor must give reasonable notice to determine a licence. It was this rule which was applied in the *Canadian Pacific Railway* case and, in applying it, Lord Russell of Killowen said ([1931] AC at p. 432):

> Whether any and what restrictions exist on the power of a licensor to determine a revocable licence must, their Lordships think, depend upon the circumstances of each case.

And, as I read the decision, it was the circumstances of that case and nothing else, certainly not any general rule, which led him to say that (ibid., at p.433):

> it will be for the Crown to determine the licence by service of a notice the sufficiency of which, if called in question, will have to be decided, upon proper evidence, in subsequent proceedings. It will be for the Crown, at its risk, to fix the length of notice.

The circumstances of that case were very unusual, and I do not doubt that they fully justified the rule being applied in that way. But so, also, in the present case the circumstances are very unusual: it is hardly possible that they should be repeated, and, even if I apply in the amplest way to the termination of the equitable arrangement between the parties in the case the rule applicable to the revocation of licence, I find nothing in the *Canadian Pacific Railway* case which precludes me from reaching the conclusion which I have already stated, viz., that the appellants gave sufficient notice that the suspensory period was at an end and allowed enough time to elapse before seeking to enforce their rights. For these reasons, I think that this defence fails and that the judgment of the Court of Appeal cannot, on this ground, be upheld. . . .

Lord Oaksey, Lord Tucker, and Lord Cohen concurred.

2.1.4.3 'Shield not a sword'

COMBE v *COMBE* [1951] 1 All ER 767 (CA)

DENNING LJ: In this case a wife who has divorced her husband claims maintenance from him – not in the Divorce Court, but in the King's Bench on an agreement which is said to be embodied in letters. The parties were married in 1915. They separated in 1939. On February 1, 1943, on the wife's petition, a decree *nisi* of divorce was pronounced. Shortly afterwards letters passed between the solicitors with regard to maintenance. On February 9, 1943 (eight days after the decree *nisi*), the solicitor for the wife wrote to the solicitor for the husband:

With regard to permanent maintenance, we understand that your client is prepared to make [the wife] an allowance of £100 per year free of income tax.

In answer, on February 19, 1943, the husband's solicitors wrote:

The respondent has agreed to allow your client £100 per annum free of tax.

On August 11, 1943, the decree was made absolute. On August 26, 1943, the wife's solicitors wrote to the husband's solicitors, saying:

Referring to your letter of February 19 last, our client would like the £100 per annum agreed to be paid to her by your client to be remitted to us on her behalf quarterly. We shall be glad if you will kindly let us have a cheque for £25 for the first quarterly instalment and make arrangements for a similar remittance to us on November 11, February 11, May 11 and August 11 in the future.

A reply did not come for nearly two months because the husband was away, and then he himself, on October 18, 1943, wrote a letter which was passed on to the wife's solicitors:

. . . regarding the sum of £25 claimed on behalf of Mrs Combe . . . I would point out that whilst this is paid quarterly as from August 11, 1943, the sum is not due till November 11, 1943, as I can hardly be expected to pay this allowance in advance.

He never paid anything. The wife pressed him for payment, but she did not follow it up by an application to the divorce court. It is to be observed that she herself has an income of her own of between £700 and £800 a year, whereas her husband has only £650 a year. Eventually, after nearly seven years had passed since the decree absolute, she brought this action in the King's Bench Division on July 28, 1950, claiming £675 being arrears for six years and three quarters at £100 a year. Byrne J held that the first three quarterly instalments of £25 were barred by the Limitation Act 1939, but he gave judgment for £600 in respect of the instalments which accrued within the six years before the action was brought. He held, on the authority of *Gaisberg* v *Storr* [1949] 2 All ER 411, that there was no consideraton for the husband's promise to pay his wife £100, but, nevertheless, he held that the promise was enforceable on the principle stated in *Central London Property Trust Ltd* v *High Trees House Ltd* [1947] KB 130 and *Robertson* v *Minister of Pensions* [1948] 2 All ER 767, because it was an unequivocal acceptance of liability, intended to be binding, intended to be acted on, and, in fact, acted on.

Much as I am inclined to favour the principle of the *High Trees* case, it is important that it should not be stretched too far lest it should be endangered. It does not create new causes of action where none existed before. It only prevents a party from insisting on his strict legal rights when it would be unjust to allow him to do so, having regard to the dealings which have taken place between the parties. That is the way it was put in the case in the House of Lords which first stated the principle – *Hughes* v *Metropolitan Ry. Co.* (1877) 2 App Cas 439 – and in the case in the Court of Appeal which enlarged it – *Birmingham and District Land Co.* v *London & North Western Ry. Co.* (1888) 40 ChD 268. It is also implicit in all the modern cases in which the principle has been developed. Sometimes it is a plaintiff who is not allowed to insist on his strict legal rights.

Seeing that the principle never stands alone as giving a cause of action in itself, it can never do away with the necessity of consideration when that is an essential part of the cause of action. The doctrine of consideraton is too firmly fixed to be overthrown by a side-wind. Its ill effects have been largely mitigated of late, but it still remains a cardinal necessity of the formation of a contract, although not of its modification or discharge. I fear that it was my failure to make this clear in *Central London Property Trust Ltd* v *High Trees House Ltd* which misled Byrne J in the present case. He held that the wife could sue on the husband's promise as a separate and independent cause of action by itself, although, as he held, there was no consideration for it. That is not correct. The wife can only enforce the promise if there was consideration for it. That is, therefore, the real question in the case: Was there sufficient consideration to support the promise?

If it were suggested that, in return for the husband's promise, the wife expressly or impliedly promised to forbear from applying to the court for maintenance – that is, a promise in return for a promise – there would clearly be no consideration because the wife's promise would not be binding on her and, therefore, would be worth nothing. Notwithstanding her promise, she could always apply to the divorce court for maintenance – perhaps, only with leave – but nevertheless she could apply. No agreement by her could take away that right: *Hyman v Hyman* [1929] AC 601, as interpreted by this court in *Gaisberg v Storr* [1949] 2 All ER 411. There was, however, clearly no promise by the wife, express or implied, to forbear from applying to the court. All that happened was that she did, in fact, forbear – that is, she did an act in return for a promise. Is that sufficient consideration? Unilateral promises of this kind have long been enforced so long as the act or forbearance is done on the faith of the promise and at the request of the promisor, express or implied. The act done is then in itself sufficient consideration for the promise, even though it arises *ex post facto*, as Parker J pointed out in *Wigan v English and Scottish Law Life Assurance Assocn* [1909] 1 Ch 298. If the findings of Byrne J are accepted, they are sufficient to bring this principle into play. His finding that the husband's promise was intended to be binding, intended to be acted on, and was, in fact, acted on – although expressed to be a finding on the principle of the *High Trees House* case – is equivalent to a finding that there was consideration within this long-settled rule, because it comes to the same thing expressed in different words: see *Oliver v Davis* [1949] 2 All ER 353. My difficulty, however, is to accept the findings of Byrne J that the promise was 'intended to be acted on'. I cannot find any evidence of any intention by the husband that the wife should forbear from applying to the court for maintenance, or, in other words, any request by the husband, express or implied, that the wife should so forbear. He left her to apply, if she wished to do so. She did not do so, and I am not surprised, because it is very unlikely that the divorce court would have made any order in her favour, since she had a bigger income than her husband. Her forbearance was not intended by him, nor was it done at his request. It was, therefore, no consideration.

It may be that the wife has suffered some detriment because, after forbearing to apply to the court for seven years, she might not now get leave to apply: *Scott v Scott* [1921] P 107. The court, however, is, nowadays much more ready to give leave than it used to be: *Fisher v Fisher* [1942] 1 All ER 438; *Hasting v Hasting* [1947] 2 All ER 744; and I should have thought that, if the wife fell on hard times, she would still get leave. Assuming, however, that she has suffered some detriment by her forbearance, nevertheless, as the forbearance was not at the husband's request, it is no consideration. In *Scott v Scott* where a maintenance agreement was made during divorce proceedings, Scrutton LJ said ([1921] P 127) that he had no doubt about there being consideration for it, but this must now be taken to be erroneous, having regard to *Hyman v Hyman* and *Gaisberg v Storr*.

The doctrine of consideration is sometimes said to work injustice, but I see none in this case, nor was there any in *Oliver v Davis* or *Gaisberg v Storr*. I do not think it would be right for this wife, who is better off than her husband, to take no action for six or seven years and then demand from him the whole £600. The truth is that in these maintenance cases the real remedy of the wife is, not by action in the King's Bench Division, but by application in the Divorce Court. I have always understood that no agreement for maintenance, which is made in the course of divorce proceedings prior to decree absolute, is valid unless it is sanctioned by the court – indeed, I said so in *Emanuel v Emanuel* [1945] 2 All ER 496. I know that such agreements are often made, but their only valid purpose is to serve as a basis for a consent application to the court. The reason why such agreements are invalid, unless approved, is because they are so apt to be collusive. Some wives are tempted to stipulate for extortionate maintenance as the price of giving their husbands their freedom. It is to remove this temptation that the sanction of the court is required. It would be a great pity if this salutory requirement could be evaded by taking action in the King's Bench Division. The Divorce Court can order the husband to pay whatever maintenance is just. Moreover, if justice so requires, it can make the order retrospective to decree absolute. That is the proper remedy of the wife here, and I do not think she has a right to any other. For these reasons I think the appeal should be allowed.

BIRKETT LJ: I agree. There were two points before the learned judge, both clearly stated and both clearly argued. . . .

With regard to the second point, we have had the great advantage of hearing Denning LJ deal with *Central London Property Trust Ltd* v *High Trees House Ltd* and *Robertson* v *Minister of Pensions* which formed such a prominent part of the judgment of the court below. I am bound to say that reading them for myself I think the description which was given by counsel for the husband in this court, namely, that the doctrine there enunciated was, so to speak, a doctrine which would enable a person to use it as a shield and not as a sword, is a very vivid way of stating what, I think, is the principle underlying both those cases. Denning J in *Central London Property Trust Ltd* v *High Trees House Ltd* concluded his judgment with these words ([1947] KB 136):

I prefer to apply the principle that a promise intended to the binding, intended to be acted on and in fact acted on, is binding so far as its terms properly apply.

If a husband who had entered into an agreement of this kind was to try to take advantage of it, I think the doctrine would then apply, but, so far as the wife is concerned, her right to apply to the court for maintenance is still, theoretically, in full force, because I see that in *Fisher* v *Fisher* Lord Greene MR dealing with *Scott* v *Scott*, which had formed such a prominent part in the argument, said ([1942] 1 All ER 441):

. . . Scrutton LJ expressed his conclusion ([1921] P 126): 'Without going through the other cases, seven or eight of which I have referred to while counsel have been arguing this case, I think in this particular case the application ought to have been made within a reasonable time after the decree for dissolution; and I see nothing whatever in the circumstances of this case to justify an application being made seven years after the decree.' He carefully refrained from saying that in any circumstances seven years would have been too long. Warrington LJ is equally cautious in the language which he used. In my view that authority does not in any way preclude us from saying that, on the facts of any particular case, a reasonable time may be as much as seven years, or even more.

It was said in the course of the argument of counsel for the husband that, if an application was made to the court at this date for maintenance, it would be necessary to explain the long delay in the making of the application. As one of the material circumstances for the court to consider, I cannot conceive of a better ground to be put forward by the wife than that mistakenly she had relied on an agreement which was to fulfil for her all that she could ever hope to acquire by making an application for maintenance, but, much to her surprise, when that agreement came before the court, it was held to be invalid. In those circumstances I agree with the judgment which has been given and I agree with its conclusion. The learned judge was certainly right in saying that there was no consideration for the agreement, and I think he misunderstood and misapplied the principles in *Central London Property Trust Ltd* v *High Trees House Ltd* and *Robertson* v *Minister of Pensions*. For those reasons I think the appeal ought to be allowed.

ASQUITH LJ: I agree. The learned judge decided that while the husband's promise was unsupported by any valid consideration, yet the principle in *Central London Property Trust Ltd* v *High Trees House Ltd* entitled the wife to succeed. It is unnecessary to express any view as to the correctness of the decision in the *High Trees* case, although I certainly must not be taken to be questioning it. I would, however, remark in passing that it seems to me a complete misconception to suppose that it struck at the roots of the doctrine of consideration. Assuming, without deciding, that it is good law, I do not think it helps the wife at all. What that case decides is that when a promise is given which (i) is intended to create legal relations, (ii) is intended to be acted on by the promisee, and (iii) is, in fact, so acted on, the promisor cannot bring an action against the promisee which involves the repudiation of his promise or is inconsistent with it. It does not, as I read it, decide that a promisee can sue on the promise. Denning J expressly states the contrary. Neither in the *High Trees* case nor in *Robertson* v *Minister of Pensions* (another decision of my Lord which is relied on by the plaintiff) was an action brought by the promisee on the promise. In the first of those two cases the plaintiff was, in effect, the promisor or a person standing in the shoes of the promisor, while in the second the action, although brought by the promisee, was brought on a cause of action which was not the promise, but was an alleged statutory right.

It is said for the wife that the husband's agreement to pay £100 a year was supported by good consideration, which consisted either of an implied undertaking by the wife not to apply to the court for an order for permanent maintenance or of an actual forbearance so to apply. As to the first of these, if the agreement was made before the decree absolute, *Hyman* v *Hyman*, beyond question, decided that such an agreement to abstain from resorting to the court is not valid consideration. It is said, however, first, that the material agreement was not made before the decree absolute, but was made after, and that such an agreement made after the decree is not open to objection and is made for valid consideration. Alternatively, it is argued that, even if such an agreement is not good consideration, an actual forbearance to apply to the court is good consideration.

As to the first of these points, the material agreement was made shortly after the decree *nisi* and long before the decree absolute, by the letters of February 9 and 19, 1943. The correspondence after the decree absolute is merely a request by the wife that an agreement, assumed to have been validly made in the previous February, shall be carried out by means of quarterly payments, followed by a consent by the husband to pay quarterly with a suggestion of different quarter days. This cannot, in my view, constitute a contract made after the decree absolute, but, if it were so, I consider on the whole that *Hyman* v *Hyman* (a decision of the House of Lords) is not to be construed as applying only to agreements made before decree absolute. I think its application is general. It contains no such limitation in time as has been suggested. I am of opinion, further that *Hyman* v *Hyman* is incidentally inconsistent with the *dicta* of Scrutton LJ in *Scott* v *Scott*. Finally, I do not think an actual forbearance, as opposed to an agreement to forbear to approach the court, is a good consideration unless it proceeds from a request, express or implied, on the part of the promisor. If not moved by such a request, the forbearance is not in respect of the promise. For these reasons and the others given by my Lords, I agree that the appeal should be allowed.

2.2   Privity of Contract

TWEDDLE v *ATKINSON* (1861) 1 B&S 393 (QB)

The declaration stated that the plaintiff was the son of John Tweddle, deceased, and before the making of the agreement hereafter mentioned, married the daughter of William Guy, deceased . . . the said William Guy and John Tweddle made and entered into an agreement in writing in the words following, that is to say:

High Coniscliffe, July 11th, 1855

Memorandum of an agreement made this day between William Guy, of &c., of the one part, and John Tweddle, of &c., of the other part. Whereas it is mutually agreed that the said William Guy shall and will pay the sum of 200*l.* to William Tweddle, his son-in-law; and the said John Tweddle, father to the aforesaid William Tweddle, shall and will pay the sum of 100*l.* to the said William Tweddle, each and severally the said sums on or before the 21st day of August, 1855. And it is hereby further agreed by the aforesaid William Guy and the said John Tweddle that the said William Tweddle has full power to sue the said parties in any Court of law or equity for the aforesaid sums hereby promised and specified.

And the plaintiff says that afterwards and before this suit, he and his said wife, who is still living, ratified and assented to the said agreement, and that he is the William Tweddle therein mentioned. And the plaintiff says that the said 21st day of August, A.D. 1855, elapsed, and all things have been done and happened necessary to entitle the plaintiff to have the said sum of 200*l.* paid by the said William Guy or his executor: yet neither the said William Guy nor his executor has paid the same, and the same is in arrear and unpaid, contrary to the said agreement.

WIGHTMAN J: Some of the old decisions appear to support the proposition that a stranger to the consideration of a contract may maintain an action upon it, if he stands in such a near relationship to the party from whom the consideration proceeds, that he may be considered a party to the consideration. The strongest of those cases is that cited in *Bourne* v *Mason* (1 Ventr. 6), in which it was held that the daughter of a physician might maintain assumpsit upon a promise to her father to give her a sum of money if he performed a certain cure. But there is no modern case in which the proposition has been supported. On the contrary, it is now established that no stranger to the consideration can take advantage of a contract, although made for his benefit.

CROMPTON J: It is admitted that the plaintiff cannot succeed unless this case is an exception to the modern and well established doctrine of the action of assumpsit. At the time when the cases which have been cited were decided the action of assumpsit was treated as an action of trespass upon the case, and therefore in the nature of a tort; and the law was not settled, as is now is, that natural love and affection is not a sufficient consideration for a promise upon which an action may be maintained; nor was it settled that the promisee cannot bring an action unless the consideration for the promise moved from him. The modern cases have, in effect, overruled the old decisions; they shew that the consideration must move from the party entitled to sue upon the contract. It would be a monstrous proposition to say that a person was a party to the contract for the purpose of suing upon it for his own advantage, and not a party to it for the purpose of being sued. It is said that the father in the present case was agent for the son in making the contract, but that argument ought also to make the son liable upon it. I am prepared to overrule the old decisions, and to hold that, by reason of the principles which now govern the action of assumpsit, the present action is not maintainable.

BLACKBURN J: The earlier part of the declaration shews a contract which might be sued on, except for the enactment in s. 4 of the Statute of Frauds, 29 Car. 2, c. 3. The declaration then sets out a new contract, and the only point is whether, that contract being for the benefit of the children, they can sue upon it. Mr Mellish admits that in general no action can be maintained upon a promise, unless the consideration moves from the party to whom it is made. But he says that there is an exception; namely, that when the consideration moves from a father, and the contract is for the benefit of his son, the natural love and affection between the father and son gives the son the right to sue as if the consideration had proceeded from himself. And *Dutton and Wife* v *Poole* (1678) 1 Free KB 471 was cited for this. We cannot overrule a decision of the Exchequer Chamber; but there is a distinct ground on which that case cannot be supported. The cases upon stat. 27 El. c. 4, which have decided that, by s. 2, voluntary gifts by settlement after marriage are void against subsequent purchasers for value, and are not saved by s. 4, shew that natural love and affection are not a sufficient consideration whereon an action of assumpsit may be founded.

Judgment for the defendant.

BESWICK v BESWICK [1968] AC 58 (HL)

LORD REID: My Lords, before 1962 the respondent's deceased husband carried on business as a coal merchant. By agreement of March 14, 1962, he assigned to his nephew, the appellant, the assets of the business and the appellant undertook first to pay to him £6 10s. per week for the remainder of his life and then to pay to the respondent an annuity of £5 per week in the event of her husband's death. The husband died in November, 1963. Thereupon, the appellant made one payment of £5 to the respondent but he refused to make any further payment to her. The respondent now sues for £175 arrears of the annuity and for an order for specific performance of the continuing obligation to pay the annuity. The Vice-Chancellor of the County Palatine of Lancaster decided against the respondent but the Court of Appeal reversed this decision and, besides ordering payment of the arrears, ordered the appellant to pay to the respondent for the remainder of her life an annuity of £5 per week in accordance with the agreement.

It so happens that the respondent is administratrix of the estate of her deceased husband and she sues both in that capacity and in her personal capacity. So it is necessary to consider her rights in each capacity.

For clarity I think it best to begin by considering a simple case where, in consideration of a sale by A to B, B agrees to pay the price of £1,000 to a third party X. Then the first question appears to me to be whether the parties intended that X should receive the money simply as A's nominee so that he would hold the money for behoof of A and be accountable to him for it, or whether the parties intended that X should receive the money for his own behoof and be entitled to keep it. That appears to me to be a question of construction of the agreement read in light of all the circumstances which were known to the parties. There have been several decisions involving this question. I am not sure that any conflicts with the view which I have expressed: but if any does, for example, *In re Engelbach's Estate* [1924] Ch 348. I would not agree with it. I think that *In re Schebsman* [1944] Ch 83, was rightly decided and that the reasoning of Uthwatt J and the Court of Appeal supports what I have just said. In the present case I think it clear that the parties to the agreement intended that the respondent should receive the weekly sums of £5 in her own behoof and should not be accountable to her deceased husband's estate for them. Indeed the contrary was not argued.

Reverting to my simple example the next question appears to me to be: Where the intention was that X should keep the £1,000 as his own, what is the nature of B's obligation and who is entitled to enforce it? It was not argued that the law of England regards B's obligation as a nullity, and I have not observed in any of the authorities any suggestion that it would be a nullity. There may have been a time when the existence of a right depended on whether there was any means of enforcing it, but today the law would be sadly deficient if one found that, although there is a right, the law provides no means for enforcing it. So this obligation of B must be enforceable either by X or by A. I shall leave aside for the moment the question whether section 56 (1) of the Law of Property Act, 1925, has any application to such a case, and consider the position at common law.

Lord Denning's view, expressed in this case not for the first time, is that X could enforce this obligation. But the view more commonly held in recent times has been that such a contract confers no right on X and that X could not sue for the £1,000. Leading counsel for the respondent based his case on other grounds, and as I agree that the respondent succeeds on other grounds, this would not be an appropriate case in which to solve this question. It is true that a strong Law Revision Committee recommended so long ago as 1937 (Cmd. 5449):

That where a contract by its express terms purports to confer a benefit directly on a third party it shall be enforceable by the third party in his own name . . . (p. 31).

And, if one had to contemplate a further long period of Parliamentary procrastination, this House might find it necessary to deal with this matter. But if legislation is probable at any early date I would not deal with it in a case where that is not essential. So for the purposes of this case I shall proceed on the footing that the commonly accepted view is right.

What then is A's position? I assume that A has not made himself a trustee for X, because it was not argued in this appeal that any trust had been created. So, if X has no right, A can at any time grant a discharge to B or make some new contract with B. If there were a trust the position would be different. X would have an equitable right and A would be entitled and, indeed, bound to recover the money and account for it to X. And A would have no right to grant a discharge to B. If there is no trust and A wishes to enforce the obligation, how does he set about it? He cannot sue B for the £1,000 because under the contract the money is not payable to him, and, if the contract were performed according to its terms, he would never have any right to get the money. So he must seek to make B pay X.

The argument for the appellant is that A's only remedy is to sue B for damages for B's breach of contract in failing to pay the £1,000 to X. Then the appellant says that A can only recover nominal damages of 40s. because the fact that X has not received the money will generally cause no loss to A: he admits that there may be cases where A would suffer damage if X did not receive the money but says that the present is not such a case.

Applying what I have said to the circumstances of the present case, the respondent in her personal capacity has no right to sue, but she has a right as administratrix of her husband's estate to require the appellant to perform his obligation under the agreement.

He has refused to do so and he maintains that the respondent's only right is to sue him for damages for breach of his contract. If that were so, I shall assume that he is right in maintaining that the administratrix could then only recover nominal damages because his breach of contract has caused no loss to the estate of her deceased husband.

If that were the only remedy available the result would be grossly unjust. It would mean that the appellant keeps the business which he bought and for which he has only paid a small part of the price which he agreed to pay. He would avoid paying the rest of the price, the annuity to the respondent, by paying a mere 40s. damages.

The respondent's first answer is that the common law has been radically altered by section 56(1) of the Law of Property Act, 1925, and that that section entitles her to sue in her personal capacity and recover the benefit provided for her in the agreement although she was not a party to it. Extensive alterations of the law were made at that time but it is necessary to examine with some care the way in which this was done. That Act was a consolidation Act and it is the invariable practice of Parliament to require from those who have prepared a consolidation Bill an assurance that it will make no substantial change in the law and to have that checked by a committee. On this assurance the Bill is then passed into law, no amendment being permissible. So, in order to pave the way for the consolidation Act of 1925, earlier Acts were passed in 1922 and 1924 in which were enacted all the substantial amendments which now appear in the Act of 1925 and these amendments were then incorporated in the Bill which became the Act of 1925. Those earlier Acts contain nothing corresponding to section 56 and it is therefore quite certain that those responsible for the preparation of this legislation must have believed and intended that section 56 would make no substantial change in the earlier law, and equally certain that Parliament passed section 56 in reliance on an assurance that it did make no substantial change.

In construing any Act of Parliament we are seeking the intention of Parliament and it is quite true that we must deduce that intention from the words of the Act. If the words of the Act are only capable of one meaning we must give them that meaning no matter how they got there. But if they are capable of having more than one meaning we are, in my view, well entitled to see how they got there. For purely practical reasons we do not permit debates in either House to be cited: it would add greatly to the time and expense involved in preparing cases involving the construction of a statute if counsel were expected to read all the debates in *Hansard*, and it would often be impracticable for counsel to get access to at least the older reports of debates in Select Committees of the House of Commons; moreover, in a very large proportion of cases such a search, even if practicable, would throw no light on the question before the court. But I can see no objection to investigating in the present case the antecedents of section 56.

Section 56 was obviously intended to replace section 5 of the Real Property Act 1845 (8 and 9 Vict. c. 106). That section provided:

That, under an indenture, executed after October 1, 1845, an immediate estate or interest, in any tenements or hereditaments, and the benefit of a condition or covenant, respecting any tenements or hereditaments, may be taken, although the taker thereof be not named a party to the same indenture. . . .

Section 56 (1) now provides:

A person may take an immediate or other interest in land or other property, or the benefit of any condition, right of entry, covenant or agreement over or respecting land or other property, although he may not be named as a party to the conveyance or other instrument: . . .

If the matter stopped there it would not be difficult to hold that section 56 does not substantially extend or alter the provisions of section 5 of the Act of 1845. But more difficulty is introduced by the definition section of the Act of 1925 (section 205) which provides:

(1) In this Act unless the context otherwise requires, the following expressions have the meanings hereby assigned to them respectively, that is to say:– . . . (xx) 'Property' includes any thing in action, and any interest in real or personal property.

Before further considering the meaning of section 56 (1) I must set out briefly the views which have been expressed about it in earlier cases. *White v Bijou Mansions Ltd* [1937] 3 All ER 269 dealt with a covenant relating to land. The interpretation of section 56 was not the main issue. Simonds J rejected an argument that section 56 enabled anyone to take advantage of a covenant if he could show that if the covenant were enforced it would redound to his advantage. He said:

> Just as under section 5 of the Act of 1845 only that person could call it in aid who, although not a party, yet was a grantee or convenantee, so under section 56 of this Act only that person can call it in aid who, although not named as a party to the conveyance or other instrument, is yet a person to whom that conveyance or other instrument purports to grant something or with which some agreement or covenant is purported to be made.

He was not concerned to consider whether or in what way the section could be applied to personal property. In the Court of Appeal Sir Wilfred Greene MR said, in rejecting the same argument as Simonds J had rejected:

> Before he can enforce it he must be a person who falls within the scope and benefit of the covenant according to the true construction of the document in question.

Again he was not considering an ordinary contract and I do not think that he can be held to have meant that every person who falls within the 'scope and benefit' of any contract is entitled to sue, though not a party to the contract.

In *In re Miller's Agreement* [1947] 2 All ER 78 two partners covenanted with a retiring partner that on his death they would pay certain annuities to his daughters. The Revenue's claim for estate duty was rejected. The decision was clearly right. The daughters, not being parties to the agreement, had no right to sue for their annuities. Whether they received them or not depended on whether the other partners were willing to pay or, if they did not pay, whether the deceased partner's executor was willing to enforce the contract. After citing the earlier cases Wynn-Parry J said:

> I think it emerges from these cases that the section has not the effect of creating rights, but only of assisting the protection of rights shown to exist.

I am bound to say I do not quite understand that. I had thought from what Lord Simonds said in *White's* case that section 5 of the Act of 1845 did enable certain persons to take benefits which they could not have taken without it. If so, it must have given them rights which they did not have without it. And, if that is so, section 56 must now have the same effect. In *Smith and Snipes Hall Farm Ltd v River Douglas Catchment Board* [1949] 2 All ER 179 Denning LJ, after stating his view that a third person can sue on a contract to which he is not a party, referred to section 56 as a clear statutory recognition of this principle, with the consequence that *Miller's* case was wrongly decided. I cannot agree with that. And in *Drive Yourself Hire Co. (London) Ltd v Strutt* [1953] 2 All ER 1475 Denning LJ again expressed similar views about section 56.

I can now return to consider the meaning and scope of section 56. It refers to any 'agreement over or respecting land or other property'. If 'land or other property' means the same thing as 'tenements or hereditaments' in the Act of 1845 then this section simply continues the law as it was before the Act of 1925 was passed, for I do not think that the other differences in phraseology can be regarded as making any substantial change. So any obscurities in section 56 are obscurities which originated in 1845. But if its scope is wider, then two points must be considered. The section refers to agreements 'over or respecting land or other property'. The land is something which existed before and independently of the agreement and the same must apply to the other property. So an agreement between A and B that A will use certain personal property for the benefit of X would be within the scope of the section, but an agreement that if A performs certain services for B, B will pay a sum to X would not be within the scope of the section. Such a capricious distinction would alone throw doubt on this interpretation.

Perhaps more important is the fact that the section does not say that a person may take the benefit of an agreement although he was not a party to it: it says that he may do so although he was not named as a party in the instrument which embodied the agreement. It is true that section 56 says 'although he may not be named'; but section 5 of the Act of 1845 says although he 'be not named a party'. Such a change of phraseology in a consolidation Act cannot involve a change of meaning. I do not profess to have a full understanding of the old English law regarding deeds. But it appears from what Lord Simonds said in *White's* case and from what Vaisey J said in *Chelsea and Waltham Green Building Society* v *Armstrong* [1951] 2 All ER 250 that being in fact a party to an agreement might not be enough; the person claiming a benefit had to be named a party in the indenture. I have read the explanation of the old law given by my noble and learned friend, Lord Upjohn. I would not venture to criticise it, but I do not think it necessary for me to consider it if it leads to the conclusion that section 56 taken by itself would not assist the present respondent.

But it may be that additional difficulties would arise from the application to section 56 of the definition of property in the definition section. If so, it becomes necessary to consider whether that definition can be applied to section 56. By express provision in the definition section a definition contained in it is not to be applied to the word defined if in the particular case the context otherwise requires. If application of that definition would result in giving to section 56 a meaning going beyond that of the old section, then, in my opinion, the context does require that the definition of 'property' shall not be applied to that word in section 56. The context in which this section occurs is a consolidation Act. If the definition is not applied the section is a proper one to appear in such an Act because it can properly be regarded as not substantially altering the pre-existing law. But if the definition is applied the result is to make section 56 go far beyond the pre-existing law. Holding that the section has such an effect would involve holding that the invariable practice of Parliament has been departed from *per incuriam* so that something has got into this consolidation Act which neither the draftsman nor Parliament can have intended to be there. I am reinforced in this view by two facts. The language of section 56 is not at all what one would have expected if the intention had been to bring in all that the application of the definition would bring in. And, secondly, section 56 is one of 25 sections which appear in the Act under the cross-heading 'Conveyances and other Instruments'. The other twenty-four sections come appropriately under that heading and so does section 56 if it has a limited meaning: but, if its scope is extended by the definition of property, it would be quite inappropriately placed in this part of the Act. For these reasons I am of opinion that section 56 has no application to the present case.

The respondent's second argument is that she is entitled in her capacity of administratrix of her deceased husband's estate to enforce the provision of the agreement for the benefit of herself in her personal capacity, and that a proper way of enforcing that provision is to order specific performance. That would produce a just result, and, unless there is some technical objection, I am of opinion that specific performance ought to be ordered. For the reasons given by your Lordships I would reject the arguments submitted for the appellant that specific performance is not a possible remedy in this case. I am therefore of opinion that the Court of Appeal reached a correct decision and that this appeal should be dismissed.

Lord Hodson, Lord Guest, Lord Pearce and Lord Upjohn concurred.

SWISS BANK CORPORATION v *LLOYDS BANK LTD* [1979] 2 All ER 853 (HC)

BROWNE-WILKINSON J: This action is concerned with a loan in Swiss francs made by the plaintiffs, the Swiss Bank Corpn (which I will call 'SBC'), to the third defendants, Israel Financial Trust Ltd (which I will call 'IFT'). IFT is a subsidiary, indirectly of the fourth defendants, Triumph Investment Trust Ltd (which I will call 'Triumph'). Before the loan was made IFT had to obtain from the Bank of England exchange control consent to the borrowing. The consent was granted subject to stringent conditions including in particular conditions requiring that the borrowed moneys should be applied in acquiring certain foreign investments, and that the servicing of the loan and its eventual repayment was to be made out of the income or capital of the investments so acquired. Under the loan agreement between SBC and IFT, IFT covenanted to observe the conditions imposed by the Bank of England. Subsequently the Triumph group got into serious financial difficulties, and in an attempt to rescue it the first defendants, Lloyds Bank Ltd (which I will call 'Lloyds'), advanced very large sums of money to the group, such advances being made on the security, inter alia, of a charge granted by IFT over the investments purchased with the loan from SBC.

The main issues in this case revolve around the difficult question whether SBC has a legal right to require its loan to be repaid out of the proceeds of sale of the investments acquired with the loan (as required by the Bank of England conditions) and if so whether such right of SBC prevails over Lloyd's rights under the charge. Triumph is insolvent and in liquidation. IFT has not yet gone into liquidation, although I was told that a petition to wind it up had been presented during the hearing before me. There is, to put it at its lowest, great doubt whether the assets of IFT will be sufficient to satify the debts owed by it both to SBC and to Lloyds. The case therefore raises questions of priorities. . . .

The De Mattos v Gibson argument
In De Mattos v Gibson (1859) 4 De G & J 276 Knight Bruce LJ said:

> Reason and justice seem to prescribe that, at least as a general rule, where a man, by gift or purchase, acquires property from another, with knowledge of a previous contract, lawfully and for valuable consideration made by him with a third person, to use and employ the property for a particular purpose in a specified manner, the acquirer shall not, to the material damage of the third person, in opposition to the contract and inconsistently with it, use and employ the property in a manner not allowable to the giver or seller. This rule, applicable alike in general as I conceive to moveable and immoveable property, and recognized and adopted, as I apprehend, by the English law, may like other general rules, be liable to exceptions arising from special circumstances; but I see at present no room for any exception in the instances before us.

SBC allege that when the Lloyds charge was created Lloyds had constructive notice of the terms of the loan agreement: for the moment I will assume that to be correct. There is no allegation that at the date of the charge Lloyds had actual notice of SBC's contractual claim to have its loan serviced and repaid out of the FIBI securities; but it is common ground that before the FIBI securities were sold and the dollar proceeds converted into sterling, Lloyds had actual knowledge of SBC's claim.

In these circumstances counsel for SBC argues, in reliance on the passage in *De Mattos v Gibson* that, even if the loan agreement did not confer on SBC a property interest in the FIBI securities, SBC is entitled to an injunction restraining Lloyds from applying the proceeds of the FIBI securities in repayment of the moneys owed by IFT to Lloyds, since this would constitute the tort of a knowing interference by Lloyds with SBC's contractual right to have the proceeds applied in discharging the debt owed by IFT to SBC. I will in future refer to such knowing interference as 'the tort'. Counsel for SBC emphasises that he does not claim that Lloyds's constructive notice of SBC's rights is sufficient to found a claim that Lloyds committed the tort when it took the charge; he accepts that actual knowledge of the contract is a necessary ingredient of the tort. The question of constructive notice comes in in this way; counsel for SBC accepts that if at the present time Lloyds repays itself out of the FIBI securities in exercise of a lawful proprietary right acquired by Lloyds under its charge, then, even though Lloyds now has actual knowledge, it is not liable to SBC for the tort: the tort is not committed if Lloyds is acting in reliance on lawful proprietary rights acquired under the charge. But, says counsel, Lloyds cannot rely on any lawful proprietary interest acquired under its charge since, at the time it acquired the charge, Lloyds had constructive notice of SBC's contractual rights.

Counsel's answer for Lloyds to these contentions is twofold. First he says that the principle enunciated by Knight Bruce LJ, which I have read, is not good law and, secondly, that, even if it is good law, actual, as opposed to constructive, notice of the plaintiff's contractual rights is required.

Before considering the authorities I will again look at the matter in principle. There are many types of contract affecting property which do not confer on the parties to that contract any legal or equitable interest in the property. For example, contracts which are not, for some reason, specifically enforceable or which merely restrain one of the parties from using the property in a particular way without purporting to give the other party any right to enjoy the property or its fruits, e.g. a restrictive covenant. The question is to what extent, if any, does such a contract affect third parties who subsequently acquire the property. In the case before me three different types of case have been considered (though there may well be others), viz: (a) restrictive covenants affecting land and resale price maintenance conditions affecting chattels; (b) cases which may raise a constructive trust; (c) cases, such as *De Mattos* v *Gibson*, where the proposed actions of the third party who has subsequently acquired the property will cause a breach of the original contract by one of the contracting parties.

I will first say a word about categories (a) and (b) which to my mind involve quite different considerations from those involved in *De Mattos* v *Gibson*.

In restrictive covenant and resale price maintenance cases, the plaintiff is seeking directly to enforce a contract against a defendant who is not a contracting party: the plaintiff is not seeking to restrain the defendant from causing a breach of the contract by one of the contracting parties. Suppose there is a covenant by A, the owner of Blackacre, with B that Blackacre will not be built on, and that A subsequently sells Blackacre to C. In restrictive covenant cases B (or his successor in title) is seeking to force C to perform the contract entered into between A and B. B is not seeking to restrain C from interfering in the performance by A of his contract with B since A, having parted with the land, has put it out of his power to perform the contract. Courts of equity could have made C liable to perform the contract if he took with notice of it, and indeed for the first 20 years after *Tulk* v *Moxhay* [1848] 2 Ph 774 notice was thought to be the basis on which the restrictive covenants were enforced: see *London County Council* v *Allen* [1914] 3 KB 642, and *Barker* v *Stickney* [1919] 1 KB 121. But as those decisions show, the law of restrictive covenants (both as affecting realty and personalty) developed on wholly different lines, said to be analogous to the doctrine in *Spencer's Case* (1583) 5 Co Rep 16a or negative easements. In my judgment the authorities on attempts to enforce performance of restrictive covenants by third parties do not bear directly on the question whether or not third parties can be restrained from interfering with the original contract. So far as I can see, no argument along those lines was raised in any of the reported decisions I was referred to, and in most of the cases the particular facts did not raise even the possibility of such an argument. In restrictive covenant cases often the plaintiff is not himself one of the original contracting parties or even a legal assignee of the benefit of the contracts: even if the plaintiff is entitled at law to enforce the original contract, the other original contracting party is usually dead or untraced.

Category (b) is best illustrated by an example. Suppose that P has contracted to allow Q to use some property owned by P. P then sells that property to R expressly subject to the terms of the contract between P and Q. There is some authority to suggest that R, by expressly agreeing to buy the property subject to Q's contractual rights is, as a constructive trustee, bound to give effect to those rights: see *Binions* v *Evans* [1972] 2 All ER 70 per Lord Denning MR. The fiduciary relationship is apparently created by R taking the property expressly subject to Q's rights. Similar reasoning seems to have been one of the bases of the decision in *Lord Strathcona Steamship Co. Ltd* v *Dominion Coal Co. Ltd* [1926] AC 108, to which I will have to return. Since in this case there is no question of Lloyds having taken the charge expressly subject to SBC's rights, that principle has no application before me.

Having sought to put those two categories on one side, I can turn to the *De Mattos* v *Gibson* principle itself. When that case was decided, it had already been recognised at common law that it was a legal wrong or tort for someone knowingly to interfere with the contractual rights of others: see *Lumley* v *Gye* (1853) 2 E & B 216. It has subsequently been established that equity will intervene to restrain such a tort and such jurisdiction is frequently exercised at the present day: see, for example, *Earl of Sefton* v *Tophams Ltd* [1964] 3 All ER 876 (the injunction against the second defendants). It follows that, if at the date of the Lloyds charge, Lloyds had had *actual* notice of SBC's rights in relation to the FIBI securities and SBC had been informed of IFT's intention to grant the Lloyds charge, SBC could, in my judgment, have obtained an injunction restraining Lloyds from taking the charge since by so doing they would have been committing the tort. If Lloyds had taken the charge with actual knowledge of SBC's rights (no injunction having been applied for in time because of SBC's ignorance of what was going on) in my judgment Lloyds could not be in any better position. The taking of the charge with that state of knowledge being itself a tort by Lloyds could not put Lloyds in a better position just because the charge had been completed before the threat of the tort was known to SBC: a man cannot rely on his own wrong.

Therefore I would accept counsel for SBC's argument as being right in principle if, but only if, Lloyds had had actual notice of SBC's rights when the charge was granted. But Lloyds did not have actual notice of SBC's rights when it took its charge and therefore committed no legal wrong by so doing since actual knowledge of the other contract is an essential ingredient of the tort. Having acquired its charge otherwise than by means of a legal wrong, I can see no ground in principle for saying that Lloyds is not entitled to rely on its rights under the charge as justification at the present time for applying the proceeds of the FIBI securities in paying its own secured debt, even though to Lloyds's knowledge that involves a breach of the contract between SBC and IFT. To say, as counsel for SBC urges, that a person acquiring a property right with constructive notice of a contract affecting it cannot rely on such property right to justify future interference with that contract is to introduce into the question 'has a legal tort been committed?' equitable concepts of notice designed to regulate the priority of conflicting property interests. Unless there are compelling authorities requiring me to do so, I would not be prepared to bedevil the tort with such equitable refinements.

How then do the authorities stand? In *De Mattos* v *Gibson* itself the plaintiff had chartered a ship from its owner Curry. Curry had subsequently charged the ship to Gibson, who had actual notice of the charterparty. Curry got into financial difficulties and was unable to continue the voyage. Gibson was proposing to sell the ship of which he had taken possession. In the action the plaintiff claimed an injunction against Gibson restraining him from interfering with the charterparty. The plaintiff applied for an interim injunction, which was granted on appeal. The grounds for the decision of Knight Bruce LJ were those set out in the passage I have already read. The decision of Turner LJ was founded entirely on balance of convenience, but one of the three questions he said would have to be decided at the trial was whether the plaintiff, even if not entitled to specific performance of the charterparty, was entitled to an injunction to restrain a breach of the charterparty. In due course the action came on for trial before Page Wood V-C (from whose decision there was an appeal to the Lord Chancellor). Lord Chelmsford LC held that no injunction should be granted against Gibson. He referred expressly to the three questions posed by Turner LJ, and after holding that the charterparty could not be specifically performed, said that Gibson having taken with full knowledge of the charter could be restrained from doing any act which would have the immediate effect of preventing its performance. But Lord Chelmsford LC went on to show that on the facts there was no real possibility of Curry performing the charterparty whatever Gibson did, and therefore there was no question of any act by Gibson constituting an interference by Gibson with the plaintiff's contractual rights. In my judgment that case is an authority binding on me that a person taking a charge on property which he knows to be subject to a contractual obligation can be restrained from exercising his rights under the charge in such a way as to interfere with the performance of that contractual obligation. In my judgment the *De Mattos* v *Gibson* principle is merely the equitable counterpart of the tort. But two points have to be emphasised about the decision in *De Mattos* v *Gibson*; first, the ship was acquired with actual knowledge of the plaintiff's contractual rights; secondly, that no such injunction will be granted against the third party if it is clear that the original contracting party cannot in any event perform his contract. It is this second point which in my judgment accounts for the fact that the *De Mattos* v *Gibson* principle is not applicable to restrictive covenants: the original contracting party (even if traceable) could not carry out his contract relating to the land, or the chattel once he had parted with it.

In *Lord Strathcona Steamship Co. Ltd* v *Dominion Coal Co.* the facts were that a ship which was the subject-matter of a charterparty to Dominion was sold to Strathcona expressly subject to the rights of Dominion under the charterparty. The Privy Council held that an injunction could be granted restraining Strathcona from interfering with Dominion's rights under the charterparty. It will be noted that the *Strathcona* case is of the type I considered under category (b) above, ie Strathcona bought expressly subject to Dominion's rights. And certainly one ground of decision is that, in the circumstances, Strathcona was a constructive trustee. It is not clear to me whether this was the only ground of decision since the passages in the judgment dealing with *De Mattos* v *Gibson* (which was held to be good law) certainly seem to proceed on the basis of knowing interference with another's contract. The Privy Council accepted that, in order to get an injunction, the plaintiff had to have a continuing interest in the property but undoubtedly held that a bare contractual right, as opposed to a property interest, was a sufficient interest for this purpose.

There are parts of the judgment in the *Strathcona* case which I find difficult to follow but in my judgment it certainly decides (i) that *De Mattos* v *Gibson* is good law and (ii) that an injunction can be granted to restrain a subsequent purchaser of a chattel from using it so as to cause a breach of a contract of which he has express notice.

In *Port Line Ltd* v *Ben Line Steamers Ltd* [1958] 1 All ER 787 Diplock J stated that he thought the *Strathcona* case was wrongly decided and refused to follow it. In that case Port had chartered a vessel from Silver. Silver then sold to Ben but subject to an immediate recharter by Ben to Silver. Under the charterparty between Port and Silver the requisitioning of the vessel did not determine the charter; under the charterparty between Ben and Silver it did. The vessel was requisitioned and Port was claiming from Ben compensation received by Ben for the requisition. It is important to notice that Port could only succeed if it showed either that it had a positive right to possession of the vessel or that Ben was accountable for the compensation as constructive trustee. Diplock J was not concerned with the question whether Port was entitled to a negative injunction to restrain the tort.

It is not necessary for me to express any view as to whether the *Strathcona* case was rightly decided so far as it was a decision based on constructive trusteeship, which was all that Diplock J was concerned with: the *Strathcona* case itself decided that there was no right to specific performance of the charterpartry. However, although I of course differ from Diplock J with diffidence, in my judgment the *Strathcona* case was rightly decided on the basis that Dominion was entitled to an injunction against Strathcona to prevent Strathcona from interfering with the contract between Dominion and the original charterer. Diplock J explained *De Mattos* v *Gibson* on that ground and gave as an alternative ground for his decision that actual, as opposed to constructive, notice was necessary in such a case. To that extent his decision supports my own view.

In my judgment there is in any event a decision of the Court of Appeal which is binding on me, namely *Manchester Ship Canal Co.* v *Manchester Racecourse Co.* [1901] 2 Ch 37. In that case the racecourse company had granted the canal company a right of first refusal over certain land. The racecourse company, without giving proper effect to such a right of first refusal, had entered into a contract to sell the land to a third party, Trafford. The Court of Appeal held (whether rightly or wrongly does not for this purpose matter) that the right of first refusal did not create any property interests in the land, but even so granted an injunction against Trafford restraining them from completing their contract to purchase. The Court of Appeal founded its decision expressly on the basis that Trafford, having full knowledge, was proposing to do something which would cause a breach of the contract between the canal company and the racecourse company, ie to commit the tort. In my judgment this is a decision of the Court of Appeal that the court will restrain a person from enforcing his contractual rights so as to cause a breach of another contract of which he had full knowledge when he entered into his own contract. As such, it covers the present case. But it is to be noted that Trafford in that case had actual knowledge, as opposed to contructive notice, of the contract between the canal company and the racecourse company.

In *Binions* v *Evans* Megaw LJ indicated that he thought the case could properly have been decided on the basis that an injunction to restrain the tort should be granted. This again supports the existence of the jurisdiction.

What then are the authorities which suggest that the *De Mattos* v *Gibson* principle is not good law? In my judgment apart from the *Port Line* case they are all cases falling within category (a) above; that is to say not cases in which the plaintiff sought an injunction to restrain the defendant from committing the tort but cases where the plaintiff was seeking to make the defendant positively perform a contract to which he was not a party. In particular, it is in my judgment, clear that the remarks of Scrutton J (as he then was) in *London County Council* v *Allen* and Scrutton LJ in *Barker* v *Stickney* are to be read in their context as cases where the plaintiff was seeking to enforce performance of the contract against the defendant who was not a party to the contract. So far as I can see, in neither of those cases was there any consideration of the rights of the plaintiff to a negative injunction restraining the defendant from causing someone else to breach the contract with the plaintiff.

Therefore, in my judgment the authorities establish the following propositions. (i) The principle stated by Knight Bruce LJ in *De Mattos* v *Gibson* is good law and represents the counterpart in equity of the tort of knowing interference with contractual rights. (ii) A person proposing to deal with property in such a way as to cause a breach of a contract affecting that property will be restrained by injunction from so doing if when he acquired that property he had actual knowledge of that contract. (iii) A plaintiff is entitled to such an injunction even if he has no proprietary interest in the property: his right to have his contract performed is a sufficient interest. (iv) There is no case in which such an injunction has been granted against a defendant who acquired the property with only constructive, as opposed to actual, notice of the contract. In my judgment constructive notice is not sufficient, since actual knowledge of the contract is a requisite element in the tort.

Accordingly, on this argument I conclude that, even assuming that Lloyds had constructive notice of SBC's claim when the Lloyds charge was granted, no injunction lies against Lloyds to restrain the application of the FIBI securities in payment of the debt due from IFT to Lloyds in reliance on the rights granted by the charge: Lloyds did not at the date of the charge have actual knowledge. Therefore, if the charge is valid, no injunction lies against Lloyds on this ground since they can properly rely on the charge to justify interfering with SBC's rights. However, if the Lloyds charge is invalid (on the grounds of illegality) an injunction should be granted against Lloyds since, at this stage, to apply the moneys in paying Lloyds's debt will amount to a knowing interference with SBC's rights without any lawful justification.

In this part of my judgment I have assumed, in favour of SBC, that Lloyds had constructive notice of SBC's rights. In the light of my conclusions there is no need for me to find whether or not there was such constructive notice or whether, in law, the doctrine has any application to commercial transactions such as these were. Since no evidence was called by Lloyds on this issue, the Court of Appeal will be in as good a position to find the facts of the matter as I am . . .

2.3   End of Chapter Assessment Question

Hartwell agrees to make all the costumes for Leonard's play, 'The Black Panther', which has its first night on 7 May. The price is £30,000 payable on 1 May, the delivery date under the contract. Early in April Leonard is alarmed to discover that Hartwell's seamstresses are substantially behind with their work, and in consequence his first night may be in jeopardy. Leonard therefore promises the seamstresses that he will pay them a bonus of £50 each if the work on his costumes is hastened. He also promises to pay Hartwell an extra £5,000 if he can ensure delivery of the costumes by 1 May. All other work is put to one side in favour of Leonard's costumes. On 30 April Leonard tells the seamstresses that his promise to pay the bonus is withdrawn.

On 1 May Leonard's costumes are delivered in accordance with the contract and Hartwell demands the sum of £35,000 from Leonard. Leonard explains that the costs of the play are far in excess of his expectations and that in consequence he is in financial difficulties. He offers to pay Hartwell £25,000 as this is all he can afford. Knowing that he will get less if Leonard goes bankrupt, Hartwell accepts this sum in full and final settlement.

On 1 June, learning that 'The Black Panther' is an outstanding success, Hartwell wishes to sue for the balance of £10,000 which he believes that Leonard owes him, and the seamstresses wish to sue Leonard for their promised bonuses.

Advise Hartwell and the seamstresses.

2.4   End of Chapter Assessment Outline Answer

Leonard is potentially contractually bound here by two separate promises of additional payment: (a) a £50 bonus to each of the seamstresses; and (b) £5,000 to Hartwell.

(a) *Leonard–seamstresses agreement*. What consideration have the seamstresses furnished in return for Leonards promise?

They have performed an existing contractual duty owed to a third party (Hartwell), which is sufficient consideration (*Shadwell* v *Shadwell*; *Scotson* v *Pegg*; *New Zealand Shipping Co. Ltd* v *Satterthwaite & Co. Ltd* (*The Eurymedon*)). *The Eurymedon* suggests that this is so even though the seamstresses have incurred no additional detriment because they have conferred a benefit on Leonard (costumes completed on time, and the first night can take place).

Leonard's attempt to revoke his promise on 30 April probably constitutes a breach of a collateral contract not to revoke until the seamstresses have had a reasonable opportunity to complete their task (*Errington* v *Errington & Woods*).

(b) *Leonard–Hartwell agreement*.

Hartwell has performed an existing contractual duty owed to Leonard by meeting the contractual delivery date. Prima facie this is insufficient consideration (*Stilk* v *Myrick*).

It might be argued, tenuously, that he has exceeded his obligation by putting all other work to one side (*Hartley* v *Ponsonby*).

However, the strongest argument comes from *Williams* v *Roffey Bros* which has refined *Stilk* v *Myrick*, probably on policy grounds. Even though Hartwell has incurred no additional detriment he has conferred a benefit in fact upon Leonard by ensuring that his first night can take place.

At common law Hartwell can go back on his promise to accept £25,000 in full and final settlement since Leonard prima facie has furnished no consideration in return (*Pinnel's Case*; *Foakes* v *Beer*).

However, one might have thought that *Williams* v *Roffey Bros* could be extended to debtor–creditor relationships. Has not Hartwell received a benefit in fact if he has received more than he would have obtained by proving in Leonard's bankruptcy? Unfortunately, the Court of Appeal in *Re Selectmove Ltd* has ruled that the *Williams* v *Roffey Bros* principle is not to be extended to debtor–creditor situations.

Since this argument is not acceptable Leonard must fall back upon the equitable doctrine of promissory estoppel as espoused by Denning J in the *High Trees* case, relying on a slim line of authority stemming from *Hughes* v *Metropolitan Railway Co.*

Can this doctrine apply here? Leonard and Hartwell are parties to an existing legal relationship; Hartwell, presumably intending legal consequences, makes an unequivocal promise to accept less than his strict contractual rights in full and final settlement; Leonard has altered his position in reliance upon the promise by going ahead with the play which presumably he would not otherwise have done. This would satisfy either the detriment requirement as per *Hughes*, or the more modern approach that the change of position must be such as to make it inequitable for the promisor to go back on his promise, at least until he has served reasonable notice of an intention to do so (*Tool Metal Case*, the *Post Chaser*). The effect of Hartwell's promise depends upon the view adopted: (a) according to Lord Denning obiter in *High Trees* and in *D & C Builders* v *Rees* Hartwell's rights have been extinguished and he can never reclaim the balance. This is controversial because it effectively ignores the doctrine of consideration; it does however give effect to the nature of Hartwell's promise; (b) according to the orthodox view (*Ajayi* v *Briscoe Ltd, The Tool Metal Case*), Hartwell's rights are merely suspended and can be revived by serving reasonable notice of such intention. This does not reflect the nature of Hartwell's promise, but cannot be said to be an inequitable result if the outstanding success of 'The Black Panther' has raised so much money that Leonard can easily afford to pay the outstanding £10,000.

CHAPTER THREE

TERMS OF A CONTRACT

3.1 Express Terms

3.1.1 THE PAROL EVIDENCE RULE

COUCHMAN v HILL [1947] 1 All ER 103 (CA)

The plaintiff was trying to enforce an oral promise that a heifer sold by auction was 'unserved'.

Scott LJ: It is a striking feature of county court appeals that they so often present features of great interest, whether of law or of practical importance to the community, and also raise quite difficult problems for solution by the court. The present appeal presents all three features.

On December 15, 1945, the plaintiff purchased at an auction sale held at Grove Farm, Castle Cary, Somerset, a heifer, the property of the defendant, for the sum of £29. The heifer in question was one of two heifers comprised in lots 26/27 in the sale catalogue described as 'two red and white stirk heifers, unserved'. There can be no question on the facts found by the county court judge but that, in the absence of some special agreement to the contrary, when the hammer fell the resulting contract was subject to the printed conditions of sale exhibited at the auction and to the stipulations contained in the sale catalogue. The latter document contained these words:

Note – The sale will be subject to the auctioneers' usual conditions, copies of which will be exhibited. The auctioneers will not be responsible for any error or misstatement in this catalogue, or in the dates of calving of any cattle. The information contained herein is supplied by the vendor and is believed to be correct, but its accuracy is not guaranteed, and all lots must be taken subject to all faults or errors of description (if any), and no compensation will be paid for the same.

No. 3 of the printed conditions of sale was as follows:

The lots are sold with all faults, imperfections, and errors of description, the auctioneers not being responsible for the correct description, genuineness, or authenticity of, or any fault or defect in, any lot, and giving no warranty whatever.

On February 6, 1946, a six months old foetus was removed from the heifer in question, and on February 26 the heifer died as a result of the strain of carrying a calf at too young an age for breeding. There was no suggestion that at the time of the sale either the defendant or the auctioneer did not honestly believe that the heifer was unserved. On the other hand, the plaintiff's evidence, which was accepted by the judge, was that he would not have bought it had he had any reason to doubt the accuracy of the description as he required an unserved heifer for service by his own bull at a time of his own choosing.

So far it is, in my opinion, clear that the plaintiff, by reason of the stipulations in the catalogue and conditions of sale, would have had no remedy by way of damages for breach of contract or warranty against the defendant unless the plaintiff is right in his contention that the language of these documents is effective only to protect the auctioneer from personal liability and affords no defence to the defendant in respect of any misstatements in the catalogue for which he would otherwise be liable. It is, no doubt, true that some of the printed conditions of sale deal only with the position of the auctioneer, and that the first part of the note in the catalogue is to the same effect, but it is, in my view, impossible to say that the words 'the lots are sold with all faults, imperfections, and errors of description,' and the words 'and all lots must be taken subject to all faults or errors of description (if any), and no compensation will be paid for the same' are not to be incorporated as terms of the contract as between the vendor and purchaser when the hammer falls. Whether the word 'unserved' amounts to a warranty or a condition is immaterial, because it is, I think, clear that it was, in any event, an error of description and as such expressly protected by the words to which I have referred. For those reasons it appears to me that, in so far as the plaintiff relied on the statement in the catalogue to support his claim for damages for breach of warranty, he necessarily failed.

The plaintiff, however, also alleged in his further particulars as follows: 'The said warranty was also confirmed verbally both by the auctioneer and by the defendant on inquiry by the plaintiff prior to the sale'. As to this the county court judge has accepted the plaintiff's evidence which was to the effect that at the sale and when the heifers were in the ring he asked both the defendant and the auctioneer: 'can you confirm heifers unserved?' and received from both the answer 'Yes'. There was no contract at that moment. There was an announcement of an auction of specific chattels. It was to the effect, first, that the auctioneer was about to make auction offers of the things and animals in the catalogue on behalf of the vendor to the public attending the auction on the terms of sale contained in the two documents, viz., the catalogue and the printed advertisement of the terms of sale hung up at the auction, and, secondly, that the vendor had given authority to the auctioneer to sell the chattels by auction in those terms. There was no contract in existence until the hammer fell. The offer was defined, the auctioneer's authority was defined, but it was in law open to any would-be purchaser to intimate in advance before bidding for any particular heifer offered from the rostrum that he was not willing to bid for the lot unless the defendant modified the terms of sale contained in the two documents in some way specified by him. There is no doubt that the plaintiff did make some attempt of the kind in order to protect himself from the risk of buying an animal that was not of the kind described.

The real question is: What did the parties understand by the question addressed to and the answer received from both the defendant and the auctioneer? It is contended by the defendant that the question meant 'having regard to the onerous stipulations which I know I shall have to put up with if I bid and the lot is knocked down to me, can you give me your honourable assurance that the heifers have in fact not been served? If so, I will risk the penalties of the catalogue'. The alternative meaning is: 'I am frightened of contracting on your published terms, but I will bid if you will tell me by word of mouth that you accept full responsibility for the statement in the catalogue that the heifers have not been served, or, in other words, give me a clean warranty. That is the only condition on which I will bid'. If that was the meaning there was clearly an oral offer of a warranty which over-rode the stultifying condition in the printed terms, that offer was accepted by the plaintiff when he bid, and the contract was made on that basis when the lot was knocked down to him. In some circumstances I concede that such a question might on its face be somewhat ambiguous, but I think in the present case the only inference that could properly be drawn by the judge or jury charged with the duty of finding the facts – and this is a question of fact as to the intention of the parties – is that the question was asked and answered with the alternative meaning indicated. That this is so follows, I think, conclusively from the plaintiff's evidence which was accepted by the judge, taken in conjunction with the admissions of the defendant that the words if used – which he denied – would have bound him. It is obvious that it was the stipulations that prompted the question. The plaintiff was not a lawyer, but he knew what he wanted. So did the defendant, and he got it. What the plaintiff wanted was to know where he stood before he made an offer which the fall of the hammer would turn into a contract.

The county court judge in a careful reserved judgment has found that this oral statement was made, and he refers to it as a warranty, but holds that its value was destroyed by the qualifying stipulations. He has not in terms put the question to himself: 'Did the parties by this question and answer intend to exclude the stipulations from the contract that resulted on the fall of the hammer?' I have, accordingly, felt some doubt whether or not the proper course was to order a new trial. On reading his judgment as a whole I have, however, arrived at the conclusion that it is implicit therein that it was not the intention of the parties to exclude the stipulation. As we are of opinion that on the facts found by him he could not properly arrive at this conclusion, I think we are not compelled to put the parties to the expense of a further trial.

There was a good deal of discussion whether the description 'unserved' constituted a warranty or a condition. I have, in what I have said so far, deliberately refrained from expressing a view thereon, but as a matter of law I think every item in a description which constitutes a substantial ingredient in the 'identity' of the thing sold is a condition, although every such condition can be waived by the purchaser who thereon becomes entitled to treat it as a warranty and recover damages.

I think there was here an unqualified condition which, on its breach, the plaintiff was entitled to treat as a warranty and recover the damages claimed. One final word. The printed condition that the vendor will take no responsibility for errors of description of things or animals specifically offered for sale on inspection is reasonable for visible defects, but for qualities or attributes which are invisible it is not reasonable. It may well become a mere trap for the unwary. The point deserves consideration by the Auctioneers' Associations.

The appeal should, therefore, in my opinion be allowed with costs here and below, the latter on Scale B.

Tucker and Bucknill LJJ concurred.

3.1.1.1 Collateral contracts

CITY AND WESTMINSTER PROPERTIES v MUDD [1958] 2 All ER 733 (Ch)

HARMAN J: This is a landlords' action for forfeiture of a lease on the ground of the breach by the defendant, the tenant, of a covenant which is said to forbid him to reside as he has been doing on the demised property, a ground floor shop and basement known as No. 4, New Cavendish Street, W.1. The defences are first that, on the true construction of the lease, residence on the property is no breach of covenant; secondly that if the tenant be wrong on construction the landlords, by reason of the promises made to him before he signed the lease, are disentitled from relying on their rights; thirdly that the landlords' acquiescence in the breach has been such that a release of the covenant must be assumed and that the landlords have waived its observance. . . .

The tenant began his connexion with the property in 1941, when he took over the shop and basement for a term of three years. No written agreement was produced covering this period, during which it is admitted that he was allowed to sleep in the ground floor back room behind the shop. This was a wartime arrangement. The tenant was engaged in civil defence activities and it was thought a useful protection against incendiaries that he should be on the property at night. No inference, in my judgment, ought to arise from this. During this period the tenant fitted up a room in the basement in an elaborate style as a sitting room.

On April 5, 1944, a lease was granted by the landlords to the tenant by a document under seal whereby the landlords let 'the shop on the ground floor and the basement floor all as now in his occupation' of No. 4, New Cavendish Street for a term of three years from Lady Day, 1944, at a rent of £170 payable monthly. There were covenants by the lessee, who was described in the lease as an antique dealer 'not to use or permit the use of the said premises except as the shop of the lessee for his business as hereinbefore described'; also 'not to do or suffer to be done anything . . . which may render the said premises . . . liable . . . to be assessed as a dwelling-house'. The tenant continued to carry on his business of an antique dealer in the ground floor shop and to sleep in an office behind the shop where he had a divan bed covered in the day with a velvet counterpane. During the term of this lease the tenant fitted up another room in the basement as a dining room. Both the basement rooms had an appearance consistent with being showrooms for antique furniture, but the tenant alleges that in fact this furniture was not for sale and that he did not take customers down to the basement. He says that he used these rooms to live in and to entertain his friends. He had an electric cooker in the front area of the basement and a wash basin with an Ascot water heater in a lavatory at the back. He says that he made no secret of the fact that he was living on the premises and that the landlords, particularly through their property manager, one Jones, were well aware of the fact. In my judgment, the landlords were aware that the tenant from time to time slept on the ground floor, but I was not satisfied on the evidence that they knew that the property was his principal or only residence or that he used the basement rooms as his home.

In January, 1947, the tenant asked for a new lease and was offered a further lease for seven years from Lady Day, 1947. Negotiations proceeded in a dilatory fashion. A draft lease was sent to the tenant in May, 1947 . . . By this document as it then stood, the landlords were expressed to demise to the tenant the ground floor shop and basement for the term of fourteen years from Lady Day, 1947, at an annual rent rising to £325 in the last seven years of the term, payable quarterly on the usual quarter days, together with fire insurance premiums. The lessee's covenants included covenants to repair and paint and a clause in the following terms (cl. 2(9)):

> To use the demised premises as and for showrooms, workrooms and offices only and not to use exercise or carry on or permit or suffer to be used excercised or carried on in or upon the said premises or any part thereof the trades or businesses of [then follows a long list of prohibited trades and businesses] . . . and not to permit or suffer the demised premises or any part thereof to be used as a place for lodging dwelling or sleeping.

There was a proviso for re-entry by the landlords on breach of any of the lessee's covenants. At the time when the red ink revisions were made, the tenant's solicitor did not know that he had been residing on the property and intended to continue so to do. On October 23, 1947, the landlords' solicitors returned the draft with various amendments in yellow ink not here relevant. The draft in this condition was submitted by the tenant's solicitors to him, when he pointed out to them the words at the end of cl. 2(9) which I have read, and took objection to them on the ground that he was in fact residing on the premises and intended so to continue. On October 29, 1947, they returned the draft with the words at the end of cl. 2(9) struck out and a side-note in green ink in these terms:

> The lessee has in fact been residing at the premises for some years and has spent a large sum of money on decorations.

The covering letter was in these terms:

> We have your letter returning draft lease revised, and our client accepts your revisions [in yellow ink]. We are informed by our client that he has been living at the premises for some considerable time and has spent a large sum of money on decorating the rooms he occupies. Our client lives entirely alone and he points out that unless he resides at the premises he cannot obtain any burglary insurance of his very valuable stock of antiques. We have seen the premises the lessee occupies for his own use and they are most expensively decorated and furnished and we consider, therefore, that your clients are not in any way prejudiced by our client's user. We have, therefore, amended cl. 2(9) in green ink and shall be glad to know that your clients will accept this. If so, perhaps you will let us have engrossment for execution.

On this the landlords' solicitors consulted their clients and advised them that permission to the tenant to reside on the premises might bring the shop and basement within the Rent Restrictions Acts. Accordingly, on November 28 the landlords' solicitors wrote this letter to the tenant's solicitors:

> With reference to your letter of the 29th of last month and the enclosure mentioned as accompanying it, we have now received our clients' instructions that notwithstanding

such user to which these premises may have been put in the past, they must insist upon the retention of the restriction in cl. 2(9) which you have deleted in green ink. On hearing from you that this is agreed, we will proceed to engross the lease and counterpart. We cannot agree with your contention that our clients are in no way prejudiced by the premises being used for residential purposes; such user would probably be construed as bringing the letting within the provisions of the Rent Restrictions Acts.

The draft was not returned to the landlords' solicitors, but the tenant's solicitors replied as follows on December 1:

We have your letter of the 28th of last month and note what you say, but our client will, of course, require an assurance that upon completion of the lease, your clients will take no steps to prevent his using the premises for residential purposes. As the primary letting is for business use, we do not think the letting would be brought within the provisions of the Rent Restrictions Acts, but our client cannot run the risk of being stopped from residing on the premises while he is the lessee.

There follows a gap in the correspondence until December 31, 1947. During this interval, according to the tenant, he telephoned to Mr Jones and told him he would not sign the lease with a clause about not sleeping there. He adds that he asked Mr Jones to have a clause inserted stating expressly that he could sleep there, but that Mr Jones replied that this was impossible because it was against the terms of the head-lease. This was in fact untrue, but it is clear that Mr Jones believed his own statement. According to the tenant Mr Jones added that the landlords would make no objection to his continuing to reside there if he would sign the lease. Mr Jones, who has left the employment of the landlords and was only called at an adjourned hearing, stated that he had no recollection of this conversation. He admitted in cross-examination that the landlords must have known that the tenant was living on the premises and said that the landlords' object was to avoid the mischief of the Rent Restrictions Acts. He added that on paper his attitude was 'business premises only', but that he was less emphatic when dealing with the tenant personally. On December 31, 1947, the tenant's solicitors wrote to the landlords' solicitors as follows:

We have now taken our client's instructions on your letter to us of November 28 and we understand that he himself has spoken to your clients with reference to this. Our client is now willing to complete the lease and we shall be glad to receive the counterpart for execution.

In due course, the lease and counterpart were exchanged, and bear date February 10, 1948. Clause 2(9) omits the words at the end expressly excluding lodging, dwelling or sleeping. Mr Byford, the landlords' solicitor, stated that he read the letter of December 31, 1947, as meaning that the tenant had given way, but that the words at the end of cl. 2(9) were omitted by inadvertence in his office. Doubt is thrown on this statement by a Mr Turner, then the tenant's solicitor, who deposed to a conversation on the telephone with Mr Byford. This is said to have been held just after the Christmas holiday and to have been to the effect that the tenant had spoken to his landlords and was 'quite happy he would not be disturbed' and had nothing to worry about. . . . I accept Mr Turner's evidence on this point.

After the execution of this lease the tenant carried on business as before and continued to live on the property. In the spring of 1950 war damage repairs were done by the landlords and in connexion with these Mr Jones and one Northover came down and inspected the basement, and a little later one Kingscote, a director of the landlords, also came down and inspected damage done. According to the tenant, he made it clear to them that he was living on the premises. Mr Jones for his part said that this was far from clear to him, though he recognised that the tenant was sleeping there from time to time. So things went on till June, 1953, when the tenant applied for leave to instal a bath in the basement. This was promptly refused in a letter of June 18, 1953, in these terms.

We understand from our surveyors who called upon you yesterday that you are contemplating installing a bath in the basement at these premises but we regret that we are unable to agree to this matter proceeding. These premises are let solely for business purposes, as clearly defined in the lease under which they are held dated February 10, 1948, and any use of the premises for residential purposes can in no way be allowed.

In May, 1956, the tenant applied to the landlords for a further twenty-one years' lease of the property and in connexion with this there was considerable negotiations in the course of which one Nixon, then the managing director of the landlords, interviewed the tenant on the property on October 1, 1956. This witness said that he had visited the property with Mr Jones in 1950, but in this he was mistaken. In the course of the interview Mr Nixon noticed signs of residence on the property and asked the tenant if he was living there, to which the tenant replied he was and why should not he. High words ensued and as a result a letter was written by Mr Nixon on the landlords' behalf which contained the following passage:

It was noticed that you are using the premises for residential purposes, which is not in accordance with the terms of your lease as this particularly specifies that the premises are to be used for business purposes. We therefore request that you cease to live in the premises forthwith and give your assurance that they will not be used for this purpose at any time in the future. This was made perfectly clear in our letter to you of June 18, 1953.

That is the letter about the bath. As a result, a notice was served and the present proceedings were begun. . . .

I cannot think that anything proved here amounts to a release by the landlord of his rights. He knew, indeed, that the tenant was using the property to sleep in, but I do not think that he knew more than that. At that he was willing to wink, but I am unable to find a release of the covenant or an agreement for new letting. In my judgment, therefore, the plea of waiver fails.

There remains the so-called question of estoppel. This, in my judgment, is a misnomer and the present case does not raise the controversial issue of *Central London Property Trust Ltd* v *High Trees House Ltd* [1956] 1 All ER 256n. This is not a case of a representation made after contractual relations existed between the parties to the effect that one party to the contract would not rely on his rights. If the tenant's evidence is to be accepted, as I hold that it is, it is a case of a promise made to him before the execution of the lease that if he would execute it in the form put before him, the landlords would not seek to enforce against him personally the covenant about using the property as a shop only. The tenant says that it was in reliance on this promise that he executed the lease and entered on the onerous obligations contained in it. He says, moreover, that but for the promise made he would not have executed the lease, but would have moved to other premises available to him at the time. If these be the facts, there was a clear contract acted on by the tenant to his detriment and from which the landlords cannot be allowed to resile. The case is truly analogous to *Re William Porter & Co. Ltd* [1937] 2 All ER 361. This is a decision of Simonds J. He said (ibid., at p. 363):

I come to the final point, the point which has given me difficulty in this case, and it is this. [Then he states some of the facts, which were very different from the facts here, but he goes on in this way:] It was an act intended to induce the company to take a certain course of action, to carry on its business, to enter into transactions and to incur obligations which, but for that resolution, it might not have done. It appears to me that there is some direct evidence here, and, in my judgment, I am entitled to apply the rule, stated nowhere better than in the old case of *Cairncross* v *Lorimer* (1860) 3 LT 130. This case was a Scottish appeal to the House of Lords, where Lord Campbell LC said, after some observations which are not material to the present case (ibid., at p. 130): 'The doctrine will apply which is to be found, I believe, in the laws of all civilised nations, that if a man, either by words or by conduct, has intimated that he consents to an act which has been done, and that he will offer no opposition to it, although it could not have been lawfully done without his consent, and he thereby induces others to do that from which they otherwise might have abstained, he cannot question the legality of the act he had so sanctioned, to the prejudice of those who have so given faith to his words, or to the fair inference to be drawn from his conduct'. Also, a little further on (ibid., at p. 131): 'I am of opinion that, generally speaking, if a party having an interest to prevent an act being done, has full notice of its having been done, and acquiesces in it, so as to induce a reasonable belief that he consents to it, and the position of others is altered by their giving credit to his sincerity, he has no more right to challenge the act, to their prejudice, than he would have had if it had been done by his previous licence'.

In my judgment, the tenant's evidence is to be accepted on this point. No alternative explanation of his change of mind between the beginning and the end of December, 1947, is available, and I think that he was a witness of truth. His evidence was uncontradicted, for Mr Jones remembered nothing about it.

The plea that this was a mere licence retractable at the landlords' will does not bear examination. The promise was that so long as the tenant personally was tenant, so long would the landlords forbear to exercise the rights which they would have as to residence if he signed the lease. He did sign the lease on this promise and is therefore entitled to rely on it so long as he is personally in occupation of the shop.

The result is that on this point the defence succeeds; and I propose to dismiss the action.

3.2   Terms and Representations

3.2.1   DISTINGUISHING BETWEEN TERMS AND REPRESENTATIONS

3.2.1.1   At what time was the statement made?

ROUTLEDGE v McKAY [1954] 1 All ER 855 (CA)

SIR RAYMOND EVERSHED MR: The question is whether or not, on a sale of a motor bicycle with a side-car combination, there was a warranty as to the date when the machine was originally put on the market . . .

In the present case by a certain amount of mechanical ingenuity an earlier possessor of this motor cycle combination, which first left the works of the makers in October, 1930, proceeded to re-condition and, in a measure, re-make it so that, although substantially it remained the old model, it had acquired certain characteristics which, this ingenious mechanic thought, justified him in attributing to it a later origin. The registration books, which were renewed from time to time, eventually showed on their face that this motor cycle combination was what is called 'a late 1941 or 1942 model'. . . .

The fourth party said in evidence that on October 23, 1949, the fifth party called at the former's house with this motor cycle combination, and continued:

[The fifth party] told me it was a 600 c.c. machine instead of 500 c.c. It says 500 c.c. in registration book. I asked the model. He told me it was a late 1941 or 1942. He produced the registration book which was dated late 1941. This was outside the house . . . Two or three days later [the fifth party] came back. I had had a document drafted. He said he had thought it over and the transaction could go through. I produced the money and he produced the registration book.

It was suggested to him in cross-examination that the fifth party had added to the statements made about the date of origin a statement that he had heard from the manufacturers that the date of the model was not 1941 or 1942, but 1936 or 1938. The fourth party denied that suggestion, and the judge on that matter disbelieved the fifth party. Except on this point, the fifth party said nothing which could be taken to controvert or add to the evidence of the fourth party. On the oral evidence, therefore, the judge found, in effect, that, before the bargain was eventually made, the fifth party specifically stated, in answer to a question, that it was a 1942 model, and pointed to the corroboration of that statement to be found in the registration book, and that he knew, from what the manufacturers told him, the true date to be 1936 or 1938. Of course, it does not follow that the fifth party was deliberately trying to deceive the fourth party, and in any case we are not here trying any action based on fraud.

The fourth party had caused to be prepared a written memorandum or contract which was signed by himself and the fifth party on October 30, 1949. The significant point is made that there the motor cycle combination is expressly referred to as being of the capacity of 600 c.c., when on the registration book it is stated as having only 500 c.c. capacity. From the evidence I have read the true cubic capacity, according to the fifth party, was 600, and that fact was carefully pointed out by him by showing the discrepancy in that respect in the registration book. This written memorandum represents prima facie the record of what the parties intended to agree when the actual transaction took place. Counsel for the fifth party contended that the terms of it necessarily exclude any warranty, that is to say, any collateral bargain, either contemporary or earlier in date. I am not sure that I would go so far as that. But I think that as a matter of construction it would be difficult to say that such an agreement was consistent with a warranty being given at the same time time so as to be intended to form a part of the bargain then made. I think, with counsel for the fifth party, that the last words 'It is understood that when the £30 is paid . . . this transaction is closed' would make such a contention difficult. But I will assume that the warranty was given, not when the bargain was struck, but on October 23, 1949, on which date alone, according to the evidence, any representation about the date of the motor cycle combination was made at all.

If that representation is to be a warranty it has to be contractual in form. In other words, so far as I can see, once the existence of a warranty as part of the actual bargain is excluded, it must be a separate contract, and the overwhelming difficulty which faces the fourth party is that when the representation was made there was then no bargain, and it is, therefore, in my view, impossible to say that it could have been collateral to some other contract. Even apart from that, it seems to me that on the evidence there is nothing to support the conclusion, as a matter of law and bearing in mind Lord Moulton's observations, that in answering the question posed about the date of the motor cycle combination there was anything more intended than a mere representation.

If that is right analysis, the problem which the county court judge felt he had to consider never arose. It was not a question whether or not on its construction this agreement negatived or excluded the possibility of an earlier warranty. In my view, there was no evidence before the judge capable of supporting the existence of any earlier warranty, and I prefer to base my conclusion on that ground rather than on the ground that the agreement, according to its language, necessarily excluded a warranty. I have felt compelled to the conclusion that the learned judge here had not before him any evidence which entitled him to conclude that there was given, and intended to be given, a warranty (in the proper sense of that word) when the reference to the date of origin of the motor cycle was made by the fifth party. I add that the written agreement tends to support that view rather than to controvert it. In my judgment, this appeal must be allowed.

Denning and Romer LJJ concurred.

3.2.1.2 Importance of the alleged term

BANNERMAN v WHITE (1861) 10 CB (NS) 844 (Court of Common Bench)

The seller of some hops wrongly stated that they had not been treated with sulphur. Was this part of the subsequent contract of sale?

ERLE CJ: In this case the plaintiff obtained a rule to set aside the verdict for the defendants, and enter it for the plaintiff, on the ground that the stipulation that no sulphur had been used in the growth of the hops did not amount to a condition that the hops might be rejected if sulphur had been used. The plaintiff argued that the contract must be so construed because it related to a specifically ascertained chattel; and for this he cited some expressions in the judgment of *Street* v *Blay* 2 B & Ad 456. The defendants, on the other hand, contended, that the contract here in question was an executory contract; that the intention of the parties governs in all contracts whatsoever; that, upon the evidence, it was clear that the stipulation in question was intended by these parties to be a condition; and that the case of *Street* v *Blay* had no application.

We propose to state the evidence in some detail, so as to shew the meaning of the finding of the jury.

At the close of the trial, the jury were requested to give specific answers to certain questions. Those questions comprised all that was in contest between the parties, and cannot be properly understood without taking them in combination with all that was uncontested, and keeping present to the mind the issue to which they relate.

The action was for hops sold and delivered. The first plea was, in effect, fraud, viz. that the plaintiff induced the defendants to buy by making a false representation that no sulphur had been used, and so forth. The second plea was non assumpsit. The evidence in support of the first plea consisted of these facts – that, in 1854, sulphur had been used in the growth of hops, and the brewers affirmed that the hops had been injured thereby and their beer spoiled; and the hop-merchants had given notice to the hop-growers of their objection to buy hops in the growth of which any sulphur had been used: and the plaintiff and defendants, each knowing these facts, met and treated for the contract in question, the samples being produced. There was no substantial variance in the account given of that which passed at the interview when the contract was made. There were six witnesses present. All agreed that, before the price was asked, the defendant inquired if sulphur had been used in the growth. The three witnesses for the defendants stated that the plaintiff answered distinctly 'no', and that the defendants said they would not ask the price if sulphur had been used. The plaintiff's witnesses did not contradict them, but said the answer was, 'There was no mould this year, and no occasion to use any sulphur', and did not remember that the defendants had said they would not ask the price if any sulphur had been used. The treaty then went on, and eventuated in a contract to sell and deliver the bulk in accordance with the samples after some days should have elapsed. The hops were accordingly sent, and corresponded with sample, and were weighed and delivered into the defendants' possession. Afterwards, the defendants repudiated the hops, and proved that sulphur had been used.

The uncontroverted facts were that sulphur had been used on five acres out of three hundred; that these sulphured hops were so mixed with the unsulphured as to be undistinguishable; that the plaintiff represented that no sulphur had been used; that the defendants would not have bought the hops if they had known that fact, and could not sell them as they were, in the ordinary course of their dealings with their customers.

The counsel agreed with the judge that there were two principal questions for the jury. On the first, the contest was in substance confined to the point whether the representation was wilfully false: and this question was answered by the jury in the negative. The second question then became material; and it was framed with reference to the same evidence, and on the assumption that the same facts were undisputed, – the term 'affirmation' being substituted for 'representation', as more appropriate to a matter of contract, to the minds of all concerned in the trial.

Thus, the question was, – 'Was the affirmation that no sulphur had been used intended between the parties to be part of the contract of sale, and a warranty by the plaintiff?'

As to this, it was contended on one side that the conversation relating to the sulphur was preliminary to entering on the contract, and no part thereof, both from the form of expression and also from the written guarantee which was shewn to have been given. On the other side it was contended that the whole interview was one transaction, that the intention of the parties was alone to be regarded, that the defendants had declared the importance they attached to the inquiry, and that the plaintiff must have known it. And the jury answered this question in the affirmative.

The effect of this finding of the jury, taken with the evidence, is now to be considered. We avoid the term 'warranty', because it is used in two senses, and the term 'condition', because the question is whether that term is applicable. Then, the effect is that the defendants required, and that the plaintiff gave his undertaking that no sulphur had been used. This undertaking was a preliminary stipulation; and if it had not been given, the defendants would not have gone on with the treaty which resulted in the sale. In this sense it was the condition upon which the defendants contracted; and it would be contrary to the intention expressed by this stipulation that the contract should remain valid if sulphur had been used.

The intention of the parties governs in the making and in the construction of all contracts. If the parties so intend, the sale may be absolute, with a warranty superadded; or the sale may be conditional, to be null if the warranty is broken. And, upon this statement of facts, we think that the intention appears that the contract should be null if sulphur had been used: and upon this ground we agree that the rule should be discharged.

Rule discharged.

3.2.1.3 Significance of special knowledge

OSCAR CHESS LTD v *WILLIAMS* [1957] All ER 325 (CA)

The plaintiff had given the defendant an allowance of £290 on a car given in part exchange, on the basis that it was a 1948 model, as stated in the registration book.

LORD DENNING MR: . . . Eight months later the plaintiffs discovered that the Morris car was made, not in 1948, as they thought, but in 1939. They discovered this by taking the chassis and engine numbers and sending those numbers to Morris Motors Ltd, who looked up their card index and found that the car left the factory on February 3, 1939. Strange to relate, the style and finish of Morris cars had not been changed between 1939 and 1948. Outwardly a 1948 model looked the same as a 1939 model, but the price was of course very different. If the plaintiffs had known that it was a 1939 model they would have given only £175 for it, and not £290. In describing it as a 1948 Morris, the defendant was perfectly innocent. He honestly believed that it was a 1948 model, and so, no doubt, did the previous sellers. Someone far back in 1948 must have fraudulently altered the log-book, but he cannot be traced now.

In these circumstances the plaintiffs claim as damages from the defendant the sum of £115, the difference in value between a 1939 Morris car and a 1948 Morris car. The question depends on whether the defendant gave a binding promise to Mr Ladd that the car was made in 1948. The evidence on this point was very short. Mr Ladd said in examination in chief: 'He offered me a 1948 10 h.p. Morris in part exchange. He produced the registration book'. In cross-examination he said: 'I had often had lifts in the defendant's car. I thought it looked like a 1948 model. I checked up in the registration book'.

Mr Ladd's evidence was accepted. Indeed, the defendant did not go into the witness-box to contradict him. On those simple facts counsel for the plaintiffs submitted to the judge that the defendant's representation that the car was a 1948 model was an essential term of the contract, that is, a condition. Alternatively, he submitted that the representation was a warranty, intended as such. The judge found that it was a condition. He said that the allowance of £290 was made by Mr Ladd 'on the assumption that the Morris was a 1948 model', and that:

> . . . this assumption was fundamental to the contract, a condition which, if not satisfied, would have caused him to rescind the contract if he had known it to be unsatisfied before the property in the Morris car passed to his principals.

Thereupon the judge awarded £115 to the plaintiffs and did not go on to consider the alternative claim on a warranty.

I entirely agree with the judge that both parties assumed that the Morris car was a 1948 model and that this assumption was fundamental to the contract. This does not prove, however, that the representation was a term of the contract. The assumption was based by both of them on the date given in the registration book as the date of first registration. They both believed that the car was a 1948 model, whereas it was only a 1939 one. They were both mistaken and their mistake was of fundamental importance.

The effect of such a mistake is this: It does not make the contract a nullity from the beginning, but it does in some circumstances enable the contract to be set aside in equity. If the buyer had come promptly, he might have succeeded in getting the whole transaction set aside in equity on the ground of this mistake (see *Solle* v *Butcher* [1949] 2 All ER 1107), but he did not do so and it is now too late for him to do it (see *Leaf* v *International Galleries* [1950] 1 All ER 693). His only remedy is in damages, and to recover these he must prove a warranty.

In saying that he must prove a warranty, I use the word 'warranty' in its ordinary English meaning to denote a binding promise. Everyone knows what a man means when he says, 'I guarantee it', or 'I warrant it', or 'I give you my word on it'. He means that he binds himself to it. That is the meaning which it has borne in English law for three hundred years from the leading case of *Chandelor* v *Lopus* (1603), Cro Jac 4 onwards. During the last hundred years, however, the lawyers have come to use the word 'warranty' in another sense. They use it to denote a subsidiary term in a contract as distinct from a vital term which they call a 'condition'. In so doing they depart from the ordinary meaning, not only of the word 'warranty', but also of the word 'condition'. There is no harm in their doing this, so long as they confine this technical use to its proper sphere, namely, to distinguish between a vital term, the breach of which gives the right to treat the contract as at an end, and a subsidiary term which does not. The trouble comes, however, when one person uses the word 'warranty' in its ordinary meaning and another uses it in its technical meaning. When Holt CJ made his famous ruling that 'An affirmation at the time of the sale is a warranty, provided it appear on evidence to be so intended', he used the word 'warranty' in its ordinary English meaning of a binding promise. When Viscount Haldane LC and Lord Moulton in 1913, in *Heilbut, Symons & Co.* v *Buckleton* [1913] AC 30, adopted this ruling (ibid., at pp.38,49), they used the word likewise in its ordinary meaning. These different uses of the word seem to have been the source of confusion in the present case. The judge did not ask himself, 'Was the representation (that the car was a 1948 Morris car) intended to be a warranty?' He asked himself, 'Was it fundamental to the contract?' He answered it by saying that it was fundamental, and, therefore, it was a condition and not a warranty. By concentrating on whether it was fundamental, he seems to me to have missed the crucial point in the case which is whether it was a term of the contract at all. The crucial question is: Was it a binding promise or only an innocent misrepresentation? The technical distinction between a 'condition' and a 'warranty' is quite immaterial in this case, because it is far too late for the buyer to reject the car. He can, at best, only claim damages. The material distinction here is between a statement which is a term of the contract and a statement which is only an innocent misrepresentation. This distinction is best expressed by the ruling of Holt CJ, 'Was it intended as a warranty or not?', using the word 'warranty' there in its ordinary English meaning: because it gives the exact shade of meaning that is required. It is something to which a man must be taken to bind himself.

In applying this test, however, some misunderstanding has arisen by the use of the word 'intended'. It is sometimes supposed that the tribunal must look into the minds of the parties to see what they themselves intended. That is a mistake. Lord Moulton made it quite clear, in *Heilbut, Symons & Co.* v *Buckleton* [1913] AC 30 at p. 51, that 'The intention of the parties can only be deduced from the totality of the evidence . . .'. The question whether a warranty was intended depends on the conduct of the parties, on their words and behaviour, rather than on their thoughts. If an intelligent bystander would reasonably infer that a warranty was intended, that will suffice. And this, when the facts are not in dispute, is a question of law. That is shown by *Heilbut, Symons & Co.* v *Buckleton* itself, where the House of Lords upset the jury's finding of a warranty. . . .

Turning now to the present case, much depends on the precise words that were used. If the seller says: 'I believe the car is a 1948 Morris. Here is the registration book to prove it', there is clearly no warranty. It is a statement of belief, not a contractual promise. If, however, the seller says: 'I guarantee that it is a 1948 Morris. This is borne out by the registration book, but you need not rely solely on that. I give you my own guarantee that it is', there is clearly a warranty. The seller is making himself contractually responsible, even though the registration book is wrong.

In this case much reliance was placed by the judge on the fact that the buyer looked up 'Glass's Guide' and paid £290 on the footing that the car was a 1948 model, but that fact seems to me to be neutral. Both sides believed the car to have been made in 1948 and in that belief the buyer paid £290. That belief can be just as firmly based on the buyer's own inspection of the log-book as on a contractual warranty by the seller.

Once that fact is put on one side, I ask myself: What is the proper inference from the known facts? It must have been obvious to both that the seller had himself no personal knowledge of the year when the car was made. He only became owner after a great number of changes. He must have been relying on the registration book. It is unlikely that such a person would warrant the year of manufacture. The most that he would do would be to state his belief, and then produce the registration book in verification of it. In these circumstances the intelligent bystander would, I suggest, say that the seller did not intend to bind himself so as to warrant that the car was a 1948 model. If the seller was asked to pledge himself to it, he would at once have said 'I cannot do that. I have only the log-book to go by, the same as you'. . .

One final word. It seems to me clear that the plaintiffs, the motor dealers who bought the car, relied on the year stated in the log-book. If they had wished to make sure of it, they could have checked it then and there, by taking the engine number and chassis number and writing to the makers. They did not do so at the time, but only eight months later. They are experts, and, as they did not make the check at the time, I do not think that they should now be allowed to recover against the innocent seller who produced to them all the evidence which he had, namely, the registraton book. I agree that it is hard on the plaintiffs to have paid more than the car is worth, but it would be equally hard on the seller to make him pay the difference. He would never have bought the Hillman car unless he had received the allowance of £290 for the Morris car. The best course in all those cases would be to 'shunt' the difference down the train of innocent sellers until one reached the rogue who perpetrated the fraud; but he can rarely be traced, or if he can, he rarely has the money to pay the damages. Therefore, one is left to decide between a number of innocent people who is to bear the loss. That can only be done by applying the law about representations and warranties as we know it, and that is what I have tried to do. If the rogue can be traced, he can be sued by whosoever has suffered the loss: but, if he cannot be traced, the loss must lie where it falls. It should not be inflicted on innocent sellers, who sold the car many months, perhaps years before, and have forgotten all about it and have conducted their affairs on the basis that the transaction was concluded. Such a seller would not be able to recollect after all this length of time the exact words which he used, such as whether he said 'I believe it is a 1948 model', or 'I warrant it is a 1948 model'. The right course is to let the buyer set aside the transaction if he finds out the mistake quickly and comes promptly before other interests have irretrievably intervened, otherwise the loss must lie where it falls: and that is, I think, the course prescribed by law. I would allow this appeal accordingly.

Hudson and Morris LJJ concurred.

DICK BENTLEY PRODUCTIONS LTD v HAROLD SMITH MOTORS LTD
[1965] 2 All ER 65 (CA)

LORD DENNING MR: The second plaintiff, Mr Charles Walter Bentley, sometimes known as Dick Bentley, brings an action against Harold Smith (Motors) Ltd, for damages for breach of warranty on the sale of a car. Mr Bentley had been dealing with Mr Smith (to whom I shall refer in the stead of the defendant company) for a couple of years and told Mr Smith he was on the look-out for a well vetted Bentley car. In January, 1960, Mr Smith found one and bought it for £1,500 from a firm in Leicester. He wrote to Mr Bentley and said: 'I have just purchased a Park Ward power operated hood convertible. It is one of the nicest cars we have had in for quite a long time'. Mr Smith had told Mr Bentley earlier that he was in a position to find out the history of cars. It appears that with a car of this quality the makers do keep a complete biography of it.

Mr Bentley went to see the car. Mr Smith told him that a German baron had had this car. He said that it had been fitted at one time with a replacement engine and gearbox, and had done twenty thousand miles only since it had been so fitted. The speedometer on the car showed only twenty thousand miles. Mr Smith said the price was £1,850, and he would guarantee the car for twelve months, including parts and labour. That was on the morning of January 23, 1960. In the afternoon Mr Bentley took his wife over to see the car. Mr Bentley repeated to his wife in Mr Smith's presence what Mr Smith had told him in the morning. In particular that Mr Smith said it had done only twenty thousand miles since it had been refitted with a replacement engine and gearbox. Mr Bentley took it for a short run. He bought the car for £1,850, gave his cheque and the sale was concluded. The car was a considerable disappointment to him. He took it back to Mr Smith from time to time . . . Eventually he brought this action for breach of warranty. The county court judge found that there was a warranty, that it was broken, and that the damages were more than £400, but as the claim was limited to £400, he gave judgment for the plaintiffs for that amount.

The first point is whether this representation, namely that the car had done twenty thousand miles only since it had been fitted with a replacement engine and gearbox, was an innocent misrepresentation (which does not give rise to damages) or whether it was a warranty. It was said by Holt CJ and repeated in *Heilbut, Symons & Co.* v *Buckleton*: 'An affirmation at the time of the sale is a warranty, provided it appear on evidence to be so intended'.

But that word 'intended' has given rise to difficulties. I endeavoured to explain in *Oscar Chess Ltd* v *Williams* that the question whether a warranty was intended depends on the conduct of the parties, on their words and behaviour, rather than on their thoughts. If an intelligent bystander would reasonably infer that a warranty was intended, that will suffice. What conduct then? What words and behaviour, lead to the inference of a warranty?

Looking at the cases once more, as we have done so often, it seems to me that if a representation is made in the course of dealings for a contract for the very purpose of inducing the other party to act on it, and it actually induces him to act on it by entering into the contract, that is prima facie ground for inferring that the representation was intended as a warranty. It is not necessary to speak of it as being collateral. Suffice it that the representation was intended to be acted on and was in fact acted on. But the maker of the representation can rebut this inference if he can show that it really was an innocent misrepresentation, in that he was in fact innocent of fault in making it, and that it would not be reasonable in the circumstances for him to be bound by it. In the *Oscar Chess* case the inference was rebutted. There a man had bought a second-hand car and received with it a log-book, which stated the year of the car, 1948. He afterwards resold the car. When he resold it he simply repeated what was in the log-book and passed it on to the buyer. He honestly believed on reasonable grounds that is was true. He was completely innocent of any fault. There was no warranty by him but only an innocent misrepresentation. Whereas in the present case it is very different. The inference is not rebutted. Here we have a dealer, Mr Smith, who was in a position to know, or at least to find out, the history of the car. He could get it by writing to the makers. He did not do so. Indeed it was done later. When the history of this car was examined, his statement turned out to be quite wrong. He ought to have known better. There was no reasonable foundation for it.

[His Lordship summarised the history of the car, and continued:] The county court judge found that the representations were not dishonest. Mr Smith was not guilty of fraud. But he made the statement as to twenty thousand miles without any foundation. And the judge was well justified in finding that there was a warranty. He said:

I have no hesitation that as a matter of law the statement was a warranty. Mr Smith stated a fact that should be within his own knowledge. He had jumped to a conclusion and stated it as a fact. A fact that a buyer would act on.

That is ample foundation for the inference of a warranty. So much for this point.
I hold that the appeal fails and should be dismissed.

DANCKWERTS LJ: I agree with the judgment of Lord Denning MR

SALMON LJ: I agree. I have no doubt at all that the learned county court judge reached a correct conclusion when he decided that Mr Smith gave a warranty to the second plaintiff, Mr Bentley, and that that warranty was broken. Was what Mr Smith said intended and understood as a legally binding promise? If so, it was a warranty and as such may be part of the contract of sale or collateral to it. In effect, Mr Smith said: 'If you will enter into a contract to buy this motor car from me for £1,850, I undertake that you will be getting a motor car which has done no more than twenty thousand miles since it was fitted with a new engine and a new gearbox'. I have no doubt at all that what was said by Mr Smith was so understood and was intended to be so understood by Mr Bentley.

I accordingly agree that the appeal should be dismissed.

3.3 Implied Terms

3.3.1 IMPLIED BY CUSTOM AND PRACTICE

BRITISH CRANE HIRE CORPORATION LTD v IPSWICH PLANT HIRE LTD
[1975] QB 303 (CA)

LORD DENNING MR: In June 1970, a big earth-moving machine got stuck in the mud. It sank so far as to be out of sight. It cost much money to get it out. Who is to pay the cost?

The defendants, Ipswich Plant Hire Ltd were doing drainage and other engineering works in the marshy land next the River Stour, near Cattawade Bridge in Essex. They are themselves in the hiring business, letting out cranes and so forth. But on this occasion they were doing the work themselves. They needed a dragline crane urgently. They got in touch with the plaintiffs, the British Crane Hire Corporation Ltd and asked if they could hire a dragline crane. The plaintiffs responded quickly. They delivered it on Sunday, June 28, 1970. They let it on hire to the defendants, together with the driver, Mr Humphrey. No doubt the driver remained the servant of the plaintiffs when he was driving the crane. The plaintiffs took it as far as they could by road. Then it was unloaded.

On the next day, Monday, June 29, 1970, the defendants' site agent, a Mr Meadows, directed the driver the way to go across the marsh. When they got to a particularly bad patch, Mr Meadows warned the driver that he ought to have 'navimats', that is, sets of timber baulks which could be laid out on the marsh and form a kind of roadway for the machine. The defendants ought to have supplied the 'navimats', but they had not yet arrived. Mr Meadows told the driver to wait for the 'navimats'. But the driver did not wait. He took his chance. He went on without 'navimats'. He got over that patch safely. Further on there was another bad patch of marsh. The driver took his chance again. This time he fared worse. The dragline crane sank into the marsh. That was the 'first mishap'. They got it out after a good deal of work. There was no doubt that it was the fault of the driver, Mr Humphrey, in not waiting for the 'navimats'. His negligence was the cause of that first mishap. His employers, the plaintiffs, must bear the cost of it.

On the next day, Tuesday, June 30, 1970, the 'navimats' arrived. But there was a second mishap. On that day the dragline crane had to cross another bad patch. The driver, Mr Humphrey, was this time using the 'navimats'. He had to make a turning movement or 'spragging'. He had just completed it when, in spite of the 'navimats', this machine sank into the marsh. It went out of sight. Great efforts were needed to get it out. Heavy equipment was brought in. Eventually, at great expense, the machine was got out.

The question arises on the second mishap. Who is to bear the expense of recovering the machine from the marsh? The judge found that the sinking into the marsh was not the fault of the driver, Mr Humphrey, but the fault of Mr Meadows, the site agent of the defendants. The judge thought that Mr Meadows ought to have directed the crane by a safer route across the marshy ground. On that account he held the defendants liable for the expense. That finding was challenged before us by Mr McCowan for the defendants. He pointed out that the driver and the site agent had gone together over the ground and decided on this route. I was impressed by Mr McCowan's submissions on this point. I doubt whether it would be right to hold the site agent guilty of negligence. It seems to me that this second mishap may have been a piece of bad luck which occurred without the fault of anyone. It was a hazard due to the nature of the marsh itself at that point.

But it does not follow that the plaintiffs fail on their claim. Even though the defendants were not negligent, nevertheless the plaintiffs say that the defendants are liable in contract for the costs of recovering the machine from the marsh. The plaintiffs say that the contract incorporated the conditions on a printed form under which the defendants are liable for the costs.

The judge found that the printed conditions were not incorporated into the contract. The plaintiffs appeal from that finding. The facts are these: the arrangements for the hire of the crane were all on the telephone. The plaintiffs agreed to let the defendants this crane. It was to be delivered on the Sunday. The hiring charges and transport charges were agreed. Nothing was said about conditions. There was nothing in writing. But soon after the crane was delivered, the plaintiffs, in accordance with their practice, sent forward a printed form to be signed by the hirer. It set out the order, the work to be done, and the hiring fee, and that it was subject to the conditions set out on the back of the form. The defendants would ordinarily have sent the form back signed: but this time they did not do so. The accident happened before they signed it. So they never did so. But the plaintiffs say that nevertheless, from the previous course of dealing, the conditions on the form govern the relationship between the parties. They rely on no. 6:

> Site conditions: The hirer shall take all reasonable precautions to ensure that the crane can safely be taken onto and kept upon or at the site and in particular to ensure that the ground is in a satisfactory condition to take the weight of the crane and/or its load. The hirer shall where necessary supply and lay timber on other suitable material for the crane to travel over and work upon and shall be responsible for the recovery of the crane from soft ground.

Also on no. 8:

> The hirer shall be responsible for and indemnify the owner against . . . all expenses in connection with or arising out of the use of the plant.

In support of the course of dealing, the plaintiffs relied on two previous transactions in which the defendants had hired cranes from the plaintiffs. One was February 20, 1969; and the other October 6, 1969. Each was on a printed form which set out the hiring of a crane, the price, the site, and so forth; and also setting out the conditions the same as those here. There were thus only two transactions many months before and they were not known to the defendants' manager who ordered this crane. In the circumstances, I doubt whether those two would be sufficient to show a course of dealing.

In *Hollier* v *Rambler Motors (A.M.C.) Ltd* [1972] 2 QB 71, 76, Salmon LJ said he knew of no case:

> In which it has been decided or even argued that a term could be implied into an oral contract on the strength of a course of dealing (if it can be so called) which consisted at the most of three or four transactions over a period of five years.

That was a case of a private individual who had had his car repaired by the defendants and had signed forms with conditions on three or four occasions. The plaintiff there was not of equal bargaining power with the garage company which repaired the car. The conditions were not incorporated.

But here the parties were both in the trade and were of equal bargaining power. Each was a firm of plant hirers who hired out plant. The defendants themselves knew that firms in the plant-hiring trade always imposed conditions in regard to the hiring of plant: and that their conditions were on much the same lines. The defendants' manager, Mr Turner (who knew the crane), was asked about it. He agreed that he had seen these conditions or similar ones in regard to the hiring of plant. He said that most of them were, to one extent or another, variations of a form which he called 'the Contractors' Plant Association form'. The defendants themselves (when they let out cranes) used the conditions of that form. The conditions on the plaintiffs' form were in rather different words, but nevertheless to much the same effect. He was asked one or two further questions which I would like to read.

(Q) If it was a matter of urgency, you would hire that machine out, and the conditions of hire would no doubt follow? (A) They would. (Q) Is it right that, by the very nature of your business, this is not something that happens just once a year, nor does it happen every day either, but it happens fairly regularly? (A) It does. (Q) You are well aware of the condition that it is the hirer's responsibility to make sure that soft ground is suitable for a vehicle or machine? (A) It is; it is also the owner's responsibility to see that the machine is operated competently.

Then the judge asked:

But it is the hirer's job to see what in relation to the ground? (A) That suitable timber was supplied for the machine to operate on in relation to the soft ground.

Then counsel asked:

And in fact it is the hirer's job to recover the crane from the soft ground, if it should go into it? (A) If the crane sank overnight of its own accord, I dare say it would be.

From that evidence it is clear that both parties knew quite well that conditions were habitually imposed by the supplier of these machines: and both parties knew the substance of those conditions. In particular that if the crane sank in soft ground it was the hirer's job to recover it: and that there was an indemnity clause. In these circumstances, I think the conditions on the form should be regarded as incorporated into the contract. I would not put it so much on the course of dealing, but rather on the common understanding which is to be derived from the conduct of the parties, namely, that the hiring was to be on the terms of the plaintiffs' usual conditions.

As Lord Reid said in *McCutcheon* v *David Macbrayne Ltd* [1964] 1 WLR 125, 128 quoting from the Scottish textbook, *Gloag on Contract*, 2nd edn, 1929, p. 7:

The judicial task is not to discover the actual intentions of each party; it is to decide what each was reasonably entitled to conclude from the attitude of the other.

It seems to me that, in view of the relationship of the parties, when the defendants requested this crane urgently and it was supplied at once – before the usual form was received – the plaintiffs were entitled to conclude that the defendants were accepting it on the terms of the plaintiffs' own printed conditions – which would follow in a day or two. It is just as if the plaintiffs had said 'We will supply it on our usual conditions' and the defendants said 'Of course, that is quite understood'. . . .

Megaw LJ and Sir Eric Sachs concurred.

3.3.2 IMPLIED BY STATUTE

SALE OF GOODS ACT 1979

Section 12. Implied terms about title, etc.
(1) In a contract of sale, other than one to which subsection (3) below applies, there is an implied term on the part of the seller that in the case of a sale he has a right to sell the goods, and in the case of an agreement to sell he will have such a right at the time when the property is to pass.
(2) In a contract of sale, other than one to which subsection (3) below applies, there is also an implied term that—
(a) the goods are free, and will remain free until the time when the property is to pass, from any charge or encumbrance not disclosed or known to the buyer before the contract is made; and
(b) the buyer will enjoy quiet possession of the goods except so far as it may be disturbed by the owner or other person entitled to the benefit of any charge or encumbrance so disclosed or known.

(3)   This subsection applies to the contract of sale in the case of which there appears from the contract or is to be inferred from its circumstances an intention that the seller should transfer only such title as he or a third person may have.

(4)   In a contract to which subsection (3) above applies there is an implied term that all charges or encumbrances known to the seller and not known to the buyer have been disclosed to the buyer before the contract is made.

(5)   In a contract to which subsection (3) above applies there is also an implied term that none of the following will disturb the buyer's quiet possession of the goods, namely—

(a)   the seller;

(b)   in a case where the parties to the contract intend that the seller should transfer only such title as a third person may have, that person;

(c)   anyone claiming through or under the seller or that third person otherwise than under a charge or encumbrance disclosed or known to the buyer before the contract is made.

(5A)   As regards England and Wales and Northern Ireland, the term implied by subsection (1) above is a condition and the terms implied by subsections (2), (4) and (5) above are warranties.

Section 13.   Sale by description

(1)   Where there is a contract for the sale of goods by description, there is an implied term that the goods will correspond with the description.

(1A)   As regards England and Wales and Northern Ireland, the term implied by subsection (1) above is a condition.

(2)   If the sale is by sample as well as by description it is not sufficient that the bulk of the goods corresponds with the sample if the goods do not also correspond with the description.

(3)   A sale of goods is not prevented from being a sale by description by reason only that, being exposed for sale or hire, they are selected by the buyer.

Section 14.   Implied terms about quality or fitness

(1)   Except as provided by this section and section 15 below and subject to any other enactment, there is no implied term about the quality or fitness for any particular purpose of goods supplied under a contract of sale.

(2)   Where the seller sells goods in the course of a business, there is an implied term that the goods supplied under the contract are of satisfactory quality.

(2A)   For the purposes of this Act, goods are of satisfactory quality if they meet the standard that a reasonable person would regard as satisfactory, taking account of any description of the goods, the price (if relevant) and all the other relevant circumstances.

(2B)   For the purposes of this Act, the quality of goods includes their state and condition and the following (among others) are in appropriate cases aspects of the quality of goods—

(a)   fitness for all the purposes for which goods of the kind in question are commonly supplied,

(b)   appearance and finish,

(c)   freedom from minor defects,

(d)   safety, and

(e)   durability.

(2C)   The term implied by subsection (2) above does not extend to any matter making the quality of goods unsatisfactory—

(a)   which is specifically drawn to the buyer's attention before the contract is made,

(b)   where the buyer examines the goods before the contract is made, which that examination ought to reveal, or

(c)   in the case of a contract for sale by sample, which would have been apparent on a reasonable examination of the sample.

(3)   Where the seller sells goods in the course of a business and the buyer, expressly or by implication, makes known—

(a)   to the seller, or

(b)   where the purchase price or part of it is payable by instalments and the goods were previously sold by a credit-broker to the seller, to that credit-broker,
any particular purpose for which the goods are being bought, there is an implied term that the goods supplied under the contract are reasonably fit for that purpose, whether or not that is a purpose for which such goods are commonly supplied, except where the circumstances show that the buyer does not rely, or that it is unreasonable for him to rely, on the skill or judgment of the seller or credit-broker.

(4)   An implied term about quality or fitness for a particular purpose may be annexed to a contract of sale by usage.

(5)   The preceding provisions of this section apply to a sale by a person who in the course of a business is acting as agent for another as they apply to a sale by a principal in the course of a business, except where that other is not selling in the course of a business and either the buyer knows that fact or reasonable steps are taken to bring it to the notice of the buyer before the contract is made.

(6)   As regards England and Wales and Northern Ireland, the terms implied by subsections (2) and (3) above are conditions.

BALDRY v MARSHALL [1925] 1 KB 260 (CA)

The plaintiff had inquired about Bugatti cars, explaining that he wanted a car that was 'comfortable and suitable for the ordinary purposes of a touring car'.

BANKES LJ: This is an appeal from a judgment of Greer J and upon the facts as found by the learned judge his conclusion was in my opinion quite right. It appears that the plaintiff wrote to the defendants, 'Can you tell me if the Bugatti eight cylinder is likely to be on the market this year, if so will you send particulars?' indicating that according to his impression this was a new type of car that was going to be put on the market. In their reply the defendants said: 'As no doubt you are already aware, we specialize in the sale of these cars, and are in a position to supply you with all information necessary', thereby intimating that the plaintiff might regard them as persons upon whose skill and judgment he could safely rely. Those letters were followed by an interview at which the plaintiff made plain to the defendants the purpose for which he required the car. Then came the contract, which was on a printed form. It was in the form of a request by the plaintiff to the defendants to supply him with 'one eight cylinder Bugatti car fully equipped and finished to standard specification as per the car inspected'. On the back of the contract there was printed 'The company reserves the right to withdraw any model or alter specifications or prices without notice. Illustrations and specifications must be taken as a general guide and not as binding in detail', and under the heading 'Guarantee' the words 'The same as received by us from the maufacturers'. The guarantee which they had so received from the manufacturers was expressed to be 'against any breakage of parts due to faulty material', and contained the following clause: 'Cars are sold on condition that the foregoing guarantee is accepted instead of and expressly excludes any other guarantee or warranty, statutory or otherwise'. It is said that by the use of that language the defendants meant to exclude conditions as well as warranties; but they have not done so, and if there is one thing more clearly established than another it is the distinction which the law recognizes between a condition and a warranty. In *Wallis v Pratt* [1911] AC 394 the sellers by a clause stating that 'Sellers give no warranty express or implied' endeavoured to exclude the condition implied under s. 13 of the Sale of Goods Act, that the goods sold should correspond with the description, but the House of Lords held that they had not used apt words to effect that purpose. So here the defendants have not used the necessary language to exclude the implied condition which arises under s. 14 as to fitness for the particular purpose of which the plaintiff had given them notice . . .

In my opinion the appeal must be dismissed.

WILSON v RICKETT COCKERELL & CO. LTD [1954] 1 QB 598 (CA)

DENNING LJ: In June, 1951, Mrs Wilson ordered one ton of Coalite from Rickett Cockerell & Co. Ltd and it was delivered and paid for. In November, 1951, she took from the bin some of the material which they had delivered to her and which she thought was Coalite. She made up the fire with it on November 26 at about 7.30 p.m., because she and her husband wanted to listen to an item on the wireless which lasted from 7.30 p.m. until 8 p.m. Shortly before eight o'clock there was an explosion in the grate. A thick cloud of black smoke came out, the whole basket which held the Coalite was shot forward, the heavy curb was pushed forward, and most of the Coalite was scattered about the room, some of it falling on to Mrs Wilson's dress. Bits of Coalite were found sticking to the wallpaper. The damage was considerable: it cost £117 4s. 1d. to put right. Fortunately, the plaintiffs were themselves uninjured. They now claim from Messrs Rickett Cockerell & Co. Ltd for the damage done to the room and the furniture.

The judge has found that the explosion was due to something in the consignment which the defendants delivered. It was not a piece of Coalite itself, but something that came with it, such as a piece of coal, in which was embedded an explosive. The offending piece had not come from the manufacturers of the Coalite, but it had got mixed with it in the course of transit, such as in a coal truck or in a lorry. It was certainly in the consignment before it was delivered to the plaintiffs. The judge has found that neither of the coalmen employed by the defendants was negligent, nor were the plaintiffs negligent, in not detecting it; but, nevertheless, it did the damage, and the question is whether the plaintiffs can recover their loss from the coal merchants.

The judge for himself would have held that the plaintiffs could have recovered, but he felt that he ought to follow a decision of the Court of Session in Scotland, *Duke* v *Jackson* 1921 SC 362. In that case a bag of household coal purchased from a coal merchant contained a detonator which exploded while the coal was being burned in the kitchen fire. The householder lost his eye, but the Court of Session held that on the facts alleged in the pleadings, there was no breach of the condition implied under section 14(1) of the Sale of Goods Act, 1894. The reasoning of the Court of Session was after this wise: the coal, as coal, was all right; it was fit for its purpose; the trouble was that there was something in it which the householder did not purchase, namely, a detonator; and as he did not purchase it, he could not complain of it as a breach of contract under section 14(1); but only for negligence, if there was any.

With all respect to the Court of Session, I must confess that I do not understand this line of reasoning. Coal is not bought by the lump. It is bought by the sack or by the hundredweight or by the ton. The consignment is delivered as a whole and must be considered as a whole; not in bits. A sack of coal, which contains hidden in it a detonator, is not fit for burning, and no sophistry should lead us to believe that it is fit. . . . The principal point made before us was that section 14 does not apply to this case, because both subsections (1) and (2), it was said, only refer to the contract goods, that is, to the goods which are the subject of the contract of sale: and, so here, it refers only to the Coalite proper and not to the explosive piece which was in it.

The answer to that argument lies in the opening words of section 14, which show that the section refers to the 'goods supplied under a contract of sale'. In my opinion that means the goods delivered in purported pursuance of the contract. The section applies to all goods so delivered, whether they conform to the contract or not: that is, in this case, to the whole consignment, including the offending piece, and not merely to the Coalite alone. . . .

In my opinion, therefore, this consignment was unmerchantable because of the presence in it of this explosive piece. That is sufficient to decide the case, but I would like to express my concurrence with what the Master of the Rolls observed during the course of the argument, that the more Mr Mocatta sought to escape from section 14, the more he became impaled on section 13. Mrs Wilson ordered Coalite from the coal merchants but they did not supply what she ordered; they delivered, not Coalite alone, but Coalite mixed with a dangerous piece of explosive.

I need not say more about that because section 13 was not pleaded, nor relied upon. Suffice it to say that section 14(2), in my judgment, clearly covers this case. It is a subsection which was not relied on before the Court of Session in Scotland, but it covers this case. I would allow the appeal on that ground and let judgment be entered for the plaintiffs for the sum claimed.

Lord Evershed MR and Romer LJ concurred.

SALE OF GOODS ACT 1979

Section 15.   Sale by sample
   (1)   A contract of sale is a contract for sale by sample where there is an express or implied term to that effect in the contract.
   (2)   In the case of a contract for sale by sample there is an implied term—
      (a)   that the bulk will correspond with the sample in quality;
      (b)   that the buyer will have reasonable opportunity of comparing the bulk with the sample;
      (c)   that the goods will be free from any defect, making their quality unsatisfactory, which would not be apparent on reasonable examination of the sample
   (3)   As regards England and Wales and Northern Ireland, the term implied by subsection (2) above is a condition.

3.3.4   IMPLIED AT COMMON LAW

LIVERPOOL CITY COUNCIL v IRWIN [1976] 2 All ER 39 (HL)

The appellants argued that a term should be implied into their tenancy agreements obliging the local authority landlords to keep the common parts of their blocks of flats in good repair.

LORD WILBERFORCE: My Lords, this case is of general importance, since it concerns the obligations of local authority, and indeed other, landlords as regards high-rise or multi-storey dwellings towards the tenants of these dwellings. This is a comparatively recent problem though there have been some harbingers of it in previous cases.
   50 Haigh Heights, Liverpool, is one of several recently erected tower blocks in the district of Everton. It has some 70 dwelling units in it. It was erected ten years ago, following a slum clearance programme at considerable cost, and was then, no doubt, thought to mark an advance in housing standards. Unfortunately, it has since turned out that effective slum clearance depends on more than expenditure on steel and concrete. There are human factors involved too, and it is these which seem to have failed. The appellants moved into one of the units in this building in July 1966; this was a maisonette of two floors, corresponding to the ninth and tenth floors of the block. Access to it was provided by a staircase and by two electrically operated lifts. Another facility provided was an internal chute into which tenants in the block could discharge rubbish or garbage for collection at the ground level.
   There has been a consistent history of trouble in this block, due in part to vandalism, in part to non-cooperation by tenants, in part, it is said, to neglect by the corporation. The appellants, with other tenants, stopped payment of rent so that in May 1973 the corporation had to start proceedings for possession. The appellants put in a counterclaim for damages and for an injunction, alleging that the corporation was in breach of its implied covenant for quiet enjoyment, that it was in breach of the statutory covenant implied by s. 32 of the Housing Act 1961 and that it was in breach of an obligation implied by law to keep the 'common parts' in repair. The case came for trial in the Liverpool County Court before his Honour Judge T A Cunliffe. A good deal of evidence was submitted, both orally and in the form of reports. The judge himself visited the block and inspected the premises; he said in his judgment that he was appalled by the general condition of the property. On 10th April 1974 he gave a detailed and careful judgment granting possession to the corporatioon on the claim and, on the counterclaim, judgment for the appellants for £10 nominal damages. He found that the defects alleged by the appellants were established. These can be summarised as consisting of (i) a number of defects in the maisonette itself – these were significant but not perhaps of major importance; (ii) defects in the common parts, which may be summarised as continual failure of the lifts, sometimes of both at one time, lack of lighting on the stairs, dangerous condition of the staircase with unguarded holes giving access to the rubbish chutes and frequent blockage of the chutes. He found that these had existed or been repeated with considerable frequency throughout the tenancy, had gone from bad to worse, and that

while some defects in the common parts could be attributed to vandalism, not all could be so attributed. No doubt also some defects, particularly the blocking of the rubbish chutes, were due to irresponsible action by the tenants themselves. The learned judge decided that there was to be implied a covenant by the corporation to keep the common parts in repair and properly lighted, and that the corporation was in breach of this implied covenant, of the covenant for quiet enjoyment and of the repairing covenant implied by the Housing Act 1961, s. 32.

The corporation appealed to the Court of Appeal, which allowed the corporation's appeal against the judgment on the counterclaim. While agreeing in the result, the members of that court differed as to their grounds. Roskill and Ormrod LJJ held that no covenant to repair the common parts ought to be implied. Lord Denning MR held that there should be implied a covenant to take reasonable care, not only to keep the lifts and stairs reasonable safe, but also to keep them reasonably fit for use by the tenant and his family and visitors. He held, however, that there was no evidence of any breach of this duty. The court was agreed in holding that there was no breach of the covenant implied under s. 32 of the Housing Act 1961; the appellants did not seek to uphold the judge's decision on the covenant for quiet enjoyment, and have not done so in the House.

I consider first the appellants' claim insofar as it is based on contract. The first step must be to ascertain what the contract is. This may look elementary, even naive, but it seems to me to be the essential step and to involve, from the start, an approach different, if simpler, from that taken by the members of the Court of Appeal. We look first at documentary material. As is common with council lettings there is no formal demise or lease or tenancy agreement. There is a document headed 'Liverpool Corporation, Liverpool City Housing Department' and described as 'Conditions of Tenancy'. This contains a list of obligations on the tenant – he shall do this, he shall not do that, or he shall not do that without the corporation's consent. This is an amalgam of obligations added to from time to time, no doubt, to meet complaints, emerging situations, or problems as they appear to the council's officers. In particular there have been added special provisions relating to multi-storey flats which are supposed to make the conditions suitable to such dwellings. We may note under 'Further special notes' some obligations not to obstruct staircases and passages, and not to permit children under ten to operate any lifts. I mention these as a recognition of the existence and relevance of these facilities. At the end there is a form for signature by the tenant stating that he accepts the tenancy. On the landlords' side there is nothing, no signature, no demise, no covenant; the contract takes effect as soon as the tenants sign the form and are let into possession.

We have then a contract which is partly, but not wholly, stated in writing. In order to complete it, in particular to give it a bilateral character, it is necessary to take account of the actions of the parties and the circumstances. As actions of the parties, we must note the granting of possession by the corporation and reservation by it of the 'common parts' – stairs, lifts, chutes etc. As circumstances we must include the nature of the premises, viz a maisonette for family use on the ninth floor of a high block, one which is occupied by a large number of other tenants, all using the common parts and dependent on them, none of them have any expressed obligation to maintain or repair them.

To say that the construction of a complete contract out of these elements involves a process of 'implication' may be correct: it would be so if implication means the supplying of what is not expressed. But there are varieties of implications which the courts think fit to make and they do not necessarily involve the same process. Where there is, on the face of it, a complete, bilateral contract, the courts are sometimes willing to add terms to it, as implied terms; this is very common in mercantile contracts where there is an established usage; in that case the courts are spelling out what both parties know and would, if asked, unhesitatingly agree to be part of the bargain. In other cases, where there is an apparently complete bargain, the courts are willing to add a term on the ground that without it the contract will not work – this is the case, if not of *The Moorcock* (1889) 14 PD 64 itself on its facts, at least of the doctrine of *The Moorcock* as usually applied. This is, as was pointed out by the majority in the Court of Appeal, a strict test – though the degree of strictness seems to vary with the current legal trend, and I think that they were right not to accept it as applicable here. There is a third variety of implication, that which I think Lord Denning MR favours, or at least did favour in this case, and that is the implication of reasonable terms. But though I agree with many of his instances, which in fact fall under one or other of the preceding heads, I cannot go so far as to endorse his principle; indeed, it seems to me, with respect, to extend a long, and undesirable way beyond sound authority.

The present case, in my opinion, represents a fourth category or, I would rather say, a fourth shade on a continuous spectrum. The court here is simply concerned to establish what the contract is, the parties not having themselves fully stated the terms. In this sense the court is searching for what must be implied.

What then should this contract be held to be? There must first be implied a letting, i.e. a grant of the right of exclusive possession to the tenants. With this there must, I would suppose, be implied a covenant for quiet enjoyment, as a necessary incident of the letting. The difficulty begins when we consider the common parts. We start with the fact that the demise is useless unless access is obtained by the staircase; we can add that, having regard to the height of the block, and the family nature of the dwellings, the demise would be useless without a lift service; we can continue that there being rubbish chutes built in to the structures and no other means of disposing of light rubbish there must be a right to use the chutes. The question to be answered – and it is the only question in this case – is what is to be the legal relationship between landlord and tenant as regards these matters.

There can be no doubt that there must be implied (i) an easement for the tenants and their licencees to use the stairs, (ii) a right in the nature of an easement to use the lifts and (iii) an easement to use the rubbish chutes.

But are these easements to be accompanied by any obligation on the landlord, and what obligation? There seem to be two alternatives. The first, for which the corporation contends, is for an easement coupled with no legal obligation, except such as may arise under the Occupiers' Liability Act 1957 as regards the safety of those using the facilities, and possibly such other liability as might exist under the ordinary law of tort. The alternative is for easements coupled with some obligation on the part of the landlords as regards the maintenance of the subject of them, so that they are available for use.

My Lords, in order to be able to choose between these, it is necessary to define what test is to be applied, and I do not find this difficult. In my opinion such obligation should be read into the contract as the nature of the contract itself implicitly requires, no more, no less; a test in other words of necessity. The relationship accepted by the corporation is that of landlord and tenant; the tenant accepts obligations accordingly, in relation, inter alia, to the stairs, the lifts and the chutes. All these are not just facilities, or conveniences provided at discretion; they are essentials of the tenancy without which life in the dwellings, as a tenant, is not possible. To leave the landlord free of contractual obligation as regards these matters, and subject only to administrative or political pressure, is, in my opinion, totally inconsistent with the nature of this relationship. The subject-matter of the lease (high-rise blocks) and the relationship created by the tenancy demands, of its nature, some contractual obligation on the landlord. . . .

I accept, of course, the argument that a mere grant of an easement does not carry with it any obligation on the part of the servient owner to maintain the subject-matter. The dominant owner must spend the necessary money, eg in repairing a drive leading to his house. And the same principle may apply when a landlord lets an upper floor with access by a staircase; responsibility for maintenance may well rest on the tenant. But there is a difference between that case and the case where there is an essential means of access, retained in the landlord's occupation, to units in a building of multi-occupation; for unless the obligation to maintain is, in a defined manner, placed on the tenants, individually or collectively, the nature of the contract, and the circumstances, require that it be placed on the landlord.

It remains to define the standard. My Lords, if, as I think, the test of the existence of the term is necessity the standard must surely not exceed what is necessary having regard to the circumstances. To imply an absolute obligation to repair would go beyond what is a necessary legal incident and would indeed be unreasonable. An obligation to take reasonable care to keep in reasonable repair and usability is what fits the requirements of the case. Such a definition involves – and I think rightly – recognition that the tenants themselves have their responsibilities. What it is reasonable to expect of a landlord has a clear relation to what a reasonable set of tenants should do for themselves.

I add one word as to lighting. In general I would accept that a grant of an easement of passage does not carry with it an obligation on the grantor to light the way. The grantee must take the way accompanied by the primaeval separation of darkness from light and if he passes during the former must bring his own illumination. I think that *Huggett* v *Miers* [1908] 2 KB 278 was decided on this principle and possibly also *Devine* v *London Housing Society Ltd* [1950] 2 All ER 1173. But the case may be different when the means of passage are constructed, and when natural light is either absent or insufficient. In such a case, to the extent that the easement is useless without some artificial light being provided, the grant should carry with it an obligation to take reasonable care to maintan adequate lighting – comparable to the obligation as regards the lifts. To impose an absolute obligation would be unreasonable; to impose some might be necessary. We have not sufficient material before us to see whether the present case on its facts meets these conditions.

I would hold therefore that the corporation's obligation is as I have described. And in agreement, I believe, with your Lordships, I would hold that it has not been shown in this case that there was any breach of that obligation. On the main point therefore I would hold that the appeal fails.

My Lords, it will be seen that I have reached exactly the same conclusion as that of Lord Denning MR, with most of whose thinking I respectfully agree. I must only differ from the passage in which, more adventurously, he suggested that the courts had power to introduce into contracts any terms they thought reasonable or to anticipate legislative recommendations of the Law Commission. A just result can be reached, if I am right, by a less dangerous route.

As regards the obligation under the Housing Act 1961, s. 32, again I am in general agreement with Lord Denning MR. The only possible item which might fall within the covenant implied by this section is that of defective cisterns in the maisonette giving rise to flooding or, if this is prevented, to insufficient flushing. I do not disagree with those of your Lordships who would hold that a breach of the statutory covenant was committed in respect of the matter for which a small sum of damages may be awarded. I would allow the appeal as to this matter and dismiss it for the rest.

Lords Cross, Salmon, Edmund-Davies and Fraser concurred.

SHELL UK LTD v LOSTOCK GARAGES [1977] 1 All ER 481 (CA)

The defendants argued that an agreement to buy petrol exclusively from the plaintiffs should contain an implied term that the plaintiffs would not discriminate against them in the terms of the supply.

LORD DENNING MR: . . .

Implied terms
It was submitted by counsel for Lostock that there was to be implied in the solus agreement a term that Shell, as the supplier, should not abnormally discriminate against the buyer and/or should supply petrol to the buyer on terms which did not abnormally discriminate against him. He said that Shell had broken that implied term by giving support to the two Shell garages and refusing it to Lostock; that, on that ground, Shell were in breach of the solus agreement; and that Lostock were entitled to terminate it.

This submission makes it necessary once again to consider the law as to implied terms. I ventured with some trepidation to suggest that terms implied by law could be brought within one comprehensive category, in which the courts could imply a term such as was just and reasonable in the circumstances: see *Greaves & Co. (Contractors) Ltd* v *Bayham Meikle & Partners* [1975] 3 All ER 99; *Liverpool City Council* v *Irwin* [1975] 3 All ER 658. But, as I feared, the House of Lords have rejected it as quite unacceptable. As I read the speeches, there are two broad categories of implied terms.

(i) The first category
The first category comprehends all those relationships which are of common occurrence, such as the relationship of seller and buyer, owner and hirer, master and sevant, landlord

and tenant, carrier by land or by sea, contractor for building works, and so forth. In all those relationships the courts have imposed obligations on one party or the other, saying they are implied tems. These obligations are not founded on the intention of the parties, actual or presumed, but on more general considerations: see *Luxor (Eastbourne) Ltd v Cooper* [1941] 1 All ER 33 per Lord Wright: *Lister v Romford Ice and Cold Storage Co.* [1957] 1 All ER 125 per Viscount Simonds and Lord Tucker (both of whom give interesting illustrations); *Liverpool City Council v Irwin* per Lord Cross of Chelsea and Lord Edmund-Davies. In such relationships the problem is not solved by asking: what did the parties intend? or, would they have unhesitatingly agreed to it, if asked? It is to be solved by asking: has the law already defined the obligation or the extent of it? If so, let it be followed. If not, look to see what would be reasonable in the general run of such cases (see per Lord Cross of Chelsea) and then say what the obligation shall be. The House in *Liverpool City Council v Irwin* went through that very process. They examined the existing law of landlord and tenant, in particular that relating to easements, to see if it contained the solution to the problem; and having found that it did not, they imposed an obligation on the landlord to use reasonable care. In these relationships the parties can exclude or modify the obligation by express words, but unless they do so, the obligation is a legal incident of the relationship which is attached by the law itself and not by reason of any implied term.

Likewise, in the general law of contract, the legal effect of frustration does not depend on an implied term. It does not depend on the presumed intention of the parties, nor on what they would have answered, if asked, but simply on what the court itself declares to amount to a frustration; see *Davis Contractors v Fareham Urban District Council* [1956] 2 All ER 145 per Lord Radcliffe; *Ocean Tramp Tankers Corpn v V/O Sovfracht, The Eugenia* [1964] 1 All ER 161.

(ii)   The second category

The second category comprehends those cases which are not within the first category. These are cases, not of common occurrence, in which from the particular circumstances a term is to be implied. In these cases the implication is based on an intention imputed to the parties from their actual circumstances; see *Luxor (Eastbourne) Ltd v Cooper* per Lord Wright. Such an imputation is only to be made when it is necessary to imply a term to give efficacy to the contract and make it a workable agreement in such manner as the parties would clearly have done if they had applied their mind to the contingency which has arisen. These are the 'officious bystander' type of case: see *Lister v Romford Ice & Cold Storage Co.* per Lord Tucker. In such cases a term is not to be implied on the ground that it would be reasonable, but only when it is necessary and can be formulated with a sufficient degree of precision. This was the test applied by the majority of this court in *Liverpool City Council v Irwin*; and they were emphatically upheld by the House on this point; see per Lord Cross of Chelsea and Lord Edmund-Davies.

There is this point to be noted about *Liverpool City Council v Irwin*. In this court the argument was only about an implication in the second category. In the House of Lords that argument was not pursued. It was only the first category.

Into which of the two categories does the present case come? I am tempted to say that a solus agreement between supplier and buyer is of such common occurrence nowadays that it could be put into the first category; so that the law could imply a term based on general considerations. But I do not think this would be found acceptable. Nor do I think the case can be brought within the second category. If Shell had been asked at the beginning: 'Will you agree not to discriminate abnormally against the buyer?' I think they would have declined. It might be a reasonable term, but it is not a necessary term. Nor can it be formulated with sufficient precision. On this point I agree with Kerr J. It should be noticed that in *Esso Petroleum Co. Ltd v Harper's Garage (Stourport) Ltd* [1967] 1 All ER 699 Mocatta J also refused to make such an implication and there was no appeal from his decision.

In the circumstances, I do not think any term can be implied.

Ormond LJ concurred; Bridge LJ dissented.

3.4   Conditions, Warranties and Intermediate Terms

POUSSARD v SPIERS AND POND [1876] 1 QB 410 (QB)

The issue here was whether the plaintiff's failure to perform was sufficiently serious to justify the defendant's treating it as a basis for repudiation of the whole agreement.

BLACKBURN J: This was an action for the dismissal of the plaintiff's wife from a theatrical engagement. On the trial before my Brother Field it appeared that the defendants, Messrs Spiers & Pond, had taken the Criterion Theatre, and were about to bring out a French opera, which was to be produced simultaneously in London and Paris. Their manager, Mr Hingston, by their authority, made a contract with the plaintiff's wife, which was reduced to writing in the following letter –

<blockquote>

Criterion Theatre, October 16th, 1874

To Madame Poussard.

On behalf of Messrs Spiers & Pond I engage you to sing and play at the Criterion Theatre on the following terms:–

You to play the part of Friquette in Lecocq's opera of Les Pres Saint Gervais, commencing on or about the fourteenth of November next, at a weekly salary of eleven pounds (11*l*.), and to continue on at that sum for a period of three months, providing the opera shall run for that period. Then, at the expiration of the said three months, I shall be at liberty to re-engage you at my option, on terms then to be arranged, and not to exceed fourteen pounds per week for another period of three months. Dresses and tights requisite for the part to be provided by the management, and the engagement to be subject to the ordinary rules and regulations of the theatre.

Ratified: E. P. Hingston, Manager.

Spiers & Pond.

Madame Poussard, 46, Gunter Grove, Chelsea.

</blockquote>

The first performance of the piece was announced for Saturday, the 28th of November. No objection was raised on either side as to this delay, and Madame Poussard attended rehearsals, and such attendance, though not expressed in the written engagement, was an implied part of it. Owing to delays on the part of the composer, the music of the latter part of the piece was not in the hands of the defendants till a few days before that announced for the production of the piece, and the latter and final rehearsals did not take place till the week on the Saturday of which the performance was announced. Madame Poussard was unfortunately taken ill, and though she struggled to attend the rehearsals, she was obliged on Monday, the 23rd of November, to leave the rehearsal, go home and go to bed, and call in medical attendance. In the course of the next day or two an interview took place between the plaintiff and Mr Leonard (Madame Poussard's medical attendant) and Mrs Liston, who was the defendants' stage manager, in reference to Madame Poussard's ability to attend and undertake her part. . . .

There was no substantial conflict as to what was in fact done by Mrs Liston. Upon learning, on the Wednesday (the 25th of November), the possibility that Madame Poussard might be prevented by illness from fulfilling her engagement, she sent to a theatrical agent to inquire what artistes of position were disengaged, and learning that Miss Lewis had no engagement till the 25th of December, she made a provisional arrangement with her, by which Miss Lewis undertook to study the part and be ready on Saturday to take the part, in case Madame Poussard was not then recovered so far as to be ready to perform. If it should turn out that this labour was thrown away, Miss Lewis was to have a douceur for her trouble. If Miss Lewis was called on to perform, she was to be engaged at 15*l*. a week up to the 25th of December, if the piece ran so long. Madame Poussard continued in bed and ill, and unable to attend either the subsequent rehearsals or the first night of the performance on the Saturday, and Miss Lewis's engagement became absolute, and she performed the part on Saturday, Monday, Tuesday, Wednesday, and up to the close of her engagement, the 25th of December. The piece proved a success, and in fact ran for more than three months.

On Thursday, the 4th of December, Madame Poussard, having recovered, offered to take her place, but was refused, and for this refusal the action was brought.

On the 2nd of January Madame Poussard left England.

My Brother Field, at the trial, expressed his opinion that the failure of Madame Poussard to be ready to perform, under the circumstances, went so much to the root of the consideration as to discharge the defendants, and that he should therefore enter judgment for the defendants; but he asked the jury five questions

The first three related to the supposed rescission and waiver. The other questions were in writing and were: 4. Whether the non-attendance on the night of the opening was of such material consequence to the defendants as to entitle them to rescind the contract? To which the jury said 'No'. And, 5. was it of such consequence as to render it reasonable for the defendants to employ another artiste, and whether the engagement of Miss Lewis, as made, was reasonable; to which the jury said 'Yes'. Lastly, he left the question of damages, which the jury assessed at 83*l.*

On these answers he reserved leave to the plaintiff to move to enter judgment for 83*l.*

A cross rule was obtained on the ground that the verdict was against evidence and that the damages were excessive.

We think that, from the nature of the engagement to take a leading, and, indeed the principal female part (for the prima donna sang her part in male costume as the Prince de Conti) in a new opera which (as appears from the terms of the engagement) it was known might run for a longer or shorter time, and so be a profitable or losing concern to the defendants, we can, without the aid of the jury, see that it must have been of great importance to the defendants that the piece should start well, and consequently that the failure of the pliaintiff's wife to be able to perform on the opening and early performances was a very serious detriment to them.

This inability having been occasioned by sickness was not any breach of contract by the plaintiff, and no action can lie against him for the failure thus occasioned. But the damage to the defendants and the consequent failure of consideration is just as great as if it had been occasioned by the plaintiff's fault, instead of by his wife's misfortune. The analogy is complete between this case and that of charterparty in the ordinary terms, where the ship is to proceed in ballast (the act of God, &c., excepted) to a port and there load a cargo. If the delay is occasioned by excepted perils, the shipowner is excused. But if it is so great as to go to the root of the matter, it frees the charterer from his obligation to furnish a cargo : see per Bramwell B, delivering the judgment of the majority of the Court of Exchequer Chamber in *Jackson* v *Union Marine Insurance Co.* (1874) LR 10 CP 125.

And we think that the question, whether the failure of a skilled and capable artiste to perform in a new piece through serious illness is so important as to go to the root of the consideration, must to some extent depend on the evidence; and is a mixed question of law and fact. Theoretically, the facts should be left to and found separately by the jury, it being for the judge or the court to say whether they, being found so, shew a breach of a condition precedent or not. But this course is often (if not generally) impracticable; and if we can see that the proper facts have been found, we should act on these without regard to the form of the questions.

Now, in the present case, we must consider what were the courses open to the defendants under the circumstances. They might, it was said on the argument before us (though not on the trial), have postponed the bringing out of the piece till the recovery of Madame Poussard, and if her illness had been a temporary hoarseness incapacitating her from singing on the Saturday, but sure to be removed by the Monday, that might have been a proper course to pursue. But the illness here was a serious one, of uncertain duration, and if the plaintiff had at the trial suggested that this was the proper course, it would, no doubt, have been shewn that it would have been a ruinous course; and that it would have been much better to have abandoned the piece altogether than to have postponed it from day to day for an uncertain time, during which the theatre would have been a heavy loss.

The remaining alternatives were to employ a temporary subsitute until such a time as the plaintiff's wife should recover; and if a temporary substitute capable of performing the part adequately could have been obtained upon such a precarious engagement on any reasonable terms, that would have been a right course to pursue; but if no substitute capable of performing the part adequately could be obtained, except on the terms that she should be permanently engaged at higher pay than the plaintiff's wife, in our opinion it follows, as a matter of law, that the failure on the plaintiff's part went to the root of the matter and discharged the defendants.

We think, therefore, that the fifth question put to the jury, and answered by them in favour of the defendants, does find all the facts necessary to enable us to decide as a matter of law that the defendants are discharged.

Quain and Field JJ concurred.

BETTINI v GYE (1876) 1 QBD 183 (QB)

BLACKBURN J: In this case the parties have entered into an agreement in writing, which is set out on the record.

The court must ascertain the intention of the parties, as is said by Parke B in delivering the judgment of the court in *Graves* v *Legg* (1854) 9 Exch 709, 'to be collected from the instrument and the circumstances legally admissible in evidence with reference to which it is to be construed'. He adds: 'One particular rule well acknowledged is, that where a covenant or agreement goes to part of the consideraton on both sides, and may be compensated in damages, it is an independent covenant or contract'. There was no averment of any special circumstances existing in this case, with reference to which the agreement was made, but the court must look at the general nature of such an engagement. By the 7th paragraph of the agreement, 'Mr Bettini agrees to be in London without fail at least six days before the commencement of his engagement for the purpose of rehearsals'. The engagement was to begin on the 30th of March, 1875. It is admitted on the record that the plaintiff did not arrive in London till the 28th of March, which is less than six days before the 30th, and therefore it is clear that he has not fulfilled this part of the contract.

The question raised by the demurrer is, not whether the plaintiff has any excuse for failing to fulfil this part of his contract, which may prevent his being liable in damages for not doing so, but whether his failure to do so justified the defendant in refusing to proceed with the engagement, and fulfill his, the defendant's part. And the answer to that question depends on whether this part of the contract is a condition precedent to the defendant's liability, or only an independent agreement, a breach of which will not justify a repudiation of the contract, but will only be a cause of action for a compensation in damages. . . .

We think the answer to this question depends on the true construction of the contract taken as a whole.

Parties may think some matter, apparently of very little importance, essential; and if they sufficiently express an intention to make the literal fulfilment of such a thing a condition precedent, it will be one; or they may think that the performance of some matter, apparently of essential importance and prima facie a condition precedent, is not really vital, and may be compensated for in damages, and if they sufficiently expressed such an intention, it will not be a condition precedent.

In this case, if to the 7th paragraph of the agreement there had been added words to this effect: 'And if Mr Bettini is not there at the stipulated time Mr Gye may refuse to proceed further with the agreement', or if, on the other hand, it had been said, 'And if not there, Mr Gye may postpone the commencement of Mr Bettini's engagement for as many days as Mr Bettini makes default, and he shall forfeit twice his salary for that time', there could have been no question raised in the case. But there is no such declaration of the intention of the parties either way. And in the absence of such an express declaration, we think that we are to look to the whole contract, and . . .see whether the particular stipulation goes to the root of the matter, so that a failure to perform it would render the performance of the rest of the contract by the plaintiff a thing different in substance from what the defendant has stipulated for; or whether it merely partially affects it and may be compensated for in damages. Accordingly, as it is one or the other, we think it must be taken to be or not to be intended to be a condition precedent.

If the plaintiff's engagement had been only to sing in operas at the theatre, it might very well be that previous attendance at rehearsals with the actors in company with whom he was to perform was essential. And if the engagement had been only for a few performances, or for a short time, it would afford a strong argument that attendance for the purpose of rehearsals during the six days immediately before the commencement of the engagement was a vital part of the agreement. But we find, on looking to the agreement, that the plaintiff was to sing in theatres, halls, and drawing-rooms, both public and private, from the 30th of March to the 13th of July, 1875, and that he was to sing in concerts as well as in operas, and was not to sing anywhere out of the theatre in Great Britain or Ireland from the 1st of January to the 31st of December, 1875, without the written permission of the defendant, except at a distance of more than fifty miles from London.

The plaintiff, therefore, has, in consequence of this agreement, been deprived of the power of earning anything in London from the 1st of January to the 30th of March; and though the defendant has, perhaps, not received any benefit from this, so as to preclude him from any longer treating as a condition precedent what had originally been one, we think this at least affords a strong argument for saying that subsequent stipulations are not intended to be conditions precedent, unless the nature of the thing strongly shews they must be so.

And, as far as we can see, the failure to attend at rehearsals during the six days immediately before the 30th of March could only affect the theatrical performances and, perhaps, the singing in duets or concerted pieces during the first week or fortnight of this engagement, which is to sing in theatres, halls, and drawing-rooms, and concerts for fifteen weeks.

We think, therefore, that it does not go to the root of the matter so as to require us to consider it a condition precedent.

The defendant must, therefore, we think, seek redress by a cross-claim for damages.

Judgment must be given for the plaintiff.

Quain and Archibald JJ concurred.

3.4.1 IMPORTANCE OF THE PARTIES' INTENTIONS

F. L. SCHULER AG v WICKMAN MACHINE TOOL SALES LTD [1974] AC 235 (HL)

A term in a contract was labelled as a 'condition'. Was this an indication of the parties' intention as to the consequences of a breach?

LORD REID: My Lords, the appellants are a German company which manufactures machine tools and other engineering products. The respondents are a selling organisaton. On May 1, 1963, they entered into an elaborate 'distributorship agreement' under which the appellants (whom I shall call Schuler) granted to the respondents (called Sales in the agreement but whom I shall call Wickman) the sole right to sell Schuler products in territory which included the United Kingdom. These products included 'panel presses' defined in clause 2 and general products. The panel presses are large machine tools used by motor manufacturers. Wickman were to act as agents for Schuler in selling the panel presses but were to purchase and re-sell the general products.

Wickman's obligation with regard to the promotion of sales of Schuler products is contained in clauses 7 and 12(b), which are in the following terms:

7. *Promotion by Sales*
  (a) Subject to clause 17 Sales will use its best endeavours to promote and extend the sale of Schuler products in the territory.
  (b) It shall be [a] condition of this agreement that : – (i) Sales shall send its representatives to visit the six firms whose names are listed in the Schedule hereto at least once in every week for the purpose of soliciting orders for panel presses; (ii) that the same representative shall visit each firm on each occasion unless there are unavoidable reasons preventing the visit being made by that representative in which case the visit shall be made by an alternate representative and Sales will ensure that such a visit is always made by the same alternate representative.
  Sales agrees to inform Schuler of the names of the representatives and alternate representatives instructed to make the visits required by this clause . . .

12(b) Sales undertakes, at its expense, to look after Schuler's interests carefully and will visit Schuler customers regularly particularly those customers principally in the motor car and electrical industries whose names are set out on the list attached hereto and initialled by the parties hereto and will give all possible technical advice to customers.

The six firms referred to in clause 7 are six of the largest motor manufacturers in this country. The agreement was to last until the end of 1967 so that clause 7(b) (i) required Wickman to make a total of some 1,400 visits during the period of the agreement. Wickman failed in their obligation. At first there were fairly extensive failures to make these visits. Then there were negotiations with a view to improving the position and Schuler have been held to have waived any right arising out of those failures. Thereafter there was an improvement but there were still a considerable number of failures.

After some correspondence Schuler wrote to Wickman in October 1964 terminating the agreement on the ground that failure to fulfil their obligation for weekly visits to the six firms entitled Schuler to treat that failure as a repudiation of the agreement by Wickman. In accordance with clause 19 of the agreement this question was referred to arbitration. In spite of the apparently simple and limited nature of the question in dispute, proceedings before the arbitrator were elaborate and protracted. Ultimately the arbitrator issued his award in the form of a special case on October 6, 1969. He held that Schuler were not entitled to terminate the agreement. This finding was reversed by Mocatta J but restored by the Court of Appeal.

In order to explain the contention of the parties, I must now set out clause 11 of the agreement.

11.   *Duration of Agreement*
   (a)   This agreement and the rights granted hereunder to Sales shall commence on May 1, 1963, and shall continue in force (unless previously determined as hereinafter provided) until December 31, 1967, and thereafter unless and until determined by either party upon giving to the other not less than 12 months' notice in writing to that effect expiring on the said December 31, 1967, or any subsequent anniversary thereof provided that Schuler or Sales may by notice in writing to the other determine this agreement forthwith if: – (i) the other shall have committed a material breach of its obligations hereunder and shall have failed to remedy the same within 60 days of being required in writing so to do or (ii) the other shall cease to carry on business or shall enter into liquidation (other than a members' voluntary liquidation for the purposes of reconstruction or amalgamation) or shall suffer the appointment of a receiver of the whole or a material part of its undertaking; and provided further that Schuler may by notice determine this agreement forthwith if Sales shall cease to be a wholly-owned subsidiary of Wickman Ltd.
   (b)   The termination of this agreement shall be without prejudice to any rights or liabilities accrued due prior to the date of termination and the terms contained herein as to discount commission or otherwise will apply to any orders placed by Sales with Schuler and accepted by Schuler before such termination.

Wickman's main contention is that Schuler were only entitled to determine the agreement for the reasons and in the manner provided in clause 11. Schuler, on the other hand, contend that the terms of clause 7 are decisive in their favour: they say that 'It shall be a condition of this agreement' in clause 7(b) means that any breach of clause 7(b)(i) or 7(b)(ii) entitles them forthwith to terminate the agreement. So as there were admittedly breaches of clause 7(b)(i) which were not waived they were entitled to terminate the contract. . . .

Schuler maintains that the word 'condition' has now acquired a precise legal meaning; that, particularly since the enactment of the Sale of Goods Act 1893, its recognised meaning in English law is a term of a contract any breach of which one party gives to the other party an immediate right to rescind the whole contract. Undoubtedly the word is frequently used in that sense. There may, indeed, be some presumption that in a formal legal document it has that meaning. But it is frequently used with a less stringent meaning. One is familiar with printed 'conditions of sale' incorporated into a contract and with the words 'For conditions see back' printed on a ticket. There it simply means that the 'conditions' are terms of the contract.

In the ordinary use of the English language 'condition' has many meanings, some of which have nothing to do with agreements. In connection with an agreement it may mean a pre-condition: something which must happen or be done before the agreement can take effect. Or it may mean some state of affairs which must continue to exist if the agreement is to remain in force. The legal meaning on which Schuler relies is, I think, one which would not occur to a layman; a condition in that sense is not something which has an automatic effect. It is a term the breach of which by one party gives to the other an option either to terminate the contract or to let the contract proceed and, if he so desires, sue for damages for the breach.

Sometimes a breach of a term gives that option to the aggrieved party because it is of a fundamental character going to the root of the contract, sometimes it gives that option because the parties have chosen to stipulate that it shall have that effect. Blackburn J said in *Bettini v Gye* (1876) 1 QBD 183, 187: 'Parties may think some matter, apparently of very little importance, essential; and if they sufficiently express an intention to make the literal fulfilment of such a thing a condition precedent, it will be one; . . .'

In the present case it is not contended that Wickman's failures to make visits amounted in themselves to fundamental breaches. What is contended is that the terms of clause 7 'sufficiently express an intention' to make any breach, however small, of the obligation to make visits a condition so that any breach shall entitle Schuler to rescind the whole contract if they so desire.

Schuler maintains that the use of the word 'condition' is in itself enough to establish this intention. No doubt some words used by lawyers do have a rigid inflexible meaning. But we must remember that we are seeking to discover intention as disclosed by the contract as a whole. Use of the word 'condition' is an indication – even a strong indication – of such an intention but it is by no means conclusive.

The fact that a particular construction leads to a very unreasonable result must be a relevant consideration. The more unreasonable the result the more unlikely it is that the parties can have intended it, and if they do intend it the more necessary it is that they shall make that intention abundantly clear.

Clause 7(b) requires that over a long period each of the six firms shall be visited every week by one or other of two named representatives. It makes no provision for Wickman being entitled to substitute others even on the death or retirement of one of the named representatives. Even if one could imply some right to do this, it makes no provision for both representatives being ill during a particular week. And it makes no provision for the possibility that one or other of the firms may tell Wickman that they cannot receive Wickman's representative during a particular week. So if the parties gave any thought to the matter at all they must have realised the probability that in a few cases out of the 1,400 required visits a visit as stipulated would be impossible. But if Schuler's contention is right, failure to make even one visit entitle them to terminate the contract however blameless Wickman might be.

This is so unreasonable that it must make me search for some other possible meaning of the contract. If none can be found then Wickman must suffer the consequences. But only if that is the only possible interpretation.

If I have to construe clause 7 standing by itself then I do find difficulty in reaching any other interpretation. But if clause 7 must be read with clause 11 the difficulty disappears. The word 'condition' would make any breach of clause 7(b), however excusable, a material breach. That would then entitle Schuler to give notice under clause 11(a)(i) requiring the breach to be remedied. There would be no point in giving such a notice if Wickman were clearly not in fault but if it were given Wickman would have no difficulty in showing that the breach had been remedied. If Wickman were at fault then on receiving such a notice they would have to amend their system so that they could show that the breach had been remedied. If they did not do that within the period of the notice then Schuler would be entitled to rescind.

In my view, that is a possible and reasonable construction of the contract and I would therefore adopt it. The contract is so obscure that I can have no confidence that this is its true meaning but for the reasons which I have given I think that it is the preferable construction. It follows that Schuler was not entitled to rescind the contract as it purported to do. So I would dismiss this appeal.

Lords Morris, Wilberforce, Simon and Kilbrandon concurred.

3.4.2 IMPORTANCE OF THE CONSEQUENCES OF THE BREACH

HONG KONG FIR SHIPPING CO. LTD v KAWASAKI KISEN KAISHA LTD
[1962] 1 All ER 474 (CA)

The term broken was that of 'seaworthiness', which can lead to a wide range of consequences.

DIPLOCK L J: . . . No doubt there are many simple contractual undertakings, sometimes express, but more often because of their very simplicity ('It goes without saying') to be implied, of which it can be predicated that every breach of such an undertaking must give rise to an event which will deprive the party not in default of substantially the whole benefit which it was intended that he should obtain from the contract. And such a stipulation, unless the parties have agreed that breach of it shall not entitle the non-defaulting party to treat the contract as repudiated, is a 'condition'. So, too, there may be other simple contractual undertakings of which it can be predicated that *no* breach can give rise to an event which will deprive the party not in default of substantially the whole benefit which it was intended that he should obtain from the contact; and such a stipulation, unless the parties have agreed that breach of it shall entitle the non-defaulting party to treat the contract as repudiated, is a 'warranty'. There are, however, many contractual undertakings of a more complex character which cannot be categorised as being 'conditions' or 'warranties' if the late nineteenth century meaning adopted in the Sale of Goods Act, 1893, and used by Bowen LJ in *Bentsen v Taylor, Sons & Co.* [1893] 2 QB 274, be given to those terms. Of such undertakings, all that can be predicated is that some breaches will, and others will not, give rise to an event which will deprive the party not in default of substantially the whole benefit which it was intended that he should obtain from the contract; and the legal consequences of a breach of such an undertaking, unless provided for expressly in the contract, depend on the nature of the event to which the breach gives rise and do not follow automatically from a prior classification of the undertaking as a 'condition' or a 'warranty'. For instance, to take the example of Bramwell B in *Jackson v Union Marine Insurance Co.* (1874) LR 10 CP 125, by itself breach of an undertaking by a shipowner to sail with all possible despatch to a named port does not necessarily relieve the charterer of further performance of his obligation under the charterparty, but, if the breach is so prolonged that the contemplated voyage is frustrated, it does have this effect.

In 1874, when the doctrine of frustration was being foaled by 'impossibility of performance' out of 'condition precedent', it is not surprising that the explanation give by Bramwell B should give full credit to the dam by suggesting that in addition to the express *warranty* to sail with all possible dispatch there was an implied *condition precedent* that the ship should arrive at the named port in time for the voyage contemplated. In *Jackson v Union Marine Insurance Co.* there was no breach of the express warranty; but, if there had been, to engraft the implied condition on the express warranty would have been merely a more complicated way of saying that a breach of a shipowner's undertaking to sail with all possible dispatch may, but will not necessarily, give rise to an event which will deprive the charterer of substantially the whole benefit which it was intended that he should obtain from the charter. Now that the doctrine of frustration has matured and flourished for nearly a century and the old technicalities of pleading 'conditions precedent' are more than a century out of date, it does not clarify, but on the contrary obscures, the modern principle of law where such an event *has* occurred as a result of a breach of an express stipulation in a contract, to continue to add the now unnecessary colophon 'therefore it was an implied *condition* of the contract that a particular kind of breach of an express *warranty* should not occur'.

The common law evolves not merely by breeding new principles but also, when they are fully grown, by burying their ancestors.

As my brethren have already pointed out, the shipowner's undertaking to tender a seaworthy ship has, as a result of numerous decisions as to what can amount to 'unseaworthiness', become one of the most complex of contractual undertakings. It embraces obligations with respect to every part of the hull and machinery, stores and equipment and the crew itself. It can be broken by the presence of trivial defects easily and rapidly remediable as well as by defects which must inevitably result in a total loss of the vessel. Consequently, the problem in this case is, in my view, neither solved nor soluble by debating whether the owners' express or implied undertaking to tender a seaworthy ship is a 'condition' or a 'warranty'. It is, like so many other contractual terms, an undertaking one breach of which may give rise to an event which relieves the charterer of further performance of his undertakings if he so elects, and another breach of which may not give rise to such an event but entitle him only to monetary compensation in the form of damages. It is, with all deference to counsel for the charterers' skilful argument, by no means surprising that, among the many hundreds of previous cases about the shipowner's undertaking to deliver a seaworthy ship, there is none where it was found profitable to discuss in the judgments the question whether that undertaking is a 'condition' or a 'warranty'; for the true answer, as I have already indicated, is that it is neither but one of that large class of contractual undertakings, one breach of which may have the same effect as that ascribed to a breach of 'condition' under the Sale of Goods Act, 1893, and a different breach of which may have only the same effect as that ascribed to a breach of 'warranty' under that Act. The cases referred to by Sellers LJ illustrate this, and I would only add that, in the dictum which he cites from *Kish v Taylor* [1912] AC 617 it seems to me from the sentence which immediately follows it as from the actual decision in the case and the whole tenor of Lord Atkinson's speech itself that the word 'will' was intended to be 'may'.

What the learned judge had to do in the present case as in any other case where one party to a contract relies on a breach by the other party as giving him a right to elect to rescind the contract, was to look at the events which had occurred as a result of the breach at the time at which the charterers purported to rescind the charterparty, and to decide whether the occurrence of those events deprived the charterers of substantially the whole benefit which it was the intention of the parties as expressed in the charterparty that the charterers should obtain from the further performance of their own contractual undertakings. One turns, therefore, to the contract, the Baltime 1939 Charter. Clause 13, the 'due diligence' clause, which exempts the shipowners from responsibility for delay or loss or damage to goods on board due to unseaworthiness unless such delay or loss or damage has been caused by want of due diligence of the owners in making the vessel seaworthy and fitted for the voyage, is in itself sufficient to show that the mere occurrence of the events that the vessel was in some respect unseaworthy when tendered or that such unseaworthiness had caused some delay in performance of the charterparty would not deprive the charterer of the whole benefit which it was the intention of the parties he should obtain from the performance of his obligations under the contract – for he undertakes to continue to perform his obligations notwithstanding the occurrence of such events if they fall short of frustration of the contract and even deprives himself of any remedy in damages unless such events are the consequence of want of due diligence on the part of the shipowner.

The question which the learned judge had to ask himself was, as he rightly decided, whether or not, at the date when the charterers purported to rescind the contract, namely June 6, 1957, or when the owners purported to accept such rescission, namely August 8, 1957, the delay which had already occurred as a result of the incompetence of the engine-room staff, and the delay which was likely to occur in repairing the engines of the vessel and the conduct of the owners by that date in taking steps to remedy these two matters, were, when taken together, such as to deprive the charterers of substantially the whole benefit which it was the intention of the parties they should obtain from further use of the vessel under the charterparty. In my view, in his judgment – on which I would not seek to improve – the learned judge took into account and gave due weight to all the relevant considerations and arrived at the right answer for the right reasons.

Sellers and Upjohn LJJ concurred.

REARDON SMITH LINE LTD v *HANSEN-TANGEN* [1976] 3 All ER 570 (HL)

A tanker was built at a different yard to that specified in the contract. Did this entitle the charterer to reject it?

LORD WILBERFORCE: . . . What was the commercial purpose of these charterparties and what was the factual background against which they were made? The purpose is clear: it was to make available (1) to Hansen-Tangen and (2) to Reardon Smith a medium sized tanker suitable for use as such, this tanker not being in existence, or even under construction, at the date of either charter and, at the date of the intermediate charter, not even the subject of contracts made by the supplying company. The vessel was to be constructed in a Japanese yard and made available on charter to Sanko as part of a programme. At the date of the sub-charter the vessel was identified in contracts for its construction in Japan and had a serial number. In order to ensure that the tanker was suitable for its purpose, a detailed specification was drawn up, by way of a warranted description with which, of course, the vessel must strictly comply. In addition, since at the time of either charterparty the vessel was not in existence or under construction, some means had to be agreed on for identifying the particular vessel – one out of a programme – which would form the subject-matter of the charters. This was indispensable so as to enable those committing themselves to hire the vessel, to sub-hire it, if they wished, and if necessary to arrange finance. This necessary indentification was to be effected by nomination, by Sanko in the first place and then by Hansen-Tangen.

The text of the charterparties confirms beyond doubt that this was what was intended and done. The preamble, in the Shelltime 3 form, provides for the insertion of a name – 'being owners of the good . . . tank vessel called . . .'. The box insertion in the sub-charter was made in this place – 'called Yard No. 354 at Osaka Zosen'. The intermediate charter, entered into before Sanko had nominated any vessel, provided in its preamble – instead of 'called. . .' – for a declaration by the owners together with the hull number, and the addendum, entered into after Sanko had nominated, provided 'to be built by Osaka Shipbuilding Co. Ltd and known as Hull No. 354, until named'. What is vital about each of these insertions is that they were simple substitutes for a name, serving no purpose but to provide a means whereby the charterers could identify the ship. At the dates when these insertions were made no importance could have been attached to the matters now said to be so significant; they were not a matter of negotiation, but of unilateral declaration. What is now sought is to elevate them into strict contractual terms in the nature of 'conditions'.

The appellants sought, necessarily, to give to the 'box' and the corresponding provision in the intermediate charter contractual effect. They argued that these words formed part of the 'description' of the future goods contracted to be provided, that, by analogy with contracts for the sale of goods, any departure from the description entitled the other party to reject, that there were departures in that the vessel was not built by Osaka and was not Hull No. 354. I shall attempt to deal with each of these contentions.

In the first place, I am not prepared to accept that authorities as to 'description' in sale of goods cases are to be extended, or applied, to such a contract as we have here. Some of these cases either in themselves (*Re Moore & Co. and Landauer & Co.* [1921] 2 KB 519) or as they have been interpreted (eg *Behn* v *Burness* (1863) 3 B & S 751) I find to be excessively technical and due for fresh examination in this House. Even if a strict and technical view must be taken as regards the description of unascertained future goods (eg commodities) as to which each detail of the description must be assumed to be vital, it may be, and in my opinion is, right to treat other contracts of sale of goods in a similar manner to other contracts generally, so as to ask whether a particular item in a description constitutes a substantial ingredient of the 'identity' of the thing sold, and only if it does to treat it as a condition (see *Couchman* v *Hill* [1947] 1 All ER 103, per Scott LJ). I would respectfully endorse what was recently said by Roskill LJ in *Cehave NV* v *Bremer Handelsgesellschaft mbH*:

> In principle it is not easy to see why the law relating to contracts for the sale of goods should be different from the law relating to the performance of other contractual obligations, whether charterparties or other types of contract. Sale of goods law is but one branch of the general law of contract. It is desirable that the same legal principles should apply to the law of contract as a whole and that different legal principles should not apply to different branches of that law.

And similarly by Devlin J in *Cargo Ships 'Ei-Yam' Ltd* v *Invoer-en Transport Onderneming 'Invotra' NV* [1958] 1 Lloyd's LR 39. The general law of contract has developed, along much more rational lines (eg *Hong Kong Fir Shipping Co. Ltd v Kawasaki Kisen Kaisha Ltd* [1962] 1 All ER 474), in attending to the nature and gravity of a breach or departure rather than in accepting rigid categories which do or do not automatically give a right to rescind, and if the choice were between extending cases under the Sale of Goods Act 1893 into other fields, or allowing more modern doctrine to infect those cases, my preference would be clear. The importance of this line of argument is that Mocatta J and Lord Denning MR used it in the present case so as to reject the appellants' argument on 'description' and I agree with them. But in case it does not appeal to this House, I am also satisfied that the appellants fail to bring the present case within the strictest rules as to 'description'.

In my opinion, the fatal defect in their argument consists in their use of the words 'identity' or 'indentification' to bridge two meanings. It is one thing to say of given words that their purpose is to state (identify) an essential part of the description of the goods. It is another to say that they provide one party with a specific indication (identification) of the goods so that he can find them and if he wishes sub-dispose of them. The appellants wish to say of words which 'identify' the goods in the second sense, that they describe them in the first. I have already given reasons why I can only read the words in the second sense. The difference is vital. If the words are read in the first sense, then, unless I am right in the legal argument above, each element in them has to be given contractual force. The vessel must, as a matter of contract, and as an essential term, be built by Osaka and must bear their yard number 354; if not, the description is not complied with and the vessel tendered is not that contracted for. If in the second sense, the only question is whether the words provide a means of identifying the vessel. If they fairly do this, they have fulfilled their function. It follows that if the second sense is correct, the words used can be construed much more liberally than they would have to be construed if they were providing essential elements of the description.

The two significant elements (whether in the 'box', or in the intermediate charter) are (i) the yard number 354, (ii) the expression 'built by Osaka Shipbuilding Co. Ltd'. (These words do not appear in the 'box' but I will assume, very much in the appellants' favour, that the 'box' has the same meaning as if the word 'built' were used.) The appellants at one time placed great stress on the yard number provision. They contended that by using it the 'owners' assumed an obligation that the vessel should bear a number which would indicate that it would be constructed in the yard, where that number was appropriate, in sequence after vessels bearing earlier yard numbers (350–353). But this argument broke down in face of the fact, certainly known to Sanko which used and introduced the number into the charterparties, that the sequence through 354 was the sequence used at Osaka's yard at Osaka, which yard could not construct the vessel. Thus the use of the yard number for the contracted vessel must have had some other purpose than indicating construction at a particular yard. This turns the argument against the appellants for it shows the words to be 'labelling' words rather than words creating an obligation.

So the question becomes simply whether, as a matter of fact, it can fairly be said that – as a means of identification – the vessel was 'Yard No. 354 at Osaka Zosen' or 'built by Osaka Shipping Co. Ltd and known as Hull No. 354, until named'. To answer this, regard may be had to the actual arrangements for building the vessel and numbering it before named. My Lords, I have no doubt, for the reasons given by the Court of Appeal, that an affirmative answer must be given. I shall not set out the evidence which clearly makes this good. The fact is that the vessel always was Osaka Hull No. 354 – though also Oshima No. 004 – and equally it can fairly be said to have been 'built' by Osaka as the company which planned, organised and directed the building and contractually engaged with Sculptor to build it, though also it could be said to have been built by Oshima. For the purpose of the identificatory clause, the words used are quite sufficient to cover the facts. No other vessel could be referred to: the reference fits the vessel in question.

There are other facts not to be overlooked. (1) So long as the charterers could identify the nominated vessel they had not the slightest interest in whatever contracting or sub-contracting arrangements were made in the course of the building, a fact which no doubt explains the looseness of the language used in the 'box'. (2) In making the arrangements they did for building the vessel, Osaka acted in a perfectly straightforward and open manner. They cannot be said to be substituting one vessel for another; they have not provided any ground on which the charterers can claim that their bargain has not been fulfilled. The contracts all down the chain were closely and appropriately knitted into what Osaka did. (3) If the market had risen instead of falling, it would have been quite impossible for Osaka or Sculptor, or Sanko, to refuse to tender the vessel in accordance with the charters on the ground that it did not correspond with that contracted for. No more on a falling market is there, in my opinion, any ground on which the charterers can reject the vessel.

Viscount Dilhorne, and Lords Simon, Kilbrandon, and Russell, concurred.

SALE OF GOODS ACT 1979

Section 15A.   Modification of remedies for breach of condition in non-consumer cases
   (1)   Where in the case of a contract of sale—
     (a)   the buyer would, apart from this subsection, have the right to reject goods by reason of a breach on the part of the seller of a term implied by section 13, 14 or 15 above, but
     (b)   the breach is so slight that it would be unreasonable for him to reject them, then, if the buyer does not deal as consumer, the breach is not to be treated as a breach of condition but may be treated as a breach of warranty.
   (2)   This section applies unless a contrary intention appears in, or is to be implied from, the contract.
   (3)   It is for the seller to show that a breach fell within subsection (1)(b) above.

3.5   End of Chapter Assessment Question

'Common sense suggests and the law has long recognised that the obligations created by a contract are not all of equal importance. It is primarily for the parties to set their own value on the terms that they impose upon each other. But it is rare for them to express with any precision what, if anything, they have in their minds; and the resultant task of inferring and interpreting their intention is, as always, a matter of great difficulty.' (Cheshire, Fifoot & Furmston's *Law of Contract*, 13th edition p. 151).

Discuss.

(The answer to question 3.5 appears overleaf).

3.6   End of Chapter Assessment Outline Answer

In order to discover the obligations of the parties to a contract it is necessary to examine the terms of the contract. Some of these will relate to obligations regarded as extremely important by the parties, others to obligations regarded as less important. Traditionally, this distinction has always been dealt with by classifying terms as either conditions or warranties. A condition is a major term of the contract which goes to the root of the contract, the breach of which entitles the injured party to repudiate the contract and/or to claim damages. A warranty is a much less important term, the breach of which entitles the injured party to claim damages only. However, since the decision of the Court of Appeal in 1962 in *Hong Kong Fir Shipping Co. Ltd* v *Kawasaki Kisen Kaisha Ltd* the law has seen the emergence of the intermediate or innominate term, where the seriousness of the consequences of the breach is extremely pertinent. Additionally, a term may be implied into a contract by legislation, eg., the Sale of Goods Act 1979 and be specifically designated as either a condition or a warranty.

The traditional approach of classification as a condition or a warranty is said to depend upon an objective ascertainment of the parties intentions at the time of entering into the contract. This is often illustrated by contrasting *Poussard* v *Spiers and Pond* with *Bettini* v *Gye*. In the former, an actress, who turned up some days after the due date and after the play had started to run, was found to be in breach of condition. Whereas in the latter, a singer, who turned up four days late for rehearsals, was held to be in breach of warranty. One might ask whether this is a legitimate application of the test or whether in reality the court was looking at the seriousness of the consequences of the breach some 90 years before it became legitimate to do so.

Where the parties have expressly designated the term as a condition or a warranty there is usually no problem. However, *Wickman* v *Schuler* demonstrates that in the exceptional case even express contractual provision is not conclusive. A term of the agreement said that it was 'a condition' that a distributor should visit six named customers per week for each week of the duration of the contract. Some of the visits were not made. The House of Lords held that despite the use of the word 'condition', a breach of the term would not automatically give the right to repudiate because, taken literally, to miss just one visit would have been a breach of condition, which the parties could not have intended.

If the words used are not necessarily conclusive, we need to look for other facts which may be crucial. For example, in some areas certain terms historically always seem to be classified as conditions because of their importance in the particular trade or industry. Thus, as in *Behn* v *Burness*, time of loading in charterparties is always treated as a condition, because the parties and their insurers need to know where they stand right from the outset, particularly in import/export 'string' transactions where delay can lead to massive financial loss.

Thus, ascertaining the nature of a term on an 'intention of the parties' basis is by no means straightforward. The picture has become even more complex due to the develop-ment of a new approach to classification in 1962 in *Hong Kong Fir Shipping Co Ltd* v *Kawasaki Kisen Kaisha Ltd*, namely examination of the consequences of the breach. The term is not classified at the outset but treated as intermediate or innominate. The more serious the consequences, the more likely that the breach will entitle the innocent party to repudiate; the less serious the consequences, the less likely that the breach will entitle the innocent party to repudiate.

This seems to make good sense in the case of a term such as the one in the Hong Kong case itself: 'in every way fitted for ordinary cargo service'. Such a general term can be breached in many different ways, some having serious, some trivial consequences. However, the approach has been followed in subsequent cases involving more specific terms. In the *Hansa Nord* 'shipment to made in good condition' and in *Reardon Smith Line Ltd* v *Hansen Tangen* 'No. 354 at Osaka' were both treated as intermediate terms. In both cases the consequences of the breach were trivial, and the buyer in the *Hansa Nord* and charter in *Reardon Smith* were prevented from repudiating the contract, because their true motive was to escape a bad bargain.

This issue remains problematic in sale of goods cases involving a breach of the condition implied by s. 13 of the Sale of Goods Act 1979 that the goods must correspond with their description. For example, in *Arcos v Ronaasen* the seller delivered staves most of which were $\frac{9}{16}$ inch thick, whereas the contract required them to be $\frac{1}{2}$ inch thick. However, the buyer could have used them for the required purpose (making cement barrels) without any problem at all. Nevertheless, the buyer was entitled to reject for breach of condition, even though his real motive was probably to escape a bad bargain.

This approach was rejected by the House of Lords in *Reardon Smith* (not a sale of goods case), Lord Wilberforce stating that these sale of goods cases were ripe for review and should not be allowed to infect the general law. However, in sale of goods cases a term implied by an Act of Parliament as a condition cannot be treated as an intermediate term. Fortunately, this has probably ceased to be a major problem in non-consumer transactions due to the insertion of s. 15A into the Sale of Goods Act 1979 (operative from 5 January 1995 onwards) which prevent the buyer from rejecting where the breach is so slight that it would be unreasonable for him to do so.

Finally, it should be noted that in the context of charterparties and time of loading the historical approach has prevailed over the intermediate term approach and in *Bunge Corporation v Tradax Export SA* the House of Lords held the charterer to be entitled to repudiate for breach of condition, even though the consequences of the breach were not serious.

Overall it is not easy to predict in any given case which of the alternative approaches to classification the court will adopt. However, the availability of the traditional condition/warranty approach and the intermediate term approach, plus statutory intervention enables the courts to find a happy medium between ultra-strict interpretation on the one hand, and ultra-flexible interpretation on the other, which can often be used to achieve substantial justice in the particular circumstances of the case.

CHAPTER FOUR

EXCLUSION AND LIMITATION CLAUSES

4.1 The Position at Common Law

4.1.1 INCORPORATION

4.1.1.1 Signature

L'ESTRANGE v GRAUCOB [1934] 2 KB 394 (CA)

The plaintiff had signed a contract which contained an exclusion clause in very small print.

SCRUTTON LJ: In this case the plaintiff commenced proceedings against the defendants in the county court, her claim being for 9l. 1s. as money received by the defendants to the use of the plaintiff as part of the consideration for the delivery of an automatic slot machine pursuant to a contract in writing dated February 7, 1933, which consideration was alleged to have wholly failed by reason of the fact that the machine was delivered in a condition unfit for the purpose for which it was intended. The only document which corresponds to the contract there mentioned is a long document on brown paper headed 'Sales agreement'. . . . The defendants pleaded: no total failure of consideration; no implied conditions; and that no action would lie for breach of implied warranty, as the agreement expressly provided for the exclusion of all implied warranties. To this last defence the plaintiff contended that she was induced to sign the contract by the misrepresentation that it was an order form, and that at the time when she signed she knew nothing of the conditions. . . .

As to the defence that no action would lie for breach of implied warranty, the defendants relied upon the following clause in the contract: 'This agreement contains all the terms and conditions under which I agree to purchase the machine specified above and any express or implied condition, statement, or warranty, statutory or otherwise not stated herein is hereby excluded'. A clause of that sort has been before the courts for sometime. The first reported case in which it made its appearance seems to be *Wallis, Son & Wells v Pratt & Haynes* [1910] 2 KB 1003, where the exclusion clause mentioned only 'warranty' and it was held that it did not exclude conditions. In the more recent case of *Andrews Brothers (Bournemouth) Ltd v Singer & Co.* [1934] 1 KB 17, where the draftsman had put into the contract of sale a clause which excluded only implied conditions, warranties and liabilities, it was held that the clause did not apply to an express term describing the article, and did not exempt the seller from liability where he delivered an article of a different description. The clause here in question would seem to have been intended to go further than any of the previous clauses and to include all terms denoting collateral stipulations, in order to avoid the result of these decisions.

The main question raised in the present case is whether that clause formed part of the contract. If it did, it clearly excluded any condition or warranty. . . .

In cases in which the contract is contained in a railway ticket or other unsigned document, it is necessary to prove that an alleged party was aware, or ought to have been aware, of its terms and conditions. These cases have no application when the document has been signed. When a document containing contractual terms is signed, then, in the absence of fraud, or, I will add, misrepresentation, the party signing it is bound, and it is wholly immaterial whether he has read the document or not. . . .

In this case the plaintiff has signed a document headed 'Sales Agreement', which she admits had to do with an intended purchase, and which contained a clause excluding all conditions and warranties. That being so, the plaintiff, having put her signature to the document and not having been induced to do so by any fraud or misrepresentation, cannot be heard to say that she is not bound by the terms of the document because she has not read them.

Maugham LJ concurred.

4.1.1.2 Notice

THOMPSON v *LMS RAILWAY CO.* [1930] 1 KB 41 (CA)

A train ticket was bought on behalf of the plaintiff, who was illiterate. The issue was whether she had been given sufficient notice of the conditions on which it was sold.

LORD HANWORTH MR: The action is brought and is based on the negligence of the defendants in the course of carrying the plaintiff to her destination – Darwen from Manchester. The defendants rely upon the conditions of the contract under which they undertook to convey the plaintiff from Manchester to Darwen, and the particulars say this: The ticket issued to the plaintiff by the defendants for the said journey was an excursion ticket and on the face of the said ticket were printed (inter alia) the words 'Excursion, For conditions see back'. . . . There is no difficulty in reading those words any more than there is a difficulty in reading the words 'Third Class' or 'Manchester' down below. Then on the back of the ticket is printed also in type, which if small is easily legible: 'Issued subject to the conditions and regulations of the company's time tables and notices and excursion and other bills. Return as per bill'. In the time table at p. 552 there is this condition, which is relied upon and which I have read. The condition on the back makes the first reference to the company's time tables, but it also refers to notices and excursion and other bills. In the excursion bills, which contain some notes as to the tickets to be issued and the charges to be made and the dates on which passengers can travel at a single fare for a double journey, there is a reference to the conditions and the inquirer is directed to the time table. Ultimately therefore the time table is the place where this particular condition is found. Any person who took the trouble to follow out the plain and legible words on the ticket, 'See Conditions', would be directed without difficulty to the source of the conditions and would be able to find it. Obviously persons who are minded to go for a day journey of this sort do not take the trouble to make an examination of all the conditions, but two things are plain, first, that any person who takes this ticket is conscious that there are some conditions on which it is issued and also, secondly, that it is priced at a figure far below the ordinary price charged by the railway company, and from that it is a mere sequence of thought that one does not get from the railway company the ticket which they do provide at the higher figure of 5s. 4d.

The plaintiff in this case cannot read; but, having regard to the authorities, and the condition of education in this country, I do not think that avails her in any degree. The ticket was taken for her by her agent. The time of the train was ascertained for her by Miss Aldcroft's father, and he had made the specific inquiry in order to see at what time and under what circumstances there was an excursion train available for the intending travellers. He ascertained, therefore, and he had the notice put before him before ever the ticket was taken, that there were conditions on the issue of excursion and other reduced-fare tickets. . . .

Whether or not the father of Miss Aldcroft took the trouble to search out the conditions, or to con them over or not, it appears to me that when that ticket was taken it was taken with the knowledge that the conditions applied, and that the person who took the ticket was bound by those conditions. If that be so, the conditions render it impossible for the plaintiff to succeed in her action. . . . It appears to me important to bear in mind that we are dealing with a special contract made for a special transit by an excursion train. We are not dealing with the ordinary schedule of trains available to every one at the usual rate. We are dealing with a particular transit, in respect of which the father of Miss Aldcroft went down to the station to know if and when such transit was available, and ascertained both the time and the price; and he could have learned all the conditions if he had been so minded.

That consideration, that it was an excursion train and a special contract, must be borne in mind; for there are a number of cases which, if you do not bear that in mind, might be taken as applying and applying in a contrary sense to the present case. For instance, I think that in dealing with *Parker* v *South Eastern Ry. Co.* (1877) 2 CPD 416 it must be remembered as regards the condition which was there relied upon as to limitation of liability in respect of goods deposited in a cloak room, that the limit there arose upon a ticket which had been handed to the depositor; but it was unnecessary for the purpose of the deposit and the safe custody that there should be any terms or conditions at all, or indeed, that there should be a written contract at all. Therefore, the contract was one which could be made, and might very ordinarily be made, without any written conditions of any sort or kind; and that feature is dwelt upon as significant in the judgment of Lord Coleridge CJ in the court below, where he says:

> Regard being had to the common and ordinary course of business, it seems to me to be reasonable that a man receiving such a ticket as this should look upon it as a mere voucher for the receipt of the package deposited, and a means of identifying him as the owner when he sought to reclaim it. . .

and in that sense not containing any special condition to which his attention was to be drawn. And in the Court of Appeal observations are made which must be taken with that qualifying factor arising upon the issue of the ticket. Bramwell LJ (as he then was) there says:

> Would the depositor be bound? I might content myself by asking: Would he be, if he were told 'our conditions are on this ticket', and he did not read them. In my judgment, he would not be bound in either case. I think there is an implied understanding that there is no condition unreasonable to the knowledge of the party tendering the document and not insisting on its being read – no condition not relevant to the matter in hand. I am of opinion, therefore, that the plaintiffs, having notice of the printing, were in the same situation as though the porter had said: 'Read that, it concerns the matter in hand'; that if the plaintiffs did not read it, they were as much bound as if they had read it and had not objected.

Now there is the present case. It was quite clear, and everybody understood and knew that there would have to be a ticket issued. Without such ticket, which is the voucher showing the money has been paid, it would not be possible for the lady to go on the platform to take her train, or on reaching the end of her transit to leave the platform without giving up a ticket. It is quite clear, therefore, that it was intended there should be a ticket issued: and on that ticket plainly on its face is a reference made to the conditions under which it is issued.

Lawrence and Sankey LJJ agreed that the plaintiff was bound by the clause.

McCUTCHEON v *DAVID MacBRAYNE LTD* [1964] 1 All ER 430 (HL)

LORD REID: My Lords, the appellant is a farm grieve in Islay. While on the mainland in October, 1960, he asked his brother-in-law, Mr McSporran, a farmer in Islay, to have his car sent by the respondents to West Loch Tarbert. Mr McSporran took the car to Port Askaig. He found in the respondents' office there the purser of their vessel 'Lochiel', who quoted the freight for a return journey for the car. He paid the money, obtained a receipt and delivered the car to the respondents. It was shipped on the 'Lochiel' but the vessel never reached West Loch Tarbert. She sank owing to negligent navigation by the respondents' servants, and the car was a total loss. The appellant sues for its value, agreed at £480.

The question is, what was the contract between the parties? The contract was an oral one. No document was signed or changed hands until the contract was completed. I agree with the unanimous view of the learned judges of the Court of Session that the terms of the receipt which was made out by the purser and handed to Mr McSporran after he paid the freight cannot be regarded as terms of the contract. So the case is not one of the familiar ticket cases where the question is whether conditions endorsed on or referred to in a ticket or other document handed to the consignor in making the contract are binding on the consignor. If conditions, not mentioned when this contract was made, are to be added to or regarded as part of this contract it must be for some reason different from those principles which are now well settled in ticket cases. If this oral contract stands unqualified there can be no doubt that the respondents are liable for the damage caused by the negligence of their servants.

The respondents' case is that their elaborate printed conditions form part of this contract. If they do, then admittedly they exclude liability in this case. I think that I can fairly summarise the evidence on this matter. The respondents exhibit copies of these conditions in their office, but neither the appellant nor his agent Mr McSporran had read these notices, and I agree that they can play no part in the decision of this case. The respondents' practice was to require consignors to sign risk notes, which included these conditions, before accepting any goods for carriage, but on this occasion no risk note was signed. The respondents' clerkess, knowing that Mr McSporran was bringing the car for shipment, made out a risk note for his signature, but when he arrived she was not there and he dealt with the purser of the 'Lochiel', who was in the office. He asked for a return passage for the car. The purser quoted a charge of some £6. He paid that sum and then the purser made out and gave him a receipt which he put in his pocket without looking at it. He then delivered the car. The purser forgot to ask him to sign the risk note. The Lord Ordinary believed the evidence of Mr McSporran and the appellant. Mr McSporran had consigned goods of various kinds on a number of previous occasions. He said that sometimes he had signed a note, sometimes he had not. On one occasion he had sent his own car. A risk note for that consignment was produced signed by him. He had never read the risk notes signed by him. He says – 'I sort of just signed it at the time as a matter of form'. He admitted that he knew that he was signing in connexion with some conditions, but he did not know what they were. In particular, he did not know that he was agreeing to send the goods at owner's risk. The appellant had consigned goods on four previous occasions. On three of them he was acting on behalf of his employer. On the other occasion he had sent his own car. Each time he had signed a risk note. He also admitted that he knew there were conditions, but said he did not know what they were.

The respondents contend that, by reason of the knowledge thus gained by the appellant and his agent in these previous transactions, the appellant is bound by their conditions. But this case differs essentially from the ticket cases. There, the carrier in making the contract hands over a document containing or referring to conditions which he intends to be part of the contract. So if the consignor or passenger, when accepting the document, knows or ought as a reasonable man to know that that is the carrier's intention, he can hardly deny that the conditions are part of the contract, or claim, in the absence of special circumstances, to be in a better position than he would be if he had read the document. But here, in making the contract neither party referred to, or indeed had in mind, any additional terms, and the contract was complete and fully effective without any additional terms. If it could be said that when making the contract Mr McSporran knew that the respondents always required a risk note to be signed and knew that the purser was simply forgetting to put it before him for signature, then it might be said that neither he nor his principal could take advantage of the error of the other party of which he was aware. But counsel frankly admitted that he could not put his case as high as that. The only other ground on which it would seem possible to import these conditions is that based on a course of dealing. If two parties have made a series of similar contracts each containing certain conditions, and then they make another without expressly referring to those conditions it may be that those conditions ought to be implied. If the officious bystander had asked them whether they had intended to leave out the conditions this time, both must, as honest men, have said 'of course not'. But again the facts here will not support that ground. According to Mr McSporran, there had been no consistent course of dealing; sometimes he was asked to sign and sometimes not. And, moreover, he did not know what the conditions were. This time he was offered an oral contract without any reference to conditions, and he accepted the offer in good faith.

The respondents also rely on the appellant's previous knowledge. I doubt whether it is possible to spell out a course of dealing in his case. In all but one of the previous cases he had been acting on behalf of his employer in sending a different kind of goods and he did not know that the respondents always sought to insist on excluding liability for their own negligence. So it cannot be said that, when he asked his agent to make a contract for him, he knew that this or, indeed, any other special term would be included in it. He left his agent a free hand to contract, and I see nothing to prevent him from taking advantage of the contract which his agent in fact made.

The judicial task is not to discover the actual intentions of each party: it is to decide what each was reasonably entitled to conclude from the attitude of the other. (W. Gloag, *Law of Contract*, p. 7.)

In this case I do not think that either party was reasonably bound or entitled to conclude from the attitude of the other as known to him that these conditions were intended by the other party to be part of this contract. I would therefore allow the appeal and restore the interlocutor of the Lord Ordinary.

Lords Hodson, Guest, Devlin, and Pearce concurred.

CHAPELTON v *BARRY UDC* [1940] 1 KB 532 (CA)

SLESSER LJ: This appeal arises out of an action brought by Mr David Chapelton against the Barry Urban District Council, and it raises a question of some importance to the very large number of people who are in the habit of using deck chairs to sit by the seaside at holiday resorts.

On June 3, 1939, Mr Chapelton went on to the beach at a place called Cold Knap, which is within the area of the Barry Urban District Council, and wished to sit down in a deck chair. On the beach, by the side of a café, was a pile of deck chairs belonging to the defendants, and by the side of the deck chairs there was a notice put up in these terms: 'Barry Urban District Council. Cold Knap. Hire of chairs, 2d. per session of 3 hours.' Then followed words which said that the public were respectfully requested to obtain tickets for their chairs from the chair attendants, and that those tickets must be retained for inspection.

Mr Chapelton, having taken two chairs from the attendant, one for himself and one for a Miss Andrews, who was with him, received two tickets from the attendant, glanced at them, and slipped them into his pocket. He said in the court below that he had no idea that there were any conditions on those tickets and that he did not know anything about what was on the back of them. He took the chairs to the beach and put them up in the ordinary way, setting them up firmly on a flat part of the beach, but when he sat down he had the misfortune to go through the canvas, and, unfortunately, had a bad jar, the result of which was that he suffered injury and had to see a doctor, and in respect of that he brought his action.

The learned county court judge has found that if he had been satisfied that the plaintiff had had a valid legal claim, he would have awarded him the sum of 50*l.* in addition to the special damages claimed.

The learned county court judge also found that the accident to the plaintiff was due to the negligence on the part of the defendants in providing a chair for him which was unfit for its use which gave way in the manner which I have stated. But he nevertheless found in favour of the defendants by reason of the fact that on the ticket which was handed to Mr Chapelton when he took the chair appeared these words: 'Available for 3 hours. Time expires where indicated by cut-off and should be retained and shown on request. The Council will not be liable for any accident or damage arising from hire of chair'. . . .

Questions of this sort are always questions of difficulty and are very often largely questions of fact. In the class of case where it is said that there is a term in the contract freeing railway companies, or other providers of facilities, from liabilities which they would otherwise incur at common law, it is a question as to how far that condition has been made a term of the contract and whether it has been sufficiently brought to the notice of the person entering into the contract with the railway company, or other body, and there is a large number of authorities on that point. In my view, however, the present case does not come within that category at all. I think that the contract here, as appears from a consideration of all the circumstances, was this: The local authority offered to hire chairs to persons to sit upon on the beach, and there was a pile of chairs there standing ready for use by any one who wished to use them, and the conditions on which they offered persons the use of those chairs were stated in the notice which was put up by the pile of chairs, namely, that the sum charged for the hire of a chair was 2d. per session of three hours. I think that was the whole of the offer which the local authority made in this case. They said, in effect: 'We offer to provide you with a chair, and if you accept that offer and sit in the chair, you will have to pay for that privilege 2d. per session of three hours'.

I think that Mr Chapelton, in common with other persons who used these chairs, when he took the chair from the pile (which happened to be handed to him by an attendant, but which, I suppose, he might have taken from the pile of chairs himself if the attendant had been going on his rounds collecting money, or was otherwise away) simply thought that he was liable to pay 2d. for the use of the chair. No suggestion of any restriction of the council's liability appeared in the notice which was near the pile of chairs. That, I think, is the proper view to take of the nature of the contract in this case. Then the notice contained these further words: 'The public are respectfully requested to obtain tickets properly issued from the automatic punch in their presence from the Chair Attendants'. The very language of that 'respectful request' shows clearly, to my mind, that for the convenience of the local authority the public were asked to obtain from the chair attendants tickets, which were mere vouchers or receipts showing how long a person hiring a chair is entitled to use that chair. It is wrong, I think, to look at the circumstances that the plaintiff obtained his receipt at the same time as he took his chair as being in any way a modification of the contract which I have indicated. This was a general offer to the general public, and I think it is right to say that one must take into account here that there was no reason why anybody taking one of these chairs should necessarily obtain a receipt at the moment he took his chair – and, indeed, the notice is inconsistent with that, because it 'respectfully requests' the public to obtain receipts for their money. It may be that somebody might sit in one of these chairs for one hour, or two hours, or, if the holiday resort was a very popular one, for a longer time, before the attendant came round for his money, or it may be that the attendant would not come to him at all for payment for the chair, in which case I take it there would be an obligation upon the person who used the chair to search out the attendant, like a debtor searching for his creditor, in order to pay him the sum of 2d. for the use of the chair and to obtain a receipt for the 2d. paid.

I think the learned county court judge has misunderstood the nature of this agreement. I do not think that the notice excluding liability was a term of the contract at all, and I find it unnecessary to refer to the different authorities which were cited to us, save that I would mention a passage in the judgment of Mellish LJ in *Parker v South Eastern Ry. Co.* (1877) 2 CPD 416, where he points out that it may be that a receipt or ticket may not contain terms of the contract at all, but may be a mere voucher, where he says: 'For instance, if a person driving through a turnpike-gate received a ticket upon paying the toll, he might reasonably assume that the object of the ticket was that by producing it he might be free from paying toll at some other turnpike-gate, and might put it in his pocket unread'. I think the object of the giving and the taking of this ticket was that the person taking it might have evidence at hand by which he could show that the obligation he was under to pay 2d. for the use of the chair for three hours had been duly discharged, and I think it is altogether inconsistent, in the absence of any qualification of liability in the notice put up near the pile of chairs, to attempt to read into it the qualification contended for. In my opinion, this ticket is no more than a receipt, and is quite different from a railway ticket which contains upon it the terms upon which a railway company agrees to carry the passenger. This, therefore, is not, I think, as Mr Ryder Richardson has argued, a question of fact for the learned county court judge. I think the learned county court judge as a matter of law has misconstrued this contract, and looking at all the circumstances of the case, has assumed that this condition on the ticket, or the terms upon which the ticket was issued, has disentitled the plaintiff to recover. The class of case which Sankey LJ dealt with in *Thompson v London, Midland and Scottish Ry. Co.* [1930] 1 KB 41, which seems to have influenced the learned county court judge in his decision, is entirely different from that which we have to consider in the present appeal.

This appeal should be allowed.

Mackinnon and Goddard LJJ concurred.

4.1.1.3   Time of notice

OLLEY v MARLBOROUGH COURT LTD [1949] 1 KB 532 (CA)

The trial judge found that the defendants could rely on an exclusion clause displayed in a hotel bedroom.

SINGLETON LJ: The defendants are the keepers of an hotel known as Marlborough Court Hotel, Lancaster Gate, and the plaintiff was a guest in that hotel. She, like many others, lived there for months on end and she knew the place quite well. It was her habit to leave her key in the reception office when she left the hotel. In the reception office there was a place provided for keys – a key rack. She knew that, and she had been accustomed to putting the key in its place upon the key rack; and she knew that that rack was at the back of the reception office. Normally, in the reception office there was one of the hotel staff, and normally there was at least one porter in the hotel on duty. We were supplied with a plan of the ground floor of the hotel. When one goes in through the main entrance, the reception office is at the back of the buildings almost directly opposite the door, and on the right-hand side there is a lounge. On November 7, 1945, the plaintiff left the hotel in the morning leaving her key as usual on the rack in the reception office. When she returned later in the day her key was missing and certain articles had been stolen from her room. During the course of the afternoon another guest at the hotel had seen someone go to the reception office, enter the reception office, come out after a very short space of time, then go to the lift and apparently use the lift, and about a quarter of an hour later that same person came from the lift carrying a bag or parcel, or something of that kind. The learned judge on the evidence found that that person was the person who had taken the key of Mrs Olley from the key rack, and had then gone to her bedroom and stolen her goods. At that time of day there ought to have been someone on duty in the reception office. It may be there was. The witness, Colonel Crerer, who saw this man, could not see whether anyone was on duty in the reception office at that moment or not, by reason of his position in the lounge; but there was during the afternoon someone on duty. If that person who was in charge of the reception office left the reception office for some good purpose, she ought to have told the porter. The porter at the time was cleaning the bust of the Duke of Marlborough. Either the lady receptionist left the reception office without telling the porter or, if she was in the office, she ought to have seen the unknown man who went to the key rack and took the plaintiff's key and who later came down in the lift and disappeared with the plaintiff's goods. Those facts are, in my view, ample to support the finding of negligence against the defendants. . . . I do not think it desirable to examine in detail the question whether this was a common inn or a boarding house. In either event the defendants are responsible for negligence, subject to this further and more difficult question. Mr Berryman on behalf of the defendants raised a question as to the true effect of a document which was exhibited in the bedroom occupied by the plaintiff and her husband. That document was inside some sort of cupboard which hid the washstand in the bedroom. That began in this way: 'The proprietors will not hold themselves responsible for articles lost or stolen unless handed to the manageress for safe custody. Valuables should be deposited for safe custody in a sealed package and a receipt obtained'. I agree with what my Lord said, that the terms of that notice at its commencement are rather more like something embraced in a notice under the Innkeepers' Liability Act, 1863, than anything else. Mr Berryman submitted that those words which I have read should be read into the contract between the plaintiff and the defendants and that, if they were so read, they must be or ought to be regarded as freeing the defendants from their own negligence, and he cited a number of authorities in support of that proposititition. The most useful, perhaps, was a case in the Court of Appeal, *Rutter* v *Palmer* [1922] 2 KB 87, where Scrutton LJ, dealing with a somewhat similar question, said:

> In construing an exemption clause certain general rules may be applied: First the defendant is not exempted from liability for the negligence of his servants unless adequate words are used; secondly, the liability of the defendant apart from the exempting words must be ascertained; then the particular clause in question must be considered; and if the only liability of the party pleading the exemption is a liability for negligence, the clause will more readily operate to exempt him.

Mr Berryman submitted that upon the finding of the judge the defendants were the keepers of a guest house and their only liability could be for negligence and, therefore, the effect of the words at the head of the notice, embraced in the contract as they should be, must be to exclude the defendants from liability for negligence. I confess that I feel some difficulty about those words of Scrutton LJ, 'secondly, the liability of the defendant apart from the exempting words must be ascertained'. If one has to look back now and say what the defendants were in the year 1945 and construe the contract with that in mind, well and good; it might be necessary to consider more seriously whether they were keepers of a common inn or merely boarding house keepers; but I find it a little difficult to ascertain what the true contractual basis would be if in fact they were keepers of a boarding house, when quite clearly from the notice they exhibited in the entrance hall of the hotel they regarded themselves as keepers of a common inn; and so too might the plaintiff be expected to regard them, having regard to what they exhibited in the hotel. Thus it is not easy to see the basis of the contract. I am more attracted, I confess, in considering this matter by the earlier words of Scrutton LJ: 'First, the defendant is not exempted from liability for the negligence of his servants unless adequate words are used.' If the defendants, who would prima facie be liable for their own negligence, seek to exempt themselves by words of some kind, they must show, first, that those words form part of the contract between the parties and, secondly, that those words are so clear that they must be understood by the parties in the circumstances as absolving the defendants from the results of their own negligence. On both those points it seems to me that the defendants' argument fails. It is clear that when the plaintiff and her husband went to the hotel they had not seen the notice. Apparently, by the custom of the hotel, they were asked to pay a week in advance, and when they went to the bedroom for the first time they had not seen the notice, and the words at the head of the notice could not be part of the contract between the parties. Then when did they become so? I asked Mr Berryman, and I am afraid it was not a very easy question to answer; he might say it was at the end of the first week when the second payment was made and the notice was seen, although the plaintiff said she did not read the notice. But there ought to be some certainty in a matter of this kind, and there is none. I do not attach great importance to Mr Glyn-Jones's point as to the husband in all probability being the payer, the contracting party. If he was, I am inclined to think he would have contracted in this regard on behalf of his wife. But I do think there is more importance in his further submission that this contract when it was entered into was not a contract for a fixed period subject to renewal, but was a contract for an indeterminate period to which an end could be put by notice, and an end was not put to that contract by notice at the time this loss took place. Indeed, the conditions so fas as one knows remained the same. I do not think it is open to the defendants to place reliance upon that notice in the bedroom or, at least, I do not think they are exempt by the words at the head of that notice from their liability for negligence. I agree, if I may say so, with what my Lord said upon the subject, and I attach even more importance to the fact that this was no part of the contract at the time when the parties first went into the bedroom; and there is no evidence to show that there was ever any alteration whatever in the terms of that contract. I agree with the submission which Mr Glyn-Jones made that it is for the defendants to show that these words formed part of the contract and that they had only one clear meaning. I think they are ambiguous in more ways than one. That is all I need say upon that side of the case.

Bucknill and Denning LJJ concurred.

4.1.1.4   Course of dealing

J. SPURLING LTD v *BRADSHAW* [1956] 2 All ER 121 (CA)

DENNING LJ: In the first part of June, 1953, the defendant bought eight wooden casks of orange juice, containing sixty gallons apiece. He bought them 'to clear for £120', and he sent them to some warehousemen, the plaintiffs, J. Spurling Ltd, who on June 10, 1953, sent a receipt for them, called a 'landing account' which said:

> We have pleasure in advising you that these goods consigned to you arrived at our premises this day and are subject to either warehouse, wharfage, demurrage or other charges. . . . The company's conditions as printed on the back hereof cover the goods held in accordance with this notice. Goods will be insured if you instruct us accordingly; otherwise they are not insured.

On the back there were 'Contract conditions' and many lines of small print, which included, towards the end, these words:

> We will not in any circumstances when acting either as warehousemen, wharfingers, contractors, stevedores, carriers by land, or agents, or in any other capacity, be liable for any loss, damage or detention howsoever, whensoever, or wheresoever occasioned in respect of any goods entrusted to or carried or handled by us in the course of our business, even when such loss, damage or detention may have been occasioned by the negligence, wrongful act or default of ourselves or our servants or agents or others for whose acts we would otherwise be responsible.

On the same date, June 10, 1953, the plaintiffs sent an invoice to the defendant: 'To receiving, warehouseing and redelivery, £4', and there was a note at the bottom of it:

> All goods are handled by us in accordance with the conditions as over and warehoused at owner's risk and not insured unless specially instructed.

There were no conditions 'as over'. The defendant paid the £4 due on the invoice and he also paid the warehouse rent on these goods for a time, but he afterwards fell into arrear on these and other goods. On March 9, 1954, the plaintiffs sent to him an account for the balance owing by him which was, they said, rather old. Within three days the defendant issued a delivery order in favour of Mr Tuson directed to the plaintiffs, asking them to release to him the eight barrels of orange juice; and on April 23, 1954, Mr Tuson, who was a cartage contractor, collected these eight barrels. I will refer a little later to what Mr Tuson said was their condition when he collected them; but so far as the correspondence is concerned, there was not a word of complaint about the barrels for a long time. The plaintiffs wrote letters asking the defendant to pay their account, but he failed to do so. Over £60 was due to them and they wrote time and again, and received no reply. They put it into the hands of a debt collecting agency who wrote twice demanding the money. At last on December 17, 1954, there was a reply. The defendant by his solicitors then said that he had a counterclaim for damages in respect of the storage of these barrels. Thus it was eight months after the goods were collected before there was any written complaint. The plaintiffs issued a writ for their charges amounting to £61 12s. 6d. The defendant put in a defence admitting the charges, but he also set up a counterclaim for £180 which, as I read it, was a counterclaim for negligence in the storage of the goods. He said that, when collected, five barrels were empty and without lids, one barrel contained dirty water, and two barrels were leaking badly. The plaintiffs put in a defence to the counterclaim in which they denied the charge of negligence and further said it was an express term of the contract that they should not be liable for any loss or damage of or to in connection with the barrels, and they relied on the 'landing account' for that purpose. In all the circumstances, it was not surprising that the plaintiffs relied on the exempting clause.

When the matter came before the judge of the Mayor's and City of London Court, the counterclaim was the only matter in dispute. The cartage contractor Mr Tuson was called. He said that when he collected the barrels they were at the far end of an alley-way, with lorry wheels in front of them, girders on top, and some tarpaulin sheets. He said that he later discovered they were damaged and spoke to the crane-driver about it. When the defendant was called, he said he had received landing accounts from the plaintiffs many times before; and he said that as soon as he saw the condition of the barrels he saw the yardman in the offices. He went on to say that when he received the letters and demands for payment of the overdue account, he went and saw someone at the plaintiff's office and raised the matter of the barrels. The judge intervened before the defendant was cross-examined, and asked his counsel 'Why is not the exempting clause a complete answer to the case?' Having heard what he had to say, the judge there and then decided in favour of the plaintiffs on the ground that the exempting clause exempted them from all liability. The judge in his judgment found that the plaintiffs were negligent; that was a finding which was not open to him, seeing that the defendant had not been cross-examined and that the plaintiffs had not had an opportunity of giving their evidence. Nevertheless, assuming that they were negligent, the question for us is whether the clause excuses them from liability. . . .

This brings me to the question whether this clause was part of the contract. Counsel for the defendant urged us to hold that the plaintiffs did not do what was reasonably sufficient to give notice of the conditions within *Parker* v *South Eastern Ry. Co.* (1877) 2 CPD 416. I agree that the more unreasonable a clause is, the greater the notice which must be given of it. Some clauses which I have seen would need to be printed in red ink on the face of the document with a red hand pointing to it before the notice could be held to be sufficient. The clause in this case, however, in my judgment, does not call for such exceptional treatment, especially when it is construed, as it should be, subject to the proviso that it only applies when the warehouseman is carrying out his contract and not when he is deviating from it or breaking it in a radical respect. So construed, the judge was, I think, entitled to find that sufficient notice was given. It is to be noticed that the landing account on its face told the defendant that the goods would be insured if he gave instructions; otherwise they were not insured. The invoice, on its face, told him they were warehoused 'at owner's risk'. The printed conditions, when read subject to the proviso which I have mentioned, added little or nothing to those explicit statements taken together. Next it was said that the landing account and invoice were issued after the goods had been received and could not therefore be part of the contract of bailment: but the defendant admitted that he had received many landing accounts before. True he had not troubled to read them. On receiving this account, he took no objection to it, left the goods there, and went on paying the warehouse rent for months afterwards. It seems to me that by the course and conduct of the parties, these conditions were part of the contract.

In these circumstances, the plaintiffs were entitled to rely on this exempting condition. I think, therefore, that the counterclaim was properly dismissed, and this appeal also should be dismissed.

Morris and Parker LJJ concurred.

4.1.2 CONSTRUCTION

AILSA CRAIG FISHING CO. LTD v *MALVERN FISHING CO. LTD*
[1983] 1 All ER 101 (HL)

The House was considering a clause which *limited* rather than *excluded* liability, in relation to a contract to provide security cover in a harbour.

LORD FRASER: . . . The question whether Securicor's liability has been limited falls to be answered by construing the terms of the contract in accordance with the ordinary principles applicable to contracts of this kind. The argument for limitation depends on certain special conditions attached to the contract prepared on behalf of Securicor and put forward in their interest. There is no doubt that such conditions must be construed strictly against the proferens, in this case Securicor, and that in order to be effective they must be 'most clearly and unambiguously expressed': see *W & S Pollock & Co.* v *Macrae* 1922 SC (HL) 192 at 199 per Lord Dunedin. *Pollock* v *Macrae* was a decision on an exclusion clause but in so far as it emphasised the need for clarity in clauses to be construed contra proferentem it is in my opinion relevant to the present case also. It has sometimes apparently been regarded as laying down, as a proposition of law, that a condition excluding liability can never have any application where there has been a total breach of contract, but I respectfully agree with the Lord President (Lord Emslie) who said in his opinion in the present case that that was a misunderstanding of *Pollock* v *Macrae*. *Pollock* v *Macrae* was followed by the Second Division in *Mechans Ltd* v *Highland Marine Charters Ltd* 1964 SC 48 and there are passages in the judgments in that case which might seem to treat *Pollock* v *Macrae* as having laid down some such general proposition of law, although it is not clear that they were so intended. If they were I would regard them as being erroneous. *Mechans Ltd* v *Highland Marine Charters Ltd* appears to have been relied on by counsel for the appellants before the Second Division, but was not relied on in this House.

There are later authorities which lay down very strict principles to be applied when considering the effect of clauses of exclusion or of indemnity: see particularly the Privy Council case of *Canada Steamship Lines Ltd* v *R* [1952] 1 All ER 305 at 310, [1952] AC 192 at 208, where Lord Morton, delivering the advice of the Board, summarised the principles in terms which have recently been applied by this House in *Smith* v *UMB Chrysler (Scotland) Ltd* 1978 SC (HL) 1. In my opinion these principles are not applicable in their full rigour when considering the effect of conditions merely limiting liability. Such conditions will of course be read contra proferentem and must be clearly expressed, but there is no reason why they should be judged by the specially exacting standards which are applied to exclusion and indemnity clauses. The reason for imposing such standards on these conditions is the inherent improbability that the other party to a contract including such a condition intended to release the proferens from a liability that would otherwise fall on him. But there is no such high degree of improbability that he would agree to a limitation of the liability of the proferens, especially when, as explained in condition 4(i) of the present contract, the potential losses that might be caused by the negligence of the proferens or its servants are so great in proportion to the sums that can reasonably be charged for the services contracted for. It is enough in the present case that the condition must be clear and unambiguous.

The contract was arranged during the morning of 31 December 1971 in some haste. It is set out on a form partly printed and partly filled in in ink, which is headed 'Temporary Contract or Contract Change Request' and in which the association 'request Securicor Ltd to carry out the services detailed below subject to the Special Conditions printed overleaf'. The form requested 'continuous security cover for your [sic] vessels from 19.00 hours on 31/12/71 until 07.00 hours on 5/1/72' and stated that the area covered was to be extended to include the Fish Market area. Nothing turns on that part of the contract but I should mention that the appellants contended that this temporary contract, so long as it was in operation, entirely superseded the contract of 12 May 1971 and was the sole measure of parties' rights and obligations to one another. Having regard to condition 8 of the special conditions, I see no reason to question that contention.

The 'special conditions of contract' were elaborate and are applied to services of several types. So far as this appeal is concerned, the part which is most directly applicable is condition 2, and especially para (f) of that condition. Condition 2(f) is in the following terms:

> If, pursuant to the provisions set out herein, any liability on the part of the Company shall arise (whether under the express or implied terms of this Contract or at Common Law, or in any other way) to the customer for any loss or damage of whatever nature arising out of or connected with the provision of, or purported provision of, or failure

in provision of, the services covered by this Contract, such liability shall be limited to the payment by the Company by way of damages of a sum: (i) In the case of all services other than the Special Delivery Service (a) Not exceeding £1,000 in respect of any claim arising from any duty assumed by the Company' which involves the operation, testing, examination, or inspection of the operational condition of any machine, plant or equipment in or about the customer's premises, or which involves the provision of any service not solely related to the prevention or detection of fire or theft; (b) Not exceeding a maximum of £10,000 for the consequences of any incident involving fire, theft or any other cause of liability in the Company under the terms hereof; and further provided that the total liability of the Company shall not in any circumstances exceed the sum of £10,000 in respect of all and any incidents arising during any consecutive period of twelve months. . . .

On behalf of the appellants it was argued that condition 2(f), even if apparently clear in its own terms, is not applicable when read in the context of the contract as a whole, where there has been a total failure to perform the services contracted for or what is sometimes called a total failure of contract, and that this was such a case. It was said that condition 2(f) must be qualified by the opening words of condition 2 and of para (a) of that condition which shows that liability can only arise for some fault in the course of providing the services contracted for, and not where there has been a total failure to provide the service. I cannot accept that submission, because condition 2(f) expressly states that it applies to liability arising out of 'the provision of, or purported provision of, or *failure* in provision of' the services contracted for. If this submission had not been so persuasively presented, I would have thought it to be unarguable in face of the provisions of para (f). . . .

Having considered these particular criticisms of condition 2(f) the question remains whether in its context it is sufficiently clear and unambiguous to receive effect in limiting the liability of Securicor for its own negligence or that of its employees. In my opinion it is. It applies to any liability 'whether under the express or implied terms of this contract, or at common law, or in any other way'. Liability at common law is undoubtedly wide enough to cover liability including the negligence of the proferens itself, so that even without relying on the final words 'any other way', I am clearly of opinion that the negligence of Securicor is covered.

Lords Wilberforce, Elwyn-Jones, Salmon and Lowry concurred.

4.1.2.1 Exclusion of liability for negligence

ALDERSLADE v *HENDON LAUNDRY LTD* [1945] 1 KB 191 (CA)

LORD GREENE MR: The terms on which the defendants, the laundry company, accepted their customer's goods included a clause in the following terms: 'The maximum amount allowed for lost or damaged articles is twenty times the charge made for laundering'. The defendants relied on that clause for the purpose of limiting liability to the plaintiff in respect of certain handkerchiefs which he had sent to be laundered but which were not returned to him. It was admitted at the hearing that the handkerchiefs were sent, were not returned, and cannot now be found. That last admission seems to me to be capable of one construction only, namely, that the handkerchiefs are lost. By admitting that they cannot be found the plaintiff must I think be taken to have admitted that the defendants had taken all reasonable steps to trace them. The case must, therefore, be approached on that footing. The learned county court judge considered that the defendants had a negligent manner of carrying on their business, relying on certain evidence given by the plaintiff which showed that he had on occasions received from them articles of clothing which did not belong to him, and that on one occasion when they were informed of this they made no attempt to recover the article from him with a view to returning it to its true owner. On that footing the learned judge considered that this clause limiting liability did not apply.

It was argued before us for the defendants that the clause did apply and was effective to limit liability for lost articles; and reliance was placed on a well-known line of authority dealing with clauses of this description. The effect of those authorities can I think be stated as follows: where the head of damage in respect of which limitation of liability is sought to be imposed by such a clause is one which rests on negligence and nothing else, the clause must be construed as extending to that head of damage, because it would otherwise lack subject-matter. Where, on the other hand, the head of damage may be based on some other ground than that of negligence, the general principle is that the clause must be confined in its application to loss occurring through that other cause, to the exclusion of loss arising through negligence. The reason is that if a contracting party wishes in such a case to limit his liability in respect of negligence, he must do so in clear terms in the absence of which the clause is construed as relating to a liability not based on negligence. A common illustration of the principle is to be found in the case of common carriers. A common carrier is frequently described, though perhaps not quite accurately, as an insurer, and his liability in respect of articles entrusted to him is not necessarily based on negligence. Accordingly if a common carrier wishes to limit his liability for lost articles and does not make it quite clear that he is desiring to limit it in respect of his liability for negligence, then the clause will be construed as extending only to his liability on grounds other than negligence. If, on the other hand, a carrier not being a common carrier, makes use of such a clause, then unless it is construed so as to cover the case of negligence there would be no content for it at all seeing that his only obligation is to take reasonable care. That, broadly speaking, is the principle which falls to be applied in this case. . . .

It was argued by counsel for the plaintiff that the clause must be construed in the present case so as to exclude loss by negligence, and the learned county court judge so held. It was said that the loss of a customer's property might take place for one of two reasons, namely, negligence and mere breach of contract, and that in the absence of clear words referring to negligence, loss through negligence cannot be taken to be covered by the clause. In my opinion that argument fails. It is necessary to analyse the legal relationship between the customer and the defendants. What I may call the hard core of the contract, the real thing to which the contract is directed, is the obligation of the defendants to launder. That is the primary obligation. It is the contractual obligation which must be performed according to its terms, and no question of taking due care enters into it. The defendants undertake, not to exercise due care in laundering the customer's goods, but to launder them, and if they fail to launder them it is no use their saying 'We did our best, we exercised due care and took reasonable precautions, and we are very sorry if as a result the linen is not properly laundered.' That is the essence of the contract, and in addition there are certain ancillary obligations into which the defendants enter if they accept goods from a customer to be laundered. The first relates to the safe custody of the goods while they are in the possession of the defendants. The customer's goods may have to wait for a time in the laundry premises to be washed, and while they are so waiting there is an obligation to take care of them, but it is in my opinion not the obligation of an insurer but the obligation to take reasonable care for the protection of the goods. If while they are waiting to be washed in the laundry a thief, through no fault of the defendants, steals them, the defendants are not liable. The only way in which the defendants could be made liable for the loss of articles awaiting their turn to be washed would, I think, quite clearly be if it could be shown that they had been guilty of negligence in performing their duty to take care of the goods. That is one ancillary obligation which is inherent in a contract of this kind. Another relates to the delivery of the goods. The laundry company in most cases, and indeed in this case, makes a practice of delivering the goods to the customer, and in the ordinary way the customer expects to receive that service. But what is the precise obligation of the laundry in respect of the return of the goods after the laundering has been completed? In my opinion it stands on the same footing as the other ancillary obligation that I have mentioned, namely, the obligation to take reasonable care in looking after and safeguarding the goods. It cannot I think be suggested that the obligation of the laundry company in the matter of returning the goods after they have been laundered is the obligation of an insurer. To say that they have undertaken by contract an absolute obligation to see that they are returned seems to me to go against common sense. Supposing the defendants are returning the goods by van to their customer and while the van is on its way a negligent driver of a lorry drives into it and overturns it with the result that it is set on fire and the goods destroyed. No action would lie by the customer for damages for the loss of those goods any more than it would lie against any ordinary transport undertaking which was not a common carrier. To hold otherwise would mean that in respect of that clearly ancillary service the defendants were undertaking an absolute obligation that the goods would, whatever happened, be returned to the customer. It seems to me that the only obligation on the defendants in the matter of returning the goods is to take reasonable care.

In the present case all that we know about the goods is that they are lost. There seems to me to be no case of lost goods in respect of which it would be necessary to limit liability, unless it be a case where the goods are lost by negligence. Goods sent to the laundry will not be lost in the act of washing them. On the other hand, they may be lost while they are in the custody of the defendants before washing or after washing has been completed. They may be lost in the process of returning them to the customer after they have been washed, but in each of those two cases, if my view is right, the obligation of the defendants is an obligation to take reasonable care and nothing else. Therefore, the claim of a customer that the defendants are liable to him in respect of articles that have been lost must, I think, depend on the issue of due care on their part. If that be right, to construe this clause, so far as it relates to loss, in such a way as to exclude loss occasioned by lack of proper care, would be to leave the clause so far as loss is concerned – I say nothing about damage – without any content at all. The result is in my opinion is that the clause must be construed as applying to the case of loss through negligence. Therefore this appeal succeeds, and the appropriate reduction in damages must be made in the order.

Uthwatt J and Mackinnon LJ concurred.

GEORGE MITCHELL v *FINNEY LOCK SEEDS* [1983] 1 All ER 108 (CA)

In this extract Lord Denning gives a useful summary of the development of the common law approach to exclusion clauses. The House of Lords' decision on the facts of this particular case appears below, **p. 164**.

LORD DENNING MR:

The heyday of freedom of contract
None of you nowadays will remember the trouble we had, when I was called to the Bar, with exemption clauses. They were printed in small print on the back of tickets and order forms and invoices. They were contained in catalogues or timetables. They were held to be binding on any person who took them without objection. No one ever did object. He never read them or knew what was in them. No matter how unreasonable they were, he was bound. All this was done in the name of 'freedom of contract'. But the freedom was all on the side of the big concern which had the use of the printing press. No freedom for the little man who took the ticket or order form or invoice. The big concern said, 'Take it or leave it'. The little man had no option but to take it. The big concern could and did exempt itself from liability in its own interest without regard to the little man. It got away with it time after time. When the courts said to the big concern, 'You must put it in clear words', the big concern had no hesitation in doing so. It knew well that the little man would never read the exemption clauses or understand them.

It was a bleak winter for our law of contract. It is illustrated by two cases, *Thompson* v *London Midland and Scottish Rly. Co.* [1930] 1 KB 41, [1929] All ER Rep 474 (in which there was exemption from liability, not on the ticket, but only in small print at the back of the timetable, and the company were held not liable) and *L'Estrange* v *F Graucob Ltd* [1934] 2 KB 394, [1934] All ER Rep 16 (in which there was complete exemption in small print at the bottom of the order form, and the company were held not liable).

The secret weapon
Faced with this abuse of power, by the strong against the weak, by the use of the small print of the conditions, the judges did what they could to put a curb on it. They still had before them the idol, 'freedom of contract'. They still knelt down and worshipped it, but

they concealed under their cloaks a secret weapon. They used it to stab the idol in the back. This weapon was called 'the true construction of the contract'. They used it with great skill and ingenuity. They used it so as to depart from the natural meaning of the words of the exemption clause and to put on them a strained and unnatural construction. In case after case, they said that the words were not strong enough to give the big concern exemption from liability, so that in the circumstances the big concern was not entitled to rely on the exemption clause. If a ship deviated from the contractual voyage, the owner could not rely on the exemption clause. If a warehouseman stored the goods in the wrong warehouse, he could not pray in aid the limitation clause. If the seller supplied goods different in kind from those contracted for, he could not rely on any exemption from liability. If a shipowner delivered goods to a person without production of the bill of lading, he could not escape responsibility by reference to an exemption clause. In short, whenever the wide words, in their natural meaning, would give rise to an unreasonable result, the judges either rejected them as repugnant to the main purpose of the contract or else cut them down to size in order to produce a reasonable result. This is illustrated by these cases in the House of Lords: *Glynn v Margetson & Co.* [1893] AC 351, [1891–4] All ER Rep 693, *London and North Western Rly. Co. v Neilson* [1922] 2 AC 263, [1922] All ER Rep 395, *Cunard Steamship Co. Ltd v Buerger* [1927] AC 1, [1926] All ER Rep 103; and by these in the Privy Council: *Canada Steamship Lines Ltd v R* [1952] 1 All ER 305, [1952] AC 192, *Sze Hai Tong Bank Ltd v Rambler Cycle Co. Ltd* [1959] 3 All ER 182, [1959] AC 576; and innumerable cases in the Court of Appeal, culminating in *Levison v Patent Steam Carpet Cleaning Co. Ltd* [1977] 3 All ER 498, [1978] QB 69. But when the clause was itself reasonable and gave rise to a reasonable result, the judges upheld it, at any rate when the clause did not exclude liability entirely but only limited it to a reasonable amount. So, where goods were deposited in a cloakroom or sent to a laundry for cleaning, it was quite reasonable for the company to limit their liability to a reasonable amount, having regard to the small charge made for the service. These are illustrated by *Gibaud v Great Eastern Rly. Co.* [1921] 2 KB 426, [1921] All ER Rep 35, *Alderslade v Hendon Laundry Ltd* [1945] 1 All ER 244, [1945] KB 189 and *Gillespie Bros & Co. Ltd v Roy Bowles Transport Ltd* [1973] 1 All ER 193, [1973] QB 400.

Fundamental breach

No doubt had ever been cast thus far by anyone. But doubts arose when in this court, in a case called *Karsales (Harrow) Ld v Wallis* [1956] 2 All ER 866, 1 WLR 936, we ventured to suggest that if the big concern was guilty of a breach which went to the 'very root' of the contract, sometimes called a 'fundamental breach', or at other times a 'total failure' of its obligations, then it could not rely on the printed clause to exempt itself from liability. This way of putting it had been used by some of the most distinguished names in the law, such as Lord Dunedin in *W & S Pollock & Co. v Macrae* 1922 SC (HL) 192 Lord Atkin and Lord Wright in *Hain Steamship Co. Ltd v Tate & Lyle Ltd* [1936] 2 All ER 597 at 603, 601, 607–608 and Devlin J in *Smeaton Hanscomb & Co. Ltd v Sassoon I Setty Son & Co. (No 1)* [1953] 2 All ER 1471 at 1473, [1953] 1 WLR 1468 at 1470. But we did make a mistake, in the eyes of some, in elevating it, by inference, into a 'rule of law'. That was too rude an interference with the idol of 'freedom of contract'. We ought to have used the secret weapon. We ought to have said that in each case, on the 'true construction of the contract' in that case, the exemption clause did not avail the party where he was guilty of a fundamental breach or a breach going to the root. That is the lesson to be learnt from the 'indigestible' speeches in *Suisse Atlantique Société d' Armement Maritime SA v NV Rotterdamsche Kolen Centrale* [1966] 2 All ER 61, [1967] 1 AC 361. They were all obiter dicta. The House were dealing with an agreed damages clause and not an exemption clause and the point had never been argued in the courts below at all. It is noteworthy that the House did not overrule a single decision of the Court of Appeal. Lord Wilberforce appears to have approved them (see [1966] 2 All ER 61 at 92–93, [1967] 1 AC 361 at 433). At any rate, he cast no doubt on the actual decision in any case.

The change in climate

In 1969 there was a change in climate. Out of winter into spring. It came with the first report of the Law Commission on Exemption Clauses in Contracts (Law Com no 24), which was implemented in the Supply of Goods (Implied Terms) Act 1973. In 1975 there was a further change. Out of spring into summer. It came with their second report on Exemption Clauses (Law Com no 69) which was implemented by the Unfair Contract Terms Act 1977. No longer was the big concern able to impose whatever terms and conditions it liked in a printed form, no matter how unreasonable they might be. These reports showed most convincingly that the courts could and should only enforce them if they were fair and reasonable in themselves and it was fair and reasonable to allow the big concern to rely on them. So the idol of 'freedom of contract' was shattered. In cases of personal injury or death, it was not permissible to exclude or restrict liability at all. In consumer contracts any exemption clause was subject to the test of reasonableness.

These reports and statutes have influenced much the thinking of the judges. At any rate, they influenced me as you will see if you read *Gillespie Bros & Co. Ltd v Roy Bowles Transport Ltd* [1973] 1 All ER 193 at 200, [1973] 1 QB 400 at 416 and *Photo Production Ltd v Securicor Transport Ltd* [1978] 3 All ER 146 at 153, [1978] 1 WLR 856 at 865:

> Thus we reach, after long years, the principle which lies behind all our striving: the court will not allow a party to rely on an exemption or limitation clause in circumstances in which it would not be fair or reasonable to allow reliance on it; and, in considering whether it is fair and reasonable, the court will consider whether it was in a standard form, whether there was equality of bargaining power, the nature of the breach, and so forth.

The effect of the changes

What is the result of all this? To my mind it heralds a revolution in our approach to exemption clauses; not only where they exclude liability altogether and also where they limit liability; not only in the specific categories in the Unfair Contract Terms Act 1977, but in other contracts too. Just as in other fields of law we have done away with the multitude of cases on 'common employment', 'last opportunity', 'invitees' and 'licensees' and so forth, so also in this field we should do away with the multitude of cases on exemption clauses. We should no longer have to go through all kinds of gymnastic contortions to get round them. We should no longer have to harass our students with the study of them. We should set about meeting a new challenge. It is presented by the test of reasonableness.

The two Securicor cases

The revolution is exemplified by the recent two *Securicor* cases in the House of Lords (*Photo Production Ltd v Securicor Transport Ltd* [1980] 1 All ER 556, [1980] AC 827 and *Ailsa Craig Fishing Co. Ltd v Malvern Fishing Co. Ltd* [1983] 1 All ER 101). In each of them the Securicor company provided a patrolman to keep watch on premises so as to see that they were safe from intruders. They charged very little for the service. In the *Photo Production* case it was a factory with a lot of paper in it. The patrolman set light to it and burnt down the factory. In the *Ailsa Craig* case it was a quay at Aberdeen where ships were berthed. The patrolman went off for the celebrations on New Year's Eve. He left the ships unattended. The tide rose. A ship rose with it. Its bow got 'snubbed' under the deck of the quay. It sank. In each case the owners were covered by insurance. The factory owners had their fire insurance. The shipowners had their hull insurance. In each case the Securicor company relied on a limitation clause. Under it they were protected from liability beyond a limit which was quite reasonable and their insurance cover was limited accordingly. The issue in practical terms was: which of the insurers should bear the loss? The question in legal terms in each case was whether Securicor could avail themselves of the limitation clause. In each case the House held that they could.

In the first case the House made it clear that the doctrine of 'fundamental breach' was no longer applicable. They replaced it by the test of reasonableness. That was the test applied by the trial judge MacKenna J which I myself quoted with approval (see [1978] 3 All ER 146 at 154, [1978] 1 WLR 856 at 865). He said:

> Condition 1, as I construe it, is, I think, a reasonable provision. . . . Either the owner of the premises, or the person providing the service, must bear the risk. Why should the parties not agree to its being borne by the [owner of the premises]? He is certain to be insured against fire and theft, and is better able to judge the cover needed than the party providing the service. . . . That is only another way of shifting the risk from

the party who provides the service to the party who receives it. There is, as I have said, nothing unreasonable, nothing impolitic, in such a contract.

His judgment was approved by the House of Lords, who themselves held that the limitation clause was valid because it was a reasonable way of apportioning the risks, as between the insurers on either side. I would set out two passages to prove it. Lord Wilberforce said ([1980] 1 All ER 556 at 564, [1980] AC 827 at 846):

> Securicor undertook to provide a service of periodical visits for a very modest charge which works out at 26p per visit. It did not agree to provide equipment. It would have no knowledge of the value of Photo Production's factory; that, and the efficacy of their fire precautions, would be known to Photo Productions. In these circumstances nobody could consider it unreasonable that as between these two equal parties the risk assumed by Securicor should be a modest one, and that Photo Productions should carry the substantial risk of damage or destruction.

And Lord Diplock said ([1980] 1 All ER 556 at 568, [1980] AC 827 at 851):

> For the reasons given by Lord Wilberforce it seems to me that this apportionment of the risk of the factory being damaged or destroyed by the injurious act of an employee of Securicor while carrying out a visit to the factory is one which reasonable businessmen in the position of Securicor and Photo Productions might well think was the most economical. An analogous apportionment of risk is provided for by the Hague Rules in the case of goods carried by sea under bills of lading.

I do hope, however, that we shall not often have to consider the new-found analysis of contractual obligations into 'primary obligations', 'secondary obligations', 'general secondary obligations' and 'anticipatory secondary obligations'. No doubt it is logical enough, but it is too esoteric altogether. It is fit only for the rarified atmosphere of the House of Lords. Not all for the chambers of the practitioner. Let alone for the student at the university.

In the second case the House made a distinction between clauses which excluded liability altogether, and those which only limited liability to a certain sum. Exclusion clauses were to be construed strictly contra proferentem, whereas limitation clauses were to be construed naturally. This must be because a limitation clause is more likely to be reasonable than an exclusion clause. If you go by the plain, natural meaning of the words (as you should do) there is nothing to choose between them. As Lord Summer said fifty years ago in *Atlantic Shipping and Trading Co.* v *Louis Dreyfus & Co.* [1922] 2 AC 250 at 260, [1922] All ER Rep 559 at 563:

> There is no difference in principle between words which save them from having to pay at all and words which save them from paying as much as they would otherwise have had to pay.

If you read the speeches in the *Ailsa Craig* case, it does look as if the House of Lords were relying on the reasonableness of the limitation clause. They held it was applicable even though the failure of the Securicor company was a 'total failure' to provide the service contracted for. They also said, obiter, that they would construe an exclusion clause much more strictly, just as was done in the old cases decided in the winter time. But I would suggest that the better reason is because it would not be fair or reasonable to allow the propounder of them to rely on them in the circumstances of the case.

4.1.2.2   Third parties and exclusion clauses

ADLER v *DICKSON* [1955] 1 QB 158 (CA)

The issue here was whether an exclusion clause in a contract between the plaintiff and a shipping company could protect the company's employees, whose negligence had caused the plaintiff's injuries.

DENNING LJ: In June, 1952, Mrs Adler, a widow, who keeps a shop, decided to go for a cruise upon the P. & O. Steamship *Himalaya*. She booked her passage through the travel agents, Thomas Cook & Son. She travelled first-class and paid £188 for the trip. In return the steamship company issued her with a first-class passage ticket by virtue of which she joined the ship at Southampton and sailed on the cruise. On July 16, 1952, the ship reached Trieste and Mrs Adler went ashore. A gangway was placed horizontally from the ship to a gantry on the quay. She went ashore across that gangway. When she returned to the ship, she was walking along the gangway and had got about half-way across when suddenly the gangway came adrift from the gantry at the shore end, and it fell down against the side of the ship. She was thrown on to the wharf below, a distance of 16 feet, and suffered severe injuries, including a broken leg, broken pelvis, and broken ribs. She claims damages against the master and the boatswain of the ship alleging that they were negligent in that they failed to see that the gangway was properly secured. They deny this and say that the gangway was properly placed and secured and that the cause of the accident was that there was an exceptionally violent gust of wind which suddenly blew the ship several feet off the quay, dragging the gangway with it. . . .

We must assume for the purposes of the argument that the master and the boatswain were personally guilty of negligence and are, prima facie, liable in tort for their wrongdoing. The question is whether they are protected by the exemption clause. It is an important question, because the steamship company say that, as good employers, they will stand behind the master and boatswain and meet any damages or costs that may be awarded against them. They say that if Mrs Adler's claim is admissible, it means that a way has been found of getting round the exemption clause which no one has ever thought of before.

I pause to say that if a way round has been found it would not shock me in the least. I am much more shocked by the extreme width of this exemption clause, which exempts the company from all liability whatsoever to the passenger. It exempts the company from liability for any acts, default or negligence of their servants under any circumstances whatsoever, which includes, I suppose, their wilful misconduct. And this exemption is imposed on the passenger by a ticket which is said to constitute a contract, but which she has no real opportunity of accepting or rejecting. It is a standard printed form upon which the company insist and from which they would not depart, I suppose, in favour of any individual passenger. The effect of it is that, if the passenger is to travel at all, she must travel at her own risk. She is not even given the option of travelling at the company's risk on paying a higher fare. She pays the highest fare, first-class, and yet has no remedy against the company for negligence. Nearly 100 years ago Blackburn J, in a memorable judgment, said that a condition exempting a carrier wholly from liability for the neglect and default of his servants was unreasonable: see *Peek* v *North Staffordshire Railway Co.* (1863) 10 HLC 473. I think so too.

Nevertheless, no matter how unreasonable it is, the law permits a carrier by special contract to impose such a condition (see *Ludditt* v *Ginger Coote Airways Ltd* [1947] AC 233) except in those cases where Parliament has intervened to prevent it. Parliament has not so intervened in the case of carriers by sea. . . .

My conclusion therefore is that, in the carriage of passengers as well as of goods, the law permits a carrier to stipulate for exemption from liability not only for himself but also for those whom he engages to carry out the contract: and this can be done by necessary implication as well as by express words. When such a stipulation is made, it is effective to protect those who render services under the contract, although they were not parties to it, subject however to this important qualification: The injured party must assent to the exemption of those persons. His assent may be given expressly or by necessary implication, but assent he must before he is bound: for it is clear law that an injured party is not to be deprived of his rights at common law except by a contract freely and deliberately entered into by him; and all the more so when the wrongdoer was not a party to the contract, but only participated in the performance of it.

In all cases where the wrongdoer has escaped it will be found that the injured party assented expressly or by necessary implication to forgo his remedy against him. In the case of goods it is not difficult to infer an assent because the owner of the goods habitually insures them against loss or damage in transit. If the carrier is protected by an exemption clause, so should his servants be, leaving the owner to recover against the insurance company. As Scrutton LJ said in the *Elder Dempster* [1924] AC 522 case: 'Were it otherwise there would be an easy way round the bill of lading'; and as Lord Finlay said: 'It would be absurd that the owner of the goods could get rid of the protective clauses of the bill of lading . . . by suing . . . in tort'. In the case of passengers, however, it is not so easy to infer an assent. It was inferred in *Hall v North Eastern Railway Co.* (1875) LR 10 QB 437 but not in *Cosgrove v Horsfall* (1945) 62 TLR 140, even though the clause there purported expressly to exempt the servant. At least, that seems to me the correct explanation of those cases.

Applying those principles to the present case, the important thing to notice is that the steamship company only stipulated for exemption from liability for themselves. They did not in terms stipulate for exemption for their servants or agents, and I see no reason to imply any such exemption. The servants or agents are therefore not excused from the consequences of their personal negligence: compare *The City of Lincoln (Masters and Owners) v Smith* [1904] AC 250.

In any case, even if the company intended that the stipulation should cover their servants, nevertheless I see nothing whatever to suggest that Mrs Adler knew of their intention or assented to it. If she read the conditions of the ticket (which she probably did not) and considered the possibility of being injured by the negligence or default of the company's servants (which I trust she thought unlikely) she might well think that her remedy against the company was barred, but she would not think her remedy against the servants was also barred. Suppose a steward on a liner were to strike a passenger or falsely to imprison her, or injure her by some wilful misconduct, then, albeit it was done in the course of his employment, he could not claim the protection of the clause, for the simple reason that the passenger never agreed to his being exempted. She could sue the steward personally, even though her remedy against the company was barred. So also if the steward is negligent in the course of his employment, for there is no difference in principle between the cases. The passenger has not agreed to forgo his remedy against the actual wrongdoer and can still pursue it.

The result in my opinion is that Mrs Adler can pursue her claim against the master and the boatswain without being defeated by the exemption clause. I think the appeal should be dismissed.

JENKINS LJ: . . . The plaintiff's right of action against the company is clearly taken away by the exempting provisions of the contract, but I fail to see how that can have the effect of depriving her also of her separate and distinct right of action against the defendants as the actual tortfeasors. There is certainly no express provision purporting so to deprive her, and in the absence of any express provision to that effect I see no justification for implying one. The exempting provisions in terms apply only to the liability of the company, without any reference to the liability of servants of the company for the consequences of their own tortious acts. Even if these provisions had contained words purporting to exclude the liability of the company's servants, non constat that the company's servants could successfully rely on that exclusion in proceedings brought against them by some party injured by their tortious conduct, for the company's servants are not parties to the contract. But as it is, not only are the company's servants not parties to the contract but the contract does not even mention their liability. I find it quite impossible to accept the suggestion that the contract between the company and the plaintiff must be taken to have been entered into by the company not only on its own behalf but also on behalf of all its servants. There is nothing whatever in the terms of the contract to support this theory, and even if it were tenable I do not see how it would assist the defendants, inasmuch as the only liability it excludes is the liability of the company.

Morris LJ agreed with Jenkins LJ.

NEW ZEALAND SHIPPING CO. LTD v A. M. SATTERTHWAITE & CO. LTD
[1974] 1 All ER 1015 (PC)

LORD WILBERFORCE: The facts of this case are not in dispute. An expensive drilling machine was received on board the ship *Eurymedon* at Liverpool for transhipment to

Wellington pursuant to the terms of a bill of lading no. 1262 dated June 5, 1964. The shipper was the maker of the drill, Ajax Machine Tool Co. Ltd ('the consignor'). The bill of lading was issued by agents for the Federal Steam Navigation Co. Ltd of Christchurch, New Zealand ('the consignee'). For several years before 1964 the New Zealand Shipping Co. Ltd ('the stevedore') had carried out all stevedoring work in Wellington in respect of the ships owned by the carrier, which was a wholly owned subsidiary of the stevedore. In addition to this stevedoring work the stevedore generally acted as agent for the carrier in New Zealand; and in such capacity as general agent (not in the course of their stevedoring functions) the stevedore received the bill of lading at Wellington on July 31, 1964. Clause 1 of the bill of lading, on the construction of which this case turns, was in the same terms as bills of lading usually issued by the stevedore and its associated companies in respect of ordinary cargo carried by their ships from the United Kingdom to New Zealand. The consignee became the holder of the bill of lading and owner of the drill prior to August 14, 1964. On that date the drill was damaged as a result of the stevedore's negligence during unloading.

At the foot of the first page of the bill of lading the following words were printed in small capitals:

In acccepting this bill of lading the shipper, consignee and the owners of the goods, and the holders of this bill of lading agree to be bound by all of its conditions, exceptions and provisions whether written, printed or stamped on the front or back hereof.

On the back of the bill of lading a number of clauses were printed in small type. It is only necessary to set out the following. The first and third paragraph of clause 1 provided:

This bill of lading shall have effect (a) subject to the provisions of any legislation giving effect to the International Convention for the unification of certain rules relating to bills of lading dated Brussels, August 25, 1924, or to similar effect which is compulsorily applicable to the contract of carriage evidenced hereby and (b) where no such legislation is applicable as if the Carriage of Goods by Sea Act 1924, of Great Britain and the rules scheduled thereto applied hereto and were incorporated herein. Nothing herein contained shall be deemed to be a surrender by the carrier of any of his rights or immunities or an increase of any of his responsibilities or liabilities under the provisions of the said legislation or Act and rules (as the case may be) and the said provisions shall not (unless and to the extent that they are by law compulsorily applicable) apply to that portion of the contract evidenced by this bill of lading which relates to forwarding under clause 4 hereof. If anything herein contained be inconsistent with or repugnant to the said provisions, it shall be to the extent of such inconsistency or repugnance and no further be null and void. . . .

It is hereby expressly agreed that no servant or agent of the carrier (including every independent contractor from time to time employed by the carrier) shall in any circumstances whatsoever be under any liability whatsoever to the shipper, consignee or owner of the goods or to any holder of this bill of lading for any loss or damage or delay of whatsoever kind arising or resulting directly or indirectly from any act neglect or default on his part while acting in the course of or in connection with his employment and, without prejudice to the generality of the foregoing provisions in this clause, every exemption, limitation, condition and liberty herein contained and every right, exemption from liability, defence and immunity of whatsoever nature applicable to the carrier or to which the carrier is entitled hereunder shall also be available and shall extend to protect every such servant or agent of the carrier acting as aforesaid and for the purpose of all the foregoing provisions of this clause the carrier is or shall be deemed to be acting as agent or trustree on behalf of and for the benefit of all persons who are or might be his servants or agents from time to time (including independent contractors as aforesaid) and all such persons shall to this extent be or be deemed to be parties to the contract in or evidenced by this bill of lading.

Clause 11 provided:

The carrier will not be accountable for goods of any description beyond £100 in respect of any one package or unit unless the value thereof shall have been stated in writing both on the broker's order which must be obtained before shipment and on the shipping note presented on shipment and extra freight agreed upon and paid and bills of lading signed with a declaration of the nature and value of the goods appearing thereon. When the value is declared and extra freight agreed as aforesaid the carrier's liability shall not exceed such value or pro rata on that basis in the event of partial loss or damage.

No declaration as to the nature and value of the goods having appeared in the bill of lading, and no extra freight having been agreed upon or paid, it was acknowledged by the consignee that the liability of the carrier was accordingly limited to £100 by the application of clause 11 of the bill of lading. Moreover, the incorporation in the bill of lading of the rules scheduled to the Carriage of Goods by Sea Act 1924 meant that the carrier and the ship were discharged from all liability in respect of damage to the drill unless suit was brought against them within one year after delivery. No action was commenced until April 1967, when the consignee sued the stevedore in negligence, claiming £880 the cost of repairing the damaged drill.

The question in the appeal is whether the stevedore can take the benefit of the time limitation provision. The starting point, in discussion of this question, is provided by the House of Lords' decision in *Midland Silicones Ltd* v *Scruttons Ltd* [1962] AC 446. There is no need to question or even to qualify that case in so far as it affirms the general proposition that a contract between two parties cannot be sued on by a third person even though the contract is expressed to be for his benefit. Nor is it necessary to disagree with anything which was said to the same effect in the Australian case of *Wilson* v *Darling Island Stevedoring and Lighterage Co. Ltd* (1956) 95 CLR 43. Each of these cases was dealing with a simple case of a contract the benefit of which was sought to be taken by a third person not a party to it, and the emphatic pronouncements in the speeches and judgments were directed to this situation. But *Midland Silicones* left open the case where one of the parties contracts as agent for the third person: in particular Lord Reich's speech spelt out, in four propositions, the prerequisites for the validity of such an agency contract. There is of course nothing unique to this case in the conception of agency contracts: well known and common instances exist in the field of hire purchase, of bankers' commercial credits and other transactions. Lord Reid said, at p. 474:

I can see a possibility of success of the agency argument if (first) the bill of lading makes it clear that the stevedore is intended to be protected by the provisions in it which limit liability, (secondly) the bill of lading makes it clear that the carrier, in addition to contracting for these provisions on his own behalf, is also contracting as agent for the stevedore that these provisions should apply to the stevedore, (thirdly) the carrier has authority from the stevedore to do that, or perhaps later ratification by the stevedore would suffice, and (fourthly) that any difficulties about consideration moving from the stevedore were overcome. And then to affect the consignee it would be necessary to show that the provisions of the Bills of Lading Act 1855 apply.

The question in this appeal is whether the contract satisfies these propositions.

Clause 1 of the bill of lading, whatever the defects in its drafting, is clear in its relevant terms. The carrier, on his own account, stipulates for certain exemptions and immunities: among these is that conferred by article III, rule 6, of the Hague Rules which discharges the carrier from all liability for loss or damage unless suit is brought within one year after delivery. In addition to these stipulations on his own account, the carrier as agent for, inter alios, independent contractors stipulates for the same exemptions.

Much was made of the fact that the carrier also contracts as agent for numerous other persons; the relevance of this argument is not apparent. It cannot be disputed that among such independent contractors, for whom, as agent, the carrier contracted, is the appellant company which habitually acts as stevedore in New Zealand by arrangement with the carrier and which is, moreover, the parent company of the carrier. The carrier was, indisputably, authorised by the appellant to contract as its agent for the purposes of clause 1. All of this is quite straightforward and was accepted by all the judges in New

Zealand. The only question was, and is, the fourth question presented by Lord Reid, namely that of consideration.

It was on this point that the Court of Appeal differed from Beattie J, holding that it had not been shown that any consideration for the shipper's promise as to exemption moved from the promisee, i.e., the appellant company.

If the choice, and the antithesis, is between a gratuitous promise, and a promise for consideration, as it must be in the absence of a tertium quid, there can be little doubt which, in commercially reality, this is. The whole contract is of a commercial character, involving service on one side, rates of payment on the other, and qualifying stipulations as to both. The relations of all parties to each other are commercial relations entered into for business reasons of ultimate profit. To describe one set of promises, in this context, as gratuitous, or nudum pactum, seems paradoxical and is prima facie implausible. It is only the precise analysis of this complex of relations into the classical offer and acceptance, with identifiable consideration, that seems to present difficulty, but this same difficulty exists in many situations of daily life, e.g., sales at auction; supermarket purchases; boarding an omnibus; purchasing a train ticket; tenders for the supply of goods; offers of rewards; acceptance by post; warranties of authority by agents; manufacturers' guarantees; gratuitous bailments; bankers' commercial credits. These are all examples which show that English law, having committed itself to a rather technical and schematic doctrine of contract, in application takes a practical approach, often at the cost of forcing the facts to fit uneasily into the market slots of offer, acceptance and consideration.

In their Lordships' opinion the present contract presents much less difficulty than many of those above referred to. It is one of carriage from Liverpool to Wellington. The carrier assumes an obligation to transport the goods and to discharge at the port of arrival. The goods are to be carried and discharged, so the transaction is inherently contractual. It is contemplated that a part of this contract, viz. discharge, may be performed by independent contractors – viz. the appellant. By clause 1 of the bill of lading the shipper agrees to exempt from liability the carrier, his servants and independent contractors in respect of the performance of this contract of carriage. Thus, if the carriage, including the discharge, is wholly carried out by the carrier, he is exempt. If part is carried out by him, and part by his servants, he and they are exempt. If part is carried out by him and part by an independent contractor, he and the independent contractor are exempt. The exemption is designed to cover the whole carriage from loading to discharge, by whomsoever it is performed: the performance attracts the exemption or immunity in favour of whoever the performer turns out to be. There is possibly more than one way of analysing this business transaction into the necessary components; that which their Lordships would accept is to say that the bill of lading brought into existence a bargain initially unilateral but capable of becoming mutual, between the shipper and the appellant, made through the carrier as agent. This became a full contract when the appellant performed services by discharging the goods. The performance of these services for the benefit of the shipper was the consideration for the agreement by the shipper that the appellant should have the benefit of the exemptions and limitations contained in the bill of lading. The conception of a 'unilateral' contract of this kind was recognised in *Great Northern Railway Co. v Witham* (1873) LR 9 CP 16 and is well established. This way of regarding the matter is very close to if not identical to that accepted by Beattie J in the Supreme Court: he analysed the transaction as one of an offer open to acceptance by action such as was found in *Carlill v Carbolic Smoke Ball Co.* [1893] 1 QB 256. But whether one describes the shipper's promise to exempt as an offer to be accepted by performance or as a promise in exchange for an act seems in the present context to be a matter of semantics. The words of Bowen LJ in *Carlill v Carbolic Smoke Ball Co.* [1893] 1 QB 256, 268: 'why should not an offer be made to all the world which is to ripen into a contract with anybody who comes forward and performs the condition?' seem to bridge both conceptions: he certainly seems to draw no distinction between an offer which matures into a contract when accepted and a promise which matures into a contract after performance, and, though in some special contexts (such as in connection with the right to withdraw) some further refinement may be needed, either analysis may be equally valid. On the main point in the appeal, their Lordships are in substantial agreement with Beattie J.

The following points require mention. 1. In their Lordships' opinion, consideration may quite well be provided by the appellant, as suggested, even though (or if) it was already under an obligation to discharge to the carrier. (There is no direct evidence of the existence or nature of this obligation, but their Lordships are prepared to assume it.) An agreement to do an act which the promisor is under an existing obligation to a third party to do, may quite well amount to valid consideration and does so in the present case: the promisee obtains the benefit of a direct obligation which he can enforce. This proposition is illustrated and supported by *Scotson v Pegg* (1861) 6 H & N 295 which their Lordships consider to be good law.

2.   The consignee is entitled to the benefit of, and is bound by, the stipulations in the bill of lading by his acceptance of it and request for delivery of the goods thereunder. This is shown by *Brandt v Liverpool, Brazil and River Plate Steam Navigation Co. Ltd* [1924] 1 KB 575 and a line of earlier cases. The Bills of Lading Act 1855, section 1 (in New Zealand the Mercantile Law Act 1908, section 13) gives partial statutory recognition to this rule, but, where the statute does not apply, as it may well not do in this case, the previously established law remains effective.

3.   The appellant submitted, in the alternative, an argument that, quite apart from contract, exemptions from, or limitation of, liability in tort may be conferred by mere consent on the part of the party who may be injured. As their Lordships consider that the appellant ought to succeed in contract, they prefer to express no opinion upon this argument: to evaluate it requires elaborate discussion.

4.   A clause very similar to the present was given effect by a United States District Court in *Carle & Montanari Inc v American Export Isbrandtsen Lines Inc* [1968] 1 Lloyd's Rep 260. The carrier in that case contracted, in an exemption clause, as agent, for, inter alios, all stevedores and other independent contractors, and although it is no doubt true that the law in the United States is more liberal than ours as regards third party contracts, their Lordships see no reason why the law of the Commonwealth should be more restrictive and technical as regards agency contracts. Commercial considerations should have the same force on both sides of the Pacific.

In the opinion of their Lordships, to give the appellant the benefit of the exemptions and limitations contained in the bill of lading is to give effect to the clear intentions of a commercial document, and can be given within existing principles. They see no reason to strain the law or the facts in order to defeat these intentions. It should not be overlooked that the effect of denying validity to the clause would be to encourage actions against servants, agents and independent contractors in order to get round exemptions (which are almost invariable and often compulsory) accepted by shippers against carriers, the existence, and presumed efficacy, of which is reflected in the rates of freight. They see no attraction in this consequence.

Their Lordships will humbly advise Her Majesty that the appeal be allowed and the judgment of Beattie J restored. The respondent must pay the costs of the appeal and in the Court of Appeal.

Lords Hodson and Salmon concurred; Viscount Dilhorne and Lord Simons dissented.

4.1.2.3   Fundamental breach

PHOTO PRODUCTIONS LTD v *SECURICOR TRANSPORT LTD* [1980] All ER 556 (HL)

LORD WILBERFORCE: My Lords, this appeal arises from the destruction by fire of a factory owned by the respondents ('Photo Productions') involving loss and damage agreed to amount to £615,000. The question is whether the appellants ('Securicor') are liable to the respondents for this sum.

Securicor are a company which provides security services. In 1968 they entered into a contract with Photo Productions by which for a charge of £8 15s 0d (old currency) per week it agreed to 'provide their Night Patrol Service whereby four visits per night shall be made seven nights per week and two visits shall be made during the afternoon of Saturday and four visits shall be made during the day of Sunday'. The contract incorporated printed standard conditions which, in some circumstances, might exclude or limit Securicor's liability. The questions in this appeal are (i) whether these conditions can be invoked at all in the events which happened and (ii) if so, whether either the exclusion provision, or a provision limiting liability, can be applied on the facts. The trial judge (MacKenna J) decided these issues in favour of Securicor. The Court of Appeal decided issue (i) in Photo Productions' favour invoking the doctrine of fundamental breach. Waller LJ in addition would have decided for Photo Productions on issue (ii).

What happened was that on a Sunday night the duty employee of Securicor was one Musgrove. It was not suggested that he was unsuitable for the job or that Securicor were negligent in employing him. He visited the factory at the correct time, but when inside he deliberately started a fire by throwing a match onto some cartons. The fire got out of control and a large part of the premises was burnt down. Though what he did was deliberate, it was not established that he intended to destroy the factory. The judge's finding was in these words:

> Whether Musgrove intended to light only a small fire (which was the very least he meant to do) or whether he intended to cause much more serious damage, and, in either case, what was the reason for his act, are mysteries I am unable to solve.

This, and it is important to bear it in mind when considering the judgments in the Court of Appeal, falls short of a finding that Musgrove deliberately burnt or intended to burn Photo Productions' factory.

The conditions on which Securicor relies reads, relevantly, as follows:

> Under no circumstances shall the Company [Securicor] be responsible for any injurious act or default by any employee of the Company unless such act or default could have been foreseen and avoided by the exercise of due diligence on the part of the Company as his employer; nor, in any event, shall the Company be held responsible for; (a) Any loss suffered by the customer through burglary, theft, fire or any other cause, except insofar as such loss is solely attributable to the negligence of the Company's employees acting within the course of their employment . . .

There are further provisions limiting to stated amounts the liability of Securicor on which it relies in the alternative if held not to be totally exempt.

It is first necessary to decide on the correct approach to a case such as this where it is sought to invoke an exception or limitation clause in the contract. The approach of Lord Denning MR in the Court of Appeal was to consider first whether the breach was 'fundamental'. If so, he said, the court itself deprives the party of the benefit of an exemption or limitation clause. Shaw and Waller LJJ substantially followed him in this argument.

Lord Denning MR in this was following the earlier decision of the Court of Appeal, and in particular his own judgment in *Harbutt's Plasticine Ltd v Wayne Tank and Pump Co. Ltd* [1970] 1 All ER 225. In that case Lord Denning MR distinguished two cases: (a) the case where as the result of breach of contract the innocent party has, and exercises, the right to bring the contract to an end; and (b) the case where the breach automatically brings the contract to an end, without the innocent party having to make an election whether to terminate the contract or to continue it. In the first case Lord Denning MR, purportedly applying this House's decision in *Suisse Atlantique Société d'Armement Maritime SA v NV Rotterdamsche Kolen Centrale* [1966] 2 All ER 61, but in effect two citations from two of their Lordships' speeches, extracted a rule of law that the 'termination' of the contract brings it, and with it the exclusion clause, to an end. The *Suisse Atlantique* case in his view –

> affirms the long line of cases in this court that when one party has been guilty of a fundamental breach of the contract . . . and the other side accepts it, so that the contract comes to an end . . . then the guilty party cannot rely on an exception or limitation clause to escape from his liability for the breach.

See (*Harbutt's* case). He then applied the same principle to the second case.

My Lords, whatever the intrinsic merit of this doctrine, as to which I shall have something to say later, it is clear to me that so far from following this House's decision in the *Suisse Atlantique* case it is directly opposed to it and that the whole purpose and tenor of the *Suisse Atlantique* case was to repudiate it. The lengthy, and perhaps I may say sometimes indigestible speeches of their Lordships, are correctly summarised in the headnote –

> (3) That the question whether an exceptions clause was applicable where there was a fundamental breach of contract was one of the true construction of the contract.

That there was any rule of law by which exception clauses are eliminated, or deprived of effect, regardless of their terms, was clearly not the view of Viscount Dilhorne, Lord Hodson or myself. The passages invoked for the contrary view of a rule of law consist only of short extracts from two of the speeches, on any view a minority. But the case for the doctrine does not even go so far as that. Lord Reid, in my respectful opinion, and I recognise that I may not be the best judge of this matter, in his speech read as a whole, cannot be claimed as a supporter of a rule of law. Indeed he expressly disagreed with Lord Denning MR's observations in two previous cases (*Karsales (Harrow) Ltd* v *Wallis* [1956] 2 All ER 866 and *UGS Finance Ltd* v *National Mortgage Bank of Greece* [1964] 1 Lloyd's Rep 446) in which he had put forward the 'rule of law' doctrine. In order to show how close the disapproved doctrine is to that sought to be revived in *Harbutt's* case I shall quote one passage from the *Karsales* case:

> Notwithstanding earlier cases which might suggest the contrary, it is now settled that exempting clauses of this kind, no matter how widely they are expressed, only avail the party when he is carrying out his contract in its essential respects. He is not allowed to use them as a cover for misconduct or indifference or to enable him to turn a blind eye to his obligations. They do not avail him when he is guilty of a breach which goes to the root of the contract.

Lord Reid comments as to this that he could not deduce from the authorities cited in the *Karsales* case that the proposition stated in the judgments could be regarded as in any way 'settled law'. His conclusion is stated thus: 'In my view no such rule of law ought to be adopted', adding that there is room for legislative reform.

My Lords, in the light of this, the passage from the *Suisse Atlantique* case cited by Lord Denning MR has to be considered. For convenience I restate it:

> If fundamental breach is established, the next question is what effect, if any, that has on the applicability of other terms of the contract. This question has often arisen with regard to clauses excluding liability, in whole or in part, of the party in breach. I do not think that there is generally much difficulty where the innocent party has elected to treat the breach as a repudiation, bring the contract to an end and sue for damages. Then the whole contract has ceased to exist including the exclusion clause, and I do not see how that clause can then be used to exclude an action for loss which will be suffered by the innocent party after it has ceased to exist, such as loss of the profit which would have accrued if the contract had run its full term.

It is with the utmost reluctance that, not forgetting the 'beams' that may exist elsewhere, I have to detect here a mote of ambiguity or perhaps even of inconsistency. What is referred to is 'loss which will be suffered by the innocent party after [the contract] has ceased to exist' and I venture to think that all that is being said, rather elliptically, relates only to what is to happen in the future, and is not a proposition as to the immediate consequences caused by the breach; if it were, that would be inconsistent with the full and reasoned discussion which follows.

It is only because of Lord Reid's great authority in the law that I have found it necessary to embark on what in the end may be superfluous analysis. For I am convinced that, with the possible exception of Lord Upjohn whose critical passage, when read in full, is somewhat ambiguous, their Lordships, fairly read, can only be taken to have rejected those suggestions for a rule of law which had appeared in the Court of Appeal and to have firmly stated that the question is one of construction, not merely of course of the exclusion clause alone, but of the whole contract.

Much has been written about the *Suisse Atlantique* case. Each speech has been subjected to various degrees of analysis and criticism, much of it constructive. Speaking for myself I am conscious of imperfections of terminology, though sometimes in good company. But I do not think that I should be conducing to the clarity of the law by adding to what was already too ample a discussion a further analysis which in turn would have to be interpreted. I have no second thoughts as to the main proposition that the question whether, and to what extent, an exclusion clause is to be applied to a fundamental breach, or a breach of a fundamental term, or indeed to any breach of contract, is a matter of construction of the contract. Many difficult questions arise and will continue to arise in the infinitely varied situations in which contracts come to be breached: by repudiatory breaches, accepted or not, anticipatory breaches, by breaches of conditions or of various terms and whether by negligent, or deliberate, action or otherwise. But there are ample resources in the normal rules of contract law for dealing with these without the superimposition of a judicially invented rule of law. I am content to leave the matter there with some supplementary observations.

1. The doctrine of 'fundamental breach' in spite of its imperfections and doubtful parentage has served a useful purpose. There were a large number of problems, productive of injustice, in which it was worse than unsatisfactory to leave exception clauses to operate. Lord Reid referred to these in the *Suisse Atlantique* case, pointing out at the same time that the doctrine of fundamental breach was a dubious specific. But since then Parliament has taken a hand: it has passed the Unfair Contract Terms Act 1977. This Act applies to consumer contracts and those based on standard terms and enables exception clauses to be applied with regard to what is just and reasonable. It is significant that Parliament refrained from legislating over the whole field of contract. After this Act, in commercial matters generally, when the parties are not of unequal bargaining power, and when risks are normally borne by insurance, not only is the case for judicial intervention undemonstrated, but there is everything to be said, and this seems to have been Parliament's intention, for leaving the parties free to apportion the risks as they think fit and for respecting their decisions.

At the stage of negotiation as to the consequences of a breach, there is everything to be said for allowing the parties to estimate their respective claims according to the contractual provisions they have themselves made, rather than for facing them with a legal complex so uncertain as the doctrine of fundamental breach must be. What, for example, would have been the position of Photo Productions' factory if instead of being destroyed it had been damaged, slightly or moderately or severely? At what point does the doctrine (with what logical justification I have not understood) decide, ex post facto, that the breach was (factually) fundamental before going on to ask whether legally it is to be regarded as fundamental? How is the date of 'termination' to be fixed? Is it the date of the incident causing the damage, or the date of the innocent party's election, or some other date? All these difficulties arise from the doctrine and are left unsolved by it.

At the judicial stage there is still more to be said for leaving cases to be decided straightforwardly on what the parties have bargained for rather than on analysis, which becomes progressively more refined, of decisions in other cases leading to inevitable appeals. The learned judge was able to decide this case on normal principles of contractual law with minimal citation of authority. I am sure that most commercial judges have wished to be able to do the same (cf. *The Angelia, Trade and Transport Inc* v *Iino Kaiun Kaisha Ltd* [1973] 2 All ER 144, per Kerr J). In my opinion they can and should.

2. *Harbutt's Plasticine Ltd* v *Wayne Tank and Pump Co. Ltd* must clearly be overruled. It would be enough to put that on its radical inconsistency with the *Suisse Atlantique* case. But even if the matter were res integra I would find the decision to be based on unsatisfactory reasoning as to the 'termination' of the contract and the effect of 'termination' on the plaintiff's claim for damage. I have, indeed, been unable to understand how the doctrine can be reconciled with the well accepted principle of law, stated by the highest modern authority, that when in the context of a breach of contract one speaks of 'termination' what is meant is no more than that the innocent party or, in some cases, both parties are excused from further performance. Damages, in such cases, are then claimed under the contract, so what reason in principle can there be for disregarding what the contract itself says about damages, whether it 'liquidates them', or limits them, or excludes them? These difficulties arise in part from uncertain or

inconsistent terminology. A vast number of expressions are used to describe situations where a breach has been committed by one party of such a character as to entitle the other party to refuse further performance: discharge, rescission, termination, the contract is at an end, or dead, or displaced; clauses cannot survive, or simply go. I have come to think that some of these difficulties can be avoided; in particular the use of 'rescission', even if distinguished from rescission ab initio, as an equivalent for discharge, though justifiable in some contexts (see *Johnson v Agnew* [1979] 1 All ER 883) may lead to confusion in others. To plead for complete uniformity may be to cry for the moon. But what can and ought to be avoided is to make use of these confusions in order to produce a concealed and unreasoned legal innovation: to pass, for example from saying that a party, victim of a breach of contract, is entitled to refuse further performance, to saying that he may treat the contract as at an end, or as rescinded, and to draw from this the proposition, which is not analytical but one of policy, that all or (arbitrarily) some of the clauses of the contract lose, automatically, their force, regardless of intention.

If this process is discontinued the way is free to use such words as 'discharge' or 'termination' consistently with principles as stated by modern authority which *Harbutt's* case disregards. I venture with apology to relate the classic passages. In *Heyman* v *Darwins Ltd* [1942] 1 All ER 337 Lord Porter said:

> To say that the contract is rescinded or has come to an end or has ceased to exist may in individual cases convey the truth with sufficient accuracy, but the fuller expression that the injured party is thereby absolved from future performance of his obligations under the contract is a more exact description of the position. Strictly speaking, to say that, upon acceptance of the renunciation of a contract, the contract is rescinded is incorrect. In such a case the injured party may accept the renunciation as a breach going to the root of the whole of the consideration. By that acceptance he is discharged from further performance and may bring an action for damages, but the contract itself is not rescinded.

Similarly Lord Macmillan; see also *Boston Deep Sea Fishing and Ice Co. Ltd* v *Ansell* (1888) 39 ChD 339 per Bowen LJ. In *Moschi* v *Lep Air Services Ltd* [1972] 2 All ER 393 my noble and learned friend Lord Diplock drew a distinction (relevant for that case) between primary obligations under a contract, which on 'rescission' generally come to an end, and secondary obligations which may then arise. Among the latter he included an obligation to pay compensation, ie damages. And he stated in terms that this latter obligation 'is just as much an obligation arising from the contract as are the primary obligations that it replaces'. My noble and learned friend has developed this line of thought in an enlightening manner in his opinion which I have now had the benefit of reading.

These passages I believe to state correctly the modern law of contract on the relevant respects; they demonstrate that the whole foundation of *Harbutt's* case is unsound. A fortiori, in addition to *Harbutt's* case there must be overruled *Wathes (Western) Ltd* v *Austins (Menswear) Ltd* [1976] 1 Lloyd's Rep 14 which sought to apply the doctrine of fundamental breach to a case where, by election of the innocent party, the contract had not been terminated, an impossible acrobatic, yet necessarily engendered by the doctrine. Similarly, *Charterhouse Credit Co. Ltd* v *Tolly* [1963] 2 All ER 432 must be overruled, though the result might have been reached on construction of the contract.

3. I must add to this, by way of exception to the decision not to 'gloss' the *Suisse Atlantique*, a brief observation on the deviation cases, since some reliance has been placed on them, particularly on the decision of this House in *Hain Steamship Co. Ltd* v *Tate & Lyle Ltd* [1936] 2 All ER 597 (so earlier that the *Suisse Atlantique*) in the support of the *Harbutt* doctrine. I suggest in the *Suisse Atlantique* that these cases can be regarded as proceeding on normal principles applicable to the law of contract generally, viz that is a matter of the parties' intentions whether and to what extent clauses in shipping contracts can be applied after a deviation, ie a departure from the contractually agreed voyage or adventure. It may be preferable that they should be considered as a body of authority sui generis with special rules derived from historical and commercial reasons. What on either view they cannot do is to lay down different rules as to contracts generally from those later stated by this House in *Heyman* v *Darwins Ltd* [1942] 1 All ER 337. The

ingenious use by Donaldson J in *Kenyon, Son & Craven Ltd* v *Baxter Hoare & Co. Ltd* [1971] 2 All ER 708 of the doctrine of deviation in order to reconcile the *Suisse Atlantique* case with *Harbutt's* case, itself based in part on the use of the doctrine of deviation, illustrates the contortions which that case has made necessary and would be unnecessary if it vanished as an authority.

4. It is not necessary to review fully the numerous cases in which the doctrine of fundamental breach has been applied or discussed. Many of these have now been superseded by the Unfair Contract Terms Act 1977. Others, as decisions, may be justified as depending on the construction of the contract (cf *Levison* v *Patent Steam Carpet Cleaning Co. Ltd* [1977] 3 All ER 498 in the light of well-known principles such as that stated in *Alderslade* v *Hendon Laundry Ltd* [1945] 1 All ER 244.

In this situation the present case has to be decided. As a preliminary, the nature of the contract has to be understood. Securicor undertook to provide a service of periodical visits for a very modest charge which works out at 26p per visit. It did not agree to provide equipment. It would have no knowledge of the value of Photo Productions' factory; that, and the efficacy of their fire precautions, would be known to Photo Productions. In these circumstances nobody could consider to unreasonable that as between these two equal parties the risk assumed by Securicor should be a modest one, and that Photo Productions should carry the substantial risk of damage or destruction.

The duty of Securicor was, as stated, to provide a service. There must be implied an obligation to use care in selecting their patrolmen, to take care of the keys and, I would think, to operate the service with due and proper regard to the safety and security of the premises. The breach of duty committed by Securicor lay in a failure to discharge this latter obligation. Alternatively it could be put on a vicarious responsibility for the wrongful act of Musgrove, viz starting a fire on the premises; Securicor would be responsible for this on the principle stated in *Morris* v *CW Martin & Sons Ltd* [1965] 2 All ER 725. This being the breach, does condition 1 apply? It is drafted in strong terms, 'Under no circumstances, any injurious act or default by any employee'. These words have to be approached with the aid of the cardinal rules of construction that they must be read contra proferentem and that in order to escape from the consequences of one's own wrongdoing, or that of one's servant, clear words are necessary. I think that these words are clear. Photo Productions in fact relied on them for an argument that since they exempted from negligence they must be taken as not exempting from the consequence of deliberate acts. But this is a perversion of the rule that if a clause can cover something other than negligence it will not be applied to negligence. Whether, in addition to negligence, it covers other, eg deliberate, acts, remains a matter of construction requiring, of course, clear words. I am of opinion that it does and, being free to construe and apply the clause, I must hold that liability is excluded. On this part of the case I agree with the judge and adopt his reasons for judgment. I would allow the appeal.

Lords Diplock, Salmon, Keith and Scarman concurred.

4.2 Unfair Contract Terms Act 1977

UNFAIR CONTRACT TERMS ACT 1977

Section 1. Scope of Part I
(1) For the purposes of this Part of this Act, 'negligence' means the breach—
(a) of any obligation, arising from the express or implied terms of a contract, to take reasonable care to exercise reasonable skill in the performance of the contract;
(b) of any common law duty to take reasonable care or exercise reasonable skill (but not any stricter duty);
(c) of the common duty of care imposed by the Occupiers' Liability Act 1957 or the Occupiers' Liability Act (Northern Ireland) 1957.
(2) This part of the Act is subject to Part III; and in relation to contracts, the operation of sections 2 to 4 and 7 is subject to the exceptions made by Schedule 1.
(3) In the case of both contract and tort, sections 2 to 7 apply (except where the contrary is stated in section 6(4)) only to business liability, that is liability for breach of obligations or duties arising—

(a)   from things done or to be done by a person in the course of a business (whether his own business or another's); or

(b)   from the occupation of premises used for business purposes of the occupier; and references to liability are to be read accordingly but liability of an occupier of premises for breach of an obligation or duty towards a person obtaining access to the premises for recreational or educational purposes, being liability for loss or damage suffered by reason of the dangerous state of the premises, is not a business liability of the occupier unless granting that person such access for the purposes concerned falls within the business purposes of the occupier.

(4)   In relation to any breach of duty or obligation, it is immaterial for any purpose of this Part of this Act whether the breach was inadvertent or intentional, or whether liability for it arises directly or vicariously.

Section 2.   Negligence liability

(1)   A person cannot by reference to any contract term or to a notice given to persons generally or to particular persons exclude or restrict his liability for death or personal injury resulting from negligence.

(2)   In the case of other loss or damage, a person cannot so exclude or restrict his liability for negligence except in so far as the term or notice satisfies the requirement of reasonableness.

(3)   Where a contract term or notice purports to exclude or restrict liability for negligence a person's agreement to or awareness of it is not of itself to be taken as indicating his voluntary acceptance of any risk.

Section 3.   Liability arising in contract

(1)   This section applies as between contracting parties where one of them deals as consumer or on the other's written standard terms of business.

(2)   As against that party, the other cannot by reference to any contract term—

(a)   when himself in breach of contract, exclude or restrict any liability of his in respect of the breach; or

(b)   claim to be entitled—

(i)   to render a contractual performance substantially different from that which was reasonably expected of him, or

(ii)   in respect of the whole or any part of his contractual obligation, to render no performance at all,

except in so far as (in any of the cases mentioned above in this subsection) the contract term satisfies the requirement of reasonableness.

Section 6.   Sale and hire purchase

(1)   Liability for breach of the obligation arising from—

(a)   section 12 of the Sale of Goods Act 1979 (seller's implied undertakings as to title, etc);

(b)   section 8 of the Supply of Goods (Implied Terms) Act 1973 (the corresponding thing in relation to hire-purchase),

cannot be excluded or restricted by reference to any contract term.

(2)   As against a person dealing as consumer, liability for breach of the obligations arising from—

(a)   section 13, 14 or 15 of the 1979 Act (seller's implied undertakings as to conformity of goods with description or sample, or as to their quality or fitness for a particular purpose);

(b)   section 9, 10 or 11 of the 1973 Act (the corresponding things in relation to hire-purchase),

cannot be excluded or restricted by reference to any contract term.

(3)   As against a person dealing otherwise than as consumer, the liability specified in subsection (2) above can be excluded or restricted by reference to a contract term, but only in so far as the term satisfies the requirement of reasonableness.

(4)   The liabilities referred to in this section are not only the business liabilities defined by section 1(3), but include those arising under any contract of sale of goods or hire-purchase agreement.

Section 7. Miscellaneous contracts under which goods pass

(1) Where the possession or ownership of goods passes under or in pursuance of a contract not governed by the law of sale of goods or hire-purchase, subsections (2) to (4) below apply as regards the effect (if any) to be given to contract terms excluding or restricting liability for breach of obligation arising by implication of law from the nature of the contract.

(2) As against a person dealing as consumer, liability in request of the goods' correspondence with description or sample, or their quality or fitness for any particular purpose, cannot be excluded or restricted by reference to any such term.

(3) As against a person dealing otherwise than as consumer, that liability can be excluded or restricted by reference to such a term, but only in so far as the term satisfies the requirement of reasonableness.

(3A) Liability for breach of the obligations arising under section 2 of the Supply of Goods and Services Act 1982 (implied terms about title etc in certain contracts for the transfer of the property in goods) cannot be excluded or restricted by reference to any such term.

(4) Liability in respect of—

(a) the right to transfer ownership of the goods, or give possession; or

(b) the assurance of quiet possession to a person taking goods in pursuance of the contract,

cannot (in a case to which subsection (3A) above does not apply) be excluded or restricted by reference to any such term except in so far as the term satisfies the requirement of reasonableness.

Section 11. The 'reasonableness' test

(1) In relation to a contract term, the requirement of reasonableness for the purpose of this Part of this Act, section 3 of the Misrepresentation Act 1967 and section 3 of the Misrepresentation Act (Northern Ireland) 1967 is that the term shall have been a fair and reasonable one to be included having regard to the circumstances which were, or ought reasonably to have been, known to or in the contemplation of the parties when the contract was made.

(2) In determining for the purposes of section 6 or 7 above whether a contract term satisfies the requirement of reasonableness, regard shall be had in particular to the matters specified in Schedule 2 to this Act; but this subsection does not prevent the court or arbitrator from holding, in accordance with any rule of law, that a term which purports to exclude or restrict any relevant liability is not a term of the contract.

(3) In relation to a notice (not being a notice having contractual effect), the requirement of reasonableness under this Act is that it should be fair and reasonable to allow reliance on it, having regard to all the circumstances obtaining when the liability arose or (but for the notice) would have arisen.

(4) Where by reference to a contract term or notice a person seeks to restrict liability to a specified sum of money, and the question arises (under this or any other Act) whether the term or notice satisfies the requirement of reasonableness, regard shall be had in particular (but without prejudice to subsection (2) above in the case of contract terms) to—

(a) the resources which he could expect to be available to him for the purpose of meeting the liability should it arise; and

(b) how far it was open to him to cover himself by insurance.

(5) It is for those claiming that a contract term or notice satisfies the requirement of reasonableness to show that it does.

Section 12. 'Dealing as a consumer'

(1) A party to a contract 'deals as consumer' in relation to another party if—

(a) he neither makes the contract in the course of a business nor holds himself out as doing so; and

(b) the other party does make the contract in the course of a business; and

(c) in the case of a contract governed by the law of sale of goods or hire-purchase, or by section 7 of this Act, the goods passing under or in pursuance of the contract are of a type ordinarily supplied for private use or consumption.

(2) But on a sale by auction or by competitive tender the buyer is not in any circumstances to be regarded as dealing as consumer.

(3) Subject to this, it is for those claiming that a party does not deal as consumer to show that he does not.

Section 13. Varieties of exemption clause
(1) To the extent that this Part of this Act prevents the exclusion or restriction of any liability it also prevents—

(a) making the liability or its enforcement subject to restrictive or onerous conditions;

(b) excluding or restricting any right or remedy in respect of the liability, or subjecting a person to any prejudice in consequence of his pursuing any such right or remedy;

(c) excluding or restricting rules of evidence or procedure;

and (to that extent) sections 2 and 5 to 7 also prevent excluding or restricting liability by reference to terms and notices which exclude or restrict the relevant obligation or duty.

(2) But an agreement in writing to submit present or future differences to arbitration is not to be treated under this Part of this Act as excluding or restricting any liability.

Section 14. Interpretation of Part I
In this Part of this Act—

'business' includes a profession and the activities of any government department or local or public authority;

'goods' has the same meaning as in the Sale of Goods Act 1979;

'hire-purchase agreement' has the same meaning as in the Consumer Credit Act 1974;

'negligence' has the meaning given by section 1(1);

'notice' includes an announcement, whether or not in writing, and any other communication or pretended communication; and

'personal injury' includes any disease and any impairment of physical or mental condition.

Schedule 2
The matters to which regard is to be had in particular for the purposes of sections 6(3), 7(3) and (4), 20 and 21 are any of the following which appear to be relevant—

(a) the strength of the bargaining positions of the parties relative to each other, taking into account (among other things) alternative means by which the customer's requirements could have been met;

(b) whether the customer received an inducement to agree to the term, or in accepting it had an opportunity of entering into a similar contract with other persons, but without having to accept a similar term;

(c) whether the customer knew or ought reasonably to have known of the existence and extent of the term (having regard, among other things, to any custom of the trade and any previous course of dealing between the parties);

(d) where the term excludes or restricts any relevant liability if some condition is not complied with, whether it was reasonable at the time of the contract to expect that compliance with that condition would be practicable;

(e) whether the goods were manufactured, processed or adapted to the special order of the customer.

SUPPLY OF GOODS AND SERVICES ACT 1982

Section 13. Implied terms about care and skill
In a contract for the supply of a service where the supplier is acting in the course of a business, there is an implied term that the supplier will carry out the service with reasonable care and skill.

R & B CUSTOMS BROKERS CO. LTD v UNITED DOMINIONS TRUST LTD
[1988] 1 All ER 847 (CA)

The issue here was whether the plaintiff company was 'dealing as a consumer' when buying a car.

DILLON LJ: The third party in these proceedings, Saunders Abbott (1980) Ltd, a motor dealer, appeals with the support of the defendants, United Dominions Trust Ltd, a finance company, against a decision of his Honour D McDonnell sitting as a deputy circuit judge in the Mayor's and City of London Court on 31 March 1987 whereby he awarded the plaintiffs, R&B Customs Brokers Ltd (the company), judgment against the defendants and awarded the defendants a corresponding judgment against the third party.

The matter concerns a Colt Shogun hard-top four-wheel drive motor vehicle (the car) which was sold to the company in 1984, but proved, as the judge found, and the finding is not disputed, to be not reasonably fit for the purpose for which it was sold, viz the purpose of ordinary use on the roads in England. The appeal raises questions as to the terms to be implied in a contract of sale under s. 14 of the Sale of Goods Act 1979 and also questions of some general importance in relation to the Unfair Contract Terms Act 1977.

The events in question happened in 1984. The company had by then, it seems, been in business for some five or six years. It was a private company whose only directors and shareholders were a Mr Roy Bell and his wife. Its business was that of shipping brokers and freight forwarding agents. It owned a Volvo car and in September 1984 Mr Bell was minded to exchange the Volvo for another vehicle. He saw the car offered for sale secondhand at the motor dealer's showrooms. The motor dealer had taken the car into stock on 18 September, cleaned it up and put it out for resale. The motor dealer did not know, and had no reason for knowing, that the car suffered from the serious defect which later became apparent.

Mr Bell saw the car on 20 and 21 September and decided that the company should buy it and hand in the Volvo in part exchange. In his evidence he said that the four-wheel drive vehicle would be more appropriate to his needs. The intention was that the car would be bought for personal and company use. . . . I agree with the judge (subject to the questions in relation to the Unfair Contract Terms Act 1977 to which I have yet to come) that there is to be implied in the contract between the company and the defendants an implied condition, under sub-s. (3), that the car was reasonably fit for the purpose for which it was being bought and that that condition was broken. . . .

I come therefore to the Unfair Contract Terms Act 1977 and the defendants' printed conditions on their form of contract with the company. It is not in dispute that those conditions were sufficiently drawn to Mr Bell's attention although he did not trouble to read them and therefore, in so far as they were applicable and valid, they are part of the conditional sale agreement of 3 November between the defendants and the company.

The relevant condition of the defendants' form, printed on the back of the form of conditional sale agreement, reads as follows:

IF THE BUYER DEALS AS A CONSUMER WITHIN THE MEANING OF SECTION 12 OF THE UNFAIR CONTRACT TERMS ACT 1977 OR ANY STATUTORY MODIFI-CATION OR RE-ENACTMENT THEREOF ('THE STATUTE')THE BUYER'S STATU-TORY RIGHTS ARE NOT AFFECTED BY SUB-CLAUSE (a) OF THE FOLLOWING CLAUSE.
EXCLUSION OF WARRANTIES AND CONDITIONS–2.(a) The seller not being the manufacturer of the goods nor at any time prior to the making of this agreement being in actual possession or control of them does not let the goods subject to any warranty or condition whether express or implied as to condition description quality or fitness for any particular purpose or at all. . . .

The 1977 Act provides by sub-ss. (2) and (3) of s. 6 as follows:

(2) As against a person dealing as consumer, liability for breach of the obligations arising from — (a) section 13, 14 or 15 of the 1979 Act (seller's implied undertakings as to conformity of goods with description of sample, or as to their quality or fitness for a particular purpose); (b) section 9, 10 or 11 of the 1973 Act (the corresponding things in relation to hire-purchase), cannot be excluded or restricted by reference to any contract term.

(3) As against a person dealing otherwise than as consumer, the liability specified in subsection (2) above can be excluded or restricted by reference to a contract term, but only in so far as the term satisfies the requirement of reasonableness.

Two questions therefore arise, amd success on either of them is sufficient for the company's purposes, namely: (1) in entering into the conditional sale agreement with the defendants, was the company 'dealing as consumer'? If it was then, on the wording of the defendants' printed conditions, cl. 2(a) did not apply, no doubt because under s. 6(2) of the 1977 Act the liability could not be excluded; (2) if the company was dealing otherwise than as a consumer, does the defendants' cl. 2(a) excluding liability under s. 14(3) satisfy 'the requirement of reasonableness'?

'Dealing as a consumer' is defined in s. 12 of the 1977 Act, which provides as follows:

(1) A party to a contract 'deals as consumer' in relation to another party if — (a) he neither makes the contract in the course of a business nor holds himself out as doing so; and (b) the other party does make the contract in the course of a business; and (c) in the case of a contract governed by the law of sale of goods or hire-purchase, or by section 7 of this Act, the goods passing under or in pursuance of the contract are of a type ordinarily supplied for private use or consumption.

(2) But on a sale by auction or by competitive tender the buyer is not in any circumstances to be regarded as dealing as consumer.

(3) Subject to this, it is for those claiming that a party does not deal as consumer to show that he does not.

It is accepted that the conditions in paras. (b) and (c) in s. 12(1) are satisfied. This issue turns on the condition in para. (a). Did the company neither make the contract with the defendants in the course of a business nor hold itself out as doing so?

In the present case there was no holding out beyond the mere facts that the contract and the finance application were made in the company's corporate name and in the finance application the section headed 'Business Details' was filled in to the extent of giving the nature of the company's business as that of shipping brokers, giving the number of years trading and the number of employees, and giving the names and addresses of the directors. What is important is whether the contract was made in the course of business.

In a certain sense, however, from the very nature of a corporate entity, where a company which carried on a business makes a contract it makes that contract in the course of its business; otherwise the contract would be ultra vires and illegal. Thus, where a company which runs a grocer's shop buys a new delivery van, it buys it in the course of its business. Where a merchant bank buys a car as a 'company car' as a perquisite for a senior executive, it buys it in the course of its business. Where a farming company buys a Landrover for the personal and company use of a farm manager, it again does so in the course of its business. Possible variations are numerous. In each case it would not be legal for the purchasing company to buy the vehicle in question otherwise than in the course of its business. Section 12 does not require that the business in the course of which the one party, referred to in the condition in para. (a), makes the contract must be of the same nature as the business in the course of which the party, referred to in the condition in para. (b), makes the contract, eg that they should both be motor dealers.

We have been referred to one decision at first instance under the 1977 Act, *Peter Symmons & Co.* v *Cook* (1981) 131 NLJ 758, but the note of the judgment is too brief to be of real assistance. More helpfully, we have been referred to decisions under the Trade Descriptions Act 1968, and in particular to the decision of the House of Lords in *Davies* v *Sumner* [1984] 3 All ER 831, [1984] 1 WLR 1301.

Under the Trade Descriptions Act 1968 any person who in the course of a trade or business applies a false trade description to goods is, subject to the provisions of that Act, guilty of an offence. It is a penal Act, whereas the 1977 Act is not, and it is accordingly submitted that decisions on the construction of the 1968 Act cannot assist on the construction of s. 12 of the 1977 Act. Also the legislative purposes of the two Acts are not the same. The primary purpose of the 1968 Act is consumer protection, and the course of business referred to is the course of the alleged wrongdoer. But the provisions as to dealing as a consumer in the 1977 Act are concerned with differentiating between two classes of innocent contracting parties (those who deal as consumers and those who do not) for whom differing degrees of protection against unfair contract terms are afforded by the 1977 Act. Despite these distinctions, however, it would, in my judgment, be unreal and unsatisfactory to conclude that the fairly ordinary words 'in the course of business' bear a significantly different meaning in, on the one hand, the 1968 Act and, on the other hand, s. 12 of the 1977 Act. In particular, I would be very reluctant to conclude that these words bear a significantly wider meaning in s. 12 than in the 1968 Act.

I turn therefore to *Davies v Sumner* [1984] 3 All ER 831, [1984] 1 WLR 1301. That case was not concerned with a company, but with an individual who had used a car for the purposes of his business as a self-employed courier. When he sold the car by trading it in in part exchange for a new one, he had applied a false trade description to it by falsely representing the mileage the car had travelled to have been far less than it actually was. Lord Keith who delivered the only speech in the House of Lords, commented that it was clear that the transaction (sc of trading in the car on the purchase of a new one) was reasonably incidental to the carrying on of the business, but he went on to say ([1984] 3 All ER 831 at 833–834, [1984] 1 WLR 1301 at 1305]):

> Any disposal of a chattel held for the purposes of a business may, in a certain sense, be said to have been in the course of that business, irrespective of whether the chattel was aquired with a view to resale or for consumption or as a capital asset. But in my opinion s. 1(1) of the 1968 Act is not intended to cast such a wide net as this. The expression 'in the course of business' in the context of an Act having consumer protection as its primary purpose conveys the concept of some degree of regularity, and it is to be observed that the long title to the Act refers to 'misdescriptions of goods, services, accommodation and facilities provided in the course of trade'. Lord Parker CJ in the *Havering* case [*Havering London Borough v Stevenson* [1970] All ER 609, [1970] 1 WLR 1375] clearly considered that the expression was not used in the broadest sense. The reason why the transaction there in issue was caught was that in his view it was 'an integral part of the business carried on as a car-hire firm'. That would not cover the sporadic selling off of pieces of equipment which were no longer required for the purposes of a business. The vital feature of the *Havering* case appears to have been, in Lord Parker's view, that the respondent's business *as part of its normal practice* bought and disposed of cars. The need for some degree of regularity does not, however, involve that a one-off adventure in the nature of trade, carried through with a view to profit, would not fall within s. 1(1) because such a transaction would itself constitute a trade. (Lord Keith's emphasis).

Lord Keith then held that the requisite degree of regularity had not been established on the facts of *Davies v Sumner* because a normal practice of buying and disposing of cars had not yet been established at the time of the alleged offence. He pointed out for good measure that the disposal of the car was not a disposal of stock in trade of the business, but he clearly was not holding that only a disposal of stock in trade could be a disposal in the course of a trade or business.

Lord Keith emphasised the need for some degree of regularity, and he found pointers to this in the primary purpose and long title of the 1968 Act. I find pointers to a similar need for regularity under the 1977 Act, where matters merely incidental to the carrying on of a business are concerned, both in the words which I would emphasise, 'in the course of' in the phrase 'in the course of a business' and in the concept, or legislative purpose, which must underlie the dichotomy under the 1977 Act between those who deal as consumers and those who deal otherwise than as consumers.

This reasoning leads to the conclusion that, in the 1977 Act also, the words 'in the course of business' are not used in what Lord Keith called 'the broadest sense'. I also find helpful the phrase used by Lord Parker CJ and quoted by Lord Keith, 'an integral part of the business carried on'. The reconciliation between that phrase and the need for some degree of regularity is, as I see it, as follows: there are some transactions which are clearly integral parts of the business concerned, and these should be held to have been carried out in the course of those businesses; this would cover, apart from much else, the instance of a one-off adventure in the nature of trade where the transaction itself would constitute a trade or business. There are other transactions, however, such as the purchase of the car in the present case, which are at the highest only incidental to the carrying on of the relevant business; here a degree of regularity is required before it can be said that they are an integral part of the business carried on and so entered into in the course of that business.

Applying the test thus indicated to the facts of the present case, I have no doubt that the requisite degree of regularity is not made out on the facts. Mr Bell's evidence that the car was the second or third vehicle acquired on credit terms was in my judgment and in the context of this case not enough. Accordingly, I agree with the judge that, in entering into the conditional sale agreement with the defendants, the company was 'dealing as consumer'. The defendants' cl. 2(a) is thus inapplicable and the defendants are not absolved from liability under s. 14(3).

Neill LJ concurred.

4.3   The Reasonableness Test

PHILLIPS PRODUCTS LTD v HYLAND [1987] 2 All ER 620 (CA)

In this extract Slade LJ is considering the scope of the Unfair Contract Terms Act 1977, Schedule 2 'guidelines'.

SLADE LJ: . . . Before reverting to the conclusions and reasoning of the judge, it is unfortunately necessary to deviate from the arguments as they were presented to us. Schedule 2 to the 1977 Act contains what are called 'Guidelines for Application of Reasonableness Test'. . . . We were told that the guidelines in Sch. 2 to the Act were not applicable in this case. It would seem, on a study of the provisions of the Act to which we were not referred in argument, that this may have been wrong. The contract here was a contract of hire. Normally in such a contract, and, it would seem consistently with the provisions of the general conditions in this case, the hirer takes possession of the article hired. Therefore, it appears to us that s. 7(3) (which we do not think it necessary to quote) would apply and thus render Sch. 2 applicable. On this basis the guidelines *would* fall to be considered. Fortunately, however, in view of the way in which the case has been argued on both sides, no difficulty arises on this account. The guideline in para. (d) is, on any footing, irrelevant. The guidelines in paras (a), (b) and (c) were argued as factors properly to be taken into account, even though not because of the guidelines themselves. The guideline in para. (e) would no doubt have been mentioned in argument if counsel on either side had thought that it affected the decision as to 'fair and reasonable' in this case.

SMITH v ERIC S BUSH [1989] 2 All ER 514 (HL)

LORD GRIFFITHS: My Lords, these appeals were heard together because they both raise the same two problems. The first is whether the law places a duty of care on a professional valuer of real property which he owes to the purchaser of the property although he has been instructed to value the property by a prospective mortgagee and not by the purchaser. The second problem concerns the construction and application of the Unfair Contract Terms Act 1977.

Smith v Eric S Bush (a firm)
I shall deal with this appeal first because its facts are similar to hundreds of thousands of house purchases that take place every year. It concerns the purchase of a house at the lower end of the market with the asistance of finance provided by a building society. The purchaser applies for finance to the building society. The building society is required by statute to obtain a valuation of the property before it advances any money (see s. 13 of the Building Societies Act 1986). This requirement is to protect the depositors who

entrust their savings to the building society. The building society therefore requires the purchaser to pay a valuation fee to cover or, at least, to defray the cost of obtaining a valuation. This is a modest sum and certainly much less than the cost of a full structual survey; in the present case it was £36.89. If the purchaser pays the valuation fee, the building society instructs a valuer, who inspects the property and prepares a report for the building society giving his valuation of the property. The inspection carried out is a visual one designed to reveal any obvious defects in the property which must be taken into account when comparing the value of the property with other similiar properties in the neighbourhood. If the valuation shows that the property provides adequate security for the loan, the building society will lend the money necessary for the purchaser to go ahead, but prior to its appeal by the Building Societies Act 1986 would send to the purchaser a statutory notice pursuant to s. 30 of the Building Societies Act 1962 to make clear that by making the loan it did not warrant that the purchase price of the property was reasonable.

The building society may either instruct an independent firm of surveyors to make the valuation or use one of its own employees. In the present case, the building society instructed the appellants, an independent firm of surveyors. I will consider whether it makes any difference if an 'in-house' valuer is instructed when I come to deal with the other appeal. The building society may or may not send a copy of the valuer's report to the purchaser. In this case the building society was the Abbey National and they did send a copy of the report to the purchaser, Mrs Smith. I understand that this is now common practice among building societies. The report, however, contained in red lettering and in the clearest terms a disclaimer of liability for the accuracy of the report covering both the building society and the valuer. Again, I understand that it is common practice for other building societies to incorporate such a disclaimer of liability.

Mrs Smith did not obtain a structural survey of the property. She relied on the valuer's report to reveal any obvious serious defects in the house she was purchasing. It is common ground that she was behaving in the same way as the vast majority of purchasers of modest houses. They do not go to the expense of obtaining their own structural survey; they rely on the valuation to reveal any obvious serious defects and take a chance that there are no hidden defects that might be revealed by a more detailed structural survey.

The valuer's report said 'the property has been modified to a fair standard . . . no essential repairs are required' and it valued the property at £16,500. If reasonable skill and care had been employed when the inspection took place, it would have revealed that as a result of removing the chimney breasts in the rooms the chimneys had been left dangerously unsupported. Unaware of this defect and relying on the valuer's report, Mrs Smith bought the house for £18,000 with the assistance of a loan of £3,500 from the building society.

After she had been living in the house for about 18 months, one of the chimney flues collapsed and crashed through the bedroom ceiling and floor causing damage for which Mrs Smith was awarded £4,379.97 against the surveyors who had carried out the valuation.

Counsel for the surveyors conceded that on the facts of this case the surveyors owed a duty of care to Mrs Smith unless they were protected by the disclaimer of liability. He made this concession, he said, because the surveyors knew that their report was going to be shown to Mrs Smith and that Mrs Smith would, in all probability, rely on it, which two factors would create the necessary proximity to found the duty of care. He submitted, however, that, if the surveyor did not know that his report would be shown to the purchaser, no duty of care would arise and that the decision in *Yianni* v *Edwin Evans & Sons (a firm)* [1981] 3 All ER 592, [1982] QB 438 was wrongly decided. I shall defer consideration of this question to the second appeal, for it does not arise on the facts of the present case. Suffice it to say, for the moment, that on the facts of the present case it is my view that the concession made by counsel is correct.

At common law, whether the duty to exercise reasonable care and skill is founded in contract or tort, a party is as a general rule free, by the use of appropriate wording, to exclude liability for negligence in discharge of the duty. The disclaimer of liability in the present case is prominent and clearly worded and, on the authority of *Hedley Byrne & Co. Ltd* v *Heller & Partners Ltd* [1963] 2 All ER 575, [1964] AC 465, in so far as the common law is concerned effective to exclude the surveyors' liability for negligence. The question then is whether the Unfair Contract Terms Act 1977 bites on such a disclaimer. In my view it does.

The Court of Appeal, however, accepted an argument based on the definition of negligence contained in s. 1(1) of the 1977 Act, which provides:

For the purposes of this part of this Act 'negligence' means the breach — (a) of any obligation, arising from the express or implied terms of a contract, to take reasonable care or exercise reasonable skill in the performance of the contract; (b) of any common law duty to take reasonable care or exercise reasonable skill (but not any stricter duty); (c) of the common duty of care imposed by the Occupiers' Liability Act 1957 or the Occupiers' Liability Act (Northern Ireland) 1957.

It held that, as the disclaimer of liability would at common law have prevented any duty to take reasonable care arising between the parties, the Act had no application. In my view this construction fails to give due weight to the provisions of two further sections of the Act. Section 11(3) provides:

In relation to a notice (not being a notice having contractual effect), the requirement of reasonableness under this Act is that it should be fair and reasonable to allow reliance on it, having regard to all the circumstances obtaining when the liability arose or (but for the notice) would have arisen.

And s. 13(1) provides:

To the extent that this Part of this Act prevents the exclusion or restriction of any liability it also prevents — (a) making the liability or its enforcement subject to restrictive or onerous conditions; (b) excluding or restricting any right or remedy in respect of the liability, or subjecting a person to any prejudice in consequence of his pursuing any such right or remedy; (c) excluding or restricting rules of evidence or procedure; and (to that extent) sections 2 and 5 to 7 also prevent excluding or restricting liability by reference to terms and notices which exclude or restrict the relevant obligation or duty.

I read these provisions as introducing a 'but for' test in relation to the notice excluding liability. They indicate that the existence of the common law duty to take reasonable care, referred to in s. 1(1)(b), is to be judged by considering whether it would exist 'but for' the notice excluding liability. The result of taking the notice into account when assessing the existence of a duty of care would result in removing all liability for negligent misstatements from the protection of the Act. It is permissible to have regard to the second report of the Law Commission on *Exemption Clauses* (Law Com no 69), which is the genesis of the Unfair Contract Terms Act 1977, as an aid to the construction of the Act. Paragraph 127 of that report reads:

Our recommendations in this Part of the report are intended to apply to exclusions of liability for negligence where the liability is incurred in the course of a person's business. We consider that they should apply even in cases where the person seeking to rely on the exemption clause was under no legal obligation (such as a contractual obligation) to carry out the activity. This means that, for example, conditions attached to a licence to enter on to land, and disclaimers of liability made where information or advice is given, should be subject to control. . . .

I have no reason to think that Parliament did not intend to follow this advice and the wording of the Act is, in my opinion, apt to give effect to that intention. This view of the construction of the Act is also supported by the judgment of Slade LJ in *Phillips Products Ltd v Hyland* [1987] 2 All ER 620, [1987] 1 WLR 659, when he rejected a similar argument in relation to the construction of a contractual term excluding negligence.

Finally, the question is whether the exclusion of liability contained in the disclaimer satisfies the requirement of reasonableness provided by s. 2(2) of the 1977 Act. The meaning of reasonableness and the burden of proof are both dealt with in s. 11 (3), which provides:

> In relation to a notice (not being a notice having contractual effect), the requirement of reasonableness under this Act is that it should be fair and reasonable to allow reliance on it, having regard to all the circumstances obtaining when the liability arose or (but for the notice) would have arisen.

It is clear, then, that the burden is on the surveyor to establish that in all the circumstances it is fair and reasonable that he should be allowed to rely on his disclaimer of liability.

I believe that it is impossible to draw up an exhaustive list of the factors that must be taken into account when a judge is faced with this very difficult decision. Nevertheless, the following matters should, in my view, always be considered.

(1) Were the parties of equal bargaining power? If the court is dealing with a one-off situation between parties of equal bargaining power the requirement of reasonableness would be more easily discharged than in a case such as the present where the disclaimer is imposed on the purchaser who has no effective power to object.

(2) In the case of advice, would it have been reasonably practicable to obtain the advice from an alternative source taking into account considerations of costs and time? In the present case it is urged on behalf of the surveyor that it would have been easy for the purchaser to have obtained his own report on the condition of the house, to which the purchaser replies that he would then be required to pay twice for the same advice and that people buying at the bottom end of the market, many of whom will be young first-time buyers, are likely to be under considerable financial pressure without the money to go paying twice for the same service.

(3) How difficult is the task being undertaken for which liability is being excluded? When a very difficult or dangerous undertaking is involved there may be a high risk of failure which would certainly be a pointer towards the reasonableness of excluding liability as a condition of doing the work. A valuation, on the other hand, should present no difficulty if the work is undertaken with reasonable skill and care. It is only defects which are observable by a careful visual examination that have to be taken into account and I cannot see that it places any unreasonable burden on the valuer to require him to accept responsibility for the fairly elementary degree of skill and care involved in observing, following up and reporting on such defects. Surely it is work at the lower end of the surveyor's field of professional expertise.

(4) What are the practical consequences of the decision on the question of reasonableness? This must involve the sums of money potentially at stake and the ability of the parties to bear the loss involved, which, in its turn, raises the question of insurance. There was once a time when it was considered improper even to mention the possible existence of insurance cover in a lawsuit. But those days are long past. Everyone knows that all prudent, professional men carry insurance, and the availability and cost of insurance must be a relevant factor when considering which of two parties should be required to bear the risk of a loss. We are dealing in this case with a loss which will be limited to the value of a modest house and against which it can be expected that the surveyor will be insured. Bearing the loss will be unlikely to cause significant hardship if it has to be borne by the surveyor but it is, on the other hand, quite possible that it will be a financial catastrophe for the purchaser who may be left with a valueless house and no money to buy another. If the law in these circumstances denies the surveyor the right to exclude his liability, it may result in a few more claims but I do not think so poorly of the surveyors' profession as to believe that the floodgates will be opened. There may be some increase in surveyors' insurance premiums which will be passed on to the public, but I cannot think that it will be anything approaching the figures involved in the difference between the Abbey National's offer of a valuation without liability and a valuation with liability discussed in the speech of my noble and learned friend Lord Templman. The result of denying a surveyor, in the circumstances of this case, the right to exclude liability will result in distributing the risk of his negligence among all house purchasers through an increase in his fees to cover insurance, rather than allowing the whole of the risk to fall on the one unfortunate purchaser.

I would not, however, wish it to be thought that I would consider it unreasonable for professional men in all cicumstances to seek to exclude or limit their liability for negligence. Sometimes breathtaking sums of money may turn on professional advice against which it would be impossible for the adviser to obtain adequate insurance cover and which would ruin him if he were to be held personally liable. In these circumstances it may indeed be reasonable to give the advice on a basis of no liability or possibly of liability limited to the extent of the adviser's insurance cover.

In addition to the foregoing four factors, which will always have to be considered, there is in this case the additional feature that the surveyor is only employed in the first place because the purchaser wishes to buy the house and the purchaser in fact provides or contributes to the surveyor's fees. No one has argued that if the purchaser had employed and paid the surveyor himself, it would have been reasonable for the surveyor to exclude liability for negligence, and the present situation is not far removed from that of a direct contract between the surveyor and the purchaser. The evaluation of the foregoing matters leads me to the clear conclusion that it would not be fair and reasonable for the surveyor to be permitted to exclude liability in the circumstances of this case. I would therefore dismiss this appeal.

It must, however, be remembered that this is a decision in respect of a dwelling house of modest value in which it is widely recognised by surveyors that purchasers are in fact relying on their care and skill. It will obviously be of general application in broadly similar circumstances. But I expressly reserve my position in respect of valuations of quite different types of property for mortgage purposes, such as industrial property, large blocks of flats or very expensive houses. In such cases it may well be that the general expectation of the behaviour of the purchaser is quite different. With very large sums of money at stake prudence would seem to demand that the purchaser obtain his own structural survey to guide him in his purchase and, in such circumstances with very much larger sums of money at stake, it may be reasonable for the surveyors valuing on behalf of those who are providing the finance either to exclude or limit their liability to the purchaser.

Lords Keith, Brandon, Templeman and Jauncey concurred.

GEORGE MITCHELL LTD v *FINNEY LOCK SEEDS* [1983] 2 All ER 737 (HL)

LORD BRIDGE OF HARWICH: My Lords, the appellants are seed merchants. The respondents are farmers in East Lothian. In December 1973 the respondents ordered from the appellants 30 lb of Dutch winter white cabbage seeds. The seeds supplied were invoiced as 'Finneys Late Dutch Special'. The price was £201.60. Finneys Late Dutch Special was the variety required by the respondents. It is Dutch winter white cabbage which grows particularly well in the area of East Lothian where the respondents farm, and can be harvested and sold at a favourable price in the spring. The respondents planted some 63 acres of their land with seedlings grown from the seeds supplied by the appellants to produce their cabbage crop for the spring of 1975. In the event, the crop proved to be worthless and had to be ploughed in. This was for two reasons. First, the seeds supplied were not Finneys Late Dutch Special or any other variety of Dutch winter white cabbage, but a variety of autumn cabbage. Second, even as autumn cabbage the seeds were of very inferior quality.

The issues in the appeal arise from three sentences in the conditions of sale indorsed on the appellants' invoice and admittedly embodied in the terms on which the appellants contracted. For ease of reference it will be convenient to number the sentences. Omitting immaterial words they read as follows:

[1] In the event of any seeds or plants sold or agreed to be sold by us not complying with the express terms of the contract of sale . . . or any seeds or plants proving defective in varietal purity we will, at our option, replace the defective seeds or plants, free of charge to the buyer or will refund all payments made to us by the buyer in respect of the defective seeds or plants and this shall be the limit of our obligation. [2] We hereby exclude all liability for any loss or damage arising from the use of any seeds or plants supplied by us and for any consequential loss or damage arising out of such

use or any failure in the performance of or any defect in any seeds or plants supplied by us or for any other loss or damage whatsoever save for, at our option, liability for any such replacement or refund as aforesaid. [3] In accordance with the established custom of the seed trade any express or implied condition, statement or warranty, statutory or otherwise, not stated in these Conditions is hereby excluded.

I will refer to the whole as 'the relevant condition' and to the parts as 'clauses 1, 2, and 3' of the relevant condition.

The first issue is whether the relevant condition, on its true construction in the context of the contract as a whole, is effective to limit the appellants' liability to a refund of £201.60, the price of the seeds (the common law issue). The second issue is whether, if the common law issue is decided in the appellants' favour, they should nevertheless be precluded from reliance on this limitation of liability pursuant to the provisions of the modified s. 55 of the Sale of Goods Act 1979 which is set out in para. 11 of sch. 1 to the Act and which applies to contracts made between 18 May 1973 and 1 February 1978 (the statutory issue) . . .

My Lords, it seems to me, with all due deference, that the judgments of the trial judge and of Oliver LJ on the common law issue come dangerously near to reintroducing by the back door the doctrine of 'fundamental breach' which this House in the *Photo Production* case had so forcibly evicted by the front. The judge discusses what I may call the 'peas and beans' or 'chalk and cheese' cases, ie those in which it has been held that exemption clauses do not apply where there has been a contract to sell one thing, eg a motor car, and the seller has supplied quite another thing, eg a bicycle. I hasten to add that the judge can in no way be criticised for adopting this approach since counsel appearing for the appellants at the trial had conceded 'that, if what had been delivered had been beetroot seed or carrot seed, he would not be able to rely on the clause'. Different counsel appeared for the appellants in the Court of Appeal, where that concession was withdrawn.

In my opinion, this is not a 'peas and beans' case at all. The relevant condition applies to 'seeds'. Clause 1 refers to 'seeds sold' and 'seeds agreed to be sold'. Clause 2 refers to 'seeds supplied'. As I have pointed out, Oliver LJ concentrated his attention on the phrase 'seeds agreed to be sold'. I can see no justification, with respect, for allowing this phrase alone to dictate the interpretation of the relevant condition, still less for treating cl. 2 as 'merely a supplement' to cl. 1. Clause 2 is perfectly clear and unambiguous. The reference to 'seeds agreed to be sold' as well as to 'seeds sold' in cl. 1 reflects the same dichotomy as the definition of 'sale' in the Sale of Goods Act 1979 as including a bargain and sale as well as a sale and delivery. The defective seeds in this case were seeds sold and delivered just as clearly as they were seeds supplied, by the appellants to the respondents. The relevant condition, read as a whole, unambiguously limits the appellants' liability to replacement of the seeds or refund of the price. It is only possible to read an ambiguity into it by the process of strained construction which was deprecated by Lord Diplock in the *Photo Production* case [1980] 1 All ER 556 at 568, [1980] AC 827 at 851 and by Lord Wilberforce in the *Ailsa Craig* case [1983] 1 All ER 101 at 102.

In holding that the relevant condition was ineffective to limit the appellants' liability for a breach of contract caused by their negligence, Kerr LJ applied the principles stated by Lord Morton giving the judgment of the Privy Council in *Canada Steamship Lines Ltd v R* [1952] 1 All ER 305 at 310, [1952] AC 192 at 208. Kerr LJ stated correctly that this case was also referred to by Lord Fraser in the *Ailsa Craig* case [1983] 1 All ER 101 at 105. He omitted, however, to notice that, as appears from the passage from Lord Fraser's speech which I have already cited, the whole point of Lord Fraser's reference was to express his opinion that the very strict principles laid down in the *Canada Steamship Lines* case as applicable to exclusion and indemnity clauses cannot be applied in their full rigour to limitation clauses. Lord Wilberforce's speech contains a passage to the like effect, and Lord Elwyn-Jones, Lord Salmon and Lord Lowry agreed with both speeches. Having once reached a conclusion in the instant case that the relevant condition unambiguously limited the appellants' liability, I know of no principle of construction which can properly be applied to confine the effect of the limitation to breaches of contract arising without negligence on the part of the appellants. In agreement with Lord Denning MR, I would decide the common law issue in the appellants' favour.

The statutory issue turns, as already indicated, on the application of the provisions of the modified s. 55 of the Sale of Goods Act 1979, as set out in para. 11 of sch. 1 to the Act. The 1979 Act is a pure consolidation. The purpose of the modified s. 55 is to preserve the law as it stood from 18 May 1973 to 1 February 1978 in relation to contracts made between those two dates. The significance of the dates is that the first was the date when the Supply of Goods (Implied Terms) Act 1973 came into force containing the provision now re-enacted by the modified s. 55, the second was the date when the Unfair Contract Terms Act 1977 came into force and superseded the relevant provisions of the 1973 Act by more radical and far-reaching provisions in relation to contracts made thereafter.

The relevant subsections of the modified s. 55 provide as follows:

(1)   Where a right, duty or liability would arise under a contract of sale of goods by implication of law, it may be negatived or varied by express agreement, . . . but the preceding provision has effect subject to the following provisions of this section. . . .

(4)   In the case of a contract of sale of goods, any term of that or any other contract exempting from all or any of the provisions of section 13, 14 or 15 above is void in the case of a consumer sale and is, in any other case, not enforceable to the extent that it is shown that it would not be fair or reasonable to allow reliance on the term.

(5)   In determining for the purposes of subsection (4) above whether or not reliance on any such term would be fair or reasonable regard shall be had to all the circumstances of the case and in particular to the following matters — (a) the strength of the bargaining positions of the seller and buyer relative to each other, taking into account, among other things, the availability of suitable alternative products and sources of supply; (b) whether the buyer received an inducement to agree to the term or in accepting it had an opportunity of buying the goods or suitable alternatives without it from any source of supply; (c) whether the buyer knew or ought reasonably to have known of the existence and extent of the term (having regard, among other things, to any previous course of dealing between the parties); (d) where the term exempts from all or any of the provisions of section 13, 14 or 15 above if some condition is not complied with, whether it was reasonable at the time of the contract to expect that compliance with that condition would be practicable; (e) whether the goods were manufactured, processed, or adapted to the special order of the buyer. . . .

(9)   Any reference in this section to a term exempting from all or any of the provisions of any section of this Act is a reference to a term which purports to exclude or restrict, or has the effect of excluding or restricting, the operation of all or any of the provisions of that section, or the exercise of a right conferred by any provision of that section, or any liability of the seller for breach of a condition or warranty implied by any provision of that section. . . .

The contract between the appellants and the respondents was not a 'consumer sale', as defined for the purpose of these provisions. The effect of cl. 3 of the relevant condition is to exclude, inter alia, the terms implied by ss. 13 and 14 of the Act that the seeds sold by description should correspond to the description and be of merchantable quality and to substitute therefor the express but limited obligations undertaken by the appellants under cll. 1 and 2. The statutory issue, therefore, turns on the words in s. 55(4) 'to the extent that it is shown that it would not be fair or reasonable to allow reliance on' this restriction of the appellants' liabilities, having regard to the matters referred to in subs. (5).

This is the first time your Lordships' House has had to consider a modern statutory provision giving the court power to override contracual terms excluding or restricting liability, which depends on the court's view of what is 'fair and reasonable'. The particular provision of the modified s. 55 of the 1979 Act which applies in the instant case is of limited and diminishing importance. But the several provisions of the Unfair Contract Terms Act 1977 which depend on 'the requirement of reasonableness', defined in s. 11 by reference to what is 'fair and reasonable', albeit in a different context, are likely to come before the courts with increasing frequency. It may, therefore, be appropriate to consider how an original decision what is 'fair and reasonable' made in the application of any of these provisions should be approached by an appellate court. It would not be accurate to describe such a decision as an exercise of discretion. But a decision under any of the provisions referred to will have this in common with the exercise of a discretion, that, in having regard to the various matters to which the modified s. 55(5) of the 1979 Act, or s. 11 of the 1977 Act direct attention, the court must entertain a whole range of considerations, put them in the scales on one side or the other and decide at the end of the day on which side the balance comes down. There will sometimes be room for a legitimate difference of judicial opinion as to what the answer should be, where it will be impossible to say that one view is demonstrably wrong and the other demonstrably right. It must follow, in my view, that, when asked to review such a decision on appeal, the appellate court should treat the original decision with the utmost respect and refrain from interference with it unless satisfied that it proceeded on some erroneous principle or was plainly and obviously wrong.

Turning back to the modified s. 55 of the 1979 Act, it is common ground that the onus was on the respondents to show that it would not be fair or reasonable to allow the appellants to rely on the relevant condition as limiting their liability. It was argued for the appellants that the court must have regard to the circumstances as at the date of the contract, not after the breach. The basis of the argument was that this was the effect of s. 11 of the 1977 Act and that it would be wrong to construe the modified s. 55 of the Act as having a different effect. Assuming the premise is correct, the conclusion does not follow. The provisions of the 1977 Act cannot be considered in construing the prior enactments now embodied in the modified s. 55 of the 1979 Act. But, in any event, the language of sub-ss. (4) and (5) of that section is clear and unambiguous. The question whether it is fair or reasonable to allow reliance on a term excluding or limiting liability for a breach of contract can only arise after the breach. The nature of the breach and the circumstances in which it occurred cannot possibly be excluded from 'all the circumstances of the case' to which regard must be had.

The only other question of construction debated in the course of the argument was the meaning to be attached to the words 'to the extent that' in sub-s. (4) and, in particular, whether they permit the court to hold that it would be fair and reasonable to allow partial reliance on a limitation clause and, for example, to decide in the instant case that the respondents should recover, say, half their consequential damage. I incline to the view that, in their context, the words are equivalent to 'in so far as' or 'in circumstances in which' and do not permit the kind of judgment of Solomon illustrated by the example.

But for the purpose of deciding this appeal I find it unnecessary to express a concluded view on this question.

My Lords, at long last I turn to the application of the stautory language to the circumstances of the case. Of the particular matters to which attention is directed by paras. (a) to (e) of s. 55(5), only those in paras. (a) to (c) are relevant. As to para. (c), the respondents admittedly knew of the relevant condition (they had dealt with the appellants for many years) and, if they had read it, particularly cl. 2, they would, I think, as laymen rather than lawyers, have had no difficulty in understanding what it said. This and the magnitude of the damages claimed in proportion to the price of the seeds sold are factors which weigh in the scales in the appellants' favour.

The question of relative bargaining strength under para. (a) and of the opportunity to buy seeds without a limitation of the seedsman's liability under para. (b) were interrelated. The evidence was that a similar limitation of liability was universally embodied in the terms of trade between seedsmen and farmers and had been so for very many years. The limitation had never been negotiated between representative bodies but, on the other hand, had not been the subject of any protests by the National Farmers' Union. These factors, if considered in isolation, might have been equivocal. The decisive factor, however, appears from the evidence of four witnesses called for the appellants, two independent seedsmen, the chairman of the appellant company, and a director of a sister company (both being wholly-owned subsidiaries of the same parent). They said that it had always been their practice, unsuccessfully attempted in the instant case, to negotiate settlements of farmers' claims for damages in excess of the price of the seeds, if they thought that the claims were 'genuine' and 'justified'. The evidence indicated a clear recognition by seedsmen in general, and the appellants in particular, that reliance on the limitation of liability imposed by the relevant condition would not be fair or reasonable.

Two further factors, if more were needed, weigh the scales in favour of the respondents. The supply of autumn, instead of winter, cabbage seed was due to the negligence of the appellants' sister company. Irrespective of its quality, the autumn variety supplied could not, according to the appellants' own evidence, be grown commercially in East Lothian. Finally, as the trial judge found, seedsmen could insure against the risk of crop failure caused by supply of the wrong variety of seeds without materially increasing the price of seeds.

My Lords, even if I felt doubts about the statutory issue, I should not, for the reasons explained earlier, think it right to interfere with the unanimous original decision of that issue by the Court of Appeal. As it is, I feel no such doubts. If I were making the original decision, I should conclude without hestitation that it would not be fair or reasonable to allow the appellants to rely on the contractual limitation of their liability.

I would dismiss the appeal.

Lords Diplock, Scarman, Roskill and Brightman concurred.

4.4   Regulations Concerning Unfair Terms in Consumer Contracts

THE UNFAIR TERMS IN CONSUMER CONTRACTS RELATIONS 1994
(SI 1944/3159)

1.   Citation and commencement
These Regulations may be cited as the Unfair Terms in Consumer Contracts Regulations 1994 and shall come into force on 1st July 1995.

2.   Interpretation
    (1)   In these Regulations—
'business' includes a trade or profession and the activities of any government department or local or public authority;
'the Community' means the European Economic Community and the other States in the European Economic Area;
'consumer' means a natural person who, in making a contract to which these Regulations apply, is acting for purposes which are outside his business;
'court' in relation to England and Wales and Northern Ireland means the High Court, and in relation to Scotland, the Court of Session;
'Director' means the Director General of Fair Trading;
'EEA Agreement' means the Agreement on the European Economic Area signed at Oporto on 2 May 1992 as adjusted by the protocol signed at Brussels on 17 March 1993(c);
'member State' shall mean a State which is a contracting party to the EEA Agreement but until the EEA Agreement comes into force in relation to Liechtenstein does not include the State of Liechtenstein;
'seller' means a person who sells goods and who, in making a contract to which these Regulations apply, is acting for purposes relating to his business; and
'supplier' means a person who supplies goods or services and who, in making a contract to which these Regulations apply, is acting for purposes relating to his business.
    (2)   [applies to Scotland]

3.   Terms to which these Regulations apply
    (1)   Subject to the provisions of Schedule 1, these Regulations apply to any term in a contract concluded between a seller or supplier and a consumer where the said term has not been individually negotiated.
    (2)   Insofar as it is in plain, intelligible language, no assessment shall be made of the fairness of any term which—
        (a)   defines the main subject matter of the contract, or
        (b)   concerns the adequacy of the price or remuneration, as against the goods or services sold or supplied.

(3)   For the purposes of these Regulations, a term shall always be regarded as not having been individually negotiated where it has been drafted in advance and the consumer has not been able to influence the substance of the term.

(4)   Notwithstanding that a specific term or certain aspects of it in a contract has been individually negotiated, these Regulations shall apply to the rest of a contract if an overall assessment of the contract indicates that it is a pre-formulated standard contract.

(5)   It shall be for any seller or supplier who claims that a term was individually negotiated to show that it was.

4.   Unfair terms

(1)   In these Regulations, subject to paragraphs (2) and (3) below, 'unfair term' means any term which contrary to the requirement of good faith causes a significant imbalance in the parties' rights and obligations under the contract to the detriment of the consumer.

(2)   An assessment of the unfair nature of a term shall be made taking into account the nature of the goods or services for which the contract was concluded and referring, as at the time of the conclusion of the contract, to all circumstances attending the conclusion of the contract and to all the other terms of the contract or of another contract on which it is dependent.

(3)   In determining whether a term satisfies the requirement of good faith, regard shall be had in particular to the matters specified in Schedule 2 to these Regulations.

(4)   Schedule 3 to these Regulations contains an indicative and non-exhaustive list of the terms which may be regarded as unfair.

5.   Consequence of inclusion of unfair terms in contracts

(1)   An unfair term in a contract concluded with a consumer by a seller or supplier shall not be binding on the consumer.

(2)   The contract shall continue to bind the parties if it is capable of continuing in existence without the unfair term.

6.   Construction of written contracts

A seller or supplier shall ensure that any written term of a contract is expressed in plain, intelligible language, and if there is doubt about the meaning of a written term, the interpretation most favourable to the consumer shall prevail.

. . .

8.   Prevention of continued use of unfair terms

(1)   It shall be the duty of the Director to consider any complaint made to him that any contract term drawn up for general use is unfair, unless the complaint appears to the Director to be frivolous or vexatious.

(2)   If having considered a complaint about any contract term pursuant to paragraph (1) above the Director considers that the contract term is unfair he may, if he considers it appropriate to do so, bring proceedings for an injunction (in which proceedings he may also apply for an interlocutory injunction) against any person appearing to him to be using or recommending use of such a term in contracts concluded with consumers.

(3)   The Director may, if he considers it appropriate to do so, have regard to any undertakings given to him by or on behalf of any person as to the continued use of such a term in contracts concluded with consumers.

(4)   The Director shall give reasons for his decision to apply or not to apply, as the case may be, for an injunction in relation to any complaint which these Regulations require him to consider.

(5)   The court on an application by the Director may grant an injunction on such terms as it thinks fit.

(6)   An injunction may relate not only to use of a particular contract term drawn up for general use but to any similar term, or a term having like effect, used or recommended for use by any party to the proceedings.

(7)   The Director may arrange for the dissemination in such form and manner as he considers appropriate of such information and advice concerning the operation of these Regulations as may appear to him to be expedient to give to the public and to all persons likely to be affected by these Regulations.

Regulation 3(1)   SCHEDULE 1
CONTRACTS AND PARTICULAR TERMS EXCLUDED FROM THE SCOPE OF THESE
REGULATIONS

These Regulations do not apply to—
    (a)   any contract relating to employment;
    (b)   any contract relating to succession rights;
    (c)   any contract relating to rights under family law;
    (d)   any contract relating to the incorporation and organisation of companies or
partnerships; and
    (e)   any term incorporated in order to comply with or which reflects—
        (i)   statutory or regulatory provisions of the United Kingdom; or
        (ii) the provisions or principles of international conventions to which the
member States or the Community are party.

Regulation 4(3)   SCHEDULE 2
ASSESSMENT OF GOOD FAITH

In making an assessment of good faith, regard shall be had in particular to—
    (a)   the strength of the bargaining positions of the parties;
    (b)   whether the consumer had an inducement to agree to the term;
    (c)   whether the goods or services were sold or supplied to the special order of the
consumer; and
    (d)   the extent to which the seller or supplier has dealt fairly and equitably with the
consumer.

Regulation 4(4)   SCHEDULE 3
INDICATIVE AND ILLUSTRATIVE LIST OF TERMS WHICH MAY BE REGARDED
AS UNFAIR

1.   Terms which have the object or effect of—
    (a)   excluding or limiting the legal liability of a seller or supplier in the event of the
death of a consumer or personal injury to the latter resulting from an act or omission of
that seller or supplier;
    (b)   inappropriately excluding or limiting the legal rights of the consumer vis-à-vis
the seller or supplier or another party in the event of total or partial non-performance or
inadequate performance by the seller or supplier of any of the contractual obligations
including the option of offsetting a debt owed to the seller or supplier against any claim
which the consumer may have against him;
    (c)   making an agreement binding on the consumer whereas provision of services
by the seller or supplier is subject to a condition whose realisation depends on his own
will alone;
    (d)   permitting the seller or supplier to retain sums paid by the consumer where
the latter decides not to conclude or perform the contract without providing for the
consumer to receive compensation of an equivalent amount from the seller or supplier
where the latter is the party cancelling the contract;
    (e)   requiring any consumer who fails to fulfil his obligation to pay a disproportion-
ately high sum in compensation;
    (f)   authorising the seller or supplier to dissolve the contract on a discretionary
basis where the same facility is not granted to the consumer or permitting the seller or
supplier to retain the sums paid for services not yet supplied by him where it is the seller
or supplier himself who dissolves the contract;
    (g)   enabling the seller or supplier to terminate a contract of indeterminate duration
without reasonable notice except where there are serious grounds for doing so;
    (h)   automatically extending a contract of fixed duration where the consumer does
not indicate otherwise, when the deadline fixed for the consumer to express this desire
not to extend the contract is unreasonably early;
    (i)   irrevocably binding the consumer to terms with which he had no real oppor-
tunity of becoming acquainted before the conclusion of the contract;

(j) enabling the seller or supplier to alter the terms of the contract unilaterally without a valid reason which is specified in the contract;

(k) enabling the seller or supplier to alter unilaterally without a valid reason any characteristics of the product or service to be provided;

(l) providing for the price of goods to be determined at the time of delivery or allowing a seller of goods or supplier of services to increase their price without in both cases giving the consumer the corresponding right to cancel the contract if the final price is too high in relation to the price agreed when the contract was concluded;

(m) giving the seller or supplier the right to determine whether the goods or services supplied are in conformity with the contract or giving him the exclusive right to interpret any term of the contract;

(n) limiting the seller's or supplier's obligation to respect commitments undertaken by his agents or making his commitments subject to compliance with a particular formality;

(o) obliging the consumer to fulfil all his obligations where the seller or supplier does not perform his;

(p) giving the seller or supplier the possibility of transferring his rights and obligations under the contract, where this may serve to reduce the guarantees for the consumer without the latter's agreement;

(q) excluding or hindering the consumer's right to take legal action or exercise any other legal remedy, particularly by requiring the consumer to take disputes exclusively to arbitration not covered by legal provisions, unduly restricting the evidence available to him or imposing on him a burden of proof which, according to the applicable law, should lie with another party to the contract.

2. Scope of subparagraphs 1(g), (j) and (l)

(a) Subparagraph 1(g) is without hindrance to terms by which a supplier of financial services reserves the right to terminate unilaterally a contract of indeterminate duration without notice where there is a valid reason, provided that the supplier is required to inform the other contracting party or parties thereof immediately.

(b) Subparagraph 1(j) is without hindrance to terms under which a supplier of financial services reserves the right to alter the rate of interest payable by the consumer or due to the latter, or the amount of other charges for financial services without notice where there is a valid reason, provided that the supplier is required to inform the other contracting party or parties thereof at the earliest opportunity and that the latter are free to dissolve the contract immediately. Subparagraph 1(j) is also without hindrance to terms under which a seller or supplier reserves the right to alter unilaterally the conditions of a contract of indetemminate duration, provided that he is required to inform the consumer with reasonable notice and that the consumer is free to disssolve the contract.

(c) Subparagraphs 1(g), (j) and (l) do not apply to:
— transactions in transferable securities, financial instruments and other products or services where the price is linked to fluctuations in a stock exchange quotation or index or a financial market rate that the seller or supplier does not control;
— contracts for the purchase or sale of foreign currency, traveller's cheques or international money orders denominated in foreign currency;

(d) Subparagraph 1(l) is without hindrance to price indexation clauses, where lawful, provided that the method by which prices vary is explicitly described.

4.5 End of Chapter Assessment Question

Janet, a 20-year-old law student, went to the Albert Bus Station to catch a coach home to Doncaster. She had made this journey from time to time in the past. Above the ticket-office window of the Trentshire Bus Company was a sign which stated that all tickets were issued subject to conditions displayed inside the coaches. Janet purchased a ticket which made no reference to any conditions.

While boarding the coach the driver carelessly knocked Janet's camera from her hand and the lens was broken.

One of the terms displayed inside the coach was as follows:

> Passengers travel with goods at their own risk. Neither the company nor its servants accept any liability for damage or loss to passengers' goods. The company's servants are parties to this contract.

Advise Janet.

4.6 End of Chapter Assessment Outline Answer

COMMON LAW

1. Incorporation

(a) Notice

Where the plaintiff has not signed a contractual document the basic test of incorporation is that of reasonably sufficient notice given by the defendant to the plaintiff before or at the time the contract is concluded — *Olley* v *Marlborough Court*. However, it may be reasonable merely to draw the attention of the plaintiff to where the exclusion clause may be discovered (*Thompson* v *LMS Railway Co.*), although should the clause be regarded as burdensome or unusual it should be drawn to the attention of the plaintiff in the most explicit manner possible (*Thornton* v *Shoe Lane Parking Ltd*).

Thus, in the question, the ticket does not draw Janet's attention to the existence of the clauses at all. The sign above the ticket-office window does, but does it satisfy the test? It is reasonably prominently displayed? Is it sufficiently explicit should the clause be regarded as unusual? Is circuitous reference reasonable in the circumstances? (Is there a coach available to discover the conditions? Is there sufficient time between the issue of the ticket and the coach departure for Janet to discover the conditions and decide whether to contract on that basis or not?)

(b) Previous course of dealings

If the clause was not incorporated by notice we need to consider previous course of dealings. In *Spurling* v *Bradshaw* the document containing the exclusion clause arrived too late on the occasion in question but B, nevertheless, admitted that he had received such documents in a series of previous transactions. The Court of Appeal held that 'by the course of business and the conduct of the parties' the clause had become part of the contract. The test is, therefore, were the previous dealings consistent and sufficiently regular/frequent to constitute a course of dealings?

We know that Janet had made the journey from time to time in the past. Consistency would require the conditions to have been displayed in the coaches during her previous journeys. Regularity/frequency would require more than the three or four transactions over a five-year period which was rejected by the House of Lords in *Hollier* v *Rambler Motors*.

2. Construction

(a) Janet's contract with Trentshire Bus Company (TBC) is one under which TBC agrees to provide a service and it falls within the Supply of Goods and Services Act 1982. Section 13 of the Supply of Goods and Services Act 1982 implies a term into such a contract that the service will be carried out with reasonable care and skill. The service has not been carried out with reasonable care and skill since the coach driver has carelessly knocked Janet's camera from her hand and damaged it. TBC are potentially vicariously liable for their employee's carelessness on the basis of a negligent breach of contract, subject to the efficacy of the exclusion clause. The exclusion clause must apply to negligence since this is the only possible basis of the employee's liability (*Alderslade* v *Hendon Laundry Ltd*).

(b) Liability of employees – the coach driver may well not be worth suing anyway, but if he were sued for the tort of negligence can he rely upon the exclusion clause contained in the Janet–TBC contract? An aspect of the doctrine of privity of contract is that persons who are not a party to the contract are not generally protected by such a clause (*Adler* v *Dickson*). However, the clause in *Adler* v *Dickson* did not purport to extend its immunity to third parties, nor did the clause in the leading House of Lords' decision of *Scruttons Ltd* v *Midland Silicones Ltd*. The plaintiff in that case was unaware that the carrier had contracted with the defendants on the basis that the defendants should have the benefit of the limitation clause contained in the contract between the plaintiff and the carrier. The clause in the Janet–TBC contract does purport to confer its benefit upon employees, but does not spell out that TBC is contracting as agent for its employees, as was the case in *New Zealand Shipping Co. Ltd* v *Satterthwaite & Co. Ltd* where the third parties were held to be protected. However, such agency might be inferred from the terminology used, but only if the employees were aware of and consented to the inclusion of the phrase making them parties to the contract.

STATUTE

Unfair Contract Terms Act 1977

(a) The contract is covered by the provisions of the Unfair Contract Terms Act 1977 as it concerns 'business liability' (s. 1).

(b) With regard to negligence liability, s. 2(2) provides that 'a person cannot exclude or restrict his liability for negligence except in so far as the term or notice satisfies the requirement of reasonableness'.

(c) Reasonableness means – 'the term shall have been a fair and reasonable one to be included having regard to the circumstances which were, or ought reasonably to have been known to or in the contemplation of the parties when the contract was made' (s. 11(1)).

(d) Schedule 2 to the Act contains guidelines for the application of the reasonableness test. Although the Act states that they are of relevance to cases under ss. 6 and 7, nevertheless they are considered to be of general application if relevant. Particular emphasis might be given to the following guidelines:

    (i) *Knowledge (Guideline (c))* Awareness of the clause might be a factor indicating the reasonableness of the clause, particularly where there has been a previous course of dealings (see, e.g. *R W Green Ltd* v *Cade Bros Farm*). But would this apply where there is inequality of bargaining power, the plaintiff is a consumer, and her knowledge may be purely constructive?

    (ii) *Inequality of bargaining power (Guideline (a))* It may be that where one party is using standard terms it means that he is in a better bargaining position than the other party, but this is not inevitably so. For example, were there any other bus companies available with whom Janet might have contracted whose terms were less onerous (Guideline (b))?

With regard to *Janet* v *TBC*, could TBC have insured against the type of loss in question without materially increasing the cost of the service offered to the public? (*George Mitchell Ltd* v *Finney Lock Seeds Ltd*). If so the exclusion clause may be unreasonable. Alternatively, if such insurance cover is not available to TBC or is available only at great expense, thus requiring considerable increases in the cost of the service to the public the exclusion clause may be reasonable. If Janet's camera were an extremely expensive one it is likely that the burden of insurance would fall upon the owner, i.e. Janet.

Unfair Terms in Consumer Contracts Regulations 1994

The term, if incorporated, would also fall within the scope of these regulations, since it is not individually negotiated, and is part of a contract between a consumer and a business supplier (regs 2(1) and 3(1)). If it is regarded as an 'unfair term', then it will not be binding on Janet (reg. 5(1)). The test of whether it is 'unfair' is whether it causes a 'significant imbalance in the parties' rights and obligations under the contract' to the detriment of Janet (reg. 4(1)), thus breaking the requirement of 'good faith'. This rather vague test is expanded a little by sch. 2 which refers, inter alia, to the strength of bargaining position of the parties, and the extent to which the supplier has dealt fairly and equitably with the consumer. Schedule 3 gives an illustrative list of terms which may be unfair. The only one which is relevant here, is that contained in paragraph 1(b), which refers to 'inappropriately excluding or limiting the rights of the consumer . . . in the event of . . . inadequate performance . . . by the supplier.'

From this it will be seen that the approach is going to be very similar to that taken to the issue of 'reasonableness' under UCTA 1977. Indeed, in this case, it is likely that whether applying UCTA 1977 or the 1994 Regulations, the court will come to exactly the same conclusion.

CHAPTER FIVE

DISCHARGE OF LIABILITY

5.1 Performance

BOLTON v *MAHADEVA* **[1972] 2 All ER 1322 (CA)**

The plaintiff had contracted to install a central heating system for a lump sum of £560.

CAIRNS LJ: . . . This is an appeal against a judgment of Sir Graeme Finlay, sitting as deputy county court judge at Brentford County Court. The judgment was delivered on 30th September 1971 after a hearing which had taken some 2½ days earlier in that month. It was a judgment in favour of the plaintiff in an action for work done and materials supplied in connection with central heating installation and other work at the defendant's house. The judgment was for a net sum of £431.50, with costs on county court scale 3. The defendant appeals, contending that judgment should have been given for him; and he sought to amend the notice of appeal to say that the judge was in any event wrong in awarding all the costs to the plaintiff.

The action was founded on a lump sum contract, together with certain items of extras. The defence was that the plaintiff had wholly failed to perform the main contract, and the defence set out extensive particulars of defects in the work. It was admitted that a small sum was due for extras consisting of the preparation of a bathroom suite, but the defendant contended that the consideration for the main contract had wholly failed. Alternatively, he claimed to set off a sum counterclaimed in respect of making good the defects. By his reply, the plaintiff conceded that there were some small defects for which the defendant was entitled to a set-off, but otherwise he denied all the defendant's allegations. The defence was afterwards amended to allege further defects, and the reply to make certain further concessions, but these involved no important change in the attitude of the parties. . . .

Now, the £431.50 for which judgment was given was made up in this way. The contract price for the central heating installation was £560. The judge held that because of deficiencies in the performance of the work the defendant was entitled to set off against that sum £174.50, leaving a balance of £385.50. In respect of extras, the judge held that £76 would be a reasonable price for the work, but here again there were some defects which he assessed at £15, leaving a balance of £61. Adding that to the £385.50, he arrived at a total of £446.50. Then he set off a further £15 representing damages for inconvenience to the defendant, and that left a balance of £431.50 for which judgment was given. . . .

The main question in the case is whether the defects in workmanship found by the judge to be such as to cost £174 to repair – ie between one-third and one-quarter of the contract price – were of such a character and amount that the plaintiff could not be said to have substantially performed his contract. That is, in my view, clearly the legal principle which has to be applied to cases of this kind.

The rule which was laid down many years ago in *Cutter* v *Powell* (1795) 6 Term Rep 320 in relation to lump sum contracts was that, unless the contracting party had performed the whole of his contract, he was not entitled to recover anything. That strong rule must now be read in the light of certain more recent cases to which I shall briefly refer. The first of those cases is *H Dakin & Co. Ltd* v *Lee* [1916] 1 KB 866, a decision of the Court of Appeal, in which it was held that, where the amount of work which had not been carried out under a lump sum contract was very minor in relation to the contract as a whole, the contractor was entitled to be paid the lump sum, subject to such deduction as might be proper in respect of the uncompleted work. It is necessary to observe that the headnote of *H Dakin & Co. Ltd* v *Lee* was based, not on the judgments in the Court of Appeal, but on the judgments that had been delivered in the Divisional Court; and, as was pointed out in *Vigers* v *Cook* [1919] 2 KB 475, that headnote does not properly represent the grounds of the decision of the Court of Appeal in that case. The basis on which the Court of Appeal did decide *H Dakin & Co. Ltd* v *Lee* is to be found in a passage of the judgment of Lord Cozens-Hardy MR. I do not think it is necessary to read it in full, but I read this short passage:

> But to say that a builder cannot recover from a building owner merely because some item of the work has been done negligently or inefficiently or improperly is a proposition which I should not listen to unless compelled by a decision of the House of Lords. Take a contract for a lump sum to decorate a house; the contract provides that there shall be three coats of oil paint, but in one of the rooms only two coats of paint are put on. Can anybody say that under these circumstances the building owner could go and occupy the house and take the benefit of all the decorations which had been done in the other rooms without paying a penny for all the work done by the builder, just because only two coats of paint had been put on in one room where there ought to have been three? . . .

Perhaps the most helpful case is the most recent one of *Hoeing* v *Isaacs* [1952] 2 All ER 176. That was a case where the plaintiff was an interior decorator and designer of furniture who had entered into a contract to decorate and furnish the defendant's flat for a sum of £750; and, as appears from the statement of facts, the Official Referee who tried the case at first instance found that the door of a wardrobe required replacing, that a bookshelf which was too short would have to be remade, which would require alterations being made to a bookcase, and that the cost of remedying the defects was £55 18s 2d. That is on a £750 contract. The ground on which the Court of Appeal in that case held that the plaintiff was entitled to succeed, notwithstanding that there was not complete performance of the contract, was that there was substantial performance of the contract and that the defects in the work which there existed were not sufficient to amount to a substantial degree of non-performance.

In considering whether there was substantial performance I am of opinion that it is relevant to take into account both the nature of the defects and the proportion between the cost of rectifying them and the contract price. It would be wrong to say that the contractor is only entitled to payment if the defects are so trifling as to be covered by the de minimis rule.

The main matters that were complained of in this case were that, when the heating system was put on, fumes were given out which made some of the living rooms (to put it at the lowest) extremely uncomfortable and inconvenient to use; secondly, that by reason of there being insufficient radiators and insufficient insulation, the heating obtained by the central heating system was far below what it should have been. There was conflicting evidence about those matters. The judge came to the conclusion that, because of a defective flue, there were fumes which affected the condition of the air in the living rooms, and he further held that the amount of heat given out was such that, on the average, the house was less warm than it should have been with the heating system on, to the extent of 10 per cent. But, while that was the average over the house as a whole, the deficiency in warmth varied very much as between one room and another. The figures that were given in evidence and, insofar as we heard, were not contradicted, were such as to indicate that in some rooms the heat was less than it should have been by something between 26 and 30 per cent.

The learned judge, having made those findings, came to the conclusion that the defects were not sufficient in degree to enable him to hold that there was not substantial performance of the contract. He expressed that conclusion in these terms:

> The defendant's main complaints against the plaintiff – that is, the style of radiators, fumes from the boiler flue, and inadequacy of heat provided by the system – neither

by themselves nor in combination amount to a sufficiently important part of the plaintiff's obligation to prevent there being substantial performance.

Now, certainly it appears to me that the nature and amount of the defects in this case were far different from those which the court had to consider in *H Dakin & Co. Ltd* v *Lee* and *Hoenig* v *Isaacs*. For my part, I find it impossible to say that the judge was right in reaching the conclusion that in those circumstances the contract had been substantially performed. The contract was a contract to install a central heating system. If a central heating system when installed is such that it does not heat the house adequately and is such, further, that fumes are given out, so as to make living rooms uncomfortable, and if the putting right of those defects is not something which can be done by some slight amendment of the system, then I think that the contract is not substantially performed.

The actual amounts of expenditure which the judge assessed as being necessary to cure those particular defects were £40 in each case. Taking those matters into account and the other matters making up the total of £174, I have reached the conclusion that the judge was wrong in saying that this contract had been substantially completed; and, on my view of the law, it follows that the plaintiff was not entitled to recover under that contract . . .

Buckley and Sachs LJJ concurred.

5.1.1 SUBSTANTIAL PERFORMANCE

H DAKIN & CO. LTD v *LEE* [1916] 1 KB 577 (CA)

LORD COZENS-HARDY MR: This is an appeal from a decision of the Divisional Court reversing the finding of the official referee in a dispute between builders and a building owner. The building owner was a lady who was engaged in school work, and whose house required certain alterations and improvements.

A specification was prepared in August, 1913, by which the builders agreed to do a great deal. They were to examine the roof and renew the decayed parts of it and the gutter pipes, to repair the gutters and rainwater pipes in the roof over the conservatory, to examine the main roof, to underpin, where necessary, the piers and walls of the conservatory, and rebuild any portions where found necessary, to repair or renew the wood staircase, to take down the bay window and rebuild it, to reconstruct the arches over the first and second floor windows, to alter the porch roof, to repair the basement area window, to cut out the cracks in the flank wall, to excavate as required and underpin the flank wall and chimney breasts with solid Portland cement concrete base, the concrete underpinning to be composed of one part of Portland cement concrete to six parts of clean Thames ballast, to test and examine the drains, to take down the brick arches in the back elevation, to alter the front gate, and to do a number of other things. It will be observed that one of the matters which is mentioned more than once is the underpinning of a wall, which was to be done with solid Portland cement concrete base. The work was finished – and when I say this I do not wish to prejudice matters, but I cannot think of a better word to use at the moment.

There were then disputes, as I have said, between the building owner and the builders. An action was commenced by the builders and referred to the official referee, and the official referee heard arguments extending over some seven or eight days, and he went twice to look at the house. He has made a finding to the effect that the obligation on the plaintiffs was to put down concrete 4 feet in depth throughout the part to be underpinned; I am not quite sure whether that is true. There is, in the specification itself, no clause binding them to put concrete to the depth of 4 feet. It is true that, in the letter of even date which enclosed the estimate for doing the work comprised in the specification, it is said that the estimate was on the basis of concrete being 4 feet deep; but there is not an express contract that the concrete should be of that depth. However, the official referee has found that the plaintiffs were under the obligation to put down 4 feet of concrete, and the builders swore at the trial that 4 feet of concrete had in fact been put in. The official referee went to the house on two occasions and tested it, and he has found as a fact 'that in no parts was there the contract depth, 1 foot 7 inches to 2 feet was the average depth'. He also said 'It is immaterial that the plaintiffs considered and that the defendant considered the depth to be safe'. He has also found that the builders put in two solid columns 4 inches in diameter when, according to the specification, they were to be 5 inches in diameter, hollow; but that is a trivial matter, and so trivial that I do not propose to say another word about it. He then says that certain rolled steel joists ought to have been bolted to caps and to each other, and that this was quite ignored. That may or may not have been a matter of importance. Lastly, he finds that the concrete was not properly mixed.

In these circumstances it has been argued before us that, in a contract of this kind to do work for a lump sum, the defect in some of the items in the specification, or the failure to do every item contained in the specification, puts an end to the whole contract, and prevents the builders from making any claim upon it; and therefore, where there is no ground for presuming any fresh contract, he cannot obtain any payment. The matter has been teated in the argument as though the omission to do every item perfectly was an abandonment of the contract. That seems to me, with great respect, to be absolutely and entirely wrong. An illustration of the abandonment of a contract which was given from one of the authorities was that of a builder who, when he had half finished his work, said to the employer 'I cannot finish it, because I have no money', and left the job undone at that stage. That is an abandonment of the contract, and prevents the builder, therefore, from making any claim, unless there be some other circumstances leading to a different conclusion. But to say that a builder cannot recover from a building owner merely because some item of the work has been done negligently or inefficiently or improperly is a proposition which I should not listen to unless compelled by a decision of the House of Lords. Take a contract for a lump sum to decorate a house; the contract provides that there shall be three coats of oil paint, but in one of the rooms only two coats of paint are put on. Can anybody seriously say that under these circumstances the building owner could go and occupy the house and take the benefit of all the decorations which had been done in the other rooms without paying a penny for all the work done by the builder, just because only two coats of paint had been put on in one room where there ought to have been three?

I regard the present case as one of negligence and bad workmanship, and not as a case where there has been an omission of any one of the items in the specification. The builders thought apparently, or so they have sworn, that they had done all that was intended to be done in reference to the contract; and I suppose the defects are due to carelessness on the part of some of the workmen or of the foreman: but the existence of these defects does not amount to a refusal by them to perform part of the contract; it simply shows negligence in the way in which they have done the work. Thus, in regard to the rolled steel joists they have not apparently bolted them together in some particular way, the precise nature of which I confess I do not understand.

Then what is the result? It seems to me that the result is that the builders are entitled to recover the contract price, less so much as it is found ought to be allowed in respect of the items which the official referee has found to be defective. There is no finding by the referee as to what the precise figures should be, and, unless they are agreed, the matter must go back to him to decide what ought to be allowed in respect of the concrete not being 4 feet and the wrong joining of the rolled steel joists, and what, if anything, ought to be allowed in respect of the concrete not having been properly mixed.

The appeal substantially fails and must be dismissed; but the case must go back, if necessary, to the official referee to find what allowance ought to be made from the sum to be paid the builders in respect of those items. The appellant must pay the costs of this appeal.

Pickford and Warrington LJJ concurred.

5.1.2   ACCEPTANCE OF PARTIAL PERFORMANCE

SUMPTER v HEDGES [1898] 1 QB 673 (CA)

SMITH LJ: In this case the plaintiff, a builder, entered into a contract to build two houses and stables on the defendant's land for a lump sum. When the buildings were still in an unfinished state the plaintiff informed the defendant that he had no money, and was not going on with the work any more. The learned judge has found as a fact that he abandoned the contract. Under such circumstances, what is a building owner to do? He cannot keep the buildings on his land in an unfinished state for ever. The law is that, where there is a contract to do work for a lump sum, until the work is completed the price of it cannot be recovered. Therefore the plaintiff could not recover on the original contract. It is suggested however that the plaintiff was entitled to recover for the work he did on a quantum meruit. But, in order that that may be so, there must be evidence of a fresh contract to pay for the work already done. With regard to that, the case of *Munro v Butt* (1858) 8 E & B 738 appears to be exactly in point. That case decides that, unless the building owner does something from which a new contract can be inferred to pay for the work already done, the plaintiff in such a case as this cannot recover on a quantum meruit. In the case of *Lysaght v Pearson, The Times*, 3 March 1879, to which we have been referred, the case of *Munro v Butt* does not appear to have been referred to. There the plaintiff had contracted to erect on the defendant's land two corrugated iron roofs. When he had completed one of them, he does not seem to have said that he abandoned the contract, but merely that he would not go on unless the defendant paid him for what he had already done. The defendant thereupon proceeded to erect for himself the second roof. The Court of Appeal held that there was in that case something from which a new contract might be inferred to pay for the work done by the plaintiff. That is not this case. In the case of *Whitaker v Dunn* (1887) 3 Times LR 602 there was a contract to erect a laundry on defendant's land, and the laundry erected was not in accordance with the contract, but the official referee held that the plaintiff could recover on a quantum meruit. The case came before a Divisional Court, consisting of Lord Coleridge CJ and myself, and we said that the decision in *Munro v Butt* applied, and there being no circumstances to justify an inference of a fresh contract the plaintiff must fail. My brother Collins thinks that that case went to the Court of Appeal, and that he argued it there, and the court affirmed the decision of the Queen's Bench Division. I think the appeal must be dismissed.

COLLINS LJ: I agree. I think the case is really concluded by the finding of the learned judge to the effect that the plaintiff had abandoned the contract. If the plaintiff had merely broken his contract in some way so as not to give the defendant the right to treat him as having abandoned the contract, and the defendant had then proceeded to finish the work himself, the plaintiff might perhaps have been entitled to sue on a quantum meruit on the ground that the defendant had taken the benefit of the work done. But that is not the present case. There are cases in which, though the plaintiff has abandoned the performance of a contract, it is possible for him to raise the inference of a new contract to pay for the work done on a quantum meruit from the defendant's having taken the benefit of that work, but, in order that that may be done, the circumstances must be such as to give an option to the defendant to take or not to take the benefit of the work done. It is only where the circumstances are such as to give that option that there is any evidence on which to ground the inference of a new contract. Where, as in the case of work done on land, the circumstances are such as to give the defendant no option whether he will take the benefit of the work or not, then one must look to other facts than the mere taking the benefit of the work in order to ground the inference of a new contract. In this case I see no other facts on which such an inference can be founded. The mere fact that a defendant is in possession of what he cannot help keeping, or even has done work upon it, affords no ground for such an inference. He is not bound to keep unfinished a building which in an incomplete state would be a nuisance on his land. I am therefore of opinion that the plaintiff was not entitled to recover for the work which he had done. I feel clear that the case of *Whitaker v Dunn*, to which reference has been made, was the case which as counsel I argued in the Court of Appeal, and in which the court dismissed the appeal on the ground that the case was concluded by *Munro v Butt*.

Chitty LJ concurred.

5.1.3 PREVENTION OF PERFORMANCE

PLANCHÉ v COLBURN (1831) 8 Bing 14 (Court of Common Pleas)

The defendants had commenced a periodical publication, under the name of 'The Juvenile Library', and had engaged the plaintiff to write for it a volume upon Costume and Ancient Armour. The declaration stated, that the defendant had engaged the plaintiff for 100*l*. to write this work for publication in 'The Juvenile Library'; and alleged for breach, that though the author wrote a part, and was ready and willing to complete and deliver the whole for insertion in that publication, yet that the defendants would not publish it there, and refused to pay the plaintiff the sum of 100*l*., which they had previously agreed he should receive. There were then the common counts for work and labour.

At the trial before Tindal CJ, Middlesex sittings after last term, it appeared that the plaintiff, after entering into the engagement stated in the declaration, commenced and completed a considerable portion of the work; performed a journey to inspect a collection of ancient armour, and made drawings therefrom; but never tendered or delivered his performance to the defendants, they having finally abandoned the publication of 'The Juvenile Library', upon the ill success of the early numbers of the work. An attempt was made to shew that the plaintiff had entered into a new contract.

The Chief Justice left it to the jury to say, whether the work had been abandoned by the defendants, and whether the plaintiff had entered into any new contract; and a verdict having been found for him, with 50*l*. damages.

Spankie Serjt moved to set it aside, on the ground that the plaintiff could not recover on the special contract, for want of having tendered or delivered the work pursuant to the contract; and he could not resort to the common courts for work and labour, when he was bound by the special contract to deliver the work. If the plaintiff had delivered the work, or so much of it as he had completed at the time 'The Juvenile Library' was abandoned, the defendants might have turned it to account in some other way.

TINDALL CJ: In this case a contract had been entered into for the publication of a work on Costume and Ancient Armour in 'The Juvenile Library'. The considerations by which an author is generally actuated in undertaking to write a work are pecuniary profit and literary reputation. Now, it is clear that the latter may be sacrificed, if an author, who has engaged to write a volume of a popular nature, to be published in a work intended for a juvenile class of readers, should be subject to have his writings published as a separate and distinct work, and therefore liable to be judged of by more severe rules than would be applied to a familiar work intended merely for children. The fact was, that the defendants not only suspended, but actually put an end to, 'The Juvenile Library'; they had broken their contract with the plaintiff; and an attempt was made, but quite unsuccessfully, to shew that the plaintiff had afterwards entered into a new contract to allow them to publish his book as a separate work.

I agree that, when a special contract is in existence and open, the plaintiff cannot sue on a quantum meruit: part of the question here, therefore, was, whether the contract did exist or not. It distinctly appeared that the work was finally abandoned; and the jury found that no new contract had been entered into. Under these circumstances the plaintiff ought not to lose the fruit of his labour; and there is no ground for the application which has been made.

Gaselee, Bosanquet and Alderson JJ concurred.

5.1.4   TIME OF PERFORMANCE

CHARLES RICKARDS LTD v OPPENHEIM [1950] 1 All ER 420 (CA)

DENNING LJ: Early in 1947 the defendant, Mr Oppenheim, wanted a new Rolls Royce car, and he placed an order in two parts with the plaintiffs Charles Rickards, Ltd, who are motor car traders. He first ordered the chassis a Rolls Royce Silver Wraith chassis, for estimated delivery in June, 1947, but he also wanted a body built on the chassis, and he particularly wanted to know the time within which that body could be made. The plaintiffs made inquiries of various firms for an estimated time for building a body on to the chassis. In July, 1947, Rolls Royce themselves estimated twenty-one months, and Park Ward at about the same time estimated fifteen months. Those times were too long for the defendant's satisfaction, so the plaintiffs obtained an estimate from Jones Brothers (Coachbuilders) Ltd, who said that they could do it within 'six months or, at the most, seven months'. Thereupon, the plaintiffs gave the same time to the defendant and he gave them the order for the body on that footing. The order was placed in July. The plaintiffs sub-contracted it and put out the work with Jones Brothers (Coachbuilders) Ltd. The actual time from which the six or seven months started is not precisely ascertained. The chassis was actually delivered to the sub-contractors on July 30, 1947, and, if that is taken as the date from which the time ran, the seven months would be up at the end of February, 1948, but the specification for the body work was not finally agreed until August 20, 1947. If that date is taken, the latest time for delivery would be March 20, 1948. Whichever date is taken, though, is immaterial, for the time was plainly exceeded. The body was not built on to the chassis by March 20, nor, indeed, until many months later – not until October 18, 1948, was the car completed. . . .

It is clear on the findings of the judge that there was an initial stipulation making time of the essence of the contract between the plaintiffs and the defendant, namely, that it was to be completed 'in six, or, at the most, seven months'. Counsel for the plaintiffs did not seek to disturb that finding – indeed, he could not successfully have done so – but he said that that stipulation was waived. His argument was that, the stipulated time having been waived, the time became at large, and that thereupon the plaintiffs' only obligation was to deliver within a reasonable time. He said that, in accordance with well-known authorities, 'a reasonable time' meant a reasonable time in the circumstances as they actually existed, i.e. that the plaintiffs would not exceed a reasonable time if they were prevented from delivering by causes outside their control, such as strikes or the impossibility of getting parts, and so forth, and that, on the evidence in this case, it could not be said that a reasonable time was in that sense exceeded. He cited the well-known words of Lord Watson ([1893] AC 32, 33) in *Hick v Raymond and Reid* to support the view that in this case, on the evidence, a reasonable time had not been exceeded. If this had been originally a contract without any stipulation in regard to time, and, therefore, with only the implication of reasonable time, it may be that the plaintiffs could have said that they had fulfilled the contract, but, in my opinion, the case is very different when there was an initial contract, making time of the essence, of 'six or, at the most, seven months'. I agree that that initial time was waived by reason of the requests for delivery which the defendant made after March, 1948, and that, if delivery had been tendered in compliance with those requests, the defendant could not have refused to accept. Supposing, for instance, delivery had been tendered in April, May, or June 1948, the defendant would have had no answer. It would be true that the plaintiffs could not aver and prove that they were ready and willing to deliver in accordance with the original contract. They would have had, in effect, to rely on the waiver almost as a cause of action. At one time there would have been theoretical difficulties about their doing that. It would be said that there was no consideration, or, if the contract was for the sale of goods, that there was nothing in writing to support the variation. *Plevins v Downing* (1876) 1 CPD 220, coupled with what was said in *Besseler, Waechter Glover & Co. v South Derwent Coal Co. Ltd* [1937] 4 All ER 552 gave rise to a good deal of difficulty on that score, but all those difficulties are swept away now. If the defendant, as he did, led the plaintiffs to believe that he would not insist on the stipulation as to time, and that, if they carried out the work, he would accept it, and they did it, he could not afterwards set up the stipulation in regard to time against them. Whether it be called waiver or forbearance on his part, or an agreed variation or substituted performance, does not matter. It is a kind of estoppel. By his conduct he made a promise not to insist on his strict legal rights. That promise was intended to be binding, intended to be acted on, and was in fact, acted on. He cannot afterwards go back on it. That, I think, follows from *Panoutsos v Raymond Hadley Corpn of New York* [1917] 2 KB 473, a decision of this court, and it was also anticipated in *Bruner v Moore* [1904] 1 Ch 305. It is a particular application of the principle which I endeavoured to state in *Central London Property Trust Ltd v High Trees House Ltd* [1947] KB 130.

Therefore, if the matter stopped there, the plaintiffs could have said that, notwithstanding that more than seven months had elapsed, the defendant was bound to accept, but the matter does not stop there, because delivery was not given in compliance with the requests of the defendant. Time and time again the defendant pressed for delivery, time and time again he was assured that he would have early delivery, but he never got satisfaction, and eventually at the end of June he gave notice saying that, unless the car was delivered by July 25, he would not accept it. The question thus arises whether he was entitled to give such a notice, making time of the essence, and that is the question which counsel for the plaintiffs has argued before us. He agrees that, if this is a contract for the sale of goods, the defendant could give such a notice. He accepted the statement of McCardie J ([1920] 3 KB 495), in *Hartley* v *Hymans*, as accurately stating the law in regard to the sale of goods, but he said that that statement did not apply to contracts for work and labour. He said that no notice making time of the essence could be given in regard to contracts for work and labour. The judge thought that the contract was one for the sale of goods, but, in my view, it is unnecessary to determine whether it was a contract for the sale of goods or a contract for work and labour, because, whichever it was, the defendant was entitled to give notice bringing the matter to a head. It would be most unreasonable if, having been lenient and having waived the initial expressed time, he should thereby have prevented himself from ever thereafter insisting on reasonably quick delivery. In my judgment, he was entitled to give a reasonable notice making time of the essence of the matter. Adequate protection to the suppliers is given by the requirement that the notice should be reasonable.

The next question, therefore, is: Was this a reasonable notice? Counsel for the plaintiffs argued that it was not. He said that a reasonable notice must give sufficient time for the work outstanding to be completed, and that, on the evidence in this case, four weeks was not a reasonable time because it would, and did, in fact, require three-and-a-half months to complete it. In my opinion, however, the words of Lord Parker of Waddington in *Stickney* v *Keeble* apply to such a case as the present, just as much as they do to a contract for the sale of land. Lord Parker said ([1915] AC 419):

In considering whether the time so limited is a reasonable time the court will consider all the circumstances of the case. No doubt what remains to be done at the date of the notice is of importance, but it is by no means the only relevant fact. The fact that the purchaser has continually been pressing for completion, or has before given similar notices which he has waived, or that it is specially important to him to obtain early completion, are equally relevant facts.

To that statement I would add, in the present case, the fact that the original contract made time of the essence. In this case, not only did the defendant press continually for delivery, not only was he given promises of speedy delivery, but, on the very day before he gave notice, he was told by the sub-contractors' manager, who was in charge of the work, that it would be ready within two weeks. He then gave a four weeks' notice. The judge found that it was a reasonable notice and, in my judgment, there is no ground on which this court could in any way differ from that finding. The reasonableness of the notice must, of course, be judged at the time at which it is given. It cannot be held to be a bad notice because, after it is given, the suppliers find themselves in unanticipated difficulties in making delivery.

The notice of June 29, 1948, was, therefore, a perfectly good notice so as to make time of the essence of the contract. . . .

The case, therefore, comes down to this. There was a contract by the plaintiffs to supply and fix a body on the chassis within six or seven months. They did not do it. The defendant waived that stipulation. For three months after the time had expired he pressed them for delivery, asking for it first for Ascot and then for his holiday abroad. But still they did not deliver it. Eventually at the end of June, being tired of waiting any longer, he gave a four weeks' notice and said: 'At all events, if you do not supply it at the end of four weeks I must cancel', and he did cancel. I see no injustice to the plaintiffs in saying that that was a reasonable notice. Having originally stipulated for six to seven months, having waited eleven months, and still not getting delivery, the defendant was entitiled to cancel the contract.

Bucknill and Singleton LJJ concurred.

5.2 Breach

5.2.1 ANTICIPATORY BREACH

HOCHSTER v *DE LA TOUR* (1853) 2 E & B 678 (KB)

In April the defendant contracted for the plaintiff to act as a courier on a foreign tour, starting on 1 June. On 11 May the defendant cancelled the arrangement. Was the plaintiff entitled to sue immediately, or only on 1 June?

LORD CAMPBELL CJ: On this motion in arrest of judgment, the question arises, whether, if there be an agreement between A and B, whereby B engages to employ A on and from a future day for a given period of time, to travel with him into a foreign country as a courier, and to start with him in that capacity on that day, A being to receive a monthly salary during the continuance of such service, B may, before the day, refuse to perform the agreement and break and renounce it, so as to entitle A before the day to commence an action against B to recover damages for breach of the agreement; A having been ready and willing to perform it, till it was broken and renounced by B. The defendant's counsel very powerfully contended that, if the plaintiff was not contented to dissolve the contract, and to abandon all remedy upon it, he was bound to remain ready and willing to perform it till the day when the actual employment as courier in the service of the defendant was to begin; and that there could be no breach of the agreement, before that day, to give a right of action. But it cannot be laid down as a universal rule that, where by agreement an act is to be done on a future day, no action can be brought for a breach of the agreement till the day for doing the act has arrived. If a man promises to marry a woman on a future day, and before that day marries another woman, he is instantly liable to an action for breach of promise of marriage; *Short* v *Stone* (8 Q B 358). If a man contracts to execute a lease on and from a future day for a certain term, and, before that day, executes a lease to another for the same term, he may be immediately sued for breaking the contract; *Ford* v *Tiley* (6 B & C 325). So, if a man contracts to sell and deliver specific goods on a future day, and before the day he sells and delivers them to another, he is immediately liable to an action at the suit of the person with whom he first contracted to sell and deliver them; *Bowdell* v *Parsons* (10 East, 359). One reason alleged in support of such an action is, that the defendant has before the day, rendered it impossible for him to perform the contract at the day: but this does not necessarily follow; for, prior to the day fixed for doing the act, the first wife may have died, a surrender of the lease executed might be obtained, and the defendant might have repurchased the goods so as to be in a situation to sell and deliver them to the plaintiff. Another reason may be, that, where there is a contract to do an act on a future day, there is a relation constituted between the parties in the meantime by the contract, and that they impliedly promise that in the meantime neither will do anything to the prejudice of the other inconsistent with that relation. As an example, a man and woman engaged to marry are affianced to one another during the period between the time of the engagement and the celebration of the marriage. In this very case, of traveller and courier, from the day of the hiring till the day when the employment was to begin, they were engaged to each other; and it seems to be a breach of an implied contract if either of them renounces the engagement. This reasoning seems in accordance with the unanimous decision of the Exchequer Chamber in *Elderton* v *Emmens* (1848) 6 CB 160 which we have followed in subsequent cases in this court. The declaration in the present case, in alleging a breach, states a great deal more than a passing intention on the part of the defendant which he may repent of, and could only be proved by evidence that he had utterly renounced the contract, or done some act which rendered it impossible for him to perform it. If the plaintiff has no remedy for breach of the contract unless he treats the contract as in force, and acts upon it down to the 1st June 1852, it follows that, till then, he must enter into no employment which will interfere with his promise 'to start with the defendant on such travels on the day and year', and that he must then be properly equipped in all respects as a courier for a three months' tour on the continent of Europe. But it is surely much more rational, and more for the benefit of both parties, that, after the renunciation of the agreement by the defendant, the plaintiff should be at liberty to consider himself absolved from any future performance of it, retaining his right to sue for any damage he has suffered from the breach of it. Thus, instead of remaining idle and laying out money in preparations which must be useless, he is at liberty to seek service under another employer, which would go in mitigation of the damages to which he would otherwise be entitled for a breach of the contract. It seems strange that the defendant, after renouncing the contract, and absolutely declaring that he will never act under it, should be permitted to object that faith is given to his assertion, and that an opportunity is not left to him of changing his mind. If the plaintiff is barred of any remedy by entering into an engagement inconsistent with starting as a courier with the defendant on the 1st June, he is prejudiced by putting faith in the defendant's assertion: and it would be more consonant with principle, if the defendant were precluded from saying that he had not broken the contract when he declared that he entirely renounced it. Suppose that the defendant, at the time of his renunciation, had embarked on a voyage for Australia, so as to render it physically impossible for him to employ the plaintiff as a courier on the continent of Europe in the months of June, July and August 1852: according to decided cases, the action might have been brought before the 1st June; but the renunciation may have been founded on other facts, to be given in evidence, which would equally have rendered the defendant's performance of the contract impossible. The man who wrongfully renounces a contract into which he has deliberately entered cannot justly complain if he is immediately sued for a compensation in damages by the man whom he has injured: and it seems reasonable to allow an option to the injured party, either to sue immediately, or to wait till the time when the act was to be done, still holding it as prospectively binding for the exercise of this option, which may be advantageous to the innocent party, and cannot be prejudicial to the wrongdoer. An argument against the action before the 1st of June is urged from the difficulty of calculating the damages: but this argument is equally strong against an action before the 1st of September, when the three months would expire. In either case, the jury in assessing the damages would be justified in looking to all that had happened, or was likely to happen, to increase or mitigate the loss of the plaintiff down to the day of trial. We do not find any decision contrary to the view we are taking of this case. . . .

5.2.2 BREACH DURING PERFORMANCE

MERSEY STEEL AND IRON CO. LTD v *NAYLOR, BENZON & CO.* (1884) 9 App Cas
434 (HL)

Five thousand tons of steel was to be delivered and paid for in instalments. Shortly before the second payment was due the sellers were the subject of a petition for winding-up. The buyers, acting on erroneous legal advice, withheld payment. The sellers treated this as a repudiatory breach.

EARL OF SELBORNE LC : . . . Upon the other point, I do not think it desirable to lay down larger rules than the case may require, or than former authorities may have laid down for my guidance, or to go into possible cases differing from the one with which we have to deal. I am content to take the rule as stated by Lord Coleridge in *Freeth* v *Burr* (1874) LR 9 CP 208, which is in substance, as I understand it, that you must look at the actual circumstances of the case in order to see whether the one party to the contract is relieved from its future performance by the conduct of the other; you must examine what that conduct is, so as to see whether it amounts to a renunciation, to an absolute refusal to perform the contract, such as would amount to a rescission if he had the power to rescind, and whether the other party may accept it as a reason for not performing his part; and I think that nothing more is necessary in the present case than to look at the conduct of the parties, and see whether anything of that kind has taken place here. Before doing so, however, I must say one or two words in order to shew why I cannot adopt Mr Cohen's argument, as far as it is represented the payment by the respondents for the iron delivered as in this case a condition precedent, and coming within the rules of law applicable to conditions precedent. If it were so, of course there would be an end of the case; but to me it is plain beyond the possibility of controversy, that upon the proper construction of this contract it is not and cannot be a condition precedent. The contract is for the purchase of 5,000 tons of steel blooms of the company's manufacture; therefore it is one contract for the purchase of that quantity of steel blooms. No doubt there are subsidiary terms in the contract, as to the time of delivery, 'Delivery 1,000 tons monthly commencing January next'; and as to the time of payment, 'Payment nett cash within three days after receipt of shipping documents'; but that does not split up the contract into as many contracts as there shall be deliveries for the purpose, of so many distinct quantities of iron. It is quite consistent with the natural meaning of the contract, that it is to be one contract for the purchase of that quantity of iron, to be delivered at those times and in that manner, and for which payment is so to be made. It is perfectly clear that no particular payment can be a condition precedent of the entire contract, because the delivery under the contract was most certainly to precede payment; and that being so, I do not see how, without express words, it can possibly be made a condition precedent to the subsequent fulfilment of the unfulfilled part of the contract, by the delivery of the undelivered steel.

But, quite consistently with that view, it appears to me, according to the authorities and according to sound reason and principle that the parties might have so conducted themselves as to release each other from the contract, and that one party might have so conducted himself as to leave it at the option of the other party to relieve himself from a future performance of the contract. The question is whether the facts here justify that conclusion? Now the facts relied upon, without reading all the evidence, are these. The company at the time when the money was about to become payable for the steel actually delivered fell into difficulties, and a petition was presented against them. There was a section in the Companies Act 1862 (s. 153), which appeared to the advisers of the purchasers to admit of the construction, that until in those circumstances the petition was disposed of by an order for the company to be wound up or otherwise, there would be no one who could receive, and could give a good discharge for, the amount due. There is not, upon the letters and documents, the slightest ground for supposing either that the purchasers could not pay, or that they were unwilling to pay, the amount due; but they acted as they did, evidently bona fide, because they doubted, on the advice from their solicitor, whether that section of the Act, as long as the petition was pending, did not make it impossible for them to obtain the discharge to which they had an unquestionable right. And therefore the case which I put during the argument is analogous to that which according to the advice they received they supposed to exist, namely, the case of a man who has died between the delivery and the time when payment ought to be made, he being the only person to whom payment is due; and of course until there is a legal personal representative of that person no receipt can be given for the money. By the Act of Parliament, in the event of a winding-up order being made, it would date from the time when the petition was presented; and this clause, which no doubt, according to its true construction, only deals with alienations of the property of the company, was supposed by the solicitor of the purchasers to make it questionable whether the payment of a debt due to the company, to the persons who if there had been no petition would have had a right to receive it, might not be held, in the event of a winding-up order being made, to be a payment of the property of the company to a wrong person and therefore an alienation.

I cannot ascribe to their conduct, under these circumstances, the character of a renunciation of the contract, a repudiation of the contract, a refusal to fulfil the contract. It is just the reverse; the purchasers were desirous of fulfilling the contract; they were advised that there was a difficulty in the way, and they expressed anxiety that the difficulty should be as soon as possible removed, by means which were suggested to them, and which they pointed out to the solicitors of the company. The company evidently took up the attitude, in that state of things, of treating the default as one which released them from all further obligation. On the 10th of February, which was before the winding-up order was made, and while that state of things still continued, the company by their secretary wrote to say that they thought (being so far correct and thinking rightly) that the objection was not well founded in law; and they added 'We shall therefore consider your refusal to pay for the goods already delivered as a breach of contract on your part and as releasing us from any further obligations on our part'. I think that they were wrong in that conclusion; and that there is no principle deducible from any of the authorities which supports that view of such – I hardly like to call it a refusal – of such a demur, such a delay or postponement, under those circumstances.

The company, until they were wound up, never receded from that position which they took up on the 10th of February 1881; and it appears to me to be clear that the liquidator adopted it, and never departed from it; and that the repudiation of the contract on insufficient grounds on the part of the company, which had taken place while the petition was pending and before the winding-up order was made, was adhered to after the winding–up order was made, on the part of the liquidator. On the other hand, it seems to me that, fairly and reasonably considered, the conduct of the respondents was justifiable. Upon the 17th of February 1881, after the making of the winding-up order, they state that there are instalments which ought to have been delivered but which have not been delivered, in respect of which they would have a claim for damages, and they apprehend that they would have a right to deduct those damages from any payments then due from them; and, according to the view which has been taken in the Court of Appeal of the effect of the 10th section of the Act of 1875, and in which view I believe your Lordships agree, that was the right way of looking at the matter. Then the respondents go on to say, that they are prepared to accept all the deliveries that the liquidator may make under the contract and to pay everything due, only requesting that those payments may be considered as made upon this understanding, in substance, that the right to the set-off which exists in law for the damages shall not be prejudiced – a perfectly reasonable, defensible, and justifiable proposal. And the solicitor who writes the letter adds, 'Or I think it probable that my clients would consent to accept delivery now and waive the damages' a thing which in a later letter they express their willingness to do. In my judgment, they have not in any portion of the proceeding acted so as to shew an intention to renouce or to repudiate the contract, or to fail in its performance on their part.

Lords Blackburn, Watson, Bramwell and Fitzgerald concurred.

5.3   Frustration

TAYLOR v *CALDWELL* (1863) 3 B & S 826 (QB)

BLACKBURN J: In this case the plaintiffs and defendants had, on the 27th May, 1861, entered into a contract by which the defendants agreed to let the plaintiffs have the use of The Surrey Gardens and Music Hall on four days then come, viz, the 17th June, 15th July, 5th August and 19th August, for the purpose of giving a series of four grand concerts, and day and night fêtes at the Gardens and Hall on those days respectively; and the plaintiffs agreed to take the Gardens and Hall on those days, and pay 100*l*. for each day.

The parties inaccurately call this a 'letting', and the money to be paid a 'rent'; but the whole agreement is such as to shew that the defendants were to retain the possession of the Hall and Gardens so that there there was to be no demise of them, and that the contract was merely to give the plaintiffs the use of them on those days. Nothing however, in our opinion, depends on this. The agreement then proceeds to set out various stipulations between the parties as to what each was to supply for these concerts and entertainments, and as to the manner in which they should be carried on. The effect of the whole is to shew that the existence of the Music Hall in the Surrey Gardens in a state fit for a concert was essential for the fulfilment of the contract – such entertainments as the parties contemplated in their agreement could not be given without it.

After the making of the agreement, and before the first day on which a concert was to be given, the Hall was destroyed by fire. This destruction, we must take it on the evidence, was without the fault of either party, and was so complete that in consequence the concerts could not be given as intended. And the question we have to decide is whether, under these circumstances, the loss which the plaintiffs have sustained is to fall upon the defendants. The parties when framing their agreement evidently had not present to their minds the possibility of such a disaster, and have made no express stipulation with reference to it, so that the answer to the question must depend upon the general rules of law applicable to such a contract.

There seems no doubt that where there is a positive contract to do a thing, not in itself unlawful, the contractor must perform it or pay damages for not doing it, although in consequence of unforeseen accidents, the performance of his contract has become unexpectedly burthensome or even impossible. The law is so laid down in 1 Roll Abr 450, Condition (G), and in the note to *Walton v Waterhouse* (2 Wms Saund 421 a 6th ed), and is recognised as the general rule by all the judges in the much discussed case of *Hall v Wright* (E B & E 746). But this rule is only applicable when the contract is positive and absolute, and not subject to any condition either express or implied: and there are authorities which, as we think, establish the principle that where, from the nature of the contract, it appears that the parties must from the beginning have known that it could not be fulfilled unless when the time for the fulfilment of the contract arrived some particular specified thing continued to exist, so that, when entering into the contract, they must have contemplated such continuing existence as the foundation of what was to be done; there, in the absence of any express or implied warranty that the thing shall exist, the contract is not to be construed as a positive contract, but as subject to an implied condition that the partries shall be excused in case, before breach, performance becomes impossible from the perishing of the thing without default of the contractor.

There seems little doubt that this implication tends to further the great object of making the legal construction such as to fulfil the intention of those who entered into the contract. For in the course of affairs men in making such contracts in general would, if it were brought to their minds, say that there should be such a condition. . . .

There is a class of contracts in which a person binds himself to do something which requires to be performed by him in person; and such promises, e.g. promises to marry, or promises to serve for a certain time, are never in practice qualified by an express exception of the death of the party; and therefore in such cases the contract is in terms broken if the promisor dies before fulfilment. Yet it was very early determined that, if the performance is personal, the executors are not liable; *Hyde v The Dean of Windsor* (Cro Eliz 552, 553). See 2 Wms Exors 1560, 5th ed, where a very apt illustration is given. 'Thus', says the learned author, 'if an author undertakes to compose a work, and dies before completing it, his executors are discharged from this contract: for the undertaking is merely personal in its nature, and by the intervention of the contractor's death, has become impossible to be performed'. . . .

It seems that in those cases the only ground on which the parties or their executors, can be excused from the consequences of the breach of the contract is, that from the nature of the contract there is an implied condition of the continued existence of the life of the contractor, . . . These are instances where the implied condition is of the life of a human being, but there are others in which the same implication is made as to the continued existence of a thing. For example, where a contract of sale is made amounting to a bargain and sale, transferring presently the property in specific chattels, which are to be delivered by the vendor at a future day; there, if the chattels, without the fault of the vendor, perish in the interval, the purchaser must pay the price and the vendor is excused from performing his contract to deliver, which has thus become impossible.

That this is the rule of the English law is established by the case of *Rugg* v *Minett* (11 East, 210), where the article that perished before delivery was turpentine, and it was decided that the vendor was bound to refund the price of all those lots in which the property had not passed; but was entitled to retain without deduction the price of those lots in which the property had passed, though they were not delivered, and though in the conditions of sale, which are set out in the report, there was no express qualification of the promise to deliver on payment. It seems in that case rather to have been taken for granted than decided that the destruction of the thing sold before delivery excused the vendor from fulfilling his contract to deliver on payment. . . . The principle seems to us to be that, in contracts in which performance depends on the continued existence of a given person or thing, a condition is implied that the impossibility of performance arising from the perishing of the person or thing shall excuse the performance.

In none of these cases is the promise in words other than positive, nor is there any express stipulation that the destruction of the person or thing shall excuse the

performance; but that excuse is by law implied, because from the nature of the contract
it is apparent that the parties contracted on the basis of the continued existence of the
particular person or chattel. In the present case, looking at the whole contract, we find
that the parties contracted on the basis of the continued existence of the Music Hall at
the time when the concerts were to be given; that being essential to their performance.

We think, therefore, that the Music Hall having ceased to exist, without fault of either
party, both parties are excused, the plaintiffs from taking the gardens and paying the
money, the defendants from performing their promise to give the use of the Hall and
Gardens and other things. Consequently the rule must be absolute to enter the verdict
for the defendants.

5.3.1   NON-OCCURRENCE OF EVENT

KRELL v HENRY [1903] 2 KB 740 (CA)

VAUGHAN WILLIAMS LJ: . . . Now what are the facts of the present case? The contract
is contained in two letters of June 20 which passed between the defendants and the
plaintiff's agent, Mr Cecil Bisgood. These letters do not mention the coronation, but speak
merely of the taking of Mr Krell's chambers, or, rather, of the use of them, in the daytime
of June 26 and 27, for the sum of 75l., 25l. then paid, balance 50l. to be paid on the 24th.
But the affidavits, which by agreement between the parties are to be taken as stating the
facts of the case, shew that the plaintiff exhibited on his premises, third floor, 56A, Pall
Mall, an announcement to the effect that windows to view the Royal coronation
procession were to be let, and that the defendant was induced by that announcement to
apply to the housekeeper on the premises, who said that the owner was willing to let
the suite of rooms for the purpose of seeing the Royal procession for both days, but not
nights, of June 26 and 27. In my judgment the use of the rooms was let and taken for the
purpose of seeing the Royal procession. It was not a demise of the rooms, or even an
agreement to let and take the rooms. It is a licence to use rooms for a particular purpose
and none other. And in my judgment the taking place of those processions on the days
proclaimed along the proclaimed route, which passed 56A, Pall Mall, was regarded by
both contracting parties as the foundation of the contract; and I think that it cannot
reasonably be supposed to have been in the contemplation of the contracting parties,
when the contract was made, that the coronation would not be held on the proclaimed
days, or the processions not take place on those days along the proclaimed route; and I
think that the words imposing on the defendant the obligation to accept and pay for the
use of the rooms for the named days, although general and unconditional, were not used
with reference to the possibility of the particular contingency which afterwards occurred.
It was suggested in the course of the argument that if the occurrence, on the proclaimed
days, of the coronation and the procession in this case were the foundation of the
contract, and if the general words are thereby limited or qualified, so that in the event
of the non-occurrence of the coronation and procession along the proclaimed route they
would discharge both parties from further performance of the contract, it would follow
that if a cabman was engaged to take someone to Epsom on Derby Day at a suitable
enhanced price for such a journey, say 10l., both parties to the contract would be
discharged in the contingency of the race at Epsom for some reason becoming impossible; but I do not think this follows, for I do not think that in the cab case the happening
of the race would be the foundation of the contract. No doubt the purpose of the engager
would be to go to see the Derby, and the price would be proportionately high; but the
cab had no special qualifications for the purpose which led to the selection of the cab for
this particular occasion. Any other cab would have done as well. Moreover, I think that,
under the cab contract, the hirer, even if the race went off, could have said, 'Drive me to
Epsom; I will pay you the agreed sum; you have nothing to do with the purpose for
which I hired the cab', and that if the cabman refused he would have been guilty of a
breach of contract, there being nothing to qualify his promise to drive the hirer to Epsom
on a particular day. Whereas in the case of the coronation, there is not merely the
purpose of the hirer to see the coronation procession, but it is the coronation procession
and the relative position of the rooms which is the basis of the contract as much for the

lessor as the hirer; and I think that if the King, before the coronation day and after the contract, had died, the hirer could not have insisted on having the rooms on the days named. It could not in the cab case be reasonably said that seeing the Derby race was the foundation of the contract, as it was of the licence in this case. Whereas in the present case, where the rooms were offered and taken, by reason of their peculiar suitability from the position of the rooms for a view of the coronation procession, surely the view of the coronation procession was the foundation of the contract, which is a very different thing from the purpose of the man who engaged the cab – namely, to see the race – being held to be the foundation of the contract. Each case must be judged by its own circumstances. In each case one must ask oneself, first, what, having regard to all the circumstances, was the foundation of the contract? Secondly, was the performance of the contract prevented? Thirdly, was the event which prevented the performance of the contract of such a character that it cannot reasonably be said to have been in the contemplation of the parties at the date of the contract? If all those questions are answered in the affirmative (as I think they should be in this case), I think both parties are discharged from futher performance of the contract. I think that the coronation procession was the foundation of this contract, and that the non-happening of it prevented the performance of the contract; and, secondly, I think that the non-happening of the procession, to use the words of Sir James Hannen in *Baily v De Crespigny* (1869) LR 4 QB 180, was an event 'of such a character that it cannot reasonably be supposed to have been in the contemplation of the contractig parties when the contract was made, and that they are not to be held bound by general words which, though large enough to include, were not used with reference to the possibility of the particular contingency which afterwards happened'. The test seems to be whether the event which causes the impossibility was or might have been anticipated and guarded against. It seems difficult to say, in a case where both parties anticipate the happening of an event, which anticipation is the foundation of the contract, that either party must be taken to have anticipated, and ought to have guarded against, the event which prevented the performance of the contract. . . . I myself am clearly of opinion that in this case, where we have to ask ourselves whether the object of the contract was frustrated by the non-happening of the coronation and its procession on the days proclaimed, parol evidence is admissible to shew that the subject of the contract was rooms to view the coronation procession, and was so to the knowledge of both parties. When once this is established, I see no difficulty whatever in the case. It is not essential to the application of the principle of *Taylor v Caldwell* (1863) 3 B & S 826 that the direct subject of the contract should perish or fail to be in existence at the date of performance of the contract. It is sufficient if a state of things or condition expressed in the contract and essential to its performance perishes or fails to be in existence at that time. In the present case the condition which fails and prevents the achievement of that which was, in the contemplation of both parties, the foundation of the contract, is not expressly mentioned either as a condition of the contract or the purpose of it; but I think for the reasons which I have given that the principle of *Taylor v Caldwell* ought to be applied. This disposes of the plaintiff's claim for 50*l.* unpaid balance of the price agreed to be paid for the use of the rooms. The defendant at one time set up a cross-claim for the return of the 25*l.* he paid at the date of the contract. As that claim is now withdrawn it is unnecessary to say anything about it. I have only to add that the facts of this case do not bring it within the principle laid down in *Stubbs v Holywell Ry. Co.* (1867) LR 2 Exch 311; that in the case of contracts falling directly within the rule of *Taylor v Caldwell* the subsequent impossibility does not affect rights already acquired, because the defendant had the whole of June 24 to pay the balance, and the public announcement that the coronation and processions would not take place on the proclaimed days made early in the morning of the 24th, and no cause of action could accrue till the end of that day. I think this appeal ought to be dismissed.

Romer and Stirling LJJ concurred.

HERNE BAY STEAM BOAT COMPANY v HUTTON [1903] 2 KB 683 (CA)

A boat had been hired to take passengers to see the coronation naval review by Edward VII at Spithead, and to tour the fleet. The review was cancelled, owing to the King's illness.

VAUGHAN WILLIAMS LJ: In my opinion this appeal must be allowed.

I wish first to call attention to this, that what the plaintiffs originally claimed in this action was the sum of *200l.*, being the balance of the price of *250l.* which was agreed to be paid. That actual sum, in my judgment, the plaintiffs are not entitled to recover: I do not think Mr Lush could have borne in mind that that was the original claim, and, therefore, he regarded some of the observations of Grantham J, dealing with the original claim, as if they were applicable to the subsequent claim. In my judgment there was, in this case, before the time came for the performance of the contract, a plain repudiation by the defendant of his obligations under it; and this is in fact admitted. He refused to carry out the contract on his part, and the plaintiffs, acting very properly in the circumstances, employed the steamer on her usual daily services, and made what profit they could out of her during the two days they intended by the contract that the defendant should have the use of the vessel. Under these circumstances the plaintiffs' claim is really for damages for the defendant's refusal to carry out the contract, and it is agreed that these damages are not *200l.*, but that sum less the profit made by the plaintiffs from having the use of the ship after the repudiation of the contract by the defendant. These damages, I think, the plaintiffs are entitled to recover. In my opinion, this contract really placed the vessel at the disposal of the defendant for these particular days. . . .

According to my understanding of this contract, this ship was placed at the disposal of Mr Hutton really for those two days. Mr Hansell says this does not constitute a demise of the ship, and with that I agree. It is very rarely that a charterparty does contain a demise of a ship. Generally speaking, the ship is not demised at all, but remains under the management and control of her owner. But at the same time this contract does, in my opinion, place the ship at the disposal of Mr Hutton, just as a charterparty places the vessel, the subject of it, at the disposal of the charterers.

That being so, what is there besides in the present case? Only this, that Mr Hutton, in hiring this vessel, had two objects in view: first, of taking people to see the naval review, and secondly, of taking them round the fleet. Those, no doubt, were the purposes of Mr Hutton, but it does not seem to me that because, as it is said, those purposes became impossible, it would be a very legitimate inference that the happening of the naval review was contemplated by both parties as the basis and foundation of this contract, so as to bring the case within the doctrine of *Taylor v Caldwell* (1863) 3 B & S 826. On the contrary, when the contract is properly regarded, I think the purpose of Mr Hutton, whether of seeing the naval review or of going round the fleet with a party of paying guests, does not lay the foundation of the contract within the authorities.

Having expressed that view, I do not know that there is any advantage to be gained by going on in any way to define what are circumstances which might or might not constitute the happening of a particular contingency as the foundation of a contract. I will content myself with saying this, that I see nothing that makes this contract differ from a case where, for instance, a person has engaged a brake to take himself and a party to Epsom to see the races there, but for some reason or other, such as the spread of an infectious disease, the races are postponed. In such a case it could not be said that he could be relieved of his bargain. So in the present case it is sufficient to say that the happening of the naval review was not the foundation of the contract.

Romer and Stirling LJJ concurred.

AMALGAMATED INVESTMENT & PROPERTY CO. LTD v JOHN WALKER & SONS LTD [1976] 3 All ER 509 (CA)

A property sold for £1,710,000 was then listed as a building of 'architectural or historic' interest. This limited the possibility of development, and reduced the value by £1,500,000.

BUCKLEY LJ: . . . I now turn to the alternative argument which has been presented to us in support of this appeal, which is on frustration. Counsel for the plaintiffs has relied on what was said in the speeches in the House of Lords in *Davis Contractors Ltd v Fareham Urban District Council* [1956] 2 All ER 145, and it may perhaps be useful if I refer to what was said by Lord Radcliffe:

So, perhaps, it would be simpler to say at the outset that frustration occurs whenever the law recognises that, without default of either party, a contractual obligation has become incapable of being performed because the circumstances in which performance is called for would render it a thing radically different from that which was undertaken by the contract.

That is a passage which was referred to by Plowman V-C in the course of his judgment. Then, a little later on, after referring to *Denny, Mott and Dickson Ltd* v *James B Fraser & Co. Ltd* [1944] 1 All ER 678, Lord Radcliffe said:

It is for that reason that special importance is necessarily attached to the occurrence of any unexpected event that, as it were, changes the face of things. But, even so, it is not hardship or inconvenience or material loss itself which calls the principle of frustration into play. There must be as well such a change in the significance of the obligation that the thing undertaken would, if performed, be a different thing from that contracted for.

Now, the obligation undertaken to be performed in this case by the defendants was to sell this property for the contract price and, of course, to show a good title and so forth. The defendants did not warrant in any way that planning permission could be obtained for the development of the property. No doubt both parties considered that the property was property which could advantageously be developed and was property for which planning permission would probably be satisfactorily obtained. But there was no stipulation in the contract relating to anything of that kind; nor, as I say, was there any warranty on the part of the defendants. I am prepared to assume for the purposes of this judgment that the law relating to frustration of contracts is capable of being applied in the case of a contract for sale of land, though that is not one of the matters which has been debated before us. But, making that assumption I have reached the conclusion that there are not here the necessary factual bases for holding that this contract has been frustrated. It seems to me that the risk of property being listed as property of architectural or historical interest is a risk which inheres in all ownership of buildings. In many cases it may be an extremely remote risk. In many cases it may be a marginal risk. In some cases it may be a substantial risk. But it is a risk, I think, which attaches to all buildings and it is a risk that every owner and every purchaser of property must recognise that he is subject to. The purchasers in the present case bought knowing that they would have to obtain planning permission in order to develop the property. The effect of listing under the sections of the 1971 Act to which I have referred makes the obtaining of planning permission, it may be, more difficult, and it may also make it a longer and more complicated process. But still, in essence, the position is that the would-be developer has to obtain the appropriate planning permissions, one form of permission being the 'listed building permission'. The plaintiffs, when they entered into the contract, must obviously be taken to have known that they would need to get planning permission. They must also, in my judgment, be taken to have known that there was the risk, although they may not have regarded it as a substantial risk, that the building might at some time be listed, and that their chances of obtaining planning permission might possibly be adversely affected to some extent by that, or at any rate their chances of obtaining speedy planning permission. But, in my judgment, this is a risk of a kind which every purchaser should be regarded as knowing that he is subject to when he enters into his contract of purchase. It is a risk which I think the purchaser must carry, and any loss that may result from the maturing of that risk is a loss which must lie where it falls. Moreover, the plaintiff's have not yet established that they will be unable to obtain all the necessary planning permissions, including 'listed building permission'. So it has not yet, I think, been established that the listing of this building has had the drastic effect which the figures I have mentioned suggest that it may have had. It may well turn out to be the case that 'listed building permission' will be obtainable here and the purchasers will be able to carry into effect the development which they desire.

For these reasons I reach the conclusion, as I say, that the necessary facts have not been established in this case to found a claim that the contract has been frustrated.

For these reasons, I would dismiss this appeal.

Lawton LJ and Sir John Pennycuick concurred.

5.3.1.1   Answer to Activity 21

Krell v *Henry* is clearly a very unusual and exceptional case and would require exceptional circumstances for it to be followed in subsequent cases. Nevertheless, the distinction drawn between *Krell and Herne Bay* by Vaughan Williams LJ is probably justifiable.

The contract in *Krell* was not merely for the hire of a room in Pall Mall, it was for the provision of a view of a particular procession. The provision of the view was at the foundation of the contract as far as *both* parties were concerned. This was evidenced by the fact that the owner of the flat as a private individual who did not regularly hire out his flat (i.e. it was a 'one-off' transaction), and by the fact that the flat was available only during the day (night-time occupation was expressly excluded).

In *Herne Bay* the naval review and inspection by Edward VII were regarded as vital by *one* of the parties only, i.e. the hirer of the boat. The owner of the boat was in the business of hiring out boats and presumably would have hired out his boat on the days in question to anyone prepared to pay the asking price, for whatever legitimate purposes they may have required it. In other words, it was a contract for the hire of a boat only.

5.3.2   ILLNESS

CONDOR v *BARRON KNIGHTS LTD* [1966] 1 WLR 87 (QB)

THOMPSON J: . . . The plaintiff, Edward Lottian Condor, an infant, who was born on March 29, 1946, was a talented drummer. In 1962, when he was aged 16, he began to work for the defendant, Barron Knights Ltd, a company controlling the Barron Knights group of performers. . . . The engagement as a drummer with the Barron Knights necessitated the plaintiff leaving his home at Darlington, where he lived with his mother, and going to Leighton Buzzard, the headquarters of the group. The group was engaged in 'one-night stands', performing in one place one night, travelling later in a bus to the next place where they were to perform, with one member of the group taking his turn at driving and the others taking the chance to sleep when they could, and performing the following night, and, in the meantime, getting in as much rehearsal as they could. The plaintiff was required to be more than a mere instrumentalist, for the group was not merely a band but did comic performances and acting, and the drummer was a key figure in the timing of the various acting performances. By December 8, 1962, when the contract of employment was entered into, the members of the group and the defendants knew what the plaintiff was capable of and how good he was and the plaintiff knew what the life with the group was like.

During the severe weather of December, 1962, to January, 1963, the plaintiff lived on his own in a caravan. He was not having proper food and had been working in that strenuous way when, on January 16, 1963, when the group was performing at a ballroom in Hitchin, although not in the actual course of a performance, he collapsed and was taken by a member of the group to a local hospital. From there he was taken to the Three Counties or Fairfield General Hospital, a mental hospital, where he was detained for three days. While he was in that hospital the manager of the group, Tony Avern went to see him, and before seeing him was told by the doctor treating him, in effect, that it was inhuman that a young lad of 16, living away from his home, should have been employed on the basis of seven nights a week in that way, with sometimes a double engagement in a night, and that he needed a rest and, after that, when he returned to work, he should not be employed for more than three or four nights a week; otherwise he would be liable to have another, and worse, breakdown. In his records the doctor entered that the plaintiff might well develop schizophrenic symptoms if under strain again.

The group was a co-operative group in that the decisions were taken by each member expressing at a meeting, either formally or informally held, his views as to what course they should take. After Tony Avern had seen the doctor and the plaintiff, the group met to discuss the plaintiff's case. Tony Avern himself informed them of what the doctor had said and the terms on which the plaintiff could sensibly and fairly be re-employed; being satisfied that he was a first-class drummer, the group regarded it as something of a calamity, but the issue before them was whether they were prepared to accept that he was fit to be employed on the basis of seven days a week, as the plaintiff had expressly or impliedly professed, or for three or four nights a week, with deputies filling in for him the engagements on the other nights. The group concluded that the latter course would not be possible. . . . First, there was the difficulty of having someone on tap on the nights when the plaintiff would not be working for them and there would be the problem of getting engagements with not one drummer with a built-up reputation to offer but one or other of two or more drummers. There would be in their rehearsing the increased difficulty that there would be in their performance of their synchronised act the problem of someone who was imported as a substitute getting to know how they did their business and when he came in or when he instructed them to come in with such business as they did.

The group did not, and I think reasonably did not, regard that variation of the contractual position as being reasonable or sensible. That it would have been a variation is not denied or controverted by Mr Rich, who accepts that the engagement of the plaintiff, both by the express words of the agreement and by the clear basis on which he and the defendants knew that the group was working, was an availability by the plaintiff to perform on seven nights a week if there were engagements on seven nights a week and more than once on such of them as they were offered and were able to accept double engagements. Therefore, in my judgment, it was quite a reasonable and proper conclusion for the group to take that it was not from their point of view a business proposition to employ the plaintiff on the only basis on which the doctor had said he might reasonably and safely be employed.

That brings one accordingly to the question whether at that date the plaintiff was capable of and available to work as the contract contemplated, that is to say, not merely to play drums, but to play drums on seven nights a week, if need be travelling from one one-night stand to another. The plaintiff thought he was and the plaintiff said that at a later date in the year he did, but I am satisfied that at the time when the defendants had to consider the situation, not merely was it a reasonable view for them to take that he was not then fit, but that he was not in fact fit, that is to say, fit to work, as the contract contemplated, seven days a week. In my judgment for this purpose fitness involves not merely being able to do the work, though with the virtual certainty that at the end of a week or a very short period such as a month there will be a breakdown of a worse kind, but it does involve the ability to do it without the likelihood of such damage to health and so as, within the contract, to continue with the continuity which the contract contemplated. I am satisfied that at the date when Tony Avern saw him, which was February 1, and said what I accept Tony Avern said, because I do not accept what the plaintiff told me he had said (namely, that the plaintiff had become too expensive), in my judgment on February 1, 1963, the situation was that the plaintiff was not fit to perform his part of the contract and at that date there was no reasonable likelihood that he would in the near future become so able.

Accordingly in my judgment, by reason of the impact upon his health and well-being of this life, far too strenuous and exhausting for a boy of 16, talented though he was and ambitious though he was, the impact was such in my judgment that that had in a business sense made it impossible for him to perform or for the defendants have him perform the terms of the contract as a member of their group. It follows that in my judgment there was no wrongful dismissal in this case and the defence so far as that is concerned prevails.

5.3.3 FRUSTRATION OF THE COMMON ADVENTURE

FA TAMPLIN STEAMSHIP CO. LTD v ANGLO–MEXICAN PETROLEUM PRODUCTS CO. LTD [1916] 2 AC 397 (HL)

A five-year charter of a ship was interrupted by government requisition. Was the interruption sufficient to frustrate the contract?

LORD PARKER: My Lords, the contract in the present case is contained in the charterparty of May 18, 1912, whereby the owners of the steamship *F. A. Tamplin* agreed to provide her with a full complement of officers, seamen, engineers, and firemen, and hold her at the disposition of the charterers for the voyages and other purposes therein mentioned for a period of sixty calendar months from December 4, 1912, subject, nevertheless, to the conditions therein specified. The charterers were to pay the owners monthly in advance for the first twelve calendar months 1750*l.*, and thereafter 1700*l.* per month by way of freight. By the 17th condition the freight was suspended in the event of loss of time, by reason of deficiency in men or stores, or any defect or breakdown of machinery or damage or accident preventing the working of the vessel for more than twenty-four consecutive hours. By the19th condition the payment of freight was to cease altogether in the event of the vessel being lost. By the 20th condition the act of God, perils of the sea, fire, barratry of the master crew, enemies, pirates, and thieves, arrests or restraints of princes, rulers, or peoples, and stranding and other accidents of navigation were excepted even when occasioned by negligence, default, or error of the pilot, master, mariners, or other servants of the owners.

As I read this contract, the parties are not contemplating the prosecution of any commercial adventure in which both are interested. They are not contemplating the performance of any definite adventure at all. The owners are not concerned in the charterers doing any specific thing beyond the payment of freight as it becomes due. They are only concerned that the charterers shall pay the freight and shall not use the ship contrary to the provisions of the charterparty. It would be to the interest of the owners that the charterers should not make any use of the ship at all. They would thus save the cost of repairs due to wear and tear. On the other hand, the charterers only stipulate that the vessel shall be at their disposal for certain defined purposes. If they so desire, they retain full liberty not to use the vessel for any purpose whatever. Further, the contract contemplates that, though the charterers desire to use the vessel, it may for intermittent periods of indefinite duration be impossible for them so to do. In such cases there are express provisions differing according to the particular circumstances from which such impossibility arises. In cases within condition 17 there is a suspension of freight only. In cases within condition 20, and not within condition 17, the payment of freight continues, and the owners incur no liability. Thus, if the ship cannot put to sea because of deficiency of seamen, freight will be suspended. If, however, the vessel cannot put to sea because of an embargo, the freight continues to be payable, nor are the owners liable in damages. It makes no difference at what period during the term of the charter the deficiency of seamen or embargo occurs. Whether it occurs within the first or last six months of the term the result is to be the same.

My Lords, I entertain no doubt that the requisitioning of the steamship by His Majesty's Government in the present case is a 'restraint of princes' within the 20th condition. The parties therefore have expressly contracted that for the period during which by reason of such restraint the owners are unable to keep the ship at the disposition of the charterers the freight is to continue payable, and the owners are to be free from liability. This period may be long or short. It may be certain or indefinite. It may occur towards the beginning or towards the end of the term of the charterparty. The result is to be the same, unless indeed the circumstances are such that the ship can be said to be lost within the meaning of condition 19. Moreover (and this seems to me the vital point), the charterparty does not contemplate any definite adventure or object to be performed or carried out within reasonable limits of time so as to justify a distinction being drawn between delays which may render such adventure or object impossible and delays which may not.

Under these circumstances it appears to me to be difficult, if not impossible, to frame any condition by virtue of which the contract of the parties is at an end without contradicting the express provisions of the contract and defeating the intention of the parties as disclosed by those provisions. The nearest I can get is a proviso to the 20th condition conceived as follows: 'Provided that if the period during which the ship cannot be held at the disposition of the charterers by reason of any of the matters referred to in this condition, though indefinite, be such as will in all reasonable probability extend beyond the term of the charterparty, the contract between the parties shall be determined'. But, in my opinion, even this would contradict the express terms of the contract.

It could, for example, except from its provisions cases in which the ship ran aground so near the end of the term of the charterparty that it would be impossible to get her off or ready to put to sea once more within such term. This would, in my opinion, be contrary to the provisions of condition 20. Further, even if it were permissible to imply such a proviso to the 20th condition, there is, in my opinion, no reason for holding that the Government will, in all reasonable probability, retain the vessel for the remainder of the term of the charterparty. Whether they will do so or not seems to me to depend on all sorts of circumstances as to which a Court of justice cannot speculate. They may do so or they may not. I do not think that one event is more likely than the other.

My Lords, having regard to the difficulty of framing any condition which can be implied without contradicting the express terms of the contract, having regard to the nature of the contract, which is a time charter only and does not contemplate any commercial adventure in which both parties are interested, or indeed any definite commercial adventure at all, and finally, having regard to the fact that the condition which is sought to be implied is a condition defeating a contract already part performed and not a condition precedent to a contract which remains purely executory, I have come to the conclusion that the decision of the Court of Appeal was right and ought not to be disturbed.

JACKSON v *UNION MARINE INSURANCE CO. LTD* (1874) LR 10 CP 125
(Exchequer Chamber)

A ship chartered to load a cargo for the US at Newport ran aground en route from Liverpool. This caused damage requiring six months of repairs.

BRAMWELL B: . . . The question turns on the construction and effect of the charter. By it the vessel is to sail to Newport with all possible dispatch, perils of the seas excepted. It is said this constitutes the only agreement as to time, and, provided all possible dispatch is used, it matters not when she arrives at Newport. I am of a different opinion. If this charterparty be read as a charter for a definite voyage or adventure, then it follows that there is *necessarily* an implied condition that the ship shall arrive at Newport in time for it. Thus, if a ship was chartered to go from Newport to St. Michael's in terms in time for the fruit season, and take coals out and bring fruit home, it would follow, notwithstanding the opinion expressed in *Touteng* v *Hubbard* 3 B & P 291, on which I will remark afterwards, that, if she did not get to Newport in time to get to St. Michael's for the fruit season, the charter would not be bound to load at Newport, though she had used all possible dispatch to get there, and though there was an exception of perils of the seas.

The two stipulations, to use all possible dispatch, and to arrive in time for the voyage, are not repugnant; nor is either superfluous or useless. The shipowner, in the case put, expressly agrees to use all possible dispatch: that is not a condition precedent; the sole remedy for and right consequent on the breach of it is an action. He also impliedly agrees that the ship shall arrive in time for the voyage: that *is* a condition precedent as well as an agreement; and its non-performance not only gives the charterer a cause of action, but also releases him. Of course, if these stipulations, owing to excepted perils, are not performed, there is no cause of action, but there is the same release of the charterer. The same reasoning would apply if the terms were, to 'use all possible dispatch, and further, and as a condition precedent, to be ready at the port of loading on June 1st'. That reasoning also applies to the present case. If the charter be read, as for a voyage or adventure not precisely defined by time or otherwise, but still for a particular voyage, arrival at Newport in time for it is necessarily a condition precedent. It seems to me it must be so read. I should say reason and good sense require it. The difficulty is supposed to be that there is some rule of law to the contrary. This I cannot see; and it seems to me that, in this case, the shipowner undertook to use all possible dispatch to arrive at the port of loading, and also agreed that the ship should arrive there 'at such a time that in a commercial sense the commercial speculation entered into by the shipowner and charterers should not be at an end, but in existence'. That latter agreement is also a condition precedent. Not arriving at such a time puts an end to the contract; though, as it arises from an excepted peril, it gives no cause of action.

The same result is arrived at by what is the same argument differently put. Where no time is named for the doing of anything, the law attaches a reasonable time. Now, let us suppose this charterparty had said nothing about arriving with all possible dispatch. In that case, had the ship not arrived at Newport in a reasonable time, owing to the default of the shipowner, the charterers would have had a right of action against the owner, and would have had a right to withdraw from the contract. It is impossible to hold that, in that case, the owner would have a right to say, 'I came a year after the time I might have come, because meanwhile I have been profitably employing my ship: you must load me, and bring your action for damages'. The charterers would be discharged, because the implied condition to arrive in a reasonable time was not performed. Now, let us suppose the charter contains, as here, that the ship shall arrive with all possible dispatch, – I ask again, is that so inconsistent with or repugnant to a further condition that at all events she shall arrive within a reasonable time? or is that so needless a condition that it is not to be implied? I say certainly not. I must repeat the foregoing reasoning. Let us suppose them both expressed, and it will be seen they are not inconsistent nor needless. Thus, I will use all possible dispatch to get the ship to Newport, but at all events she shall arrive in a reasonable time for the adventure contemplated. I hold, therefore, that the implied condition of a reasonable time exists in this charter. Now, what is the effect of the exception of perils of the seas, and of delay being caused thereby? Suppose it was not there, and not implied, the shipowner would be subject to an action for not arriving in a reasonable time, and the charterers would be discharged. Mr Benjamin says the exception would be implied. How that is, it is not necessary to discuss, as the words are there: but, if it is so, it is remarkable as shewing what must be implied from the necessity of the case.

The words are there. What is their effect? I think this: they excuse the shipowner, but give him no right. The charterer has no cause of action, but is released from the charter. When I say *he* is, I think *both* are. The condition precedent has not been performed, but by default of neither. It is as though the charter were conditional on peace being made between countries A and B, and it was not; or as though the charterer agreed to load a cargo of coals, strike of pitmen excepted. If a strike of probably long duration began, he would be excused from putting the coals on board, and would have no right to call on the shipowner to wait till the strike was over. The shipowner would be excused from keeping his ship waiting, and have no right to call on the charter to load at a future time. This seems in accordance with general principles. The exception is an excuse for him who is to do the act, and operates to save him from an action and make his non-performance not a breach of contract, but does not operate to take away the right the other party would have had, if the non-performance had been a breach of contract, to retire from the engagement: and, if one party may, so may the other. Thus, A enters the service of B, and is ill and cannot perform his work. No action will lie against him; but B may hire a fresh servant, and not wait his recovery, if his illness would put an end, in a business sense, to their business engagement, and would frustrate the object of that engagement: a short illness would not suffice, if consistent with the object they had in view. So, if A engages B to make a drawing, say, of some present event, for an illustrated paper, and B is attacked with blindness which will disable him for six months, it canot be doubted that, though A could maintain no action against B, he might procure someone else to make the drawing. So, of an engagement to write a book, and insanity of the intended author. So, of the case I have put, of an exception of a strike of pitmen.

There is, then, a condition precedent that the vessel shall arrive in a reasonable time. On failure of this, the contract is at an end and the charterers discharged, though they have no cause of action, as the failure arose from an excepted peril. The same result follows, then, whether the implied condition is treated as one that the vessel shall arrive in time for that adventure, or one that it shall arrive in a reasonable time, that time being, in time for the adventure cotemplated. And in either case, as in the express cases supposed, and in the analogous cases put, non-arrival and incapacity by that time ends the contract; the principle being that, though non-performance of a condition may be excused, it does not take away the right to rescind from him for whose benefit the condition was introduced.

On these grounds, I think that, in reason, in principle, and for the convenience of both parties, it ought to be held in this case that the charterers were, on the finding of the jury, discharged.

Blackburn, Mellor and Lush JJ concurred; Cleasby B dissented.

5.3.4   INCREASE IN DIFFICULTY OR EXPENSE INSUFFICIENT

TSAKIROGLOU & CO. LTD v *NOBLEE & THORL GMBH* [1962] AC 93 (HL)

A contract to ship ground nuts from the Sudan to Hamburg was affected by the closure of the Suez Canal.

VISCOUNT SIMONDS: . . . It is put in the forefront of the appellants' case that the contract was a contract for the shipment of goods via Suez. This contention can only prevail if a term is implied, for the contract does not say so. To say that that is nevertheless its meaning is to say in other words that the term must be implied. For this I see no ground. It has been rejected by the learned trial judge and each of the members of the Court of Appeal; and in two other cases, *Carapanayoti & Co. Ltd* v *E. T. Green Ltd* [1959] 1 QB 131 and *Gaon (Albert D.) & Co.* v *Société Interprofessionelle des Oléagineux Fluides Alimentaires* [1959] 2 All ER 693, where the same question arose, it was rejected by McNair J and Ashworth J respectively. A variant of this contention was that there should be read into the contract by implication the words 'by the usual and customary route' and that, as the only usual and customary route at the date of the contract was via Suez, the contractual obligation was to carry the goods via Suez. Though this contention has been viewed somewhat differently. I see as little ground for the implication. In this I agree with Harman LJ, for it seems to me that there are precisely the same grounds for rejecting the one as the other. Both of them assume that sellers and buyers alike intended and would have agreed that, if the route via Suez became impossible, the goods should not be shipped at all. Inasmuch as the buyers presumably wanted the goods and might well have resold them, the assumption appears wholly unjustified. Freight charges may go up or down. If the parties do not specifically protect themselves against change, the loss must lie where it falls.

For the general proposition that in a c.i.f. contract the obligation, in the absence of express terms, is to follow the usual or customary route there is a significant absence of authority. Some reliance was placed on *In re L. Sutro & Co. and Heilbut, Symons & Co.* [1917] 2 KB 348. But the facts and the question arising upon them were widely different from those in the present case. The decision was that since the contract clearly contemplated carriage by sea from the loading port to the ultimate port of discharge it could not be performed by carriage partly by sea and partly by rail, though the arbitrators had found that that method of transport had become a usage in the trade. It is possible that, if the decision was reviewed in this House, it might not stand: it is unnecessary now to determine that question. For as I have said, the decisive fact there was that the actual route was different in kind from the contractual route. Apart from this authority the appellants relied on a passage in Kennedy on C.I.F. Contracts, 1st ed, p.39: 'In the absence of express terms in the contract the customary or usual route must be followed'. I cannot accept this general proposition without some qualification. In particular, since it is, in any case, clear that it is not the date of the contract but the time of performance that determines what is customary, the proposition must be qualified by adding to it some such words as 'unless at the time of performance there is no customary or usual route'. If those words are implied, the question arises: 'What then?'. The answer must depend on the circumstances of each case. This leads me directly to section 32(2) of the Sale of Goods Act 1893, which provides that 'Unless otherwise authorised by the buyer, the seller must make such contract with the carrier on behalf of the buyer as may be reasonable having regard to the nature of the goods and the other circumstances of the case'. If there is no customary route, that route must be chosen which is reasonable. If there is only one route, that must be taken if it is practicable: see *Evans, Sons & Co.* v *Cunard Steamship Co. Ltd* (1902) 18 TLR 374, *per* Wills J.

I turn now to what was the main argument for the appellants: that the contract was frustrated by the closure of the Canal from November 2, 1956, till April 1957. Were it not for the decision of McNair J in *Green's* case I should not have thought this contention arguable and I must say with the greatest respect to that learned judge that I cannot think he has given full weight to the decisions old and new of this House upon the doctrine of frustration. He correctly held upon the authority of *Reardon Smith Line Ltd* v *Black Sea and Baltic General Insurance Co. Ltd* [1939] 3 All ER 444 that 'where a contract, expressly or by necessary implication, provides that performance, or a particular part of the performance, is to be carried out in a customary manner, the performance must be carried out in a manner which is customary at the time when the performance is called for'. But he concluded that the continued availability of the Suez route was a fundamental assumption at the time when the contract was made and that to impose upon the sellers the obligation to ship by an emergency route via the Cape would be to impose upon them a fundamentally different obligation which neither party could at the time when the contract was performed have dreamed that the sellers would be required to perform. Your Lordships will observe how similar this line of argument is to that which supports the implication of a term that the route should be via Suez and no other. I can see no justification for it. We are concerned with a c.i.f. contract for the sale of goods, not a contract of affreightment, though part of the sellers' obligation will be to procure a contract of affreightment. There is no evidence that the buyers attached any importance to the route. They were content that the nuts should be shipped at any date in November or December. There was no evidence, and I suppose could not be, that the nuts would deteriorate as the result of a longer voyage and a double crossing of the Equator, nor any evidence that the market was seasonable. In a word, there was no evidence that the buyers cared by what route or, within reasonable limits, when the nuts arrived. What, then, of the sellers? I recall the well-known passage in the speech of Lord Atkinson in *Johnson* v *Taylor Bros. & Co. Ltd* [1902] AC 144 where he states the obligations of the vendor of goods under a c.i.f. contract, and ask which of these obligations is (to use McNair J's word) 'fundamentally' altered by a change of route. Clearly the contract of affreightment will be different and so may be the terms of insurance. In both these respects the sellers may be put to greater cost: their profit may be reduced or even disappear. But it hardly needs reasserting that an increase of expense is not a ground of frustration: see *Larrinaga & Co. Ltd* v *Société Franco-Américaine des Phosphates de Médulla, Paris* (1922) 38 TLR 739.

Nothing else remains to justify the view that the nature of the contract was 'fundamentally' altered. That is the word used by Viscount Simon in *British Movietonews Ltd* v *London and District Cinemas Ltd* [1951] 2 All ER 617 and by my noble and learned friend Lord Reid in *Davis Contractors Ltd* v *Fareham Urban District Council* [1956] 2 All ER 145. In the latter case my noble and learned friend Lord Radcliffe used the expression 'radically different' and I think that the two expressions mean the same thing, as perhaps do other adverbs which have been used in this context. Whatever expression is used, I venture to say what I have said myself before and others more authoritatively have said before me: that the doctrine of frustration must be applied within very narrow limits. In my opinion this case falls far short of satisfying the necessary conditions. Reluctant as I am to differ from a judge so experienced in commercial law as McNair J, I am glad to find that my view is shared by Ashworth J and all the members of the Court of Appeal.

Lords Reid, Radcliffe, Hodson and Guest concurred.

5.3.5   SELF-INDUCED FRUSTRATION

MARITIME NATIONAL FISH LTD v *OCEAN TRAWLERS LTD* **[1935] AC 524 (PC)**

LORD WRIGHT: The appellants were charterers of a steam trawler the *St. Cuthbert* which was the property of the respondents. The charterparty, dated October 25, 1928, had originally been entered into between the respondents and the National Fish Company Ltd, but was later by agreement taken over by the appellants. It was for twelve calendar months, but was to continue from year to year unless terminated by three months' notice from either party, the notice to take effect at the end of one of the years. It was expressly agreed that the trawler should be employed in the fishing industry only; the amount of monthly hire was to be fixed on a basis to include a percentage of the purchase price, and also operating expenses. There was an option given to the charterers to purchase the trawler. . . .

The appellants, in addition to the *St. Cuthbert*, also operated four other trawlers, all fitted with otter trawling gear.

On March 11, 1933, the appellants applied to the Minister of Fisheries for licences for the trawlers they were operating, and in so doing complied with all the requirements of the Regulations, but on April 5, 1933, the Acting Minister replied that it had been decided (as had shortly before been announced in the House of Commons) that licences were only to be granted to three of the five trawlers operated by the appellants: he accordingly requested the appellants to advise the Department for which three of the five trawlers they desired to have licences. The appellants thereupon gave the names of three trawlers other than the *St. Cuthbert,* and for these three trawlers licences were issued, but no licence was granted for the *St. Cuthbert.* In consequence, as from April 30, 1933, it was no longer lawful for the appellants to employ the *St. Cuthbert* as a trawler in their business. On May, 1 1933, the appellants gave notice that the *St. Cuthbert* was available for re-delivery to the respondents; they claimed that they were no longer bound by the charter. . . .

The main defence was that through no fault, act or omission on the part of the appellants, the charterparty contract became impossible of performance on and after April 30, 1933, and thereupon the appellants were wholly relieved and discharged from the contract, including all obligations to pay the monthly hire which was stipulated.

The defence succeeded before the trial judge, Doull J. His opinion was that there had been a change in the law, including the Regulations, which completely changed the basis on which the parties were contracting. He thought it 'not unreasonable to imply a condition to the effect that if the law prohibits the operation of this boat as a trawler the obligation to pay hire will cease'. He also thought the appellants were not bound to lay up another boat instead of the *St. Cuthbert.*

It seems that the learned judge proceeeded on the footing that the change of law was subsequent to the making of the contract, whereas it was in fact anterior to the agreement of 1932, under which the trawler was being employed at the time the licence was refused.

This judgment was unanimously reversed by the judges in the Supreme Court En Banco. The judges of that court rightly pointed out that the discharge of a contract by reason of the frustration of the contemplated adventure follows automatically when the relevant event happens and does not depend on the volition or election of either party. They held that there was in this case no discharge of the contract for one or both of two reasons. In the first place they thought that the appellants when they renewed the charter in 1932 were well informed of the legislation, and when they renewed the charter at a reduced rate and inserted no protecting clause in this regard, must be deemed to have taken the risk that a licence would not be granted. They also thought that if there was frustration of the adventure, it resulted from the deliberate act of the appellants in selecting the three trawlers for which they desired licences to be issued.

Their Lordships are of opinion that the latter ground is sufficient to determine this appeal. . . .

It is clear that the appellants were free to select any three of the five trawlers they were operating and could, had they willed, have selected the *St. Cuthbert* as one, in which event a licence would have been granted to her. It is immaterial to speculate why they preferred to put forward for licences the three trawlers which they actually selected. Nor is it material, as between the appellants and the respondents, that the appellants were operating other trawlers to three of which they gave the preference. What matters is that they could have got a licence for the *St. Cuthbert* if they had so minded. If the case be figured as one in which the *St. Cuthbert* was removed from the category of privileged trawlers, it was by the appellants' hand that she was so removed, because it was their hand that guided the hand of the Minister in placing the licences where he did and thereby excluding the *St. Cuthbert.* The essence of 'frustration' is that it should not be due to the act or election of the party. . . .

It cannot in their Lordships' judgment be predicated that what is here claimed to be a frustration, that is, by reason of the withholding of the licence, was a matter for which the appellants were not responsible or which happened without any default on their part. In truth, it happened in consequence of their election. If it be assumed that the performance of the contract was dependent on a licence being granted, it was that election which prevented performance, and on that assumption it was the appellants' own default which frustrated the adventure: the appellants cannot rely on their own default to excuse them from liability under the contract.

5.3.6   EFFECTS OF FRUSTRATION

5.3.6.1   Common law

APPLEBY v *MYERS* [1867] LR 2 CP 651 (Exchequer Chamber)

The plaintiffs contracted to erect machinery on the defendant's premises, the price being payable on completion. Before the work was completed, the factory and the machinery were destroyed by an accidental fire.

BLACKBURN J: . . . The whole question depends upon the true construction of the contract between the parties. We agree with the court below in thinking that it sufficiently appears that the work which the plaintiffs agreed to perform could not be performed unless the defendant's premises continued in a fit state to enable the plaintiffs to perform the work on them; and we agree with them in thinking that, if by any default on the part of the defendant, his premises were rendered unfit to receive the work, the plaintiffs would have had the option to sue the defendant for this default, or to treat the contract as rescinded, and sue on a quantum meruit. But we do not agree with them in thinking that there was an absolute promise or warranty by the defendant that the premises should at all events continue so fit. We think that where, as in the present case, the premises are destroyed without fault on either side, it is a misfortune equally affecting both parties; excusing both from further performances of the contract, but giving a cause of action to neither.

Then it was argued before us, that, inasmuch as this was a contract of that nature which would in pleading be described as a contract for work, labour, and materials, and not as one of bargain and sale, the labour and materials necessarily became the property of the defendant as soon as they were worked into his premises and became part of them, and therefore were at his risk. We think that, as to a great part of the work done in this case, the materials had not become the property of the defendant; for, we think that the plaintiffs, who were to complete the whole for a fixed sum, and keep it in repair for two years, would have had a perfect right, if they thought that a portion of the engine which they had put up was too slight, to change it and substitute another in their opinion better calculated to keep in good repair during the two years, and that without consulting or asking the leave of the defendant. But, even on the supposition that the materials had become unalterably fixed to the defendant's premises, we do not think that, under such a contract as this, the plaintiffs could recover anything unless the whole work was completed. It is quite true that materials worked by one into the property of another become part of that property. This is equally true, whether it be fixed or movable property. Bricks built into a wall become part of the house; thread stiched into a coat which is under repair, or planks and nails and pitch worked into a ship under repair, become part of the coat or the ship; and therefore, generally, and in the absence of something to shew a contrary intention, the bricklayer, or tailor, or shipwright, is to be paid for the work and materials he has done and provided, although the whole work is not complete. It is not material whether in such a case the non-completion is because the shipwright did not choose to go on with the work, as was the case in *Roberts* v *Havelock* (1832) 3 B & Ad 404, or because in consequence of a fire he could not go on with it, as in *Menetone* v *Athawes* (1746) 3 Burr 1592. But, though this is the prima facie contract between those who enter into contracts for doing work and supplying materials, there is nothing to render it either illegal or absurd in the workman to agree to complete the whole, and be paid when the whole is complete, and not till then: and we think that the plaintiffs in the present case had entered into such a contract. Had the accidental fire left the defendant's premises untouched, and only injured a part of the work which the plaintiffs had already done, we apprehend that it is clear the plaintiffs under such a contract as the present must have done that part over again, in order to fulfil their contract to complete the whole and 'put it to work for the sums above named respectively'. As it is, they are, according to the principle laid down in *Taylor* v *Caldwell* (1863) 3 B & S 826, excused from completing the work; but they are not therefore entitled to any compensation for what they have done, but which has, without any fault of the defendant, perished. The case is in principle like that of a shipowner who has been excused from the performance of his contract to carry goods to their destination, because his ship has been disabled by one of the excepted perils, but who is not therefore entitled to any payment on account of the part-performance of the voyage, unless there is something to justify the conclusion that there has been a fresh contract to pay freight pro ratâ.

On the argument, much reference was made to the Civil law. The opinions of the great lawyers collected in the Digest afford us very great assistance in tracing out any question of doubtful principle; but they do not bind us: and we think that, on the principles of English law laid down in *Cutter* v *Powell* (1795) 6 TR 320, *Jesse* v *Roy* (1834) 1 CM & R 316, *Munro* v *Butt* (1858) 8 E & B 738, *Sinclair* v *Bowles* (1829) 9 B & C 92, and other cases, the plaintiffs, having contracted to do an entire work for a specific sum, can recover nothing unless the work be done, or it can be shewn that it was the defendant's fault that the work was incomplete, or that there is something to justify the conclusion that the parties have entered into a fresh contract.

We think, therefore, as already said, that the judgment should be reversed.

FIBROSA SPOLKA AKCYJNA v FAIRBAIRN LAWSON [1942] 2 All ER 122 (HL)

Could the appellants reclaim the £1,000 paid under a subseqently frustrated contract, contrary to the view expressed in *Chandler* v *Webster*?

VISCOUNT SIMON LC: . . . The respondents are a limited company carrying on at Leeds the business of manufacturing textile machinery, and by a contract in writing dated July 12, 1939, they agreed to supply the appellants with certain flaxhackling machines as therein specified and described, at a lump-sum price of £4,800. The machines were of a special kind, and there is no suggestion that the respondents were not to manufacture them themselves. By the terms of the contract, delivery was to be in 3 to 4 months from the settlement of final details. The machines were to be packed and delivered by the respondents c.i.f. Gdynia; the services of a skilled monteur to superintend erection were to be provided by the respondents and included in the price; and payment was to be made by cheque on London, one-third of the price (£1,600) with the order and the balance (£3,200) against shipping documents.

On July 18, 1939, the appellants paid to the respondents £1,000 on account of the initial payment of £1,600 due under the contract. On September 1, 1939, Germany invaded Poland and on September 3, Great Britain declared was on Germany. On September 7, the appellants' agents in this country wrote to the respondents:

> Owing to the outbreak of hostilities it is now evident that the delivery of the machines for Poland cannot take place. Under the circumstances we shall be obliged if you will kindly arrange to return our initial payment of £1,000 at your early convenience.

To this request, the respondents replied on the next day refusing to return the sum and stating that:

> considerable work has been done on these machines and we cannot consent to the return of this payment. After the war the matter can be reconsidered.

On September 23, by order in council made under the provisions of the Trading with the Enemy Act, 1939, it was declared that Poland (including that part in which the port of Gdynia is situated) was enemy territory.

There was further correspondence between the parties or their agents which failed to produce agreement, and on May 1, 1940, the appellant company issued a writ and by its statement of claim alleged that the respondents had broken the contract by refusing to deliver the machines while the appellants 'are and have at all material times been ready and willing to take delivery and pay for the machines'. The prayer of the claim was (a) for damages for breach of contract, (b) for specific performance – an obviously hopeless claim – or, alternatively, return of the £1,000 with interest, and (c) for further or other relief. The substantial defence of the respondents was that the contract had been frustrated by the German occupation of Gdynia on September 23, 1939, and that in these circumstances the appellants had no right to the return of the £1,000. . . .

Counsel for the appellants admitted that, if the point with which I have already dealt was decided against him, the only other issues to be determined was whether, when this contract became frustrated, the appellants could, in the circumstances of the present case, claim back from the respondents the £1,000 which they have paid when placing the order. As to this, MacKinnon LJ in delivering the judgment of the Court of Appeal, said at p. 306:

> Tucker J held that, having regard to the principle laid down in *Chandler v Webster* [1904] 1 KB 493, and other like cases, this claim must fail. We think he was right, and, further, that that principle must equally bind this court to reject the claim. Whether the principle can be overruled is a matter which can only concern the House of Lords.

This alleged principle is to the effect that where a contract has been frustrated by such a supervening event as releases from further performance, 'the loss lies where it falls', with the result that sums paid or rights accrued before that event are not to be surrendered, but that all obligations falling due for performance after that event are discharged. . . .

The *locus classicus* for the view which has hitherto prevailed is to be found in the judgment of Sir Richard Collins MR in *Chandler v Webster*. It was not a considered judgment, but it is hardly necessary to say that I approach this pronouncement of the then Master of the Rolls, with all the respect due to so distinguished a common lawyer. When his judgment is studied, however, one cannot but be impressed by the circumstance that he regarded the proposition that money in such cases could not be recovered back as flowing from the decision in *Taylor v Caldwell* (1863) 3 B & S 826. *Taylor v Caldwell*, however, was not a case in which any question arose as to whether money could be recovered back, for there had been no payment in advance, and there is nothing in the judgment of Blackburn J which, at any rate in terms, affirms the general proposition that 'the loss lies where it falls'. The application of *Taylor v Caldwell* to the actual problem with which he had to deal in *Chandler v Webster*, by Sir Richard Collins MR, deserves close examination. He said, at p. 499:

> The plaintiff contends that he is entitled to recover the money which he has paid on the ground that there has been a total failure of consideration. He says that the condition on which he paid the money was that the procession should take place, and that, as it did not take place, there has been a total failure of consideration. That contention does no doubt raise a question of some difficulty, and one which has perplexed the courts to a considerable extent in several cases. The principle on which it has been dealt with is that which was applied in *Taylor v Caldwell* – namely, that, where, from causes outside the volition of the parties, something which was the basis of, or essential to the fulfilment of, the contract has become impossible, so that, from the time when the fact of that impossibility has been ascertained, the contract can no further be performed by either party, it remains a perfectly good contract up to that point, and everything previously done in pursuance of it must be treated as rightly done, but the parties are both discharged from further performance of it. If the effect were that the contract were wiped out altogether, no doubt the result would be that the money paid under it would have to be repaid as on a failure of consideration. But that is not the effect of the doctrine; it only releases the parties from further performance of the contract. Therfore, the doctrine of failure of consideration does not apply.

It appears to me that the reasoning in this crucial passage is open to two criticisms:

(a) The claim of a party who has paid money under a contract to get the money back, on the ground that the consideration for which he paid it has totally failed, is not based upon any provision contained in the contract, but arises because, in the circumstances which have happened, the law gives a remedy, in quasi-contract to the party who has not got that for which he bargained. It is a claim to recover money to which the defendant has no further right because, in the circumstances which have happened, the money must be regarded as received to the plaintiff's use. It is true that the effect of frustration is that, while the contract can no further be performed, 'it remains a perfectly good contract up to that point, and everything previously done in pursuance of it must be treated as rightly done'; but it by no means follows that the situation existing at the moment of frustration is one which leaves the party that has paid money and has not received the stipulated consideration without any remedy. To claim the return of money paid on the ground of total failure of consideration is not to vary the terms of the contract in any way. The claim arises not because the right to be repaid is one of the stipulated conditions of the contract, but because, in the circumstances which have happened, the law gives the remedy. It is the failure to distinguish between (i) the action of *assumpsit* for money had and received in a case where the consideration has wholly failed, and (ii) an action on the contract itself, which explains the mistake which I think has been made in applying English law to this subject-matter. Thus, in *Blakeley* v *Muller & Co.* [1903] 2 KB 760, Lord Alverstone LCJ said, at p. 761, n.:

> I agree that *Taylor* v *Caldwell* applies, but the consequence of that decision is that neither party here could have sued on the contract is respect of anything which was to be done under it after the procession had been abandoned.

That is true enough, but it does not follow that because the plaintiff cannot sue 'on the contract', he cannot sue *dehors* the contract for the recovery of a payment in respect of which consideration has failed. In the same case Wills J relied on *Appleby* v *Myers* (1867) LR 2 CP 651, where a contract was made for the erection by A of machinery upon the premises of B, to be paid for upon completion. There was no prepayment, and in the course of the work the premises were destroyed by fire. It was held that both parties were excused from futher performance, and that no liability accrued on either side. The liability referred to, however, was liability under the contract, and the judge seems to have thought that no action to recover money in such circumstances as the present could be conceived of unless there was a term of the contract, express or implied, which so provided. Once it is realised that the action to recover money for a consideration that has wholly failed rests not upon a contractual bargain between the parties but, as Lord Sumner said in *Sinclair* v *Brougham* [1914] AC 398, at p. 452, upon a notional or implied 'promise to repay', or, if it is preferred to omit reference to a fictitious promise, on an obligation to repay arising from the circumstances, the difficulty in the way of holding that a pre-payment made under a contract which has been frustrated can be recovered back appears to me to disappear.

(b)   There is, no doubt, a distinction between cases in which a contract is 'wiped out altogether', e.g., because it is void as being illegal from the start, or as being due to fraud which the innocent party has elected to treat as avoiding the contract, and cases in which intervening impossibility 'only releases the parties from further performance of the contract'. Does the distinction between these two classes of case, however, justify the deduction of Sir Richard Collins MR that 'the doctrine of failure of consideration does not apply, where the contract remains a perfectly good contract up to the date of frustration? This conclusion seems to be derived from the view that, if the contract remains good and valid up to the moment of frustration, money which has already been paid under it cannot be regarded as having been paid for a consideration which has wholly failed. The party who has paid the money has had the advantage, whatever it may be worth, of the promise of the other party. That is true, but it is necessary to draw a distinction. In English law, an enforceable contract may be formed by an exchange of a promise for a promise, or by the exchange of a promise for an act – I am excluding contracts under seal – and thus, in the law relating to the formation of contract, the promise to do a thing may often be the consideration; but, when one is considering the law of failure of consideration and of the quasi-contractual right to recover money on that ground, it is, generally speaking, not the promise which is referred to as the consideration, but the performance of the promise. The money was paid to secure performance and, if performance fails, the inducement which brought about the payment is not fulfilled.

If this were not so, there could never be any recovery of money, for failure of consideration, by the payer of the money in return for a promise of future performance. Yet there are endless examples which show that money can be recovered, as for a complete failure of consideration, in cases where the promise was given but could not be fulfilled: see the notes in Bullen and Leake, 9th edn, p. 263. In this connection the decision in *Rugg* v *Minett* (1809) 11 East 210 is instructive. There the plaintiff had bought at auction a number of casks of oil; the contents of each cask was to be made up after the auction by the seller to the prescribed quantity so that the property in a cask did not pass to the plaintiff until this had been done. The plaintiff paid in advance a sum of money on account of his purchases generally, but a fire occurred after some of the casks had been filled up, while the others had not. The plaintiff's action was to recover the money he had paid as money received by the defendants to the use of the plaintiff. The Court of King's Bench ruled that this cause of action succeeded in respect of the casks which at the time of the fire had not been filled up to the prescribed quantity. A simple illustration of the same result is an agreement to buy a horse, the price to be paid down, but the horse not to be delivered and the property not to pass until the horse has been shod. If the horse dies before the shoeing, the price can unquestionably be recovered as for a total failure of consideration, notwithstanding that the promise to deliver was given. This is the case of a contract *de certo corpore* where the *certum corpus* perishes after the contract is made; but, as the judgment of Vaughan Williams LJ, in *Krell* v *Henry* [1903] 2 KB 740, at p. 748, explained, the same doctrine applies:

> . . . to cases where the event which renders the contract incapable of performance is the cessation or non-existence of an express condition or state of things, going to the root of the contract, and essential to its performance.

I can see no valid reason why the right to recover pre-paid money should not equally arise on frustration arising from supervening circumstances as it arises on frustration from destruction of a particular subject-matter.

The conclusion is that the rule in *Chandler* v *Webster* is wrong, and that the appellants can recover their £1,000.

While this result obviates the harshness with which the previous view in some instances treated the party who had made a prepayment, it cannot be regarded as dealing fairly between parties in all cases, and must sometimes have the result of leaving the recipient who has to return the money at a grave disadvantage. He may have incurred expenses in connection with the partial carrying out of the contract which are equivalent, or more than equivalent, to the money which he prudently stipulated should be prepaid, but which he now has to return for reasons which are no fault of his. He may have to repay the money, though he has executed almost the whole of the contractual work, which will be left on his hands. These results follow from the fact that the English common law does not undertake to apportion a prepaid sum in such circumstances – contrast the provision, now contained in the Partnership Act, 1894, s. 40, for apportioning a premium if a partnership is prematurely dissolved. It must be for the legislature to decide whether provision should be made for an equitable apportionment of prepaid monies which have to be returned by the recipient in view of the frustration of the contract in respect of which they were paid.

I move that the appeal be allowed and that judgment be entered for the appellants.

Lords Atkin, Russell, Macmillan, Roche and Porter concurred.

5.3.6.2   The Law Reform (Frustrated Contracts) Act 1943

LAW REFORM (FRUSTRATED CONTRACTS) ACT 1943

Section 1.   Adjustment of rights and liabilities of parties to frustrated contracts

(1)   Where a contract governed by English law has become impossible of performance or been otherwise frustrated, and the parties thereto have for that reason been discharged from the further performance of the contract, the following provisions of this section shall, subject to the provisions of section 2 of this Act, have effect in relation thereto.

(2)   All sums paid or payable to any party in pursuance of the contract before the time when the parties were so discharged (in this Act referred to as 'the time of discharge') shall, in the case of sums so paid, be recoverable from him as money received by him

for the use of the party by whom the sums were paid, and in the case of sums so payable, cease to be so payable:

Provided that, if the party to whom the sums were so paid or payable incurred expenses before the time of discharge in, or for the purpose of, the performance of the contract, the court may, if it considers it just to do so having regard to all the circumstances of the case, allow him to retain or, as the case may be, recover the whole or any part of the sums so paid or payable, not being an amount in excess of the expenses so incurred.

(3) Where any party to the contract has, by reason of anything done by any other party thereto in, or for the purpose of, the performance of the contract, obtained a valuable benefit (other than a payment of money to which the last foregoing subsection applies) before the time of discharge, there shall be recoverable from him by the said other party such sum (if any), not exceeding the value of the said benefit to the party obtaining it, as the court considers just, having regard to all the circumstances of the case and, in particular –

(a) the amount of any expenses incurred before the time of discharge by the benefited party in, or for the purpose of, the performance of the contract, including any sums paid or payable by him to any other party in pursuance of the contract and retained or recoverable by that party under the last foregoing subsection, and

(b) the effect, in relation to the said benefit, of the circumstances giving rise to the frustration of the contract.

(4) In estimating, for the purposes of the foregoing provisions of this section, the amount of any expenses incurred by any party to the contract, the court may, without prejudice to the generality of the said provisions, include such sum as appears to be reasonable in respect of overhead expenses and in respect of any work or services performed personally by the said party.

(5) In considering whether any sum ought to be recovered or retained under the foregoing provisions of this section by any party to the contract, the court shall not take into account any sums which have, by reason of the circumstances giving rise to the frustration of the contract, become payable to that party under any contract of insurance unless there was an obligation to insure imposed by an express term of the frustrated contract or by or under any enactment.

(6) Where any person has assumed obligations under the contract in consideration of the conferring of a benefit by any other party to the contract upon any other person, whether a party to the contract or not, the court may, if in all the circumstances of the case it considers it just to do so, treat for the purposes of subsection (3) of this section any benefit so conferred as a benefit obtained by the person who has assumed the obligations as aforesaid.

Section 2. Provisions as to the application of this Act

(1) This Act shall apply to contracts, whether made before or after the commencement of this Act, as respects which the time of discharge is on or after the first day of July, nineteen hundred and forty-three, but not to contracts as respects which the time of discharge is before the said date.

(2) This Act shall apply to contracts to which the Crown is a party in like manner as to contracts between subjects.

(3) Where any contract to which this Act applies contains any provision which, upon the true construction of the contract, is intended to have effect in the event of circumstances arising which operate, or would but for the said provision operate, to frustrate the contract, or is intended to have effect whether such circumstances arise or not, the court shall give effect to the said provision and shall only give effect to the foregoing section of this Act to such extent, if any, as appears to the court to be consistent with the said provision.

(4) Where it appears to the court that a part of any contract to which this Act applies can properly be severed from the remainder of the contract, being a part wholly performed before the time of discharge, or so performed except for the payment in respect of that part of the contract of sums which are or can be ascertained under the contract, the court shall treat that part of the contract as if it were a separate contract and

had not been frustrated and shall treat the foregoing section of this Act as only applicable to the remainder of that contract.

(5)   This Act shall not apply—

(a)   to any charterparty, except a time charterparty or a charterparty by way of demise, or to any contract (other than a charterparty) for the carriage of goods by sea; or

(b)   to any contract of insurance, save as is provided by subsection (5) of the foregoing section; or

(c)   to any contract to which section 7 of the Sale of Goods Act 1979 (which avoids contracts for the sale of specific goods which perish before the risk has passed to the buyer) applies, or to any other contract for the sale, or for the sale and delivery, of specific goods, where the contract is frustrated by reason of the fact that the goods have perished.

Section 3.   Short title and interpretation

(1)   This Act may be cited as the Law Reform (Frustrated Contracts) Act 1943.

(2)   In this Act the expression 'court' means, in relation to any matter, the court or arbitrator by or before whom the matter falls to be determined.

BP EXPLORATION CO. (LIBYA) LTD v HUNT (No. 2) [1982] 1 All ER 925 (QB)

ROBERT GOFF J: . . . *The principles governing claims under the 1943 Act*
The Law Reform (Frustrated Contracts) Act 1943 is described as an Act to amend the law relating to the frustration of contracts. In fact, it is concerned not with frustration itself, but with the consequences of frustration; and it creates statutory remedies, enabling the court to award restitution in respect of benefits conferred under contracts thereafter frustrated. . . .

(1)   *The principle of recovery*
The principle, which is common to both s. 1(2) and (3), and indeed is the fundamental principle underlying the Act itself, is prevention of the unjust enrichment of either party to the contract at the other's expense. It was submitted by counsel, on behalf of BP that the principle common to both subsections was one of restitution for net benefits received, the net benefit being the benefit less an appropriate deduction for expenses incurred by the defendant. This is broadly correct so far as s. 1(2) is concerned; but under s. 1(3) the net benefit of the defendant simply provides an upper limit to the award: it does not measure the amount of the award to be made to the plaintiff. This is because in s. 1(3) a distinction is drawn between the plaintiff's performance under the contract, and the benefit which the defendant has obtained by reason of that performance, a distinction about which I shall have more to say later in this judgment; and the net benefit obtained by the defendant from the plaintiff's performance may be more than a just sum payable in respect of such performance, in which event a sum equal to the defendant's net benefit would not be an appropriate sum to award to the plaintiff. I therefore consider it better to state the principle underlying the Act as being the principle of unjust enrichment, which underlies the right of recovery in very many cases in English law, and indeed is the basic principle of the English law of restitution, of which the Act forms part.

Although s. 1(2) and (3) is concerned with restitution in respect of different types of benefit, it is right to construe the two subsections as flowing from the same basic principle and therefore, so far as their different subject matters permit, to achieve consistency between them. Even so, it is always necessary to bear in mind the difference between awards of restitution in respect of money payments and awards where the benefit conferred by the plaintiff does not consist of a payment of money. Money has the peculiar character of a universal medium of exchange. By its receipt, the recipient is inevitably benefited; and (subject to problems arising from such matters as inflation, change of position and the time value of money) the loss suffered by the plaintiff is generally equal to the defendant's gain, so that no difficulty arises concerning the amount to be repaid. The same cannot be said of other benefits, such as goods or services. By their nature, services cannot be restored; nor in many cases can goods be restored, for example where they have been consumed or transferred to another. Furthermore the identity and value of the resulting benefit to the recipient may be debatable. From the very nature of things, therefore, the problem of restitution in respect of such benefits is more complex than in cases where the benefit takes the form of a money payment; and the solution of the problem has been made no easier by the form in which the legislature has chosen to draft s. 1(3) of the Act.

The Act is *not* designed to do certain things. (i) It is not designed to apportion the loss between the parties. There is no general power under either s. 1(2) or s. 1(3) to make any allowance for expenses incurred by the plaintiff (except, under the proviso to s. 1(2), to enable him to enforce pro tanto payment of a sum payable but unpaid before frustration); and expenses incurred by the defendant are only relevant in so far as they go to reduce the net benefit obtained by him and thereby limit any award to the plaintiff. (ii) It is not concerned to put the parties in the position in which they would have been if the contract had been performed. (iii) It is not concerned to restore the parties to the position they were in before the contract was made. A remedy designed to prevent unjust enrichment may not achieve that result; for expenditure may be incurred by either party under the contract which confers no benefit on the other, and in respect of which no remedy is available under the Act.

An award under the Act may have the effect of rescuing the plaintiff from an unprofitable bargain. This may certainly be true under s. 1(2), if the plaintiff has paid the price in advance for an expected return which, if furnished, would have proved unprofitable; if the contract is frustrated before any part of that expected return is received, and before any expenditure is incurred by the defendant, the plaintiff is entitled to the return of the price he has paid, irrespective of the consideration he would have recovered had the contract been performed. Consistently with s. 1(2), there is nothing in s. 1(3) which necessarily limits an award to the contract consideration. But the contract consideration may nevertheless be highly relevant to the assessment of the just sum to be awarded under s. 1(3); this is a matter to which I will revert later in this judgment.

(2) *Claims under s. 1(2)*

Where an award is made under s. 1(2), it is, generally speaking, simply an award for the repayment of money which has been paid to the defendant in pursuance of the contract, subject to an allowance in respect of expenses incurred by the defendant. It is not necessary that the consideration for the payment should have wholly failed: claims under s. 1(2) are not limited to cases of total failure of consideration, and cases of partial failure of consideration can be catered for by a cross-claim by the defendant under s. 1(2) or (3) or both. There is no discretion in the court in respect of a claim under s. 1(2), except in respect of the allowance for expenses; subject to such an allowance (and, of course, a crossclaim) the plaintiff is entitled to repayment of the money he has paid. The allowance for expenses is probably best rationalised as a statutory recognition of the defence of change of position. True, the expenses need not have been incurred by reason of the plaintiff's payment; but they must have been incurred in, or for the purpose of, the performance of the contract under which the plaintiff's payment has been made, and for that reason it is just that they should be brought into account. No provision is made in the subsection for any increase in the sum recoverable by the plaintiff, or in the amount of expenses to be allowed to the defendant, to allow for the time value of money. The money may have been paid, or the expenses incurred, many years before the date of frustration; but the cause of action accrues on that date, and the sum recoverable under the Act at that date can be no greater than the sum actually paid, though the defendant may have had the use of the money over many years, and indeed may have profited from its use. Of course, the question whether the court may award interest from the date of the accrual of the cause of action is an entirely different matter, to which I shall refer later in this judgment.

(3) *Claims under s. 1(3)*

General. In contract, where an award is made under s. 1(3), the process is more complicated. First, it has to be shown that the defendant has, by reason of something done by the plaintiff in, or for the purpose of, the performance of the contract, obtained a valuable benefit (other than a payment of money) before the time of discharge. That benefit has to be identified, and valued, and such value forms the upper limit of the award. Secondly, the court may award to the plaintiff such sum, not greater than the value of such benefit, as it considers just having regard to all the circumstances of the case, including in particular the matters specified in s. 1(3)(a) and (b). In the case of an award under s. 1(3) there are, therefore, two distinct stages: the identification and valuation of the benefit, and the award of the just sum. The amount to be awarded is the just sum, unless the defendant's benefit is less, in which event the award will be limited to the amount of that benefit. The distinction between the identification and valuation of the defendant's benefit, and the assessment of the just sum, is the most controversial part of the Act. It represents the solution adopted by the legislature of the problem of restitution in cases where the benefit does not consist of a payment of money; but the solution so adopted has been criticised by some commentators as productive of injustice, and it certainly gives rise to considerable problems, to which I shall refer in due course.

Identification of the defendant's benefit.   In the course of the argument before me, there was much dispute whether, in the case of services, the benefit should be identified as the services themselves, or as the end product of the services. One example canvassed (because it bore some relationship to the facts of the present case) was the example of prospecting for minerals. If minerals are discovered, should the benefit be regarded (as counsel for Mr Hunt contended) simply as the services of prospecting, or (as counsel for BP contended) as the minerals themselves being the end product of the successful exercise? Now, I am satisfied that it was the intention of the legislature, to be derived from s. 1(3) as a matter of contruction that the benefit should in an appropriate case be identified as the end product of the services. This appears, in my judgment, not only from the fact that s. 1(3) distinguishes between the plaintiff's performance and the defendant's benefit, but also from s. 1(3)(b) which clearly relates to the product of the plaintiff's performance. Let me take the example of a building contract. Suppose that a contract for work on a building is frustrated by a fire which destroys the building and which, therefore, also destroys a substantial amount of work already done by the plaintiff. Although it might be thought just to award the plaintiff a sum assessed on a quantum meruit basis, probably a rateable part of the contract price, in respect of the work he has done, the effect of s. 1(3)(b) will be to reduce the award to nil, because of the effect, in relation to the defendant's benefit, of the circumstances giving rise to the fustration of the contract. It is quite plain that, in s. 1(3)(b), the word 'benefit' is intended to refer, in the example I have given, to the actual improvement to the building, because that is what will be affected by the frustrating event; the subsection therefore contemplates that, in such a case, the benefit is the end product of the plaintiff's services, not the services themselves. This will not be so in every case, since in some cases the services will have no end product; for example, where the services consist of doing such work as surveying, or transporting goods. In each case it is necessary to ask the question: what benefit has the defendant obtained by reason of the plaintiff's contractual performance? But is must not be forgotten that in s. 1(3) the relevance of the value of the benefit is to fix a ceiling to the award. If, for example, in a building contract, the building is only partially completed, the value of the partially completed building (ie the product of the services) will fix a ceiling for the award; but the stage of the work may be such that the uncompleted building may be worth less than the value of the work and materials that have gone into it, particularly as completion by another builder may cost more than completion by the original builder would have cost. In other cases, however, the actual benefit to the defendant may be considerably more than the appropriate or just sum to be awarded to the plaintiff, in which event the value of the benefit will not in fact determine the quantum of the award. I should add, however, that, in a case of prospecting it would usually be wrong to identify the discovered mineral as the benefit. In such a case there is always (whether the prospecting is successful or not) the benefit of the prospecting itself, ie of knowing whether or not the land contains any deposit of the relevant minerals; if the prospecting is successful, the benefit may include also the enhanced value of the land by reason of the discovery; if the prospector's contractual task goes beyond discovery and includes development and production, the benefit will include the further enhancement of the land by reason of the installation of the facilities, and also the benefit of in part transforming a valuable mineral deposit into a marketable commodity.

I add by way of footnote that all these difficulties would have been avoided if the legislature had thought it right to treat the services themselves as the benefit. In the opinion of many commentators, it would be more just to do so; after all, the services in question have been requested by the defendant, who normally takes the risk that they may prove worthless, from whatever cause. In the example I have given of the building destroyed by fire, there is much to be said for the view that the builder should be paid for the work he has done, unless he has (for example by agreeing to insure the works) taken on himself the risk of destruction by fire. But my task is to construe the Act as it stands. On the true construction of the Act, it is in my judgment clear that the defendant's benefit must, in an appropriate case, be indentified as the end product of the plaintiff's services, despite the difficulties which this construction creates, difficulties which are met again when one comes to value the benefit.

Apportioning the benefit.   In all cases, the relevant benefit must have been obtained by the defendant by reason of something done by the plaintiff. Accordingly, where it is appropriate to identify the benefit with an end product and it appears that the defendant has obtained the benefit by reason of work done both by the plaintiff and by himself, the court will have to do its best to apportion that benefit, and to decide what proportion is attributable to the work done by the plaintiff. That proportion will then constitute the relevant benefit for the purposes of s. 1(3) of the Act.

Valuing the benefit.   Since the benefit may be identified with the product of the plaintiff's performance, great problems arise in the valuation of the benefit. First, how does one solve the problem which arises from the fact that a small service may confer an enormous benefit, and conversely, a very substantial service may confer only a very small benefit? The answer presumably is that at the stage of valuation of the benefit (as opposed to assessment of the just sum) the task of the court is simply to assess the value of the benefit to the defendant. For example, if a prospector after some very simple prospecting discovers a large and unexpected deposit of a valuable mineral, the benefit to the defendant (namely, the enhancement in the value of the land) may be enormous; it must be valued as such, always bearing in mind that the assessment of a just sum may very well lead to a much smaller amount being awarded to the plaintiff. But conversely, the plaintiff may have undertaken building work for a substantial sum which is, objectively speaking, of little or no value, for example, he may commence the redecoration, to the defendant's execrable taste, of rooms which are in good decorative order. If the contract is frustrated before the work is complete, and the work is unaffected by the frustrating event, it can be argued that the defendant has obtained no benefit, because the defendant's property has been reduced in value by the plaintiff's work; but the partial work must be treated as a benefit to the defendant, since he requested it, and valued as such. Secondly, at what point in time is the benefit to be valued? If there is a lapse of time between the date of the receipt of the benefit, and the date of frustration, there may in the meanwhile be a substantial variation in the value of the benefit. If the benefit had simply been identified as the services rendered, this problem would not arise; the court would simply award a reasonable remuneration for the services rendered at the time when they were rendered, the defendant taking the risk of any subsequent depreciation and the benefit of any subsequent appreciation in value. But that is not what the Act provides: s. 1(3)(b) makes it plain that the plaintiff is to take the risk of depreciation or destruction by the frustrating event. If the effect of the frustrating event on the value of the benefit is to be measured, it must surely be measured on the benefit as at the date of frustration. For example, let it be supposed that a builder does work which doubles in value by the date of frustration, and is then so severely damaged by fire that the contract is frustrated; the valuation of the residue must surely be made on the basis of the value as at the date of frustration. However, does this mean that, for the purposes of s. 1(3), the benefit is always to be valued as at the date of frustration? For example, if goods are transferred and retained by the defendant till frustration when they have appreciated or depreciated in value, are they to be valued as at the date of frustration? The answer must, I think, generally speaking, be in the affirmative, for the sake of consistency. But this raises an acute problem in relation to the time value of money. Suppose that goods are supplied and sold, long before the date of frustration; does the principle that a benefit is to be valued as at the date of frustration require that allowance must be made for the use in the meanwhile of the money obtained by the disposal of the goods, in order to obtain a true valuation of the benefit as at the date of frustration? This was one of the most hotly debated matters before me, for the very good reason that in the present case it affects the valuation of the parties' respective benefits by many millions of dollars. It is very tempting to conclude that an allowance should be made for the time value of money, because it appears to lead to a more realistic valuation of the benefit as at the date of frustration; and, as will appear hereafter, an appropriate method for making such an allowance is available in the form of the net discounted cash flow system of accounting. But I have come to the conclusion that, as a matter of construction, this course is not open to me. First, the subsection limits the award to the value of the benefit obtained by the defendant; and it does not follow that, because the defendant has had the money over a period of time, he has in fact derived any benefit from it. Secondly, if an allowance was to be made for the time value of the money obtained by the defendant, a comparable allowance should be made in respect of expenses incurred by the defendant, ie in respect of the period between the date of incurring the expenditure and the date of frustration, and s. 1(3)(a) only contemplates that the court, in making an allowance for expenses, shall have regard to the 'amount of [the] expenses'. Thirdly, as I have already indicated, no allowance for the time value of money can be made under s. 1(2); and it would be inconsistent to make such an allowance under s. 1(3) but not under s. 1(2).

Other problems can arise from the valuation of the defendant's benefit as the end product; I shall come to these later in the consideration of the facts of the present case. But there is a further problem which I should refer to, before leaving this topic. Section 1(3)(a) requires the court to have regard to the amount of any expenditure incurred before the time of discharge by the benefited party in, or for the purpose of, the performance of the contract. The question arises: should this matter be taken into account at the stage of valuation of the benefit, or of assessment of the just sum? Take a simple example. Suppose that the defendant's benefit is valued at £150 and that a just sum is assessed at £100, but that there remains to be taken into account defendant's expenses of £75: is the award to be £75 or £25? The clue to this problem lies, in my judgment in the fact that the allowance for expenses is a statutory recognition of the defence of change of position. Only to the extent that the position of the defendant has so changed that it would be unjust to award restitution, should the court make an allowance for expenses. Suppose that the plaintiff does work for the defendant which produces no valuable end product or a benefit no greater in value than the just sum to be awarded in respect of the work, there is then no reason why the whole of the relevant expenses should not be set off against the just sum. But suppose that the defendant has reaped a large benefit from the plaintiff's work, far greater in value than the just sum to be awarded for the work. In such circumstances it would be quite wrong to set off the whole of the defendant's expenses against the just sum. The question whether the defendant has suffered a change of position has to be judged in the light of all the circumstances of the case. Accordingly, on the Act as it stands, under s. 1(3) the proper course is to deduct the expenses from the value of the benefit, with the effect that only in so far as they reduce the value of the benefit below the amount of the just sum which would otherwise be awarded will they have any practical bearing on the award.

Finally, I should record that the court is required to have regard to the effect, in relation to the defendant's benefit, of the circumstances giving rise to the frustration of the contract. I have already given an example of how this may be relevant, in the case of building contracts; and I have recorded the fact that this provision has been the subject of criticism. There may, however, be circumstances where it would not be just to have regard to this fact or, for example, if, under a building contract, it was expressly agreed that the work in progress should be insured by the building-owner against risks which include the event which had the effect of frustrating the contract and damaging or destroying the work.

Assessment of the just sum.   The principle underlying the Act is prevention of the unjust enrichment of the defendant at the plaintiff's expense. Where, as in cases under s. 1(2), the benefit conferred on the defendant consists of payment of a sum of money, the plaintiff's expense and the defendant's enrichment are generally equal; and, subject to other relevant factors, the award of restitution will consist simply of an order for repayment of a like sum of money. But where the benefit does not consist of money, then the defendant's enrichment will rarely be equal to the plaintiff's expense. In such cases, where (as in the case of a benefit conferred under a contract thereafter frustrated) the benefit has been requested by the defendant, the basic measure of recovery in restitution is the reasonable value of the plaintiff's performance: in a case of services, a quantum meruit or reasonable remuneration, and in a case of goods, a quantum valebat or reasonable price. Such cases are to be contrasted with cases where such a benefit has not been requested by the defendant. In the latter class of case, recovery is rare in restitution; but if the sole basis of recovery was that the defendant had been incontrovertibly benefited, it might be legitimate to limit recovery to the defendant's actual benefit, a limit which has (perhaps inappropriately) been imported by the legislature into s. 1(3) of the Act. However, under s. 1(3) as it stands, if the defendant's actual benefit is less than the just or reasonable sum which would otherwise be awarded to the plaintiff, the award must be reduced to a sum equal to the amount of the defendant's benefit.

A crucial question, on which the Act is surprisingly silent, is this: what bearing do the terms of the contract, under which the plaintiff has acted, have on the assessment of the just sum? First, the terms on which the work was done may serve to indicate the full scope of the work done, and so be relevant to the sum awarded in respect of such work. For example, if I do work under a contract under which I am to receive a substantial prize if successful, and nothing if I fail, and the contract is frustrated before the work is complete but not before a substantial benefit has been obtained by the defendant, the element of risk taken by the plaintiff may be held to have the effect of enhancing the amount of any sum to be awarded. Secondly, the contract consideration is always relevant as providing some evidence of what will be a reasonable sum to be awarded in respect of the plaintiff's work. Thus if a prospector, employed for a fee, discovers a goldmine before the contract under which he is employed is frustrated (for example, by illegality or by his illness or disablement) at a time when his work was incomplete, the court may think it just to make an award in the nature of a reasonable fee for what he has done (though of course the benefit obtained by the defendant will be far greater), and a rateable part of the contract fee may provide useful evidence of the level of sum to be awarded. If, however, the contract had provided that he was to receive a stake in the concession, then the just sum might be enhanced on the basis that, in all the circumstances, a reasonable sum should take account of such a factor: cf *Way* v *Latilla* [1937] 3 All ER 759. Thirdly, however, the contract consideration, or a rateable part of it, may provide a limit to the sum to be awarded. To take a fairly extreme example, a poor householder or a small businessman may obtain a contract for building work to be done to his premises at considerably less than the market price, on the basis that he cannot afford to pay more. In such a case, the court may consider it just to limit the award to a rateable part of the contract price, on the ground that it was the understanding of the parties that in no circumstances (including the circumstances of the contract being frustrated) should the plaintiff recover more than the contract price or a rateable part of it. Such a limit may properly be said to arise by virtue of the operation of s. (2)3 of the Act. But it must not be forgotten that, unlike money, services can never be restored, nor usually can goods, since they are likely to have been either consumed or disposed of, or to have depreciated in value; and since, ex hypothesi, the defendant will only have been prepared to contract for the goods or services on the basis that he paid no more than the contract consideration, it may be unjust to compel him, by an award under the Act, to pay more than that consideration, or a rateable part of it, in respect of the services or goods he has received. It is unnecessary for me to decide whether this will always be so; but it is likely that in most cases this will impose an important limit on the sum to be awarded: indeed it may well be the most relevant limit to an award under s. 1(3) of the Act. The legal basis of the limit may be s. 2(3) of the Act; but even if that subsection is inapplicable, it is open to the court, in an appropriate case, to give effect to such a limit in assessing the just sum to be awarded under s. 1(3), because in many cases it would be unjust to impose on the defendant an obligation to make restitution under the subsection at higher than the contract rate.

The Court of Appeal and House of Lords affirmed the judgment of Robert Goff J, without any detailed discussion of the above issues.

5.4   End of Chapter Assessment Question

In order to promote tourism in the town of Accrington, Stanley, a prominent business-man, organises a 'May Day Marathon' running race to be held on the May Day national holiday .

Stanley agrees to purchase 20,000 sheets of foil (to be used to wrap around the runners at the end of the race) from Tin Ltd at a price of £20,000. He pays £10,000 immediately and is to pay the remaining £10,000 after the race. Tin Ltd subsequently delivers 15,000 sheets 'with 5,000 to follow'.

Parliament then passes an Act which states that May Day will no longer be a national holiday. As a result, the vast majority of the runners withdraw their entries for the race.

Stanley cancels the race and claims repayment from Tin Ltd of his £10,000, saying that the contract is frustrated.

Alf, an enthusiastic jogger, who had paid his £10 entry fee in order to run in the race, claims compensation from Stanley for his 'loss of enjoyment'.

Advise Stanley.

5.5   End of Chapter Assessment Outline Answer

(a)   The contract between Stanley and Tin Ltd

The doctrine of frustration arises where the contract, after its formation, becomes impossible to perform due to some subsequent event which occurs due to the fault of neither party. The event may cause the contract to become literally impossible to perform (*Taylor* v *Caldwell*), or produce such radically changed circumstances that if the parties were required to continue they would be performing a fundamentally different contract and so should be released from their obligations (*Krell* v *Henry*).

Stanley's claim against Tin Ltd for repayment of £10,000 on the basis that the contract is frustrated would no doubt be resisted by way of counterclaim by Tin Ltd for the contract price, on the basis that the race taking place on May Day was not at the foundation of the contract as far as Tin Ltd was concerned. The outcome of this dispute depends upon the distinction between *Krell* v *Henry*, where the Court of Appeal inferred from the circumstances that the proximity of the flat to Edward VII's proposed coronation procession route was at the foundation of the contract as far as both parties were concerned, and *Herne Bay Steamboat Co.* v *Hutton*, where the Court of Appeal inferred that the venture was undertaken at the defendant's risk. That is, the tour of the fleet and the fleet's inspection by Edward VII were not at the foundation of the contract as far as both parties were concerned. (The two objects to the contract approach put forward by Stirling LJ in this case is not particularly helpful in the context of the facts of the question.)

It is submitted that either view is tenable dependent upon circumstances. No doubt the May Day race is at the foundation for Stanley with his desire to promote tourism in Accrington, but can the same be said for Tin Ltd? This might be the case if the foil were of special manufacture or the order was an exceptionally large one. Thus, the contract may be frustrated by the passing of the subsequent Act of Parliament, but the issue is not clear-cut.

If the contract is frustrated, the parties' financial positions will be determined by the provisions of the Law Reform (Frustrated Contracts) Act 1943. Under s. 1(2) Stanley has a prima facie right to recover his £10,000 pre-payment but this is subject to Tin Ltd's possible retention of up to £10,000 on the basis of having incurred expenditure before the time of discharge for the purpose of performance of the contract. The sum retainable rests at the discretion of the court and will be whatever is just in all the circumstances of the case. If, for example, Tin Ltd were allowed to retain £10,000 on the basis of 15,000 sheets delivered, it would have to pursue its claim for the additional £5,000 under s. 1(3). This would be on the basis of its having conferred a valuable non-monetary benefit upon Stanley (the additional 5,000 sheets) before the time of discharge. Again the court has a discretion to award such sum as is just in all the circumstances of the case. Thus, if the additional 5,000 sheets were valued at £5,000 (which is not necessarily the case) this would fix the maximum possible 'just sum'. However, in calculating the 'just sum' the court is required to take into account the circumstances giving rise to the frustration of the contract, e.g. the fact that the sheets of foil after cancellation may well be virtually useless to Stanley. This may lead to a much reduced 'just sum', although the principles behind such a calculation cannot be precisely defined, according to the House of Lords in *BP Exploration Co. (Libya) Ltd* v *Hunt*. An additional complicating factor would arise if Robert Goff J was correct at first instance in *BP* v *Hunt* in valuing the benefit immediately after, rather than immediately before, the occurrence of the frustrating event. In this problem the outcome is, in fact, likely to be similar, whichever point in time is chosen.

(b)   The contract between Alf and Stanley

Whether this contract were frustrated or not would depend again upon the *Krell* v *Henry*, *Herne Bay Steamboat Co.* v *Hutton* distinction explained above. If it were frustrated then under the Law Reform (Frustrated Contracts) Act 1943, s. 1(2) Alf's right to recover his £10 entry fee might be set off against the just sum to be retained by Stanley, on the basis that it constitutes expenses incurred in performing the contract before the time of discharge.

If the contract is not frustrated then Stanley is in breach of contract. However, damages for 'loss of enjoyment' are generally not recoverable (*Bliss* v *SE Thames Regional Health Authority*). Damages may be recoverable, however, the object of the contract is the conferment of a pleasurable experience (*Jarvis* v *Swans Tours*). Whilst a contract to run a marathon is hardly akin to a holiday contract, and the reasonable person might not regard this as a loss of an enjoyable experience, this is, nonetheless, a possible ruling.

CHAPTER SIX

VITIATING FACTORS

6.1 Misrepresentation

6.1.1 FALSE STATEMENT OF FACT

6.1.1.1 Statements of opinion or belief

BISSET v WILKINSON [1927] AC 177 (PC)

A statement was made as to the number of sheep which a piece of land would support.

LORD MERRIVALE: The appellant in this litigation brought his action in the Supreme Court of New Zealand to recover a sum of money payable to him under an agreement for sale and purchase of land. The defendants by way of defence and counterclaim alleged misrepresentation by the appellant in a material particular as to the character and quality of the land in question and claimed rescission of the agreement with consequential relief or alternatively damages for fraudulent misrepresentation or breach of warranty. Upon the trial of the action judgment was given for the plaintiff on the claim and the counterclaim. The Court of Appeal of New Zealand, by a majority, set aside the judgment of the trial judge and decreed rescission of the contract between the parties with consequential relief as prayed. The appellant claims to have the judgment of the Supreme Court reinstated.

The contract between the parties was an agreement in writing made in May, 1919, whereby the respondents agreed for the purchase by them of two adjoining blocks of land at Avondale, in the Southern Island of New Zealand, called 'Homestead' and 'Hogans', containing respectively 2,062 acres and 348 acres or thereabouts, for 13,260*l.* 10*s.*; 2000*l.* payable – and it was in fact paid – on the signing of the agreement, and the balance payable in May, 1924, interest to be paid half-yearly in the meantime. . . .

Sheep-farming was the purpose for which the respondents purchased the lands of the plaintiff. One of them had no experience of farming. The other had been before the war in charge of sheep on an extensive sheep-farm carried on by his father, who had accompanied and advised him in his negotiation with the appellant and had carefully inspected the lands at Avondale. In the course of coming to his agreement with the respondents the appellant made statements as to the property which, in their defence and counterclaim, the respondents alleged to be misrepresentations.

At an early period after the respondents went into occupation and commenced their farming operations they found themselves in difficulties. They sought and obtained extensions of time for payment of the interest which fell due to the appellant. Sheep-farming became very unprofitable and they changed their user of the land. One of them withdrew from the partnership. The other made an assignment of the valuable part of his property to his wife, and on being eventually pressed by the appellant for payments under the agreement disclosed this assignment as an answer to the practical enforcement by the appellant of his demands. The appellant brought his action for a half-year's interest on the unpaid purchase money and the respondents set up their case of misrepresentation.

By their defence and counterclaim the respondents alleged that the appellant had 'represented and warranted that the land which was the subject of the agreement had a carrying capacity of two thousand sheep if only one team were employed in the agricultural work of the said land'. It was common ground at the hearing and in the Court of Appeal that the carrying capacity of a sheep-farm is its capacity the year round. As was said by Reed J in the Court of Appeal: 'The meaning of the representation as alleged was that the carrying capacity of the farm during the winter, with such special food and new pasture as could be grown by the proper use in ploughing of one team of horses regularly employed throughout the year was two thousand sheep'. 'It is also common ground', said the same learned judge, 'that to bring a farm to its full carrying capacity skilled management is required. It is admitted that the appellants were not experienced farmers'.

The appellant made these admissions at the hearing: 'I told them that if the place was worked as I was working it, with a good six-horse team, my idea was that it would carry two thousand sheep. That was my idea and still is my idea'. Further, he said: 'I do not dispute that they bought it believing it would carry two thousand sheep'. . . .

In an action for rescission, as in an action for specific performance of an executory contract, when misrepresentation is the alleged ground of relief of the party who repudiates the contract, it is, of course, essential to ascertain whether that which is relied upon is a representation of a specific fact, or a statement of opinion, since an erroneous opinion stated by the party affirming the contract, though it may have been relied upon and have induced the contract on the part of the party who seeks rescission, gives no title to relief unless fraud is established. The application of this rule, however, is not always easy, as is illustrated in a good many reported cases, as well as in this. A representation of fact may be inherent in a statement of opinion and, at any rate, the existence of the opinion in the person stating it is a question of fact. In *Karberg's Case* [1892] 3 Ch 1 Lindley LJ, in course of testing a representation which might have been, as it was said to be by interested parties, one of opinion or belief, used this inquiry: 'Was the statement of expectation a statement of things not really expected?'. The Court of Appeal applied this test and rescinded the contract which was in question. In *Smith v Land and House Property Corporation* (1884) 28 ChD 7 there came in question a vendor's description of the tenant of the property sold as 'a most desirable tenant' – a statement of his opinion, as was argued on his behalf in an action to enforce the contract of sale. This description was held by the Court of Appeal to be a misrepresentation of fact, which, without proof of fraud, disentitled the vendor to specific performance of the contract of purchase. 'It is often fallaciously assumed', said Bowen LJ, 'that a statement of opinion cannot involve the statement of fact. In a case where the facts are equally well known to both parties, what one of them says to the other is frequently nothing but an expression of opinion. The statement of such opinion is in a sense a statement of fact, about the condition of the man's own mind, but only of an irrelevant fact, for it is of no consequence what the opinion is. But if the facts are not equally well known to both sides, then a statement of opinion by one who knows the facts best involves very often a statement of a material fact, for he impliedly states that he knows facts which justify his opinion'. The kind of distinction which is in question is illustrated again in a well known case of *Smith v Chadwick* (1884) 9 App Cas 187. There the words under consideration involved the inquiry in relation to the sale of an industrial concern whether a statement of 'the present value of the turnover or output' was of necessity a statement of fact that the produce of the works was of the amount mentioned, or might be and was a statement that the productive power of the works was estimated at so much. The words were held to be capable of the second of these meanings. The decisive inquiries came to be: what meaning was actually conveyed to the party complaining; was he deceived, and, as the action was based on a charge of fraud, was the statement in question made fraudulently?

In the present case, as in those cited, the material facts of the transaction, the knowledge of the parties respectively, and their relative positions, the words of representation used, and the actual condition of the subject-matter spoken of, are relevant to the two inquiries necessary to be made: What was the meaning of the representation? Was it true?

In ascertaining what meaning was conveyed to the minds of the now respondents by the appellant's statement as to the two thousand sheep, the most material fact to be remembered is that, as both parties were aware, the appellant had not and, so far as appears, no other person had at any time carried on sheep-farming upon the unit of land in question. That land as a distinct holding had never constituted a sheep-farm. The two blocks comprised in it differed substantially in character. Hogan's block was described by one of the respondents' witnesses as 'better land'. 'It might carry', he said, 'one sheep or perhaps two or even three sheep to the acre'. He estimated the carrying capacity of the land generally as little more than half a sheep to the acre. And Hogan's land had been allowed to deteriorate during several years before the respondents purchased. As was said by Sim J: 'In ordinary circumstances, any statement made by an owner who has been occupying his own farm as to its carrying capacity would be regarded as a statement of fact. . . . This, however, is not such a case. The defendants knew all about Hogan's block and knew also what sheep the farm was carrying when they inspected it. In these circumstances . . . the defendants were not justified in regarding anything said by the plaintiff as to the carrying capacity as being anything more than an expression of his opinion on the subject'. In this view of the matter their Lordships concur.

Whether the appellant honestly and in fact held the opinion which he stated remained to be considered. This involved examination of the history and condition of the property. If a reasonable man with the appellant's knowledge could not have come to the conclusion he stated, the description of that conclusion as an opinion would not necessarily protect him against rescission for misrepresentation. But what was actually the capacity in competent hands of the land the respondents purchased had never been, and never was, practically ascertained. The respondents, after two years trial of sheep-farming, under difficulties caused in part by their inexperience, found themselves confronted by a fall in the values of sheep and wool which would have left them losers if they could have carried three thousand sheep. As is said in the judgment of Ostler J: 'Owing to sheep becoming practically valueless, they reduced their flock and went in for cropping and dairy-farming in order to make a living'.

The opinions of experts and of their neighbours, on which the respondents relied, were met by the appellant with evidence of experts admitted to be equally competent and upright with those of his opponents, and his own practical experience upon part of the land, as to which his testimony was unhesitatingly accepted by the judge of first instance. It is of dominant importance that Sim J negatived the respondents' charge of fraud.

After attending to the close and very careful examination of the evidence which was made by learned counsel for each of the parties their Lordships entirely concur in the view which was expressed by the learned judge who heard the case. The defendants failed to prove that the farm if properly managed was not capable of carrying two thousand sheep.

Questions of laches and of affirmance of the contract on the part of the respondents which were argued at the hearing, are not material for further consideration, and in view of the course of the proceedings and the finding of Sim J as to the honesty of the appellant in the statements he in fact made, it would be improper to accede to the application which was made at the Board on behalf of the respondents for leave to proceed anew upon the charge of fraudulent misrepresentation.

Their Lordships will humbly advise His Majesty that the appeal should be allowed, and the judgment of Sim J restored. The respondents must bear the appellant's costs here and below.

SMITH v LAND AND HOUSE PROPERTY CORPORATION (1884) 28 ChD 7 (CA)

BAGGALLAY LJ: On the 4th of May, 1882, the plaintiffs entered into a contract with the defendants for the sale to them of certain property described in particulars of sale. The property had been offered for sale by auction, but no sale was effected, and immediately afterwards this contract was entered into. The purchasers declined to complete, saying that they had been induced by misrepresentation to enter into the contract. Early in October, 1882, this action was commenced by the vendors for specific performance. It was met by a statement of defence, accompanied by a counter-claim for rescission of the contract or compensation. The foundation of the counter-claim is that the property was first described in the particulars as held by Fleck, 'a very desirable tenant', and then again as 'let to Mr F. Fleck a most desirable tenant, at a rental of £400 per annum, for an unexpired term of twenty-seven and a half years, thus offering a first-class investment'. It is alleged that this was a false representation, for that it was not true that Fleck was a 'very desirable' or a 'most desirable' tenant. The vendors entered into receipt of the rents in January, 1882. We have no evidence as to the receipt of rent which accrued before Lady Day, 1882, but as to the quarter's rent which accrued on that day it is in evidence that it was not paid at once; that a distress was threatened, but not put in, and that the tenant paid £30 on the 6th of May, £40 on the 13th of June, and the balance of £30 some time before August, but at what precise time it does not appear. At the date of the auction, on the 4th of August, the Midsummer rent had been applied for, but no part of it had been paid. Under this state of things the representation in question was made. It is said that these are words of course put in by the auctioneer, but I hold it to be the duty of a vendor to see that the property is not untruly described, and I cannot hold him to be excused because a description which the property will not bear has been inserted by the auctioneer without his instructions. Nor can the auctioneer excuse himself for inserting a false representation by saying that he did not know it to be untrue. I think that Mr Justice Denman came to a correct conclusion as to there having been a material misrepresentation, for the vendors must have known perfectly well that the tenant did not pay his rent properly, and they therefore were not justified in describing him as a very desirable tenant.

Bowen and Fry LJJ concurred.

6.1.1.2   Statement of future conduct or intention

EDGINGTON v *FITZMAURICE* (1885) 29 ChD 459 (CA)

BOWEN LJ: This is an action for deceit, in which the plaintiff complains that he was induced to take certain debentures by the misrepresentations of the defendants, and that he sustained damage thereby. The loss which the plaintiff sustained is not disputed. In order to sustain his action he must first prove that there was a statement as to facts which was false; and secondly, that it was false to the knowledge of the defendants, or that they made it not caring whether it was true or false. For it is immaterial whether they made the statement knowing it to be untrue, or recklessly, without caring whether it was true or not, because to make a statement recklessly for the purpose of influencing another person is dishonest. It is also clear that it is wholly immaterial with what object the lie is told. That is laid down in Lord Blackburn's judgment in *Smith* v *Chadwick* (1884) 9 App Cas 187, but it is material that the defendant should intend that it should be relied on by the person to whom he makes it. But, lastly, when you have proved that the statement was false, you must further shew that the plaintiff has acted upon it and has sustained damage by so doing: you must shew that the statement was either the sole cause of the plaintiff's act, or materially contributed to his so acting. So the law is laid down in *Clarke* v *Dickson* (1858) EB & E 148, and that is the law which we have now to apply.

The alleged misrepresentations were three. First, it was said that the prospectus contained an implied allegation that the mortgage for £21,500 could not be called in at once, but was payable by instalments. I think that upon a fair construction of the prospectus it does so allege; and therefore that the prospectus must be taken to have contained an untrue statement on that point; but it does not appear to me clear that the statement was fraudulently made by the defendants. It is therefore immaterial to consider whether the plaintiff was induced to act as he did by that statement.

Secondly, it is said that the prospectus contains an implied allegation that there was no other mortgage affecting the property except the mortgage stated therein. I think there was such an implied allegation, but I think it is not brought home to the defendants that it was made dishonestly; accordingly, although the plaintiff may have been damnified by the weight which he gave to the allegation, he cannot rely on it in this action: for in an action of deceit the plaintiff must prove dishonesty. Therefore if the case had rested on these two allegations alone, I think it would be too uncertain to entitle the plaintiff to succeed.

But when we come to the third alleged misstatement I feel that the plaintiff's case is made out. I mean the statement of the objects for which the money was to be raised.

These were stated to be to complete the alterations and additions to the buildings, to purchase horses and vans, and to develop the supply of fish. A mere suggestion of possible purposes to which a portion of the money might be applied would not have formed a basis for an action of deceit. There must be a misstatement of an existing fact: but the state of a man's mind is as much a fact as the state of his digestion. It is true that it is very difficult to prove what the state of a man's mind at a particular time is, but if it can be ascertained it is as much a fact as anything else. A misrepresentation as to the state of a man's mind is, therefore, a misstatement of fact. Having applied as careful consideration to the evidence as I could, I have reluctantly come to the conclusion that the true objects of the defendants in raising the money were not those stated in the circular. I will not go through the evidence, but looking only to the cross-examination of the defendants, I am satisfied that the objects for which the loan was wanted were misstated by the defendants, I will not say knowingly, but so recklessly as to be fraudulent in the eye of the law.

Then the question remains – did this misstatement contribute to induce the plaintiff to advance his money. Mr Davey's argument has not convinced me that they did not. He contended that the plaintiff admits that he would not have taken the debentures unless he had thought they would give him a charge on the property, and therefore he was induced to take them by his own mistake, and the misstatement in the circular was not material. But such misstatement was material if it was actively present to his mind when he decided to advance his money. The real question is, what was the state of the plaintiff's mind, and if his mind was disturbed by the misstatement of the defendants, and such disturbance was in part the cause of what he did, the mere fact of his also making a mistake himself could make no difference. It resolves itself into a mere question of fact. I have felt some difficulty about the pleadings, because in the statement of claim this point is not clearly put forward, and I had some doubt whether this contention as to the third misstatement was not an afterthought. But the balance of my judgment is weighed down by the probability of the case. What is the first question which a man asks when he advances money? It is, what is it wanted for? Therefore I think that the statement is material, and that the plaintiff would be unlike the rest of his race if he was not influenced by the statement of the objects for which the loan was required. The learned judge in the Court below came to the conclusion that the misstatement did influence him, and I think he came to a right conclusion.

Cotton and Fry LJJ concurred.

6.1.2   INDUCEMENT

REDGRAVE v *HURD* (1881) 20 ChD 1 (CA)

Did the fact that the representee could have checked the truth of the representor's statement mean that it did not induce the contract?

BAGGALLAY LJ: Upon the hearing of this action, Mr Justice Fry held, as a conclusion of fact, from the evidence before him, that a misrepresentation was made by the plaintiff to the defendant as to the amount of his professional business. The learned judge had the opportunity of hearing and seeing the witnesses, and of observing the manner in which their evidence was given, and it must be a very strong case indeed in which the Court of Appeal, upon a question of fact, entirely depending upon oral testimony, will dissent from the finding of the court below. Mr Justice Fry also held that the defendant ought not to be considered as having been influenced by those misrepresentations to enter into the contract but I am unable to concur in this conclusion. The facts from which that conclusion was drawn were partly proved by oral testimony and partly by written documents. As regards the oral testimony, according to the judgment of Mr Justice Fry, it amounted to this, that opportunities were afforded to the defendant to ascertain the inaccuracy of the representation made to him, and that to some extent, at least, he had availed himself of these opportunities. The mere fact that a party has the opportunity of investigating and ascertaining whether a representation is true or false is not sufficient to deprive him of his right to rely on a misrepresentation as a defence to an action for specific performance. The person who has made the misrepresentation cannot be heard to say to the party to whom he has made that representation, 'You chose to believe me when you might have doubted me, and gone further'. The representation once made relieves the party from an investigation, even if the opportunity is afforded. I do not mean to say that there may not be certain circumstances of suspicion, which might put a person upon inquiry, and make it his duty to inquire, but under ordinary circumstances, the mere fact that he does not avail himself of the opportunity of testing the accuracy of the representation made to him will not enable the opposing party to succeed on that ground. The case of *Rawlins v Wickham* (1858) 3 De G & J 304 is a very strong illustration of the application of that principle. There, a person who had been induced by false representations to enter into a partnership continued in that partnership for four years, and then for the first time discovered the fraud which had been practised upon him. He was held entitled to relief, though at any time during that period he might have investigated matters for himself. It is true that in the present case there was some investigation, but it was an investigation of a most cursory character, which could not have enabled the defendant to ascertain the truth or the falsity of the representation that had been made. So far, therefore, as the conclusions arrived at by the learned judge, upon consideration of the oral testimony on that second point are concerned, I am unable to agree with him.

Lord Jessel MR, and Lush LJ concurred.

6.1.3 TYPES OF MISREPRESENTATION

6.1.3.1 Fraudulent

DERRY v PEEK (1889) 14 App Cas 337 (HL)

LORD HERSCHELL: My Lords, in the statement of claim in this action the respondent, who is the plaintiff, alleges that the appellants made in a prospectus issued by them certain statements which were untrue, that they well knew that the facts were not as stated in the prospectus, and made the representations fraudulently, and with the view to induce the plaintiff to take shares in the company.

'This action is one which is commonly called an action of deceit, a mere common law action'. This is the description of it given by Cotton LJ in delivering judgement. I think it important that it should be borne in mind that such an action differs essentially from one brought to obtain rescission of a contract on the ground of misrepresentation of a material fact. The principles which govern the two actions differ widely. Where rescission is claimed it is only necessary to prove that there was a misrepresentation; then, however honestly it may have been, however free from blame the person who made it, the contract, having been obtained by misrepresentation, cannot stand. In an action of deceit, on the contrary, it is not enough to establish misrepresentation alone; it is conceded on all hands that something more must be proved to cast liability upon the defendant, though it has been a matter of controversy what additional elements are requisite. I lay stress upon this because observations made by learned judges in actions for rescission have been cited and much relied upon at the bar by counsel for the respondent. Care must obviously be observed in applying the language used in relation to such actions to an action of deceit. Even if the scope of the language used extend beyond the particular action which was being dealt with, it must be remembered that the learned judges were not engaged in determining what is necessary to support an action of deceit, or in discriminating with nicety the elements which enter into it. . . .

In the court below Cotton LJ said: 'What in my opinion is a correct statement of the law is this, that where a man makes a statement to be acted upon by others which is false, and which is known by him to be false, or is made by him recklessly, or without care whether it is true or false, that is, without any reasonable ground for believing it to be true, he is liable in an action of deceit at the suit of anyone to whom it was addressed or anyone of the class to whom it was addressed and who was materially induced by the misstatement to do an act to his prejudice'. About much that is here stated there cannot, I think, be two opinions. But when the learned Lord Justice speaks of a statement made recklessly or without care whether it is true or false, *that is* without any reasonable ground for believing it to be true, I find myself, with all respect, unable to agree that these are convertible expressions. To make a statement careless whether it to be true or false, and therefore without any real belief in its truth, appears to me to be an essentially different thing from making, through want of care, a false statement, which is nevertheless honestly believed to be true. And it is surely conceivable that a man may believe that what he states is the fact, though he has been so wanting in care that the court may think that there were no sufficient grounds to warrant his belief. I shall have to consider hereafter whether the want of reasonable ground for believing the statement made is sufficient to support an action of deceit. I am only concerned for the moment to point out that it does not follow that it is so, because there is authority for saying that a statement made recklessly, without caring whether it be true or false, affords sufficient foundation for such an action.

That the learned Lord Justice thought that if a false statement were made without reasonable ground for believing it to be true an action of deceit would lie, is clear from a subsequent passage in his judgment. He says that when statements are made in a prospectus like the present, to be circulated amongst persons in order to induce them to take shares, 'there is a duty cast upon the director or other persons who makes those statements to take care that there are no expressions in them which in fact are false; to take care that he has reasonable ground for the material statements which are contained in that document which he prepares and circulates for the very purpose of its being acted upon by others'. . . .

In my opinion making a false statement through want of care falls far short of, and is a very different thing from, fraud, and the same may be said of a false representation honestly believed though on insufficient grounds. Indeed Cotton LJ himself indicated, in the words I have already quoted, that he should not call it fraud. But the whole of current authorities, with which I have so long detained your Lordships, shews to my mind conclusively that fraud is essential to found an action of deceit, and that it cannot be maintained where the acts proved cannot properly be so termed. And the case of *Taylor* v *Ashton* (1843) 11 M & W 401 appears to me to be in direct conflict with the dictum of Sir George Jessel, and inconsistent with the view taken by the learned judges in the court below. I observe that Sir Frederick Pollock, in his able work on Torts (p. 243, note), referring, I presume, to the dicta of Cotton LJ and Sir George Jessel MR, says that the actual decision in *Taylor* v *Ashton* is not consistent with the modern cases on the duty of directors of companies. I think he is right. But for the reasons I have given I am unable to hold that anything less than fraud will render directors or any other persons liable to an action of deceit.

At the same time I desire to say distinctly that when a false statement has been made the questions whether there were reasonable grounds for believing it, and what were the means of knowledge in the possession of the person making it, are most weighty matters for consideration. The ground upon which an alleged belief was founded is a most important test of its reality. I can conceive many cases where the fact that an alleged belief was destitute of all reasonable foundation would suffice of itself to convince the court that it was not really entertained, and that the representation was a fraudulent one.

6.1.3.2   Negligence at common law

HEDLEY BYRNE & CO. LTD v *HELLER & PARTNERS LTD* [1964] AC 465 (HL)

The House of Lords considered whether a negligent misstatement could ever give rise to liability at common law.

LORD REID: . . . Much of the difficulty in this field has been caused by *Derry* v *Peek* (1889) 14 App Cas 337. The action was brought against the directors of a company in respect of false statements in a prospectus. It was an action of deceit based on fraud and nothing else. But it was held that the directors had believed that their statements were true although they had no reasonable grounds for their belief. The Court of Appeal held that this amounted to fraud in law, but naturally enough this House held that there can be no fraud without dishonesty and that credulity is not dishonesty. The question was never really considered whether the facts had imposed on the directors a duty to exercise care. It must be implied that on the facts of that case there was no such duty. But that was immediately remedied by the Directors' Liability Act, 1890, which provided that a director is liable for untrue statements in a prospectus unless he proves that he had reasonable ground to believe that they were true.

It must now be taken that *Derry v Peek* did not establish any universal rule that in the absence of contract an innocent but negligent misrepresentation cannot give rise to an action. It is true Lord Bramwell said: 'To found an action for damages there must be a contract and breach, or fraud'. And for the next 20 years it was generally assumed that *Derry v Peek* decided that. But it was shown in this House in *Nocton v Lord Ashburton* [1914] AC 932 that that is much too widely stated. We cannot, therefore, now accept as accurate the numerous statements to that effect in cases between 1889 and 1914, and we must now determine the extent of the exceptions to that rule.

In *Nocton v Lord Ashburton* a solicitor was sued for fraud. Fraud was not proved but he was held liable for negligence. Viscount Haldane LC dealt with *Derry v Peek* and pointed out that while the relationship of the parties in that case was not enough, the case did not decide 'that where a different sort of relationship ought to be inferred from the circumstances the case is to be concluded by asking whether an action for deceit will lie. . . . There are other obligations besides that of honesty the breach of which may give a right to damages. These obligations depend on principles which the judges have worked out in the fashion that is characteristic of a system where much of the law has always been judge-made and unwritten'. It hardly needed *Donoghue v Stevenson* [1932] AC 562 to show that that process can still operate. Then Lord Haldane quoted a passage from the speech of Lord Herschell in *Derry v Peek* where he excluded from the principle of that case 'those cases where a person within whose special province it lay to know a particular fact has given an erroneous answer to an inquiry made with regard to it by a person desirous of ascertaining the fact for the purpose of determining his course'. Then he explained the expression 'constructive fraud' and said: 'What it really means in this connection is, not moral fraud in the ordinary sense, but breach of the sort of obligation which is enforced by a court which from the beginning regarded itself as a court of conscience'. He went on to refer to 'breach of special duty' and said: 'If such a duty can be inferred in a particular case of a person issuing a prospectus, as, for instance, in the case of directors issuing to the shareholders of the company which they direct a prospectus inviting the subscription by them of further capital, I do not find in *Derry v Peek* an authority for the suggestion that an action for damages for misrepresentation without an actual intention to deceive may not lie'. I find no dissent from these views by the other noble and learned Lords. Lord Shaw also quoted the passage I have quoted from the speech of Lord Herschell, and, dealing with equitable relief, he approved a passage in an argument of Sir Roundell Palmer in *Peek v Gurney* (1871) LR 13 Eq 79 which concluded '. . . in order that a person may avail himself of relief founded on it he must show that there was such a proximate relation between himself and the person making the representaion as to bring them virtually into the position of parties contracting with each other', an interesting anticipation in 1871 of the test of who is my neighbour.

Lord Haldane gave a further statement of his view in *Robinson v National Bank of Scotland Ltd* 1916 SC 154 (HL), a case to which I shall return. Having said that in that case there was no duty excepting the duty of common honesty, he went on to say:

> In saying that I wish emphatically to repeat what I said in advising this House in the case of *Nocton v Lord Ashburton* [1914] AC 932, that it is a great mistake to suppose that, because the principle in *Derry v Peek* clearly covers all cases of the class to which I have referred, therefore the freedom of action of the courts in recognising special duties arising out of other kinds of relationship which they find established by the evidence is in any way affected. I think, as I said in *Nocton's* case, that an exaggerated view was taken by a good many people of the scope of the decision in *Derry v Peek*. The whole of the doctrine as to fiduciary relationships, as to the duty of care arising from implied as well as express contracts, as to the duty of care arising from other special relationships which the courts may find to exist in particular cases, still

remains, and I should be very sorry if any word fell from me which should suggest that the courts are in any way hampered in recognising that the duty of care may be established when such cases really occur.

This passage makes it clear that Lord Haldane did not think that a duty to take care must be limited to cases of fiduciary relationship in the narrow sense of relationships which had been recognised by the Court of Chancery as being of a fiduciary character. He speaks of other special relationships, and I can see no logical stopping place short of all those relationships where it is plain that the party seeking information or advice was trusting the other to exercise such a degree of care as the circumstances required, where it was reasonable for him to do that, and where the other gave the information or advice when he knew or ought to have known that the inquirer was relying on him. I say 'ought to have known' because in question of negligence we now apply the objective standard of what the reasonable man would have done.

A reasonable man, knowing that he was being trusted or that his skill and judgment were being relied on, would, I think, have three courses open to him. He could keep silent or decline to give the information or advice sought: or he could give an answer with a clear qualification that he accepted no responsibility for it or that it was given without that reflection or inquiry which a careful answer would require: or he could simply answer without any such qualification. If he chooses to adopt the last course he must, I think, be held to have accepted some responsibility for his answer being given carefully, or to have accepted a relationship with the inquirer which requires him to exercise such care as the circumstances require. . . .

Lords Morris, Hodson, Devlin and Pearce concurred.

ESSO PETROLEUM CO. LTD v MARDON [1976] QB 801 (CA)

Esso misrepresented to a prospective tenant the likely throughput of petrol at one of their petrol stations.

LORD DENNING MR: . . . I turn to consider the law. It is founded on the representation that the estimated throughput of the service station was 200,000 gallons. No claim can be brought under the Misrepresentation Act 1967, because that Act did not come into force until April 22, 1967: whereas this representation was made in April 1963. So the claim is put in two ways. First, that the representation was a collateral warranty. Second, that it was a negligent misrepresentation. I will take them in order.

Collateral warranty
Ever since *Heilbut, Symons & Co.* v *Buckleton* [1913] AC 30, we have had to contend with the law as laid down by the House of Lords that an innocent misrepresentation gives no right to damages. In order to escape from that rule, the pleader used to allege – I often did it myself – that the misrepresentation was fraudulent, or alternatively a collateral warranty. At the trial we nearly always succeeded on collateral warranty. We had to reckon, of course, with the dictum of Lord Moulton, at p. 47, that 'such collateral contracts must from their very nature be rare'. But more often than not the court elevated the innocent misrepresentation into a collateral warranty: and thereby did justice – in advance of the Misrepresentation Act 1967. I remember scores of cases of that kind, especially on the sale of a business. A representation as to the profits that had been made in the past was invariably held to be a warranty. Besides that experience, there have been many cases since I have sat in this court where we have readily held a representation – which induces a person to enter into a contract – to be a warranty sounding in damages. I summarised them in *Dick Bentley Productions Ltd* v *Harold Smith* (*Motors*) *Ltd* [1965] 1 WLR 623, 627, when I said:

Looking at the cases once more, as we have done so often, it seems to me that if a representation is made in the course of dealings for a contract for the very purpose of inducing the other party to act upon it, and actually inducing him to act upon it, by entering into the contract, that is prima facie ground for inferring that it was intended as a warranty. It is not necessary to speak of it as being collateral. Suffice it that it was intended to be acted upon and was in fact acted on.

Mr Ross-Munro, retaliated, however, by citing *Bisset v Wilkinson* [1927] AC 177, where the Privy Council said that a statement by a New Zealand farmer that an area of land 'would carry 2,000 sheep' was only an expression of opinion. He submitted that the forecast here of 200,000 gallons was an expression of opinion and not a statement of fact: and that it could not be interpreted as a warranty or promise.

Now I would quite agree with Mr Ross-Munro that it was not a warranty – in this sense – that it did not *guarantee* that the throughput *would be* 200,000 gallons. But, nevertheless, it was a forecast made by a party – Esso – who had special knowledge and skill. It was the yardstick (the e.a.c.) by which they measured the worth of a filling station. They knew the facts. They knew the traffic in town. They knew the throughput of comparable stations. They had much experience and expertise at their disposal. They were in a much better position than Mr Mardon to make a forecast. It seems to me that if such a person makes a forecast, intending that the other should act upon it – and he does act upon it, it can well be interpreted as a warranty that the forecast is sound and reliable in the sense that they made it with reasonable care and skill. It is just as if Esso said to Mr Mardon: 'Our forecast of throughput is 200,000 gallons. You can rely upon it as being a sound forecast of what the service station should do. The rent is calculated on that footing'. If the forecast turned out to be an unsound forecast such as no person of skill or experience should have made, there is a breach of warranty. Just as there is a breach of warranty when a forecast is made – 'expected to load' by a certain date – if the maker has no reasonable grounds for it: see *Samuel Sanday and Co. v Keighley, Maxted and Co.* (1922) 27 Com Cas 296; or bunkers 'expected 600/700 tons': see *Efploia Shipping Corporation Ltd v Canadian Transport Co. Ltd (The Pantanassa)* [1958] 2 Lloyd's Rep 449, 455–457 by Diplock J. It is very different from the New Zealand case where the land had never been used as a sheep farm and both parties were equally able to form an opinion as to its carrying capacity: see particularly *Bisset v Wilkinson* [1927] AC 177, 183–184.

In the present case it seems to me that there was a warranty that the forecast was sound, that is, Esso made it with reasonable care and skill. That warranty was broken. Most negligently Esso made a 'fatal error' in the forecast they stated to Mr Mardon, and on which he took the tenancy. For this they are liable in damages. The judge, however, declined to find a warranty. So I must go further.

Negligent misrepresentation
Assuming that there was no warranty, the question arises whether Esso are liable for negligent misstatement under the doctrine of *Hedley Byrne & Co. Ltd v Heller & Partners Ltd* [1964] AC 465. It has been suggested that *Hedley Byrne* cannot be used so as to impose liability for negligent pre-contractual statements: and that, in a pre-contract situation, the remedy (at any rate before the Act of 1967) was only in warranty or nothing. Thus in *Hedley Byrne* itself Lord Reid said, at p. 483: 'Where there is a contract there is no difficulty as regards the contracting parties: the question is whether there is a warranty'. And in *Oleificio Zucchi S.p.A. v Northern Sales Ltd* [1965] 2 Lloyd's Rep 496, 519, McNair J said:

. . . as at present advised, I consider the submission advanced by the buyers, that the ruling in [*Hedley Byrne* [1964] AC 465] applies as between contracting parties, is without foundation.

As against these, I took a different view in *McInerny v Lloyds Bank Ltd* [1964] 1 Lloyd's Rep 246, 253 when I said:

. . . if one person, by a negligent misstatement, induces another to enter into a contract – with himself or with a third person – he may be liable in damages.

In arguing this point, Mr Ross-Munro took his stand in this way. He submitted that when the negotiations between two parties resulted in a contract between them, their rights and duties were governed by the law of contract and not by the law of tort. There was, therefore, no place in their relationship for *Hedley Byrne* [1964] AC 465, which was solely on liability in tort. He relied particularly on *Clark* v *Kirby-Smith* [1964] Ch 506 where Plowman J held that the liability of a solicitor for negligence was a liability in contract and not in tort, following the observations of Sir Wilfrid Greene MR in *Groom* v *Crocker* [1939] 1 KB 194, 206. Mr Ross-Munro might also have cited *Bagot* v *Stevens Scanlan & Co. Ltd* [1966] 1 QB 197, about an architect; and other cases too. But I venture to suggest that those cases are in conflict with other decisions of high authority which were not cited in them. These decisions show that, in the case of a professional man, the duty to use reasonable care arises not only in contract, but it is also imposed by the law apart from contract, and is therefore actionable in tort. It is comparable to the duty of reasonable care which is owed by a master to his servant, or vice versa. It can be put either in contract or in tort: see *Lister* v *Romford Ice and Cold Storage Co. Ltd* [1957] AC 555, 587 by Lord Radcliffe and *Matthews* v *Kuwait Bechtel Corporation* [1959] 2 QB 57. The position was stated by Tindal CJ, delivering the judgment of the Court of Exchequer Chamber in *Boorman* v *Brown* (1842) 3 QB 511, 525–526:

> That there is a large class of cases in which the foundation of the action springs out of privity of contract between the parties, but in which, nevertheless, the remedy for the breach, or non-performance, is indifferently either assumpsit or case upon tort, is not disputed. Such are actions against attorneys, surgeons, and other professional men, for want of competent skill or proper care in the service they undertake to render: . . . The principle in all these cases would seem to be that the contract creates a duty, and the neglect to perform that duty, or the nonfeasance, is a ground of action upon a tort.

That decision was affirmed in the House of Lords in (1844) 11 Cl & Fin 1, when Lord Campbell, giving the one speech, said, at p. 44:

> . . . wherever there is a contract, and something to be done in the course of the employment which is the subject of that contract, if there is a breach of a duty in the course of that employment, the plaintiff may either recover in tort or in contract.

To this there is to be added the high authority of Viscount Haldane LC, in *Nocton* v *Lord Ashburton* [1914] AC 932, 956:

> . . . the solicitor contracts with his client to be skilful and careful. For failure to perform his obligation he may be made liable at law in contract or even in tort, for negligence in breach of a duty imposed on him.

That seems to me right. A professional man may give advice under a contract for reward; or without a contract, in pursuance of a voluntary assumption of responsibility, gratuitously without reward. In either case he is under one and the same duty to use reasonable care: see *Cassidy* v *Ministry of Health* [1951] 2 KB 343, 359–360. In the one case it is by reason of a term implied by law. In the other, it is by reason of a duty imposed by law. For a breach of that duty he is liable in damages: and those damages should be, and are, the same, whether he is sued in contract or tort.

It follows that I cannot accept Mr Ross-Munro's proposition. It seems to me that *Hedley Byrne & Co. Ltd* v *Heller & Partners Ltd* [1964] AC 465, properly understood, covers this particular proposition: if a man, who has or professes to have special knowledge or skill, makes a representation by virtue thereof to another – be it advice, information or opinion – with the intention of inducing him to enter into a contract with him, he is under a duty to use reasonable care to see that the representation is correct, and that the advice, information or opinion is reliable. If he negligently gives unsound advice or misleading information or expresses an erroneous opinion, and thereby induces the other side to enter into a contract with him, he is liable in damages. This proposition is in line with what I said in *Candler* v *Crane, Christmas & Co.* [1951] 2 KB 164, 179–180, which was approved by the majority of the Privy Council in *Mutual Life and Citizens' Assurance Co. Ltd* v *Evatt* [1971] AC 793. And the judges of the Commonwealth have shown themselves quite ready to apply *Hedley Byrne* [1964] AC 465, between contracting parties: see in Canada, *Sealand of the Pacific Ltd* v *Ocean Cement Ltd* (1973) 33 DLR (3d) 625; and in New Zealand, *Capital Motors Ltd* v *Beecham* [1975] 1 NZLR 576.

Applying this principle, it is plain that Esso professed to have – and did in fact have – special knowledge or skill in estimating the throughput of a filling station. They made the representation – they forecast a throughput of 200,000 gallons – intending to induce Mr Mardon to enter into a tenancy on the faith of it. They made it negligently. It was a 'fatal error'. And thereby induced Mr Mardon to enter into a contract of tenancy that was disastrous to him. For this misrepresentation they are liable in damages.

Ormrod and Shaw LJJ concurred.

6.1.3.2 Negligence under the Misrepresentation Act 1967

MISREPRESENTATION ACT 1967

Section 1. Removal of certain bars to rescission for misrepresentation
Where a person has entered into a contract after a misrepresentation has been made to him, and –
    (a) the misrepresentation has become a term of the contract; or
    (b) the contract has been performed;
or both, then, if otherwise he would be entitled to rescind the contract without alleging fraud, he shall be so entitled, subject to the provisions of this Act, notwithstanding the matter mentioned in paragraphs (a) and (b) of this section.

Section 2. Damages for misrepresentation
    (1) Where a person has entered into a contract after a misrepresentation has been made to him by another party thereto and as a result thereof he has suffered loss, then, if the person making the misrepresentation would be liable to damages in respect thereof had the misrepresentation been made fraudulently, that person shall be so liable notwithstanding that the misrepresentation was not made fraudulently, unless he proves that he had reasonable ground to believe and did believe up to the time the contract was made that the facts represented were true.
    (2) Where a person has entered into a contract after a misrepresentation has been made to him otherwise than fraudulently, and he would be entitled, by reason of the misrepresentation, to rescind the contract, then, if it is claimed, in any proceedings arising out of the contract, that the contract ought to be or has been rescinded, the court or arbitrator may declare the contract subsisting and award damages in lieu of rescission, if of opinion that it would be equitable to do so, having regard to the nature of the misrepresentation and the loss that would be caused by it if the contract were upheld, as well as to the loss that rescission would cause to the other party.
    (3) Damages may be awarded against a person under subsection (2) of this section whether or not he is liable to damages under subsection (1) thereof, but where he is so liable any award under the said subsection (2) shall be taken into account in assessing his liability under the said subsection (1).

6.1.4 REMEDIES FOR MISREPRESENTATION

6.1.4.1 Rescission

WHITTINGTON v *SEALE-HAYNE* (1900) 82 LT 49 (ChD)

FARWELL J: The plaintiffs' action is one of the rescission of a lease on the ground of innocent misrepresentation, and the claim also asks for damages and an indemnity against all costs and charges incurred by the plaintiffs in respect of the lease and the insanitary condition of the premises. The suggestion was made that I should assume for the purpose of argument that innocent misrepresentations were made sufficient to entitle the plaintiffs to rescission. The question then arises to what extent the doctrine, that a plaintiff who succeeds in an action for rescission on the ground of innocent misrepresentation is entitled to be placed *in statu quo ante*, is to be applied. Counsel for the plaintiffs say that in such a case the successful party is to be placed in exactly the same position as if he had never entered into the contract. The defendant admits liability so far as regards anything which was paid under the contract, but not in respect of any damages incurred by reason of the contract; and I think the defendant's view is the correct one. . . . I think Bowen LJ's is the correct view. [In *Newbigging* v *Adam*] At p. 592 of 34 Ch Div he says: 'But when you come to consider what is the exact relief to which a person is entitled in a case of misrepresentation, it seems to me to be this and nothing more, that he is entitled to have the contract rescinded, and is entitled accordingly to all the incidents and consequences of such rescission. It is said that the injured party is entitled to be placed *in statu quo*. It seems to me that when you are dealing with innocent misrepresentation that you must understand that proposition that he is to be placed *in statu quo* with this limitation – that he is not to be replaced in exactly the same position in all respects, otherwise he would be entitled to recover damages, but is to be replaced in his position so far as regards the rights and obligations which have been created by the contract into which he has been induced to enter. That seems to me to be the true doctrine, and I think it is put in the neatest way in *Redgrave* v *Hurd* (*ubi sup.*)' That case decided that you cannot recover damages for innocent misrepresentation. And at p. 594 the Lord Justice goes on to say: 'Speaking only for myself, I should not like to lay down the proposition that a person is to be restored to the position which he held before the misrepresentation was made, nor that the person injured must be indemnified against loss which arises out of the contract, unless you place upon the words 'out of the contract' the limited and special meaning which I have endeavoured to shadow forth. Loss arising out of the contract is a term which would be too wide. It would embrace damages at common law, because damages at common law are only given upon the supposition that they are damages which would naturally and reasonably follow from the injury done'. With respect, if I may say so, I agree with every word the Lord Justice said. . . . This being so, the point I have here to consider is what is the limit of the liabilities which are within the indemnity. Mr Hughes admits that the rents, rates, and repairs under the covenants in the lease ought to be made good; but he disputes, and I agree with him, that the plaintiff is entitled to what is claimed by paragraph 11 of the statement of claim, which is really damages pure and simple.

6.1.4.2 Affirmation

LEAF v *INTERNATIONAL GALLERIES* [1950] 2 KB 86 (CA)

A picture had been sold as being painted by John Constable. Five years later it was discovered that it was not by Constable.

DENNING LJ: The question is whether the plaintiff is entitled to rescind the contract on the ground that the picture in question was not painted by Constable. I emphasize that it is a claim to rescind only: there is no claim in this action for damages for breach of condition or breach of warranty. The claim is simply one for rescission. At a very late stage before the county court judge counsel did ask for leave to amend by claiming damages for breach of warranty, but it was not allowed. No claim for damages is before us at all. The only question is whether the plaintiff is entitled to rescind.

The way in which the case is put by Mr Weitzman, on behalf of the plaintiff, is this: he says that this was an innocent misrepresentation and that in equity he is, or should be, entitled to claim rescission even of an executed contract of sale on that account. He points out that the judge has found that it is quite possible to restore the parties to their original position. It can be done by simply handing back the picture to the defendants.

In my opinion, this case is to be decided according to the well known principles applicable to the sale of goods. This was a contract for the sale of goods. There was a mistake about the quality of the subject-matter, because both parties believed the picture to be a Constable; and that mistake was in one sense essential or fundamental. But such a mistake does not avoid the contract: there was no mistake at all about the subject-matter of the sale. It was a specific picture, 'Salisbury Cathedral'. The parties were agreed in the same terms on the same subject-matter, and that is sufficient to make a contract: see *Solle* v *Butcher* [1949] 2 All ER 1107.

There was a term in the contract as to the quality of the subject-matter: namely, as to the person by whom the picture was painted – that it was by Constable. That term of the contract was, according to our terminology, either a condition or a warranty. If it was a condition, the buyer could reject the picture for breach of the condition at any time before he accepted it, or is deemed to have accepted it; whereas, if it was ony a warranty, he could not reject it at all but was confined to a claim for damages.

I think it right to assume in the buyer's favour that this term was a condition, and that if he had come in proper time he could have rejected the picture; but the right to reject for breach of condition has always been limited by the rule that, once the buyer accepted, or is deemed to have accepted, the goods in performance of the contract, then he cannot thereafter reject, but is relegated to his claim for damages: see s. 11(1)(c), of the Sale of Goods Act, 1893, and *Wallis, Son & Wells* v *Pratt & Haynes* [1910] 2 KB 1003.

The circumstances in which a buyer is deemed to have accepted goods in performance of the contract are set out in s. 35 of the Act, which says that the buyer is deemed to have accepted the goods, amongst other things, 'when, after the lapse of a reasonable time, he retains the goods without intimating to the seller that he has rejected them'. In this case the buyer took the picture into his house and, apparently, hung it there, and five years passed before he intimated any rejection at all. That, I need hardly say, is much more than a reasonable time, It is far too late for him at the end of five years to reject this picture for breach of any condition. His remedy after that length of time is for damages only, a claim which he has not brought before the court.

Is it to be said that the buyer is in any better position by relying on the representation, not as a condition, but as an innocent misrepresentation? I agree that on a contract for the sale of goods an innocent material misrepresentation may, in a proper case, be ground for rescission even after the contract has been executed. The observations of Joyce J in *Seddon* v *North Eastern Salt Co. Ltd* [1905] 1 Ch 326, are in my opinion, not good law. Many judges have treated it as plain that an executed contract of sale may be rescinded for innocent misrepresentation: see, for instance, per Warrington LJ and Scrutton LJ in *T. & J. Harrison* v *Knowles and Foster* [1918] 1 KB 608; per Lord Atkin in *Bell* v *Lever Bros. Ltd* [1932] AC 161; and per Scrutton LJ and Maugham LJ in *L'Estrange* v *Graucob Ltd* [1934] 2 KB 394.

Apart from that, there is now the decision of the majority of this court in *Solle* v *Butcher*, which overrules the first ground of decision in *Angel* v *Jay* [1911] 1 KB 666. But it is unnecessary to explore these matters now.

Although rescission may in some cases be a proper remedy, it is to be remembered that an innocent misrepresentation is much less potent than a breach of condition; and a claim to rescission for innocent misrepresentation must at any rate be barred when a right to reject for breach of condition is barred. A condition is a term of the contract of a most material character, and if a claim to reject on that account is barred, it seems to me a fortiori that a claim to recission on the ground of innocent misrepresentation is also barred.

So, assuming that a contract for the sale of goods may be rescinded in a proper case for innocent misrepresentation, the claim is barred in this case for the self-same reason as a right to reject is barred. The buyer has accepted the picture. He had ample opportunity for examination in the first few days after he had bought it. Then was the time to see if the condition or representation was fulfilled. Yet he has kept it all this time. Five years have elapsed without any notice of rejection. In my judgment he cannot now claim to rescind. His only claim, if any, as the county court judge said, was one for damages, which he has not made in this action. In my judgment, therefore, the appeal should be dismissed.

Lord Evershed MR and Jenkins LJ concurred.

6.1.5 DAMAGES FOR MISREPRESENTATION

6.1.5.1 Fraudulent misrepresentation

EAST v *MAURER* [1991] 2 All ER 733 (CA)

BELDAM LJ: . . .
The plaintiff bought a hairdressing salon from the defendant, relying on the defendant's misrepresentation that he had no intention of continuing to work in the area. Mrs East

started to run the salon on 1 September 1979. It was not long before it was apparant to her, and to others who were working in the salon, that the level of business was falling away at an alarming rate. In due course she learnt that the first defendant was working full-time at his Canford Cliffs salon.

For just over three years Mrs East tried to make the salon profitable. In her attempts she spent considerable sums on advertising; she installed a solarium bed and eventually began to combine the hairdressing business with a boutique.

During this period she made several attempts to sell the business and eventually, on 6 February 1989, she succeeded in selling the lease of the premises for £7,500. The learned judge found that the plaintiffs had behaved reasonably throughout; that they could not have sold the business before they actually did. He awarded them damages totalling £33,328; interest on the sums awarded brought the total award to £55,205.

His award was made up in this way. Firstly, he took the capital expenditure by taking the cost price of the business, £20,000, and deducting from it the amount realised on the sale, thus arriving at the figure of £12,500. Secondly, he awarded the plaintiffs the fees and expenses incurred by them in buying and selling the business and in carrying out improvements in an attempt to make it profitable. The figures awarded there amounted in total to £2,390. Next, he awarded trading losses incurred during the three and a quarter years during which the plaintiffs attempted to run the business. Those amounted to £2,438.

The next head of damages he awarded has led the defendants to appeal to this court against the amount of the damages. In addition to the sums already mentioned, he awarded the plaintiffs loss of profits during the three and a quarter year period arriving at a figure of £15,000. Finally he awarded the figure of £1,000 as general damages for disappointment and inconvenience of the plaintiffs in their attempt to establish this business. It is against the award of £15,000 for loss of profit that the defendants now appeal.

Mr Shawcross, for the defendants, submits that there is a difference in the manner in which damages are assessed for breach of contract and for the tort of deceit. He says that the authorities show that no damages at all are recoverable for loss of profits in an action of deceit. Although there is no express decision which states that to be the case, in no case which has dealt with the proper measure of damage in an action of deceit has there been an award for loss of profits, although one would have expected to see one. He concedes that if his submission in this regard is correct there would have to be a compensatory factor, for the learned judge only awarded interest on the capital expended from 2 February 1983, when the plaintiffs ceased to carry on the business and sold it. So Mr Shawcross concedes that, if his submission is right, the plaintiff would be entitled to interest on the award for that three and a quarter year period. Finally, he submits that, even if damages for loss of profit are recoverable, the learned judge assessed the figure at too high a level, and on an incorrect basis.

That the measure of damages for the tort of deceit and for breach of contract are different no longer needs support from authority. Damages for deceit are not awarded on the basis that the plaintiff is to be put in as good a position as if the statement had been true; they are to be assessed on a basis which would compensate the plaintiff for all the loss he has suffered, so far as money can do it. . . .

In the present cases it seems to me that the difference can be put in this way. The first defendant did not warrant to the plaintiffs that all the customers with whom he had a professional rapport would remain customers of the salon at Exeter Road. He represented that he would not be continuing to practise as a stylist in the immediate area. . . .

So I consider that on the facts found by the learned judge in the present case, the plaintiffs did establish that they had suffered a loss due to the defendants' misrepresentation which arose from their inability to earn the profits in the business which they hoped to buy in the Bournemouth area.

I would therefore reject the submission of Mr Shawcross that loss of profits is not a recoverable head of damage in cases of this kind.

However, I am not satisfied that in arriving at the figure of £15,000 the learned judge approached the quantification of those damages on the correct basis. It seems to me that he was inclined to base his award on an assessment of the profits which the business actually bought by the plaintiffs might have made if the statement made by the first defendant had amounted to a warranty that customers would continue to patronise the salon in Exeter Road; further, that he left out of account a number of significant factors. What he did was to found his award on an evaluation which he made of the profits of the business at Exeter Road made by the first defendant in the year preceding the purchase of the business by the plaintiffs. Basing himself on figures which had been given to him by an accountant, and making an allowance for inflation he arrived at a figure for the profits which might have been made if the first defendant had continued to run the business at Exeter Road during the three and a quarter years. He then made an allowance only for the fact that the second plaintiff's experience in hair styling and hairdressing was not as extensive or as cosmopolitan as that of the first defendant. Thus he based his award on an assessment of what the profits would have been, less a deduction of 25% for the second plaintiff's lack of experience.

It seems to me that he should have begun by considering the kind of profit which the second plaintiff might have made if the representation which induced her to buy the business at Exeter Road had not been made, and that involved considering the kind of profits which *she* might have expected in another hairdressing business bought for a similar sum. Mr Nicholson has argued that on the evidence of Mr Knowles, an experienced accountant, the learned judge could have arrived at the same or an equivalent figure on that basis. I do not agree. The learned judge left out of account the fact that the second plaintiff was moving into an entirely different area and one in which she was, comparatively speaking, a stranger, secondly, that she was going to deal with a different clientele and, thirdly, that there were almost certainly in that area of Bournemouth other smart hairdressing salons which represented competition and which, in any event, if the first defendant had, as he had represented, gone to open a salon on the continent, could have attracted the custom of his former clients.

The learned judge, as Mr Nicholson has pointed out, had two clear starting points: first, that any person investing £20,000 in a business would expect a greater return than if the sum was left safely in the bank or in a building society earning interest, and a reasonable figure for that at the rates then prevailing would have been at least £6,000; secondly, that the salary of a hairdresser's assistant in the usual kind of establishment was at this time £40 per week and that the assistant could expect tips in addition. That would produce a figure of over £2,000, but the proprietor of a salon would clearly expect to earn more, having risked his money in the business. It seems to me that those are valid points from which to start to consider what would be a reasonable sum to award for loss of profits of a business of this kind. As was pointed out by Winn LJ in *Doyle* v *Olby*, this is not a question which can be considered on a mathematical basis. It has to be considered essentially in the round, making what he described as a 'jury assessment' (see [1969] 2 All ER 119 at 124, [1969] 2 QB 158 at 169).

Taking all the factors into account, I think that the learned judge's figure was too high; for my part I would have awarded a figure of £10,000 for that head of damage, and to this extent I would allow the appeal.

Butler-Sloss and Mustill LJJ concurred.

DOYLE v *OLBY LTD* [1969] 2 QB 158 (CA)

LORD DENNING MR: Mr Doyle in 1963 was minded to buy a business. He saw an advertisement in 'Daltons Weekly'. He got particulars. The business was said to belong to Olby (Ironmongers) Ltd, 12 Upper High Street, Epsom, Surrey, and the turnover £27,000. The price asked for the lease, the business and goodwill was £4,500. The stock was to be taken at valuation. Mr Doyle made further enquiries about it. On November 6, 1963, Mr Leslie Olby, a director of the company, produced accounts to him. They were for the three years ending December 31, 1962. In a covering letter Mr Olby said:

Dear Mr Doyle,
As requested we are enclosing accountant's figures covering Olby (Ironmongers] Ltd, 12 Upper High Street, Epsom, Surrey.

Those figures showed that for those three years there had been considerable profits: £1,921 net profits in 1960; £1,749 in 1961; and £1,361 in 1962. Mr Doyle also saw Mr Cecil

Olby who worked on the premises. Mr Doyle asked Mr Cecil Olby what staff were employed. Mr Cecil Olby said: 'One manager, two assistants, one van-driver, and a part-time clerical assistant; with a wage bill of £42 a week'. He added that one of the staff was a very old man. Mr Doyle also asked Mr Cecil Olby how the trade was geared as between the retail trade and the wholesale trade. Mr Cecil said: 'Two-thirds retail; one-third wholesale – all over the counter'. In other words, it was trade which was done from the shop itself and would not need a traveller to go round and canvass for orders. On those representations, Mr Doyle agreed to buy the business.

The agreement was entered into in January, 1964. Mr Doyle agreed to pay £4,500 down in cash, which covered the goodwill, fixtures and fittings, and the remainder of the lease (which had about four years to run). The stock was to be bought on valuation. In addition, there was a restrictive covenant on the sellers, Olby (Ironmongers) Ltd, in which they covenanted that they would not for five years engage in any ironmongers' business within a radius of ten miles from 12 Upper High Steet, Epsom.

Mr Doyle paid the £4,500. He took over stock at a valuation of £5,000 which he paid. He needed a longer lease, so he surrendered the existing lease and took a longer lease at a greatly increased rent. The freeholder who benefited was Mr Cecil Olby himself.

In order to pay all the money, Mr Doyle put up all the cash he had – £7,000; and he raised £3,000 on mortgage from Askinex Ltd.

So he went into occupation. But I am afraid that things were very different from what he was led to believe. The turnover was far less than he had been told. The trade was not all over the counter. Half of the trade was wholesale business which could only be obtained by employing a traveller to go round to the customers. Mr Doyle could not afford to employ a traveller. So all that trade was lost. The whole transaction was a disaster for Mr Doyle. To add to his troubles, in February, 1964, soon after Mr Doyle went into occupation, a company called A. Olby & Son Ltd of Penge (which was closely associated with the vendor company, Olby (Ironmongers) Ltd) canvassed and sent travellers round to customers who had previously been customers of the Epsom business. The judge held that this was not a breach of the restrictive covenant, though I am not so sure about it.

Mr Doyle was most dissatisfied, and in May, 1964, he brought this action for damages for fraud and conspiracy against the company which sold him the Epsom business, that is, Olby (Ironmongers) Ltd; against Mr Cecil Olby, who was the man who worked in that business; Mr Leslie Olby, his brother, who was a director; and against A. Olby & Son Ltd, which was the company at Penge, of which Mr Leslie Olby was managing director.

Although Mr Doyle had started the action, he had to remain in occupation. He had burnt his boats and had to carry on with the business as best he could. He tried to sell it, but there were difficulties. One was that the landlord, Mr Cecil Olby, would not give him a licence to assign, and so forth. After three years he did manage to sell it for a sum of some £3,700. This cleared off the mortgage to Askinex Ltd, but he was left with many outstanding debts to the bank, to suppliers, and the like. His debts came to £4,000, and he has been sued in the county court by many of his creditors. . . . we approach the case on the accepted footing that Mr Doyle was induced by the fraud and conspiracy of the defendants to buy this business.

The judge awarded Mr Doyle £1,500 damages. Mr Doyle appeals against that award. He says it is far too small. The judge arrived at the figure of £1,500 by accepting the submissions of counsel then appearing for Mr Doyle. The judge said as to damages:

My task is simplified by the submissions of the plaintiff's counsel, which I accept, that there are two alternative bases for damages, each of which arrives at virtually the same round figure. . . . The first is that to preserve the trade custom it would have been necessary to employ a part-time traveller at about £600 a year, and I think there is a reasonable prospect that such a person could have been obtained. If two-and-a-half times this figure is taken, that being the normal basis for valuing goodwill, it actually represents, as I have said, a reduction in the value of the goodwill equivalent to the cost of making good the representation, that is, about £1,500. Secondly and alternatively, if the trade custom was 50 per cent of the turnover, its loss would result in a reduction in the value of the goodwill of 35 per cent to 40 per cent, which, applied to the accountant's figures of £4,000, again would approximate to a round figure of £1,500. Therefore, I think it is at this figure that I can best quantify the loss.

It appears, therefore, that the plaintiff's counsel submitted, and the judge accepted, that the proper measure of damages was the 'cost of making good the representation', or what came to the same thing, 'the reduction in value of the goodwill' due to the misrepresentation. In so doing, he treated the representation as if it were a contractual promise, that is, as if there were a contractual term to the effect 'The trade is all over the counter. There is no need to employ a traveller'. I think it was the wrong measure. Damages for fraud and conspiracy are assessed differently from damages for breach of contract.

It was submitted by Mr Smout that we could not or, at any rate, ought not to correct this error. I do not agree. We never allow a client to suffer for the mistake of his counsel if we can possibly help it. We will always seek to rectify it as far as we can. We will correct it whenever we are able to do so without injustice to the other side. Sometimes the error has seriously affected the course of the evidence, in which case we can at best order a new trial. But there is nothing of that kind here. The error was made at the end of the case. All the evidence had been taken on the footing that the damages were at large. It was only in the final submission that the error was made. Such an error we can, and will, correct.

The second question is what is the proper measure of damages for fraud, as distinct from damages for breach of contract. It was discussed during the argument in *Hadley* v *Baxendale* ((1854) 9 Ex 341), and finds a place in the notes to *Smith's Leading Cases*, 13th edn (1929) at p. 563, where it is suggested there is no difference. But in *McConnel* v *Wright* [1903] 1 Ch 546, 554, Lord Collins MR pointed out the difference. It was an action for fraudulent statements in a prospectus whereby a man was induced to take up shares. Lord Collins said of the action for fraud:

> It is not an action for breach of contract, and, therefore, no damages in respect of prospective gains which the person contracting was entitled by his contract to expect to come in, but it is an action of tort – it is an action for a wrong done whereby the plaintiff was tricked out of certain money in his pocket, and, therefore, prima facie, the highest limit of his damages is the whole extent of his loss, and that loss is measured by the money which was in his pocket and is now in the pocket of the company.

But that statement was the subject of comment by Lord Atkin in *Clark* v *Urquhart* [1930] AC 28, 67–68. He said:

> I find it difficult to suppose that there is any difference in the measure of damages in an action of deceit depending upon the nature of the transaction into which the plaintiff is fraudulently induced to enter. Whether he buys shares or buys sugar, whether he subscribes for shares, or agrees to enter into a partnership, or in any other way alters his position to his detriment, in principle, the measure of damages should be the same, and whether estimated by a jury or a judge. I should have thought it would be based on the actual damage directly flowing from the fraudulent inducement. The formula in *McConnel* v *Wright* [1903] 1 Ch 546 may be correct or it may be expressed in too rigid terms.

I think that Lord Collins did express himself in too rigid terms. He seems to have overlooked consequential damages. On principle the distinction seems to be this: in contract, the defendant has made a promise and broken it. The object of damages is to put the plaintiff in as good a position , as far as money can do it, as if the promise had been performed. In fraud, the defendant has been guilty of a deliberate wrong by inducing the plaintiff to act to his detriment. The object of damages is to compensate the plaintiff for all the loss he has suffered, so far, again, as money can do it. In contract, the damages are limited to what may reasonably be supposed to have been in the contemplation of the parties. In fraud, they are not so limited. The defendant is bound to make reparation for all the actual damages directly flowing from the fraudulent inducement. The person who has been defrauded is entitled to say:

> I would not have entered into this bargain at all but for your representation. Owing to your fraud, I have not only lost all the money I paid you, but, what is more, I have

been put to a large amount of extra expense as well and suffered this or that extra damages.

All such damages can be recovered: and it does not lie in the mouth of the fraudulent person to say that they could not reasonably have been foreseen. For instance, in this very case Mr Doyle has not only lost the money which he paid for the business, which he would never have done if there had been no fraud: he put all that money in and lost it; but also he has been put to expense and loss in trying to run a business which has turned out to be a disaster for him. He is entitled to damages for all his loss, subject, of course to giving credit for any benefit that he has received. There is nothing to be taken off in mitigation: for there is nothing more that he could have done to reduce his loss. He did all that he could reasonably to be expected.

This brings us to the third question: must we send the case back for a new trial for damages; or can we assess them ourselves? The difficulty is that we have not got a transcript of all the evidence. Mr Doyle is a poor man. He comes here without legal aid. He was unable to afford a transcript. The defendants, I presume, could afford it, but they have not thought fit to get one. There was a finding of fraud and conspiracy against them. They gave notice of appeal against that finding. Yet, they did not get a transcript of the evidence. It was they who ought to have done so. In these circumstances, I do not think it would be right to put either party to the expense of getting a full transcript of eight or nine days' evidence with all the delay that would entail. The court must do the best it can to put right the error which has taken place. I will not go into the details myself as to the figures. It is a case for assessing damages at large, much as a jury would do. Winn LJ has considered the matter carefully, and he will deal with it; but I say in advance that I agree with the figure which he is going to propose, that the damages should be in the sum of £5,500.

Winn and Sachs LJJ concurred.

6.1.5.2   Negligent misrepresentation

ROYSCOT TRUST LTD v *ROGERSON* [1991] 3 All ER 294 (CA)

A car dealer had misrepresented the amount of a deposit paid by a customer in order to obtain a larger loan from a finance company.

BALCOMBE LJ: This appeal, from a judgment of Judge Barr given in the Uxbridge County Court on 22 February 1990, raises an issue on the measure of damages for innocent misrepresentation under the Misrepresentation Act 1967. . . .

I turn to the issue on this appeal which the dealer submits raises a pure point of law: where (a) a motor dealer innocently misrepresents to a finance company the amount of the sale price of, and the deposit paid by the intended purchaser of, the car and (b) the finance company is thereby induced to enter into a hire-purchase agreement with the purchaser which it would not have done if it had known the true facts and (c) the purchaser thereafter dishonestly disposes of the car and defaults on the hire-purchase agreement, can the finance company recover all or part of its losses on the hire-purchase agreement, from the motor dealer?

The finance company's cause of action against the dealer is based on s. 2(1) of the Misrepresentation Act 1967. . . .

In view of the wording of the subsection it is difficult to see how the measure of damages under it could be other than the tortious measure and despite the initial aberrations referred to above, that is now generally accepted. Indeed counsel before us did not seek to argue the contrary.

The first main issue before us was: accepting that the tortious measure is the right measure, is it the measure where the tort is that of fraudulent misrepresentation, or is it the measure where the tort is negligence at common law? The difference is that in cases of fraud a plaintiff is entitled to any loss which flowed from the defendant's fraud, even if the loss could not have been foreseen: see *Doyle* v *Olby (Ironmongers) Ltd* [1969] 2 All ER 119, [1969] 2 QB 158. In my judgment the wording of the subsection is clear: the person making the innocent misrepresentation shall be 'so liable', ie liable to damages as if the representation had been made fraudulently. This was the conclusion to which Walton J came in *F & B Entertainments Ltd* v *Leisure Enterprises Ltd* (1976) 240 EG 455 at 461 (see also the decision of Sir Douglas Franks QC sitting as a deputy judge of the High Court in *McNally* v *Welltrade International Ltd* [1978] IRLR 497). In each of these cases the judge held that the basis for the assessment of damages under s. 2(1) of the 1967 Act is that established in *Doyle* v *Olby (Ironmongers) Ltd*. This is also the effect of the judgment of Eveleigh LJ in *Chesneau* v *Interhome Ltd* [1983] CA Transcript 238 already cited: 'By "so liable" I take it to mean liable as he would be if the misrepresentation had been made fraudulently'.

This was also the original view of the academic writers. In Atiyah and Treitel 'Misrepresentation Act 1967' (1967) 30 MLR 369 at 373–374 it says:

> The measure of damages in the statutory action will apparently be that in an action of deceit . . . But more probably the damages recoverable in the new action are the same as those recoverable in an action of deceit. . . .

Professor Treitel has since changed his view. In *Law of Contract* (7th edn, 1987) p. 278 he says:

> Where the action is brought under section 2(1) if the Misrepresentation Act, one possible view is that the deceit rule will be applied by virtue of the fiction of fraud. But the preferable view is that the severity of the deceit rule can only be justified in cases of actual fraud and that remoteness under section 2(1) should depend, as in actions based on negligence, on the test of foreseeability.

The only authority cited in support of the 'preferable' view is *Shepheard* v *Broome* [1904] AC 342, a case under s. 38 of the Companies Act 1867, which provided that in certain circumstances a company director, although not in fact fraudulent, should be 'deemed to be fraudulent'. As Lord Lindley said ([1904] AC 342 at 346):'. . . To be compelled by Act of Parliament to treat an honest man as if he were fraudulent is at all times painful', but he went on to say: 'but the repugnance which is naturally felt against being compelled to do so will not justify your Lordships in refusing to hold the appellant responsible for acts for which an Act of Parliment clearly declares he is to be held liable. . . .' The House of Lords so held.

It seems to me that that case, far from supporting Professor Treitel's view, is authority for the proposition that we must follow the literal wording of s. 2(1), even though that has the effect of treating, so far as the measure of damages is concerned, an innocent person as if he were fraudulent. *Chitty on Contracts* (26th edn, 1989) para. 439 says:

> . . . it is doubtful whether the rule that the plaintiff may recover even unforeseeable losses suffered as the result of fraud would be applied; it is an exceptional rule which is probably justified only in cases of actual fraud.

No authority is cited in support of that proposition save a reference to the passage in Professor Treitel's book cited above.

Professor Furmston in *Cheshire Fifoot and Furmston's Law of Contract* (11th edn, 1986) p. 286 says:

> It has been suggested [and the reference is to passage in Atiyah and Treitel's article cited above] that damages under section 2(1) should be calculated on the same principles as govern the tort of deceit. This suggestion is based on a theory that section 2(1) is based on a 'fiction of fraud'. We have already suggested that this theory is misconceived. On the other hand the action created by section 2(1) does look much more like an action in tort than one in contract and it is suggested that the rules for negligence are the natural ones to apply.

The suggestion that the 'fiction of fraud' theory is misconceived occurs in a passage which includes the following (p. 271):

Though it would be quixotic to defend the drafting of the section, it is suggested that there is no such 'fiction of fraud' since the section does not say that a negligent misrepresentor shall be treated for all purposes as if he were fraudulent. No doubt the wording seeks to incorporate by reference some of the rules relating to fraud but, for instance, nothing in the wording of the subsection requires the measure of damages for deceit to be applied to the statutory action.

With all respect to the various learned authors whose works I have cited above, it seems to me that to suggest that a different measure of damage applies to an action for innocent misrepresentation under the section than that which applies to an action for fraudulent misrepresentation (deceit) at common law is to ignore the plain words of the subsection and is inconsistent with the cases to which I have referred. In my judgment, therefore, the finance company is entitled to recover from the dealer all the losses which it suffered as a result of its entering into the agreements with the dealer and the customer, even if those losses were unforeseeable, provided that they were not otherwise too remote. . . .

Ralph Gibson LJ concurred.

HOWARD MARINE AND DREDGING v *OGDEN & SONS* [1978] 1 QB 574 (CA)

The defendant had innocently misrepresented the capacity of a barge, having relied on a figure in Lloyds Register.

BRIDGE LJ: The powerful arguments addressed to us on behalf of the defendants by Mr Anthony Lloyd have failed to persuade me that we could properly depart from the judge's primary findings of fact as to the substance of the all important conversations between the parties. Accepting those findings, there is no material in any of the communications between the parties prior to July 11, 1974, which amounted to a misrepresentation by Mr O'Loughlin, let alone to a warranty, with respect to the deadweight capacity of Howards' barges. In the course of the interview at Otley on July 11, however, Mr O'Loughlin told Mr Redpath that the barges would each carry about 1,600 tonnes subject to weather, fuel load, and time of the year. As the judge said, even with the qualification, this information was hopelessly wrong. It overstated the pay load capacity of the barges by about 50 per cent. To establish that this information was warranted as accurate by Howards, Ogdens would have to satisfy the court that Howards intended to assume such a contractual liability collateral to the main contract embodied in the charterparty. Considering the whole of the evidence of the negotiations between the parties from the initial exchange of letters through to the eventual conclusion of a contract on the terms of the charterparty and setting the Otley interview in that context it does not appear to me that Howards ever intended to bind themselves by such a collateral warranty.

Accordingly, in my judgment, Ogdens establish no claim against Howards in contract. But the remaining, and to my mind the more difficult question raised in this appeal is whether Mr O'Loughlin's undoubted misrepresentation gives rise to any liability in tort either under the provisions of the Misrepresentation Act 1967 or at common law for breach of a duty of care owed to Ogdens with respect to the accuracy of the information given. I will consider first the position under the statute. . . .

The first question then is whether Howards would be liable in damages in respect of Mr O'Loughlin's misrepresentation if it had been made fraudulently, that is to say, if he had known that it was untrue. An affirmative answer to that question is inescapable. The judge found in terms that what Mr O'Loughlin said about the capacity of the barges was said with the object of getting the hire contract for Howards, in other words, with the intention that it should be acted on. This was clearly right. Equally clearly the misrepresentation was in fact acted on by Ogdens. It follows, therefore, on the plain language of the statute that, although there was no allegation of fraud, Howards must be liable unless they proved that Mr O'Loughlin had reasonable ground to believe what he said about the barges' capacity.

It is unfortunate that the judge never directed his mind to the question whether Mr O'Loughlin had any reasonable ground for his belief. The question he asked himself, in considering liability under the Misrepresentation Act 1967, was whether the innocent misrepresentation was negligent. He concluded that if Mr O'Loughlin had given the inaccurate information in the course of the April telephone conversations he would have been negligent to do so but that in the circumstances obtaining at the Otley interview in July there was no negligence. I take it that he meant by this that on the earlier occasions the circumstances were such that he would have been under a duty to check the accuracy of his information, but on the later occasions he was exempt from any such duty. I appreciate the basis of this distinction, but it seems to me, with respect, quite irrelevant to any question of liability under the statute. If the representee proves a misrepresentation which, if fraudulent, would have sounded in damages, the onus passes immediately to the representor to prove that he had reasonable ground to believe the facts represented. In other words the liability of the representor does not depend upon his being under a duty of care the extent of which may vary according to the circumstances in which the representation is made. In the course of negotiations leading to a contract the statute imposes an absolute obligation not to state facts which the representor cannot prove he had reasonable ground to believe.

Although not specifically posing the question of whether he had reasonable ground for his belief, the judge made certain findings about Mr O'Loughlin's state of mind. He said:

> Mr O'Loughlin looked at the documents of the ships he was in charge of including HB2 and HB3's German documents. He is not a master of maritime German. He saw, but did not register, the deadweight figure of 1,055.135 tonnes. Being in the London office he went to the City and looked up Lloyd's Register. There he noted that the summer loading deadweight figure for B41 and B45, described as TM sand carriers, was 1,800 tonnes. This figure stayed in his mind. But it was one of Lloyd's Register's rare mistakes.

Later the judge said à propos of Mr O'Loughlin's state of mind at the Otley interview:

> He had in mind the 1,800 tonnes figure from the Bible [meaning Lloyd's Register] obviously an approximation and certainly subject to the Bible's caveat.

It is tempting to adopt these findings simpliciter and to conclude that the figure Mr O'Loughlin had seen in Lloyd's Register afforded reasonable ground for his belief. But the judge's summary in the passages I have cited from the judgment not only over-simplifies the effect of Mr O'Loughlin's evidence on this matter; it also embodies at one point a positive misapprehension of what Mr O'Loughlin said. In the transcript the following evidence is given:

> (Q) (by Mr Evans) Had you seen that document among the company's files prior to April 1974? (A) I would have said that I would have sighted it. (Bristow J) If you did see it, did it register? (A) Not really, my Lord.

The document, however, to which this evidence related was *not* the document containing the vital figure of the barges' deadweight capacity, but another German ship's document of earlier date. Mr O'Loughlin never said that the deadweight figure 'did not register' with him. He acknowledged that he had seen it and understood it. It is true he said that he had not noticed the discrepancy between the deadweight figure in the German ship's document and that in Lloyd's Register, though he had noticed a discrepancy in the figures for the gross and registered tonnage and he had quite correctly taken these latter figures from the German ship's documents.

He was pressed to explain how it came about that, having seen both the inaccurate figure in Lloyd's Register and the accurate figure in the German ship's documents for deadweight capacity he came to rely on the former and to disregard the latter. This certainly called for explanation since both according to the expert evidence and as a matter of common sense it would normally be expected that the original figures in the ship's documents were more reliable than the derivative figures in Lloyd's Register. This part of Mr O'Loughlin's evidence is of such importance that I will set out the crucial passages in full. He is asked about the vital document in chief:

(Q) Was this document in your possession? (A) It was, yes. (Q) Had you looked at this document at all? (A) I had, yes. Basically as soon as I started to go through it or look through it, I saw that all the measurements – all they were talking about was for work in freshwater or sweet water, they call it. (Q) I think if you looked at page 50, you would find the entry is 'Ladefähigkeit in Süsswasser' – a figure of 1,000.135 with no further measurement. Then if you turn to page 44, there is a figure for 'Tragfähigkeit' of 1,055.135 tonnes. Had you those entries in mind when you consulted Lloyd's Register? (A) Not really because, as I say, they are basically talking about a deadweight in freshwater and the other thing is that all the time when we are talking about barges of this nature, one doesn't talk about deadweight, one talks about their cubic capacity.

Then, in cross-examination:

Mr Lloyd: When you were giving your evidence yesterday, you said that you did not pay much attention to the document at 1/32 and 1/42 because the deadweight relates to freshwater? (A) That is correct. (Q) But I think you also accepted this morning that that would only make a difference of about 25/30 tonnes at the most to the deadweight cargo carrying capacity? (A) Something of that order. (Q) So that would still give you a much more accurate view of the deadweight in saltwater than anything else that was available to you? (Bristow J) Mr Lloyd, the point is made. It is there for better or for worse. It is a beautiful one, but it is made! (Mr Lloyd) Now, you based yourself you said instead – You rejected this figure because it was freshwater and you based yourself instead on the Lloyd's Register figure of 1,800 tonnes? (A) Precisely. [Finally, in cross-examination:] (Q) You knew that the figure in the German document, the deadweight, was 1,050 tonnes in freshwater? (Bristow J) He says he has seen it, but it had not registered. (Mr Lloyd) You had seen that figure? (A) I had looked at that – (Q) You had seen that figure had you not? (A) I had seen that figure among many others in German. (Q) And you rejected it, as you told my Lord yesterday, for two reasons; because it was freshwater and because you were only concerned with cubic capacity? (A) That is precisely so.

It should be pointed out that the judge's intervention in the last passage quoted reflects the same misapprehension as the passage cited from his judgment.

I am fully alive to the dangers of trial by transcript and it is to be assumed that Mr O'Loughlin was perfectly honest throughout. But the question remains whether his evidence, however benevolently viewed, is sufficient to show that he had an objectively reasonable ground to disregard the figure in the ship's documents and to prefer the Lloyd's Register figure. I think it is not. The fact that he was more interested in cubic capacity could not justify reliance on one figure of deadweight capacity in preference to another. The fact that the deadweight figure in the ship's documents was a freshwater figure was of no significance since, as he knew, the difference between freshwater and sea water deadweight capacity was minimal. Accordingly I conclude that Howards failed to prove that Mr O'Loughlin had reasonable ground to believe the truth of his misrepresentation to Mr Redpath. . . .

I would accordingly allow the appeal to the extent of holding that Ogdens establish liability against Howards under section 2(1) of the Misrepresentation Act 1967 for any damages they suffered as a result of Mr O'Loughlin's misrepresentation at the Otley interview in the terms as found by the judge.

Shaw LJ concurred; Lord Denning MR dissented.

6.2 Duress

PAO ON v LAU YIU LONG [1979] 3 All ER 65 (PC)

In this extract Lord Scarman indicates the requirements for duress, and in particular for 'economic duress'.

LORD SCARMAN: Duress, whatever form it takes, is a coercion of the will so as to vitiate consent. Their Lordships agree with the observation of Kerr J in *The Siboen and The Sibotre* [1976] 1 Lloyd's Rep 293 that in a contractual situation commercial pressure is not enough. There must be present some factor 'which could in law be regarded as a coercion of his will so as to vitiate his consent'. This conception is in line with what was said in this Board's decision in *Barton v Armstrong* [1975] 2 All ER 465 by Lord Wilberforce and Lord Simon of Glaisdale, observations with which the majority judgment appears to be in agreement. In determining whether there was a coercion of will such that there was no true consent, it is material to enquire whether the person alleged to have been coerced did or did not protest; whether, at the time he was allegedly coerced into making the contract, he did or did not have an alternative course open to him such as an adequate legal remedy; whether he was independently advised; and whether after entering the contract he took steps to avoid it. All these matters are, as recognised in *Maskell v Horner* [1915] 3 KB 106, relevant in determining whether he acted voluntarily or not.

In the present case there is unanimity amongst the judges below that there was no coercion of Lau's will. In the Court of Appeal the trial judge's finding (already quoted) that Lau considered the matter thoroughly, chose to avoid litigation, and formed the opinion that the risk in giving the guarantee was more apparent than real was upheld. In short, there was commerical pressure, but no coercion. Even if this Board was disposed, which it is not, to take a different view, it would not substitute its opinion for that of the judges below on this question of fact.

It is therefore unnecessary for the Board to embark on the enquiry into the question whether English law recognises a category of duress known as 'economic duress'. But since the question has been fully argued in this appeal, their Lordships will indicate very briefly the view which they have formed. At common law money paid under economic compulsion could be recovered in an action for money had and received: see *Astley v Reynolds* (1731) 2 Sta 915. The compulsion had to be such that the party was deprived of his 'freedom of excercising his will'. It is doubtful, however, whether at common law any duress other than duress to the person sufficed to render a contract voidable; see Blackstone's Commentaries and *Skeate v Beale* (1841) 11 Ad & E 1983. American law (Williston on Contracts) now recognises that a contract may be avoided on the ground of economic duress. The commercial pressure alleged to constitute such duress must, however, be such that the victim must have entered the contract against his will, must have had no alternative course open to him, and must have been confronted with coercive acts by the party exerting the presssure: see Williston on Contracts. American judges pay great attention to such evidential matters as the effectiveness of the alternative remedy available, the fact or absence of protest, the availability of independent advice, the benefit received, and the speed with which the victim has sought to avoid the contract. Recently two English judges have recognised that commerical pressure may constitute duress the pressure of which can render a contract voidable: see Kerr in *The Siboen and The Sibotre* and Mocatta J in *North Ocean Shipping Co. Ltd v Hyundai Construction Co. Ltd* [1978] 3 All ER 1170. Both stressed that the pressure must be such that the victim's to the contract was not a voluntary act on his part. In their Lordship's view, there is nothing contrary to principle in recognising economic duress as a factor which may render a contract voidable, provided always that the basis of such recognition is that it must amount to a coercion of will, which vitiates consent. It must be shown that the payment or the contract entered into was not a voluntary act.

ATLAS EXPRESS LTD v KAFCO (IMPORTERS AND DISTRIBUTORS) LTD
[1989] 1 All ER 641 (QB)

TUCKER J: By their statement of claim the plaintiffs, Atlas Express Ltd, claim against the defendants, Kafco (Importers and Distributors) Ltd, £17,031.83 plus interest, as outstanding payments due to them under a number of invoices submitted to the defendants. It is admitted that some of this has since been paid, and the sum now claimed is £10,970.37.

The plaintiffs are well-known carriers of goods by road in the United Kingdom. They offer a parcels delivery service. The defendant company derives its name from the first letters of the surnames of its three original directors, Messrs King, Armiger and Fox. The company imports basketware from abroad and supplies it to retailers in the United Kingdom.

On 24 June 1986 the plaintiffs entered into a general trading agreement with the defendants whereby the plaintiffs agreed to deliver cartons of the defendants' basket-ware at a rate per carton depending on the number of cartons in the load. By October 1986 the defendants had entered into an agreement to supply their basketware to Woolworth shops in the United Kingdom. The defendants wished the plaintiffs to make the deliveries for them, and the plaintiffs agreed to do so. The terms of this agreement were contained in a trading agreement signed by Mr Armiger on the defendants' behalf on 20 October 1986. The rate agreed was expressed as being £1.10 per carton. There was a minimum charge of £7.50 per consignment but this referred to the delivery to each branch. The agreement was silent as to the size of the cartons or as to the number of cartons necessary to constitute a load. The rate was expressed to be effective from 10 October 1986 to a review on 31 May 1987. The case proceeded on the basis that this was a concluded agreement. Neither the plaintiffs' nor the defendants' counsel submitted that it was not capable of giving effect to the parties' intentions, and this issue was not raised in the pleadings.

The rate agreement was that orally agreed between Mr Armiger and Mr Hope, the manager of the plaintiffs' in Wellingborough. They met at the defendants' warehouse at Tinker's Drove, Wisbech, on 10 October 1986. Mr Hope had gone there to see a sample of the goods his company were being asked to deliver. He was shown a range of cartons of the sort the defendants used. He cannot say what size the largest carton was which he then saw, because he did not take any measurements. The trailers which the plaintiffs used were 40 feet long. Mr Hope says he calculated the rate per carton on the basis that the plaintiffs would be transporting a minimum of 400 cartons, and possibly as many as 600, on each trailer, thus producing a minimum return of £440 per load. In order to achieve this quantity per load, it would be necessary that no carton should exceed a measurement of 2ft 6in in any dimension. Mr Hope said that to the best of his memory, he and Mr Armiger discussed the basis on which the rate was calculated, though later he agreed that he was not sure they had had a conversation about a load of 400. Mr Armiger was firmer in his evidence. He said that the sizes of the cartons were never discussed and nothing was said about the number of cartons which would be carried, and that he could not have agreed a figure of 400 because he never knew what revenue the plaintiffs expected, and he did not know how many cartons could be loaded onto a trailer.

I prefer Mr Armiger's evidence on this point. I think his recollection of the conversation is clearer than Mr Hope's, and I believe him. His account is confirmed to some extent by the telex which he sent to Mr Hope on 13 October, referring simply to the rate per carton and not to size or number. Further, when Mr Hope drew up the trading agreement, he made no mention of these matters. As I have already indicated, there was no reference to this in the written agreement which Mr Armiger signed on 20 October. But when Mr Hope wrote to Mr Armiger on 17 November about raising a minimum charge, he referred to the initial quote of £1.10 per carton but he did not suggest that the basis on which this figure had been agreed had ever been discussed at the initial meeting.

In any event, the plaintiffs' counsel said that he did not rely on any knowledge by Mr Armiger of the basis on which the calculation was made. This was not part of his pleaded case, and he did not submit that this was a term of the contract between the parties, or that it was a representation made by or on behalf of the defendants.

Much more important is the question of the sample or mix of cartons which Mr Hope saw at the defendants' warehouse at Tinker's Drove, Wisbech. It is agreed that he did not see any of the goods destined for Woolworth, because they were stored at another warehouse called Wisbech Roadways. But I accept the evidence of Mr Armiger, supported to a great extent by that of Mr King, that the cartons which Mr Hope did see included three kinds of the same size as those in which the Woolworth goods were contained, and that the fourth kind of carton used to pack Woolworth's goods was of a smaller size than the three kinds which Mr Hope saw. I find that the plaintiffs had already carried those three sizes of cartons for the defendants under their general agreement. I also find that the largest carton to be carried for Woolworth was a bale measuring 6 feet long by 18 inches in diameter, and that bales of that kind and size were present at Mr Hope's inspection. I find that Mr Hope saw a fair representative mix of the kind of cartons which his company was being asked to deliver, and that he was given every opportunity of inspecting what was there, so as to enable him to calculate the rate to be quoted. It may be that Mr Hope mistakenly believed that he could load more cartons onto a trailer than was physically possible but, in fixing the rate of £1.10 per carton, he was not in any way misled by the defendants and he should not have been deceived by the sample and mix of the cartons which he saw.

In pursuance of the written agreement, the plaintiffs proceeded to make the first delivery. When Mr Hope saw the load from the defendants, he said he was suprised to see how large the cartons were and how many large cartons were included in the load. He said they were far larger than the parties had contemplated and because of this there were fewer of them, only 200 instead of the 400 he had anticipated. He said he had no prior knowledge that cartons of that size would be included. I find that he is wrong about this. I accept Mr Armiger's evidence that the load was representative of the type of cartons which Mr Hope had seen at the warehouse, and that the cartons were no larger than those inspected by him.

However, Mr Hope was convinced that it would not be financially viable to carry such a load at the rate agreed. He contacted Mr Armiger about it, in an attempt to renegotiate the rate. I find that the two of them met to discuss it, and that Mr Hope made it plain to Mr Armiger that the plaintiffs would not carry any more goods under the Woolworth agreement unless the defendants agreed to pay at least a minimum rate of £440 per trailer load. I find that if the defendants had refused, the plaintiffs would not have made any further deliveries. However, I find that no agreement to renegotiate the terms of the contract was reached at this stage.

The defendants were a small company and their three directors were personally committed to its success. They had secured a large order from Woolworth and had obtained a large quantity of goods to fulfil it. It was essential to the defendants' success and to their commercial survival that they should be in a position to make deliveries. I find that this was obvious to Mr Hope, and was known by him. It was now early November, a time of year when demands on road hauliers and deliverers are heaviest.

It would have been difficult, if not impossible, for the defendants to find alternative carriers in time to meet their delivery dates.

I find that the meeting between Mr Hope and Mr Armiger took place on Friday, 14 November. I derive this date from a letter written by Mr Hope on 17 November, which would have been the following Monday. The letter is in these terms:

> Further to our conversation on Friday 14 November, I would confirm the necessity for Atlas Express Limited to raise a minimum charge of £440 per trailer for distribution to the Woolworth Stores. Our initial quote of £1.10 per carton was based purely and simply on our achieving a minimum of 400 cartons per trailer, indeed we were anticipating a far higher figure in some instances. It is unfortunate that this has added considerably to your distribution costs. However, we as a company could not accommodate your operation whilst achieving such a possibly low revenue per movement. I have, therefore, enclosed an updated trading agreement for covering this new aspect of the operation which I will require signing and handing back to my driver by return.

The following day, 18 November, one of the plaintiffs' drivers arrived at the defendants' premises with an empty trailer. He brought with him a document entitled 'Amended Transferred Account Details'. Mr Hope had written in the new rates, which now specified a minimum charge of £400 per trailer. Mr Armiger did not want to agree to this, and he had not done so at the meeting. He queried it with the driver, who said that he had instructions that if the defendants did not sign the agreement he was to take the trailer away unloaded. Mr Armiger had done his best at the meeting to persuade Mr Hope to reduce his demands, but the only concession he had achieved was that the minimum charge would not apply to deliveries within the five counties nearest to the plaintiffs' depot at Wellingborough. Mr Armiger tried to contact Mr Hope on 18 November, but he was unable to do so. Mr Hope was unavailable. I infer that this was deliberate. It prevented the defendants from protesting to him. In these circumstances, Mr Armiger justifiably felt himself to be in a situation of 'take it or leave it'. He could not afford to lose the plaintiffs' services, with all the consequences that would ensue, so he signed the agreement. Before doing so, he wrote in the concession which he had obtained.

I find that when Mr Armiger signed that agreement he did so unwillingly and under compulsion. He believed on reasonable grounds that it would be very difficult, if not impossible, to negotiate with another contractor. He did not regard the fact that he had signed the new agreement as binding the defendants to its terms. He had no bargaining power. He did not regard it as a genuine armslength renegotiation in which he had a free and equal say and, in my judgment, that view was fully justified.

In the words of the co-director, Mr Fox, he felt that he was 'over a barrel'. He tried in vain to contact Mr Hope but, as he said to Mr Armiger, they really had no option but to sign. I accept the evidence of the Woolworth manager, Mr Graham, that if the defendants had told them that they could not supply the goods Woolworth would have sued them for loss of profit and would have ceased trading with them. I find that this was well known to the defendants' directors.

After Mr Armiger signed the agreement, the plaintiff's driver agreed to load a delivery. Thereafter the plaintiffs carried the defendants' goods and delivered them to Woolworth until 29 December 1986. The plaintiffs knew that the defendants would not be paid by Woolworth until deliveries were completed, and the plaintiffs agreed that they would not expect payment from the defendants until the defendants had been paid by Woolworth. Mr Hope recognised that this would not be before 30 January 1987.

On 2 January 1987 the defendants sent to the plaintiffs a cheque for £10,000, expressed as being a payment on account. I do not regard that as an acceptance of the new terms. The defendants made their position quite clear through their solicitors, who wrote to the plaintiffs on 2 March 1987, saying that the revised contract was signed under duress. This was three months before the plaintiffs commenced proceedings.

The issue which I have to determine is whether the defendants are bound by the agreement signed on their behalf on 18 November 1986. The defendants contend that they are not bound, for two reasons: first, because the agreement was signed under duress; second, because there was no consideration for it.

The first question raises an interesting point of law, i e whether economic duress is a concept known to English law.

Economic duress must be distinguished from commercial pressure, which on any view is not sufficient to vitiate consent. The borderline between the two may in some cases be indistinct. But the authors of *Chitty on Contracts* (25th edn,1983) and of *Goff and Jones on the Law of Restitution* (3rd edn, 1986) appear to recognise that in appropriate cases economic duress may afford a defence, and in my judgment it does. It is clear to me that in a number of English cases judges have acknowleged the existence of this concept.

Thus, in *D & C Builders Ltd v Rees* [1965] 3 All ER 837 at 841, [1966] 2 QB 617 at 625 Lord Denning MR said: 'No person can insist on a settlement procured by intimidation'. And in *Occidental Worldwide Investment Corp v Skibs A/S Avanti, The Siboen and the Sibotre* [1976] 1 Lloyd's Rep 293 at 336 Kerr J appeared to accept that economic duress could operate in appropriate circumstances. A similar conclusion was reached by Mocatta J in *North Ocean Shipping Co. Ltd v Hyundai Construction Co. Ltd, The Atlantic Baron* [1978] 3 All ER 1170 at 1182, [1979] QB 705 at 719.

In particular, these are passages in the judgment of Lord Scarman in *Pao On v Lau Yui* [1979] 3 All ER 65 at 78–79, [1980] AC 614 at 635–636, which clearly indicate recognition of the concept. . . . A further case, which was not cited to me was *B & S Contracts and Design Ltd v Victor Green Publications Ltd* [1984] ICR 419 at 423, where Eveleigh LJ referred to the speech of Lord Diplock in another uncited case, *Universe Tankships Inc of Monrovia v International Transport Workers Federation* [1982] 2 All ER 67 at 75–76, [1983] AC 366 at 384:

The rationale is that his apparent consent was induced by pressure exercised on him by that other party which the law does not regard as legitimate, with the consequence that the consent is treated in law as revocable unless approbated either expressly or by implication after the illegitimate pressure has ceased to operate on his mind.

In commenting on this Eveleigh LJ said of the word 'legitimate' [(1984] ICR at 419 at 423):

For the purpose of this case it is sufficient to say that if the claimant has been influenced against his will to pay money under the threat of unlawful damage to his economic interest he will be entitled to claim the money back. . . .

Reverting to the case before me, I find that the defendants' apparent consent to the agreement was induced by pressure which was illegitimate and I find that it was not approbated. In my judgment that pressure can properly be described as economic duress, which is a concept recognised by English law, and, which in the circumstances of the present case vitiates the defendants' apparent consent to the agreement.

In any event, I find that there was no consideration for the new agreement. The plaintiffs were already obliged to deliver the defendants' goods at the rates agreed under the terms of the original agreement. There was no consideration for the increased minimum charge of £440 per trailer.

Accordingly, I find that the plaintiffs' claim fails, and there will be judgment for the defendants with costs.

6.3   Undue Influence

6.3.1   ACTUAL UNDUE INFLUENCE

WILLIAMS v *BAYLEY* (1866) LR 1 HL 200 (HL)

A bank put pressure on the father of a young man who had forged his father's signature to some promissory notes.

LORD CRANWORTH LC: My Lords, although the facts of this case are somewhat complicated, and extend over a considerable length of time, I do not think it is necessary, in giving the advise I am about to tender to your Lordships, that I should go into any details of the facts, because, having occupied the consideration of the House for two or three days, they are, I am quite sure, present to the minds of all persons concerned. It will be sufficient, I think, to start from this point, that on Friday the 17th April, 1863, the father being at a railway station, and circumstances having arisen which caused these bankers to have doubts about the signatures to certain bills or promissory notes, and the bankers wishing to satisfy themselves whether a signature was, as it purported to be, that of the father, James Bayley, they presented to him a note of £500 made by the son, and purporting to contain the father's signature, and asked him whether that was his signature. The father denied it. The bank manager, who was present, was much surprised to find that the signature was not correct, and it was arranged that the matter should be looked into, that it should stand over then, and that there should be another meeting with the parties on the following day. It appears that, in the course of the evening of that day, the son William Bayley was communicated with. He was informed of what had taken place; and, I suppose, the conclusion was come to in the family that the son had been in the habit of using his father's name without his sanction. I say 'using his father's name without his sanction', for I have no doubt at all in coming to the conclusion (there is not a tittle of evidence to the contrary) that all these signatures were forgeries. That they were not the signatures of the father is clear, and I do not think there is the smallest reason to suppose that he ever gave his son any express or implied authority to sign the bills in his name.

This matter appears to have come to the knowlege of the family on the evening of the same day. One member of the family, Thomas Abishai Bayley (another son of the respondent and brother of William), who is not at all involved in these transactions, went with his father to the bank, and then considerable negotiation took place. It is obvious that at the time the bankers must have seen that they were in great jeopardy as to the notes, and that they would probably lose their money unless the father came in and assisted the son. I cannot, however, but come to the conclusion, from the evidence, that they strongly suspected, indeed they must be said to have known, that these signatures were forgeries. If the signatures were forgeries, then the bankers were in this position, that they had the means of prosecuting the son. That was clear.

Now the question is, what was the sort of influence which they exercised on the mind of the father to induce him to take on himself the responsibility of paying these notes? Was it merely, we do not know these to be forgeries, we do not believe them to be so, but your son is responsible for them, and if you do not help him we must sue him for the amount? Or was it, if you do not pay these notes we shall be in a position to prosecute him for forgery, and we will prosecute him for forgery? What is the fair inference from what took place?

I do not know what may be the opinion of the rest of your Lordships but I very much agree with the argument of Sir Hugh Cairns, that it is not pressure in the sense in which a court of equity sets aside transactions on account of pressure, if the pressure is merely this: 'If you do not do such and such an act I shall reserve all my legal rights, whether against yourself, or against your son'. If it had only been, 'if you do not take on yourself the debt of your son, we must sue you for it', I cannot think that that amounts to pressure, when parties are at arms' length, and particularly when, as in this case, the party supposed to be influenced by pressure had the assistance of his solicitor, not, indeed, on the first occasion, but afterwards, before anything was done. But if what really takes place is this: If you do not assist your son, by taking on yourself the payment of these bills and notes on which there are signatures which are said, at least, to be forgeries, you must not be surprised at any course we shall take, meaning to insinuate, if not to say, we shall hold in our hands the means of criminally prosecuting him for forgery. I say, if it amounts to that, that it is a very different thing. When the parties met on Saturday, there was a very significant expression made use of by Mr Deakin, the manager, in the presence of one of the bankers, Henry Williams, 'We do not wish to exercise pressure on you if it can be satisfactorily arranged'. Does the 'pressure' mean a pressure arising from our exercising the power, or keeping in our hands the means of exercising the power, of instituting a criminal prosecution? Or does it mean the 'pressure' of getting you to make yourself responsible for your son's debt? It must have meant the former, because the context shews that the other was alternatively provided for. When it was said, we do not wish to exercise pressure if it can be satisfactorily arranged, that could not mean, if you take on yourself the debt, without pressure, we don't mean to press you. That would be nonsensical. But, on the other interpretation of the words, the sense is very plain. 'If you can satisfactorily arrange this, and if you choose' (according to another expression that was used) 'to treat it as a matter of business', that is, to take it upon yourself the debt, we will not exercise 'pressure'. Of course not. The 'pressure' there referred to must be something different from merely obtaining the security of the father. It amounts to this: 'Take your choice – give us security for your son's debt. If you take that on yourself, then it will go smoothly; if you do not, we shall be bound to exercise pressure'; which could only mean, to exercise those rights which remain to us, by reason of our holding signatures forged by your son.

That is what took place on the 18th. It was then arranged that there should be another meeting on the 20th. It was urged in the argument, that the bankers could not have contemplated a prosecution, because they allowed two days to elapse, during which the son might have escaped. But all parties supposed that the father could prevent the prosecution by giving what the bank required. On Monday, the 20th, the parties met the father, the son, and other members of the family, with the father's solicitor, all met at the bank office, On that occasion, farther conversation takes place. There had been some negotiations going on, to see how the debts of the son could be met or satisified, what assets he had, and so forth. The father said something about the son paying the bankers by instalments of £1,000 a-year. To which one of the bankers answered, 'We shall have nothing to do with any £1,000 a-year. If the bills are yours' (addressing the plaintiff) 'we are all right. If they are not, we have only one course to pursue; we cannot be parties to compounding a felony'. Now, according to my interpretation of the law, it does not amount to compounding a felony. But one sees clearly what the parties meant. It was this: If you choose to take on yourself the responsibility of these bills, all will be right; but if not, we cannot be parties to what they call 'compounding a felony'; but what Lord Ellenborough more correctly called 'stifling a prosecution'. I think that is the only interpretation that can possibly be put on what passed. Then, in the course of this same conversation, the solicitor of the bankers said 'Yes, it is a serious matter', and Mr Duignan remarked, 'it is a case of transportation for life'. Now that was said in the hearing of the bankers. They must have heard it. They must have known, while all these negotiations were going on, that all the parties to them understood that this was a case, not of life or death, but of transportation for life. The father, then , was acting in this matter under the notion that if he did not interfere to save his son, the latter would be liable to be prosecuted, and probably, would be prosecuted for forgery, and so be transported for life.

Then that being, as I think, the clear inference from all the evidence, the question arises: What is the law applicable to such a case? These bankers hold a number of acceptances which one can hardly suppose they did not believe to be forged acceptances. I say that because they never suggest any doubt on the subject. Although the bill of the plaintiff was amended and re-amended, and in the last re-amended bill there is a special charge that the bankers never suggested that the notes, which certainly were not in the plantiff's handwriting, were signed with the privity of the plantiff, the bankers, in answering that bill, never deny that; but, on the other hand, one of the witnesses, Thomas Bayley, I think, says that during the whole meeting no such suggestion was ever made. I asked Sir Hugh Cairns, in the course of his argument this morning, if he could point out any suggestion of that kind as having been made; but the only approach to such a suggestion that he could refer to was a question addressed to the father, as to one of the notes, to this effect: 'Why did you not answer the letter informing you that it was dishonoured?' It is very true that lawyers might fully understand what that might mean, but I cannot think that could possibly be understood by the parties as amounting to this, that we do not admit that this indorsements, though not in your handwriting, were not signed by your authority. I think that is an inference which, under all the circumstances of this case, never could be dreamt of as deducible from what so passed. That being so, I think the case in point of fact is this: – Here are several forged notes. The bankers, in the presence of the father and of the person who forged them, both being persons of apparent respectability in the country, carrying on business as tradesmen, and the father having the presence and the assistance of his solicitor, the bankers say to him what amounts to this: 'Give us security to the amount of these notes, and they shall all be delivered up to you; or do not give us security, and then we tell you we do not mean to compound a felony; in other words, we mean to prosecute'. That is the fair inference from what passed. Now is that transaction which a court of equity will tolerate, or is it not? I agree very much with a good deal of the argument of Sir Hugh Cairns as to this doctrine of pressure. Many grounds on which a court of equity has acted in such cases do not apply in this case. The parties were not standing in any fiduciary relation to one another; and if this had been a legal transaction I do not know that we should have thought that there was any pressure that would have warranted the decree made by the Vice-Chancellor. But here was a pressure of this nature. We have the means of prosecuting, and so transporting your son. Do you choose to come to his help and take on yourself the amount of his debts – the amount of these forgeries? If you do we will not prosecute; if you do not, we will. That is the plain interpretation of what passed. Is that, or is it not, legal? In my opinion, my Lords, I am bound to go the length of saying I do not think it is legal. I do not think that a transaction of that sort would have been legal even if, instead of being forced on the father, it had been proposed by him and adopted by the bankers . . .

Lords Chelmsford and Westbury concurred.

6.3.2 PRESUMED UNDUE INFLUENCE

LLOYD'S BANK v *BUNDY* [1974] 3 All ER 757 (CA)

This concerned possible undue influence of a bank over a long-standing elderly customer, who had mortgaged his house to guarantee his son's business debts.

SIR ERIC SACHS: . . . Undue influence is a phrase which is commonly regarded – even in the eyes of a number of lawyers – as relating solely to occasions when the will of one person has become so dominated by that of another that, to use the county court judge's words, 'the person acts as the mere puppet of the dominator'. Such occasions, of course, fall within what Cotton LJ in *Allcard* v *Skinner* (1887) 36 ChD 145, 171 described as the first class of cases to which the doctrine on undue influence applies. There is, however, a second class of such cases. This is referred to by Cotton LJ as follows:

In the second class of cases the court interferes, not on the ground that any wrongful act has in fact been committed by the donee, but on the ground of public policy, and to prevent the relations which existed between the parties and the influence arising therefrom being abused.

It is thus to be emphasised that as regards the second class the exercise of the court's jurisdiction to set aside the relevant transaction does *not* depend on proof of one party being 'able to dominate the other as though a puppet' (to use the words again adopted by the county court judge when testing whether the defence was established) nor any wrongful intention on the part of the person who gains a benefit from it; but on the concept that once the special relationship has been shown to exist, no benefit can be retained from the transaction unless it has been positively established that the duty of fuduciary care has been entirely fulfilled. To this second class, however, the judge never adverted and plainly never directed his mind.

It is also to be noted that what constitutes fulfilment of that duty (the second issue in the case now under consideration) depends again on the facts before the court. It may in the particular circumstances entail that the person in whom confidence has been reposed should insist on independent advice being obtained or ensuring in one way or another that the person being asked to execute a document is not insufficiently informed of some factor which could affect his judgment. The duty has been well stated as being one to ensure that the person liable to be influenced has formed 'an independent *and informed* judgment', or, to use the phraseology of Lord Evershed MR in *Zamet v Hyman* [1961] 1 WLR 1442, 1446, 'after full, free *and informed* thought'. (The underlining in each case is mine.) As to the difficulties in which a person may be placed and as to what he should do when there is a conflict of interest between him and the person asked to execute a document: see *Bank of Montreal v Stuart* [1911] AC 120, 139.

Stress was placed in argument for the bank on the effect of the word 'abused' as it appears in the above cited passage in the judgment of Cotton LJ and in other judgments and textbooks. As regards the second class of undue influence, however, that word in the context means no more than that once the existence of a special relationship has been established, then any possible use of the relevant influence is, irrespective of the intentions of the persons possessing it, regarded in relation to the transaction under consideration as an abuse – unless and until the duty of fiduciary care has been shown to be fulfilled or the transaction is shown to be truly for the benefit of the person influenced. This approach is a matter of public policy. . . . What happened on December 17, 1969, has to be assessed in the light of the general background of the existence of the long-standing relations between the Bundy family and the bank. It not infrequently occurs in provincial and country branches of great banks that a relationship is built up over the years, and in due course the senior officials may become trusted councillors of customers of whose affairs they have an intimate knowledge. Confidential trust is placed in them because of a combination of status, goodwill and knowledge. Mr Head was the last of a relevant chain of those who over the years had earned, or inherited, such trust whilst becoming familiar with the finance and business of the Bundys and the relevant company: he had taken over the accounts from Mr Bennett (a former assistant manager at Salisbury) of whom Mr Bundy said 'I always trusted him'.

The fact that Mr Bundy may later gave referred to Mr Head as being 'straight' is not inconsistent with this view – see also the statement of Mr Trethowan that 'defendant is straightforward. Agrees with anyone'. Indeed more than one passage in Mr Bundy's evidence is consistent with Mr Head's vital answer as to the implicit reliance placed on his advice.

It is, of course, plain that when Mr Head was asking Mr Bundy to sign the documents, the bank would derive benefit from the signature, that there was a conflict of interest as between the bank and Mr Bundy, that the bank gave him advice, that he relied on that advice, and that the bank knew of the reliance. The further question is whether on the evidence concerning the matters already recited there was also established that element of confidentiality which has been discussed. In my judgment it is thus established. Moreover reinforcement for that view can be derived from some of the material which it is more convenient to examine in greater detail when considering what the resulting duty of fiduciary care entailed.

What was required to be done on the bank's behalf once the existence of that duty is shown to have been established? The situation of Mr Bundy in his sitting room at Yew Tree Farm can be stated as follows. He was faced by three persons anxious for him to sign. There was his son Michael, the overdraft of whose company had been, as is shown by the correspondence, escalating rapidly; whose influence over his father was observed by the judge – and can hardly not have been realised by the bank; and whose ability to overcome the difficulties of his company was plainly doubtful, indeed its troubles were known to Mr Head to be 'deep-seated'. There was Mr Head, on behalf of the bank, coming with the documents designed to protect the bank's interest already substantially made out and in his pocket. There was Michael's wife asking Mr Head to help her husband.

The documents Mr Bundy was being asked to sign could result, if the company's troubles continued, in Mr Bundy's sole asset being sold, the proceeds all going to the bank, and his being left penniless in his old age. That he could thus be rendered penniless was known to the bank – and in particular Mr Head. That the company might come to a bad end quite soon with these results was not exactly difficult to deduce (less than four months later, on April 3, 1970, the bank were insisting that Yew Tree Farm be sold).

The situation was thus one which to any reasonably sensible person, who gave it but a moment's thought, cried aloud Mr Bundy's need for careful independent advice. Over and above the need any man has for counsel when asked to risk his last penny on even an apparently reasonable project, was the need here for informed advice as to whether there was any real chance of the company's affairs becoming viable if the documents were signed. If not, there arose questions such as, what is the use of taking the risk of becoming penniless without benefiting anyone but the bank? Is it not better both for you and your son that you, at any rate, should still have some money when the crash comes? Should not the bank at least bind itself to hold its hand for some given period? The answers to such questions could only be given in the light of a worth-while appraisement of the company's affairs – without which Mr Bundy could not come to an informed judgment as to the wisdom of what he was doing.

No such advice to get an independent opinion was given; on the contrary, Mr Head chose to give his own views on the company's affairs and to take this course, though he had at trial to admit: 'I did not explain the company's affairs very fully as I had only just taken over'. (Another answer that escaped entry in the judge's original notes).

On the above recited facts, the breach of the duty to take fiduciary care is manifest. . . .

The existence of the duty and its breach having thus been established, there remains the submission urged by Mr Rankin that whatever independent advice had been obtained, Mr Bundy would have been so obstinately determined to help his son that the documents would anyway have been signed. That point fails for more than one reason, of which it is sufficient to mention two. First, on a question of fact, it ignores the point that the independent advice might well have been to the effect that it would benefit the son better in the event of an inevitable crash if his father had some money left after it occurred – advice which could have affected the mind of Mr Bundy. Secondly, once the relevant duty is established, it is contrary to public policy that benefit of the transaction be retained by the person under that duty unless he positively shows that the duty of fiduciary care has been fulfilled: there is normally no room for debate on the issue as to what would have happened had the care been taken.

It follows that the county court judgment cannot stand. The judge having failed to direct his mind to a crucial issue and to important evidence supporting Mr Bundy's case thereon, at the very least the latter is entitled to an order for a new trial. That would produce as an outcome of this appeal a prolongation of uncertainties affecting others beside Mr Bundy, who still resides at Yew Tree Farm, and could hardly be called desirable even if one left out of account the latter's health and financial position. In my judgment, however, a breach by the bank of their duty to take fiduciary care has, upon the evidence, as a whole been so affirmatively established that this court can and should make an order setting aside the guarantee and the charge of December 17, 1969.

Cairns LJ concurred; Lord Denning agreed with the result, but on slightly different grounds.

NATIONAL WESTMINSTER BANK v MORGAN [1985] 1 All ER 821 (HL)

LORD SCARMAN: My Lords, the appellant, the National Westminster Bank plc (the bank), seeks against Mrs Janet Morgan (the wife), the respondent in the appeal, an order for the possession of a dwelling house in Taunton. The house is the wife's family home. She acquired it jointly with her husband, and since his death on 9 December 1982 has been the sole owner. The bank relies on a charge by way of legal mortgage given by her and her husband to secure a loan granted to them by the bank. The manner in which the wife came to give this charge is at the heart of the case. The only defence to the bank's action with which your Lordships are concerned is the wife's plea that she was induced to execute the charge by the exercise of undue influence on the part of the bank. The bank, she says, procured the charge by bringing to bear undue influence on her at an interview at home which Mr Barrow, the bank manager, sought and obtained in early February 1978. . . . Two issues are said to arise: the first, the substantive issue, is whether the wife has established a case of undue influence; the second, said to be procedural, is whether, if she has, she ought properly to be granted equitable relief, and the nature of any such relief. The two issues are, in truth, no more than different aspects of one fundamental question: has the wife established a case for equitable relief? For there is no longer any suggestion that she has a remedy at law. Unless the transaction can be set aside on the ground of undue influence, it is inimpeachable.

I now come to the heart of the case. It is not suggested, nor could it be, that prior to the interview at which the wife signed the charge the relationship between the bank and its two customers, the husband and the wife, had been other than the normal business one of banker and customer. It was business for profit so far as the bank was concerned; it was a rescue operation to save their house so far as the two customers were concerned.

But it is said on behalf of the wife that the relationship between the bank and herself assumed a very different character when in early February Mr Barrow called at the house to obtain her signature to the charge; the husband had already signed.

The trial judge set the scene for the critical interview by these findings of fact: husband and wife were looking for a rescue operation by the bank to save the home for themselves and their children; they were seeking from the bank only a breathing space of some five weeks; and the wife knew that there was no other way of saving the house.

Mr Barrow's visit to the house lasted 15 to 20 minutes. His conversation with the wife lasted only five minutes. The wife's concern was lest the document which she was being asked to sign might enable the husband to borrow from the bank for business purposes. She wanted the charge confined to paying off the Abbey National and to the provision of bridging finance for about five weeks. She told Mr Barrow that she had no confidence in her husband's business ability and did not want the mortgage to cover his business liabilities. Mr Barrows advised her that the cover was so limited. She expressed her gratitude to the bank for saving their home. The judge found that the bank was not seeking any advantage other than to provide on normal commercial terms but at extremely short notice the bridging finance necessary to secure their home. He rejected the suggestion that the wife had any misgivings on the basis that she would prefer the house to be sold. He accepted that it was never the intention of Mr Barrow that the charge should be used to secure any other liability of the husband.

The atmosphere in the home during Mr Barrow's visit was plainly tense. The husband was in and out of the room, 'hovering around'. The wife made it clear to Mr Barrow that she did not want him there. Mr Barrow did manage to discuss the more delicate matters when he was out of the room.

Such was the interview in which it is said that Mr Barrow crossed the line which divides a normal business relationship from one of undue influence. I am bound to say that the facts appear to me to be a far cry from a relationship of undue influence or from a transaction in which an unfair advantage was obtained by one party over the other. The trial judge clearly so thought, for he stated his reasons for rejecting the wife's case with admirable brevity. He made abundantly clear his view that the relationship between Mr Barrow and the wife never went beyond that of a banker and customer, that the wife had made up her own mind that she was ready to give the charge, and that the one piece of advice (as to the legal effect of the charge) which Mr Barrow did give, though erroneous as to the terms of the charge, correctly represented his intention and that of the bank. The judge dealt with three points. First, he ruled on the submission by the bank that the transaction of loan secured on the property was not one of manifest disadvantage to the wife since it provided what to her was desperately important, namely the rescue of the house from the Abbey National. He was pressed, of course, with the contrast between unlimited terms of the legal charge and the assurance (to which at all times the bank adhered) by Mr Barrow that the charge was limited to paying off the Abbey National and the bridging finance. He considered the balance to be between the 'enormous' advantage of preserving the home from the Abbey National and the 'essentially theoretical' disadvantage of the written charge, and accepted the submission that the transaction was not manifestly disadvantageous to the wife.

Second, he rejected the submission made on behalf of the wife that Mr Barrow put pressure on her. In his view the pressure on her was the knowledge that Abbey National were on the point of obtaining possession with a view to the sale of her home. It was, however, suggested that Mr Barrow had made a mistake in the advice which he gave her as to the nature of the charge. Mr Barrow's mistake was not as to the bank's intentions but as to the wording of the charge. He accurately stated the bank's intention and events have proved him right. I would add in passing that no case of misrepresentation by Mr Barrow was sought to be developed at the trial and the case of negligence is not pursued.

The judge recognised that Mr Barrow did not advise her to take legal advice; but he held that the circumstances did not call for any such advice and that she was not harried into signing. She was signing to save her house and to obtain short-term bridging finance. 'The decision', the judge said, 'was her own'.

Third, he rejected the submission that there was a confidential relationship between the wife and the bank such as to give rise to a presumption of undue influence. Had the relationship been such as to give rise to the presumption, he would have held, as counsel for the bank conceded, that no evidence had been called to rebut it. He concluded that the wife had failed to make out her case of undue influence.

The Court of Appeal disagreed. The two Lords Justices who constituted the court (Dunn and Slade LJJ) (surely it should have been a court of three) put an interpretation on the facts very different from that of the judge; they also differed from him on the law.

As to the facts, I am far from being persuaded that the trial judge fell into error when he concluded that the relationship between the bank and the wife never went beyond the normal business relationship of banker and customer. . . .

But further, the view of the law expressed by the Court of Appeal was, I shall endeavour to show, mistaken. Dunn LJ, while accepting that in all the reported cases to which the court was referred the transactions were disadvantageous to the person influenced, took the view that in cases where public policy requires the court to apply the presumption of undue influence there is no need to prove a disadvantageous transaction (see [1983] 3 All ER 85 at 90). Slade LJ also clearly held that it was not necessary to prove a disadvantageous transaction where the relationship of influence was proved to exist. . . . I know of no reported authority where the transaction set aside was not to the manifest disadvantage of the person influenced. It would not always be a gift: it can be a 'hard and equitable' agreement (see *Ormes* v *Beadel* (1860) 2 Giff 166 at 174, 66 ER 70 at 74); or a transaction 'immoderate and irrational' (see *Bank of Montreal* v *Stuart* [1911] AC 120 at 137) or 'unconscionable' in that it was a sale at an undervalue (see *Poosathurai* v *Kannappa Chettiar* (1919) LR 47 Ind App 1 at 3–4). Whatever the legal character of the transaction, the authorities show that it must constitute a disadvantage sufficiently serious to require evidence to rebut the presumption that in the circumstances of the relationship between the parties it was produced by the exercise of undue influence. In my judgment, therefore, the Court of Appeal erred in law in holding that the presumption of undue influence can arise from the evidence of the relationship of the parties without also evidence that the transaction itself was wrongful in that it constituted an advantage taken of the person subjected to the influence which, failing proof to the contrary, was explicable only on the basis that undue influence had been exercised to procure it. . . .

. . . The wrongfulness of the transaction must, therefore, be shown: it must be one in which an unfair advantage has been taken of another. The doctrine is not limited to transactions of gift. A commercial relationship can become a relationship in which one party assumes a role of dominating influence over the other. In *Poosathuri's case* (1919) LR 47 Ind App 1 the Board recognised that a sale at an undervalue could be a transaction which a court could set aside as unconscionable if it was shown or could be presumed to have been procured by the exercise of undue influence. Similarly, a relationship of banker and customer may become one in which the banker acquires a dominating influence. If he does and a manifestly disadvantageous transaction is proved, there would then be room for the court to presume that it resulted from the exercise of undue influence.

6.3.3 LOSS OF RIGHT TO RESCIND

ALLCARD v *SKINNER* (1887) 36 ChD 145 (CA)

The plaintiff had given money to the defendant who was the superior of a religious order of which the plaintiff was at the time a member.

BOWEN LJ: This is a case of great importance. There are no authorities which govern it; my brethren, on whose experience in matters of equity I naturally should rely, differ, and on that ground I have thought it right to express my own views upon the point. It is a question which must be decided upon broad principles, and we have to consider what is the principle, and what is the limitation of the principle, as to voluntary gifts where there is no fraud on the part of the defendant, but where there is an all-powerful religious influence which disturbs the independent judgment of one of the parties, and subordinates for all worldly purposes the will of that person to the will of the other.

It seems to me that it is of essential importance to keep quite distinct two things which in their nature seem to me to be different – the rights of the donor, and the duties of the donee and the obligations which are imposed upon the conscience of the donee by the principles of this court. As to the rights of the donor in a case like the present I entertain no doubt. It seems to me that persons who are under the most complete influence of religious feelings are perfectly free to act upon it in the disposition of their property, and not the less free because they are enthusiasts. Persons of this kind are not dead in law. They are dead indeed to the world so far as their own wishes and feelings about the things of the world are concerned; but such indifference to things external does not prevent them in law from being free agents. In the present instance there was no duress, no incompetency, no want of mental power on the part of the donor. It seems to me that, so far as regards her rights, she had the absolute right to deal with her property as she chose. Passing next to the duties of the donee, it seems to me that, although this power of perfect disposition remains in the donor under circumstances like the present, it is plain that equity will not allow a person who exercises or enjoys a dominant religious influence over another to benefit directly or indirectly by the gifts which the donor makes under or in consequence of such influence, unless it is shewn that the donor, at the time of making the gift, was allowed full and free opportunity for counsel and advice outside – the means of considering his or her worldly position and exercising an independent will about it. This is not a limitation placed on the action of the donor; it is a fetter placed upon the conscience of the recipient of the gift, and one which arises out of public policy and fair play. If this had been the gift of a chattel, therefore, the property then would have passed in law, and the gift of this stock may be treated upon a similar method of reasoning. Now, that being the rule, in the first place, was the plaintiff entitled to the benefit of it? She had vowed in the most sacred and solemn way absolute and implicit obedience to the will of the defendant, her superior, and she was bound altogether to neglect the advice of externs – not to consult those outside the convent. Now I offer no sort of criticism on institutions of this sort; no kind of criticism upon the action of those who enter them, or of those who administer them. In the abstract I respect their motives, but it is obvious that it is exactly to this class of case that the rule of equity which I have mentioned ought to be applied if it exists. It seems to me that the plaintiff, so long as she was fettered by this vow – so long as she was under the dominant influence of this religious feeling – was a person entitled to the protection of the rule. Now, was the defendant bound by this rule? I acquit her most entirely of all selfish feeling in the matter. I can see no sort of wrongful desire to appropriate to herself any worldy benefit from the gift; but, nevertheless, she was a person who benefited by it so far as the disposition of the property was concerned, although, no doubt, she meant to use it in conformity with the rules of the institution, and did so use it. I pause for one moment to say a word as to Mr Justice Kekewich's view, which is not altogether consistent with the above. He seems to have thought that the question turned on the original intention of the donor at the time she entered the convent, and that what passed subsequently could be treated as if it were a mere mechanical performance of a complete mental intention originally formed. I entirely agree with the view presented to us by the appellants as to that part of Mr Justice Kekewich's judgment. It seems to me that the case does not turn upon the fact that the standard of duty was originally created by the plaintiff herself, although her original intention is one of the circumstances, no doubt, which bear upon the case, and is not to be neglected. But it is not the crucial fact. We ought to look, it seems to me, at the time at which the gift was made, and to examine what was then the condition of the donor who made it. For these reasons I think that without any interference with the freedom of persons to deal with their property as they please, we can hold but one opinion, that in 1879 the plaintiff could have set this gift aside.

Then comes the question of the time which has elapsed since. What effect has time upon a right to the protection of this rule? The rule is an equity arising out of public policy. I do not think that the delay in itself is an absolute bar, though it is a fact to be considered in determining the inference of fact which appears to me to be the one that we must draw on one side or the other. I have described, to the best of my power, what to my mind the principle of the rule is. It is a principle arising out of public policy, and one which imposes a fetter upon the conscience of the recipient of the gift. When is that barrier removed from the conscience of the recipient of the gift. It seems to me that the common-sense answer ought to be – and I think the right answer is – as soon as the donor escapes from the religious influence which hampered her at the time, as soon as she becomes free, and has determined to leave the gift where it is. Now, if she has so acted, if her delay has been so long as reasonably to induce the recipient to think, and to act upon the belief that the gift is to lie where it has been laid, then, by estoppel, it appears to me that the donor of the gift would be prevented from revoking it. But I do not base my decision here upon the ground of estoppel. Yet a long time has elapsed. Five years is a long time in the life of anybody, and is a long time in the life of a person who has passed her life in seclusion like the plaintiff. Every day and every hour during those five years she has had the opportunity of reflecting upon her past life and upon what she has done. She has had that opportunity since she passed away from the influence of the defendant, and that she did pass away from it most completely is proved to demonstration by the fact that she entered a different religious community. Having belonged to the Church of England she at once entered the Church of Rome. The influence, therefore, ceased completely. She was surrounded by persons perfectly competent to give her proper advice. She had her solicitor. She had her brother, a barrister himself, and she had the directors of the consciences of of the community which she had entered. I draw unhesitatingly the inference, under the circumstances, that she did, in or shortly after 1879, consider this matter and determine not to interfere with her previous disposition. Was she aware of her rights at the time she formed this resolution? In my view I incline to think that she must have been, having regard to the character of the advisers who surrounded her; but I do not consider it to be essential to draw that inference. It is enough if she was aware that she might have rights and deliberately determined not to inquire what they were or to act upon them. There, again, I unhesitatingly draw the inference that she was aware that she had rights or might have them and that she deliberately made up her mind not to enforce them. In drawing this inference of fact I do no discredit to the character of the plaintiff, which is above all reproach, but on carefully considering her evidence I do not feel that I can place reliance upon her memory; and, in my view, it would be wrong to draw the inference from her evidence that she did in her own mind never form any definite view about the property she left behind in the convent.

I need hardly say that I feel great embarrassment in having to give the casting vote in a matter of such great importance, when two whose opinions and authority are far greater than my own differ in the matter. In my view, this appeal ought to be dismissed, and dismissed on the ground that the time which has elapsed, though not a bar in itself, though not accurately to be described as mere laches which disentitles the plaintiff to relief, is nevertheless, coupled with the other facts of the case, a matter from which but one reasonable inference ought to be drawn by men of the world – namely, that the lady considered her position at the time, and elected and chose not to disturb the gift which she then at that moment felt, if she had the will, she had the power to disturb.

The appeal is therefore dismissed with costs.

Lindley LJ concurred; Cotton LJ dissented.

6.4   Inequality of Bargaining Power

CRESSWELL v POTTER [1978] 1 WLR 255 (ChD)

MEGARRY J: The facts of this case lie within a narrow compass. The plaintiff, a telephonist, was formerly the wife of the defendant. They were married on October 29, 1955, a decree nisi was granted on July 1, 1959, and the decree was made absolute on October 1, 1959. The divorce was granted on the defendant's petition. A house, no. 98, St. Andrew's Avenue, Colchester, was acquired in the defendant's name at or shortly after the time of the marriage, subject to a mortgage. The plaintiff contributed nothing towards the purchase price; but certain improvements to the house were effected by the defendant, his father and friends, and it is common ground that the plaintiff paid for at least some of the materials. The defendant put the plaintiff's contribution at about £65, whereas the plaintiff says that it was some £200. It was certainly not trivial; for the defendant says that it comprised a fireplace, a bath (of second quality), a basin, a water-closet, taps, a hot-water cylinder, a radiator, piping and fitting. He explains the apparently low cost of these as being due to the purchase being made at trade prices over 10 years ago.

In 1958, when the Colchester house had been sold for a price which left a surplus of some £300 or £350 after discharging the mortgage and costs, the premises which give rise to the dispute were bought and conveyed to the plaintiff and the defendant as joint tenants in law and in equity. No suggestion has been made that the plaintiff did not thereupon become beneficially entitled to a potential half interest. These premises, which included about an acre and a half of land, were known as Slate Hall, Wakes Colne, Essex. The conveyance was dated November 29, 1958, and so was a mortgage to the Halifax Building Society which was executed by the plaintiff and the defendant. The consideration for the conveyance was £1,500, and the loan was £1,200.

The marriage was soon in trouble, and in June 1959, the plaintiff left the defendant, having confessed to him some while earlier that she was pregnant by another man. Shortly after the decree absolute she remarried. The divorce was undefended, and evidence of the plaintiff's adultery was obtained by Mr Thomas Olyott, an inquiry agent. On August 6, 1959, the plaintiff executed the document upon which this case turns. It was stated to be a conveyance, and by it, in return for an indemnity against the liabilities under the mortgage but for no other consideration, the plaintiff released and conveyed to the defendant all her interest in Slate Hall. I shall call this deed 'the release'.

On December 9, 1960, the defendant sold part of Slate Hall for £1,950. On September 12, 1961, aided by a planning permission for the erection of houses on the land which he obtained a year or more after the execution of the release, the defendant made a contract to sell the remainder of Slate Hall for £1,400; and this later sale was completed. The total obtained for the property was thus £3,350. After allowing for costs, moving expenses and the like, the defendant's view is that he made a 'profit' of some £1,400 on the whole deal.

The plaintiff does not seek to upset these dispositions, but claims that the release is ineffective as regards the proceeds of sale, and that she is entitled to half of these. No point has been taken upon the jurisdiction to set aside the release in this qualified manner. What the defendant says is, quite simply, that the release is valid. The whole case turns on whether or not the release was executed in circumstances which, the plaintiff alleges, amount to unfair dealing. The release was drafted by Mr Puxon, an experienced solicitor who was acting for the defendant in the divorce. He drafted it in consequence of messages that he had received from the defendant that the plaintiff would give up her interest in the house. Looking back, Mr Puxon agrees that it would have been better if the plaintiff had been separately advised. As it was, he had the release given to Mr Olyott with instructions to get it executed by the plaintiff.

On August 4, 1959, Mr Olyott called at the house where the plaintiff was staying. He had seen the plaintiff at least twice before in connection with the divorce. As on previous occasions, he asked the plaintiff to come out into his car; for there was illness in the house. He can remember very little about the execution of the release. He could not remember the document, or whether he asked the plaintiff to read it; and he did not know what was in it. He was not interested. The plaintiff signed it, and Mr Olyott added his name and address to the attestation clause, describing himself as a retired police inspector, as, indeed, he was, in addition to being an inquiry agent.

According to the plaintiff, Mr Olyott said that the document was for the sale of the house. She made some inquiry about whether she would get her money back, and Mr Olyott said that so far as he knew she would. The reference to getting her money back was to what she had spent on the Colchester house. She did not read the release, and thought that she was signing a document which would make it possible to sell the property without affecting her rights in it.

The defendant asserts that at some stage before the divorce the plaintiff had said to him that she did not want anything to do with Slate Hall, or that it was not any good to her if she could not live there. He said that he had had Slate Hall put into their joint names because, having been employed as a carpenter, he was going to start up on his own as a builder, and if he went bankrupt he would still have the house to live in. It has very properly not been suggested that this in any way prevented the plaintiff from becoming entitled to a beneficial interest in the premises.

Mr Sunnucks, for the plaintiff, has put before me a considerable number of authorities on setting aside transactions at an undervalue. I think I can go straight to the well-known case of *Fry v Lane* (1888) 40 ChD 312. In his judgment, Kay J considered many of the authorities, and then said at p. 322:

> The result of the decisions is that where a purchase is made from a poor and ignorant man at a considerable undervalue, the vendor having no independent advice, a Court of Equity will set aside the transaction. This will be done even in the case of property in possession, and a fortiori if the interest be reversionary. The circumstances of poverty and ignorance of the vendor, and absense of independent advice, throw upon the purchaser, when the transaction is impeached, the onus of proving, in Lord Selborne's words, that the purchase was 'fair, just, and reasonable'.

The reference to Lord Selborne LC's words is a reference to his judgment in *Earl of Aylesford* v *Morris* (1873) 8 Ch App 484, 491.

The judge thus laid down three requirements. What has to be considered is, first, whether the plaintiff is poor and ignorant; second, whether the sale was at a considerable undervalue; and third, whether the vendor had independent advice. I am not, of course, suggesting that these are the only circumstances which will suffice; thus there may be circumstances of oppression or abuse of confidence which will invoke the aid of equity. But in the present case only these three requirements are in point. Abuse of confidence, though pleaded, is no longer relied on; and no circumstances of oppression or other matters are alleged. I must therefore consider whether the three requirements laid down in *Fry v Lane* are satisfied.

I think that the plaintiff may fairly be described as falling within whatever is the modern equivalent of 'poor and ignorant'. Eighty years ago, when *Fry v Lane* was decided, social conditions were very different from those which exist today. I do not, however, think that the principle has changed, even though the euphemisms of the 20th century may require the word 'poor' to be replaced by 'a member of the lower income group' or the like, and the word 'ignorant' by 'less highly educated'. The plaintiff has been a van driver for a tobacconist, and is a Post Office telephonist. The evidence of her means is slender. The defendant told me that the plaintiff probably had a little saved, but not much; and there was evidence that her earnings were about the same as the defendant's, and that these were those of a carpenter. The plaintiff also has a legal aid certificate.

In those circumstances I think the plaintiff may properly be described as 'poor' in the sense used in *Fry v Lane*, where it was applied to a laundryman who, in 1888, was earning £1 a week. In this context, as in others, I do not think that 'poverty' is confined to destitution. Further, although no doubt it requires considerable alertness and skill to be a good telephonist, I think that a telephonist can properly be described as 'ignorant' in the context of property transactions in general and the execution of conveyancing documents in particular. I have seen and heard the plaintiff giving evidence, and I have reached the conclusion that she satisfies the requirements of the first head.

The second question is whether the sale was at a 'considerable undervalue'. Slate Hall cost £1,500, £1,200 of the price being provided by the mortgage. The release recited that £1,196 13s. 5d. remained outstanding on the mortgage, so that very little had been paid off the capital sum due. Nevertheless, all that the plaintiff was getting for giving up her half interest in Slate Hall was the release from her liability under the mortgage. If Slate Hall was worth no more than it cost, she was giving up her half share in an equity worth £300; and, after all, the mortgage was a recent mortgage to a well-known building society. If she had sought advice it is unlikely in the extreme that she would have been told that there was any real probability that the value of the property would be less than the sum due under the mortgage. There can be little doubt that she was getting virtually nothing for £150. . . .

The defendant's view of the transaction was that the plaintiff was giving him nothing. He had lost so much, he said. He had lost his wife and his young child (who left with the plaintiff), and his home had been broken up. I find it hard, however, to treat the execution of the release by the plaintiff as amounting in effect to conscience money, conferring upon the defendant merely some compensation in respect of the plaintiff having left him for another man, or anything like it. What was done by the release was, in substance, that a gift was made by a wife who was being divorced to the husband who was divorcing her; and such a transaction, though by no means impossible, is at least not very usual, and would, I think, have to be established by evidence a good deal more convincing than anything I have heard.

At the end of the day, my conclusion is that this transaction cannot stand. In my judgment the plaintiff has made out her case, and so it is for the defendant to prove that the transaction was 'fair, just, and reasonable'. This he has not done. The whole burden of his case has been that the requirements of *Fry v Lane*, 40 ChD 312, were not satisfied, whereas I have held that they were. I fully accept that the plaintiff's claim is open to some justifiable criticisms. It was brought none too promptly, and it took some time for the full claim to be formulated. The plaintiff's idea initially seems to have been that she ought to recover the money expended by her in materials for the Colchester house; and this, guided no doubt by legal advice, later became a claim to half the proceeds of sale of Slate Hall.

I give full weight to these and other criticisms that Mr Balcombe has so cogently put forward. Yet having seen and heard the witnesses, I accept the plaintiff's evidence in its essentials. I would, of course, be reluctant to do anything to weaken the security given by solemn conveyancing documents executed under seal. Nevertheless, although Mr Puxon at no time acted for the plaintiff, in acting for the defendant I think he ought to have realised that if he did no more than send an inquiry agent round to get the release executed by the plaintiff, with no explanation of its effect, no discussion of its contents, and no attempt to warn her that she ought to get independent advice unless she understood it, questions as to its validity might well arise. The document abounds in terms which, though speaking to the conveyancer in language of precision, can hardly be expected to speak to a van driver and telephonist lucidly or, indeed, at all.

It would not have been very difficult to send to the plaintiff a short covering letter which explained that by signing the release the plaintiff would be giving up her half-share in Slate Hall to the defendant in return for nothing except an agreement by him that she would never have to pay anything under the mortgage, adding that she ought to consider getting independent advice before signing the document. If in the teeth of that information the plaintiff had executed the release without obtaining such advice, I think that the requirement that there should be independent advice might well have been discharged. In other words, I do not think that the requirement of independent advice should be regarded as an absolute. But here there was no attempt whatever to comply with the requirement, whether absolute or qualified.

Accordingly, it seems to me that this action ought to succeed, and, subject to discussion of the terms of the appropriate order, I so hold.

NATIONAL WESTMINSTER BANK LTD v *MORGAN* [1985] 1 All ER 821 (HL)

In this further extract from this case (see also above, **p. 246**), Lord Scarman deals with Lord Denning's argument for a broad doctrine of 'unconscionable transactions' based on 'inequality of bargaining power'.

LORD SCARMAN: . . . This brings me to *Lloyd's Bank Ltd* v *Bundy* [1974] 3 All ER 757, [1975] QB 326. It was, as one would expect, conceded by counsel for the wife that the relationship between banker and customer is not one which ordinarily gives rise to a presumption of undue influence; and that in the ordinary course of banking business a banker can explain the nature of the proposed transaction without laying himself open to a charge of undue influence. This proposition has never been in doubt, though some, it would appear, have thought that the Court of Appeal held otherwise in *Lloyd's Bank Ltd* v *Bundy*. If any such view has gained currency, let it be destroyed now once and for all time (see [1974] 3 All ER 757 at 763, 766, 767, [1975] QB 326 at 336, 340, 341–342 per Lord Denning MR, Cairns LJ and Sir Eric Sachs). Your Lordships are, of course, not concerned with the interpretation put on the facts in that case by the Court of Appeal; the present case is not a rehearing of that case. The question which the House does have to answer is: did the court in *Lloyd's Bank Ltd* v *Bundy* accurately state the law?

Lord Denning MR believed that the doctrine of undue influence could be subsumed under a general principle that English courts will grant relief where there has been 'inequality of bargaining power' (see [1974] 3 All ER 757 at 765, [1975] QB 326 at 339). He deliberately avoided reference to the will of one party being dominated or overcome by another. The majority of the court did not follow him; they based their decision on the orthodox view of the doctrine as expounded in *Allcard* v *Skinner* (1887) 36 ChD 145, [1886–90] All ER Rep 90. This opinion of Lord Denning MR, therefore, was not the ground of the court's decision, which has to be found in the view of the majority, for whom Sir Eric Sachs delivered the leading judgment.

Nor has counsel for the wife sought to rely on Lord Denning MR's general principle; and, in my view, he was right not to do so. The doctrine of undue influence has been sufficiently developed not to need the support of a principle which by its formulation in the language of the law of contract is not appropriate to cover transactions of gift where there is no bargain. The fact of an unequal bargain will, of course, be a relevant feature in some cases of undue influence. But it can never become an appropriate basis of principle of an equitable doctrine which is concerned with transactions 'not to be reasonably accounted for on the ground of friendship, relationship, charity, or other ordinary motives on which ordinary men act . . .' (see *Allcard* v *Skinner* (1887) 36 ChD 145 at 185, [1886–90] All ER Rep 90 at 100–101 per Lindley LJ). And even in the field of contract I question whether there is any need in the modern law to erect a general principle of relief against inequality of bargaining power. Parliament has undertaken the task (and it is essentially a legislative task) of enacting such restrictions on freedom of contract as are in its judgment necessary to relieve against the mischief: for example, the hire-purchase and consumer protection legislation, of which the Supply of Goods (Implied Terms) Act 1973, the Consumer Credit Act 1974, the Consumer Safety Act 1978, the Supply of Goods and Services Act 1982 and the Insurance Companies Act 1982 are examples. I doubt whether the courts should assume the burden of formulating further restrictions.

6.5 Undue Influence by a Third Party

BARCLAYS BANK PLC v *O'BRIEN* [1993] 4 All ER 417 (HL)

LORD BROWNE-WILKINSON: My lords, in this appeal your Lordships for the first time have to consider a problem which has given rise to reported decisions of the Court of

Appeal on no less than 11 occasions in the last eight years and which has led to a difference of judicial view. Shortly stated the question is whether a bank is entitled to enforce against a wife an obligation to secure a debt owed by her husband to the bank where the wife has been induced to stand as surety for her husband's debt by the undue influence or misrepresentation of the husband.

The facts

The facts of the present case are very fully set out in the judgment of Scott LJ in the Court of Appeal ([1992] 4 All ER 983, [1993] QB 109). I will only state them in summary form. Mr and Mrs O'Brien were husband and wife. The matrimonial home, 151 Farnham Lane, Slough, was in their joint names subject to a mortgage of approximately £25,000 to a building society. Mr O'Brien was a chartered accountant and had an interest in a company, Heathrow Fabrications Ltd. The company's bank account was at the Woolwich branch of Barclays Bank. In the first three months of 1987 the company frequently exceeded its overdraft facility of £40,000 and a number of its cheques were dishonoured on presentation. In discussions in April 1981 between Mr O'Brien and the manager of the Woolwich branch, Mr Tucker, Mr O'Brien told Mr Tucker that he was remortgaging the matrimonial home: Mr Tucker made a note that Mrs O'Brien might be a problem. The overdraft limit was raised at that stage to £60,000 for one month. Even though no additional security was provided, by 15 June 1987 the company's overdraft had risen to £98,000 and its cheques were again being dishonoured.

On 22 June 1987 Mr O'Brien and Mr Tucker agreed (1) that the company's overdraft limit would be raised to £135,000 reducing to £120,000 after three weeks, (2) that Mr O'Brien would guarantee the company's indebtedness and (3) that Mr O'Brien's liability would be secured by a second charge on the matrimonial home.

The necessary security documents were prepared by the bank. They consisted of an unlimited guarantee by Mr O'Brien of the company's liability and a legal charge by both Mr and Mrs O'Brien of the matrimonial home to secure any liability of Mr O'Brien to the bank. Mr Tucker arranged for the documents, together with a side letter, to be sent to the Burnham branch of the bank for execution by Mr and Mrs O'Brien. In a covering memorandum Mr Tucker requested the Burnham branch to advise the O'Briens as to the current level of the facilities afforded to the bank (£107,000) and the projected increase to £135,000. The Burnham branch was also asked to ensure that the O'Briens were 'fully aware of the nature of the documentation to be signed and advised that if they are in any doubt they should contact their solicitors before signing'.

Unfortunately the Burnham branch did not follow Mr Tucker's instructions. On 1 July Mr O'Brien alone signed the guarantee and legal charge at the Burnham branch, the document simply being produced for signature and witnessed by a clerk. On the following day Mrs O'Brien went to the branch with her husband. There were produced for signature by Mrs O'Brien the legal charge on the matrimonial home together with a side letter, which reads:

> We hereby agree acknowledge and confirm as follows: (1) That we have each received from you a copy of the guarantee dated 3 July 1987 (a copy of which is attached hereto) under which Nicholas Edward O'Brien guarantees the payment and discharge of all moneys and liabilities now or hereafter due owing or incurred by Heathrow Fabrications Ltd to you. (2) That the liability of the said Nicholas Edward O'Brien to you pursuant to the said guarantee is and will be secured by the legal charge dated 3 July 1987 over the property described above made between (1) Nicholas Edward O'Brien (2) Nicholas Edward O'Brien and Bridget Mary O'Brien and (3) Barclays Bank Plc. (3) That you recommended that we should obtain independent legal advice before signing this letter.

In fact the Burnham branch gave Mrs O'Brien no explanation of the effect of the documents. No one suggested that she should take independent legal advice. She did not read the documents or the side letter. She simply signed the legal charge and side letter and her signature was witnessed by the clerk. She was not given a copy of the guarantee.

The company did not prosper and by October 1987 its indebtedness to the bank was over £154,000. In November 1987 demand was made against Mr O'Brien under his guarantee. When the demand was not met possession proceedings under the legal charge were brought by the bank against Mr and Mrs O'Brien. Mrs O'Brien seeks to defend these proceedings by alleging that she was induced to execute the legal charge on the matrimonial home by the undue influence of Mr O'Brien and by his misrepresentation. The trial judge, Judge Marder QC, and the Court of Appeal rejected the claim based on undue influence: on the appeal to this House the claim based on undue influence is not pursued. However, the judge did find that Mr O'Brien had falsely represented to Mrs O'Brien that the charge was to secure only £60,000 and that even this liability would be released in a short time when the house was remortgaged. On those findings of fact the trial judge granted an order for possession against Mrs O'Brien holding that the bank could not be held responsible for the misrepresentation made by Mr O'Brien. . . .

Policy considerations
The large number of cases of this type coming before the courts in recent years reflects the rapid changes in social attitudes and the distribution of wealth which have recently occurred. Wealth is now more widely spread. Moreover a high proportion of privately owned wealth is invested in the matrimonial home. Because of the recognition by society of the equality of the sexes, the majority of matrimonial homes are now in joint names of both spouses. Therefore in order to raise finance for the business enterprises of one or other of the spouses, the jointly owned home has become a main source of security. The provision of such security requires the consent of both spouses.

In parallel with these financial developments, society's recognition of the equality of the sexes has led to a rejection of the concept that the wife is subservient to the husband in the management of the family's finances. A number of the authorities reflect an unwillingness in the court to perpetuate law based on this outmoded concept. Yet, as Scott LJ in the Court of Appeal rightly points out, although the concept of the ignorant wife leaving all financial decisions to the husband is outmoded, the practice does not yet coincide with the ideal (see [1992] 4 All ER 983 at 1008, [1993] QB 109 at 139). In a substantial proportion of marriages it is still the husband who has the business experience and the wife is willing to follow his advice without bringing a truly independent mind and will to bear on financial decisions. The number of recent cases in this field shows that in practice many wives are still subjected to, and yield to, undue influence by their husbands. Such wives can reasonably look to the law for some protection when their husbands have abused the trust and confidence reposed in them.

On the other hand, it is important to keep a sense of balance in approaching these cases. It is easy to allow sympathy for the wife who is threatened with the loss of her home at the suit of a rich bank to obscure an important public interest, viz the need to ensure that the wealth currently tied up in the matrimonial home does not become economically sterile. If the rights secured to wives by the law renders vulnerable loans granted on the security of matrimonial homes, institutions will be unwilling to accept such security, thereby reducing the flow of loan capital to business enterprises. It is therefore essential that a law designed to protect the vulnerable does not render the matrimonial home unacceptable as security to financial institutions.

With these policy considerations in mind I turn to consider the existing state of the law. The whole of the modern law is derived from the decision of the Privy Council in *Turnbull & Co. v Duval* [1902] AC 429 which, as I will seek to demonstrate, provides an uncertain foundation. Before considering that case however, I must consider the law of undue influence which (though not directly applicable in the present case) underlies both *Turnbull v Duval* and most of the later authorities.

Undue influence
A person who has been induced to enter into a transaction by the undue influence of another (the wrongdoer) is entitled to set that transaction aside as against the wrongdoer. Such undue influence is either actual or presumed. In *Bank of Credit and Commerce International SA v Aboody* (1988) [1992] 4 All ER 955 at 964, [1990] 1 QB 923 at 953 the Court of Appeal helpfully adopted the following classification.

Class 1: actual undue influence. In these cases it is necessary for the claimant to prove affirmatively that the wrongdoer exerted undue influence on the complainant to enter into the particular transaction which is impugned.

Class 2: presumed undue influence. In these cases the complainant only has to show, in the first instance, that there was a relationship of trust and confidence between the complainant and the wrongdoer of such a nature that it is fair to presume that the wrongdoer abused that relationship in procuring the complainant to enter into the impugned transaction. In class 2 cases therefore there is no need to produce evidence that actual undue influence was exerted in relation to the particular transaction impugned: once a confidential relationship has been proved, the burden then shifts to the wrongdoer to prove that the complainant entered into the impugned transaction freely, for example by showing that the complainant had independent advice. Such a confidential relationship can be established in two ways, viz:

Class 2A. Certain relationships (for example solicitor and client, medical advisor and patient) as a matter of law raise the presumption that undue influence has been exercised.

Class 2B. Even if there is no relationship falling within class 2A, if the complainant proves the de facto existence of a relationship under which the complainant generally reposed trust and confidence in the wrongdoer, the existence of such relationship raises the presumption of undue influence. In a class 2B case therefore, in the absence of evidence disproving undue influence, the complainant will succeed in setting aside the impugned transaction merely by proof that the complainant reposed trust and confidence in the wrongdoer without having to prove that the wrongdoer exerted actual undue influence or otherwise abused such trust and confidence in relation to the particular transaction impugned.

As to dispositions by a wife in favour of her husband, the law for long remained in an unsettled state. In the nineteenth century some judges took the view that the relationship was such that it fell into class 2A, ie as a matter of law undue influence by the husband over the wife was presumed. It was not until the decisions in *Howes* v *Bishop* [1909] 2 KB 390 and *Bank of Montreal* v *Stuart* [1911] AC 120 that it was finally determined that the relationship of husband and wife did not as a matter of law raise a presumption of undue influence within class 2A. It is to be noted therefore that when *Turnbull* v *Duval* was decided in 1902 the question whether there was a class 2A presumption of undue influence as between husband and wife was still unresolved.

An invalidating tendency?
Although there is no class 2A presumption of undue influence as between husband and wife, it should be emphasised that in any particular case a wife may well be able to demonstrate that de facto she did leave decisions on financial affairs to her husband thereby bringing herself within class 2B, ie that the relationship between husband and wife in the particular case was such that the wife reposed confidence and trust in her husband in relation to their financial affairs and therefore undue influence is to be presumed. Thus, in those cases which still occur where the wife relies in all financial matters on her husband and simply does what he suggests, a presumption of undue influence within class 2B can be established solely from the proof of such trust and confidence without proof of actual undue influence.

In the appeal in *CIBC Mortgages plc* v *Pitt* [1993] 4 All ER 433 (judgment in which is to be given immediately after that in the present appeal) Mr Price QC for the wife argued that in the case of transactions between husband and wife there was an 'invalidating tendency', ie although there was no class 2A presumption of undue influence, the courts were more ready to find that a husband had exercised undue influence over his wife than in other cases. Scott LJ in the present case also referred to the law treating married women 'more tenderly' than others. This approach is based on dicta in early authorities. In *Grigby* v *Cox* (1750) 1 Ves Sen 517, 27 ER 1178 Lord Hardwicke LC, whilst rejecting any presumption of undue influence, said that a court of equity 'will have more jealousy' over dispositions by a wife to a husband. In *Yerkey* v *Jones* (1939) 63 CLR 649 at 675 Dixon J refers to this 'invalidating tendency'. He also refers (at 677) to the court recognising 'the opportunities which a wife's confidence in her husband gives him of unfairly or improperly procuring her to become surety'.

In my judgment this special tenderness of treatment afforded to wives by the courts is properly attributable to two factors. First, many cases may well fall into the class 2B category of undue influence because the wife demonstrates that she placed trust and confidence in her husband in relation to her financial affairs and therefore raises a presumption of undue influence. Secondly, the sexual and emotional ties between the parties provide a ready weapon for undue influence: a wife's true wishes can easily be overborne because of her fear of destroying or damaging the wider relationship between her and her husband if she opposes his wishes.

For myself, I accept that the risk of undue influence affecting a voluntary disposition by a wife in favour of a husband is greater than in the ordinary run of cases where no sexual or emotional ties affect the free exercise of the individual's will.

Undue influence, misrepresentation and third parties
Up to this point I have been considering the right of a claimant wife to set aside a transaction as against the wrongdoing husband when the transaction has been procured by his undue influence. But in surety cases the decisive question is whether the claimant wife can set aside the transaction, not against the wrongdoing husband, but against the creditor bank. Of course, if the wrongdoing husband is acting as agent for the creditor bank in obtaining the surety from the wife, the creditor will be fixed with the wrongdoing of its own agent and the surety contract can be set aside as against the creditor. Apart from this, if the creditor bank has notice, actual or constructive, of the undue influence exercised by the husband (and consequentially of the wife's equity to set aside the transaction) the creditor will take subject to that equity and the wife can set aside the transaction against the creditor (albeit a purchaser for value) as well as against the husband: see *Bainbrigge v Browne* (1881) 18 ChD 188 and *BCCI v Aboody* [1992] 4 All ER 955 at 980, [1990] 1 QB 923 at 973. Similarly, in cases such as the present where the wife has been induced to enter into the transaction by the husband's misrepresentation, her equity to set aside the transaction will be enforceable against the creditor if either the husband was acting as the creditor's agent or the creditor had actual or constructive notice. . . . [T]he present law is built on the unsure foundations of *Turnbull v Duval*. Like most law founded on obscure and possibly mistaken foundations it has developed in an artificial way, giving rise to artificial distinctions and conflicting decisions. In my judgment your Lordships should seek to restate the law in a form which is principled, reflects the current requirements of society and provides as much certainty as possible.

Conclusions
(a) *Wives* My starting point is to clarify the basis of the law. Should wives (and perhaps others) be accorded special rights in relation to surety transactions by the recognition of a special equity applicable only to such persons engaged in such transactions? Or should they enjoy only the same protection as they would enjoy in relation to their other dealings? In my judgment, the special equity theory should be rejected. First, I can find no basis in principle for affording special protection to a limited class in relation to one type of transaction only. Second, to require the creditor to prove knowledge and understanding by the wife in all cases is to reintroduce by the back door either a presumption of undue influence of class 2A (which has been decisively rejected) or the Romilly heresy (which has long been treated as bad law). Third, although Scott LJ found that there were two lines of cases one of which supported the special equity theory, on analysis although many decisions are not inconsistent with that theory the only two cases which support it are *Yerkey v Jones* and the decision of the Court of Appeal in the present case. Finally, it is not necessary to have recourse to a special theory for the proper protection of the legitimate interests of wives as I will seek to show.

In my judgment, if the doctrine of notice is properly applied, there is no need for the introduction of a special equity in these types of cases. A wife who has been induced to stand as a surety for the husband's debts by his undue influence, misrepresentation or some legal wrong has an equity as against him to set aside that transaction. Under the ordinary principles of equity, her right to set aside that transaction will be enforceable against third parties (eg against a creditor) if either the husband was acting as the third party's agent or the third party had actual or constructive notice of the facts giving rise to her equity. Although there may be cases where, without artificiality, it can properly be held that the husband was acting as the agent of the creditor in procuring the wife to stand as surety, such cases will be of very rare occurrence. The key to the problem is to identify the circumstances in which the creditor will be taken to have had notice of the wife's equity to set aside the transaction.

The doctrine of notice lies at the heart of equity. Given that there are two innocent parties, each enjoying rights, the earlier right prevails against the later right if the acquirer of the later right knows of the earlier right (actual notice) or would have discovered it had he taken proper steps (constructive notice). In particular, if the party asserting that he takes free of the earlier rights of another knows of certain facts which put him on inquiry as to the possible existence of the rights of that other and he fails to make such inquiry or take such other steps as are reasonable to verify whether such earlier right does or does not exist, he will have constructive notice of the earlier right and take subject to it. Therefore where a wife has agreed to stand surety for her husband's debts as a result of undue influence or misrepresentation, the creditor will take subject to the wife's equity to set aside the transaction if the circumstances are such as to put the creditor on inquiry as to the circumstances in which she agreed to stand surety.

It is at this stage that, in my view, the 'invalidating tendency' or the law's 'tender treatment' of married women, becomes relevant. As I have said above in dealing with undue influence, this tenderness of the law towards married women is due to the fact that, even today, many wives repose confidence and trust in their husbands in relation to their financial affairs. This tenderness of the law is reflected by the fact that voluntary dispositions by the wife in favour of her husband are more likely to be set aside than other dispositions by her: a wife is more likely to establish presumed undue influence of class 2B by her husband than by others because, in practice, many wives do repose in their husbands trust and confidence in relation to their financial affairs. Moreover the informality of business dealings between spouses raises a substantial risk that the husband has not accurately stated to the wife the nature of the liability she is undertaking, ie he has misrepresented the position, albeit negligently.

Therefore, in my judgment a creditor is put on inquiry when a wife offers to stand surety for her husband's debts by the combination of two factors: (a) the transaction is on its face not to the financial advantage of the wife; and (b) there is a substantial risk in transactions of that kind that, in procuring the wife to act as surety, the husband has committed a legal or equitable wrong that entitles the wife to set aside the transaction.

It follows that, unless the creditor who is put on inquiry takes reasonable steps to satisfy himself that the wife's agreement to stand surety has been properly obtained, the creditor will have constructive notice of the wife's rights.

What, then are the reasonable steps which the creditor should take to ensure that it does not have constructive notice of the wife's rights, if any? Normally the reasonable steps necessary to avoid being fixed with constructive notice consist of making inquiry of the person who may have the earlier right (ie the wife) to see if whether such right is asserted. It is plainly impossible to require of banks and other financial institutions that they should inquire of one spouse whether he or she has been unduly influenced or misled by the other. But in my judgment the creditor, in order to avoid being fixed with constructive notice, can reasonably be expected to take steps to bring home to the wife the risk she is running by standing as surety and to advise her to take independent advice. As to past transactions, it will depend on the facts of each case whether the steps taken by the creditor satisfy this test. However, for the future in my judgment a creditor will have satisfied these requirements if it insists that the wife attend a private meeting (in the absence of the husband) with a representative of the creditor at which she is told of the extent of her liability as surety, warned of the risk she is running and urged to take independent legal advice. If these steps are taken in my judgment the creditor will have taken such reasonable steps as are necessary to preclude a subsequent claim that it had constructive notice of the wife's rights. I should make it clear that I have been considering the ordinary case where the creditor knows only that the wife is to stand surety for her husband's debts. I would not exclude exceptional cases where a creditor has knowledge of further facts which render the presence of undue influence not only possible but probable. In such cases, the creditor to be safe will have to insist that the wife is separately advised.

I am conscious that in treating the creditor as having constructive notice because of the risk of class 2B undue influence or misrepresentation by the husband I may be extending the law as stated by Fry J in *Bainbrigge* v *Browne* (1881) 18 ChD 188 at 197 and the Court of Appeal in *BCCI* v *Aboody* [1992] 4 All ER 955 at 980, [1990] 1 QB 923 at 973. Those cases suggest that for a third party to be affected by constructive notice of presumed undue influence the third party must actually know of the circumstances which give rise to a presumption of undue influence. In contrast, my view is that the risk of class 2B undue influence or misrepresentation is sufficient to put the creditor on inquiry. But my statement accords with the principles of notice: if the known facts are such as to indicate the possibility of an adverse claim that is sufficient to put a third party on inquiry.

If the law is established as I have suggested, it will hold the balance fairly between on the one hand the vulnerability of the wife who relies implicitly on her husband and, on the other hand, the practical problems of financial institutions asked to accept a secured or unsecured surety obligation from the wife for her husband's debts. In the context of suretyship, the wife will not have any right to disown her obligations just because subsequently she proves that she did not fully understand the transaction: she will, as in all other areas of her affairs, be bound by her obligations unless her husband has, by misrepresentation, undue influence or other wrong, committed an actionable wrong against her. In the normal case, a financial institution will be able to lend with confidence in reliance on the wife's surety obligation provided that it warns her (in the absence of the husband) of the amount of her potential liability and of the risk of standing surety and advises her to take independent advice.

Mr Jarvis QC for the bank urged that this is to impose too heavy a burden on financial institutions. I am not impressed by this submission. The report by Professor Jack's Review Committee on *Banking Services: Law and Practice* (1989), (Cmnd 622) recommended that prospective guarantors should be adequately warned of the legal effects and possible consequences of their guarantee and of the importance of receiving independent advice. Pursuant to this recommendation, the Code of Banking Practice (adopted by banks and building societies in March 1992) provides in para. 12.1 as follows:

> Banks and building socities will advise private individuals proposing to give them guarantee or other security for another person's liabilities that: (i) by giving the guarantee or third party security he or she might become liable instead of or as well as that other person; (ii) he or she should seek independent legal advice before entering into the guarantee or third party security. Guarantees and other third party security forms will contain a clear and prominent notice to the above effect.

Thus good banking practice (which applies to all guarantees, not only those given by a wife) largely accords with what I consider the law should require when a wife is offered as surety. The only further substantial step required by law beyond that good practice is that the position should be explained by the bank to the wife in a personal interview. I regard this as being essential because a number of the decided cases show that written warnings are often not read and are sometimes intercepted by the husband. It does not seem to me that the requirement of a personal interview imposes such an additional administrative burden as to render the bank's position unworkable.

(b) Other persons I have hitherto dealt only with the position where a wife stands surety for her husband's debts. But in my judgment the same principles are applicable to all other cases where there is an emotional relationship between cohabitees. The 'tenderness' shown by the law to married women is not based on the marriage ceremony but reflects the underlying risk of one cohabitee exploiting the emotional involvement and trust of the other. Now that unmarried cohabitation, whether heterosexual or homosexual, is widespread in our society, the law should recognise this. Legal wives are not the only group which are now exposed to the emotional pressure of cohabitation. Therefore if, but only if, the creditor is aware that the surety is cohabiting with the principal debtor, in my judgment the same principles should apply to them as apply to husband and wife.

In addition to the cases of cohabitees, the decision of the Court of Appeal in *Avon Finance Co. Ltd* v *Bridger* [1985] 2 All ER 281 shows (rightly in my view) that other relationships can give rise to a similar result. In that case a son, by means of misrepresentation, persuaded his elderly parents to stand surety for his debts. The surety obligation was held to be unenforceable by the creditor inter alia because to the bank's knowledge the parents trusted the son in their financial dealings. In my judgment that case was rightly decided: in a case where the creditor is aware that the surety reposes trust and confidence in the principal debtor in relation to his financial affairs, the creditor is put on inquiry in just the same way as it is in relation to husband and wife.

Summary
I can therefore summarise my views as follows. Where one cohabitee has entered into an obligation to stand as surety for the debts of the other cohabitee and the creditor is aware that they are cohabitees: (1) the surety obligation will be valid and enforceable by the creditor unless the suretyship was procured by the undue influence, misrepresentation or other legal wrong of the principal debtor; (2) if there has been undue influence, misrepresentation or other legal wrong by the principal debtor, unless the creditor has taken reasonable steps to satisfy himself that the surety entered into the obligation freely and in knowledge of the true facts, the creditor will be unable to enforce the surety obligation because he will be fixed with constructive notice of the surety's right to set aside the transaction; (3) unless there are special exceptional circumstances, a creditor will have taken such reasonable steps to avoid being fixed with constructive notice if the creditor warns the surety (at a meeting not attended by the principal debtor) of the amount of her potential liability and of the risks involved and advises the surety to take independent legal advice.

I should make it clear that in referring to the husband's debts I include the debts of a company in which the husband (but not the wife) has a direct financial interest.

The decision of this case
Applying those principles to this case, to the knowledge of the bank Mr and Mrs O'Brien were man and wife. The bank took a surety obligation from Mrs O'Brien, secured on the matrimonial home, to secure the debts of a company in which Mr O'Brien was interested but in which Mrs O'Brien had no direct pecuniary interest. The bank should therefore have been put on inquiry as to the circumstances in which Mrs O'Brien had agreed to stand as surety for the debt of her husband. If the Burham branch had properly carried out the instructions from Mr Tucker of the Woolwich branch Mrs O'Brien would have been informed that she and the matrimonial home were potentially liable for the debts of a company which had an existing liability of £107,000 and which was to be afforded an overdraft facility of £135,000. If she had been told this, it would have counteracted Mr O'Brien's misrepresenation that the liability was limited to £60,000 and would last for only three weeks. In addition according to the side letter she would have been recommended to take independent legal advice.

Unfortunately Mr Tucker's instructions were not followed and to the knowledge of the bank (through the clerk at the Burnham branch) Mrs O'Brien signed the documents without any warning of the risks or any recommendation to take legal advice. In the circumstances the bank (having failed to take reasonable steps) is fixed with constructive notice of the wrongful misrepresentation made by Mr O'Brien to Mrs O'Brien. Mrs O'Brien is therefore entitled as against the bank to set aside the legal charge on the matrimonial home securing her husband's liability to the bank.

For these reasons I would dismiss the appeal with costs.

Lords Templeman, Lowry, Slynn and Woolf concurred.

6.6   Mistake

6.6.1   COMMON MISTAKE

6.6.1.1   *Res extincta*

COUTURIER v HASTIE (1856) 5 HLC 673 (HL)

A cargo of corn had begun to deteriorate en route and had therefore been sold to a third party at the time that the defendant purported to sell it to the plaintiff.

THE LORD CHANCELLOR: . . . I have no hesitation in advising your Lordships, and at once moving that the judgment of the court below should be affirmed. It is hardly necessary, and it has not ordinarily been usual for your Lordships to go much into the merits of a judgment which is thus unanimously affirmed by the judges who are called in to consider it, and to assist the House in forming its judgment. But I may state shortly that the whole question turns upon the construction of the contract which was entered into between the parties. I do not mean to deny that many plausible and ingenious arguments have been passed by both the learned counsel who have addressed your Lordships, showing that there might have been a meaning attached to that contract different from that which the words themselves impart. If this had depended not merely upon the construction of the contract but upon evidence, which, if I recollect rightly, was rejected at the trial, of what mercantile usage had been, I should not have been prepared to say that a long-continued mercantile usage interpreting such contracts might not have been sufficient to warrant, or even to compel your Lordships to adopt a different construction. But in the absence of any such evidence, looking to the contract itself alone, it appears to me clearly that what the parties contemplated, those who bought and those who sold, was that there was an existing something to be sold and bought, and if sold and bought, then the benefit of insurance should go with it. I do not feel pressed by the latter argument, which has been brought forward very ably by Mr Wilde, derived from the subject of insurance. I think the full benefit of the insurance was meant to go as well to losses and damage that occurred previously to the 15th of May, as to losses and damage that occurred subsequently, always assuming that something passed by the contract of the 15th of May. If the contract of the 15th of May had been an operating contract, and there had been a valid sale of cargo at that time existing, I think the purchaser would have had the benefit of insurance in respect of all damage previously occurring. The contract plainly imports that there was something which was to be sold at the time of the contract, and something to be purchased. No such thing existing, I think the Court of Exchequer Chamber has come to the only reasonable conclusion upon it, and consequently that there must be judgment given by your Lordships for the Defendants in Error.

AMALGAMATED INVESTMENT PROPERTY CO. LTD v JOHN WALKER & SONS LTD
[1976] 3 All ER 509 (CA)

BUCKLEY LJ: This is an appeal from a decision of Plowman V-C on 5th March 1975 relating to a contract for sale of some land in the Commercial Road, London E1. The property was advertised by estate agents, in particulars prepared by them, as being for sale 'For occupation or redevelopment'. It consisted of a site on which stood a large warehouse building which had been purpose-built to be used as a bonded warehouse and bottling factory for the defendant company, who are manufacturers of whisky. They had ceased to use it for that purpose, and it was for sale vacant. A company called Gladdings had written to the defendants expressing interest in the property as possible purchasers and mentioning the fact that Gladdings had an office development permit which might be used in connection with a redevelopment of the site. The property had been advertised in the press as suitable for redevelopment and occupation.

On 13th July 1973 Gladdings wrote to estate agents acting for the defendants making an offer of £1,710,000, subject to contract, for the freehold with vacant possession. On the same day the company which is now the plaintiff company in the action made an offer of £1,460,000. Five days later the plaintiffs wrote to say that they had agreed to join forces with Gladdings and associated themselves with the offer of £1,710,000. On 19th July the defendants' agent wrote accepting that offer, subject to contract.

Enquiries were made before contract in the ordinary way, and amongst other questions asked was this:

> Although the Purchaser will be making the usual searches and enquiries of the local and planning authorities, the Vendor is asked specifically to state whether he is aware of any order, designation or proposal of any local or other authority or body having compulsory powers involving any of the following. . . .

Then there are a number of sub-paragraphs, the only relevant one being (iv), which reads: 'The designation of the property as a building of special architectual or historic interest'. A negative answer was given to that question by the vendors on 14th August.

With the approval of Gladdings, it was arranged that the contract should be taken in the name of the plaintiffs, and on 25th September 1973 the contract was signed. It incorporated the Law Society's General Conditions of Sale (1973 Revision), which contained, amongst other provisions, a condition that nothing in the conditions should entitle the vendor to compel the purchaser to accept or the purchaser to compel the vendor to convey (with or without compensation) property which differed substantially from the property agreed to be sold and purchased, whether in quantity, quality, tenure or otherwise, if the purchaser or the vendor respectively would be prejudiced by reason of such difference.

On 26th September 1973, that is the day after the contract, the Department of the Environment wrote a letter to the defendants notifying them that the property, the subject-matter of the contract, had been selected for inclusion on the statutory list of buildings of special architectural or historic interest compiled by the Secretary of State, and that that list was about to be given legal effect . . .

The judge found as a fact that the value of the property with no redevelopment potential was probably £1,500,000 less than the contract price. So the effect of the building being put into the list was this: that so long as it remained listed and 'listed building consent' could not be obtained, the value of the property was depreciated from the £1,700,000 odd, which was the sale price, to something of the order of £200,000. The judge also found as a fact that the defendants knew at all material times that the purchasers were buying the property for redevelopment.

On 12th December 1973 the plaintiffs issued their writ against the defendants claiming rescission of the agreement on the ground of common mistake, a declaration that the agreement was void and of no effect and a declaration that the agreement was voidable, and an order rescinding the agreement. Those were, of course, alternative remedies. On 14th December the defendants issused a writ against the plantiffs claiming specific performance on the contract and alternatively a declaration that the plaintiffs had wrongfully repudiated the contract, and forefeiture of the deposit and damages, with ancillary relief. Those two actions were consolidated on 19th July 1974, and the action came on with Amalgamated Investment and Property Co. Ltd as plaintiffs and John Walker & Sons Ltd as defendants. There was a counterclaim raised by the defendants for the relief sought in their action, specific performance and so forth. . . . [T]he alleged common mistake was the property was properly suitable for and capable of being developed.

For the application of the doctrine of mutual mistake as a ground for setting the contract aside, it is of course necessary to show that the mistake existed at the date of the contract; and so counsel for the plantiffs relies in that respect not on the signing of the list by the officer who alone was authorised to sign it on behalf of the Secretary of State, but on the decision of Miss Price to include the property in the list. That decision, although in fact it led to the signature of the list in the form in which it was eventually signed, was merely an administrative step in the carrying out of the operations of the branch of the Ministry. It was a personal decision on the part of Miss Price that the list should contain the particular property with which we are concerned. But there was still the possibility that something else might arise before the list was signed. Some communication might have been received from some outside body which threw some light on the qualifications of this building for listing, which might have resulted in its being excluded from the list as it was actually signed. Indeed, the head of the department might himself, had he known of the circumstances, have formed a different opinion from the opinion formed by Miss Price or Miss Price might, I suppose, herself have changed her mind during the time between preparing the list, sending it to the typing pool and eventually laying it before her superior for signature. Although she accepts the responsibility for the decision and says it was her decision, it was (as I say) no more than an administrative step leading to the ultimate signature of the list, just as the obtaining of the information that was eventually included in the report of the investigating officer was an administrative step or the prepartion of the report of the investigating officer. It seems to me that it is no more justifiable to point to that date as being the crucial date than it is to point to other earlier dates or later dates. The crucial date, in my judgment, is the date when the list was signed. It was then that the building became a listed building, and it was only then that the expectations of the parties (who no doubt both expected that this property would be capable of being developed, subject always of course to obtaining planning permission, without it being necessary to obtain listed building permission) were disappointed. For myself, I entirely agree with the conclusion which the learned judge reached on this part of the case. In my judgment, there was no mutual mistake as to the circumstances surrounding the contract at the time when the contract was entered into. The only mistake that there was was one which related to the expectation of the parties. They expected that the building would be subject only to ordinary town planning consent procedures, and that expectation has been disappointed. But at the date when the contract was entered into I cannot see that there is any ground for saying that the parties were then subject to some mutual mistake of fact relating to the circumstances surrounding the contract. Accordingly, for my part, I think that the learned judge's decision on that part of the case is one which should be upheld. . . .

Lawton J and Sir John Pennycuick concurred.

MCRAE v COMMONWEALTH DISPOSALS COMMISSION (1950) 84 CLR 377
(High Court of Australia)

The contract concerned an oil tanker supposedly lying on the 'Jourmand Reef'. In fact, neither the tanker nor the reef existed.

DIXON and FULLAGAR JJ: . . . The position so far, then, may be summed up as follows. It was not decided in *Couturier* v *Hastie* (1856) 5 HLC 673 that the contract in that case was void. The question whether it was void or not did not arise. If it had arisen, as in an action by the purchaser for damages, it would have turned on the ulterior question whether the contract was subject to an implied condition precedent. Whatever might then have been held on the facts of *Couturier* v *Hastie*, it is impossible in this case to imply any such term. The terms of the contract and the surrounding circumstances clearly exclude any such implication. The buyers relied upon, and acted upon, the assertion of the seller that there was a tanker in existence. It is not a case in which the parties can be seen to have proceeded on the basis of a common assumption of fact so as to justify the conclusion that the correctness of the assumption was intended by both parties to be a condition precedent to the creation of contractual obligations. The officers of the Commission made an assumption, but the plaintiffs did not make an assumption in the same sense. They knew nothing except what the Commission had told them. If they had been asked, they would certainly not have said: 'Of course, if there is no tanker, there is no contract'. They would have said: 'We shall have to go and take possession of the tanker. We simply accept the Commissioner's assurance that there is a tanker and the Commission's promise to give us that tanker'. The only proper construction of the contract is that it included a promise by the Commission that there was a tanker in the position specified. The Commission contracted that there was a tanker there. 'The sale in this case of a ship implies a contract that the subject of the transfer did exist in the character of a ship' (*Barr* v *Gibson* (1838) 3 M & W 390). If, on the other hand, the case of *Couturier* v *Hastie* and this case ought to be treated as cases raising a question of 'mistake', then the Commission cannot in this case rely on any mistake as avoiding the contract, because any mistake was induced by the serious fault of their own servants, who asserted the existence of a tanker recklessly and without any reasonable ground. There was a contract, and the Commission contracted that a tanker existed in the position specified. Since there was no such tanker, there has been a breach of contract, and the plaintiffs are entitled to damages for that breach.

6.6.1.2 *Res sua*

COOPER v PHIBBS (1887) LR 2 HL 149 (HL)

LORD CRANWORTH: My Lords, this is an appeal against a decree of the Lord Chancellor of Ireland, of the 14th of June, 1865, dismissing a cause petition which had been filed by the Appellant on the 9th of April, 1864, pursuant to the Chancery Regulation Act of 1850. The object of the petition was to be relieved from an agreement, dated on the 14th of October, 1863, by which the petitioner agreed to become tenant to the respondent Phibbs, for three years, of the salmon fishery of Ballysadare, in the county of Sligo. The ground of the relief asked was, that the petitioner had entered into an agreement in mistake as to his rights. He thought that the fishery belonged to the other respondents, for whom Phibbs acted as trustee; but he was in truth himself the owner of the fishery as tenant thereof in tail. . . .

The consequence was, that the present appellant, when, after the death of his uncle, he entered into the agreement to take a lease of this property, entered into an agreement to take a lease of what was, in truth, his own property – for, in truth, this fishery was bound by the covenant, and belonged to him, just as much as did the lands of Ballysadare; therefore, he says, I entered into the agreement under a common mistake, and I am entitled to be relieved from the consequence of it.

In support of that proposition he relied upon a case which was decided in the time of Lord Hardwicke, not by Lord Hardwicke himself, but by the then Master of the Rolls, *Bingham v Bingham* (1748) 1 Ves Sen 126, where that relief was expressly administered. I believe that the doctrine there acted upon was perfectly correct doctrine; but even if it had not been, that will not at all shew that this appellant is not entitled to this relief, because in this case the appellant was led into the mistake by the misinformation given to him by his uncle, who is now represented by the respondents. It is stated by him in his Cause Petition, which is verified, and to which there is no contradiction, and in all probability it seems to be the truth, that his uncle told him, not intending to misrepresent anything, but being in fact in error, that he was entitled to this fishery as his own fee simple property; and the appellant, his nephew, after his death acting on the belief of the truth of what his uncle had so told him, entered into the agreement in question. It appears to me, therefore, that it is impossible to say that he is not entitled to the relief which he asks, namely, to have the agreement delivered up and the rent repaid.

Lords Colonsay and Westbury concurred.

6.6.1.3 Mistake as to quality

BELL v LEVER BROTHERS LTD [1932] AC 161 (HL)

An agreement to compensate an employee on termination of his contract was made in ignorance of earlier conduct which would have justified termination without compensation.

LORD ATKIN: . . . My Lords, the rules of law dealing with the effect of mistake on contract appear to be established with reasonable clearness. If mistake operates at all it operates so as to negative or in some cases to nullify consent. The parties may be mistaken in the identity of the contracting parties, or in the existence of the subject-matter of the contract at the date of the contract, or in the quality of the subject-matter of the contract. These mistakes may be by one party, or by both, and the legal effect may depend upon the class of mistake above mentioned. Thus a mistaken belief by A that he is contracting with B, whereas in fact he is contracting with C, will negative consent where it is clear that the intention of A was to contract only with B. So the agreement of A and B to purchase a specific article is void if in fact the article had perished before the date of sale. In this case, though the parties in fact were agreed about the subject-matter, yet a consent to transfer or take delivery of something not existent is deemed useless, the consent is nullified. As codified in the Sale of Goods Act the contract is expressed to be void if the seller was in ignorance of the destruction of the specific chattel. I apprehend that if the seller with knowledge that a chattel was destroyed purported to sell it to a purchaser, the latter might sue for damages for non-delivery though the former could not sue for non-acceptance, but I know of no case where a seller has so committed himself. This is a case where mutual mistake certainly and unilateral mistake by the seller of goods will prevent a contract from arising. Corresponding to mistake as to the existence of the subject-matter is mistake as to title in cases where, unknown to the parties, the buyer is already the owner of that which the seller purports to sell to him. The parties intended to effectuate a transfer of ownership: such a transfer is impossible: the stipulation is naturali ratione inutilis. This is the case of *Cooper* v *Phibbs* (1887) LR 2 HL 149, where A agreed to take a lease of a fishery from B, though contrary to the belief of both parties at the time A was tenant for life of the fishery and B appears to have had no title at all. . . .

Mistake as to quality of the thing contracted for raises more difficult questions. In such a case a mistake will not affect assent unless it is the mistake of both parties, and is as to the existence of some quality which makes the thing without the quality essentially different from the thing as it was believed to be. Of course it may appear that the parties contracted that the article should possess the quality which one or other or both mistakenly believed it to possess. But in such a case there is a contract and the inquiry is a different one, being whether the contract as to quality amounts to a condition or a warranty, a different branch of the law. . . .

We are now in a position to apply to the facts of this case the law as to mistake so far as it has been stated. It is essential on this part of the discussion to keep in mind the finding of the jury acquitting the defendants of fraudulent misrepresentation or concealment in procuring the agreements in question. Grave injustice may be done to the defendants and confusion introduced into the legal conclusion, unless it is quite clear that in considering mistake in this case no suggestion of fraud is admissible and cannot strictly be regarded by the judge who has to determine the legal issues raised. The agreement which is said to be void is the agreement contained in the letter of March 19th, 1929, that Bell would retire from the Board of the Niger Company and its subsidiaries, and that in consideration of his doing so Levers would pay him as compensation for the termination of his agreements and consequent loss of office the sum of 30,000*l.* in full satisfaction and discharge of all claims and demands of any kind against Lever Brothers, the Niger Company or its subsidiaries. The agreement, which as part of the contract was terminated, had been broken so that it could be repudiated. Is an agreement to terminate a broken contract different in kind from an agreement to terminate an unbroken contract, assuming that the breach has given the one party the right to declare the contract at an end? I feel the weight of the plaintiffs' contention that a contract immediately determinable is a different thing from a contract for an unexpired term, and that the difference in kind can be illustrated by the immense price of release from the longer contract as compared with the shorter. And I agree that an agreement to take an assignment of a lease for five years is not the same thing as to take an assignment of a lease for three years, still less a term for a few months. But, on the whole, I have come to the conclusion that it would be wrong to decide that an agreement to terminate a definite specified contract is void if it turns out that the agreement has already been broken and could have been terminated otherwise. The contract released is the identical contract in both cases, and the party paying for release gets exactly what he bargains for. It seems immaterial that he could have got the same result in another way, or that if he had known the true facts he would not have entered into the bargain. A buys B's horse; he thinks the horse is sound and he pays the price of a sound horse; he would certainly not have bought the horse if he had known as the fact is that the horse is unsound. If B has made no respresentation as to soundness and has not contracted that the horse is sound, A is bound and cannot recover back the price. A buys a picture from B; both A and B believe it to be the work of an old master, and a high price is paid. It turns out to be a modern copy. A has no remedy in the absence of representation or warranty. A agrees to take on lease or to buy from B an unfinished dwelling-house. The house is in fact uninhabitable. A would never have entered into the bargain if he had known the fact. A has no remedy, and the position is the same whether B knew the facts or not, so long as he made no representation or gave no warranty. A buys a roadside garage business from B abutting on a public thoroughfare: unknown to A, but known to B, it has already been decided to construct a byepass road which will divert substantially the whole of the traffic from passing A's garage. Again A has no remedy. All these cases involve hardship on A and benefit B, as most people would say, unjustly. They can be supported on the ground that it is of paramount importance that contracts should be observed, and that if parties honestly comply with the essentials of the formation of contracts – i.e., agree in the same terms on the same subject-matter – they are bound, and must rely on the stipulations of the contract for protection from the effect of facts unknown to them.

Lords Blanesburgh and Thankerton concurred; Viscount Hailsham and Lord Warrington dissented.

LEAF v INTERNATIONAL GALLERIES [1950] 2 KB 86 (CA)

See above, **p. 226**, for Lord Denning's judgment in this case.

ASSOCIATED JAPANESE BANK v CREDIT DU NORD [1988] 3 All ER 902 (QB)

The defendant guaranteed the obligations of a third party under a contract with the plaintiff. The guarantee assumed that four machines were in the third party's possession, but they did not in fact exist.

STEYN J: . . .
The common law regarding mutual or common mistake
There was a lively debate about the common law rules governing a mutual or common mistake of the parties as to some essential quality of the subject matter of the contact. Counsel for CDN submitted that *Bell v Lever Bros Ltd* [1932] AC 161, [1931] All ER Rep 1 authoritatively established that a mistake by both parties as to the existence of some quality of the subject matter of the contract, which makes the subject matter of the contract without the quality essentially different from the subject matter as it was believed to be, renders the contract void ab initio. Counsel for AJB contested this proposition. He submitted that at common law a mistake even as to an essential quality of the subject matter of the contract will not affect the contract unless it resulted in a total failure of consideration. It was not clear to me that this formulation left any meaningful and independent scope for the application of common law rules in this area of the law. In any event, it is necessary to examine the legal position in some detail.

The landmark decision is undoubtedly *Bell v Lever Bros Ltd*. Normally a judge of first instance would simply content himself with applying the law stated by the House of Lords. There has, however, been substantial controversy about the rule established in that case. It seems right therefore to examine the effect of that decision against a somewhat wider framework. In the early history of contract law, the common law's peoccupation with consideration made the development of a doctrine of mistake impossible. Following the emergence in the nineteenth century of the theory of consensus ad idem it became possible to treat misrepresentation, undue influence and mistake as factors vitiating consent. Given that the will theory in English contract law was cast in objective form, judging matters by the external standard of the reasonable man, both as to contract formation and contractual interpretation, it nevertheless became possible to examine in what circumstances mistake might nullify or negative consent. But even in late Victorian times there was another powerful policy consideration militating against upsetting bargains on the ground of unexpected circumstances which occurred before or after the contract. That was the policy of caveat emptor which held sway outside the field of contract law subsequently codified by the Sale of Goods Act in 1893. Nevertheless, principles affecting the circumstances in which consent may be vitiated gradually emerged. The most troublesome areas proved to be two related areas, viz common mistake as to an essential quality of the subject matter of the contract and post-contractual frustration. Blackburn J, an acknowledged master of the common law, who yielded to no one in his belief in the sanctity of contract, led the way in both areas.

In *Taylor v Caldwell* (1863) 3 B & S 826, [1861–73] All ER Rep 24 Blackburn J first stated the doctrine of frustration in terms which eventually led to the adoption of the 'radical change in obligation' test of commercial frustration in modern law: see *Davis Contractors Ltd v Fareham UDC* [1956] 2 All ER 145, [1956] AC 696; *National Carriers Ltd v Panalpina (Northern) Ltd* [1981] 1 All ER 161, [1981] AC 675. In the field of mistake as to the essential quality of the subject matter Blackburn J also gave the lead. In *Kennedy v Panama New Zealand and Australian Royal Mail Co. Ltd* (1867) LR 2 QB 580 the issue was whether a contract for the purchase of shares was vitiated by an untrue representation that the company had secured a contract to carry mail for the New Zealand government. The court upheld the contract. In passing it must be noted that the case was decided on a restrictive approach as to the circumstances in which a contract can be rescinded for innocent misrepresentation; that, of course, was remedied in due course by equity. But in the present context the importance of the case lies in the remarks of Blackburn J about mistakes as to quality (at 586–590). Given the fact that there was no direct authority on the point (and certainly none which could not be explained on other grounds) he turned to the civil law. He referred to the civilian doctrine of error in substantia. That doctrine seeks to categorise mistakes into two categories, viz mistakes as to the substance of the subject matter or mistakes as to attributes (sometimes classified as mistakes in motive). Blackburn J, delivering the judgment of the court, held (at 588):

> . . . the principle of our law is the same as that of the civil law; and the difficulty in every case is to determine whether the mistake or misapprehension is as to the substance of the whole consideration, going, as it were, to the root of the matter, or only to some point, even though a material point, an error as to which does not affect the substance of the whole consideration.

That test did not avail the plaintiff, for it was held that he got what he bought.

None of the cases between the decisions in *Kennedy* v *Panama New Zealand and Australian Royal Mail Co. Ltd* and *Bell* v *Lever Bros Ltd* significantly contributed to the development of this area of the law. But *Bell* v *Lever Bros Ltd* was a vitally important case. The facts of that case are so well known as to require no detailed exposition. Lever Bros had, in the modern phrase, given two employees 'golden handshakes' of £30,000 and £20,000 in consideration of the early termination of their service contracts. Subsequently, Lever Bros discovered that the contracts of service had been voidable by reason of the two employees' breach of fiduciary duties in trading for their own account. Lever Bros argued that the contracts pursuant to which the service agreements were terminated were void ab initio for common mistake, and sought recovery of the sums paid to the employees. The claim succeeded at first instance and in the Court of Appeal but by a three to two majority the House of Lords held that the claim failed. Lord Atkin held ([1932] AC 161 at 218, [1931] All ER Rep 1 at 28):

> a mistake will not affect assent unless it is the mistake of both parties, and is as to the existence of some quality which makes the thing without the quality essentially different from the thing as it was believed to be.

In my view none of the other passages in Lord Atkin's speech detract from that statement of the law. . . .

It seems to me that the better view is that the majority in *Bell* v *Lever Bros Ltd* had in mind only mistake at common law. That appears to be indicated by the shape of the argument, the proposed amendment placed before the House of Lords (see [1932] AC 161 at 191, [1931] All ER Rep 1 at 15) and the speeches of Lord Atkin and Lord Thankerton. But, if I am wrong on this point, it is nevertheless clear that mistake at common law was in the forefront of the analysis in the speeches of the majority.

The law has not stood still in relation to mistake in equity. Today, it is clear that mistake in equity is not circumscribed by common law definitions. A contract affected by mistake in equity is not void but may be set aside on terms: see *Solle* v *Butcher* [1949] 2 All ER 1107, [1950] 1 KB 671; *Magee* v *Pennine Insurance Co. Ltd* [1969] 2 All ER 891, [1969] 2 QB 507; *Grist* v *Bailey* [1966] 2 All ER 875, [1967] Ch 532. It does not follow, however, that *Bell* v *Lever Bros Ltd* is no longer an authoritative statement of mistake at common law. On the contrary, in my view the principles enunciated in that case clearly still govern mistake at common law. It is true that in *Solle* v *Butcher* [1949] 2 All ER 1107 at 1119, [1950] 1 KB 671 at 691 Denning LJ interpreted *Bell* v *Lever Bros Ltd* differently. He said that a common mistake, even on a most fundamental matter, does not make the contract void at law. That was an individual opinion. Neither Bucknill LJ (who agreed in the result) nor Jenkins LJ (who dissented) even mentioned *Bell* v *Lever Bros Ltd*. In *Magee* v *Pennine Insurance Co. Ltd* [1969] 2 All ER 891 at 893, [1969] 2 QB 507 at 514 Lord Denning MR returned to the point. About *Bell* v *Lever Bros Ltd* he simply said: 'I do not propose . . . to go through the speeches in that case. They have given enough trouble to commentators already.' He then repeated his conclusion in *Solle* v *Butcher*. Winn LJ dissented. Fenton Atkinson LJ agreed in the result but it is clear from his judgment that he did not agree with Lord Denning MR's interpretation of *Bell* v *Lever Bros Ltd* (see [1969] 2 All ER 891 at 896, [1969] 2 QB 507 at 517–518). Again, Lord Denning MR's observation represented only his own view. With the profoundest respect to the former Master of the Rolls, I am constrained to say that in my view his interpretation of *Bell* v *Lever Bros Ltd* does not do justice to the speeches of the majority.

When Lord Denning MR referred in *Magee* v *Pennine Insurance Co. Ltd* to the views of commentators he may have had in mind comments in Cheshire and Fifoot *Law of Contract* (6th edn, 1964) p 196. In substance the argument was that the actual decision in *Bell* v *Lever Bros Ltd* contradicts the language of the speeches. If the test was not satisfied there, so the argument runs, it is difficult to see how it could ever be satisfied: see the latest edition of this valuable textbook for the same argument (Cheshire, Fifoot and Furmston *Law of Contract* (11th edn, 1986) pp 225–226). This is a point worth examining because at first glance it may seem persuasive. *Bell* v *Lever Bros Ltd* was a quite exceptional case; all their Lordships were agreed that common mistake had not been pleaded and would have required an amendment in the House of Lords if it were to succeed. The speeches do not suggest that the employees were entitled to keep both the gains secretly made and the golden handshakes. The former were clearly recoverable from them. Nevertheless, the golden handshakes were very substantial. But there are indications in the speeches that the so-called 'merits' were not all in favour of Lever Bros. The company was most anxious, because of a corporate merger, to terminate the two service agreements. There was apparently a doubt whether the voidability of the service agreements if revealed to the company *at the time of the severance contact* would have affected the company's decision. Lord Thankerton said ([1932] AC 161 at 236, [1931] All 1 ER Rep 1 at 37):

> . . . I do not find sufficient material to compel the inference that the appellants, at the time of the contract, regarded the indefeasibility of the service agreements as an essential and integral element in the subject-matter of the bargain.

Lord Atkin clearly regarded it as a hard case on the facts, but concluded 'on the whole' that the plea of common mistake must fail (see [1932] AC 161 at 223, [1931] All ER Rep 1 at 30). It is noteworthy that Lord Atkin commented on the scarcity of evidence as to the subsidiaries from the boards of which the two employees resigned (see [1932] AC 161 at 212, [1931] All ER Rep 1 at 25). Lord Blanesburgh's speech was directed to his conclusion that the amendment ought not to be allowed. He did, however, make clear that 'the mistake must go to the whole consideration', and pointed to the advantages (other than the release from the service agreements) which Lever Bros received (see [1932] AC 161 at 181, 197, [1931] All ER Rep 1 at 10, 18). Lord Blanesburgh emphasised that Lever Bros secured the *future* co-operation of the two employees for the carrying through of the amalgamation (see [1932] AC 161 at 181, [1931] All ER Rep 1 at 10). And the burden, of course, rested squarely on Lever Bros. With due reference to the distinguished authors who have argued that the actual decision in *Bell* v *Lever Bros Ltd* contradicts the principle enunciated in the speeches it seems to me that their analysis is altogether too simplistic, and that the actual decision was rooted in the particular facts of the case. In my judgment there is no reason to doubt the substantive reasons emerging from the speeches of the majority.

No one could fairly suggest that in this difficult area of the law there is only one correct approach or solution. But a narrow doctrine of common law mistake (as enunciated in *Bell* v *Lever Bros Ltd*), supplemented by the more flexible doctrine of mistake in equity (as developed in *Solle* v *Butcher* and later cases), seems to me to be an entirely sensible and satisfactory state of the law: see *Sheikh Bros Ltd* v *Ochsner* [1957] AC 136. And there ought to be no reason to struggle to avoid its application by artificial interpretations of *Bell* v *Lever Bros Ltd*.

It might be useful if I now summarised what appears to me to be a satisfactory way of approaching this subject. Logically, before one can turn to the rules as to mistake, whether at common law or in equity, one must first determine whether the contract itself, by express or implied condition precedent or otherwise, provides who bears the risk of the relevant mistake. It is at this hurdle that many pleas of mistake will either fail or prove to have been unnecessary. Only if the contract is silent on the point is there scope for invoking mistake. That brings me to the relationship between common law mistake and mistake in equity. Where common law mistake has been pleaded, the court must first consider this plea. If the contract is held to be void, no question of mistake in equity arises. But, if the contract is held to be valid, a plea of mistake in equity may still have to be considered : see *Grist v Bailey* [1966] 2 All ER 875, [1967] Ch 532 and the analysis in *Anson's Law of Contract* (26th edn, 1984) pp 290–291. Turning now to the approach to common law mistake, it seems to me that the following propositions are valid although not necessarily all entitled to be dignified as propositions of law.

The first imperative must be that the law ought to uphold rather than destroy apparent contracts. Second, the common law rules as to a mistake regarding the quality of the subject matter, like the common law rules regarding commercial frustration, are designed to cope with the impact of unexpected and wholly exceptional circumstances on apparent contracts. Third, such a mistake in order to attract legal consequences must substantially be shared by both parties, and must relate to facts as they existed at the time the contract was made. Fourth, and this is the point established by *Bell v Lever Bros Ltd*, the mistake must render the subject matter of the contract essentially and radically different from the subject matter which the parties believed to exist. While the civilian distinction between the substance and attributes of the subject matter of a contract has played a role in the development of our law (and was cited in the speeches in *Bell v Lever Bros Ltd*), the principle enunciated in *Bell v Lever Bros Ltd* is markedly narrower in scope than the civilian doctrine. It is therefore no longer useful to invoke the civilian distinction. The principles enunciated by Lord Atkin and Lord Thankerton represent the ratio decidendi of *Bell v Lever Bros Ltd*. Fifth, there is a requirement which was not specifically discussed in *Bell v Lever Bros Ltd*. What happens if the party who is seeking to rely on the mistake had no reasonable grounds for his belief? An extreme example is that of the man who makes a contract with minimal knowledge of the facts to which the mistake relates but is content that it is a good speculative risk. In my judgment a party cannot be allowed to rely on a common mistake where the mistake consists of a belief which is entertained by him without any reasonable grounds for such belief: cf *McRae v Commonwealth Disposals Commission* (1951) 84 CLR 377 at 408. That is not because principles such as estoppel or negligence require it, but simply because policy and good sense dictate that the positive rules regarding common mistake should be so qualified. Curiously enough this qualification is similar to the civilian concept where the doctrine of error in substantia is tempered by the principles governing culpa in contrahendo. More importantly, a recognition of this qualification is consistent with the approach in equity where fault on the part of the party adversely affected by the mistake will generally preclude the granting of equitable relief: see *Solle v Butcher* [1949] 2 All ER 1107 at 1120, [1950] 1 KB 671 at 693.

Applying the law to the facts

It is clear, of course, that in this case both parties, the creditor and the guarantor, acted on the assumption that the lease related to existing machines. If they had been informed that the machines might not exist, neither AJB nor CDN would for one moment have contemplated entering into the transaction. That, by itself, I accept, is not enough to sustain the plea of common law mistake. I am also satisfied that CDN had reasonable grounds for believing that the machines existed. That belief was based on CDN's discussions with Mr Bennett, information supplied by National Leasing, a respectable firm of lease brokers, and the confidence created by the fact that AJB were the lessors.

The real question is whether the subject matter *of the guarantee* (as opposed to the sale and lease) was essentially different from what it was reasonably believed to be. The real security of the guarantor was the machines. The existence of the machines, being profit-earning chattels, made it more likely that the debtor would be able to service the debt. More importantly, if the debtor defaulted and the creditor repossessed the machines, the creditor had to give credit for 97½% of the value of the machines. If the creditor sued the guarantor first, and the guarantor paid, the guarantor was entitled to be subrogated to the creditor's rights in respect of recovery against the debtor: see Goff and Jones *Law of Restitution* (3rd edn, 1986) pp 533–536). No doubt the guarantor relied to some extent on the creditworthiness of Mr Bennett. But I find that the prime security to which the guarantor looked was the existence of the four machines as described to both parties. For both parties the guarantee of obligations under a lease with non-existent machines was essentially different from a guarantee of a lease with four machines which both parties at the time of the contract believed to exist. The guarantee is an accessory contract. The non-existence of the subject matter of the principal contract is therefore of fundamental importance. Indeed the analogy of the classic res extinca cases, so much discussed in the authorities, is fairly close. In my judgment, the stringent test of common law mistake is satisfied; the guarantee is void ab initio.

6.6.1.4 Common mistake in equity

SOLLE v *BUTCHER* [1950] 1 KB 671 (CA)

A landlord sought to avoid a lease on the basis of a mistake as to whether it was subject to statutory rent controls.

DENNING LJ: . . . The only ground on which he can avoid it is on the ground of mistake. It is quite plain that the parties were under a mistake. They thought that the flat was not tied down to a controlled rent, whereas in fact it was. In order to see whether the lease can be avoided for this mistake it is necessary to remember that mistake is of two kinds: first, mistake which renders the contract void, that is a nullity from the beginning, which is the kind of mistake which was dealt with by the courts of common law: and secondly, mistake which renders the contract not void, but voidable, that is, liable to be set aside on such terms as the court thinks fit, which is the kind of mistake which was dealt with by the courts of equity. Much of the difficulty which has attended this subject has arisen because, before the fusion of law and equity, the courts of common law, in order to do justice in the case in hand, extended this doctrine of mistake beyond its proper limits and held contracts to be void which were really only voidable, a process which was capable of being attended with much injustice to third persons who had bought goods or otherwise committed themselves on the faith that there was a contract. In the well-known case of *Cundy* v *Lindsay* (1878) 3 App Cas 459, Cundy suffered such an injustice. He bought the handkerchiefs from the rogue, Blenkarn, before the Judicature Acts came into operation. Since the fusion of law and equity, there is no reason to continue this process, and it will be found that only those contracts are now held void in which the mistake was such as to prevent the formation of any contract at all.

Let me first consider mistakes which render a contract a nullity. All previous decisions on this subject must now be read in the light of *Bell* v *Lever Bros Ltd* [1932] AC 161. The correct interpretation of that case, to my mind, is that, once a contract has been made, that is to say, once the parties, whatever their inmost states of mind, have to all outward appearances agreed with sufficient certainty in the same terms on the same subject matter, then the contract is good unless and until it is set aside for failure of some condition on which the existence of the contract depends, or for fraud, or on some equitable ground. Neither party can rely on his own mistake to say it was a nullity from the beginning, no matter that it was a mistake which to his mind was fundamental, and no matter that the other party knew that he was under a mistake. A fortiori, if the other party did not know of the mistake, but shared it. . . .

Applying these principles, it is clear that here there was a contract. The parties agreed in the same terms on the same subject-matter. It is true that the landlord was under a mistake which was to him fundamental: he would not for one moment have considered letting the flat for seven years if it meant that he could only charge 140*l*. a year for it. He made the fundamental mistake of believing that the rent he could charge was not tied down to a controlled rent; but, whether it was his own mistake or a mistake common to both him and the tenant, it is not a ground for saying that the lease was from the beginning a nullity. Any other view would lead to remarkable results, for it would mean that, in the many cases where parties mistakenly think a house is outside the Rent Restriction Acts when it is really within them, the tenancy would be a nullity, and the tenant would have to go; with the result that the tenants would not dare to seek to have their rents reduced to the permitted amounts lest they should be turned out. . . .

A contract is also liable in equity to be set aside if the parties were under a common misapprehension either as to facts or as to their relative and respective rights, provided that the misapprehension was fundamental and that the party seeking to set it aside was not himself at fault. That principle was first applied to private rights as long ago as 1730 in *Lansdown* v *Lansdown* (1730) Mos 364 . . . . Eighteen years later, in the time of Lord Hardwicke, the same principle was applied in *Bingham* v *Bingham* (1748) 1 Ves Sen 126.

If and in so far as those cases were compromises of disputed rights, they have been subjected to justifiable criticism, but in cases where there is no element of compromise, but only of mistaken rights, the House of Lords in 1867 in the great case of *Cooper* v *Phibbs* (1867) LR 2 HL 149, affirmed the doctrine there acted on as correct. . . . The mistake there as to the title to the fishery did not render the tenancy agreement a nullity. If it had done, the contract would have been void at law from the beginning and equity would have had to follow the law. There would have been no contract to set aside and no terms to impose. The House of Lords, however, held that the mistake was only such as to make it voidable, or in Lord Westbury's words, 'liable to be set aside' on such terms as the court thought fit to impose; and it was so set aside.

The principle so established by *Cooper* v *Phibbs* has been repeatedly acted on: see for instance, *Earl Beauchamp* v *Win* (1873) LR 6 HL 223, and *Huddersfield Banking Co. Ltd* v *Lister* [1895] 2 Ch 273. . . .

Applying that principle to this case, the facts are that the plaintiff, the tenant, was a surveyor who was employed by the defendant, the landlord, not only to arrange finance for the purpose of the building and to negoiate with the rating authorities as to the new rateable values, but also to let the flats. He was the agent for letting, and he clearly formed the view that the building was not controlled. He told the valuation officer so. He advised the defendant what were the rents which could be charged. He read to the defendant an opinion of counsel relating to the matter, and told him that in his opinion he could charge 250*l*. and that there was no previous control. He said that the flats came joutside the Act and that the defendant was 'clear'. The defendant relied on what the plaintiff told him, and authorized the plaintiff to let at the rentals which he had suggested. The plaintiff not only let the four other flats to other people for a long period of years at the new rentals, but also took himself for seven years at 250*l*. a year. Now he turns round and says, quite unashamedly, that he wants to take advantage of the mistake to get the flat at 140*l*. a year for seven years instead of the 250*l*. a year, which is not only the rent he agreed to pay but also a fair and economic rent; and it is also the rent permitted by the Acts on compliance with the necessary formalities. If the rules of equity have become so rigid that they cannot remedy such an injustice, it is time we had a new equity, to make good the omissions of the old. But, in my view, the established rules are amply sufficient for this case.

On the defendant's evidence, which the judge preferred, I should have thought there was a good deal to be said for the view that the lease was induced by an innocent material misrepresentation by the plaintiff. . . . But it is unneccessary to come to a firm conclusion on this point, because, as Bucknill LJ has said, there was clearly a common mistake, or, as I would prefer to describe it, a common misapprehension, which was fundamental and in no way due to any fault of the defendant; and *Cooper* v *Phibbs* affords ample authority for saying that, by reason of the common misapprehension, this lease can be set aside on such terms as the court thinks fit. . . .

In the ordinary way, of course, rescission is only granted when the parties can be restored to substantially the same position as that in which they were before the contract was made; but, as Lord Blackburn said in *Erlanger* v *New Sombrero Phosphate Co.* (1878) 3 App Cas 1218. 'The practice has always been for a court of equity to give this relief whenever, by the exercise of its powers, it can do what is practically just, though it cannot restore the parties precisely to the state they were in before the contract'. That indeed was what was done in *Cooper* v *Phibbs*. Terms were imposed so as to do what was practically just. What terms then, should be imposed here? If the lease were set aside without any terms being imposed, it would mean that the plaintiff, the tenant, would have to go out and would have to pay a reasonable sum for his use and occupation. That would, however, not be just to the tenant.

The situation is similar to that of a case where a long lease is made at the full permitted rent in the common belief that notices of increase have previously been served, whereas in fact they have not. In that case, as in this, when the lease is set aside, terms must be imposed so as to see that the tenant is not unjustly evicted. When Sir John Romilly MR was faced with a somewhat similar problem, he gave the tenant the option to agree to pay the proper rent or to go out: see *Garrard* v *Frankel* (1862) 30 Bear 445; and when Bacon V-C had a like problem before him he did the same, saying 'the object of the court is, as far as it can, to put the parties into the position in which they would have been in if the mistake had not happened': see *Paget* v *Marshall* (1884) 28 ChD 255. If the mistake here had not happened, a proper notice of increase would have been given and the lease would have been executed at the full permitted rent. I think that this court should follow these examples and should impose terms which will enable the tenant to choose either to stay on at the proper rent or to go out.

Bucknill LJ concurred; Jenkins LJ dissented.

6.6.2   MUTUAL MISTAKE

SCRIVEN BROTHERS & CO. v *HINDLEY & CO.* [1913] 3 KB 564 (KB)

The defendants bid an extravagant price for a lot consisting of tow under the misapprehension that it consisted of more valuable hemp.

AT LAWRENCE: In this case the plaintiffs brought an action for 476*l*. 12*s*. 7*d*., the price of 560 cwt. 2 qrs. 27 lbs of Russian tow, as being due for goods bargained and sold. The defendants by their defence denied that they agreed to buy this Russian tow, and alleged that they bid for Russian hemp and that the tow was knocked down to them under a mistake of fact as to the subject-matter of the supposed contract. . . . A number of cases were cited upon either side. I do not propose to examine them in detail because I think that the findings of the jury determine what my judgment should be in this case.

The jury have found that hemp and tow are different commodities in commerce. I should suppose that no one can doubt the correctness of this finding. The second and third findings of the jury shew that the partiess were never ad idem as to the subject-matter of the proposed sale, there was therefore in fact no contract of bargain and sale. The plaintiffs can recover from the defendants only if they can shew that the defendants are estopped from relying upon what is now admittedly the truth. Mr Hume Williams for the plaintiffs argued very ingeniously that the defendants were estopped; for this he relied upon findings 5 and 7, and upon the fact that the defendants had failed to prove the allegation in paragraph 4 of the defence to the effect that Northcott knew at the time he knocked down the lot that Macgregor was bidding for hemp and not for tow.

I must, of course, accept for the purposes of this judgment the findings of the jury, but I do not think they create any estoppel. Question No. 7 was put to the jury as a supplementary question, after they had returned into court with their answers to the other questions, upon the urgent insistence of the learned junior counsel for the plaintiffs. It begs an essential question by using the word 'negligence' and assuming that the purchaser has a duty towards the seller to examine goods that he does not wish to buy, and to correct any latent defect there may be in the sellers' catalogue.

Once it was admitted that Russian hemp was never before known to be consigned or sold with the same shipping marks as Russian tow from the same cargo, it was natural for the person inspecting the 'S.L.' goods and being shewn hemp to suppose that the 'S.L.' bales represented the commodity hemp. Inasmuch as it is admitted that some one had perpetrated a swindle upon the bank which made advances in respect of this shipment of goods it was peculiarly the duty of the auctioneer to make it clear to the bidder either upon the face of his catalogue or in some other way which lots were hemp and which lots were tow,

To rely upon a purchaser's discovering chalk marks upon the floor of the show-room seems to me unreasonable as demanding an amount of care upon the part of the buyer which the vendor had no right to exact. A buyer when he examines a sample does so for his own benefit and not in the discharge of any duty to the seller; the use of the word 'negligence' in such a connection is entirely misplaced, it should be reserved for cases of want of due care where some duty is owed by one person to another. No evidence was tendered of the existence of any such duty upon the part of buyers of hemp. In so far as there was any evidence upon the point it was given by a buyer called as a witness for the plaintiffs who said he had marked the word 'tow' on his catalogue when at the show-rooms 'for his own protection'. I ought probably to have refused to leave the seventh question to the jury; but neither my complaisance nor their answer can create a duty. In my view it is clear that the finding of the jury upon the sixth question prevents the plaintiffs from being able to insist upon a contract by estoppel. Such a contract cannot arise when the person seeking to enforce it has by his own negligence or by that of those for whom he is responsible caused, or contributed to cause, the mistake.

I am therefore of opinion that judgment should be entered for the defendants.

6.6.3 UNILATERAL MISTAKE

SMITH v *HUGHES* (1871) LR 6 QB 597 (QB)

The defendant thought he was buying old oats, whereas in fact they were new.

HANNEN J: . . . It appears from the evidence on both sides that the plaintiff sold the oats in question by a sample which the defendant's agent took away for examination. The bargain was only completed after this sample had been in the defendant's possession for two days. This, without more, would lead to the conclusion that the defendant bought on his own judgment as to the quality of the oats represented by the sample and with the usual warranty only, that the bulk should correspond with it. There might, however, be super-added to this warranty an express condition that the oats should be old, and the defendant endeavoured by his evidence to establish that there was such an express bargain between him and the plaintiff. This was the first question which the jury had to consider; but as they have not stated whether they answered it in favour of the defendant, it is possible – and, from the judge's report, it is most probable – that they did not so answer it, and the case must be considered on the assumption that there was no express stipulation that the oats were old.

There might have been an implied term in the contract arising from previous dealings or other circumstances, that the oats should be old; but the learned judge probably thought the evidence did not make it necessary that he should leave this question to the jury. And the second question, which he did leave to them, seems intended to ascertain whether there was any contract at all between the parties.

It is essential to the creation of a contract that both parties should agree to the same thing in the same sense. Thus, if two persons enter into an apparent contract concerning a particular person or ship, and it turns out that each of them, misled by a similarity of name, had a different person or ship in his mind, no contract would exist between them: *Raffles* v *Wichelhaus* (1864) 2 H & C 906.

But one of the parties to an apparent contract may, by his own fault, be precluded from setting up that he had entered into it in a different sense to that in which it was understood by the other party. Thus in the case of a sale by sample where the vendor, by mistake, exhibited a wrong sample, it was held that the contract was not avoided by this error of the vendor: *Scott* v *Littledale* (1858) 8 E & B 815.

But if in the last-mentioned case the purchaser, in the course of the negotiations preliminary to the contract, had discovered that the vendor was under a misapprehension as to the sample he was offering, the vendor would have been entitled to shew that he had not intended to enter into the contract by which the purchaser sought to bind him. The rule of law applicable to such a case is a corollary from the rule of morality which Mr Pollock cited from Paley, that a promise is to be performed 'in that sense in which the promiser apprehended at the time the promisee received it', and may be thus expressed: 'The promiser is not bound to fulfil a promise in a sense in which the promisee knew as the time the promiser did not intend it'. And in considering the question, in what sense a promisee is entitled to enforce a promise, it matters not in what way the knowledge of the meaning in which the promiser made it is brought to the mind of the promisee, whether by express words, or by conduct, or previous dealings, or other circumstances. If by any means he knows that there was no real agreement between him and the promiser, he is not entitled to insist that the promise shall be fulfilled in a sense to which the mind of the promiser did not assent.

If, therefore, in the present case, the plaintiff knew that the defendant, in dealing with him for oats, did so on the assumption that the plaintiff was contracting to sell him old oats, he was aware that the defendant apprehended the contract in a different sense to that in which he meant it, and he is thereby deprived of the right to insist that the defendant shall be bound by that which was only the apparent, and not the real bargain.

This was the question which the learned judge intended to leave to the jury; and, as I have already said, I do not think it was incorrect in its terms, but I think that it was likely to be misunderstood by the jury. The jury were asked, 'whether they were of opinion, on the whole of the evidence, that the plaintiff believed the defendant to believe, or to be under the impression that he was contracting for the purchase of old oats? If so, there would be a verdict for the defendant.' The jury may have understood this to mean that, if the plaintiff believed the defendant to believe that he was buying old oats, the defendant would be entitled to the verdict; but a belief on the part of the plaintiff that the defendant was making a contract to buy the oats, of which he offered him a sample, under a mistaken belief that they were old, would not relieve the defendant from liability unless his mistaken belief were induced by some misrepresentation of the plaintiff, or concealment by him of a fact which it became his duty to communicate. In order to relieve the defendant it was necessary that the jury should find not merely that the plaintiff believed the defendant to believe that he was buying old oats, but that he believed the defendant to believe that he, the plaintiff, was contracting to sell old oats.

I am the more disposed to think that the jury did not understand the question in this last sense because I can find very little, if any, evidence to support a finding upon it in favour of the defendant. It may be assumed that the defendant believed the oats were old, and it may be suspected that the plaintiff thought he so believed, but the only evidence from which it can be inferred that the plaintiff believed that the defendant thought that the plaintiff was making it a term of the contract that the oats were old is that the defendant was a trainer, and that trainers, as a rule, use old oats; and that the price given was high for new oats, and more than a prudent man would have given.

Having regard to the admitted fact that the defendant bought the oats after two days' detention of the sample, I think that the evidence was not sufficient to justify the jury in answering the question put to them in the defendant's favour, if they rightly understood it; and I therefore think there should be a new trial.

Cockburn CJ and Blackburn J concurred.

6.6.4 MISTAKE AS TO IDENTITY

CUNDY v LINDSAY (1873) 3 App Cas 459 (HL)

Blenkarn duped the plaintiffs, by means of a fraudulent signature and letters, into thinking that they were contracting with Blenkiron & Co., a firm with an address in the same street as Blenkarn.

LORD HATHERLEY: . . . Now the case is simply this, as put by the learned judge in the court below; it was most carefully stated, as one might expect it would be by that learned judge; 'Is it made out to your satisfaction that Alfred Blenkarn, with a fraudulent intent to induce customers generally, and Mr Thomson in particular, to give him the credit of the good character which belonged to William Blenkiron & Sons, wrote those letters in the way you have heard, and had those invoices headed as you have heard', and farther than that, 'did he actually by that fraud induce Mr Thomson to send the goods' 'to 37, Wood Street?'.

Both these questions were answered in the affirmative by the jury. What, then, was the result? It was, that there were letters written by a man endeavouring by contrivance and fraud, as appears upon the face of the letters themselves, to obtain the credit of the well-known firm of Blenkiron & Co., Wood Street. That was done by a falsification of the signature of the Blenkirons, writing his own name in such a manner as that it appeared to represent the signature of that firm. And farther, his letters and invoices were headed 'Wood Street', which was not an accurate way of heading them; for he occupied only a room on a third floor, looking into Little Love lane on one side, and looking into Wood Street on the other. He headed them in that way, in order that by these two devices he might represent himself to the respondents as Blenkiron of Wood Street. He did that purposely; and it is found that he induced the respondents by that device to send the goods to Blenkiron of Wood Street. I apprehend, therefore, that if there could be said to have been any sale at all, it failed for want of a purchaser. The sale, if made out upon such a transaction as this, would have been a sale to the Blenkirons of Wood Street, if they had chosen to adopt it, and to no other person whatever – not to this Alfred Blenkarn, with whom the respondents had not, and with whom they did not wish to have, any dealings whatever.

My Lords, it appears to me that that brings the case completely within the authority of *Hardman* v *Booth* (1863) 1 H & C 803, where it was held that there was no real contract between the parties by whom the goods were delivered and the concoctor of the fraud who obtained possession of them, because they were not *to him* sold. Exactly in the same way here, there was no real contract whatever with Alfred Blenkarn; no goods had been delivered to anybody except for the purpose of transferring the property to Blenkiron (not Blenkarn); therefore the case really in substance is the identical case of *Hardman* v *Booth* over again. . . .

We have been pressed very much with an ingenious mode of putting the case on the part of the counsel who have argued with eminent ability for the appellants in this case, namely, suppose this fraudulent person had gone himself to the firm from whom he wished to obtain the goods, and had represented that he was a member of one of the largest firms in London. Suppose on his making that representation the goods had been delivered to him. Now I am very far, at all events on the present occasion, from seeing my way to this, that the goods being sold to him as representing that firm he could be treated in any other way than as an agent of that firm, or suppose he had said: 'I am as rich as that firm. I have transactions as large as those of that firm. I have a large balance at my bankers'; then the sale would have been a sale to a fraudulent purchaser on fraudulent representations, and a sale which would have been capable of being set aside, but still a sale would have been made to the person who made those false representations; and the parting with the goods in that case might possibly – I say no more – have passed the property.

But this case is an entirely different one. The whole case, as represented here is this; from beginning to end the respondents believed they were dealing with Blenkiron & Co., they made out their invoices to Blenkiron & Co., they supposed they sold to Blenkiron & Co., they never sold in any way to Alfred Blenkarn; and therefore Alfred Blenkarn cannot, by so obtaining the goods, have by possibility made a good title to a purchaser, as against the owners of the goods, who had never in any shape or way parted with the property nor with anything more than the possession of it.

Lords Cairns and Penzance concurred.

INGRAM v *LITTLE* [1961] 1 QB 31 (CA)

SELLERS LJ: In August, 1957, the plaintiffs were the joint owners of a Renault Dauphine motor-car, ULJ 101.

On August 3, 1957, the Saturday before the August Bank Holiday of that year, in a transaction with a man not inappropriately called 'the rogue Hutchinson' by the judge, the plaintiffs parted with the car to him. By August 6 the car was in Blackpool and there was a purported sale of it to the defendant by the rogue, as the judge found, then using the name Hardy. . . .

The decision in the present case turns solely on whether 'Hutchinson' entered into a contract which gave him a title to the car which would subsist until it was avoided in the undoubted fraud being discovered. . . . The plaintiffs, Miss Elsie Ingram, Miss Hilda Ingram and Mrs Mary Ann Maud Badger, advertised their Renault Dauphine motor-car, registration number ULJ 101, for sale in the issue of the 'Bournemouth Echo' for August 2, 1957. . . . About 2.15 pm on August 3 the rogue Hutchinson called at the house where the plaintiffs were living. He was admitted by Miss Hilda Ingram; he told her he was Hutchinson, and Miss Hilda Ingram accordingly introduced him to her sister Miss Elsie

Ingram as Hutchinson. He looked at the car, and asked Miss Elsie Ingram to take him for a run in it, and she did so.

After the drive they came back to the house and discussed the sale of the car. Hutchinson offered Miss Elsie Ingram, who conducted the negotiations for the plaintiffs, £700 and she refused. After some bargaining he offered £717, which she said she was prepared to accept. The rogue then pulled out a cheque book and she immediately realised that he was proposing to pay £717 by cheque. She told him that she would not in any circumstances accept a cheque, and that she was only willing to sell the car for cash. She said that she was not prepared to accept a cheque. She had expected cash, and she made as though to walk out of the room.

The rogue started to talk and try to convince her that he was a most reputable person, and then for the first time he gave his initials. He said that he was P. G. M. Hutchinson. He said that he had business interests in Guildford, and that he lived at Stanstead House, Stanstead Road, Caterham.

Miss Hilda Ingram, who had been in the room, slipped out of the room and after a short time returned. She had gone to the Parkstone post office, which was only about two minutes away from the plaintiffs' house, and had looked in the main telephone directory covering the district of Caterham. In that directory she had seen the entry 'Hutchinson, P. G. M., Stanstead House, Stanstead Road, Caterham 4665', and she believed that that was the man who, at that moment, was with her sister in their house. On her return to the house she told her sister, Miss Elsie Ingram, who was still discussing the proposed sale, that she had checked with the telephone directory at the post office and that there was such a person as P. G. M. Hutchinson living at Stanstead House, Stanstead Road, Caterham. Having received that information, the two sisters decided that they would let the rogue have the car in exchange for the cheque. The decision was reached because they believed that the rogue was the person he said he was. When he gave the cheque, the rogue wrote on the back 'P. G. M. Hutchinson, Stanstead House, Stanstead Road, Caterham'. . . .

During the conversation, from which a contract, if any, has to be derived, the rogue 'Hutchinson' knew he was not the person the plaintiffs believed him to be and to whom alone they made their offer to sell the car and to whom alone they intended to give possession of it in exchange for his cheque.

'Hutchinson' knew that the offer to sell the car in exchange for a cheque was not made to him as he was, but only to an existing person whom he represented himself to be. If the plaintiffs are to be regarded as the acceptors of 'Hutchinson's' offer to pay by cheque, he knew full well that it was not his cheque they were accepting but the cheque of the man they thought he was by reason of his persuasion and deceit.

The judge found that Miss Elsie Ingram intended to part not merely with possession but with the property in the car, but that she did so believing that the person to whom she was selling the car was P. G. M. Hutchinson of Stanstead House, Stanstead Road, Caterham, with a number in the telephone directory, and he further held that, if the entry in the telephone directory had not been confirmed by Miss Hilda Ingram, the two sisters would not have accepted the cheque in payment or parted with the car.

If 'Hutchinson' had paid cash for the car, then it seems clear that there would have been a concluded and unimpeachable transaction in which the identity and financial stability of the buyer would have been of no moment. This is not a case where the plaintiffs wished to withhold their car from any particular person or class of persons. Their desire, made quite obvious in the negotiations, was to ensure that they received payment and, unless cash was paid, the person with whom they were dealing was of major importance truly as to his credit worthiness and this fact was equally clear to 'Hutchinson' from the course which the negotiations took.

It does not seem to me to matter whether the right view of the fact is, as the judge held and as I would agree, that there was no concluded contract before the cheque book was produced and before the vital fraudulent statements were made or that there was a concluded contract which 'Hutchinson' at once repudiated by refusing to pay cash and that this repudiation was accepted by the plaintiffs and the transaction was then and there at an end. The property would not have passed until cash had been paid and it never was paid or intended to be paid.

Was there a contract of sale subsequently made which led to the plaintiffs taking 'Hutchinson's' cheque and in exchange for it handing over the car and its log book?

The judgment held that there never was a concluded contract, applying, as I understand it, the elementary factors required by law to establish a contract.

The judge, treating the plaintiffs as the offerors and the rogue 'Hutchinson' as the offeree, found that the plaintiffs in making their offer to sell the car not for cash but for a cheque (which in the circumstances of the Bank Holiday week-end could not be banked before the following Tuesday, August 6, 1957) were under the belief that they were dealing with, and therefore making their offer to, the honest P. G. M. Hutchinson of Caterham, whom they had reason to believe was a man of substance and standing.

'Hutchinson', the offeree, knew precisely what was in the minds of the two ladies for he had put it there and he knew that their offer was inteded for P. G. M. Hutchinson of Caterham and that they were making no offer to and had no intention to contract with him, as he was. There was no offfer which he 'Hutchinson' could accept and, therefore, there was no contract.

The judge pointed out that the offer which the plaintiffs made was one which was capable of being accepted only by the honest P. G. M. Hutchinson of Caterham and was incapable of acceptance by 'Hutchinson'.

In all the circumstances of the present case I would accept the judges findings. Indeed the conclusion so reached seems self-evident.

Is the conclusion to be held wrong in law? If it is, then, as I see it, it must be on the sole ground that as 'Hutchinson' was present, albeit making fraudulent statements to induce the plaintiffs to part with their car to him on exchange for his worthless cheque and was successful in so doing, then a bargain must have been struck with him personally, however much he deceived the plaintiffs into thinking they were dealing with someone else.

Where two parties are negotiating together and there is no question of one or the other purporting to act as an agent for another, and an agreement is reached, the normal and obvious conclusion would no doubt be that they are the contracting parties. A contrary finding would not be justified unless very clear evidence demanded it. The unfortunate position of the defendant is this case illustrates how third parties who deal in good faith with the fraudulent person may be prejudiced.

The mere presence of an individual cannot, however, be conclusive that an apparent bargain he may make is made with him. If he were disguised in appearance and in dress to represent someone else and the other party, deceived by the disguise, dealt with him on the basis that he was that person and would not have contracted had he known the truth then, it seems clear, there would be no contract established. If words are substituted for outward disguise so as to depict a different person from the one physically present, in what circumstances would the result be different?

Whether the person portrayed, by disguise or words, is known to the other party or not is important in considering whether the identity of the person is of any moment or whether it is a matter of indifference. If a man said his name was Brown when it was in fact Smith, and both were unknown to the other party, it would be difficult to say that there was any evidence that the contract was not made and intended to be made with the person present. In *King's Norton Metal Co. Ltd* v *Edridge, Merrett & Co. Ltd* (1897) 14 TLR 98 one Wallis fraudulently described himself as Hallam & Co., making it appear a substantial firm with a large factory. The court held that the use of an assumed name by the buyer did not prevent a finding that the plaintiffs, the sellers of some brass rivet wire, had contracted with him.

But personal knowledge of that person fraudulently represented cannot, I think, be an essential feature. It might be a very strong factor but the qualities of a person not personally known might be no less strong. If a man misrepresented himself to be a Minister of the Crown or a stockbroker, confidence in the person so identified might arise although the individual so described was wholly unknown personally or by sight to the other party.

It would seem that there is an area of fact in cases of the type under consideration where a fraudulent person is present purporting to make a bargain with another and that the circumstances may justify a finding that, notwithstanding some fraud and deceit, the correct view may be that a bargain was struck with the person present, or on the other hand they may equally justify, as here, a finding the other way.

Some of the difficulties and perhaps confusion which have arisen in some of the cases do not, in my view, arise here.

If less had been said by the rogue, and if nothing had been done to confirm his statements by Miss Hilda Ingram, who communicated what she had learnt to Miss Elsie who was doing the main negotiation, the result might have been different, for the sellers' concern about the stability and standing of the buyer might not have been revealed and it might have been held that an offer in such circumstances was to the party present, whatever his true identity would be.

In *Phillips v Brooks Ltd* [1919] 2 KB 243 the rogue North had apparently been in the shop some time inspecting goods which were brought and displayed for sale to him without any regard to his identity – he was a 'customer' only. The judgment of Horridge J is, as I read it, based on a finding of the fact that Phillips intended to deal with North as a customer. Viscount Haldane, in *Lake v Simmons* [1927] AC 487, has taken the view that the case could be explained on the ground that the fraudulent misrepresentation was not made until after the parties had agreed upon a sale.

That opinion has been criticised, mainly, I think, by academic writers, but if, as must be conceded, it is a possible view, and as *Phillips v Brooks Ltd* has stood for so long and is, as I think, a decision within an area of fact, I would not feel justified in saying it was wrong.

Pearce LJ agreed that the plaintiffs should succeed; Devlin LJ dissented.

LEWIS v AVERAY [1972] 1 QB 198 (CA)

LORD DENNING MR: This is another case where one of two innocent persons has to suffer for the fraud of a third. It will no doubt interest students and find its place in the textbooks.

Mr Lewis is a young man who is a post-graduate student of chemistry. He lives at Clifton near Bristol. He had an Austin Cooper 'S' motor car. He decided to sell it. He put an advertisement in the newspaper offering it for £450. On May 8, 1969, in reply to the advertisement a man – I will simply call him the 'rogue', for so he was – telephoned and asked if he could come and see the car. He did not give his name. He said he was speaking from Wales, in Glamorganshire. Mr Lewis said he could come and see it. He came in the evening to Mr Lewis's flat. Mr Lewis showed him the car, which was parked outside. The rogue drove it and tested it. He said he liked it. They then went along to the flat of Mr Lewis's fiancée, Miss Kershaw (they have since married). He told them he was Richard Green and talked much about the film world. He led both of them to believe that he was the well-known film actor, Richard Greene, who played Robin Hood in the 'Robin Hood' series. They talked about the car. He asked to see the logbook. He was shown it and seemed satisfied. He said he would like to buy the car. They agreed a price of £450. The rogue wrote out a cheque for £450 on the Beckenham Branch of the Midland Bank. He signed it 'R. A. Green'. He wanted to take the car at once. But Mr Lewis was not willing for him to have it until the cheque was cleared. To hold him off, Mr Lewis said there were one or two small jobs he would like to do on the car before letting him have it, and that would give time for the cheque to be cleared. The rogue said 'Don't worry about those small jobs. I would like to take the car now'. Mr Lewis said: 'Have you anything to prove that you are Mr Richard Green?'. The rogue thereupon brought out a special pass of admisson to Pinewood Studios, which had an official stamp on it. It bore the name of Richard A. Green and the address, and also a photograph which was plainly the photograph of the man, who was the rogue.

On seeing this pass, Mr Lewis was satisfied. He thought this man was really Mr Richard Greene, the film actor. By that time it was 11 'clock at night. Mr Lewis took the cheque and let the rogue have the car and the logbook and the Ministry of Transport test certificate. . . .

Next day, May 9, 1969, Mr Lewis put the cheque into the bank. A fews days later the bank told him it was worthless. The rogue had stolen a cheque book and written this £450 on a stolen cheque.

Meanwhile, while the cheque was going through, the rogue sold the car to an innocent purchaser. He sold it to a young man called Mr Averay. He was at the time under 21. He was a music student in London at the Royal College of Music. . . .

Now Mr Lewis, the orginal owner of the car, sues young Mr Averay. Mr Lewis claims that the car is still his. He claims damages for conversion. The judge found in favour of Mr Lewis and awarded damages of £330 for conversion.

The real question in the case is whether on May 8, 1969, there was a contract of sale under which the property in the car passed from Mr Lewis to the rogue. If there was such a contract, then, even though it was voidable for fraud, nevertheless Mr Averay would get a good title to the car. But if there was no contract of sale by Mr Lewis to the rogue – either because there was, on the face of it, no agreement between the parties, or because any apparent agreement was a nullity and void ab initio for mistake, then no property would pass from Mr Lewis to the rogue. Mr Averay would not get a good title because the rogue had no property to pass to him.

There is no doubt that Mr Lewis was mistaken as to the identity of the person who handed him the cheque. He thought that he was Richard Greene, a film actor of standing and worth: whereas in fact he was a rogue whose identity is quite unknown. It was under the influence of that mistake that Mr Lewis let the rogue have the car. He would not have dreamed of letting him have it otherwise.

What is the effect of this mistake? There are two cases in our books which cannot, to my mind, be reconciled the one with the other. One of them is *Phillips v Brooks Ltd* [1919] 2 KB 243, where a jeweller had a ring for sale. The other is *Ingram v Little* [1961] 1 QB 31, where two ladies had a car for sale. In each case the story is very similar to the present. A plausible rogue comes along. The rogue says he likes the ring, or the car, as the case be. He asks the price. The seller names it. The rogue says he is prepared to buy it at that price. He pulls out a cheque book. He writes, or prepares to write, a cheque for the price. The seller hestitates. He has never met this man before. He does not want to hand over the ring or the car not knowing whether the cheque will be met. The rogue notices the seller's hesitation. He is quick with his next move. He says to the jeweller, in *Phillips v Brooks:* 'I am Sir George Bullough of 11 St James's Square'; or to the ladies in *Ingram v Little* 'I am P. G. M. Hutchinson of Stanstead House, Stanstead Road, Caterham'; or to the post-graduate student in the present case: 'I am Richard Greene, the film actor of the Robin Hood series'. Each seller checks up the information. The jeweller looks up the directory and finds there is a Sir George Bullough at 11 St James's Square. The ladies check up too. They look at the telephone directory and find there is a 'P.G.M. Hutchinson of Stanstead House, Stanstead Road, Caterham'. The post-graduate student checks up too. He examines the official pass of the Pinewood Studios and finds that it is a pass for 'Richard A. Green' to the Pinewood Studios with this man's photograph on it. In each case the seller feels that this is sufficient confirmation of the man's identity. So he accepts the cheque signed by the rogue and lets him have the ring, in the one case, and the car and logbook in the other two cases. The rogue goes off and sells the goods to a third person who buys them in entire good faith and pays the price to the rogue. The rogue disappears. The original seller presents the cheque. It is dishonoured. Who is entitled to the goods? The original seller? Or the ultimate buyer? The courts have given different answers. In *Phillips v Brooks*, the ultimate buyer was held to be entitled to the ring. In *Ingram v Little* the original seller was held to be entitled to the car. In the present case the deputy county court judge has held the original seller entitled.

It seems to me that the material facts in each case are quite indistinguishable the one from the other. In each case there was, to all outward appearance, a contract: but there was a mistake by the seller as to the identity of the buyer. This mistake was fundamental. In each case it led to the handing over of the goods. Without it the seller could not have parted with them.

This case therefore raises the question: What is the effect of a mistake by one party as to the identity of the other? It has sometimes been said that if a party makes a mistake as to the identity of the person with whom he is contracting there is no contract, or, if there is a contract, it is a nullity and void, so that no property can pass under it. This has been supported by a reference to the French jurist Pothier; but I have said before, and I repeat now, his statement is no part of English law. I know that it was quoted by Lord Haldane in *Lake v Simmons* [1927] AC 487, 501, and, as such, misled Tucker J in *Sowler v Potter* [1940] 1 KB 271, into holding that a lease was void whereas it was really voidable. But Pothier's statement has given rise to such refinements that it is time it was dead and buried together.

For instance, in *Ingram* v *Little* [1961] 1 QB 31 the majority of the court suggested that the difference between *Phillips* v *Brooks* [1919] 2 KB 243 and *Ingram* v *Little* was that in *Phillips* v *Brooks* the contract of sale was concluded (so as to pass the property to the rogue) before the rogue made the fraudulent misrepresentation: see [1961] 1 QB 31, 51, 60: whereas in *Ingram* v *Little* the rogue made the fraudulent misrepresentation before the contract was concluded. My own view is that in each case the property in the goods did not pass until the seller let the rogue have the goods.

Again it has been suggested that a mistake as to the identity of a person is one thing: and a mistake as to his attributes is another. A mistake as to identity, it is said, avoids a contract; whereas a mistake as to attributes does not. But this is a distinction without a difference. A man's very name is one of his attributes. It is also a key to his identity. If then, he gives a false name, is it a mistake as to his identity? or a mistake as to his attributes? These fine distinctions do no good to the law.

As I listened to the argument in this case, I felt it wrong that an innocent purchaser (who knew nothing of what passed between the seller and the rogue) should have his title depend on such refinements. After all, he has acted with complete circumspection and in entire good faith: whereas it was the seller who let the rogue have the goods and thus enabled him to commit the fraud. I do not, therefore, accept the theory that a mistake as to identity renders a contract void. I think the true principle is that which underlies the decision of this court in *King's Norton Metal Co. Ltd* v *Edridge Merrett & Co. Ltd* (1897) 14 TLR 98 and of Horridge J in *Phillips* v *Brooks* [1919] 2 KB 243, which has stood for these last 50 years. It is this: When two parties have come to a contract – or rather what appears, on the face of it, to be a contract – the fact that one party is mistaken as to the identity of the other does not mean that there is no contract, or that the contract is a nullity and void from the beginning. It only means that the contract is voidable, that is, liable to be set aside at the instance of the mistaken person, so long as he does so before third parties have in good faith acquired rights under it.

Applied to the cases such as the present, this principle is in full accord with the presumption stated by Pearce LJ and also Devlin LJ in *Ingram* v *Little* [1961] 1 QB 31, 61, 66. When a dealing is had between a seller like Mr Lewis and a person who is actually there present before him, then the presumption in law is that there is a contract, even though there is a fraudulent impersonation by the buyer representing himself as a different man than he is. There is a contract made with the very person there, who is present in person. It is liable no doubt to be avoided for fraud, but it is still a good contract under which title will pass unless and until it is avoided. In support of that presumption, Devlin LJ quoted, at p. 66, not only the English case of *Phillips* v *Brooks*, but other cases in the United States where 'the courts hold that if A appeared in person before B, impersonating C, an innocent purchaser from A gets the property in the goods against B'. That seems to me to be right in principle in this country also.

In this case Mr Lewis made a contract of sale with the very man, the rogue, who came to the flat. I say that he 'made a contract' because in this regard we do not look into his intentions, or into his mind to know what he was thinking or into the mind of the rogue. We look to the outward appearances. On the face of the dealing, Mr Lewis made a contract under which he sold the car to the rogue, delivered the car and the logbook to him, and took a cheque in return. The contract is evidenced by the receipts which were signed. It was, of course, induced by fraud. The rogue made false representations as to his identity. But it was still a contract, though voidable for fraud. It was a contract under which this property passed to the rogue, and in due course passed from the rogue to Mr Averay, before the contract was avoided.

Though I very much regret that either of these good and reliable gentlemen should suffer, in my judgment it is Mr Lewis who should do so. I think the appeal should be allowed and judgment entered for the defendant.

Phillimore and Megaw LJJ concurred.

KING'S NORTON METAL COMPANY LTD v EDRIDGE, MERRETT AND COMPANY LTD (1879) 14 TLR 98 (CA)

SMITH LJ: . . . the case was a plain one. The question was whether the plaintiffs, who had been cheated out of their goods by a rogue called Wallis, or the defendants were to bear the loss. The law seemed to him to be well settled. If a person, induced by false pretences, contracted with a rogue to sell goods to him and the goods were delivered the rogue could until the contract was disaffirmed give a good title to the goods to a *bona fide* purchaser for value. The facts here were that Wallis, for the purpose of cheating, set up in business as Hallam and Co., and got note-paper prepared for the purpose, and wrote to the plaintiffs representing that he was carrying on business as Hallam & Co. He got the goods in question and sold them to the defendants, who bought them *bona fide* for value. The question was, With whom, upon this evidence, which was all one way, did the plaintiffs contract to sell the goods? Clearly with the writer of the letters. If it could have been shown that there was a separate entity called Hallam & Co. and another entity called Wallis then the case might have come within the decision in *Cundy v Lindsay* (1878) 3 App Cas 459. In his opinion there was a contract by the plaintiffs with the person who wrote the letters, by which the property passed to him. There was only one entity, trading it might be under an *alias,* and there was a contract by which the property passed to him. Mr Justice Cave said that this was nothing more than a long firm fraud. Did anyone ever hear of an attempt being made by a person who had delivered his goods to a long firm to get his goods back on the ground that he had made no contract with the long firm? The indictment against a long firm was always for obtaining the goods by false pretences, which presupposed the passing of the property. For these reasons there was no question to go to the jury, and the non-suit was right.

Collins and Rigby LJJ concurred.

6.6.5   *NON EST FACTUM*

SAUNDERS v *ANGLIA BUILDING SOCIETY (SUB NOM GALLIE v LEE)*
[1971] AC 1004 (HL)

LORD HODSON: My Lords, on June 25, 1962, the appellant executed an assignment of her leasehold interest in 12, Dunkeld Road, Dagenham, to one Lee, the first defendant in the action.

Her case is that her intention was to give the house to her nephew Walter William Parkin upon condition that he was to permit her to reside there for the rest of her life and that she handed the title deeds to her nephew believing that the house thereupon became his property. She admits that she signed the deed of assignment to Lee but says that she believed that this was a deed of gift giving effect to the transaction in favour of her nephew. She claims accordingly that the deed is void just as if she had not signed it at all, for example as if her signature had been forged. She pleads non est factum.

On the day when the deed was signed by her she was 78 years of age and her pleaded case was that Lee came to her house with Parkin and produced a document to her. This he asked her to sign saying words to the effect that he was asking her to sign it as a deed of gift to Wally (Parkin) and everything was in order. The appellant had broken her spectacles so that she could not use them. She could not read without them so did not read the document. Giving her evidence on commission she said that she thought Parkin and Lee were getting money on the house and that the whole purpose of giving the house to Parkin was so that he could get money on it. She said: 'When they came and spoke to me about the house, I said to my nephew "I don't mind what I do to help you along" '.

As against Lee the deed was voidable as having been induced by fraud and the learned judge accordingly held it to be void against him. Lee has not appealed.

The position of the second defendant, the Anglia Building Society, which is the respondent to the appeal, is entirely different. The society has advanced £2,000 on a deed which on its face is good security for their loan. The learned judge, however, held that the appellant was entitled to succeed against this defendant also. He held that the deed was void, accepting the plea non est factum put forward by the appellant on the basis that she was misled as to the character, not only as to the contents, of the deed. He held that the assignment for consideration to her was of a different character from a deed of gift to Parkin. Relying upon the long-accepted distinction between character and contents he gave judgment against the respondent as well as against Lee.

This distinction stems from the case of *Howatson* v *Webb* [1907] 1 Ch 537 (affirmed in the Court of Appeal [1908] 1 Ch 1), a decision of Warrington J.

The majority of the Court of Appeal in this case applying the same test as the trial judge arrived at a different conclusion. Russell LJ, accepting an argument which had been rejected by the trial judge, said that the essential character of the document which the appellant was intending to execute was such as to divest herself of her leasehold property by transferring it to another so that the transferee should be in a position to deal with the property, in particular by borrowing money on the security of the property. Her evidence showed that she understood that Lee and Parkin were jointly concerned in raising money on the security of the property. It was her intention that this should be done. This was, as Russell LJ said, [1969] 2 Ch 17, 38, 'the whole object of the exercise'. I agree with him that the identity of the transferee (namely Lee instead of Parkin) does not make the deed of a totally different character from that which she intended to sign. On this ground the plea of non est factum must fail. Salmon LJ put the matter somewhat differently, but to the same effect, in concluding from the appellant's evidence that she would have executed the assignment to Lee even if the transaction had been properly explained to her. The Master of the Rolls reached the same conclusion but was not prepared to be fettered by the distinction between character and contents.

The distinction is a valid one in that it emphasises that points of detail in the contents of a document are not to be relied upon in support of a plea of non est factum. The Master of the Rolls did, however, demonstrate that using the words as terms of art for test purposes may produce ludicrous results, for example, a mistake as to the amount of money involved may be described as a mistake as to contents although the difference between two figures may be so great as to produce a document of an entirely different character from the one the signer intended.

It is better to adopt the test which is supported by the authorities prior to *Howatson* v *Webb* and is sound in principle. This is that the difference to support a plea of non est factum must be in a particular which goes to the substance of the whole consideration or to the root of the matter. Where, as in this case, there is an error of personality it may or may not be fundamental; the question cannot be answered in isolation. There is a distinction between a deed and a contract in that the former does not require consensus and the latter does. Hence, in the case of deeds error of personality is not necessarily so vital as in the case of contracts.

The plea of non est factum requires clear and positive evidence before it can be established. As Donovan LJ said, delivering the judgment of the Court of Appeal in *Muskham Finance Ltd* v *Howard* [1963] 1 QB 904, 912: 'The plea of non est factum is a plea which must necessarily be kept within narrow limits'. To take an example, the man who in the course of his business signs a pile of documents without checking them takes the responsibility for them by appending his signature. It would be surprising if he was allowed to repudiate one of those documents on the ground of non est factum.

I agree with the robust conclusion reached by the Master of the Rolls on the facts of this case that the appellant having signed the questioned document, obviously a legal document, upon which the building society advanced money on the faith of its being her document, cannot now be allowed to disavow her signature.

I should have arrived at this conclusion even if I had thought that the law applicable was that which had previously been accepted, namely, that the distinction between character and contents should be maintained.

Want of care on the part of the person who signs a document which he afterwards seeks to disown is relevant. The burden of proving non est factum is on the party disowning his signature; this includes proof that he or she took care. There is no burden on the opposite party to prove want of care. The word 'negligence' in this connection does not involve the proposition that want of care is irrelevant unless there can be found a specific duty to the opposite party to take care. *Carlisle and Cumberland Banking Co. Ltd* v *Bragg* [1911] 1 KB 489 was on this point, in my opinion, wrongly decided and seems to be due to a confusion of thought by introducing the kind of negligence which founds an action in tort for injury.

A person may be precluded by his own negligence, carelessness or inadvertence from averring his mistake. The word 'estoppel' has often been used in this context but, for my part, I agree with Salmon LJ that this is not a true estoppel but an illustration of the principle that no man may take advantage of his own wrong. If it were treated as estoppel one would have to face the argument put forward by the appellant that if there is no deed there can be no estoppel established by the document itself. If there was no estoppel by deed there was no other foundation for that doctrine to be invoked since there was no conduct by way of representation to the building society that the questioned deed was good.

The plea of non est factum was originally available, it seems, only to the blind and the illiterate (compare *Thoroughgood's Case* (1582) 2 Co Rep 9b) but by the middle of the last century the modern approach to the matter is illustrated by the leading case of *Foster* v *Mackinnon* (1869) LR 4 CP 704, 711–12, in which the judgment of the court was delivered by Byles J. I need not cite the whole passage but note that the judgment, at p. 711, extends the scope of the doctrine to a person:

> . . . who for some reason (not implying negligence) forbears to read, has a written contract falsely read over to him, the reader misreading to such a degree that the written contract is of a nature altogether different from the contract pretended to be read from the paper which the blind or illiterate man afterwards signs: then, at least if there be no negligence, the signature so obtained is of no force. And it is invalid not merely on the ground of fraud, where fraud exists, but on the ground that the mind of the signer did not accompany the signature.

It is, I think, plain that the word 'negligence' is not used in this passage in the restricted sense of breach of duty.

The case for the appellant stands or falls by her evidence. On no reasonable interpretation of this can she, in my opinion, succeed. I would dismiss the appeal.

Viscount Dilhorne, and Lords Reid, Wilberforce and Pearson concurred.

6.7 Contracts in Restraint of Trade

NORDENFELT v *MAXIM NORDENFELT GUNS AND AMMUNITION CO.*
[1894] AC 535 (HL)

LORD MACNAGHTEN: . . . The true view at the present time I think, is this: The public have an interest in every person's carrying on his trade freely: so has the individual. All interference with individual liberty of action in trading, and all restraints of trade of themselves, if there is nothing more, are contrary to public policy, and therefore void. That is the general rule. But there are exceptions: restraints of trade and interference with individual liberty of action may be justified by the special circumstances of a particular case. It is a sufficient justification, and indeed it is the only justification, if the restriction is reasonable – reasonable, that is, in reference to the interests of the parties concerned and reasonable in reference to the interests of the public, so framed and so guarded as to afford adequate protection to the party in whose favour it is imposed, while at the same time it is in no way injurious to the public.

6.7.1 RESTRAINTS OVER EMPLOYEES

MARION WHITE LTD v *FRANCIS* [1972] 1 WLR 1423 (CA)

The defendant had agreed not to be in any way engaged in the business of a ladies' hairdresser within one half mile of the plaintiffs' premises for 12 months after leaving their employment.

BUCKLEY LJ: . . . It is accepted by the employers that the burden rests upon them to establish that this covenant is one which is reasonable in the interests of the parties and reasonable in the public interest, and that it is for the protection of some interest of theirs in respect of which they are entitled to protection.

It is obvious that in an establishment such as a ladies' hairdresser's establishment the assistants who actually deal with the customers, who dress their hair, wash their hair, and do whatever else they do for the customers, provide a very important part of the personal contact between those engaged in the business and the customers of the business. That constitutes an important element of the goodwill of the business; and that is an interest which the employer is entitled to have protected.

It is well established by authority that, in the case of a covenant in restraint of the trade between employer and employee, the employer is not entitled to a covenant against all types of competition but is only entitled to such a covenant as will protect such interest of the employer as it is legitimate for him to protect. In *Home Counties Dairies Ltd v Skilton* [1970] 1 WLR 526 Harman LJ said this, which is à propos to what I have just been saying, dealing in that case with a milk roundsman and the nature of his employment, at p 530:

> . . . he has been throughout the years, one way or another, a familiar and probably influential character well known to every householder in the road. It is natural in the circumstances that he acquires, usually on behalf of a master, a clientele along his round who, if he is an agreeable and competent man, will tend to rely on him for his arrival and to follow his departure to serve another employer. In these circumstances it is natural that employers should make great efforts to retain the goodwill so acquired and to restrain, so far as they can, the employee who leaves their service from taking his clients with him. This is very much a part of the employer's goodwill which he is entitled to protect, for it is his most saleable asset.

And, just as the milk roundsman may endear himself to the housewives on his round, so an assistant in a ladies' hairdressing establishment may very well endear herself, either by her personality or her skill, to the customers of the establishment who come there for services; and that constitutes part of the goodwill of the employer's business which the employer is fully entitled to protect. It is that aspect of the matter to which this covenant is directed.

Mr Addison has contended on behalf of the employee that the judge was justified in taking the view that he did, in the passage that I have read from his judgment, that this covenant is too wide in its operation and that it would extend to activities in which the employee would not be brought into connection with customers at all. He suggested that she might be employed as a bookkeeper in a back room and never see a customer; or she might be merely a shareholder or a director in a company concerned with a hairdressing establishment within the prohibited area. The example taken by the judge was that she might become or be employed as a receptionist. It is not absolutely clear, on the language he used in the judgment, whether he was there thinking of a receptionist in a hairdresser's salon or a receptionist in some other kind of establishment, perhaps a dentist's place of business or an hotel or something of that sort. I think that upon a fair reading of what the judge said he was thinking on employment as a receptionist in a hairdressing establishment. If that was what he had in mind, I would myself think that that would be likely to be just as damaging or almost as damaging to the goodwill of the employers as employment in the actual processes of attending to people's hair; for if a customer of the employers became aware that the employee, who used to serve her at the employers' shop and with whom she had become friendly, had moved to a nearby competitor hairdresser as receptionist or as manageress of the business in that shop, I think that there would be almost as great a risk of custom being lost by the employers as if the employee had merely entered the employment of the competitor as an assistant carrying out the operations of dressing hair.

I have stressed already that I think that this covenant is aimed at active participation by the employee in a hairdressing business within the prohibited area, and I think that it is aimed at active participation in a way that is directly connected with the hairdressing aspects of the business. I do not think it was within the contemplation of the parties to this agreement that the employee would would either be likely to be employed as a bookkeeper in another hairdressing establishment or as a cleaner or in any other capacity that one can think of that has nothing to do with dressing hair, although it may have to do with the administrative or domestic arrangements of the business. As was pointed out in *Home Counties Dairies v Skilton* [1970] 1 WLR 526, an agreement of this kind and a clause of this kind must be read in the context of the business in relation to which the covenant is entered into and of the relation between the parties; and I think that it is giving too wide an interpretation to this covenant to say that it would extend to any such activities as being employed as a bookkeeper or as a cleaner or anything of that sort.

In my judgment, this covenant, which cannot be criticised on the basis of either area or period, is a good and valid and effective covenant, and I think that the deputy judge was in error in arriving at the contrary conclusion.

Stephenson and Davies LJJ concurred.

FITCH v *DEWES* [1920] 2 Ch 159 (ChD)

EVE J: This action has been brought at the instigation of the defendant with the object of having it determined whether a restrictive covenant entered into by him is binding upon and enforceable against him, or whether it is void as being in the nature of an excessive restraint on trade. . . .

The first thing to do is to construe the restriction. I do not think this presents much difficulty. It is a restriction which, in effect, restrains the defendant for the rest of his life from practising as a solicitor either as a principal or agent within the area included in a radius of seven miles from the Town Hall of Tamworth. The draftsmanship may be open to a suggestion of verbosity, but the meaning and effect of the clause are in my opinion tolerably plain. The question then arises, is this restriction reasonable both in reference to the interests of the contracting parties and in reference to the interests of the public?

. . . I cannot bring myself to hold that the restraint affords more than adequate protection to the party in whose favour it is imposed, or that it was not in the interest of the covenantor to so restrict himself for the sake of the advantages he has obtained by so doing. He has been adequately and properly educated and trained in his profession; he has been introduced to a large body of clients and given every opportunity of learning their affairs, and of disclosing to them the skill and ability of which he is possessed. This equipment of these advantages he carries away with him, and the only restriction imposed upon him is that he shall not employ his objective knowledge within the restricted area. Outside that area he can act for clients, whether resident within the area or not, with whom and with whose business he has become acquainted solely by reason of his employment by the plaintiff; in other words, he is left free to use for his own purposes outside the restricted area the whole of his subjective knowledge, and so much of his objective knowledge as relates to the affairs of clients of his former employer who elect to employ him.

It is said that the restriction is not reasonable in the interests of the contracting parties, because it is imposed for the whole of the defendant's life, but when attempts were made by counsel appearing for him to suggest what would be a reasonable limit from their point of view their proposals did not agree, and in the end the objection on this ground resolved itself into this, that if the plaintiff's business were wholly discontinued, either in consequence of the defection of clients, or of the plaintiff relinquishing it or for some other cause, the restriction would become superfluous and of no use to anybody; and it was urged this possible result proves that the restraint is more than is requisite for the plaintiff's protection. I cannot agree with this. Agreements of this nature are entered into on the supposition that the owner of the business will not abandon it, and that if and when it exhibits symptoms of anaemia he will take steps to revive it by the infusion of new blood. I think the argument founded on the possible demise of the business is too far fetched, and in the absence of authority to support the suggestion that a duration extending during the whole life of the covenantor is sufficient in itself to make a restrictive agreement relating to a profession unreasonably wide, I am content to adopt the reasoning of Tindal CJ in *Hitchcock* v *Coker* [1894] AC 535 as affording sufficient reasons for coming to the opposite conclusion.

I come therefore to the conclusion that the contract is reasonable in the interests of the parties.

Eve J's judgment was affirmed by the Court of Appeal and House of Lords [1921] 2 AC 158.

6.7.2 CONSTRUCTION OF RESTRAINT CLAUSES

THE LITTLEWOODS ORGANISATION LTD v HARRIS [1978] 1 All ER 1026 (CA)

The defendant who had been employed in a senior position in the plaintiffs' mail order business was subject to a 12-month restriction against working for GUS, the plaintiffs' main rival.

LORD DENNING: . . .
The present clause
This brings me to the clause in the present case. It is said to be too wide in that it prevents Mr Harris being concerned or interested in the businesses of Great Universal Stores and its subsidiaries, and those businesses are infinitely varied and are worldwide; whereas Littlewoods are confined to the United Kingdom and operate in the two fields only of a mail order business and a chain of retail stores.

I would first consider the phrase 'Great Universal Stores or any company subsidiary thereto'. It appears that Great Universal Stores have 200 or more subsidiaries all over the world, carrying on all sorts of businesses. An instance given in argument was a restaurant in Alice Springs in the centre of Australia. Does that invalidate the clause? Is the introduction of 'subsidiaries' a ground for not enforcing it? This is an important point in these days when so many companies are multinational in their operations. The answer is, I think, the law today has regard to the realities of big business. It takes the group as being one concern under one supreme control. It does not regard each subsidiary as being a separate and independent entity. As Professor Gower says in his book on companies:

> . . . it has become a habit to create a pyramid of inter-related companies, each of which is theoretically a separate entity but in reality part of one concern represented by the group as a whole. The separation of the group into distinct companies is not necessarily in any way improper; it may well be the most economical and convenient arrangement when the concern carries on a number of separate businesses . . . [Then he goes on to say that] there is evidence of a general tendency to ignore the separate legal entities of various companies within a group, and to look instead at the economic unity of the whole group. The courts are here following the lead of the legislature.

A recent illustration of this tendency is *DHN Food Distributors Ltd* v *London Borough of Tower Hamlets* [1976] 3 All ER 462 when the group was regarded virtually as a partnership in which all the subsidiaries are partners. Likewise in the present case the phrase 'Great Universal Stores or any company subsidiary thereto' denotes in reality one group in which the individual subsidiaries cannot usefully be distinguished one from the other. The group is under one unified control. Those in charge of the group are able to switch a servant from one subsidiary to another without any difficulty whatever. They can lend his services or transmit his information and knowledge, as they please, within the group. If the clause is to afford any protection to Littlewoods at all, it must cover the whole GUS group, that is, not only the parent company but also its subsidiaries.

The next point is that the business of Littlewoods is within the United Kingdom whereas the businesses of the Great Universal Stores group are worldwide. In this regard the clause should, I think, be limited by relation to its object. It should be limited to such part of the business of the GUS group as operates within the United Kingdom.

Then there is this point. The only business of Littlewoods which can reasonably require protection is their mail order business, not their retail chain stores. The clause should, I think, be limited to the mail order business of both concerns – and for this reason. When the clause was introduced into Mr Harris's agreement of January 1974 and continued on his promotion in 1976 his concern was with the mail order side of the business of Littlewoods. And the protection should be regarded as limited to that side.

In summary I think that limiting words ought to be read into the clause so as to limit it to the part of the business for which Littlewoods are reasonably entitled to protection. It should be construed in relation to the surrounding circumstances at the time of renewal in 1976 when Mr Harris was made executive director of the mail order business.

The object was to protect Littlewoods in respect of the mail order business. Great Universal Stores should not be allowed to entice or induce this servant away so as to be in their mail order business for 12 months after he left the employment of Littlewoods.

Megaw and Browne LJJ concurred.

GREER v SKETCHLEY LTD [1979] IRLR 445 (CA)

LORD DENNING MR: Mr Greer is now 42 years of age. He has been with Sketchleys, the well-known dry cleaning service, for nearly all his working life. When he was 21, after he had done his National Service, he went to them as a management trainee in 1957. He gradually worked his way up. In 1974, when he was still under 40, he was made a director of their dry cleaning division. The activities of Sketchley Ltd in England and Wales are all south of a line from Grimsby to Chester. They cover all the Midlands and the London area, but they do not include Devon and Cornwall. They include Cardiff but do not include the greater part of Wales. That is the area where the Sketchley dry cleaning services operate with all their many shops which are used and valued by the public so much.

Mr Greer's special responsibility, as director of the dry cleaning division, was the Midlands area.

On 1 February 1974 when he was made a director, he was given a written agreement. It was determinable on 12 months' notice on either side. He was getting what would be a reasonable salary at that time, some £5,000-odd a year but with many fringe benefits. In the agreement there was a covenant restricting his activities after he left the company's service. I will read it a little later because a question arises as to its validity. It restrained him for a period of 12 months from engaging in any part of the United Kingdom in any similar dry cleaning business. I will come later on to the question of whether that is a valid restriction or not.

It appears that in 1976 and 1977 Sketchleys came under new management. For instance, Mr Richardson, who was the managing director, had only been with Sketchleys for some 18 months. This new management brought difficulties between the personnel. Mr Greer found himself unhappy and at variance with his superiors at Sketchley. He felt that he wanted to change his job. He did not do it, he said, for any financial gain at all. He went to the other big firm in the dry cleaning business, a firm of which the holding company is Johnsons. They operate on a much wider scale than Sketchleys. They have shops all over England, Wales and Scotland, right up to Inverness. They cover the whole of the country with their various shops, not under the name of 'Johnson' but under various subsidiary names.

Mr Greer approached Johnsons. By that time his salary at Sketchleys was £9,000-odd with fringe benefits like a car and so forth; and, if he went to Johnsons, he would get much the same – only a little more – about £10,000 a year with fringe benefits. Johnsons were ready to employ him if he left Sketchleys, and that is what he decided to do.

He told Sketchleys of his proposal at the end of August 1977. He wrote to them and told them that he was proposing to join Johnsons. Sketchleys were upset about it. They did not want him to do any more work for them in the dry cleaning division. His service agreement would expire at the end of the year, December 1977. So he spent about four months with them on full pay. They offered to find him work in some other division, but he did not think that would help him. So he declined any offers by them. Sketchleys said quite clearly that they intended to insist on the 12 months' restraint clause and said he could not go into any other similar business – he could not go into Johnsons – for 12 months from the end of December 1977 until the end of 1978.

Mr Greer found himself in a difficulty then because it is quite plain on the evidence that the one trade in which he has spent his life is the dry cleaning trade. It is the one trade he knows as an expert. We all know that senior executives find it difficult to get jobs these days. He has no prospect of getting a senior executive job except this one with Johnsons. He went to management consultants. They told him that it would be very difficult for him to get another job outside this business. In the words of one consultant: 'You have 'dry cleaning 20 years' stamped on your back'.

In those circumstances Mr Greer did not go off to work for Johnsons at once. He did a very courteous and sensible thing, which I have never come across before in these cases. He said: 'I want to know my legal position'. He himself issued a writ, a fortnight after he left, on 16 December 1977 claiming a declaration that the restrictive clause was invalid. When that writ was issued on his behalf, Sketchleys countered it and said that the clause was valid and claimed an injunction to restrain him for 12 months from going into any other similar business and in particular from going into Johnsons.

It was arranged very wisely that the matter should be dealt with expeditiously. It was dealt with as a trial of an action by Fox J in January 1978. He refused to grant an injunction and he declared that the clause was invalid. Now there is an appeal by Sketchleys to this court. We have heard argument on the first question in the case: whether this clause is valid or not.

The law as to covenants of restraint of trade between master and servant has been with us for years and years. The approach to it varies from one generation to another. At one time such clauses were very rarely held valid. They were held invalid if they were too wide, either in regard to the area they covered or in the length of time the restraint was to operate. That trend has altered in recent years, and especially since the recent case of *Littlewoods Organisation Ltd* v *Harris* [1977] 1 WLR 1472. There it does appear that the courts will not strain to hold these clauses invalid. If they are reasonable, the courts will seek to interpret them reasonably and to hold the restraint good if it is reasonable between the parties. They would not hold them unreasonable simply because one can find some far-fetched examples of how they might operate unreasonably.

There are clauses about not soliciting customers or trade connections. They do not arise in this case. There is no suggestion that Mr Greer would take any customers or trade connections of Sketchleys and hand them over to Johnsons. The important clause is clause 16 of the agreement of February 1974. It reads as follows:

In view of the access to trade secrets and secret processes which the Employee may have during the course of his employment hereunder he shall not within a period of twelve months from the termination thereof either directly or indirectly and either alone or in association with any other person firm or company engage in any part of the United Kingdom in any business which is similar to any business involving such trade secrets and/or secret processes carried on by the Company or any of its subsidiaries during the course of his employment hereunder.

There it is: he will not engage in any part of the United Kingdom in any business similar to dry cleaning.

Is that too wide in geographical area? One must remember that in the cases between master and servant the master cannot protect himself from competition at the hands of an outgoing servant. He cannot prevent the outgoing servant from using the skill and experience he has acquired over the years, perhaps in the master's business. Those are the servant's own property. He is not to be denied the use of his own skill and experience even though he has acquired them in the course of the master's business. He can be prevented from soliciting the master's customers or trade connections. He can be prevented from using the employer's trade secrets. Also the master can be protected from the servant using confidential information which he acquired in the course of the master's business.

As Mr Buckley rightly pointed out to us, in many of the earlier cases the courts were only concerned with subordinate servants – clerks, tally-men, and the like. Here we have a senior executive, a director of the dry cleaning division, a director who sat on the board at all the meetings in control of his division. He knew all the confidential information as to the conduct of the business, as to the management research, and so forth. Mr Greer very fairly in cross-examination answered questions by Mr Buckley in which he admitted as much. He said:

I had acquired and been a party to seeing normal business confidential reports and information during my time at Sketchley, as had every other businessman in the course of his business. (Q) . . . virtually everything about that particular business, plans for the future, profit margins – everything, you know about it all, do you not? (A) Yes, I do indeed.

Mr Greer admitted that he knew about matters which would be regarded as confidential by the company. So a senior executive of this kind does, as I think we all know, acquire a great deal of confidential information about the business; and, in these circumstances, certainly the employer can have a covenant which is reasonable to protect himself against any disclosure of it.

In a way, as the *Littlewoods* case illustrated, it is often difficult to sort out what is confidential and what is not. Sometimes it is permissible to make an agreement, as in that particular case, saying that the man is not to go to a rival concern for 12 months. That is what happened in the *Littlewoods* case. The Great Universal Stores in effect approached Mr Harris and offered him all sorts of better terms and induced him to go to them. That was a breach of the restrictive covenant which Littlewoods had expressly made saying that Mr Harris was not to go to their rival the Great Universal Stores for 12 months. That clause was held valid because it was the one way of protecting the position. But in this particular case it seems to me, for all Mr Buckley's admirable arguments, this is a much wider clause which says that he shall not engage in any part of the United Kingdom in any similar business. If Sketchleys operated all over England, Scotland and Wales, it might be reasonable to have such a covenant; but Sketchleys do not operate as widely. In 1974 their operations were confined to the Midlands and the South of England, excluding Wales, Cornwall and Devon and Lancashire right up to the north. Sketchleys did not cover any of that area. Was it reasonable for them to have a covenant restraining Mr Greer from going to any of these other parts of England, Scotland and Wales? Suppose, for instance, there had been a group of dry cleaning shops in the Tyne and Wear conurbation or in the Lancashire conurbation or Glasgow and Edinburgh or down in Devon? Sketchleys had not any kind of operation in those areas then. Was it reasonable to restrain him from engaging in any of those businesses or with any of those groups which were in those areas in which Sketchleys did not operate at all? It is said by Mr Buckley that they might expand into those areas in the future. Now over three years later they have not expanded into Devon and Cornwall or into Yorkshire or Lancashire or into the north of England or into Scotland. It seems to me that that problematical and possible expansion into all these other areas is much too vague and much too wide to justify restraint over every part of the United Kingdom.

I may add this further difficulty which emerged in the course of the case: What is the confidential information which can be protected in this regard? The employers' general organisation and method of business, certainly on the cases, would not be regarded as the subject of protection by a restrictive clause in such a case as this. In the course of the case, these were the sorts of things which were suggested as being confidential information: Mr Greer was especially concerned in a project which is called 'Clean X service'. That is to meet the needs of young people between 18 and 35. Apparently in these shops – and they have them on the continent – they have background music, and the staff wear white T-shirts and blue jeans, and the whole emphasis is on youth, and they call it a 'Clean X service'. That idea came from the continent in the beginning – perhaps from France. That could not be called confidential information. Another project Mr Greer was concerned with was 'household services', which are centres where household furnishings and curtains can be dry-cleaned, but that cannot be called confidential information. The judge made many inquiries into many things which were being done. He came to the conclusion that there were only two or three matters which could be classed as confidential information, such as the names of the towns where Sketchley shops might be opened and where certain shops might be closed, and a proposed promotional calendar which was being issued. Upon that Mr Greer and his advisers undertook that they would not make use of such information as that. That is the sort of thing which might be protected, but not this wide range of activities such as have been dealt with here. That only shows the difficulty with dealing with a clause such as this.

The essential point to my mind, following the many earlier cases about it, is that the clause is geographically too wide. It covers the whole of the United Kingdom, whereas the areas which Sketchley could at the most stipulate for are the areas of their activities.

There is one last point. Mr Buckley did urge that we should limit the operation of this clause by writing in the word 'competing'. He said: 'If you only write in the words 'competing business' in this clause, all will be well.' He said that the actual words should be, 'will not engage in any part of the United Kingdom in any competing business'. He urged us this afternoon to read the word 'competing' in just as it appears to be read in in a case which was heard long ago in this court, *Moenich* v *Fenestre* (1892) 67 LTR 602, which was quoted by Megaw LJ in the *Littlewoods* case at p. 1479. I must say that I can see no justification as a matter of construction for reading in the word 'competing', quite apart from the difficulty of saying what is a competing business. It may only be one shop in one town. It seems to me that this is not a case where we can read in any such limitation as Mr Buckley would urge us to do.

I am afraid on that short ground (but it is a decisive ground) of geographical area it seems to me that this covenant is too wide and is on that account invalid, and I would support the judge's judgment on the simple ground on which he made a declaration that the covenant is invalid.

In those circumstances, there is no need to go on to the further question of whether, if it were valid, an injunction should be granted. It is sufficient that it is not valid, and I would dismiss the appeal accordingly.

Shaw and Waller LJJ concurred.

6.7.3   RESTRAINTS FOLLOWING THE SALE OF A BUSINESS

BRITISH REINFORCED CONCRETE v *SCHELFF* [1921] 2 Ch 563 (ChD)

ASTBURY J: . . . This raises the most important legal question in the case – namely, whether in an agreement for sale of a business the reasonableness of a vendor's restrictive covenant is to be judged by the extent and circumstances of the business sold or by the extent and range of any business of the purchaser of which after transfer to him it is to form a part.

The plaintiffs' claim here is based on the hypothesis that the legitimate subject of protection is the plaintiffs' business, and there can, I think, be no doubt that the restrictive covenant is framed with reference to the requirements of that business and no other. Its extragavance in range as applied to the altogether insignificant business sold hardly requires statement.

Now but for one unreported case before Sargant J I should have thought that the law on this subject was clear. It is the business sold which is the legitimate subject of protection, and it is for its protection in the hands of its purchaser, and for its protection only, that the vendor's restrictive covenant can be legitimately exacted. A restrictive covenant by a grocer on the sale of his business in a country town, if it would be unreasonable and void when the purchaser was acquiring it as his sole business, does not become valid if the purchasers are, say, Messrs Lipton, with branches everywhere. The point is perhaps most clearly brought out in those recent cases in the House of Lords in which the essential distinction between vendors' and employees' restrictive covenants has been so clearly laid down. Take, for instance, the justification for a wider vendor's covenant in Lord Shaw's speech in *Mason's Case* [1913] AC 724 : 'If the contract, for instance, be for the sale of a business to another for full consideration or price, there may be elements going in the strongest degree to shew that such a contract – in so far as it restrains the vendor from becoming a rival of the business whose goodwill he has sold and which he has bargained he shall not oppose . . . is enforceable, and, indeed, that a declinature by the law to enforce it would amount to a denial of justice'. Again in *Saxelby's Case* [1916] 1 AC 688 Lord Parker says: 'In the *Nordenfelt Case* [1894] AC 535 that which it was required to protect was the goodwill of a business transferred by the covenantor to the covenantee, and that against which protection was sought was competition by the covenantor throughout the area in which such business was carried on'. He does not say 'going to be carried on'. Take again Lord Watson's observations in the *Nordenfelt Case* 'I think it is now generally conceded that it is to the advantage of the public to allow a trader who has established a lucrative business to dispose of it to a successor by whom it may be efficiently carried on. That object could not be accomplished if, upon the score of public policy, the law reserved to the seller an absolute and indefeasible right to start a rival concern the day after he sold. Accordingly it has been determined judicially, that in cases where the purchaser, for his own protection, obtains an obligation restraining the seller from competing with him, within bounds which having regard to the nature of the business are reasonable and are limited in respect of space, the obligation is not obnoxious to public policy, and is therefore capable of being enforced. Whether – when the circumstances of the case are such that a restraint unlimited in space becomes reasonably necessary in order to protect the purchaser against any attempt by the seller to resume the business which he sold – a covenant imposing that restraint must be invalidated by the principle of public policy is the substance of the question which your Lordships have to consider in this appeal.' Lord Herschell in the same case says: 'I think that a covenant entered into in connection with the sale of the goodwill of a business must be valid where the full benefit of the purchase cannot be otherwise secured to the purchaser'. In all these cases the business sold is treated as the subject of permissible protection; and similar judicial utterances could be indefinitely multiplied.

6.7.4 EXCLUSIVE DEALING AGREEMENTS

ESSO PETROLEUM v HARPER'S GARAGE [1967] 1 All ER 699 (HL)

LORD REID: My Lords, the appellants are a large company whose most important product is Esso petrol, most of which is sold by them to garages and filling stations for resale to the public. The respondent company own two garages: they contracted with the appellants under what are known as solus agreements and bound themselves for the periods of those agreements, inter alia, to sell at their garages Esso petrol and no other. When cheaper 'cut price' petrol came on the market they began to sell it and ceased to sell Esso petrol. The appellants then raised two actions, now consolidated, to prevent this: they sought injunctions to restrain the respondents from buying other than from them any motor fuel for resale at those garages. Mocatta J granted an injunction, but on appeal the Court of Appeal set aside this order on the ground that the ties in these agreements were in restraint of trade and were unenforceable. The appellants now maintain first that these ties were not in restraint of trade and secondly that, if they were, they were in the circumstances valid and enforceable.

The earlier agreement related to the Corner Garage, Stourport, and was to remain in force for twenty-one years from July 1, 1962. As the case with regard to it is complicated, however, by there being a mortgage as security for money lent by the appellants to the respondents, I shall first consider the second agreement which related to the Mustow Green Garage near Kidderminster. This agreement was to remain in force for four years and five months from July 1, 1963. It appears that the appellants had a similar agreement with the previous owners of that garage and that this period was chosen because it was the unexpired period of that earlier agreement.

The main provisions of the Mustow Green agreement are that while it remained in force the respondents agreed to buy from the appellants their total requirements of motor fuels for resale at that garage and agreed to keep it open at all reasonable hours for the sale of Esso motor fuels and Esso motor oils, and in return the appellants agreed to sell to the respondents at their wholesale schedule price at the time of delivery, and to allow a rebate from that price of one penny farthing per gallon payable quarterly. There were a number of other provisions with regard to advertising, service at the garage, etc., which I shall not specify because they do not appear to me to assist in determining the questions at issue; but there are two other provisions which I must notice. If the respondents wished to dispose of the garage they were not to do so except to a person who agreed to be substituted for them for all purposes of this agreement. If the agreement is otherwise unobjectionable, I do not think that this provision can invalidate it, because it was only by some such means that the appellants could ensure that their petrol would continue to be sold at this garage for the full period of the agreement. The other is a provision for retail price maintenance which the appellants at that time inserted in all their numerous tying agreements with garages and filling stations. Shortly before the present action was raised the appellants intimated that they would not enforce this clause against any of their tied customers. The respondents were in favour of retail price maintenance and their original defence was that this change of policy by the appellants entitled them to rescind the whole agreement for the tie. This defence was rejected by Mocatta J, and it has not been maintained before your lordships.

So I can now turn to the first question in this appeal – whether this agreement is to be regarded in law as an agreement in restraint of trade. . . .

In my view this agreement is within the scope of the doctrine of restraint of trade, as it had been developed in English law. Not only have the respondents agreed negatively not to sell other petrol, but also they have agreed positively to keep the garage open for the sale of the appellants' petrol at all reasonable hours throughout the period of the tie. It was argued that this was merely regulating the respondent's trading and rather promoting than restraining his trade; but regulating a person's existing trade, may be a greater restraint than prohibiting him from engaging in a new trade. Further a contract to take one's whole supply from one source may be much more hampering than a contract to sell one's whole output to one buyer. I would not attempt to define the dividing line between contracts which are and contracts which are not in restraint of trade, but in my view this contract must be held to be in restraint of trade. So it is necessary to consider whether its provisions can be justified.

Before considering this question I must deal briefly with the other agreement tying the Corner Garage for twenty-one years. The rebate and other advantages to the respondents were similar to those in the Mustow Green agreement, but in addition the appellants made a loan of £7,000 to the respondents to enable them to improve their garage and this loan was to be repaid over the twenty-one years of the tie. As security they took a mortgage of this garage. The agreement provided that the loan should not be paid off earlier than at the dates stipulated; but the respondents now tender the unpaid balance of the loan, and they say that the appellants have no interest to refuse to accept repayment now except in order to maintain the tie for the full twenty-one years

The appellants argue that the fact that there is a mortgage excludes any application of the doctrine of restraint of trade; but I agree with your Lordships in rejecting that argument. I am prepared to assume that, if the respondents had not offered to repay the loan so far as it is still outstanding, the appellants would have been entitled to retain the tie. As they have tendered repayment, however, I do not think that the existence of the loan and the mortgage puts the appellants in any stronger position to maintain the tie than they would have been in if the original agreements had permitted repayment at an earlier date. The appellants must show that, in the circumstances when the agreement was made, a tie for twenty-one years was justifiable.

It is now generally accepted that a provision in a contract which is to be regarded as in restraint of trade must be justified if it is to be enforceable, and that the law on this matter was correctly stated by Lord Macnaghten in the *Nordenfelt* case. He said:

> Restraints of trade and interference with individual liberty of action, may be justified by the special circumstances of a particular case. It is a sufficient justification, and indeed, it is the only justification, if the restriction is reasonable – reasonable, that is, in reference to the parties concerned and reasonable in reference to the interests of the public, so framed and so guarded as to afford adequate protection to the party in whose favour it is imposed, while at the same time it is in no way injurious to the public.

So in every case, it is necessary to consider, first whether the restraint went farther than to afford adequate protection to the party in whose favour it was granted, secondly whether it can be justified as being in the interests of the party restrained, and thirdly whether it must be held contrary to the public interest. . . .

When petrol rationing came to an end in 1950 the large producers began to make agreements, now known as solus agreements, with garage owners under which the garage owner, in return for certain advantages, agreed to sell only the petrol of the producer with whom he made the agreement. Within a short time three-quarters of the filling stations in this country were tied in that way, and by the dates of the agreement in this case over ninety per cent. had agreed to ties. It appears that the garage owners were not at a disavantage in bargaining with the large producing companies as there was intense competition between these companies to obtain these ties. So we can assume that both the garage owners and the companies thought that such ties were to their advantage: and it is not said in this case that all ties are either against the public interest or against the interests of the parties. The respondents' case is that the ties with which we are concerned are for too long periods.

The advantage to the garage owner is that he gets a rebate on the wholesale price of the petrol which he buys and also may get other benefits or financial assistance. The main advantages for the producing company appear to be that distribution is made easier and more economical, and that it is assured of a steady outlet for its petrol over a period. As regards distribution it appears that there were some thirty-five thousand filling stations in this country at the relevant time, of which about a fifth were tied to the appellants. So they have to distribute only to some seven thousand filling stations instead of to a very much larger number if most filling stations sold several brands of petrol. The main reason why the producing companies want ties for five years and more instead of ties for one or two years only seems to be that they can organise their business better if on the average only one-fifth or less of their ties came to an end in any one year. The appellants make a point of fact that, they have invested some £200 millions in refineries and other plant, and that they could not have done that unless they could foresee a steady and assured level of sales of their petrol. Most of their ties appear to have been made for periods between five and twenty years: but we have no evidence as to the precise additional advantage which they derive from a five-year tie as compared with a two-year tie or from a twenty-year tie as compared with a five-year tie.

The Court of Appeal held that these ties were for unreasonably long periods. They thought that, if for any reason the respondents ceased to sell the appellants' petrol, the appellants could have found other suitable outlets in the neighbourhood within two or three years. I do not think that that is the right test. In the first place there was no evidence about this, and I do not think that it would be practicable to apply this test in practice. It might happen that, when the respondents ceased to sell their petrol, the appellants would find such an alternative outlet in a very short time; but looking to the fact that well over ninety per cent. of existing filling stations are tied and that there may be great difficulty in opening a new filling station, it might take a very long time to find an alternative. Any estimate of how long it might take to find suitable alternatives for the respondents' filling stations could be little better than guesswork.

I do not think the appellants' interest can be regarded so narrowly. They are not so much concerned with any particular outlet as with maintaining a stable system of distribution throughout the country, so as to enable their business to run efficiently and economically. In my view there is sufficient material to justify a decision that ties of less than five years were insufficient, in the circumstances of the trade when these agreements were made, to afford adequate protection to the appellants' legitimate interests. If that is so, I cannot find anything in the details of the Mustow Green agreement which would indicate that it is unreasonable. It is true that, if some of the provisions were operated by the appellants in a manner which would be commercially unreasonable, they might put the respondents in difficulties. I think, however, that a court must have regard to the fact that the appellants must act in such a way that they will be able to obtain renewals of the great majority of their very numerous ties, some of which will come to an end almost every week. If in such circumstances a garage owner chooses to rely on the commercial probity and good sense of the producer, I do not think that a court should hold his agreement unreasonable because it is legally capable of some misuse. I would therefore allow the appeal as regards the Mustow Green agreement.

The Corner Garage agreement, however, involves much more difficulty. Taking first the legitimate interests of the appellants, a new argument was submitted to your Lordships that, apart from any question of security for their loan, it would be unfair to the appellants if the respondents, having used the appellants' money to build up their business, were entitled after a comparatively short time to be free to seek better terms from a competing producer. There is no material, however, on which I can assess the strength of this argument, and I do not find myself in a position to determine whether it has any validity. A tie for twenty-one years stretches far beyond any period for which developements are reasonably foreseeable. Restrictions on the garage owner which might seem tolerable and reasonable in reasonably foreseeable conditions might come to have a very different effect in quite different conditions; the public interest comes in here more strongly. Moreover, apart from a case where he gets a loan, a garage owner appears to get no greater advantage from a twenty year tie than he gets from a five year tie. So I would think that there must at least be some clearly established advantage to the producing company – something to show that a shorter period would not be adequate – before so long a period could be justified: but in this case there is no evidence to prove anything of the kind. Moreover, the other material which I have thought it right to consider does not appear to me to assist the appellant here. I would therefore dismiss the appeal as regards the Corner Garage agreement.

I would add the decision in this case – particularly in view of the paucity of evidence – ought not in my view to be regarded as laying down any general rule as to the length of tie permissible in a solus agreement. I do not think that the case of *Petrofina* (*Gt. Britain*) *Ltd* v *Martin* [1966] 1 All ER 126 can be regarded as laying down a general rule. The agreement there was in unusual terms. I think that the decision was right, although I do not agree with all the reasons; but I must not be taken as expressing any opinion as to the validity of ties for periods mid-way between the two periods with which the present case is concerned.

Lords Morris, Hodson, Pearce and Wilberforce concurred.

SCHROEDER MUSIC PUBLISHING CO. LTD v MACAULAY [1974] 3 All ER 1308 (HL)

LORD REID: My Lords, the appellants are publishers of music. The repondent is a writer of songs. On 12th July 1966 they entered into a somewhat elaborate agreement under which the appellants engaged the exclusive services of the respondent for a term of five years which in a certain event was to be extended to ten years. In 1970 the respondent raised the present action claiming a declaration that the agreement is contrary to public policy and void. He also made various alternative claims which your Lordships have found it unnecessary to consider. Plowman J made the declaration claimed and his decision was affirmed by the Court of Appeal.   In 1966 the respondent was aged about 21. He and Mr McLeod had collaborated in writing a few songs, but it appears that none of them had been published. He obtained an interview with Mr Schroeder who, with Mrs Schroeder, controls an American music publishing corporation with world wide connections. The appellant company is a subsidiary of the corporation. The respondent wished to get a different kind of contract but agreed to sign this agreement which is in the appellants' standard form with a few alterations. . . .

Clauses 1 and 9(a) determine the duration of the agreement. It was to last for five years in any event and for ten years if the royalties for the first five years exceeded £5,000. There is little evidence about this extension. Five thousand pounds in five years appears to represent a very modest success, and so if the respondent's work became well know and popular he would be tied by the agreement for ten years. The duration of an agreement in restraint of trade is a factor of great importance in determining whether the restrictions in the agreement can be justified but there was no evidence as to why so long a period was necessary to protect the appellants' interests. Clause 2 requires the respondent to give the exclusive services to and obey all lawful orders of the appellants. It is not very clear what this means. Read in conjunction with cl. 2(c) it probably does not prevent him from doing non-musical work so long as that does not interfere with his obligations to the appellants. I do not attach importance to this clause as being at all unduly rstrictive. Clause 3 is of importance but I shall return to it later. Clauses 5 to 8 deal with remuneration. Some parts are not very clear but it was not argued that this was un unreasonable basis for the remuneration of a composer unknown when the agreement was made. Clause 9(b) entitles the appellants to terminate the agreement but there is no corresponding provision in favour of the respondent. I shall have to deal with this later. Clause 10(b) could be rather oppressive but no serious objection was taken to it and the same may be said of cl. 13. Clause 16 appears to me to be important. There may sometimes be room for an argument that although on a strict legal construction restrictions could be enforced oppressively, one is entitled to have regard to the fact that a large organisation could not afford to act oppressively without damaging the goodwill of its business. But the power to assign leaves no room for that argument. We cannot assume that an assignee would always act reasonably.

The public interest requires both of the public and of the individual that everyone should be free so far as practicable to earn a livelihood and to give to the public the fruits of his particular abilities. The main question to be considered is whether and how far the operation of the terms of this agreement is likely to conflict with this objective. The respondent is bound to assign to the appellants during a long period the fruits of his musical talent. But what are the appellants bound to do with those fruits? Under the contract nothing. If they do use the songs which the respondent composes they must pay in terms of the contract. But they need not do so. As has been said they may put them in a drawer and leave them there. No doubt the expectation was that if the songs were of value they would be published to the advantage of both parties. But if for any reason the appellants chose not to publish them the respondent would get no remuneration and he could not do anything. Inevitably the respondent must take the risk of misjudgment of the merits of his work by the appellants. But that is not the only reason which might cause the appellants not to publish. There is no evidence about this so we must do the best we can with common knowledge. It does not seem fanciful and it was not argued that it is fanciful to suppose that purely commercial consideration might cause a publisher to refrain from publishing and promoting promising material. He might think it likely to be more profitable to promote work by other composers with whom he had agreements and unwise or too expensive to try to publish and popularise the repondent's work in addition. And there is always the possibility that less legitimate reasons might influence a decision not to publish the respondent's work.

It was argued that there must be read into this agreement an obligation on the publisher to act in good faith. I take that to mean that he would be in breach of contract if by reason of some oblique or malicious motive he refrained from publishing work which he would otherwise have published. I very much doubt this but even if it were so it would make little difference. Such a case would seldom occur and then would be difficult to prove.

I agree with the appellants' argument to this extent. I do not think that a publisher could reasonably be expected to enter into any positive commitment to publish future work by an unknown composer. Possibly there might be some general undertaking to use his best endeavours to promote the composer's work. But that would probably have to be in such general terms as to be of little use to the composer.

But if no satisfactory positive undertaking by the publisher can be devised, it appears to me to be an unreasonable restraint to tie the composer for this period of years so that his work will be sterilised and he can earn nothing from his abilities as a composer if the publisher chooses not to publish. If there had been in cl. 9 any provision entitling the composer to terminate the agreement is such an event the case might have had a very different appearance. But as the agreement stands, not only is the composer tied but he cannot recover the copyright of the work which the publisher refuses to publish. . . .

Any contract by which a person engages to give his exclusive services to another for a period necessarily involves extensive restrictions during that period of the common law right to exercise any lawful activity he chooses in such manner as he thinks best. Normally the doctrine of restraint of trade has no application to such restrictions: they require no justification. But if contractual restrictions appear to be unnecessary or to be reasonably capable of enforcement in an oppressive manner, then they must be justified before they can be enforced.

In the present case the respondent assigned to the appellants 'the full copyright for the whole world' in every musical composition 'composed created or conceived' by him alone or in collaboration with any other person during a period of five or it might be ten years. He received no payment (apart from an initial £50) unless his work was published and the appellants need not publish unless they chose to do so. And if they did not publish he had no right to terminate the agreement or to have any copyrights re-assigned to him. I need not consider whether in any cirumstances it would be possible to justify such a one-sided agreement. It is sufficient to say that such evidence as there is falls far short of justification. It must therefore follow that the agreement so far as unperformed is unenforceable.

I would dismiss this appeal.

Viscount Dilhorne, Lords Simon, Kilbrandon and Diplock concurred.

6.7.5 SEVERANCE

GOLDSOLL v *GOLDMAN* [1915] 1 Ch 292 (CA)

LORD COZENS-HARDY MR: This is an appeal from Neville J, and the question is whether a covenant entered into between Goldsoll and Goldman is unreasonable as it stands, and, if it is, whether it is severable, so that it may be good in part and bad in part. The plaintiffs are carrying on the business of dealers in imitation jewellery. They do not carry on business in real jewellery, and I say this although some of the articles they deal in are made of real gold in which Tecla pearls are set and occasionally the pearls are set in small diamonds. Substantially the business is in imitation jewellery. In 1912 Goldman was carrying on a business in competition with Goldsoll, and the agreement in question was entered into with the object of putting an end to the competition. There was ample consideration for the agreement, and by the clause of the deed which we have to consider Goldman covenanted with Goldsoll that he would not for a period of ten years (which was reduced by a subsequent agreement of two years) 'either solely or jointly with or as agent or employee for any person or company directly or indirectly carry on or be interested in the business of a vendor of or dealer in real or imitation jewellery in the county of London, England, Scotland, Ireland, Wales, or any part of the United Kingdom of Great Britian and Ireland and the Isle of Man or in France, the United States of America, Russia, or Spain, or within twenty-five miles of Potsdamerstrasse, Berlin, or St Stefans Kirche, Vienna'. Notwithstanding this covenant Goldman has, according to the finding of the learned judge, been assisting and rendering services to a confederate who is carrying on a business identical to that of the plaintiffs in the same street. It is perfectly clear that there has been a breach of the covenant; but that is not conclusive of the case, for what we have to consider is whether the covenant he has broken can be treated as good either in whole or in part, and can be enforced. On the question of the space covered by the covenant Neville J has held, and I entirely agreed with him, that it is unnecessarily large in so far as it is intended to cover not merely the United Kingdom and the Isle of Man but also the foreign countries mentioned in the covenant. He has also held, and his decision is consistent with a long series of authorities, that the covenant can be severed as regards the space covered by it. It is clear that part of the covenant dealing with the area is reasonable, and the learned judge has limited the injunction he has granted to 'the county of London, England, Scotland, Ireland, Wales, or any part of the United Kingdom of Great Britain and Ireland and the Isle of Man'. That such a covenant is severable in this respect has been decided by authorities nearly 200 years old. No objection is taken or could be taken with regard to the limit of time, but the further difficulty has been raised that, while the business of the plaintiffs was, as I said, a business in imitation jewellery, the covenant is against carrying on or being interested in 'the business of a vendor of or dealer in real or imitation jewellery'. It is admitted that the business of a dealer in real jewellery is not the same as that of a dealer in imitation jewellery. There are many shopkeepers who would be insulted if they were asked whether they sold imitation jewellery. That being so, it is difficult to support the whole of this provision, for the covenant must be limited to what is reasonably necessary for the protection of the covenantee's business. Then comes the question whether the doctrine of severability is applicable to this part of the covenant. In my opinion it is, and the covenant is good in so far as it operates to restrain the covenantor from carrying on business in imitation jewellery.

The result is, in my opinion, that the order of Neville J is right with the exception that the words 'real or' ought to be omitted from the injunction granted by him. The appeal fails on the matter as to which alone the plaintiffs complained and must be dismissed with costs.

Kennedy and Swinfen LJJ concurred.

ATTWOOD v *LAMONT* [1920] 3 KB 571 (CA)

YOUNGER LJ: . . . Proceeding now to apply these principles to the facts of the present case, the position appears to be that the respondent is the owner of a considerable business at Kidderminster, described in the agreement in question as a business of drapers, tailors and general outfitters. The business is, I presume for convenience, divided into different departments all under the same roof, customers going from one to another, and many customers dealing in all departments. The agreement into which the appellant entered, a printed form which all managers of departments are required to sign with modifications of salary and detail appropriate to the individual case, is indorsed as 'An agreement not to trade in opposition within a radius of 10 miles of Regent House, Kidderminster', and contains a recital 'that the assistant', the appellant, 'has requested the employers to employ him as an assistant in their business at Kidderminster at an annual salary commencing at 208*l*. and two and a half per cent. commission on turnover above 1000*l*. in tailoring department and the employers are only willing to do so upon entering into the agreement not to trade in opposition with him which is hereinafter expressed' and witnesses 'that in consideration of the employers employing him in the capacity and at the salary aforesaid . . . he will not at any time thereafter . . . carry on or be in any way directly or indirectly concerned in any of the following trades or businesses, that is to say, the trade or business of a tailor, dressmaker, general draper, milliner, hatter, haberdasher, gentlemen's, ladies' or children's outfitter at any place, within a radius of 10 miles of the employers' place of business at Regent House, Kidderminster, aforesaid'. The agreement is expressed to be and is, in my opinion, nothing more than an agreement not to trade in opposition with the employers in any part of their business. It will be broken if the appellant not only carries on but is directly or indirectly concerned in any of the specified businesses; and the period of restriction is to cover the whole life of the appellant, although the employment was itself an employment only for a month certain. The appellant, while it is not so stated in the agreement, was manager of the tailoring department and was the principal or only cutter in the respondent's employ. He measured, cut, and fitted on the clothes made in that department, and in doing so, he, of course, became acquainted with the customers. He is said to be an extremely skilful cutter, and the department prospered when under his management. He has now set up in business in Worcester, beyond the ten-mile radius, but he has supplied with clothes former customers of the respondent within that radius, and has also fitted on their clothes within it. That is the breach of covenant complained of. The evidence of a Mr Middleton called to prove one such breach was that he had been measured and fitted by the appellant when he was at the respondents; that he gave him every satisfaction; that he met him in Broad Street, Worcester, one day and said: 'I hear you have started business in Worcester, I may as well give you an order, send me over some patterns'. That evidence confirms me in the conclusion which I should have drawn from the case generally, that it is the appellant's known personal skill as a cutter which attracts to him the customers to whom he attended when with the respondent, and except that they made his acquaintance when he was in the respondent's service, it was not his position there, but it is his own skill which leads them to desire to have the continued benefit of his services, now that he is in business for himself. The question accordingly is whether in these circumstances, and in view of principles applicable to them enunciated by the House of Lords, this covenant has any validity. In my opinion, as I have already said, it has none. It was apparently strongly urged in the Divisional Court that the covenant was valid as it stands. The learned judges there held that extending to businesses with which the appellant had had no connnection when in the respondent's employment it was manifestly too wide, and they so held.

But the learned judges held also that they were entitled to sever the covenant by limiting it to the business of a tailor, and this they did.

Now I agree with the Master of the Rolls that this was not a case in which upon any principle this severance was permissible. The learned judges of the Divisional Court, I think, took the view that such severance always was permissible when it could be effectively accomplished by the action of a blue pencil. I do not agree. The doctrine of severance has not, I think, gone further than to make it permissible in a case where the covenant is not really a single covenant but is in effect a combination of several distinct covenants. In that case and where the severance can be carried out without the addition or alteration of a word, it is permissible. But in that case only.

Now, here, I think, there is in truth but one covenant for the protection of the respondent's entire business, and not several covenants for the protection of his several businesses. The respondent is, on the evidence, not carrying on several businesses but one business, and, in my opinion, this covenant must stand or fall in its unaltered form.

Lord Sterndale and Atkin LJ concurred.

6.8   End of Chapter Assessment Question

Gaspers Ltd of Nottingham, cigarette manufacturers, wished to buy a new cigarette-making machine. The production manager of Gaspers, Ash, contacted Rollem Ltd who sent their sales representative, Keen, to negotiate.

Keen said, 'I reckon our machine is capable of making upwards of 5,000 cigarettes per hour'. Keen also stated that it was the type of machine that did not require fencing under the industrial safety legislation. If Ash had consulted the literature that Keen had handed to him, he would have seen that the latter statement was untrue. Three months later, Gaspers Ltd entered into a written contract to purchase the machine and the price was paid. The written contract made no reference to the statements made by Keen during negotiations, but did include a term that Gaspers' acceptance of the machine should be conclusive evidence that it was 'in all respects fit for the intended and contemplated use' by them.

After delivery, it was discovered that the machine would make only 2,000 cigarettes per hour and that it needed fencing by law. When it was installed, Ash arranged for parts of the machine to be sawn off to allow for the welding on of a safety fence.

Advise Gaspers Ltd.

6.9   End of Chapter Assessment Outline Answer

You should approach the question by asking the following four questions in the following order.

1.   Are the statements made representations or terms?

2.   Is there any actionable misrepresentation?

3.   If so, what type of misrepresentation is it?

4.   What are the remedies available?

1.   Representations or terms

Whether a statement is a representation or a term is primarily a question of intention, but the court may have regard to the following factors:

(a) Has the contract been reduced to writing so that the statements made in negotiations are excluded from the written document?
(b) Did the parties place particular importance upon the statement? (See e.g., *Bannerman* v *White* (1861) 10 CBNS 844.)
(c) Was the plaintiff discouraged from verifying the statement as in *Schawel* v *Reade* (1913) 2 IR 64? Alternatively, was he warned to verify it as in *Ecay* v *Godfrey* (1947) 80 Lloyd's Rep 286?
(d) Was there special skill and knowledge on the part of the maker of the statement which was relied on by the other party? (See *Dick Bentley Productions Ltd* v *Harold Smith (Motors) Ltd* [1965] 2 All ER 65; cf: *Oscar Chess* v *Williams* [1957] 1 All ER 325.)
(e) Was there an interval of time between the making of the statement and the date when the contract was entered into? (See, e.g., *Hopkins* v *Tanqueray* (1854) 15 CB 130; but see *Schawel* v *Reade* (supra).)

On the facts given, factors (a), (d) and (e) above are of relevance, though (d) is probably equal.
    On the assumption, then, that the statements are representations, we need to consider whether there is an actionable misrepresentation.

2: Actionable misrepresentation

An actionable misrepresentation is a *false statement of fact* which *induces* the plaintiff to enter the contract. Statements of opinion, belief, intention and law are excluded, although they could be actionable if dishonest (*Edgington* v *Fitzmaurice* (1885) 29 ChD 459).
We need to examine Keen's two statements in turn:

(a) 'I reckon our machine is capable of making upwards of 5,000 cigarettes per hour.'
A statement as to the production capacity of the machine would normally be a statement of fact. However, the use of the expression 'I reckon' suggests perhaps that it is a mere false opinion, which, as in *Bisset* v *Wilkinson* is not actionable.
If the opinion is not honestly, held, or has no factual basis, then it may be treated as a statement of fact. In *Smith* v *Land and House Properties* it was held that such a statement would be an actionable misrepresentation.
(b) The fencing of the machine.
A statement as to the application of legislation is a statement of law and thus is not actionable. It is doubtful here whether the statement could be interpreted as being as to the physical condition of the machine, like the statement about the property in *Solle* v *Butcher*.
However, the statement could be verified from the literature and is therefore not an honest and reasonable statement. Thus, again, this statement might be actionable.
It is not relevant that Ash did not verify the statement when it was possible to do so, see *Redgrave* v *Hurd*.

3. Type of misrepresentation

It can be difficult to state with certainty into which category a misrepresentation falls. There is some evidence, on the facts we are given, that Keen may have been dishonest. If this can be proved, the (heavy) burden of proof will fall on Ash. It might be better to advise Ash to base his claim on negligent misrepresentation under s. 2(1) of the Misrepresentation Act 1967; i.e., that Keen had no reasonable grounds for believing in the truth of his statements.

4. Remedies

Actionable misrepresentation renders the contract voidable at the option of the misrepresentee. This means that Ash may be able to obtain the remedy of rescission – the effect of this will be to put the parties in their original position and restore the *status quo ante*.

(a) *Rescission*
The right to rescind may be lost if one of the bars to rescission exists. If Ash seeks rescission he must enforce his rights as soon as he learns of the falsity of the representation – otherwise he may be considered to have affirmed the contract. However, there may be no affirmation if the plaintiff is aware of the falsity but is unaware of his right to rescind (*Peyman* v *Lanjani* [1984] 3 All ER 703). Lapse of time may be evidence of affirmation; in this regard see *Leaf* v *International Galleries* [1950] 2 KB 86.
More importantly here, parts of the machine have been sawn off. Thus, 'restitutio in integrum' is not possible as Ash cannot give back exactly what he has received under the contract.
However, this is an equitable rule which applies if one is attempting to give back something in a worse condition than when received. Here, the machine has been improved as it now conforms with the safety legislation. Perhaps, therefore, this is no bar to rescission here.
(b) *Damages*
Ash will be able to recover damages for misrepresentation whether or not he has lost his right to rescind the contract. In this respect whether Ash relies on fraud or negligent misrepresentation under s. 2(1), both the measure of damages and remoteness rule will be the same as fraud. (See *Royscot Trust* v *Rogerson* [1991]

3 All ER 294.) Ash will be able to recover by way of damages the full amount by which he is out of pocket as a result of entering the contract.

5. Exclusion clause

A clause similar to that in the written contract, that acceptance of the machine should be conclusive evidence that it was fit for their use, was held to constitute an exclusion clause in *Howard Marine and Dredging Co. Ltd* v *Ogden & Sons*. Both the Misrepresentation Act 1967 and the Unfair Contract Terms Act 1977 provide that exclusion of liability for misrepresentation is subject to a test of reasonableness. In the *Howard Marine* case the clause was considered to be reasonable because of the equality of bargaining power of the parties. This could seriously affect the chance of success of Gaspers Ltd.

CHAPTER SEVEN

REMEDIES FOR BREACH OF CONTRACT

7.1 Damages

7.1.1 REMOTENESS

HADLEY v BAXENDALE (1854) 9 Exch 341
(Court of Exchequer)

The defendant had delayed in delivering a mill-shaft which meant that the plaintiff's mill was idle for longer than it should have been.

ALDERSON B: We think that there ought to be a new trial in this case; but, in so doing, we deem it to be expedient and necessary to sate explicitly the rule which the judge, at the next trial, ought, in our opinion, to direct the jury to be governed by when they estimate the damages.

Now we think the proper rule in such a case as the present is this: – Where two parties have made a contract which one of them has broken, the damages which the other party ought to receive in respect of such breach of contract should be such as may fairly and reasonably be considered either arising naturally, i.e., according to the usual course of things, from such breach of contract itself, or such as may reasonably be supposed to have been in the contemplation of both parties, at the time they made the contract, as the probable result of the breach of it. Now, if the special circumstances under which the contract was actually made were communicated by the plaintiffs to the defendants, and thus known to both parties, the damage resulting from the breach of such a contract, which they would reasonably contemplate, would be the amount of injury which would ordinarily follow from a breach of contract under these special circumstances so known and communicated. But, on the other hand, if these special circumstances were wholly unknown to the party breaking the contract, he, at the most, could only be supposed to have had in his contemplation the amount of injury which would arise generally, and in the great multitude of cases not affected by any special circumstances, from such a breach of contract. For, had the special circumstances been known, the parties might have specially provided for the breach of contract by special terms as to the damages in that case; and of this advantage it could be very unjust to deprive them. Now the above principles are those by which we think the jury ought to be guided in estimating the damages arising out of any breach of contract. It is said, that other cases such as breaches of contract in the non-payment of money, or in the not making a good title to land, are to be treated as exceptions from this, and as governed by a conventional rule. But as, in such cases, both parties must be supposed to be cognisant of that well-known rule, these cases may, we think, be more properly classed under the rule above enunciated as to cases under known special circumstances, because there both parties may reasonably be presumed to contemplate the estimation of the amount of damages according to the conventional rule. Now, in the present case, if we are to apply the principles above laid down, we find that the only circumstances here communicated by the plaintiffs to the defendants at the time the contract was made, were, that the article to be carried was the broken shaft of a mill, and that the plaintiffs were the millers of that mill. But how do these circumstances shew reasonably that the profits of the mill must be stopped by an unreasonable delay in the delivery of the broken shaft by the carrier to the third person? Suppose the plaintiffs had another shaft in their possession put up or putting up at the time, and that they only wished to send back the broken shaft to the engineer who made it; it is clear that this would be quite consistent with the above circumstances, and yet the unreasonable delay in the delivery would have no effect upon the intermediate profits of the mill. Or, again, suppose that, at the time of the delivery to the carrier, the machinery of the mill had been in other respects defective, then, also, the same results would follow. Here it is true that the shaft was actually sent back to serve as a model for a new one, and that the want of a new one was the only cause of the stoppage of the mill, and that the loss of profits really arose from not sending down the new shaft in proper time, and that this arose from the delay in delivering the broken one to serve as a model. But it is obvious that, in the great multitude of cases of millers sending off broken shafts to third persons by a carrier under ordinary circumstances, such consequences would not, in all probability, have occurred; and these special circumstances were here never communicated by the plaintiffs to the defendants. It follows, therefore, that the loss of profits here cannot reasonably be considered such a consequence of the breach of contract as could have been fairly and reasonably contemplated by both the parties when they made this contract. For such loss would neither have flowed naturally from the breach of this contract in the great multitude of such cases occurring under ordinary circumstances, nor were the special circumstances, which, perhaps, would have made it a reasonable and natural consequence of such breach of contract, communicated to or known by the defendants. The judge ought, therefore, to have told the jury, that, upon the facts then before them, they ought not to take the loss of profits into consideratiion at all in estimating the damages. There must therefore be a new trial in this case.

VICTORIA LAUNDRY (WINDSOR) LTD v NEWMAN INDUSTRIES LTD
[1949] 1 All ER 997 (CA)

Delay in the delivery of a boiler meant that the plaintiffs lost some new, very lucrative, dyeing contracts.

ASQUITH LJ: . . . What propositions applicable to the present case emerge from the authorities as a whole? . . . We think they include the following: (1) It is well settled that the governing purpose of damages is to put the party whose rights have been violated in the same position, so far as money can do so, as if his rights had been observed: *Wertheim v Chicoutimi Pulp Co.* [1911] AC 301. This purpose, if relentlessly pursued, would provide him with a complete indemnity for all loss *de facto* resulting from a particular breach, however improbable, however unpredictable. This, in contract at least, is recognised as too harsh a rule. Hence: (2) In cases of breach of contract the aggrieved party is only entitled to recover such part of the loss actually resulting as was at the time of the contract reasonably foreseeable as liable to result from the breach. (3) What was at that time reasonably foreseeable depends on the knowledge then possessed by the parties, or, at all events, by the party who later commits the breach. (4) For this purpose, knowledge 'possessed' is of two kinds – one imputed, the other actual. Everyone, as a reasonable person, is taken to know the 'ordinary course of things' and consequently what loss is liable to result from a breach of that ordinary course. This is the subject-matter of the 'first rule' in *Hadley v Baxendale* (1854) 9 Exch 341, but to this knowledge, which a contract-breaker is assumed to possess whether he actually possesses it or not, there may have to be added in a particular case knowledge which he actually possesses of special circumstances outside the 'ordinary course of things' of such a kind that a breach in those special circumstances would be liable to cause more loss. Such a case attracts the operation of the 'second rule' so as to make additional loss also recoverable. (5) In order to make the contract-breaker liable under either rule it is not necessary that he should actually have asked himself what loss is liable to result from a breach. As has often been pointed out, parties at the time of contracting contemplate, not the breach of the contract, but its performance. It suffices that, if he had considered the question, he would as a reasonable man have concluded that the loss in question was liable to result: see certain observations of Lord Du Parcq in *Monarch Steamship Co. Ltd* v *A/B Karlshamns Oljefrabriker* [1949] 1 All ER 19. (6) Nor, finally, to make a particular loss recoverable, need it be proved that on a given state of knowledge the defendant could, as a reasonable man, foresee that a breach must necessarily result in that loss. It is enough if he could foresee it was likely so to result. It is enough, to borrow from the language of Lord Du Parcq in the same case, if the loss (or some factor without which it would not have occurred) is a 'serious possibility' or a 'real danger'. For short, we have used the word 'liable' to result. Possibly the colloquialism 'on the cards' indicates the shade of meaning with some approach to accuracy.

If these, indeed, are the principles applicable, what is the effect of their application to the facts of the present case? We have, at the beginning of this judgment, summarised the main relevant facts. . . . The defendants were an engineering company supplying a boiler to a laundry. We reject the submission for the defendants that an engineering company knows no more than the plain man about boilers or the purposes to which they are commonly put by different classes of purchasers, including laundries. The defendant company were not, it is true, manufacturers of this boiler or dealers in boilers, but they gave a highly technical and comprehensive description of this boiler to the plaintiffs by letter of January 19, 1946, and offered both to dismantle the boiler at Harpenden and to re-erect it on the plaintiffs' premises. Of the uses or purposes to which boilers are put, they would clearly know more than the uninstructed layman. Again, they knew they were supplying the boiler to a company carrying on the business of laundrymen and dyers, for use in that business. The obvious use of a boiler, in such a business, is surely to boil water for the purpose of washing or dyeing. A laundry might conceivably buy a boiler for some other purpose, for instance, to work radiators or warm bath water for the comfort of its employees or directors, or to use for research, or to exhibit in a museum. All these purposes are possible, but the first is the obvious purpose which, in the case of a laundry, leaps to the average eye. If the purpose then be to wash or dye, why does the company want to wash or dye, unless for purposes of business advantage, in which term we, for the purposes of the rest of this judgment, include maintenance or increase of profit or reduction of loss? We shall speak henceforward not of loss of profit, but of 'loss of business'. No commercial concern commonly purchases for the purposes of its business a very large and expensive structure like this – a boiler nineteen feet high and costing over £2,000 – with any other motive, and no supplier, let alone an engineering company, which has promised delivery of such an article by a particular date with knowledge that it was to be put into use immediately on delivery, can reasonably contend that it could not foresee that loss of business (in the sense indicated above) would be liable to result to the purchaser from a long delay in the delivery thereof. The suggestion that, for all the supplier knew, the boiler might have been needed simply as a 'stand-by', to be used in a possibly distant future, is gratuitous and was plainly negatived by the terms of the letter of April 26, 1946.

Since we are differing from a carefully reasoned judgment, we think it due to the learned judge to indicate the grounds of our dissent. In that judgment, after stressing the fact that the defendants were not manufacturers of this boiler or of any boilers (a fact which is indisputable), nor (what is disputable) people possessing any special knowledge not common to the general public of boilers or laundries as possible users thereof, he goes on to say ([1948] 2 All ER 809):

That is the general principle and I think that the principle running through the cases is that, if there is nothing unusual, if it is a normal user of the plant in question, it may well be that the parties must be taken to contemplate that a loss of profits may result from the non-delivery, or the delay in delivery, of the particular article. On the other hand, if there are – as I think there are here – special circumstances, I do not think that the defendants are liable for loss of profits unless the special circumstances were brought to their notice. In looking at the cases, I think there is a distinction between the supply of a part of the profit-making machine, as against the profit-making machine itself. . . .

Then, after referring to *Portman* v *Middleton* (1858) 4 CBND 322 he continues (*ibid*):

> It is to be observed that, not only must the circumstances be known to the supplier or the carrier, but they must be such that the object must be taken to have been within the contemplation of both parties. I do not think that on the facts it can be said that it was within the contemplation of the suppliers that any delay in the delivery of this boiler was going to lead necessarily to loss of profits. There was nothing that I know of in the evidence to indicate how the boiler was to be used or whether delivery of it by a particular day would necessarily be vital to the earning of profits. I agree that it was no part of the contract and cannot be taken to have been the basis of the contract that the laundry would be unable to work if there was a delay in the delivery of the boiler, or that the laundry was extending its business or had any special contracts which could be fulfilled only by getting delivery of this boiler. In my view, therefore, this case falls within the second rule of *Hadley* v *Baxendale* under which the defendants would not be liable for the payment of damages for loss of profits unless there were evidence before the court – which there is not – that the special purpose of this boiler was drawn to their attention and that they contracted on the basis that delay in the delivery would make them liable to payment of loss of profits.

The answer to this reasoning has largely been anticipated in what has been said above, but we would wish to add, first, that the learned judge appears to infer that because certain 'special circumstances' were, in his view, not 'drawn to the notice of' the defendants, and, therefore, in his view, the operation of the 'second rule' was excluded, *ergo*, nothing in respect of loss of business can be recovered under the 'first rule'. This inference is, in our view, no more justified in the present case than it was in *Cory* v *Thames Ironworks Co.* (1868) LR 3 QB 181. Secondly, while it is not wholly clear what were the 'special circumstances' on the non-communication of which the learned judge relied, it would seem that they were or included the following: – (a) the 'circumstance' that delay in delivering the boiler was going to lead 'necessarily' to loss of profits, but the true criterion is surely not what was bound 'necessarily' to result, but what was likely or liable to do so, and we think that it was amply conveyed to the defendants by what was communicated to them (plus what was patent without express communication) that delay in delivery was likely to lead to 'loss of business'; (b) the 'circumstance' that the plaintiffs needed the boiler 'to extend their business'. It was surely not necessary for the defendants to be specifically informed of this as a precondition of being liable for loss of business. Reasonable persons in the shoes of the defendants must be taken to foresee, without any express intimation, that a laundry which, at a time when there was a famine of laundry facilities, was paying £2,000 odd for plant and intended at such a time to put such plant 'into use' immediately, would be likely to suffer in pocket from five months' delay in delivery of the plant in question, whether they intended by means of it to extend their business, or merely to maintain it, or to reduce a loss; (c) the 'circumstance' that the plaintiffs had the assured expectation of special contracts, which they could only fulfil by securing punctual delivery of the boiler. Here, no doubt, the learned judge had in mind the particularly lucrative dyeing contracts to which the plaintiffs looked forward and which they mention in para. 10 of the statement of claim. We agree that in order that the plaintiffs should recover specifically and as such the profits expected on these contracts, the defendants would have had to know, at the time of their agreement with the plaintiffs, of the prospect and terms of such contracts. We also agree that they did not, in fact, know these things. It does not, however, follow that the plaintiffs are precluded from recovering some general (and perhaps conjectural) sum for loss of business in respect of dyeing contracts to be reasonably expected any more than in respect of laundering contracts to be reasonably expected. Thirdly, the other point on which Streatfield J largely based his judgment was that there is a critical difference between the measure of damages applicable when the defendant defaults in supplying a self-contained profit-earning whole and when he defaults in supplying a part of that whole. In our view, there is no intrinsic magic, in this connection, in the whole as against a part. The fact that a part only is involved is only significant in so far as it bears on the capacity of the supplier to foresee the consequences of non-delivery. If it is clear from the nature of the part (or the supplier of it is informed) that its non-delivery will have the same effect as non-delivery of the whole, his liability will be the same as if he had defaulted in delivering the whole. The cases of *Hadley v Baxendale, British Columbia, etc. Saw Mill Co. v Nettleship* (1868) LR 3 CP 499 and *Portman v Middleton* which were so strongly relied on for the defence and by the learned judge, were all cases in which, through want of a part, catastrophic results ensued, in that a whole concern was paralysed or sterilised – a mill stopped, a complex of machinery unable to be assembled, a threshing machine unable to be delivered in time for the harvest, and, therefore, useless. In all three cases the defendants were absolved from liability to compensate the plaintiffs for the resulting loss of business, not because what they had failed to deliver was a part, but because there had been nothing to convey to them that want of that part would stultify the whole business of the person for whose benefit the part was contracted for. There is no resemblance between these cases and the present, in which, while there was no question of a total stoppage resulting from non-delivery, yet there were ample means of knowledge on the part of the defendants that business loss of some sort would be likely to result to the plaintiffs from the defendants' default in performing their contract.

We are, therefore, of opinion that the appeal should be allowed and the issue referred to an official referee as to what damage, if any, is recoverable in addition to the £110 awarded by the learned trial judge. The official referee would assess those damages in consonance with the findings in this judgment as to what the defendants knew or must be taken to have known at the material time, either party to be at liberty to call evidence as to the *quantum* of the damage in dispute.

Tucker and Singleton LJJ concurred.

THE HERON II [1967] 3 All ER 686 (HL)

A ship deviated from its route, and the delay resulted in its cargo of sugar being sold for a lower price, because of a fall in the market price.

LORD REID: . . . In cases like *Hadley v Baxendale* (1854) 9 Exch 341 or the present case it is not enough that in fact the plaintiff's loss was directly caused by the defendant's breach of contract. It clearly was so caused in both. The crucial question is whether, on the information available to the defendant when the contract was made, he should, or the reasonable man in his position would, have realised that such loss was sufficiently likely to result from the breach of contract to make it proper to hold that the loss flowed naturally from the breach or that loss of that kind should have been within his contemplation.

The modern rule in tort is quite different and it imposes a much wider liability. The defendant will be liable for any type of damage which is reasonably foreseeable as liable to happen even in the most unusual case, unless the risk is so small that a reasonable man would in the whole circumstances feel justified in neglecting it; and there is good reason for the difference. In contract, if one party wishes to protect himself against a risk which to the other party would appear unusual, he can direct the other party's attention to it before the contract is made, and I need not stop to consider in what circumstances the other party will then be held to have accepted responsibility in that event. In tort, however, there is no opportunity for the injured party to protect himself in that way, and the tortfeasor cannot reasonably complain if he has to pay for some very unusual but nevertheless foreseeable damage which results from his wrong-doing. I have no doubt that today a tortfeasor would be held liable for a type of damage as unlikely as was the stoppage of Hadley's Mill for lack of a crank shaft: to any one with the knowledge the carrier had that may have seemed unlikely, but the chance of it happening would have been seen to be far from negligible. But it does not at all follow that *Hadley v Baxendale* would today be differently decided. . . . it has been said that the liability of defendants has been further extended by *Victoria Laundry (Windsor) Ltd v Newman Industries Ltd* [1949] 1 All ER 997. I do not think so. The plaintiffs bought a large boiler from the defendants and the defendants were aware of the general nature of the plaintiffs' business and the plaintiffs' intention to put the boiler into use as soon as possible. Delivery of the boiler was delayed in breach of contract and the plaintiffs claimed as damages loss of profit caused by the delay. A large part of the profits claimed would have resulted from some specially lucrative contracts which the plaintiffs could have completed if they had had the boiler: that was rightly disallowed because the defendants had no knowledge of these contracts. Asquith LJ, said:

> It does not, however, follow that the plaintiffs are precluded from recovering some general (and perhaps conjectural) sum for loss of business in respect of dyeing contracts to be reasonably expected, any more than in respect of laundering contracts to be reasonably expected.

It appears to me that this was well justified on the earlier authorities. It was certainly not unlikely on the information which the defendants had when making the contract that delay in delivering the boiler would result in loss of business: indeed it would seem that that was more than an even chance. And there was nothing new in holding that damages should be estimated on a conjectural basis. This House had approved of that as early as 1813 in *Hall* v *Ross* (1813) 1 Dow 201.

What is said to create a 'landmark', however, is the statement of principles by Asquith LJ. This does to some extent go beyond the older authorities and in so far as it does, I do not agree with it. In para. (2) it is said that the plaintiff is entitled to recover 'such part of the losss actually resulting as was at the time of the contract reasonably foreseeable as liable to result from the breach'. To bring in reasonable foreseeability appears to me to be confusing measure of damages in contract with measure of damages in tort. A great many extremely unlikely results are reasonably foreseeable: it is true that Asquith LJ, may have meant foreseeable as a likely result, and if that is all he meant I would not object farther than to say that I think that the phrase is liable to be misunderstood. For the same reason I would take exception to the phrase 'liable to result' in para. (5). Liable is a very vague word, but I think that one would usually say that when a person foresees a very improbable result he foresees that it is liable to happen.

I agree with the first half of para. (6). For the best part of a century it has not been required that the defendant could have foreseen that a breach of contract must necessarily result in the loss which has occurred; but I cannot agree with the second half of para. (6). It has never been held to be sufficient in contract that the loss was foreseeable as 'a serious possibility' or 'a real danger' or as being 'on the cards'. It is on the cards that one can win £100,000 or more for a stake of a few pence – several people have done that; and anyone who backs a hundred to one chance regards a win as a serious possibility – many people have won on such a chance. Moreover *The Wagon Mound* (*No. 2*) *Overseas Tankship* (*UK*) *Ltd* v *Miller Steamship Co. Pty Ltd* [1966] 2 All ER 709 could not have been decided as it was unless the extremely unlikely fire should have been foreseen by the ship's officer as a real danger. It appears to me that in the ordinary use of language there is a wide gulf between saying that some event is not unlikely or quite likely to happen and saying merely that it is a serious possibility, a real danger, or on the cards. Suppose one takes a well-shuffled pack of cards, it is quite likely or not unlikely that the top card will prove to be a diamond: the odds are only three to one against; but most people would not say that it is quite likely to be the nine of diamonds for the odds are then fifty-one to against. On the other hand I think that most people would say that there is a serious possibility or a real danger of its being turned up first and, of course, it is on the cards. If the tests of 'real danger' or 'serious possibility' are in future to be authoritative, then the *Victoria Laundry* case would indeed be a landmark because it would mean that *Hadley* v *Baxendale* would be differently decided today. I certainly could not understand any court deciding that, on the information available to the carrier in that case, the stoppage of the mill was neither a serious possibility nor a real danger. If those tests are to prevail in future, then let us cease to pay lip service to the rule in *Hadley* v *Baxendale*. But in my judgment to adopt these tests would extend liability for breach of contract beyond which I have of commercial affairs I would not expect such an extension to be welcomed by the business community, and from the legal point of view I can find little or nothing to recommend it. . . .

It appears to me that, without relying in any way on the *Victoria Laundry* case, and taking the principle that had already been established, the loss of profit claimed in this case was not too remote to be recovereable as damages.

Lords Morris, Hodson, Pearce and Upjohn concurred.

PARSONS v *UTTLEY INGHAM* [1978] 1 All ER 525 (CA)

LORD DENNING MR: . . . The plaintiffs, Parsons (Livestock) Ltd, have a fine herd of nearly 700 pigs at their farm in Derbyshire. They call it the Wayside Herd. They manage it most efficiently. They feed the pigs on special pig nuts. They use about ten tons a month of these pig nuts. In order to store and handle these pig nuts, Parsons bought in 1968 a big hopper called a bulk feed storage hopper. They bought it from the defendants, Uttley Ingham & Co Ltd, the makers, who are sheet metal workers. Parsons paid £270 for it. It was a huge round metal bin 28 feet high and eight feet six inches in diameter. It was cylindrical at the top tapering down into a cone. It had a lid on the top with a ventilator in it. The pig nuts go into the top and come out at the bottom.

The first hopper was so succesful that in 1971 Parsons ordered a second one to be just the same as the first. It cost £275. The makers accepted the order in a letter of 23 April 1971 in these terms:

> . . . we are very pleased to book your order for 1 Bulk Hopper exactly as supplied in 1968 . . . Hopper fitted with ventilated top and complete with filler and breather pipes . . . Ex Works Price £275.00 nett. Carriage charges £15.00 nett. We deliver in an upright position on your prepared concrete base and bolt down . . . tipping the hopper off the back of the vehicle.

On 2nd August 1971 the makers delivered the hopper to the site. It was exactly the same as the first, but when the delivery man erected it in position he forgot to adjust the ventilator. He left it closed. It was fastened with a piece of tape which had been put on so as to stop it rattling on the journey. No one noticed the mistake, because the ventilator was at the top of the hopper 28 feet above the ground. The delivery man went off. The pig farmers used the hopper. They put pig nuts into it just as they did with the first hopper. On 12th August 1971 they filled it with 9½ tons of pig nuts; on 10th September, 8½ tons; on 1st October 8 tons.

At first all was well. But on 28th September a small number of the nuts appeared to be mouldy. The farmers did not think this would harm the pigs. So they went on feeding them. Early in October more nuts turned mouldy. But still the farmers were not unduly concerned. As a rule, mouldy nuts do not harm pigs. On Saturday, 9th October, there was a bigger proportion of mouldy nuts; and some of the pigs were showing signs of illness. About six of the 21 sows suckling litters were very loose; and about seven or eight were not eating all their ration of nuts. Over the weekend the pig farmers became really concerned. They did not know the cause. They telephoned the suppliers of the nuts. They telephoned the veterinary surgeon. The suppliers of nuts came. The veterinary surgeon came. They stopped feeding the pigs with nuts from the hopper. They got some bagged food and fed them from the bags. They telephoned the makers. On Friday, 15th October, a representative of the makers came. He climbed up to the top of the hopper. He found the ventilator closed. He opened it. When he came down, he said to the pig farmer: 'That appears to be your trouble'.

It was indeed the trouble. After much evidence by experts, the judge found that the closed ventilator was the cause. But the effects remained so as to affect the herd greatly. A large number of the pigs suffered an attack of E coli, which is very bad for pigs. It was 'triggered' off by the eating of the mouldy nuts. The infection spread rapidly. Two hundred and fifty four pigs died, of a value of £10,000. They also lost sales and turnover resulting in big financial loss. The total claim is £20,000 of £30,000. The question is whether that damage is recoverable from the makers, or whether it is too remote. . . .

Remoteness of damage is beyond doubt a question of law. In *The Heron II, Koufos* v *C Czarnikow Ltd* [1967] 3 All ER 686, the House of Lords said that, in remoteness of damage, there is a difference between contract and tort. In the case of a *breach of contract*, the court has to consider whether the consequences were of such a kind that a reasonable man, at the time of making the contract, would *contemplate* them as being of a very substantial degree of probability. (In the House of Lords various expressions were used to describe this degree of probability, such as, not merely 'on the cards' because that may be too low: but as being 'not likely to occur'; or likely to result or at least not unlikely to result'; or 'liable to result'; or that there was a 'real danger' or 'serious possibility' of them occuring.)

In the case of a *tort*, the court has to consider whether the consequences were of such a kind that a reasonable man, at the time of the tort committed, would *foresee* them as being of a much lower degree of probability. (In the House of Lords various expressions were used to describe this, such as, it is sufficient if the consequences are 'liable to happen in the most unusual case' or in a 'very improbable' case or that 'they may happen as a result of the breach however unlikely it may be, unless it can be brushed aside as far-fetched'.)

I find it difficult to apply those principles universally to all cases of contract or to all cases of tort, and to draw a distinction between what a man 'contemplates' and what he 'foresees'. I soon begin to get out of my depth. I cannot swim in this sea of semantic exercises – to say nothing of the different degrees of probability – especially when the cause of action can be laid either in contract or in tort. I am swept under by the conflicting currents. I go back with relief to the distinction drawn in legal theory by Professors Hart and Honore in their book *Causation in the Law*. They distinguish between those cases in contract in which a man has suffered no damage to person or property, but only *economic loss*, such as, loss of profit or loss of opportunities for gain in some future transaction: and those in which he claims damages for an *injury actually done* to his person or *damage actually done* to his property (including his livestock) or for ensuing expense (damnum ermegens) to which he has actually been put. In law of *tort*, there is emerging a distinction between economic loss and physical damage: see *Spartan Steel & Alloys Ltd* v *Martin & Co. (Contractors) Ltd* [1972] 2 All ER 557. It underlies the words of Lord Wilberforce in *Anns* v *London Borough of Merton* [1977] 2 All ER 492 recently, where he classified the recoverable damage as 'material, physical damage'. It has been much considered by the Supreme Court of Canada in *Rivtow Marine Ltd* v *Washington Iron Works* [1974] SCR 1189 and by the High Court in Australia in *Calex Oil (Australia) Pty Ltd* v *The Dredge Willemstad* (1976) 11 ALR 227.

It seems to me that in the law of *contract*, too, a similar distinction is emerging. It is between loss of profit consequent on a breach of contract and physical damage consequent on it.

Loss of profit cases
I would suggest as a solution that in the former class of case, loss of profit cases, the defaulting party is only liable for the consequences if they are such as, at the time of the contract, he ought reasonably to have contemplated as a *serious* possibility or real danger. You must assume that, at the time of the contract, he had the very kind of breach in mind, such a breach as afterwards happened, as for instance, delay in transit, and then you must ask: ought he reasonably to have contemplated that there was a serious possibility that such a breach would involve the plaintiff in loss of profit? If Yes, the contractor is liable for the loss unless he has taken care to exempt himself from it by a condition in the contract as, of course, he is able to do if it was the sort of thing which he could reasonably contemplate. The law on this class of case is now covered by the three leading cases of *Hadley* v *Baxendale*, *Victoria Laundry (Windsor) Ltd* v *Newman Industries Ltd* and *The Heron II, Koufos* v *C Czarnikow Ltd*. These were all 'loss of profit' cases, and the test of 'reasonable contemplation' and 'serious possibility' should, I suggest, be kept to that type of loss or, at any rate, to economic loss.

Physical damage cases
In the second class of case, the physical injury or expense case, the defaulting party is liable for any loss or expense which he ought reasonably to have foreseen at the time of the breach as a possible consequence, even if it was only a *slight* possibility. You must assume that he was aware of his breach, and then you must ask: ought he reasonably to have foreseen, at the time of the breach, that something of this kind might happen in consequence of it? This is the test which has been applied in cases of tort, ever since *The Wagon Mound* [1966] 2 All ER 709 cases. But there is a long line of cases which support a like test case in cases of contract. One class of case which is particularly apposite here concerns latent defects in goods. In modern words: 'product liability'. In many of these cases the manufacturer is liable in contract to the immediate party for a breach of his duty to use reasonable care, and is liable in tort to the ultimate consumer for the same want of reasonable care. The ultimate consumer can either sue the retailer in contract and

pass the liability up the chain to the manufacturer, or he can sue the manufacturer in tort and thus by-pass the chain. The liability of the manufacturer ought to be the same in either case. In nearly all these cases the defects were outside the range of anything that was in fact contemplated, or could reasonably have been contemplated by the manufacturer or by anyone down the chain to the retailers. Yet the manufacturer and others in the chain have been held liable for the damage done to the ultimate user, as for instance the death of the youg pheasants in *Henry Kendall & Sons (a firm) v William Lillico & Sons Ltd* [1968] 2 All ER 444 and of the mink in *Ashington Piggeries Ltd v Christopher Hill Ltd* [1971] 1 All ER 847. Likewise the manufacturers and retailers were held liable for the dermatitis caused to the wearer in the woollen underwear case of *Grant v Australian Knitting Mills Ltd* [1936] AC 85, even though they had not the faintest suspicion of any trouble. So were the manufacturers down the chain to the sub-contractors for the disintegrating roofing-tiles in *Young v Marten Ltd v McManus Childs Ltd* [1968] 2 All ER 1169. . . .

Instances could be multiplied of injuries to persons or damage to property where the defendant is liable for his negligence to one man in contract and to another in tort. Each suffers like damage. The test of remoteness is, and should be, the same in both.

Coming to the present case, we were told that in some cases the makers of these hoppers supply them direct to the pig farmer under contract with him, but in other cases they supply them through an intermediate dealer who buys from the manufacturer and resells to the pig farmer on the self-same terms, in which the manufacturer delivers direct to the pig farmer. In the one case the pig farmer can sue the manufacturer in contract. In the other in tort. The test of remoteness should be the same. It should be the test in tort.

Conclusion
The present case falls within the class of case where the breach of contract causes physical damage. The test of remoteness in such cases is similar to that in tort. The contractor is liable for all such loss or expense as could reasonably have been foreseen, at the time of the breach, as a possible consequence of it. Applied to this case, it means that the makers of the hopper are liable for the death of the pigs. They ought reasonably to have foreseen that, if the mouldy pig nuts were fed to the pigs, there was a possibility that they might become ill. Not a serious possibility. Nor a real danger. But still a slight possibility. On that basis the makers were liable for the illness suffered by the pigs. They suffered from diarrhoea at the beginning. This 'triggered off' the deadly E coli. That was a far worse illness than could then be foreseen. But that does not lessen this liability. The type or kind of damage was foreseeable even though the extent of it was not; see *Hughes v Lord Advocate* [1963] 1 All ER 705. The makers are liable for the loss of the pigs that died and of the expenses of the vet, and such like. But not for loss of profit on future sales or future opportunities of gain; see *Simon v Pawson & Leafs Ltd* (1932) 38 Com Cas 151.

So I reach the same result as Swanwick J, but by a different route. I would dismiss the appeal.

ORR LJ: I agree with Lord Denning MR and also with Scarman LJ, whose judgment I have had the opportunity of reading, that this appeal should be dismissed, but with respect to Lord Denning MR I would dismiss it for the reasons to be given by Scarman LJ and not on the basis that a distinction is to be drawn for the present purposes between loss of profits and physical damage cases. I have not been satisfied that such a distinction is sufficiently supported by the authorities. . . .

SCARMAN LJ: . . . My conclusion in the present case is the same as that of Lord Denning MR but I reach it by a different route. I would dismiss the appeal. I agree with him in thinking it absurd that the test for remoteness of damage should, in principle, differ according to the legal classification of the cause of action, though one must reconise that parties to a contract have the right to agree on a measure of damages which may be greater or less than the law would offer in the absence of agreement. I also agree with him in thinking that, not withstanding the interpretation put on some dicta in *The Heron II, Koufos v C Czarnikow Ltd*, the law is not so absurd as to differentiate between contract and tort save in situations where the agreement, or the factual relationship of the parties with each other requires it in the interests of justice. I differ from him only to this extent: the cases do not, in my judgment support a distinction in law between loss of profit and physical damage. Neither do I think it necessary to develop the law judicially by drawing such a distinction. Of course (and this a reason for refusing to draw the distinction in law) the type of consequence, loss of profit or market or physical injury, will always be an important matter of fact in determining whether in all the circumstances the loss or injury was of a type which the parties could reasonably be supposed to have in contemplation.

In *The Heron II, Koufos* v *C Czarnikow Ltd* (a case of a contract of carriage of goods by sea) the House of Lords resolved some of the difficulties in this branch of the law. The law, which the House in that case either settled or recognised as already settled, may be stated as follows: (1) the general principle regulating damages for breach of contract is that 'where a party sustains a loss by reason of a breach of contract he is, as far as money can do it, to be placed in the same situation . . . as if the contract had been performed' (see Lord Pearce quoting Parke B in *Robinson* v *Harman* (1848) 1 Exch 850; (2) the formulation of the remoteness test is not the same in tort and in contract because the relationship of the parties in a contract situation differs from that in tort (see Lord Reid); (3) the two rules formulated by Alderson B in *Hadley* v *Baxendale* (1854) 9 Exch 341 are but two aspects of one general principle, that to be recoverable in an action for damages for breach of contract the plaintiff's loss must be such as may reasonably be supposed would have been in the contemplation of the parties as a serious possibility had their attention been directed to the possibility of the breach which has, in fact, occurred. Two problems are left unsolved by *The Heron II , Koufos* v *C Czarnikow Ltd*: (1) the law's reconciliation of the remoteness principle in contract with that in tort where as, for instance in some product liability cases, there arises the danger of differing awards, the lesser award going to the party who has a contract, even though the contract is silent as to the measure of damages and all parties are, or must be deemed to be, burdened with the same knowledge (or enjoying the same state of ignorance); (2) what is meant by 'serious possibility' (or its synonyms): is it a reference to the type of consequence which the parties might be supposed to contemplate as possible though unlikely, or must the chance of it happening appear to be likely? See the way Lord Pearce puts it.

As to the first problem, I agree with Lord Denning MR in thinking that the law must be such that, in a factual situation where all have the same actual or imputed knowledge and the contract contains no term limiting the damages recoverable for breach, the amount of damages recoverable does not depend on whether, as a matter for legal classification, the plaintiff's cause of action is breach of contract or tort. It may be that necessary reconciliation is to be found, notwithstanding the strictures of Lord Reid, in holding that the difference between 'reasonably foreseeable' (the test in tort) and 'reasonably contemplated' (the test in contract) is semantic, not substantial. Certainly Asquith LJ in *Victoria Laundry (Windsor) Ltd* v *Newman Industries Ltd* and Lord Pearce in *The Heron II, Koufos* v *C Czarnikow Ltd* thought so; and I confess I think so too. The second problem, what is meant by a 'serious possibility', is, in my judgment, ultimately a question of fact. I shall return to it, therefore, after analysing the facts since I believe it requires of the judge no more, and no less, than the application of common sense in the particular circumstances of the case. Finally, there are two legal rules relevant to the present case which were not considered in *The Heron II, Koufos* v *C Czarnikow Ltd*.

The first relates to sale of goods. Section 53(2) of the Sale of Goods Act 1893 provides that –

The measure of damages for breach of warranty is the estimated loss directly and naturally resulting, in the ordinary course of events, from the breach of warranty.

The subsection, clearly a statutory formulation of the first rule in *Hadley* v *Baxendale* is not, however, intended to oust the second rule where appropriate: see s. 54. Nevertheless it vindicates the judge's approach to this case, always assuming that the facts are such as to make the application of the first rule appropriate.

Secondly, the breach does not have to be foreseen, or contemplated. In a breach of warranty case the point may be put in this way: it does not matter if the defect is latent.

It may be unknown, even unknowable: see *Grant v Australian Knitting Mills Ltd*. The court has to assume, though it be contrary to the fact, that the parties had in mind the breach that has occurred. Thus, whenever a question of remoteness of damage arises in a contract case, its solution involves the court in making a hypothesis, which may, or may not, correspond with fact.

The court's task, therefore, is to decide what loss to the plaintiffs it is reasonable to suppose would have been in the contemplation of the parties as a serious possibility had they had in mind the breach when they made their contract. . . . I think the judge was making the approach which, according to Lord Reid, is the correct one. He was saying, in effect, that the parties to this contract must have appreciated that, if, as happened in the event, the hopper, unventilated, proved not to be suitable for the storage of pig nuts to be fed to the plaintiffs' pigs, it was not unlikely, there was a serious possibility, that the pigs would become ill. The judge put it in this way:

> The *natural* result of feeding toxic food to animals is damage to their health and maybe death, which is what occurred, albeit from a hitherto unknown disease and to particularly suspectible animals. There was therefore no need to invoke the question of *reasonable* contemplation in order to make the defendants liable. (My emphasis.)

The judge in this critical passage of his judgment is contrasting a natural result, i.e. one which people placed as these parties were would consider as a serious possibility, with a special specific result, E coli disease, which, as he later found, the parties could not at the time of contract reasonably have contemplated as a consequence. He distinguishes between 'presumed contemplation' based on a special knowledge from ordinary understanding based on general knowledge and concludes that the case falls within the latter category. He does so because he has held that the assumption, or hypothesis, to be made is that the parties had in mind at the time of contract not a breach of warranty limited to the delivery of mouldy nuts but warranty as to the fitness of the hopper for its purpose. The assumption is of the parties asking themselves not what is likely to happen if the nuts are mouldy but what is likely to happen to the pigs if the hopper is unfit for storing nuts suitable to be fed to them. While, on his finding, nobody at the time of contract could have expected E coli to ensue from eating mouldy nuts, he is clearly, and, as a matter of common sense, rightly, saying that people would contemplate, on the second assumption, the serious possibility of injury and even death among the pigs.

And so the question becomes; was he right to make the assumption he did? In my judgment, he was (see *Grant v Australian Knitting Mills Ltd*, and particularly the well-known passage in the speech of Lord Wright).

I would agree with Mr McGregor in his work on Damages that –

> . . . in contract as in tort, it should suffice that, if physical injury or damage is within the contemplation of the parties, recovery is not to be limited because the degree of physical injury or damage could not have been anticipated.

This is so, in my judgment, not because there is, or ought to be a specific rule of law governing cases of physical injury but because it would be absurd to regulate damages in such cases on the necessity of supposing the parties had a prophetic foresight as to the exact nature of the injury that does in fact arise. It is enough if on the hypothesis predicated physical injury must have been a serious possibility. Though in loss of market or loss of profit cases the factual analysis will be very different from cases of physical injury, the same principles, in my judgment, apply. Given the situation of the parties at the time of contract, was the loss of profit, or market, a serious possibility, something that would have been in their minds had they contemplated breach?

It does not matter, in my judgment, if they thought that the chance of physical injury, loss of profit, loss of market, or other loss as the case may be, was slight or that the odds were against it provided they contemplated as a serious possibility the type of consequence, not necessarily the specific consequence, that ensued on breach. Making the assumption as to breach that the judge did, no more than common sense was needed for them to appreciate that food affected by bad storage conditions might well cause illness in the pigs fed on it.

As I read the judgment under appeal, this was how the judge, whose handling of the issues at trial was such that none save one survives for our consideration, reached this decision. In my judgment, he was right, on the facts as found, to apply the first rule in *Hadley* v *Baxendale*, or, if the case be one of breach of warranty, as I think it is, the rule in s. 53(2) of the Sale of Goods Act 1893 without enquiring whether, on a juridical analysis, the rule is based on a presumed contemplation. At the end of a long and complex dispute the judge allowed common sense to prevail. I would dismiss the appeal.

7.1.2 MEASURE OF DAMAGES

7.1.2.1 Expectation interest (loss of bargain)

WL THOMPSON LTD v *R ROBINSON LTD* [1955] 1 All ER 154 (ChD)

The defendants had refused to go through with the purchase of a car.

UPJOHN J: . . . The point is whether the plaintiffs are entitled to loss of profit on the transactions or whether damages are nominal. . . . It was proved first that, in common with the other makes of motor car, dealers are only permitted to sell new Vanguard cars at a price fixed from time to time by the manufacturers, the Standard Motor Car Company. If a dealer breaks that rule he is soon put out of business. The dealer's profit on the transaction is also fixed. He would have received in this case a commission of ten per cent. on the list price of the Vanguard and accessories such as wireless and heaters supplied therewith. In this case, the amount of profit he would have made to be exact, I am told, is £61 1s. 9d.

When the defendants repudiated the transaction on March 5, the plaintiffs mitigated their damages by rescinding the contract with their suppliers. Their supplier was a company called George Thompson Ltd, who were the main distributors for the East Riding, and, as the name implies, they are closely associated with the plaintiffs, but that, I think, is irrelevant. At all events, George Thompson Ltd, took back the Vanguard car which they had already supplied to the plaintiffs, free of any claim for damages, and later sold the car on May 5, 1954, to another purchaser. It is also common ground that, at this stage, the plaintiffs lost a sale in the sense, that if another purchaser had come into the plaintiffs' premises there was available for another purchaser a Vanguard car for immediate delivery; so that the effect as a fact on the plaintiffs was that they lost their profit on a sale: they sold one Vanguard less than they would otherwise have done. The plaintiffs say that the true measure of damages in those circumstances is no more, no less, than their loss of profit, £61. The defendants say: 'No, the loss is nominal, for you could have sold the car to another customer or you could do what, in fact, you did do, which was to get your suppliers to release you, and you have suffered no damage'.

The law is not really in doubt. It is set out in the Sale of Goods Act, 1893, s. 50, which is in these terms:

(1) Where the buyer wrongfully neglects or refuses to accept and pay for the goods, the seller may maintain an action against him for damages for non-acceptance. (2) The measure of damages is the estimated loss directly and naturally resulting, in the ordinary course of events, from the buyer's breach of contract. (3) Where there is an available market for the goods in question the measure of damages is prima facie to be ascertained by the difference between the contract price and the market or current price at the time or times when the goods ought to have been accepted, or, if no time was fixed for acceptance, then at the time of the refusal to accept. . . .

The main case, however, put by the defendants is this: they submit that s. 50(3) of the Sale of Goods Act 1893, applies, because they say there is an available market for the goods in question, and in that available market we know that the price of the Vanguard is fixed. It is fixed by the manufacturers. Therefore, they say the measure of damages must necessarily be little more than nominal. Had the plaintiffs kept the car and sold it to another at a later stage, no doubt they would have been entitled to the costs of storage in the meantime, possibly interest on their money laid out, and so on, but, as they in fact mitigated damages by getting out of the contract, damages are nil.

Counsel for the defendants said that the market now must not be treated as a market or fair in a limited or technical sense. It is curious that there is a comparative absence of authority on the meaning of the phrase 'available market', because one would have thought there would have been many cases, but the researches of counsel have only disclosed one authority on s. 50(3). It is *Dunkirk Colliery Co.* v *Lever* (1878) 9 ChD 20, a decision of the Court of Appeal. The facts were far removed from the facts before me, and I do not think that I need recite them. It will be sufficient if I read an extract from the judgment of James LJ. He said (9 ChD at p. 24):

> Under those circumstances the only thing that we can do is to send it back to the referee with an intimation that we are of opinion upon the facts (agreeing with the Master of the Rolls in that respect), that the facts do not warrant the application of the principle mentioned in the award, namely, that there was what may be properly called a market. What I understand by a market in such a case as this is, that when the defendant refused to take the three hundred tons the first week or the first month, the plaintiffs might have sent it in waggons somewhere else, where they could sell it, just as they can sell corn on the Exchange, or cotton at Liverpool: that is to say, that there was a fair market where they could have found a purchaser either by themselves or through some agent at some particular place. That is my notion of the 'meaning of a market under those circumstances.

If that be the right principle to apply, it was proved that there is nothing in the nature of a market like a Cotton Exchange or Baltic or Stock Exchange, or anything of the sort, for the sale of new motor cars. . . .

I think that in that state of affairs the decision of the Court of Appeal in *Dunkirk Colliery Co.* v *Lever* is binding on me, and, therefore, unless one finds something in the nature of a market in the sense used by James LJ, s. 50(3) has no further application. However, the point seems to me of somewhat academic interest in this case, because, if one gives to the word 'market' an extended meaning, in my view on the facts which I have to consider, a precisely similar result is reached.

Had the matter been *res integra*, I think I should have found that an 'available market' merely means that the situation in the particular trade in the particular area was such that the particular goods could freely be sold, and that there was a demand sufficient to absorb readily all the goods that were thrust on it, so that if a purchaser defaulted the goods in question could readily be disposed of. Indeed, such was the situation in the motor trade until very recently. It was, of course, notorious that dealers all over the country had long waiting lists for new motor cars. People put their names down and had to wait five or six years, and whenever a car was spared by the maufacturer from export it was snatched at. If any purchaser fell out, there were many waiting to take his place, and it was conceded that if those circumstances were still applicable to the Vanguard motor car, the claim for damages must necessarily have been purely nominal. But on the assumed facts, circumstances had changed in relation to Vanguard motor cars, and in March, 1954, there was not a demand in the East Riding which could readily absorb all the Vanguard motor cars available for sale. If a purchaser defaulted, that sale was lost and there was no means of readily disposing of the Vanguard contracted to be sold, so that there was not, even on the extended definition, an available market. But there is this further consideration: even if I accepted the defendants' broad argument that one must now look at the market as being the whole conspectus of trade, organisation and marketing, I have to remember that s. 50(3) provides only a prima facie rule, and, if on investigation of the facts, one finds that it is unjust to apply that rule, in the light of the general principles mentioned above it is not to be applied. In this case, as I said in the earlier part of my judgment, it seems to me plain almost beyond argument that, in fact, the loss to the plaintiffs is £61. Accordingly, however one interprets s. 50(3), it seems to me on the facts that I have to consider one reaches the same result.

There will be judgment for the plaintiffs for £61 1s. 9d., but the order must incorporate an undertaking by the plaintiffs to indemnify the defendants against their costs of this action. There must be a mutual set-off between the costs and the sum of £61.

CHARTER v SULLIVAN [1957] 1 All ER 809 (CA)

SELLERS LJ: The judgment from which the defendant, the buyer, appeals found and established that on or about June 29 or 30, 1956, the defendant agreed to buy from the plaintiff a new Hillman Minx saloon motor car and that on July 5, 1956, when the car was licensed and ready for delivery as arranged, the defendant repudiated the agreement and refused to take delivery because he had found that he could get a better bargain elsewhere for his Commer van, which was to be taken in part payment of the price. The only question on the appeal is as to the damages the plaintiff is entitled to receive for the non-acceptance of the car by the defendant. The plaintiff claimed the loss of profit on the sale. The defendant denied that there had been in the circumstances any profit lost and alleged that nominal damages only were recoverable.

The car rejected by the defendant was put back into the plaintiff's showroom and was sold within a week or ten days to another customer at the same fixed retail price. This effective sale resulted in the normal profit to the plaintiff, but he claims that he has nevertheless lost a profit, for he would have sold and delivered, but for the defendant's default, two cars instead of one and would have made two profits instead of one. Having regard to the nature of this claim singularly little evidence was directed to the issue.

The plaintiff was the area car dealer for the Rootes Group, who manufacture the Hillman Minx cars, and he was required to sell them at not less than their fixed price for retail sale. He had only one Hillman Minx in stock, but, if the defendant had taken delivery, he would have ordered another one and would have expected a replacement within a week or ten days. The sales manager said he was certain he would have sold the new purchaser another Hillman Minx if the one in question had not been available (by reason of the defendant's default).

A seller's loss of profit on a sale may clearly directly and naturally result in the ordinary course of events from a buyer's wrongful neglect or refusal to accept and pay for the goods bought. But it may be that the seller is so circumstanced that he could sell the goods elsewhere, either at the same price as the contract price, or at some lesser price which would either extinguish or minimise the loss to the seller and therefore the damages which the defaulting buyer will have to pay.

Learned counsel for the defendant placed great reliance on s. 50(3) of the Sale of Goods Act 1893, and submitted that there was an available market for the car at the one fixed or current price, which was also the contract price, and therefore there could be no loss of profit recoverable as that sub-section established the measure of damages. No evidence was given as to anything the plaintiff might have done to bring about a resale of the rejected car except that which he did, viz., place it is his showroom and await a new buyer. Having regard to his success within ten days, the submissions on the meaning of 'available market' seem to me to be somewhat theoretical and academic.

The Act does not attempt to define a market and it may be conceded that one can exist in a variety of circumstances and apart, of necessity, from a defined place, but, since its trading has to serve as a factor in measuring the damages, it must at least be a market in which the seller could, if he wished, sell the goods left on his hands. At the time of the defendant's refusal to accept, June 5 1956, it has not been shown that there was any real market where the rejected car could have been offered for sale and sold. There was no available market. No doubt the current price was known and ascertained but there was no immediate buyer.

The plaintiff had the duty to act reasonably and mitigate the damages as far as he reasonably could. What he did resulted in a resale at the contract price but the question is whether that resale mitigated his loss and the same question would arise if a sale could have been made in an 'available market'. The plaintiff's case is that, by reason of the defendant's non-acceptance of the car he had bought, the plaintiff has lost the profit he would have earned and that the resale of the car to another customer did not and could not in the circumstances give him a substituted profit. He claims that he could have sold a Hillman Minx to the defendant and another to the new purchaser and made two profits, whereas he has made only one and lost irreplaceably the profit on the defendant's transaction (or at least on one of the two transactions).

If a seller can prove that a profit has been irretrievably lost on a sale of goods by the buyer's default, it would in my opinion be recoverable as damages in accordance with

s. 50(2). But where there has in fact been a resale of the goods, the seller has the burden of proving a loss of profit beyond that which on the face of it has been recouped in whole or in part by the resale. In my view the plaintiff has failed to give adequate proof of such a loss in this case. The sales manager for the plaintiff said that he had lost the sale of a car, but he also said that he could sell all the Hillman Minx cars he could get. It was argued that the statement that he could sell all the cars he could get ought not to be taken literally, but should be qualified in some way. Even if that is so, which I see, on the evidence, no reason to concede, it does not establish affirmative evidence that the plaintiff could get all the Hillman Minx cars he could sell.

If it could be proved that there were in effect unlimited supplies of Hillman Minx cars and a limited number of buyers in the circumstances in which a dealer was trading, then it would appear that the dealer could establish a loss of profit which could not be mitigated. On the other hand most dealers in cars (and in many other commodities) it might be visualised, have either a quota fixed by their supplier or a supply fixed by their own trading limits governed by their scope of trading. In such a case, if in a given trading period all the goods the dealer had available for sale had been sold, or would in all probability be sold, then the fact that one or more purchasers had defaulted and had been or would be replaced by others would not reduce the dealer's maximum profits . The matter cannot of course be worked out ad infinitum, but would be decided on the probabilities of the case and having regard to the nature, extent and circumstances of the dealer's trading. If a dealer had twenty cars available for sale and twenty-five potential buyers, he still would make his full profit if he sold the twenty cars notwithstanding that two or three purchasers defaulted. In *W L Thompson Ltd v R Robinson* (*Gunmakers*) *Ltd* [1955] 1 All ER 154, Upjohn J gave damages for loss of profit to dealers who had sold a Vanguard motor car to the defendants, who refused to take delivery. The dealers had returned the vehicle to their suppliers but the learned judge decided the case on the basis that the dealers had lost their bargain, that they had sold one car less than they otherwise would have done, which is the plaintiff's contention here. It is important to note in that case (*ibid*, at p. 156):

> . . . that in the East Riding of Yorkshire, the transaction taking place actually in Hull, at the time the contract of sale took place there was no shortage of Vanguard models to meet all immediate demands, at any rate in the locality.

On those facts the learned judge in my view was right in saying that the plaintiffs had lost a customer and thereby a profit. There was no point in their keeping the car and awaiting a resale, as they could acquire a Vanguard car to meet each purchaser as he presented himself. They could not, in other words, avoid their loss. The reasoning of Hamilton LJ and Buckley LJ in *Re Vic Mill Ltd* [1913] 1 Ch 465 at pp. 473, 474 quoted by the judge is singularly apt and adaptable to this case. Upjohn J ([1955] 1 All ER at p. 160) states the possible extreme situations: one, where in the case of rejection 'if any purchaser fell out, there were many waiting to take his place', the other:

> But on the assumed facts, circumstances had changed in relation to Vanguard motor cars, and in March, 1954, there was not a demand in the East Riding which could readily absorb all the Vanguard motor cars available for sale.

Whether the plaintiff could have proved a similar situation with regard to the Hillman Minx cars in his area I do not know, but I cannot find that it was either admitted or proved. It is for this reason that I would allow this appeal. There are two items in the damage claimed, loss of profit on a car heater and on wheel discs, both of which were ordered for the Hillman Minx and for which £7 12s. 6d. in all is claimed. These items might stand on a different footing from the loss of profit of £90 2s. 6d. claimed for the loss of the sale of the car, but no such distinction was made either at the trial or on the appeal and I would therefore find the plaintiff entitled to 40s. nominal damages only.

Jenkins and Hodson LJJ concurred.

LAZENBY GARAGES LTD v *WRIGHT* [1976] 2 All ER 770 (CA)

LORD DENNING MR: Mr Wright works on the land. On 19th February 1974 he went to
the showrooms of motor dealers called Lazenby Garages Ltd. He saw some secondhand
cars there. He agreed to buy a BMW 2002. He signed a contract to pay £1,670 for it. It
was to be delivered to him on 1st March 1974. He went back home to his wife and told
her about it. She persuaded him not to buy it. So next day he went back to the garage
and said he would not have it after all. They kept it there offering it for resale. Two
months later on 23rd April 1974 they resold it for £1,770, that is for £100 more than Mr
Wright was going to pay.

Notwithstanding this advantageous resale, the garage sued Mr Wright for damages.
They produced evidence that they had themselves bought the car secondhand on 14th
February 1974, that is five days before Mr Wright had come in and agreed to buy it. They
said that they had bought it for £1,325. He had agreed to buy it from them for £1,670. So
they had lost £345 and they claimed that sum as damages.

In answer Mr Wright said: 'You haven't lost anything; you've sold it for a higher price'.
The garage people said that they were dealers in secondhand cars; that they had had a
number of cars of this sort of age and type, BMW 2002s; and that they had lost the sale
of another car. They said that, if Mr Wright had taken this car, they would have been
able to sell one of those other cars to the purchaser. So they had sold one car less and
were entitled to profit accordingly.

The judge thought that they had not proved that they had sold one car less, but that
there was a 50:50 chance that they would have sold an extra car. So he gave them
damages for half the sum claimed. Instead of £345 he gave them £172.50.

Now there is an appeal to this court. The cases show that if there are a number of new
cars, all exactly of the same kind, available for sale, and the dealers can prove that they
sold one car less than they otherwise would have done, they would be entitled to
damages amounting to their loss of profit on the one car: see the judgment of Upjohn J
in *W L Thompson v Robinson (Gunmakers) Ltd* [1955] 1 All ER 184. The same has been held
in the United States: *Torkomian v Russell* and *Stewart v Hansen* (1916) 97 Atlantic Reporter
760 in Canada, *Mason & Risch Ltd v Christner*; and in Australia, *Cameron v Campbell &
Worthington* [1930] SASR 402.

But it is entirely different in the case of a secondhand car. Each secondhand car is
different from the next, even though it is the same make. The sales manager of the garage
admitted in evidence that some secondhand cars, of the same make, even of the same
year, may sell better than others of the same year. Some may sell quickly, others
sluggishly. You simply cannot tell why. But they are all different.

In the circumstances the cases about new cars do not apply. We have simply to apply
to s. 50 of the Sale of Goods Act 1893. There is no 'available market' for secondhand cars.
So it's not sub-s. (3) but sub-s. (2). The measure of damages is the estimated loss directly
and naturally resulting in the ordinary course of events from the buyer's breach of
contract. That throws us back to the test of what could reasonably be expected to be in
the contemplation of the parties as a natural consequence of the breach. The buyer in
this case could not have contemplated that the dealer would sell one car less. At most
he would contemplate that, if they resold this very car at a lower price, they would suffer
by reason of that lower price and should recover the difference. But if they resold this
very car at a higher price, they would suffer no loss. Seeing that these plaintiffs resold
this car for £100 more than the sale to Mr Wright , they clearly suffered no damage at all.

In my opinion the appeal should be allowed and judgment entered for the defendant,
Mr Wright.

LAWTON LJ: In the course of argument counsel for the plaintiffs accepted that if a dealer
was selling an article which is a unique article, for example if a secondhand car dealer
was selling a vintage car, or if an antique dealer was selling a picture, then, if there were
a repudiation by a buyer of a contract entered into, the damages would be the particular
loss which was sustained on that transaction, and nothing more.

At the other end of the scale, the courts had to consider the principles accepted in a
line of cases, of which the most recent one is probably *W L Thompson Ltd v Robinson
(Gunmakers) Ltd.* As Lord Denning MR has pointed out, when the goods are not unique,

but are mass-produced, different considerations may apply from those which apply when an article is unique.

The problem in this case is whether a secondhand car of the type with which we are concerned, namely a BMW 2002, petrol injected, was a unique article. The evidence from the plaintiffs' own sales manager shows that it was; he put the matter in this way: 'No one can say what makes a secondhand car sellable. It is the same with new cars. Cars vary as to date, mileage, sound of engine, wear and tear, upholstery etc.' Then, a few answers later, he said: 'In a secondhand showroom each car is different'. In other words, he was saying that secondhand cars are, from their very nature, unique. In those circumstances it seems to me that the *Thompson* type of case has no application to the circumstances of this particular case.

I agree that the appeal should be allowed.

Bridge LJ concurred.

7.1.2.2 Reliance interest

ANGLIA TELEVISION LTD v *REED* [1972] 1 QB 60 (CA)

LORD DENNING MR: Anglia Television Ltd, the plaintiffs, were minded in 1968 to make a film of a play for television entitled 'The Man in the Wood'. It portrayed an American man married to an English woman. The American has an adventure in an English wood. The film was to last for 90 minutes. Anglia Television made many arrangements in advance. They arranged for a place where the play was to be filmed. They employed a director, a designer and a stage manager, and so forth. They involved themselves in much expense. All this was done before they got the leading man. They required a strong actor capable of holding the play together. He was to be on the scene the whole time. Anglia Television eventually found the man. He was Mr Robert Reed, the defendant, an American who has a very high reputation as an actor. He was very suitable for this part. By telephone conversation on August 30, 1968, it was agreed by Mr Reed through his agent that he would come to England and be available between September 9 and October 11, 1968, to rehearse and play in this film. He was to get a performance fee of £1,050, living expenses of £100 a week, his first class fares to and from the United States, and so forth. It was all subject to the permit of the Ministry of Labour for him to come here. That was duly given on September 2, 1968. So the contract was concluded. But unfortunately there was some muddle with the bookings. It appears that Mr Reed's agents had already booked him in America for some other play. So on September 3, 1968, the agent said that Mr Reed would not come to England to perform in this play. He repudiated his contract. Anglia Television tried very hard to find a substitute but could not do so. So on September 11 they accepted his repudiation. They abandoned the proposed film. They gave notice to the people whom they had engaged and so forth.

Anglia Television then sued Mr Reed for damages. He did not dispute his liability, but a question arose as to the damages. Anglia Television do not claim their profit. They cannot say what their profit would have been on this contract if Mr Reed had come here and performed it. So, instead of claim for loss of profits, they claim for the wasted expenditure. They had incurred the director's fees, the designer's fees, the stage manager's and assistant manager's fees, and so on. It comes in all to £2,750. Anglia Television say that all that money was wasted because Mr Reed did not perform his contract.

Mr Reed's advisers take a point of law. They submit that Anglia Television cannot recover for expenditure incurred *before* the contract was concluded with Mr Reed. They can only recover the expenditure *after* the contract was concluded. They say that the expenditure *after* the contract was only £854.65, and that is all that Anglia Television can recover.

The master rejected that contention: he held that Anglia Television could recover the whole £2,750; and now Mr Reed appeals to this court.

Mr Butler, for Mr Reed, has referred us to the recent case of *Perestrello & Companhia Limitada* v *United Paint Co. Ltd, The Times*, 16 April, 1969, in which Thesiger J quoted the words of Tindal CJ in *Hodges* v *Earl of Litchfield* (1835) 1 Bing NC 492, 498:

The expenses preliminary to the contract ought not to be allowed. The party enters into them for his own benefit at a time when it is uncertain whether there will be any contract or not.

Thesiger J applied those words, saying: 'In my judgement pre-contract expenditure, though thrown away, is not recoverable'.

I cannot accept the proposition as stated. It seems to me that a plaintiff in such a case as this has an election: he can either claim for loss of profits; or for his wasted expenditure. But he must elect between them. He cannot claim both. If he has not sufferred any loss of profits – or if he cannot prove what his profits would have been – he can claim in the alternative the expenditure which has been thrown away, that is, wasted, by reason of the breach. That is shown by *Cullinane* v *British 'Rema' Manufacturing Co. Ltd* [1954] 1 QB 292, 303, 308.

If the plaintiff claims the wasted expenditure, he is not limited to the expenditure incurred *after* the contract was concluded. He can claim also the expenditure incurred *before* the contract, provided that it was such as would reasonably be in the contemplation of the parties as likely to be wasted if the contract was broken. Applying that principle here, it is plain that, when Mr Reed entered into this contract, he must have known perfectly well that much expenditure had already been incurred on director's fees and the like. He must have contemplated – or, at any rate, it is reasonably to be imputed to him – that if he broke his contract, all that expenditure would be wasted, whether or not it was incurred before or after the contract. He must pay damages for all the expenditure so wasted and thrown away. This view is supported by the recent decision of Brightman J in *Lloyd* v *Stanbury* [1971] 1 WLR 535. There was a contract for the sale of land. In anticipation of the contract – and before it was concluded – the purchaser went to much expense in moving a caravan to the site and in getting his furniture there. The seller afterwards entered into a contract to sell the land to the purchaser, but afterwards broke his contract. The land had not increased in value, so the purchaser could not claim for any loss of profit. But Brightman J held, at p. 547, that he could recover the cost of moving the caravan and furniture, because it was 'within the contemplation of the parties when the contract was signed'. That decision is in accord with the correct principle, namely, that wasted expenditure can be recovered when it is wasted by reason of the defendant's breach of contract. It is true that, if the defendant had never entered into the contract, he would not be liable, and the expenditure would have been incurred by the plaintiff without redress; but, the defendant having made his contract and broken it, it does not lie in his mouth to say he is not liable, when it was because of his breach that the expenditure has been wasted.

I think the master was quite right and this appeal should be dismissed.

Phillimore and Megaw LJJ concurred.

7.1.2.3 Damages for disappointment or injured feelings

JARVIS v *SWANS TOURS* [1973] QB 233 (CA)

LORD DENNING MR: Mr Jarvis is a solicitor, employed by a local authority at Barking. In 1969 he was minded to go for Christmas to Switzerland. He was looking forward to a ski-ing holiday. It is his one fortnight's holiday in the year. He prefers it in the winter rather than in the summer.

Mr Jarvis read a brochure issued by Swans Tours Ltd. He was much attracted by the description of Mörlialp, Giswil, Central Switzerland. I will not read the whole of it, but just pick out some of the principle attractions:

House Party Centre with special resident host. . . .
Mörlialp is a most wonderful little resort on a sunny plateau. Up there you will find yourself in the midst of beautiful alpine scenery, which in the winter becomes a wonderland of sun, snow and ice, with a wide variety of fine ski-runs, a skating rink and exhilarating toboggan run. . . . Why did we choose the Hotel Krone. . . mainly and most of all because of the 'Gemütlichkeit' and friendly welcome you will receive from

Herr and Frau Weibel. . . . The Hotel Krone has its own Alphütte Bar which will be open several evenings a week. . . . No doubt you will be in for a great time, when you book this house-party holiday. . . . Mr Weibel, the charming owner, speaks English.

On the same page, in a special yellow box, it was said:

Swans House Party in Morlialp. All these House Party arrangments are included in the price of your holiday. Welcome party on arrival. Afternoon tea and cake for 7 days. Swiss dinner by candlelight. Fondue party. Yodler evening. Chali farewell party in the 'Alphütte Bar'. Service of representative.

Alongside on the same page there was a special note about ski-packs. 'Hire of Skis, Sticks and Boots . . . Ski Tuition . . . 12 days £11.10'.

In August 1969, on the faith of that brochure, Mr Jarvis booked a 15-day holiday, with ski-pack. The total charge was £63.45, including Christmas supplement. He was to fly from Gatwick to Zurich on December 20, 1969, and return on January 3, 1970.

The plaintiff went on the holiday, but he was very disappointed. He was a man of about 35 and he expected to be one of a house party of some 30 or so people. Instead, he found there were only 13 during the first week. In the second week there was no house party at all. He was the only person there. Mr Weibel could not speak English. So there was Mr Jarvis, in the second week, in this hotel with no house party at all, and no one could speak English, except himself. He was very disappointed, too, with the ski-ing. It was some distance away at Giswil. There were no ordinary length skis. There were only mini-skis, about 3 ft. long. So he did not get his ski-ing as he wanted to. In the second week he did get some longer skis for a couple of days, but then, because of the boots, his feet got rubbed and he could not continue even with the long skis. So his ski-ing holiday, from his point of view, was pretty well ruined.

There were many other matters, too. They appear trivial when they are set down in writing, but I have no doubt they loomed large in Mr Jarvis's mind, when coupled with the other disappointments. He did not have the nice Swiss cakes which he was hoping for. The only cakes for tea were potato crisps and little dry nut cakes. The yodler evening consisted of one man from the locality who came in his working clothes for a little while, and sang four or five songs very quickly. The 'Alphütte Bar' was an unoccupied annexe which was only open one evening. There was a representative, Mrs Storr, there during the first week, but she was not there during the second week.

The matter was summed up by the judge: 'During the first week he got a holiday in Switzerland which was to some extent inferior . . . and, as to the second week, he got a holiday which was very largely inferior' to what he was led to expect.

What is the legal position? I think that the statements in the brochure were representations or warranties. The breaches of them give Mr Jarvis a right to damages. It is not necessary to decide whether they were representations or warranties: because since the Misrepresentation Act 1967, there is a remedy in damages for misrepresentation as well as for breach of warranty.

The one question in the case is: What is the amount of damages? The judge seems to have taken the difference in value between what he paid for and what he got. He said that he intended to give 'the difference between the two values and no other damages' under any other head. He thought that Mr Jarvis had got half of what he paid for. So the judge gave him half the amount which he had paid, namely, £31.72. Mr Jarvis appeals to this court. He says that the damages ought to have been much more.

. . .

What is the right way of assessing damages? It has often been said that on a breach of contract damages cannot be given for mental distress. Thus in *Hamlin* v *Great Northern Railway Co.* (1856) 1 H & N 408, 411 Pollock CB said that damages cannot be given 'for the disappointment of mind occasioned by the breach of contract'. And in *Hobbs* v *London & South Western Railway Co.* (1875) LR 10 QB 111, 122, Mellor J said that:

. . . for the mere inconvenience, such as annoyance and loss of temper, or vexation, or for being disappointed in a particular thing which you have set your mind upon, without real physical inconvenience resulting, you cannot recover damages.

The courts in those days only allowed the plaintiff to recover damages if he suffered physical inconvenience, such as having to walk five miles home, as in *Hobbs'* case; or to live in an over-crowded house: *Bailey* v *Bullock* [1950] 2 All ER 1167.

I think that those limitations are out of date. In a proper case damages for mental distress can be recovered in contract, just as damages for shock can be recovered in tort. One such case is a contract for a holiday, or any other contract to provide entertainment and enjoyment. If the contracting party breaks his contract, damages can be given for the disappointment, the distress, the upset and frustration caused by the breach. I know that it is difficult to assess in terms of money, but it is no more difficult than the assessment which the courts have to make every day in personal injury cases for loss of amenities. Take the present case. Mr Jarvis has only a fortnight's holiday in the year. He books it far ahead, and looks forward to it all that time. He ought to be compensated for the loss of it.

A good illustration was given by Edmund Davis LJ in the course of the argument. He put the case of a man who has taken a ticket for Glyndbourne. It is the only night on which he can get there. He hires a car to take him. The car does not turn up. His damages are not limited to the mere cost of the ticket. He is entitled to general damages for the disappointment he has suffered and the loss of the entertainment which he should have had. Here, Mr Jarvis's fortnight's winter holiday has been a grave disappointment. It is true that he was conveyed to Switzerland and back and had meals and bed in the hotel. But that is not what he went for. He went to enjoy himself with all the facilities which the defendants said he would have. He is entitled to damages for the lack of those facilities, and for his loss of enjoyment.

A similar case occurred in 1951. It was *Stedman* v *Swan's Tours* (1951) 95 SJ 727. A holiday-maker was awarded damages because he did not get the bedroom and the accommodation which he was promised. The county court judge awarded him £13.15. This court increased it to £50.

I think the judge was in error in taking the sum paid for the holiday £63.45 and halving it. The right measure of damages is to compensate him for the loss of entertainment and enjoyment which he was promised, and which he did not get.

Looking at the matter quite broadly, I think the damages in this case should be the sum of £125. I would allow the appeal, accordingly.

Edmund Davies and Stephenson LJJ concurred.

BLISS v SOUTH EAST THAMES REGIONAL HEALTH AUTHORITY
[1985] IRLR 308 (CA)

The plaintiff sought damages for 'frustration and mental distress' in action for wrongful dismissal from his post as a consultant orthopaedic surgeon.

DILLON LJ: . . . It remains to consider the final point on the cross-appeal, viz the validity of the judge's award of £2,000 with interest by way of general damages for frustration and mental distress. In making such an award, the learned judge considered that he was justified by the decision of Mr Justice Lawson in *Cox* v *Philips Industries Ltd* [1975] IRLR 344. With every respect to them, however, the views of Mr Justice Lawson in that case and of the learned judge in the present case are on this point, in my judgment, wrong.

The general rule laid down by the House of Lords in *Addis* v *Gramophone Company Ltd* [1909] AC 488 is that where damages fall to be assessed for breach of contract rather than in tort it is not permissible to award general damages for frustration, mental distress, injured feelings or annoyance occasioned by the breach. Modern thinking tends to be that the amount of damages recoverable for a wrong should be the same whether the cause of action is laid in contract or in tort. But in *Addis* Lord Loreburn regarded the rule that damages for injured feelings cannot be recovered in contact for wrongful dismissal as too inveterate to be altered, and Lord James of Hereford supported his concurrence in the speech of Lord Loreburn by reference to his own experience at the Bar.

There are exceptions now recognised where the contract which has been broken was itself a contract to provide peace of mind or freedom from distress. See *Jarvis* v *Swans*

Tours Ltd [1973] QB 233 and *Heywood* v *Wellers* [1976] QB 446. Those decisions, as decisions, do not however cover this present case.

In *Cox* v *Philips Industries Ltd* Mr Justice Lawson took the view that damages for distress, vexation and frustration, including consequent ill-health, could be recovered for breach of a contract of employment if it could be said to have been in the contemplation of the parties that the breach would cause such distress etc. For my part, I do not think that the general approach is open to this court unless and until the House of Lords has reconsidered its decision in *Addis*.

Cumming Bruce LJ, and Heilbron J concurred.

7.1.2.4 Damages for loss suffered by third parties

JACKSON v *HORIZON HOLIDAYS LTD* [1975] 1 WLR 1468 (CA)

Could a father, who had booked and paid for a disastrous family holiday, claim damages for the distress and disappointment of the rest of the family?

LORD DENNING MR: Mr Jackson is a young man, in his mid-twenties. He has been very successful in his business. He is married with three small children. In November 1970 there were twin boys of three years of age; and his wife had just had her third child. He had been working very hard. They determined to have a holiday in the sun. He decided upon Ceylon. He inquired of Horizon Holidays Ltd. He made arrangements with their agent, a Mrs Bremner, for a holiday at a hotel, the Pegasus Reef Hotel, Hendala Point, Ceylon. He wrote them a letter which shows that he wanted everything of the highest standard:

> With reference to our telephone conversation would you please confirm that you can arrange for my wife myself and my two twin boys aged three years to stay for 28 days from January 23 at the Hotel Pegasus Reef, Hendala Point, Ceylon. Would you also arrange that the children's room has an adjoining door to our room; this is essential and is a condition of me booking this holiday. Would you please make sure that the balcony is facing the sea and would you also confirm the distance the hotel is from the sea. Would you confirm that the meals are four course with a choice of three or four dishes to each course. Could you confirm that there have been arrangements made that an English speaking doctor would call on the hotel if needed. Would you please make a clear answer to all these questions appreciating that you might have difficulties in answering some of these questions and not to send an evasive answer to any of these questions.

He spoke on the telephone to Mrs Bremner. She led him to believe that the hotel would come up to his expectations. She wrote on the booking form:

> 'Remarks Twins' room with connecting door essential. Total charge £1432.

He sent it in and booked the holiday.

In the middle of January it was discovered that the Pegasus Reef Hotel would not be ready in time. So Horizon Holidays recommended a substitute. This was Brown's Beach Hotel. It was described in the advertisement as being

> superbly situated right on the beach, with all facilities for an enjoyable holiday including mini-golf, excellent restaurant, cocktail lounge, and gift shop. . . . The bedrooms are well furnished and equipped in modern style. *All rooms have private bath, shower, w.c., sea view and air-conditioning.*

Mr Jackson had some hesitation about this other hotel. But Horizon Holidays assured him that it would be up to his expectation. So Mr Jackson accepted it. But Horizon Holidays reduced the charge. Instead of the price being the total sum of £1,432 it would, because of the change of hotel, be £1,200. That included air travel to Ceylon and back and a holiday for four weeks. So they went there. The courier, Miss Redgrove, met them and took them to the Brown's Beach Hotel. But they were greatly disappointed. Their room had not got a connecting door with the room for the children at all. The room for the children was mildewed – black with mildew, at the bottom. There was fungus growing on the walls. The toilet was stained. The shower was dirty. There was no bath. They could not let the children sleep in the room. So for the first three days they had all the family in one room. The two children were put into one of the single beds and the two adults slept in the other single bed. After the first three days they were moved into what was said to be one of the best suites in the hotel. Even then they had to put the children to sleep in the sitting room and the parents in the bedroom. There was dirty linen on the bed. There was no private bath but only a shower; no mini-golf course; no swimming pool; no beauty salon; no hairdressers' salon. Worst of all was the cooking. There was no choice of dishes. On some occasions, however, curry was served as an alternative to the main dish. They found the food was very distasteful. It appeared to be cooked in coconut oil. There was a pervasive taste because of the manner of cooking. They were so uncomfortable at Brown's Beach Hotel that after a fortnight they moved to the Pegasus Reef Hotel. It appears that by that time it was nearing completion. But a lot of building work was still going on. At any rate, for the second fortnight they were in the Pegasus Reef Hotel, where things were somewhat better than at Brown's Beach Hotel. They stayed out for the four weeks, and came home.

Soon after their return, Mr Jackson wrote a letter setting out all his complaints from the beginning to the end. Then Mr Jackson brought an action for damages in respect of the loss of his holiday for himself, his wife and the two small children. Horizon Holidays admitted liability. The contest was only on the amount of damages.

In *Jarvis* v *Swans Tours Ltd* [1973] QB 233, it was held by this court that damages for the loss of a holiday may include not only the difference in value between what was promised and what was obtained, but also damages for mental distress, inconvenience, upset, disappointment and frustration caused by the loss of the holiday. The judge directed himself in accordance with the judgments in that case. He eventually awarded a sum of £1,100. Horizon Holidays Ltd appeal. They say it was far too much.

The judge did not divide up the £1,000. Counsel has made suggestions about it. Mr Cheyne for Horizon Holidays suggests that the judge gave £100 for diminution in value and £1,000 for the mental distress. But Mr Davies for Mr Jackson suggested that the judge gave £600 for the diminution in value and £500 for the mental distress. If I were inclined myself to speculate, I think Mr Davies' suggestion may well be right. The judge took the cost of the holidays at £1,200. The family only had about half the value of it. Divide it by two and you get £600. Then add £500 for the mental distress.

On this question a point of law arises. The judge said that he could only consider the mental distress to Mr Jackson himself, and that he could not consider the distress to his wife and children. He said:

> The damages are the plaintiff's. . . . I cannot consider the effect upon his mind of the wife's discomfort, vexation, and the like, although I cannot award a sum which represents her own vexation.

Mr Davies, for Mr Jackson, disputes that proposition. He submits that damages can be given not only for the leader of the party – in this case, Mr Jackson's own distress, discomfort and vexation – but also for that of the rest of the party.

We have had an interesting discussion as to the legal position when one person makes a contract for the benefit of a party. In this case it was a husband making a contract for the benefit of himself, his wife and children. Other cases readily come to mind. A host makes a contract with a restaurant for a dinner for himself and his friends. The vicar makes a contract for a coach trip for the choir. In all these cases there is only one person who makes the contract. It is the husband, the host or the vicar, as the case may be. Sometimes he pays the whole price himself. Occasionally he may get a contribution from the others. But in any case it is he who makes the contract. It would be a fiction to say that the contract was made by all the family, or all the guests, or all the choir, and that he was only an agent for them. Take this very case. It would be absurd to say that the twins of three years old were parties to the contract or that the father was making the contract on their behalf as if they were principals. It would equally be a mistake to say that in any of these instances there was a trust. The transaction bears no resemblance to a trust. There was no trust fund and no trust property. No, the real truth is that in each instance, the father, the host or the vicar, was making a contract himself for the benefit of the whole party. In short, a contract by one for the benefit of third persons.

What is the position when such a contract is broken? At present the law says that the only one who can sue is the one who made the contract. None of the rest of the party can sue, even though the contract was made for their benefit. But when that one does sue, what damages can he recover? Is he limited to his own loss? Or can he recover for the others? Suppose the holiday firm puts the family into a hotel which is only half built and the visitors have to sleep on the floor? Or suppose the restaurant is fully booked and the guests have to go away, hungry and angry, having spent so much on fares to get there? Or suppose the coach leaves the choir stranded halfway and they have to hire cars to get home? None of them individually can sue. Only the father, the host or the vicar can sue. He can, of course, recover his own damages. But can he not recover for the others? I think he can. The case comes within the principle stated by Lush LJ in *Lloyd's v Harper* (1880) 16 ChD 290, 321:

> I consider it to be an established rule of law that where a contract is made with A for the benefit of B, A can sue on the contract for the benefit of B, and recover all that B could have recovered if the contract had been made with B himself.

It has been suggested that Lush LJ was thinking of a contract in which A was trustee for B. But I do not think so. He was a common lawyer speaking of common law. His words were quoted with considerable approval by Lord Pearce in *Beswick v Beswick* [1968] AC 58, 88. I have myself often quoted them. I think they should be accepted as correct, at any rate so long as the law forbids the third person themselves from suing for damages. It is the only way in which a just result can be achieved. Take the instance I have put. The guests ought to recover from the restaurant their wasted fares. The choir ought to recover the cost of hiring the taxis home. Then is no one to recover from them except the one who made the contract for their benefit? He should be able to recover the expense to which he has been put, and pay it over to them. Once recovered, it will be money had and received to their use. (They might even, if desired, be joined as plaintiffs.) If he can recover for the expense, he should also be able to recover for the discomfort, vexation and upset which the whole party have suffered by reason of the breach of contract, recompensing them accordingly out of what he recovers.

Applying the principles to this case, I think that the figure of £1,100 was about right. It would, I think, have been excessive if it had been awarded only for the damage suffered by Mr Jackson himself. But when extended to his wife and children, I do not think it is excessive. People look forward to a holiday. They expect the promises to be fulfilled. When it fails, they are greatly disappointed and upset. It is difficult to assess in terms of money; but it is the task of the judges to do the best they can. I see no reason to interfere with the total award of £1,100. I would therefore dismiss the appeal.

Orr LJ concurred; James LJ came to the same conclusion, but on the basis that the father's own loss was increased by the problems suffered by the rest of the family.

WOODAR INVESTMENT DEVELOPMENT LTD v WIMPEY CONSTRUCTION UK LTD
[1980] 1 All ER 571 (HL)

In this case the House reconsidered the Court of Appeal's decision in *Jackson v Horizon Holidays*.

LORD WILBERFORCE: . . . The second issue in this appeal is one of damages. Both courts below have allowed Woodar to recover substantial damages in respect of condition I under which £150,000 was payable by Wimpey to Transword Trade Ltd on completion. On the view which I take of the repudiation issue, this question does not require decision, but in view of the unsatisfactory state in which the law would be if the Court of Appeal's decision were to stand I must add three observations.

1.   The majority of the Court of Appeal followed, in the case of Goff LJ with expressed reluctance, its previous decision in *Jackson v Horizon Holidays Ltd* [1975] 3 All ER 92. I am not prepared to dissent from the actual decision in that case. It may be supported either as a broad decision on the measure of damages (per James LJ) or possibly as an example of a type of contract, examples of which are persons contracting for family holidays, ordering meals in restaurants for a party, hiring a taxi for a group, calling for special treatment. As I suggested in *New Zealand Shipping Co. Ltd v A M Satterthwaite & Co. Ltd* [1974] 1 All ER 1015, there are many situations of daily life which do not fit neatly into conceptual analysis, but which require some flexibility in the law of contract. *Jackson's* case may well be one.

I cannot agree with the basis on which Lord Denning MR put his decision in that case. The extract on which he relied from the judgment of Lush LJ in *Lloyd's v Harper* (1880) 16 ChD 290 was part of a passage in which Lush LJ was stating as an 'established rule of law' that an agent (sc an insurance broker) may sue on a contract made by him on behalf of the principal (sc the assured) if the contract gives him such a right, and is no authority for the proposition required in *Jackson's* case, still less for the proposition, required here, that if Woodar made a contract for a sum of money to be paid to Transworld, Woodar can, without showing that it has itself suffered loss or that Woodar was agent or trustee for Transworld, sue for damages for non-payment of that sum. That would certainly not be an established rule of law, nor was it quoted as such authority by Lord Pearce in *Beswick v Beswick* [1967] 2 All ER 1197.

2.   Assuming that *Jackson's* case was correctly decided (as above), it does not carry the present case, where the factual situation is quite different. I respectfully think therefore that the Court of Appeal need not, and should not have followed it.

3.   Whether in a situation such as the present, viz where it is not shown that Woodar was agent or trustee for Transworld, or that Woodar itself sustained any loss, Woodar can recover any damages at all, or any but nominal damages, against Wimpey, and on what principle, is, in my opinion, a question of great doubt and difficulty, no doubt open in this House, but one on which I prefer to reserve my opinion.

. . .

LORD RUSSELL: . . . There is no question on this appeal as to quantum of damage save under the heading of damages for breach of special condition I, under which Wimpey agreed on completion of the sale to pay £150,000 to Transworld, a Hong Kong company. Transworld was in some way connected with Mr Cornwell, who died before action. No evidence connects Transworld with Woodar, the party to the contract. No evidence suggests that Woodar could suffer any damage from a failure by Wimpey to pay £150,000 to Transworld. It is clear on the authority of *Beswick v Beswick* that Woodar on completion could have secured an order for specific performance of the agreement to pay £150,000 to Transworld, which the latter could have enforced. That would not have been an order for payment to Woodar, nor (contrary to the form of order below) to Woodar for the use and benefit of Transworld. There was no suggestion of trust or agency of Woodar for Transworld. If it were necessary to decide the point, which in the light of the views of the majority of your Lordships on the first point it is not, I would have concluded that no more than nominal damages had been established by Woodar as a consequence of the refusal by Wimpey to pay Transworld in the light of the law of England as it now stands. I would not have thought that the reasoning of Oliver J in *Radford v De Froberville* [1978] 1 All ER 33 suppported Woodar's case for substantial damages. Nor do I think that on this point the Court of Appeal was correct in thinking it was constrained by *Jackson v Horizon Holidays Ltd* to award substantial damages. I do not criticize the outcome of that case: the plaintiff had bought and paid for a high class family holiday; he did not get it, and therefore he was entitled to substantial damages for the failure to supply *him* with one. It is to be observed that the order of the Court of Appeal as drawn up did not suggest that any part of the damages awarded to him were 'for the use and benefit of' any member of his family. It was a special case quite different from the instant case on the Transworld point.

I would not, my Lords, wish to leave the *Jackson* case without adverting with respectful disapproval to the reliance there placed by Lord Denning MR, not for the first time, on an extract taken from the judgment of Lush LJ in *Lloyd's* v *Harper* (1880) 16 ChD 290. That case was plainly a case in which a trustee or agent was enforcing the rights of a beneficiary or principal, there being therefore a fiduciary relationship. Lord Denning MR in *Jackson'* case said this:

> The case comes within the principle stated by Lush LJ in *Lloyd's* v *Harper*: . . . I consider it to be an established rule of law that where a contract is made with A for the benefit of B, A can sue on the contract for the benefit of B, and recover all that B could have recovered if the contract had been made with B himself. [Lord Denning continued:] It has been suggested that Lush LJ was thinking of a contract in which A was trustee for B. But I do not think so. He was a common lawyer speaking of the common law.

I have already indicated that in all the other judgments the matter proceeded on a fiduciary relationship between A and B; and Lush LJ in the same passage made it plain that he did also, for he said:

> It is true that the person [B] who employed him [the broker A] has a right, if he pleases, to take action himself and sue upon the contract made by the broker for him, for he [B] *is a principal party to the contract*. (Emphasis mine).

To ignore that passage is to divorce the passage quoted by Lord Denning MR from the fiduciary context in which it was uttered, the context of principal and agent, a field with which it may be assumed Lush LJ was familiar. I venture to suggest that the brief quotation should not be used again as support for a proposition which Lush LJ cannot have intended to advance. . . .

7.1.3 MITIGATION OF LOSS

BRACE v *CALDER* [1895] 2 QB 253 (CA)

LOPES LJ: This is a case of some difficulty, and it appears to me to be material to refer briefly to the terms of the agreement between the plaintiff and the defendants. By the terms of that agreement the plaintiff was, for the term of two years from November 1, 1892, to be the manager of the office part of the business of Scotch whisky merchants, carried on in the city of London and surrounding districts by the defendants, who were a firm consisting of four partners, and he was to receive for his services as and from November 1, 1892, the salary of 300*l.* payable monthly, together with all travelling expenses incurred by him not exceeding 25*l.* for each period of three months in each year of the engagement. It was provided by clause 5 of the agreement that the employers should be at liberty to terminate the agreement at any time during the period of two years on giving to the plaintiff one calendar month's previous notice in writing of their desire so to do, but should in such case pay to him a sum equivalent to the salary he would have received if he had been retained as manager for the full period of two years from November 1, 1892. Before the two years for which the agreement was to last had expired, two of the partners retired, the other two continuing to carry on business. Till July, 1893, the plaintiff continued to act as manager, not knowing of the change. The continuing partners were then willing to retain him in their service on the same terms as before; but he declined to serve them. The plaintiff claims in this action his whole salary for the remainder of the period of two years mentioned in the agreement. The question is, what was the effect of the dissolution of partnership? Did it operate as a wrongful dismissal of the plaintiff or a breach of the contract between the plaintiff and the defendants? There is authority to the effect that by the death of one of a firm of masters the servant is discharged unless the contrary is stipulated by the terms of the contract: see *Hoey* v *McEwan* 5 Court Sess Cas 3rd Series 814 and *Tasker* v *Shepherd* 6 H & N 575. I express no opinion, however, on the question what effect the death of one of the partners would have had. What took place here was that there was a dissolution of partnersip by reason of the retirement of two of the partners, and the business was transferred to the other two who continued to carry on business. That seems to me a stronger case than that of the death of a partner, and, according to my view, it constituted either a wrongful dismissal of the plaintiff or a breach of the contract to employ him for two years. I do not know that it matters much for the purposes of this case in which way it is put. There is nothing in this agreement which indicates that in any event, except that mentioned in clause 5, the employment was not to be for the period of two years. On the contrary the provision contained in clause 5 of the agreement appears to me strong to shew that there was an express agreement to employ the plaintiff for two years. It appears to me therefore that the plaintiff was discharged by the defendants and was entitled to damages either on the ground that he was wrongfully discharged, or that there was a breach of a contract to employ him for two years. But, in estimating the damages, it must be taken into consideration that the continuing partners were willing to keep him on in their service till the end of the two years at the same salary as before; but he declined to serve them, and therefore it was his own fault that he suffered any loss. Consequently, the damages resulting from the breach of contract would be nominal. It is true that, as the Master of the Rolls has pointed out, he did continue to serve till the end of July, and would have been entitled to claim for that service; but the action was not brought in respect of that. If it had been, the defendants might have paid into court a sum sufficient to cover that claim. Therefore I do not think that the plaintiff is entitled now to avail himself of it. In the result I am of opinion that there was a breach of the agreement; but the plaintiff is only entitled to nominal damages in respect of it, because in point of fact he did not suffer any loss through it; and the appeal must therefore be allowed and judgment entered for the plaintiff, but only for nominal damages, and with the result as to costs mentioned by the Master of the Rolls.

Rigby LJ concurred; Lord Esher MR dissented

7.1.3.1   Mitigation of loss and anticipatory breach

WHITE & CARTER (COUNCILS) LTD v MCGREGOR [1962] AC 413 (HL)

LORD REID: My Lords, the pursuers supply to local authorities litter bins which are placed in the streets. They are allowed to attach to these receptacles plates carrying advertisements, and they make their profit from payments made to them by the advertisers. The defender carried on a garage in Clydebank and in 1954 he made an agreement with the pursuers under which they displayed advertisements of his business on a number of these bins. In June, 1957, his sales manager made a further contract with the pursuers for the display of these advertisements for a further period of three years. The sales manager had been given no specific authority to make this contract and when the defender heard of it later on the same day he at once wrote to the pursuers to cancel the contract. The pursuers refused to accept this cancellation. They prepared the necessary plates for attachment to the bins and exhibited them on the bins from November 2, 1957, onwards.

The defender refused to pay any sums due under the contract and the pursuers raised the present action in the Sheriff Court craving payment of £196 4s. the full sum due under the contract for the period of three years. After sundry procedure the Sheriff-Substitute on March 15, 1960, dismissed the action. He held that the sales manager's action in renewing the contract was within his apparent or ostensible authority and that is not now disputed. The ground on which he dismissed the action was that in the circumstances an action for implement of the contract was inappropriate. He relied on the decision in *Langford & Co. Ltd* v *Dutch* 1952 SC 15, and cannot be criticised for having done so.

The pursuers appealed to the Court of Session and on November 2, 1960, the Second Division refused the appeal. The present appeal is taken against their interlocutor of that date. That interlocutor sets out detailed findings of fact and, as this case began in the Sheriff Court, we cannot look beyond those findings. The pursuers must show that on those findings they are entitled to the remedy which they seek.

The case for the defender (now the respondent) is that, as he repudiated the contract before anything had been done under it, the appellants were not entitled to go on and carry out the contract and sue for the contract price: he maintains that in the circumstances the appellants' only remedy was damages, and that, as they do not sue for damages, this action was rightly dismissed.

The contract was for the display of advertisements for a period of 156 weeks from the date when the display began. This date was not specified but admittedly the display began on November 2, 1957, which seems to have been the date when the former contract came to an end. The payment stipulated was 2s. per week per plate together with 5s. per annum per plate both payable annually in advance, the first payment being due seven days after the first display. The reason why the appellants sued for the whole sum due for the three years is to be found in clause 8 of the conditions: 'In the event of an instalment or part thereof being due for payment, and remaining unpaid for a period of four weeks or in the event of the advertiser being in any way in breach of this contract then the whole amount due for the 156 weeks or such part of the said 156 weeks as the advertiser shall not yet have paid shall immediately become due and payable'.

A question was debated whether this clause provides a penalty or liquidated damages, but on the view which I take of the case it need not be pursued. The clause merely provides for acceleration of payment of the stipulated price if the advertiser fails to pay an instalment timeously. As the respondent maintained that he was not bound by the contract he did not pay the first instalment within the time allowed. Accordingly, if the appellants were entitled to carry out their part of the contract notwithstanding the respondent's repudiation, it was hardly disputed that this clause entitled them to sue immediately for the whole price and not merely the first instalment.

The general rule cannot be in doubt. It was settled in Scotland at least as early as 1848 and it has been authoritatively stated time and again in both Scotland and England. If one party to a contract repudiates it in the sense of making it clear to the other party that he refuses or will refuse to carry out his part of the contract, the other party, the innocent party, has an option. He may accept that repudiation and sue for damages for breach of contract whether or not the time for performance has come; or he may if he chooses disregard or refuse to accept it and then the contract remains in full effect. . . .

I need not refer to the numerous authorities. They are not disputed by the respondent but he points out that in all of them the party who refused to accept the repudiation had no active duties under the contract. The innocent party's option is generally said to be to *wait* until the date of performance and then to claim damages estimated as at that date. There is no case in which it is said that he may, in face of the repudiation, go on and incur useless expense in performing the contract and then claim the contract price. The option, it is argued, is merely as to the date as at which damages are to be assessed.

Developing this argument, the respondent points out that in most cases the innocent party cannot complete the contract himself without the other party doing, allowing or accepting something, and that it is purely fortuitous that the appellants can do so in this case. In most cases by refusing co-operation the party in breach can compel the innocent party to restrict his claim to damages. Then it was said that, even where the innocent party can complete the contract without such co-operation, it is against the public interest that he should be allowed to do so. An example was developed in argument. A company might engage an expert to go abroad and prepare an elaborate report and then repudiate the contract before anything was done. To allow such an expert then to waste thousands of pounds in preparing the report cannot be right if a much smaller sum of damages would give him full compensation for his loss. It would merely enable the expert to extort a settlement giving him far more than reasonable compensation.

The respondent founds on the decision of the First Division in *Langford & Co. Ltd v Dutch* 1952 SC 15. There an advertising contractor agreed to exhibit a film for a year. Four days after this agreement was made the advertiser repudiated it but, as in the present case, the contractor refused to accept the repudiation and proceeded to exhibit the film and sue for the contract price. The Sheriff-Substitute dismissed the action as irrelevant and his decision was affirmed on appeal. In the course of a short opinion Lord President Cooper said: 'It appears to me that, apart from wholly exceptional circumstances of which there is no trace in the averments on this record, the law of Scotland does not afford to a person in the position of the pursuers the remedy which is here sought. The pursuers could not force the defender to accept a year's advertisement which she did not want, though they could of course claim damages for her breach of contract. On the averments the only reasonable and proper course, which the pursuers should have adopted, would have been to treat the defender as having repudiated the contract and as being on that account liable in damages, the measure of which we are, of course, not in a position to discuss.'

The Lord President cited no authority and I am in doubt as to what principle he had in mind. In the earlier part of the passage which I have quoted he speaks of forcing the defender to accept the advertisement. Of course, if it had been necessary for the defender to do or accept anything before the contract could be completed by the pursuers, the pursuers could not and the court would not have compelled the defender to act, the contract would not have been completed and the pursuers' only remedy would have been damages. But the peculiarity in that case, as in the present case, was that the pursuers could completely fulfil the contract without any co-operation of the defender. The Lord President cannot have meant that because of non-acceptance the contract had not been completely carried out, because that in itself would have been a complete answer to an action for the contract price. He went on to say that the only reasonable and proper course which the pursuers should have adopted would have been to treat the defender as having repudiated the contract, which must, I think, mean to have accepted the repudiation. It is this reference to 'the only reasonable and proper course' which I find difficult to explain. It might be, but it never has been, the law that a person is only entitled to enforce his contractual rights in a reasonable way, and that a court will not support an attempt to enforce them in an unreasonable way. One reason why that is not the law is, no doubt, because it was thought that it would create too much uncertainty to require the court to decide whether it is reasonable or equitable to allow a party to enforce his full rights under a contract. The Lord President cannot have meant that.

The only principle I can think of which he may have had in mind is the principle invoked by Lord Watson in a well-known passage at the beginning of his speech in *Grahame* v *Magistrates of Kirkcaldy* (1882) 9 R (HL) 91: 'It appears to me that a superior court, having equitable jurisdiction, must also have a discretion, in certain exceptional cases, to withhold from parties applying for it that remedy to which, in ordinary circumstances, they would be entitled as a matter of course.' But Lord Watson went on to say 'In order to justify the exercise of such a discretionary power there must be some very cogent reason for depriving litigants of the ordinary means of enforcing their legal rights. There are, so far as I know, only three decided cases, in which the Court of Session, there being no facts sufficient to raise a plea in bar of the action, have nevertheless denied to the pursuer the remedy to which, in strict law, he was entitled. These authorities seem to establish, if that were necessary, the proposition that the court has the power of declining, upon equitable grounds, to enforce an admittedly legal right; but they also show that the power has been very rarely exercised.'

Langford & Co. Ltd v *Dutch* is indistinguishable from the present case. Quite properly the Second Division followed it in this case as a binding authority and did not develop Lord Cooper's reasoning: they were not asked to send this case to a larger court. We must now decide whether that case was rightly decided. In my judgment it was not. It could only be supported on one or other of two grounds. It might be said that, because in most cases the circumstances are such that an innocent party is unable to complete the contract and earn the contract price without the assent or co-operation of the other party, therefore in cases where he can do so he should not be allowed to do so. I can see no justification for that.

The other ground would be that there is some general equitable principle or element of public policy which requires this limitation of the contractual rights of the innocent party. It may well be that, if it can be shown that a person has no legitimate interest, financial or otherwise, in performing the contract rather than claiming damages, he ought not to be allowed to saddle the other party with an additional burden with no benefit to himself. If a party has no interest to enforce a stipulation, he cannot in general enforce it: so it might be said that, if a party has no interest to insist on a particular remedy, he ought not to be allowed to insist on it. And, just as a party is not allowed to enforce a penalty, so he ought not to be allowed to penalise the other party by taking one course when another is equally advantageous to him. If I may revert to the example which I gave of a company engaging an expert to pepare an elaborate report and then repudiating before anything was done, it might be that the company could show that the expert had no substantial or legitimate interest in carrying out the work rather than accepting damages: I would think that the *de minimis* principle would apply in determining whether his interest was substantial, and that he might have a legitimate interest other than an immediate financial interest. But if the expert had no such interest then that might be regarded as a proper case for the exercise of the general equitable jurisdiction of the court. But that is not this case. Here the respondent did not set out to prove that the appellants had no legitimate interest in completing the contract and claiming the contract price rather than claiming damages; there is nothing in the findings of fact to support such a case, and it seems improbable that any such case could have been proved. It is, in my judgment, impossible to say that the appellants should be deprived of their right to claim the contract price merely because the benefit to them, as against claiming damages and re-letting their advertising space, might be small in comparison with the loss to the respondent: that is the most that could be said in favour of the respondent. Parliament has on many occasions relieved parties from certain kinds of improvident or oppressive contracts, but the common law can only do that in very limited circumstances. Accordingly, I am unable to avoid the conclusion that this appeal must be allowed and the case remitted so that decree can be pronounced as craved in the initial writ.

Lords Tucker and Hodson concurred; Lords Morton and Keith dissented.

ATTICA SEA CARRIERS CORPORATION v FERROSTAL POSEIDON BULK REEDEREI GMBH, THE PUERTO BUITRAGO [1976] 1 Lloyd's Rep 250 (CA)

LORD DENNING MR: This is an urgent case. A vessel – the *Puerto Buitrago* – is lying at Kiel with only a caretaker on board. She was let on a bareboat charter, which expired three months ago. She is out of repair. So much so that it would cost more to repair her than she is worth, even after the repairs have been done. The cost of repairs is said to be *twice* as much as her value when repaired. The shipowners say that it is the charterer's duty to repair her, whatever the cost, and that the charterers must pay the charter hire until she is repaired, even to the crack of doom. The charterers say that that is absurd; and that they are entitled to hand her back to the shipowners at this very moment, just as she is, out of repair: and that the shipowners should sell her for what they can get. The shipowners, they say, can get damages for the delivery up out of repair, but not the charter hire. . . .

The fourth question is as to the remedy available to the shipowners. Are they entitled to sue for the charter hire month by month for every month during which the charterers do not execute the repairs, no matter how long that may be? This question assumes that the charterers are in breach of the contract in two ways: (i) by not repairing the vessel; (ii) by attempting to redeliver her when out of repair. I do not think in the circumstances it amounts to frustration, even though it would be economic nonsense to go to the expense of repairing her. But the breach may be said to go to the root of the contract – a repudiatory beach if you like to call it so. And the fourth question asks: are the shipowners bound to accept that repudiation and treat the charter as at an end? Or, can they ignore it, and sue for the charter hire until such time – if ever – as the repairs are done?

The shipowners naturally relied on the decision of the House of Lords in *White & Carter Ltd* v *McGregor* [1962] AC 413. White & Carter were advertising agents, who put small advertising plates onto litter bins. They got Mr McGregor's manager to sign a printed form entitling them to put these small advertisements on the litter bins for three years at a weekly payment. The manager had no actual authority to make a contract. A day or two later, when Mr McGregor got to know of it, he at once cancelled the contract. The advertising agents took no notice but went on to incur the expenditure. It would be just the same as if Mr McGregor had given up his business. They put up the useless advertisements and sued for the full amount. The House of Lords, by a majority of three to two, held that they were entitled to do so. The decision has been criticized in a leading textbook (Cheshire & Fifoot, pp. 600 and 601). It is said to give a 'grotesque' result. Even though it was a Scots case, it would appear that the House of Lords, as at present constituted, would expect us to follow it in any case that is precisely on all fours with it. But I would not follow it otherwise. It has no application whatever in a case where the plaintiff ought, in all reason, to accept the repudiation and sue for damages – provided that damages would provide an adequate remedy for any loss suffered by him.

The reason is because, by suing for the money, the plaintiff is seeking to enforce specific performance of the contract – and he should not be allowed to do so when damages would be an adequate remedy. Take a servant, who has a contract for six months certain, but is dismissed after one month. He cannot sue for his wages for each of the six months by alleging that he was ready and willing to serve. His only remedy is damages. Take a finance company which lets a machine or motor-car on hire purchase, but the hirer refuses to accept it. The finance company cannot sue each month for the instalments. Its only remedy is in damages: see *National Cash Register Co.* v *Stanley* [1921] 3 KB 292; *Karsales (Harrow)* v *Wallis* [1956] 1 WLR 936 (2nd point). So here, when the charterers tendered redelivery at the end of the period of the charter – in breach of the contract to repair – the shipowners ought in all reason to have accepted it. They cannot sue for specific performance – either of the promise to pay the charter hire, or of the promise to do the repairs – because damages are an adequate remedy for the breach. What is the alternative which the shipowners present to the charterers? Either the charterers must pay the charter hire for years to come, whilst the vessel lies idle and useless for want of repair. *Or* the charterers must do repairs which would cost twice as much as the ship would be worth when repaired – after which the shipowners might sell it as scrap, making the repairs a useless waste of money. In short, on either alternative, the shipowners seek to compel specific performance of one or other of the provisions of the charter – with most unjust and unreasonable consequences – when damages would be an adequate remedy. I do not think the law allows them to do this. I think they should accept redelivery and sue for damages. The charterers are, we are told, good for the money. That should suffice.

Orr and Browne LJJ concurred.

GATOR SHIPPING CORPORATION v *TRANS-ASIATIC OIL LTD SA, THE 'ODENFELD'*
[1978] 2 Lloyd's Rep 357 (QB)

KERR J: . . . *Issue III (obligation to accept defendants' repudiation):*
   Whether, on the assumption that the defendants repudiated the charter-party, the defendants' plea that Occidental ought to have accepted the defendants' repudiation, and that thereafter the only liability of the defendants was in respect of damages, is correct: and, if so, when the repudiation ought to have been accepted.
   It is common ground that if Occidental did not repudiate the charter, as I have held in issue I, then the defendants repudiated it on or about January 6, 1976. The defendants contend that Occidental thereupon came under a duty to accept the repudiation and to treat the charter as at an end; they contend that this was the only reasonable course for Occidental to take in the circumstances. They say that thereafter Occidental were not entitled to elect to hold the defendants to the charter, that the charter must therefore be deemed to have come to an end on January 6, 1976, and that the plaintiffs accordingly cannot thereafter sue as assignees of the hire.
   But for the decision of the Court of Appeal in *Attica Sea Carriers Corporation* v *Ferrostaal Poseideon Bulk Reederei GmbH* [1976] 1 Lloyd's Rep 250, I doubt whether this issue would have been raised by the defendants. It is necessary to consider this decision against the background of other authorities and of the facts on which it was based.
   A number of other cases were cited in argument, but I think that I need only refer to two earlier authorities. The first is the decision of the House of Lords by a majority of 3 to 2 in *White and Carter (Councils) Ltd* v *McGregor* [1962] AC 413. The appellants were advertising contractors who had contracted with the respondent, a garage proprietor, to display advertisements over a period of three years. On the day when the contract had been concluded the respondent wrote to say that there had been a mistake and required the appellants to cancel the contract. They refused, and began the display of advertisements some five months later. The respondent refused to pay and the appellants then sued him for the whole sum due under the contract, as they were entitled to do if the contract was still alive. The respondent contended that the appellants were not entitled to treat the contract as remaining in force after he had required it to be cancelled, but only to sue for such damages as they might be able to establish. In the view of the majority of their Lordships this contention failed, and the appellants succeeded. I should

mention that the defendants before me expressly reserved the right, if necessary, to ask their Lordships' House to reconsider this decision if the present case should go there.

I do not propose to analyse the speeches in detail. The main divergence of views is to be found in the speech of Lord Hodson, with which Lord Tucker agreed, on the one hand, and the speeches of Lord Morton and Lord Keith on the other. The former were of the view that the innocent party, to use the convenient term, has an unfettered right to elect to keep the contract alive against the party in repudiation, unless he can only do so by invoking the assistance of the Court for an order of specific performance which the Court might then refuse under its equitable jurisdiction: see Lord Hodson at p. 445. The following passage on the same page is worth quoting in the context of the *Attica Sea Carriers* decision:

> There is no duty laid upon a party to a subsisting contract to vary it at the behest of the other party so as to deprive himself of the benefit given to him by the contract. To hold otherwise would be to introduce a novel equitable doctrine that a party was not to be held to his contract unless the court in a given instance thought it reasonable so to do. In this case it would make an action for debt a claim for a discretionary remedy.

Lord Morton and Lord Keith took an opposite view. They considered that the innocent party's primary remedy for any breach, repudiatory or otherwise, was a claim for damages, and subject to a duty to mitigate any loss suffered by it. They regarded the appellants' claim as being in effect a claim for specific implement or performance which the Court should refuse in the circumstances. Lord Reid adopted something of a middle position while arriving at the same conclusion as Lord Hodson and Lord Tucker. He stated the general rule in unequivocal terms at p. 427 as follows:

> The general rule cannot be in doubt. It was settled in Scotland at least as early as 1848, and it has been authoritatively stated time and again in both Scotland and England. If one party to a contract repudiates it in the sense of making it clear to the other party that he refuses or will refuse to carry out his part of the contract, the other party, the innocent party, has an option. He may accept that repudiation and sue for damages for breach of contract; whether or not the time for performance has come; or he may if he chooses disregard or refuse to accept it and then the contract remains in full effect.

However, at pp. 430 and 431 he envisaged the possibility of an exception to the general rule under 'some general equitable principle or element of public policy' which required limitation of the contractual rights of the innocent part. He said in this context:

> It may well be that, if it can be shown that a person has no legitimate interest, financial or otherwise, in performing the contract rather than claiming damages, he ought not to be allowed to saddle the other party with an additional burden with no benefit to himself. If a party has no interest to enforce a stipulation, he cannot in general enforce it: so it might be said that, if a party has no interest to insist on a particular remedy, he ought not to be allowed to insist on it. And, just as a party is not allowed to enforce a penalty, so he ought not to be allowed to penalise the other party by taking one course when another is equally advantageous to him.

He concluded that this was not the position in that case.

The decision in *White and Carter* was discussed by the Court of Appeal in *Decro-Wall International S A* v *Practitioners in Marketing Ltd* [1971] 1 WLR 361 in the context of a manufacturer/distributor relationship. Lord Justice Salmon (as he then was) and Lords Justices Sachs and Buckley clearly considered that the general rule was that stated in the speech of Lord Hodson and in the earlier of the passages from the speech of Lord Reid which I have cited. They wondered whether the later passage in this speech amounted to more than a restatement of the argument addressed to the House in that case. It would appear to follow from their judgments, at any rate at the level of this Court, that the general rule is not qualified by some 'general equitable principle or element of public policy' to which Lord Reid also referred. They concluded that the fetter on the rights of the innocent party only lay in what the practicalities dictated. But this was clearly not the view of the Court of Appeal in the more recent *Attica Sea Carriers* case which now binds me. The case arose out of facts which were extreme in their nature. It concerned a demise charter for 17 months under which the charterers were bound to redeliver the vessel in good repair. After six months she suffered a series of engine breakdowns which the charterers unsuccessfully attempted to repair. The vessel was then towed to her destination and surveyed. It was estimated that the cost of the repairs would be of the order of $2 million but that her value after the repairs would be only about $1 million. The charterers thereupon purported to redeliver the vessel in an unrepaired state, admitting that in doing so they would be liable in damages, but no doubt contending that on the facts the owners had suffered no loss. The owners contended that they were entitled to refuse to accept the charterers' purported termination of the charter, that the charterers were bound to carry out the repairs, and that hire continued to run until they had done so. The first question was whether on the construction of the charter the charterers were entitled to redeliver the vessel in an unrepaired state subject to a claim for damages, or whether they were bound to carry out the repairs and pay hire meanwhile. This question was answered unanimously in favour of the charterers. But there was a further question which raised the issue whether, if the first question were answered the other way, the owners would have been entitled to hold the charterers to their obligation to carry out the repairs and to claim hire meanwhile. This was also answered unanimously in favour of the charterers and is relevant for present purposes. All three judgments proceeded on the basis that the owners' contention must fail because it amounted to an attempt to enforce the charter by specific performance *and* because, on the extreme facts of that case, it was wholly unreasonable for the owners to seek to hold the charterers to the charter instead of claiming such damages as they could establish. I emphasise the latter part of what I regard as the ratio of the judgments, because I do not regard the case as any authority for a general proposition to the effect that whenever a charterer repudiates a time or demise charter, for whatever reason and in whatever circumstances, the owners are always bound to take the vessel back, because a refusal to do so would be equivalent to seeking an order for specific performance. The consequences of such a proposition would be extremely serious in many cases, and no trace of such a doctrine is to be found in our shipping law. But no such general proposition was laid down. One only has to read the judgment of Lord Denning MR, with which Lords Justices Orr and Browne agreed, to see that his conclusion was based on the extreme facts of the case. In saying this I am in no way belittling the importance of the case insofar as it is a presently binding authority on this court in limiting or qualifying the generality of the principle of a virtually unfettered right of election in favour of the innocent party. This had been stated in the speech of Lord Hodson, and was evidently accepted, subject to the practicalities of the situation, by all three members of the Court of Appeal in the *Decro-Wall* case. It must be accepted in this Court that the generality of this principle is qualified by the later *Attica Sea Carriers* decision, since all three judgments deal with the *White and Carter* case and the *Decro-Wall* case is also expressly referred to in the judgments of Lords Justices Orr and Browne. However, what was decided in the *Attica Sea Carriers* case, to use the language of Lord Justice Orr at the end of his judgment, was that the passages in the judgments in the *Decro-Wall* case did not apply 'in the very different circumstances of this case'. It follows that any fetter on the innocent party's right of election whether or not to accept a repudiation will only be applied in extreme cases, viz, where damages would be an adequate remedy *and* where an election to keep the contract alive would be wholly unreasonable.

In the light of these considerations I then turn to the facts of the present case, which are again entirely different. What was the position on January 6, 1976, when, as I have to assume for this purpose, the defendants wrongfully repudiated the charter? The vessel was at their disposal and there was nothing to prevent or hinder them from giving orders to her and employing her normally under the charter. Indeed, she was employed by the defendants without any difficulty for the two without prejudice voyage charters in May and June. Alternatively, and I regard this as a point of considerable importance, they had the express right to sub-let her or to lay her up at a reduced rate of hire. They were under no obligation to employ her; their only irreducible obligation was to make whatever were the payments due under the charter at any particular time, and to make them to the plantiffs as assignees. I confess that I am not impressed by arguments to the effect that a time or demise charter requires a degree of co-operation between the parties so as to make such charters analogous to contracts for personal services. When the freight market is at one extremity or the other, as at present, there are many and often bitter disputes between charterers and owners which come before the courts; but they do not prevent the operation of the vessels under the charters. Mr Alexander laid some stress on the fact that, if the defendants did not employ the vessel, and did not sub-let her, or lay her up, they would be liable to pay the full hire even though this would probably have been reduced by losses of time due to off-hire periods and under-performance. But the remedy lay entirely in the hands of the defendants; they could employ her, or sub-let her, or lay her up.

What then of Occidental's position? They were bound to the plaintiffs by the loan agreement and the assignment of the charter hire. I must refer to some of their provisions. One of the 'Events of Default' which entitled the plaintiffs to call in the loan at once was the termination of the time charter and the failure of Occidental within 60 days to provide alternative employment for the vessel acceptable to the plaintiffs. In the then state of the market it was clearly impossible to find any comparable employment. Secondly, Occidental were under express covenants to the plaintiffs by virtue of the assignment. These included covenants:

[(a)] to take all necessary steps to procure due performance by the Charterer of its obligations under the charter [– and (b) –] not to take or omit to take any action the taking or omission of which might result in any alteration or employment of the charter or of the assignment or of any of the rights created by the charter or the assignment.

The plaintiffs were at all material times requiring Occidental to hold the defendants to the charter. To have accepted the defendants' repudiation would have involved breaches of these convenants. Then there are other considerations. To have accepted the repudiation would clearly have caused damage to the plaintiffs, who were an entirely innocent party. I do not see how Occidental could reasonably be said to have been under a duty to the defendants, the party in repudiation, to break their contracts with the plantiffs and to cause injury to the plantiffs. Even if the concept of a duty to mitigate damages is relevant in this context, I cannot think for one moment that the duty would go as far as this. The existence of the loan agreement and of the assignment were known to the defendants and had been in the contemplation of both parties from the time when the charter was concluded.

Next, it it is said that a claim for damages would have been an adequate remedy and that this had been assigned to the plaintiffs. In practice, however, this is an oversimplification. In practice it is an extremely difficult and lengthy process to assess damages in a situation such as this. How are they to be fairly assessed, when at the time of the repudiation the charter still had about $6\frac{1}{2}$ years to run with many possible variables in the market rate and the performance of the vessel? Of course, the law provides some answer, but having to establish a claim for damages puts a shipowner into a very different position from that of being entitled to hire under a subsisting charter. In the *Attica Sea Carriers* case the position was quite different. There was no difficulty about the damages, because there were probably none. In the present case the defendants wish to confine Occidental to a claim for damages largely because they wish to be able to say that, because of the funding arrangement in the side letter, Occidental have suffered no damage. They wish to contend, because their ultimate obigation was only to pay the market rate by virtue of the side letter, that there had been no loss. But this again ignores all factors concerning the plaintiffs. In truth, it was equally open to Occidental and to the defendants to employ the vessel on the market. Whether she operated under the charter to the defendants or under a sub-charter made no practical difference to the employment of the ship, her master or crew. It only affected the question of whose agents gave the orders as to her employment. The real question is simply whether, as the result of their assumed repudiation, the defendants are to be relieved from their undertaking to the plaintiffs to pay them the hire due under the charter. To my mind this situation is fundamentally different from anything decided in the *Attica Sea Carriers* case.

Finally, Mr Alexander had two further arguments. He submitted that Occidental should in any event reasonably have accepted the repudiation after the plaintiffs had called in the loan in February, 1976. But the loan agreement continued to be binding thereafter, as did the covenants in the assignment; and all the other factors which I have mentioned continued to apply. Secondly, he submitted that it was quite unreasonable for Occidental to repudiate their obligations under the funding arrangement but at the same time to seek to hold the defendants to the charter. At first sight this appears to be a strong point. But it overlooks three things. First, Occidental were not free agents but bound to the plantiffs. Secondly, so to hold would be unfair to the plaintiffs for the reasons already discussed. Thirdly, if my conclusion on issue I is correct, then this is a risk which the defendants accepted when they entered into the charter and the separate side letter. Their position was hedged about with many protective provisions which I have already analysed. The only reason why these failed to protect the defendants was the collapse of MFC. This was the ultimate risk which they took, though no one anticipated that it might happen. But it did, and it seems to me that the defendants must bear the consequences. I do not see how the collapse of the MFC can alter what would otherwise be the legal position as between the defendants, Occidental and the plaintiffs.

I therefore answer this issue by saying that the defendants' plea is incorrect; Occidental were not obliged to accept the defendants' repudiation and treat the charter as at an end. It follows that in my judgment the last part of this issue does not arise. If it had been necessary to decide it, I would not have been able to point to any event before September, 1976, which would have altered the legal position. The laying up of the vessel in my view has different consequences to which I turn hereafter. However, in saying this I must not be thought to be implying that Occidental and the plaintiffs could necessarily have maintained the same position for a further six years. As was pointed out by the Court of Appeal in the *Decro-Wall* case, the reality is that deadlocked situations of this kind are usually resolved by the practicalities. Moreover, the passage of time might in itself alter the legal position of the parties, because an insistence to treat the contract as still in being might in time become quite unrealistic, unreasonable and untenable. I am only saying in that my view on the facts of the present case this had not happened by September, 1976.

CLEA SHIPPING CO. v BULK OIL INTERNATIONAL LTD, 'THE ALASKAN TRADER'
[1984] 1 All ER 129 (QB)

The issue was again the right of the owner of a chartered ship to continue the charter rather than treating it as at an end as a result of the charterer's repudiatory breach. The arbitrator had held that the breach should have been accepted as bringing the charter to an end.

LLOYD J: . . . Counsel for the owners now seeks to persuade me that the arbitrator was wrong in law. He submits that in a case of repudiation the innocent party has an unfettered right to elect whether to accept the repudiation or not. Here the owners chose not to accept the repudiation. Provided they continued to keep the vessel at the disposal of the charterers, as they did, they were entitled to their hire. The arbitrator was wrong in law in holding that the owners *ought* to have accepted the charterers' repudiation by midnight on 8 April 1981. . . .

It may be convenient to repeat a few sentences from para. 30 of the award:

I am satisfied that this commercial absurdity is not justified by a proper interpretation of the decided cases. I consider that the analogy of a contract between Master and servant applies more closely to a timecharter than the analogy of a simple debt. The Owner supplies the vessel and crew; the Charterer supplies fuel oil, pays disbursements and gives orders. The Charterers were also able to satisfy me that at that stage the Owners had no legitimate interest in pursuing their claim for hire rather than a claim for damages. In these respects the present case differs materially from the case of *White & Carter* v *McGregor*, and is more closely analogous to the case of *The Puerto Buitrago* [1976] 1 Lloyd's Rep 250, where the judgments of Lord Denning MR and Lord Orr are particularly in point.

It seems to me that the arbitrator is here distinguishing clearly between the two observations or limitations on the general principle to which Lord Reid had drawn attention in his speech. He is saying that a time charter is more analogous to a contract between master and servant than a simple debt, i.e. that it is a contract which calls for co-operation between both parties. He is also saying ('The charterers were *also* able to satisfy me . . .') that the owners had no legitimate interest in pursuing their claim for hire as distinct from damages. I will take the legitimate interest point first.

In addition to arguing that what Lord Reid had said about legitimate interest was only a quotation from counsel, and in any event obiter, arguments with which I have already dealt, counsel for the owners submitted that Lord Reid was, quite simply, wrong. It seems to me that it would be difficult for me to take that view in the light of what was said by all three members of the Court of Appeal in *The Puerto Buitrago*. Whether one takes Lord Reid's language, which was adopted by Orr and Browne LJJ in *The Puerto Buitrago*, or Lord Denning MR's language in that case ('in all reason'), or Kerr J's language in *The Odenfeld* ('wholly unreasonable . . . quite unrealistic, unreasonable and untenable'), there comes a point at which the court will cease, on general equitable principles, to allow the innocent party to enforce his contract according to its strict legal terms. How one defines that point is obviously a matter of some difficulty, for it involves drawing a line between conduct which is merely unreasonable (see per Lord Reid in *White & Carter* v *McGregor* [1961] 3 All ER 1178 at 1182, [1962] AC 473 at 429–430, criticising the Lord President in *Langford & Co. Ltd* v *Dutch* 1952 SC 15) and conduct which is *wholly* unreasonable (see per Kerr J in *The Odenfeld* [1978] 2 Lloyd's Rep 357 at 374. But however difficult it may be to define the point, that there is such a point seems to me to have been accepted both by the Court of Appeal in *The Puerto Buitrago* and by Kerr J in *The Odenfeld*.

I appreciate that the House of Lords has recently re-emphasised the importance of certainty in commercial contracts, when holding that there is no equitable jurisdiction to relieve against the consequences of the withdrawal clause in a time charter: see *Scandinavian Trading Tanker Co. AB* v *Flota Petrolera Ecuatoriana, The Scaptrade* [1983]] 2 All ER 763, [1983] 3 WLR 203. I appreciate, too, that the importance of certainty was one of the main reasons urged by Lord Hodson in *White & Carter* v *Mcgregor* in upholding the innocent party's unfettered right to elect. But, for reasons already mentioned, it seems to me that this court is bound to hold that there is *some* fetter, if only in extreme cases; and, for want of a better way of describing that fetter, it is safest for this court to use the language of Lord Reid, which, I have already said, was adopted by a majority of the Court of Appeal in *The Puerto Buitrago*.

I would add only two observations of my own. First, although the point is sometimes put in terms of the innocent party being obliged to accept the repudiation (it is so put by the arbitrator in the last sentence of para. 31 of his award), I think it is more accurate to say that it is the court which, on equitable grounds, refuses to allow the innocent party to enforce his full contractual rights. It is, as Sachs LJ said in *Decro-Wall*, the range of remedies which is limited, not the right to elect. The court is not exercising a dispensing power; nor is it rewriting an improvident contract. It is simply refusing a certain kind of relief. In America the courts take the uncomplicated view that whether the repudiation is accepted or not, the innocent party is *always* obliged to mitigate his damages: see *Williston on Contracts* (3rd edn, 1968) vol 11, § 1301, *Corbin on Contracts* (1951) vol 4, § 983 and Professor A L Goodhart 'Measure of damages when a contract is repudiated' (1962) 78 LQR 263 at 267.

Second, on the point of uncertainty, it is of course true that the existence of a fetter on the right to claim hire, even if it only be exercised in extreme cases, necessarily introduces an element of uncertainty. Thus it can be said with force that bankers need to know where they are when accepting an assignment of charter hire as security for their loan. On the other hand, absolute certainty can never be attained. Counsel for the charterers gave as an example the doctrine of frustration which may import a degree of uncertainty into commercial contracts of all kinds. So may the Unfair Contract Terms Act 1977 in the case of certain contracts for the sale of goods.

On the facts of *The Odenfeld*, Kerr J held on various grounds that the owners had ample justification for enforcing their claim for hire, at least until September 1976, although he went on to hold that the owners must be taken to have accepted the charterers' repudiation when they laid up the vessel in July 1976. Kerr J did not use the language of 'legitimate interest'. But he must be taken to have found that the charterers had failed to prove absence of legitimate interest on the part of the owners in claiming hire. One of the grounds on which Kerr J so found was the difficulty in calculating damages.

In the present case, by contrast, the arbitrator has found, and found clearly, that the owners had *no* legitimate interest in pursuing their claim for hire. In my view that finding is conclusive of this appeal. Counsel for the owners argued that the finding must be wrong in law. The arbitrator must have misunderstood what was said by Lord Reid, or applied the wrong test. But I could only accept that submission if the conclusion reached by the arbitrator was one which no reasonable arbitrator could have reached applying the right test. I cannot take that view. Indeed I can well understand why the arbitrator reached the conclusion he did. It is of course quite unnecessary for me to say whether I would have reached the same conclusion on the facts myself; nor by saying even that, do I mean to imply that I would have reached a different conclusion. It was the arbitrator who heard the evidence over many days, not me. It was for him to decide.

Counsel for the owners then turned to the further reasons given by the arbitrator which I have mentioned earlier in this judgment. But counsel was unable to extract any error of law or any mistake in approach. The arbitrator analysed in detail the main grounds on which it could be said that the owners were justified in continuing to claim hire, rather than damages, namely the requirements of the bank, the difficulty in assessing damages and the difficulty in obtaining alternative employment. These are all matters which were considered by Kerr J in *The Odenfeld*. For example, on the question of damages the arbitrator said:

> I did not accept that the assessment of damages in fact presented any special difficulty, or that the poor prospects of obtaining alternative employment would preclude the Owners from obtaining substantial damages. It was a matter of evidence.

On the difficulty of assessing damages therefore, as on the other matters, the arbitrator reached, as he was entitled, a different view on the facts than did Kerr J in *The Odenfeld*. I cannot begin to say that he was wrong in law.

The arbitrator also gave thought to another consideration, that the owners, being a one-ship company, might have decided to keep the charterparty on foot in order to protect their parent company from heavy claims under the charter. Counsel for the owners argued that this showed a wrong approach on the part of the arbitrator. But the arbitrator specifically stated in para. 7 of his further reasons that the consideration which I have just mentioned could not in any event be regarded as a legitimate interest in claiming hire rather than damages. So there is nothing in that point.

Finally, counsel for the owners argued that there is an inconsistency in the arbitrator's reasoning in so far as he held that the owners were not obliged to accept the charterers' repudiation in October 1980, but nevertheless were so obliged in April 1981. I see no necessary inconsistency. In October 1980 the vessel was unrepaired. She was not capable of performing any services under the charterparty. She was not costing the charterers anything, as she was off-hire and would remain off-hire for many months. In this sense the chaterers' repudiation in October 1980 was anticipatory. The position was, as the arbitrator rightly said, very different in April 1981, when the vessel was again capable of earning hire. In *The Odenfeld* Kerr J accepted that the legal position might change over time, because of changing circumstances. Even if there were an inconsistency in the arbitrator's reasoning, which I do not think there was, it would not justify me in reversing his decision as to the April repudiation.

I turn last to the alternative ground on which the arbitrator based his decision, that this was a contract which called for co-operation between the parties, and therefore fell within Lord Reid's first limitation. Counsel for the charterers argued that a time charter is a contract for services, to be performed by the owners through the master and crew, and through the use of their vessel. As a contract for services, it is, as Lord Diplock pointed out in *The Scaptrade* [1983] 2 All ER 763 at 766, [1983] 3 WLR 203 at 207:

> the very prototype of a contract of which before the fusion of law and equity a court would never grant specific performance. . . .

As in any other contract for services the owners earn their remuneration by performing the services required. If they are wrongfully prevented from performing any services, then, as in any other contract for services, the only remedy lies in damages. The fact that the owners' remuneration in this case, called hire, is payable in advance makes no difference. Counsel for the owners, on the other hand, argued that the owners earned their hire simply by holding the vessel and the services of their master and crew at the charterers' disposal. He concedes that in the case of master and servant, where the master has wrongfully dismissed the servant, the servant cannot earn remuneration by holding himself at the disposal of his master. He is confined to his remedy in damages. But counsel for the owners submits that a time charter is different. In view of my decision on the legitimate interest point, it is unnecessary for me to decide between these rival arguments, or to explore the nature of a time charter contract any further. All I will say is that, at first blush, there seemed much to be said for the argument of counsel for the charterers. I say no more, because in *The Odenfeld* Kerr J found a similar argument unimpressive.

For the reasons I have given I would dismiss the owners' appeal and uphold the award.

HOUNSLOW LONDON BOROUGH COUNCIL v TWICKENHAM GARDEN DEVELOPMENTS LTD [1971] 1 Ch 233 (ChD)

Contractors working on a building contract refused to accept the council's purported termination of it, but continued to carry out the work.

MEGARRY J: . . . Apart from any question of specific performance, Mr Neill strongly contended that the contractor had not merely a right to refuse to accept the borough's alleged repudiation of the contract as determining it, but also a right to insist upon continuing to perform the contract, despite the protests of the borough. He based his contention on *White and Carter (Councils) Ltd* v *McGregor* [1962] AC 413, a striking decision of the House of Lords. It was a Scottish appeal, but I do not think that it was suggested that English law was any different on the point. The sales manger of a garage contracted with advertising agents for the display of advertisements of the garage fixed to litter bins in the streets for three years from the first exhibition of the advertisement. Immediately after the contract had been made, the garage proprietor wrote to the agents cancelling the order; but the agents refused to accept the cancellation, and sued the proprietor for the sums due under the contract. By a majority, with Lord Morton of Henryton and Lord Keith of Avonholm dissenting, the House of Lords held that the agents were not obliged to accept the repudiation by the proprietor, with merely the right to sue for damages, but were entitled to perform the contract and sue for the contract price.

Lord Hodson, with whom Lord Tucker concurred, rested his decision on the broad principle that repudiation of a contract by one party does not discharge it, and that whether or not the contract is specifically enforceable, the contract survives. Accordingly,

> When the assistance of the court is not required the innocent party can choose whether he will accept repudiation and sue for damages for anticipatory breach or await the date of performance by the guilty party. Then, if there is a failure in performance, his rights are preserved.: p. 445

As stated in Lord Hodson's speech, this principle was subject to no qualification. The question is whether, as Mr Neill claims, this principle applies to the case before me, so that if the borough has not lawfully terminated the contract but has repudiated it, the contractor can insist on retaining possession of the site and completing the contract.

A number of examples were discussed in argument in addition to the example given by Lord Keith in his dissent, at p. 442, and mentioned by Lord Reid and Lord Morton at pp. 428 and 432. Lord Keith took the case of a contract by a man to go to Hong Kong and produce a report for a fee of £10,000. Before he goes, the other party repudiates the contract. Nevertheless, on the majority view the man is entitled to go to Hong Kong, produce the unwanted report and claim the £10,000. The examples discussed in argument before me applied the doctrine to cases concerning land. A contract to erect buildings on land is let; a few days later the landowner unexpectedly learns that he can obtain a far more advantageous planning permission for developing the land, and he thereupon repudiates the contract; but the contractor insists on performing it, even though the landowner must then either abandon the more valuable development and accept the far less profitable buildings or else pull those buildings down when they have been completed and then carry out the more fruitful scheme. Another landowner lets a contract to erect an extravagant building which his wealth can afford; before much work has been done his fortune collapses, and he can pay for the building only by using all that is left to him; yet the contractor insists on performing the contract. A third landowner contracts with an artist to paint extensive frescoes in a new building over a period of two years; the landowner then receives a handsome offer for the unadorned building, provided vacant possession is delivered forthwith; yet the artist insists on painting on for the rest of the two years.

Examples such as these suggest that there may well be limits to the doctrine. Lord Morton and Lord Keith both stressed the duty to mitigate damages: and he who is bound to mitigate can hardly be entitled to insist on aggravating. However, theirs were dissenting speeches which rejected the doctrine in toto. Accordingly, I must turn to the speech of Lord Reid. Although it was his voice, with the voices of Lord Tucker and Lord Hodson, that carried the day, two important limitations appear in Lord Reid's speech. First, he pointed out that the peculiarity of the case was that the agents could perform the contract without any co-operation by the proprietor. He said, at p. 429:

> Of course, if it had been necessary for the defender to do or accept anything before the contract could be completed by the pursuers, the pursuers could not and the court would not have compelled the defender to act, the contract would not have been completed and the pursuers' only remedy would have been damages.

This, I think, was in effect an acceptance of the argument to which Lord Reid had referred on p. 428:

> the respondent points out that in most cases the innocent party cannot complete the contract himself without the other party doing, allowing or accepting something, and that it is purely fortuitous that the appellants can do so in this case. In most cases by refusing co-operation the party in breach can compel the innocent party to restrict his claim to damages.

The other limitation, cautiously expressed at p. 431, was that 'it may well be' that if a person has no legitimate financial or other interest in performing the contract rather than claiming damages, 'he ought not to be allowed to saddle the other party with an additional burden with no benefit to himself': and this principle might apply to the example of the expert report. However, no such absence of a legitimate interest in the agents had been established, and so the possible principle did not apply.

It seems to me that the decision is one which I should be slow to apply to any category of case not fairly within the contemplation of their Lordships. The case before me is patently one in which the contractor cannot perform the contract without any co-operation by the borough. The whole machinery of the contract is geared to acts by the architect and quantity surveyor, and it is a contract that is to be performed on the borough's land. True, the contractor already has de facto possession or control of the land; there is no question of the borough being required to do the act of admitting the contractor into possession, and so in that respect the contractor can perform the contract without any 'co-operation' by the borough. But I do not think that the point can be brushed aside so simply. Quite apart from questions of active co-operation, cases where one party is lawfully in possession of property of the other seem to me to raise issues not before the House of Lords in *White and Carter (Councils) Ltd* v *McGregor* [1962] AC 413. Suppose that A, who owns a large and valuable painting, contracts with B, a picture restorer, to restore it over a period of three months. Before the work is begun, A receives a handsome offer from C to purchase the picture, subject to immediate delivery of the picture in its unrestored state, C having grave suspicions of B's competence. If the work of restoration is to be done in A's house, he can effectually exclude B by refusing to admit him to the house: without A's 'co-operation' to this extent B cannot perform his contract.

But what if the picture stands in A's locked barn, the key of which he has lent to B so that he may come and go freely, or if the picture has been removed to B's premises? In these cases can B insist on performing his contract, even though this makes it impossible for A to accept C's offer? In the case of the barn, A's co-operation may perhaps be said to be requisite to the extent of not barring B's path to the barn or putting another lock on the door: but if the picture is on B's premises, no active co-operation by A is needed. Nevertheless, the picture is A's property, and I find it difficult to believe that Lord Reid intended to restrict the concept of 'co-operation' to active co-operation. In *White and Carter (Councils) Ltd* v *McGregor* no co-operation by the proprietor, either active or passive, was required: the contract could be performed by the agents wholly without reference to the proprietor or his property. The case was far removed from that of a property owner being forced to stand impotently aside while a perhaps ill-advised contract is executed on property of his which he has delivered into the possession of the other party, and is powerless to retrieve.

Accordingly, I do not think that *White and Carter (Councils) Ltd* v *McGregor* has any application to the case before me. I say this, first, because a considerable degree of active co-operation under the contract by the borough is requisite, and second, because the work is being done to property of the borough. I doubt very much whether the *White* case can have been intended to apply where the contract is to be performed by doing acts to property owned by the party seeking to determine it. I should add that it seems to me that the ratio of the *White* case involves acceptance of Lord Reid's limitations, even though Lord Tucker and Lord Hodson said nothing of them: for without Lord Reid there was no majority for the decision of the House. Under the doctrine of precedent, I do not think that it can be said that a majority of a bare majority is itself the majority.

7.1.4 LIQUIDATED DAMAGES AND PENALTY CLAUSES

DUNLOP PNEUMATIC TYRE CO. LTD v *NEW GARAGE AND MOTOR COMPANY LTD* [1915] AC 79 (HL)

LORD DUNEDIN: . . . My Lords, the appellants, through an agent, entered into a contract with the respondents under which they supplied them with their goods, which consisted mainly of motor-tyre covers and tubes. By this contract, in respect of certain concessions as to discounts, the respondents bound themselves not to do several things, which may be shortly set forth as follows: not to tamper with the manufacturers' marks; not to sell to any private customer or co-operative society at prices less than the current price list issued by the Dunlop Company; not to supply to persons whose supplies the Dunlop Company had decided to suspend; not to exhibit or to export without the Dunlop Company's assent. Finally, the agreement concluded (clause 5), 'We agree to pay to the Dunlop Pneumatic Tyre Company Ltd the sum of 5*l*. for each and every tyre, cover or tube sold or offered in breach of this agreement, as and by the way of liquidated damages and not as a penalty'.

The appellants, having discovered that the respondents had sold covers and tubes at under the current list price, raised action and demanded damages. The case was tried and the breach in fact held proved. An inquiry was directed before the Master as to damages. The Master inquired, and assessed the damages at 250*l*., adding this explanation: 'I find that it was left open to me to decide whether the 5*l*. fixed in the agreement was penalty or liquidated damages. I find that it was liquidated damages'.

The respondents appealed to the Court of Appeal, when the majority of that court, Vaughan Williams and Swinfen Eady LJJ, held, Kennedy LJ dissenting, that the said sum of 5*l*. was a penalty, and entered judgment for the plaintiffs for the sum of 2*l*. as nominal damages. Appeal from that decision is now before your Lordships' House.

My Lords, we had the benefit of a full and satisfactory argument, and a citation of the very numerous cases which have been decided on this branch of the law. The matter has been handled, and at no distant date, in the courts of highest resort. I particularly refer to the *Clydebank Case* [1905] AC 6 in your Lordships' House and the cases of *Public Works Commissioner* v *Hills* [1906] AC 368 and *Webster* v *Bosanquet* [1912] AC 394 in the Privy Council. In both of these cases many of the previous cases were considered. In view of the fact, and of the number of the authorities available, I do not think it advisable to attempt any detailed review of the various cases, but I shall content myself with stating succinctly the various propositions which I think are deducible from the decisions which rank as authoritative:

1. Though the parties to a contract who use the words 'penalty' or 'liquidated damages' may prima facie be supposed to mean what they say, yet the expression used is not conclusive. The court must find out whether the payment stipulated is in truth a penalty or liquidated damages. This doctrine may be said to be found passim in nearly every case.

2. The essence of a penalty is a payment of money stipulated as in terrorem of the offending party; the essence of liquidated damages is a genuine covenanted pre-estimate of damage (*Clydebank Engineering and Shipbuilding Co.* v *Don Jose Ramos Yzquierdo y Castaneda*).

3. The question whether a sum stipulated is penalty or liquidated damages is a question of construction to be decided upon the terms and inherent circumstances of each particular contract, judged of as at the time of the making of the contract, not as at the time of the breach (*Public Works Commissioner* v *Hills* and *Webster* v *Bosanquet*).

4. To assist this task of construction various tests have been suggested, which if applicable to the case under consideration may prove helpful, or even conclusive. Such are:

(a) It will be held to be a penalty if the sum stipulated for is extravagant and unconscionable in amount in comparison with the greatest loss that could conceivably be proved to have followed from the breach. (Illustration given by Lord Halsbury in *Clydebank Case*).

(b) It will be held to a penalty if the breach consists only in not paying a sum of money, and the sum stipulated is a sum greater than the sum which ought to have been paid (*Kemble* v *Farren* (1829) 6 Bing 141). This though one of the most ancient instances is truly a corollary to the last test. Whether it had its historical origin in the doctrine of the common law that when A promised to pay B a sum of money on a certain day and did not do so, B could only recover the sum with, in certain cases, interest, but could never recover further damages for non-timeous payment, or whether it was a survival of the time when equity reformed unconscionable bargains merely because they were unconscionable – a subject which much exercised Jessel MR in *Wallis* v *Smith* (1804) 21 ChD 243 – is probably more interesting than material.

(c) There is a presumption (but no more) that it is penalty when a 'single lump sum is made payable by way of compensation, on the occurrence of one or more or all of several events, some of which may occasion serious and others but trifling damage' (Lord Watson in *Lord Elphinstone* v *Monkland Iron and Coal Co.* (1886) 11 App Cas 332).

On the other hand:

(d) It is no obstacle to the sum stipulated being a genuine pre-estimate of damage, that the consequences of the breach are such as to make precise pre-estimation almost an impossibility. On the contrary, that is just the situation when it is probable that pre-estimated damage was the true bargain between the parties (*Clydebank Case*, Lord Halsbury; *Webster* v *Bosanquet*, Lord Mersey).

Turning now to the facts of the case, it is evident that the damage apprehended by the appellants owing to the breaking of the agreement was an indirect and not a direct damage. So long as they got their price from the respondents for each article sold, it could not matter to them directly what the respondents did with it. Indirectly it did. Accordingly, the agreement is headed 'Price Maintenance Agreement', and the way in which the appellants would be damaged if prices were cut is clearly explained in evidence by Mr Baisley, and no successful attempt is made to controvert that evidence. But though damage as a whole from such a practice would be certain, yet damage from any one sale would be impossible to forecast. It is just, therefore, one of those cases where it seems quite reasonable for parties to contract that they should estimate that damage at a certain figure, and provided that figure is not extravagant there would seem no reason to suspect that it is not truly a bargain to assess damages, but rather a penalty to be held on terrorem.

The argument of the respondents was really based on two heads. They overpressed, in my judgment, the dictum of Lord Watson in *Lord Elphinstone's Case*, reading it as if he had said that the matter was conclusive, instead of saying, as he did, that it raised a presumption, and they relied strongly on the case of *Willson v Love* [1896] 1 QB 626.

Now, in the first place, I have considerable doubt whether the stipulated payment here can fairly be said to deal with breaches, 'some of which' – I am quoting Lord Watson's words – 'may occasion serious and others but trifling damage'. As a mere matter of construction, I doubt whether clause 5 applies to anything but sales below price. But I will assume that it does. None the less the mischief, as I have already pointed out, is an indirect mischief, and I see no data on which, as a matter of construction, I could settle in my own mind that the indirect damage from selling a cover would differ in magnitude from the indirect damage from selling a tube; or that the indirect damage from a cutting-price sale would differ from the indirect damage from supply at a full price to a hostile, because prohibited, agent. You cannot weigh such things in a chemical balance. The character of the agricultural land which was ruined by slag heaps in *Elphinstone's Case* was not all the same, but no objection was raised by Lord Watson to applying an overhead rate per acre, the sum not being in itself unconscionable.

I think *Elphinstone's Case*, or rather the dicta in it, do go this length, that if there are various breaches to which one indiscriminate sum to be paid in breach is applied, then the strength of the chain must be taken at its weakest link. If you clearly see that the loss on one particular breach could never amount to the stipulated sum, then you may come to the conclusion that the sum is penalty. But further than this it does not go; so, for the reasons already stated, I do not think the present case forms an instance of what I have just expressed.

As regards *Willson's Case*, I do not think it material to consider whether it was well decided on the facts. For it was decided on the view of the facts that the manurial value of straw and of hay were known ascertainable quantities as at the time of the bargain, and radically different, so that the damage resulting from the want of one could never be the same as the damage resulting from the want of the other.

Added to that, the parties there had said 'penalty', and the effort was to make out that that really meant liquidated damages; and lastly, if my view of the facts in the present case is correct, then Rigby LJ would have agreed with me, for the last words of his judgment are as follows: 'On the other hand it is stated that, when the damages caused by a breach of contract are incapable of being ascertained, the sum made by the contract payable on such a breach is to be regarded as liquidated damages. The question arises, What is meant in this statement by the expression "incapable of being ascertained"? In their proper sense the words appear to refer to a case where no rule or measure of damages is available for the guidance of a jury as to the amount of the damages, and a judge would have to tell them they must fix the amount as best they can'. To arrive at the indirect damage in this case, supposing no sum had been stipulated, that is just what a judge would, in my opinion, have had to do.

On the whole matter, therefore, I go with the opinion of Kennedy LJ, and I move your Lordships that the appeal be allowed, and judgment given for the sum as brought out by the Master, the appellants to have their costs in this House and in the courts below.

Lords Atkinson, Parker, and Parmoor concurred.

BRIDGE v CAMPBELL DISCOUNT CO. LTD [1962] 1 All ER 385 (HL)

LORD DENNING: My Lords, in order to determine this case it is as well to remember what is the nature of a hire-purchase transaction. It is in effect, though not in law, a mortgage of goods. Just as a man who buys land may raise the price by a mortgage of it, so, also, a man who buys goods may raise part of the price by hire-purchase of them. And just as the old mortgage of land was not what it appeared to be, so also the modern hire-purchase of goods is not what it seems to be. One might well say of a hire-purchase transaction what Maitland said of a mortgage deed: 'That is the worst of our mortgage deed . . . it is one long suppressio veri and suggestio falsi': see his Lectures on Equity (2nd edn), 1949, p. 182. Take this present transaction. If you were able to strip off the legal trappings in which it has been dressed and see it in its native simplicity, you would discover that the appellant agreed to buy a car from a dealer for £405 but he could only find £105 towards it. So he borrowed the other £300 from a finance house and got them to pay it to the dealer, and he gave the finance house a charge on the car as security for repayment. But if you tried to express the transaction in those simple terms, you would soon fall into troubles of all sorts under the Bills of Sale Acts, the Sale of Goods Act, and the Money-lenders Acts. In order to avoid these legal obstacles, the finance house has to discard the role of a lender of money on security and it has to become an owner of goods who lets them out on hire: see *Re Robertson, Ex p. Crawcour, McEntire v Crossley Brothers Ltd* (1878) 9 ChD 419. So it buys the goods from the dealer and lets them out on hire to the appellant. The appellant has to discard the role of a man who has agreed to buy goods, and he has to become a man who takes them on hire with only an option to purchase: see *Helby v Matthews* [1895] AC 471. And when these new roles have been assumed, the finance house is not a moneylender but a hire-purchase company free of the trammels of the Moneylenders Acts: see *Transport & General Credit Co. Ltd v Morgan* [1939] 2 All ER 17. So you arrive at the modern hire-purchase transaction whereby (i) the dealer sells the goods to a finance house for cash; and (ii) the finance house lets them out on hire to a hirer in return for rentals which are so calculated as to ensure that the finance house is eventually repaid the cash with interest; and (iii) when the finance house is repaid the hirer has the option of purchasing the car for a nominal sum. The dealer is the intermediary who arranges it all. The finance house supplies him with the printed forms, and he gets them signed. In the result, the finance house buys a car it has never seen, and lets it to a hirer it has never met, and the dealer seemingly drops out.

When hire-purchase transactions were first validated by this House in 1895 in *Helby v Matthews*, the contract of hire had most of the features of an ordinary hiring. In particular, the hirer was at liberty to terminate the hiring at any time without paying any penalty. He could return the goods and not be liable to make any further payments beyond the monthly sum then due. There was no clog on his right to terminate. And this was one of the reasons why the House saw nothing wrong with the transaction. Lord Macnaughten in characteristic fashion pointed out what a benefit this was to the hirer:

> . . . if a coveted treasure is becoming a burthen and an encumbrance it is something, surely, to know that the transaction may be closed at once *without further liability and without the payment of any forfeit.*

Since that time, however, the finance houses have imposed a serious clog on the hirer's right to terminate the hiring. They have introduced into their printed forms a 'minimum-payment' clause such as never appeared in *Helby v Matthews*. The clause in this case is a good example. The minimum payment is *two-thirds* of the hire-purchase price. The respondents stipulate that, if the hiring be terminated for any reason before the car has become the property of the hirer, then the hirer must deliver up the car in proper condition and also make up the payments to £321 13s. 4d. in all. Now the appellant only had this car for eight weeks. He had already paid £115 10s. He delivered it up in good condition. So the respondents have the car back. Yet they claim another £206 3s. 4d. from him, so as to make up £321 13s. 4d. altogether. In the result, it means that he must pay £321 13s. 4d. for eight weeks use of the car.

What possible justification have the finance houses for inserting this 'minimum-payment' clause? They call it 'agreed compensation for depreciation'. But it is no such thing. It is not 'agreed'. Nor is it 'compensation for depreciation'. There is not the slightest evidence that the appellant ever agreed it, and I do not suppose for a moment that he did. He simply signed the printed form. And as for 'depreciation', everyone knows that a car depreciates more and more as it gets older and older, but this sum gets less and less. It is obvious that the initial rental of £105 (which was one-quarter of the cash price) would compensate at once for a twenty-five per cent. depreciation; and the monthly rentals covered any remaining depreciation over the next three years. The truth is that this minimum-payment is not so much compensation for depreciation but rather compensation for loss of the future instalments which the respondents expected to receive, but which they had no right to receive. It is a penal sum which they exact because the hiring is terminated before two-thirds has been paid. In cases when the hiring is terminated, as it was here, within a few weeks, it is beyond doubt oppressive and unjust. Is not, this, then, a classic case for equity to intervene? The contract is contained in a printed form. Not one hirer in a thousand reads it, let alone understands it. He takes it on trust and signs it. It is binding at law but, when it comes to be examined, it is found to contain a penalty which is oppressive and unjust. It seems to me that such a case comes within the very first principles on which equity intervenes to grant relief.

> The whole system of equity jurisprudence proceeds upon the ground that a party, having a legal right, shall not be permitted to avail himself of it for the purposes of injustice, or fraud, or oppression, or harsh and vindictive injury.

See Story's Commentaries on Equity Jurisprudence (1839), Vol. II, p. 508.

The Court of Appeal acknowledge that, in some cases, there is room for the intervention of equity. They accept that, where the hiring is terminated because the hirer is in breach, equity will relieve him from payment of the penalty: see *Cooden Engineering Co. Ltd* v *Stanford* [1952] 2 All ER 915. But they say that, when it is terminated for any other reason, as for instance, if the hirer gives notice of termination himself, or if he dies, there is no equity to relieve him or his executors from the rigours of the law: see *Associated Distributors Ltd* v *Hall*. The jurisdiction of equity is confined, they say, to the relief against penalties for breach of contract and does not extend further. Applied to this case it means this: If the appellant, after a few weeks, find himself unable to keep up the instalments and, being a conscientious man, gives notice of termination and returns the car, without falling into arrear, he is liable to pay the penal sum of £206 3s. 4d. without relief of any kind; but if he is an unconscientious man who falls into arrear without saying a word, so that the respondents re-take the car for his default, he will be relieved from payment of the penalty. Let no one mistake the injustice of this. It means that equity commits itself to this absurd paradox: It will grant relief to a man who breaks his contract but will penalise the man who keeps it. If this be the state of equity today, then it is in sore need of an overhaul so as to restore its first principles. But I am quite satisfied that such is not the state of equity today. This case can be brought within long-established principles without recourse to any new equity. From the very earliest times, equity has relieved not only against penalties for breach of contract, but also against penalties for non-performance of a condition. And the stipulation for a 'minimum payment' was, it seems to me, a penalty which was payable on non-performance of a condition. The respondents said to the appellant: 'If the hiring is terminated for any reason before you have paid £321 13s. 4d., then you must make up the payments to that sum'. The condition was designed to ensure that he should pay a minimum sum of £321 13s. 4d. If he fulfilled that condition, he was not liable to pay any penalty; but, if he did not perform it, he had to pay the difference. The principal object was to secure a minimum payment of £321 13s. 4d. The condition was the means of achieving it.

To prove this point, I need not dwell on the cases of penalties for breach of contract. Their name is legion, and no one disputed them before your Lordships. A good instance is *Sloman* v *Walter* (1783) 1 Bro CC 418, to which your Lordships were referred. But I must draw attention to the cases of penalties for non-performance of a condition They, too, are legion. Take mortgages for instance. At law, the mortgagor was subject to a penalty for non-payment of this condition: 'If you repay the money on this day six months, you shall have the land back: but if you do not repay it by that date, you shall lose it for ever', see Coke on Littleton, s. 332. The court of equity always relieved the mortgagor in case of non-performance of this condition, and it did so, not by reason of any specialty about mortgages, but in pursuance of its general power to relieve against penalties: see *Kreglinger* v *New Patagonia Meat & Cold Storage Co. Ltd* [1914] AC 25 by Viscount Haldane LC. Take next the common penalty bond. It was taken in order to secure that something should be done by the obligor, such as to be of good behaviour (or to pay an annuity, or anything else). The obligor bound himself by his bond to pay a specified sum, say £20, on some such condition as this: 'If you are of good behaviour (or pay the annuity, or whatever else it might be), this obligation shall be void: but if you do not do so, then this obligation shall be of full force and effect'. In many of those cases, there was no covenant by the obligor to perform the condition; no covenant by him to be of good behaviour (or to pay the annuity or to do anything else); no covenant on which he could be sued at law; but simply a bond that, if he did not perform the condition, he would pay the specified sum. There was thus no breach of contract for which he could be sued at law for damages, but only non-performance of a condition which exposed him to payment of the sum specified in the bond. Yet equity always granted relief in such cases if the sum was a penalty: see, for instance, *Tall* v *Ryland* (1670) 1 Cas in Ch 183, *Collins* v *Collins* (1759) 2 Burr 820 and the very learned note by Mr Evans in his appendix to *Pothier* on the *Law of Obligations* (1806), p. 92; and it did so not by reason of any specialty about penalty bonds, but in pursuance of its general power to relieve against penalties. It would restrain the obligee from suing at law on the bond so long as the obligor was ready to pay him the damage he had really sustained. Likewise, even when the sum had already been paid over in the shape of a deposit to secure performance, equity would be prepared to grant restitution if it was a penal sum: see *Benson* v *Gibson* (1746) 3 Atk 395 by Lord Harwicke LC, *Steedman* v *Drinkle* [1916] 1 AC 275 by Viscount Haldane.

In my judgment, therefore, the courts have power to grant relief against the penal sum contained in this 'minimum-payment' clause, no matter for what reason the hiring is terminated. The 'minimum-payment' clause is single and indivisible, and no just distinction can be drawn between the cases where the hirer is in breach and where he is not. I find myself in entire agreement with the judgment of Lord MacDermott CJ, in *Lombank Ltd* v *Kennedy, Lombank Ltd* v *Crossan* (1961, unreported) from which I have profited much. I do not think that *Associated Distributors Ltd* v *Hall* [1938] 1 All ER 511 was rightly decided. This conclusion is not affected by the provision of the Hire-Purchase Act 1938. The legislature deliberately left transactions above £300 to the existing rules of the common law and equity; and it is these that I have considered. If I am wrong about all this, however, and there is no jurisdiction to grant relief unless the hirer is in breach, then I would be prepared to hold that, in this case, the appellant was in breach. Not that I think the point is at all clear. The pleadings are ambiguous. The evidence is scanty. But I think that any ambiguity should be resolved in his favour. His conduct should be interpreted on the assumption that he would do that which is the least burdensome to him, rather than that which is the most profitable to the hire-purchase company; cf. *Withers* v *General Theatre Co. Ltd* [1933] 2 KB 536 per Scrutton LJ. For this reason, I would be prepared, if necessary, to hold that the hiring was terminated by a repudiation which was accepted. If so, the appellant was in breach and will qualify for relief under the authority of *Cooden* v *Stanford* [1952] 2 All ER 915 which all your Lordships hold to be rightly decided. In any case, however, when relief is given, it does not mean that the hire-purchase company will recover nothing. When equity granted relief against a penalty, it always required the recipient of its favours, as a condition of relief, to pay the damage which the other party had really sustained. A *quantum damnificatus* was issued to determine it. On payment of the damage, equity granted an injunction to restrain the other party from proceeding to enforce the penalty at law. Now that equity and law are one, the hire-purchase company should recover its actual damage, and such damage should be assessed according to the realities and not according to any fiction. The respondents should recover the money they have advanced with interest at a reasonable rate up to the time when the hiring was terminated, less the instalments already received and the sum which the car might reasonably be expected to realise when it was delivered up to them.

I would, therefore, allow this appeal, and remit the case to the county court judge so that he may determine the amount of damage, if any, which the respondents have sustained, and give judgment for that sum only.

Lord Radcliffe and Devlin concurred; Viscount Simonds and Lord Morton concurred in part.

7.2 Equitable Remedies

7.2.1 SPECIFIC PERFORMANCE

RYAN v *MUTUAL TONTINE WESTMINSTER CHAMBERS ASSOCIATION*
[1893] 1 Ch 116 (CA)

A lease provided that a resident porter should be constantly in attendance on the premises. Could this obligation be 'specifically enforced'?

LORD ESHER MR: I do not think that the points on which we are about to decide this case were brought so fully before the learned judge below as they have been before us. It seems to me that this case comes within one or the other, according to the point of view from which it is regarded, of two well-recognised rules of Chancery practice, which prevent the application of the remedy by compelling specific performance. I do not myself put this case as coming within any rule as to contracts to perform personal services. It is not necessary for me therefore to express any opinion as to such a rule. The contract sought to be enforced here is not a contract with a person employed as a servant. It is a contract between a person who has to employ a servant and a person for whose benefit the employment of such servant is to take place. It is a contract between a landlord and his tenant, by which the former undertakes to employ a porter to perform certain services for the benefit of the latter. The contract, therefore, is not merely that the landlord shall employ a porter, but that he shall employ a porter who shall do certain specified work for the benefit of the tenant. Than is, in my opinion, one indivisible contract. The performance of what is suggested to be the first part of the contract, viz., the agreement to employ a porter, would be of no use whatever to the tenant unless he performed the services specified. The right of the tenant under the contract is really an entirety, viz., to have a porter employed by whom these services shall be performed; and the breach of contract substantially is that these services were not performed. The contract is that these services shall be performed during the whole term of the tenancy; it is therefore a long-continuing contract, to be performed from day to day, and under which the circumstances of non-performance might vary from day to day. I apprehend, therefore, that the execution of it would require that constant superintendence by the court, which the court in such cases has always declined to give. Therefore, if the contract is regarded as a whole, there is good ground for saying that it is not one of which the court could compel specific performance. It was contended that the court could grant specific performance of the defendants' obligation to appoint a porter. But then the case is brought within another rule, viz., that, when the court cannot compel specific performance of the contract as a whole, it will not interfere to compel specific performance of part of a contract. That clearly appears to be a rule of Chancery practice on the subject. Therefore, if it is urged that what the judge has ordered to be performed is merely the obligation to appoint a porter, the case falls within that rule, and on that ground his decision must be reversed. It was argued that the case of *Rigby* v *Great Western Railway Company* (1928) 15 LJ (Ch) 266, shewed that a contract such as this might be severed, and that performance of part of it could be enforced. But that is not what the case appears to have decided. It decided that, where in one contract there were really several wholly independent stipulations, the court could grant specific performance of one of them. It is no authority for the proposition that the court can separate part of what is really one single indivisible contract and grant specific performance of that part. Then it was said that this case fell within the exception which has been established in the railway cases. That is admitted to be an exception grafted upon the Chancery jurisdiction by decisions, in which the court, for the reasons stated, treated cases where railway companies had taken land on condition of doing works as exceptional, and granted specific performance. But being admittedly exceptions, these cases do not do away with the general rule, which appears to be applicable to the case before us. The language used by James VC, in *Wilson* v *Furness Railway Company* (1869) Law Rep 9 Eq 28, was cited to us as an authority to shew that the court ought in this case to grant specific performance.

That language, as applied by the counsel for the defendants, is really cited as an authority for the proposition that the Court of Chancery will always, regardless of any rules, do what the justice of the particular case requires. But the answer is that the Court of Chancery has never acted on any such proposition. Then the judgment of Lord Eldon in *Lane* v *Newdigate* (1804) 10 Ves 192 was cited, in which that learned judge appears on that occasion to have deliberately held that the court ought to do indirectly that which it had no power to do directly. That is a doctrine that I, for one, must decline to follow. It appears to me that the appeal must be allowed, and the judgment for the plaintiff must stand only for the damages found by the learned judge.

Lopes and Kay LJJ concurred.

TRADE UNION AND LABOUR RELATIONS (CONSOLIDATION) ACT 1992

Section 16.
No court shall, whether by way of–
  (a) an order for specific performance or specific implement of a contract of employment, or
  (b) an injunction or interdict restraining a breach or threatened breach of such a contract, compel an employee to do any work or attend at any place for the doing of any work.

7.2.2 INJUNCTIONS

LUMLEY v *WAGNER* (1852) 1 De GM & G 604

LORD ST LEONARDS LC: . . . The question which I have to decide in the present case arises out of a very simple contract, the effect of which is, that the defendant Johanna Wagner should sing at Her Majesty's Theatre for a certain number of nights, and that she should not sing elsewhere (for that is the true construction) during that period. As I understand the points taken by the defendants' counsel in support of this appeal they in effect come to this, namely, that a Court of Equity ought not to grant an injunction except in cases connected with specific performance, or where the injunction being to compel a party to forbear from committing an act (and not to perform an act), that injunction will complete the whole of the agreement remaining unexecuted. . . .

The present is a mixed case, consisting not of two correlative acts to be done – one by the plaintiff, and the other by the defendants, which state of facts may have and in some cases has introduced a very important difference – but of an act to be done by J Wagner alone, to which is supperadded a negative stipulation on her part to abstain from the commission of any act which will break in upon her affirmative covenant; the one being ancillary to, concurrent and operating together with, the other. The agreement to sing for the plaintiff during three months at his theatre, and during that time not to sing for anybody else, is not a correlative contract, it is in effect one contract; and though beyond all doubt this court could not interfere to enforce the specific performance of the whole of this contract, yet in all sound construction, and according to the true spirit of the agreement, the engagement to perform for three months at one theatre must necessarily exclude the right to perform at the same time at another theatre. It was clearly intended that J Wagner was to exert her vocal abilities to the utmost to aid the theatre to which she agreed to attach herself. I am of opinion that if she had attempted, even in the absence of any negative stipulation, to perform at another theatre, she would have broken the spirit and true meaning of the contract as much as she would now do with reference to the contract into which she has actually entered.

Wherever this court has not proper jurisdiction to enforce specific performance, it operates to bind men's consciences, as far as they can be bound, to a true and literal performance of their agreements; and it will not suffer them to depart from their contracts at their pleasure, leaving the party with whom they have contracted to the mere chance of any damages which a jury may give. The exercise of this jurisdiction has, I believe, had a wholesome tendency towards the maintenance of the good faith which exists in this country to a much greater degree perhaps than in any other; and although the jurisdiction is not to be extended, yet a judge would desert his duty who did not act up to what his predecessors have handed down as the rule for his guidance in the administration of such an equity.

It was objected that the operation of the injunction in the present case was mischievious, excluding the defendant J Wagner from performing at any other theatre while this court has no power to compel her to perform at Her Majesty's Theatre. It is true that I have not the means of compelling her to sing, but she has no cause of complaint if I compel her to abstain from the commision of an act which she has bound herself not to do, and thus possibly cause her to fulfil her engagement. The jurisdiction which I now exercise is wholly within the power of the court, and being of opinion that it is a proper case for interfering, I shall leave nothing unsatisfied by the judgment I pronounce. The effect, too, of the injunction in restraining J Wagner from singing elsewhere may, in the event of an action being brought against her by the plaintiff, prevent any such amount of vindictive damages being given against her as a jury might probably be inclined to give if she had carried her talents and exercised them at the rival theatre: the injunction may also, as I have said, tend to the fulfilment of her engagement; though, in continuing the injunction, I disclaim doing indirectly what I cannot do directly.

WARNER BROTHERS PICTURES INC v NELSON [1937] 1 KB 209 (KB)

BRANSON J: The facts of this case are few and simple. The plaintiffs are a firm of film producers in the United States of America. In 1931 the defendant, then not well known as a film actress, entered into a contract with the plaintiffs. Before the expiration of that contract the present contract was entered into between the parties. Under it the defendant received a considerably enhanced salary, the other conditions being substantially the same. This contract was for fifty-two weeks and contains options to the plaintiffs to extend if for further periods of fifty-two weeks at ever-increasing amounts of salary to the defendant. No question of construction arises upon the contract, and it is not necessary to refer to it in any great detail; but in view of some of the contentions raised it is desirable to call attention quite generally to some of the provisions contained in it. It is a stringent contract, under which the defendant agrees 'to render her exclusive services as motion picture and/or legitimate stage actress' to the plaintiffs, and agrees to perform solely and exclusively for them. She also agrees, by way of negative stipulation, that 'she will not, during such time' – that is to say, during the term of the contract – 'render any services for or in any other phonographic, stage or motion picture production or productions or business of any other person . . . . or engage in any other occupation without the written consent of the producer being first had and obtained'.

With regard to the term of the contract there is a further clause, clause 23, under which, if the defendant fails, refuses or neglects to perform her services under the contract, the plaintiffs 'have the right to extend the term of this agreement and all of its provisions for a period equivalent to the period during which such failure, refusal or neglect shall be continued'.

In June of this year the defendant, for no discoverable reason except that she wanted more money, declined to be further bound by the agreement, left the United States and in September, entered into an agreement in this country with a third person. This was a breach of contract on her part, and the plaintiffs on September 9 commenced this action claiming a declaration that the contract was valid and binding, an injunction to restrain the defendant from acting in breach of it, and damages. The defence alleged that the plaintiffs had committed breaches of the contract which entitled the defendant to treat it as at an end; but at the trial this contention was abandoned and the defendant admitted that the plaintiffs had not broken the contract and that she had; but it was contended on her behalf that no jurisdiction could as a matter of law be granted in the circumstances of the case. . . .

I turn then to the consideration of the law applicable to this case on the basis that the contract is a valid and enforceable one. It is conceded that our courts will not enforce a positive covenant of personal service; and specific performance of the positive covenants by the defendant to serve the plaintiffs is not asked in the present case. The practice of the Court of Chancery in relation to the enforcement of negative covenants is stated on the highest authority by Lord Cairns in the House of Lords in *Doherty* v *Allman* (1878) 3 App Cas 709. His Lordship says: 'My Lords, if there had been a negative covenant, I apprehend, according to well-settled practice, a Court of Equity would have had no discretion to exercise. If parties, for valuable consideration, with their eyes open, contract that a particular thing shall not be done, all that a Court of Equity has to do is say, by way of injunction, that which parties have already said by way of covenant, that the thing shall not be done; and in such a case the injunction does nothing more than give the sanction of the process of the court to that which already is the contract between the parties. It is not then a question of the balance of convenience or inconvenience, or of the amount of damage or of injury – it is specific performance, by the court, of that negative bargain which the parties have made, with their eyes open, between themselves'.

That was not a case of a contract of personal service; but the same principle had already been applied to such a contract by Lord St. Leonards in *Lumley* v *Wagner* (1852) 1 De G M & G 604. . . .

The defendant, having broken her positive undertakings in the contract without any cause or excuse which she was prepared to support in the witness-box, contends that she cannot be enjoined from breaking the negative covenants also. The mere fact that a covenant which the court would not enforce, if expressed in positive form, is expressed in the negative instead, will not induce the court to enforce it. That appears, if authority is needed for such a proposition, from *Davis* v *Foreman* [1894] 3 Ch 654; *Kirchner* v *Gruban* [1909] 1 Ch 413; and *Chapman* v *Westerby* [1913] WN 277. The court will attend to the substance and not to the form of the covenant. Nor will the court, true to the principle that specific performance of a contract of personal service will never be ordered, grant an injunction in the case of such a contract to enforce negative covenants if the effect of so doing would be to drive the defendant either to starvation or to specific performance of the positive covenants: see *Whitwood Chemical Co.* v *Hardman* [1891] 2 Ch 416, where Lindley LJ said: 'What injunction can be granted in this particular case which will not be, in substance and effect, a decree for specific performance of this agreement?'; *Ehrman* v *Bartholomew* [1898] 1 Ch 671, where the injunction was refused, firstly, on the ground that it was doubtful whether the covenant applied at all, and secondly, on the ground that to grant it would compel the defendant wholly to abstain from any business whatsoever; and *Mortimer* v *Beckett* [1920] 1 Ch 571, where there was also no negative stipulation.

The case of *Rely-a Bell Burglar and Fire Alarm Co. Ltd* v *Eisler* [1926] Ch 609, which was strongly relied upon by the defendant, falls within the same category as *Ehrman* v *Bartholomew* and *Chapman* v *Westerby*. Russell J, as he then was, said, after citing those two cases: 'It was said on the other side that there were points of distinction. It was said that the covenants in those two cases were so framed that the servant, if the covenants were enforced, could make his living neither by serving nor by carrying on business independently; whereas in the present case the covenant only prohibited serving. Therefore, it was said, he was still free to start in business on his own account, and it could not be said, if an injunction were granted in the terms of the covenant, that he would be forced to remain idle and starve. That distinction seems to me somewhat of a mockery. It would be idle to tell this defendant, a servant employed at a wage, that he must not serve anybody else in that capacity, but that the world was still open to him to start business as an independent man. It seems to me that if I were to restrain this man according to the terms of the covenant, he would be forced to remain idle and starve'. Had it not been for that view of the facts, I think that the learned judge would have granted an injunction in that case.

The conclusion to be drawn from the authorities is that, where a contract of personal service contains negative covenants the enforcement of which will not amount either to a decree of specific performance of the positive covenants of the contract or to the giving of a decree under which the defendant must either remain idle or perform those positive covenants, the court will enforce those negative covenants; but this is subject to a further consideration. An injunction is a discretionary remedy, and the court in granting it may limit it to what the court considers reasonable in all the circumstances of the case. . . .

The cases before me is, therefore, one in which it would be proper to grant an injunction unless to do so would in the circumstances be tantamount to ordering the defendant to perform her contract or remain idle or unless damages would be the more appropriate remedy.

With regard to the first of these considerations, it would, of course, be impossible to grant an injunction covering all the negative covenants in the contract. That would indeed, force the defendant to perform her contract or remain idle; but this objection is removed by the restricted form in which the injunction is sought. It is confined to forbidding the defendant without the consent of the plaintiffs, to render any services for or in any motion picture or stage production for any one other than the plaintiffs.

It was also urged that the difference between what the defendant can earn as a film artiste and what she might expect to earn by any other form of activity is so great that she will in effect be driven to perform her contract. That is not the criterion adopted in any of the decided cases. The defendant is stated to be a person of intelligence, capacity and means, and no evidence was adduced to show that, if enjoined from doing the specified acts otherwise than for the plaintiffs, she will not be able to employ herself both usefully and remuneratively in other spheres of activity, though not as remuneratively as in her special line. She will not be driven, although she may be so tempted, to peform the contract, and the fact that she may be so tempted is no objection to the grant of an injunction. . . .

With regard to the question whether damages is not the more appropriate remedy, I have the uncontradicted evidence of the plaintiffs as to the difficulty of estimating the damages which they may suffer from the breach by the defendant of her contract. I think it is not inappropriate to refer to the fact that, in the contract between the parties, in clause 22, there is a formal admission by the defendant that her services, being 'of a special, unique, extraordinary and intellectual character' gives them a particular value 'the loss of which cannot be reasonably or adequately compensated in damages' and that a breach may 'cost the producer great and irreparable injury and damage', and the artiste expressly agrees that the producer shall be entitled to the remedy of injunction. Of course, parties cannot contract themselves out of the law; but it assists, at all events, on the question of evidence as to the applicability of an injunction in the present case, to find the parties formally recognizing that in cases of this kind injunction is a more appropriate remedy than damages.

Furthermore, in the case of *Grimston v Cuningham* [1894] 1 QB 125, which was also a case in which a theatrical manager was attempting to enforce against an actor a negative stipulation against going elsewhere, Willis J granted an injunction, and used the following language: 'This is an agreement of a kind which is pre-eminently subject to the interference of the court by injunction, for in cases of this nature it very often happens that the injury suffered in consequence of the breach of the agreement would be out of all proportion to any pecuniary damages which could be proved or assessed by a jury. This circumstance affords a strong reason in favour of exercising the discretion of the court by granting an injunction'.

I think that that applies to the present case also, and that an injunction should be granted in regard to the specified services.

Then comes the question as to the period for which the injunction should operate. The period of the contract, now that the plaintiffs have undertaken not as from October 16, 1936, to exercise the rights of suspension conferred upon them by clause 23 thereof, will, if they exercise their options to prolong it, extend to about May, 1942. As I read the judgment of the Court of Appeal in *Robinson v Heuer* [1898] 2 Ch 451 the court should make the period such as to give reasonable protection and no more to the plaintiffs against the ill effects to them of the defendant's breach of contract. The evidence as to that was perhaps necessarily somewhat vague. The main difficulty that the plaintiffs apprehend is that the defendant might appear in other films whilst the films already made by them and not yet shown are in the market for sale or hire and thus depreciate their value. I think that if the injunction is in force during the continuance of the contract or for three years from now, whichever period is shorter, that will substantially meet the case.

The other matter is as to the area within which the injunction is to operate. The contract is not an English contract and the parties are not British subjects. In my opinion all that properly concerns this court is to prevent the defendant from committing the prohibited acts within the jurisdiction of this court, and the injunction will be limited accordingly.

7.3   Restitution

7.3.1   RECOVERY OF MONEY PAID

7.3.1.1   Total failure of consideration

ROWLAND v *DIVALL* [1923] 2 KB 500 (CA)

BANKES LJ: Whatever doubt there may have been in former times as to the legal rights of a purchaser in the position of the present plaintiff was settled by the Sale of Goods Act 1893, by s. 12 of which it was provided that: 'In a contract of sale, unless the circumstances of the contract are such as to show a different intention, there is (1.) An implied condition on the part of the seller that . . . he has a right to sell the goods.' The facts are shortly these. The plaintiff bought a motor car at Brighton from the defendant in May, 1922. He took possession of it at once, drove it to his place of business at Blandford, where he exhibited it for sale in his shop, and ultimately sold it to a purchaser. It was not discovered that the car was a stolen car until September, when possession was taken of it by the police. The plaintiff and his purchaser between them had possession of it for about four months. The plaintiff now brings his action to recover back the price that he paid to the defendant upon the ground of total failure of consideration. As I have said, it cannot now be disputed that there was an implied condition on the part of the defendant that he had a right to sell the car, and unless something happened to change that condition into a warranty the plaintiff is entitled to rescind the contract and recover back the money. The Sale of Goods Act itself indicates in s. 53 the circumstances in which a condition may be changed into a warranty: 'Where the buyer elects, or is compelled, to treat any breach of a condition on the part of the seller as a breach of warranty' the buyer is not entitled to reject the goods, but his remedy is in damages. Mr Doughty contends that this is a case in which the buyer is compelled to treat the condition as a warranty within the meaning of that section, because, having had the use of the car for four months, he cannot put the seller in statu quo and therefore cannot now rescind, and he has referred to several authorities in support of that contention. But when those authorities are looked at I think it will be found that in all of them the buyer got some part of what he contracted for. In *Taylor* v *Hare* (1805) 1 B & P (NR) 260 the question was as to the right of the plaintiff to recover back money which he had paid for the use of a patent which turned out to be void. But there the Court treated the parties, who had made a common mistake about the validity of the patent, as being in the nature of joint adventurers in the benefit of the patent; and Chambre J expressly pointed out that 'The plaintiff has had the enjoyment of what he stipulated for.' The language there used by Heath J, though it may have been correct as applied to the facts of that case, is much too wide to be applied to such a case as the present. In *Hunt* v *Silk* (1804) 5 East 449 Lord Ellenborough went upon the ground that the plaintiff had received part of what he bargained for. He said: 'Where a contract is to be rescinded at all, it must be rescinded in toto, and the parties put in statu quo. But here was an intermediate occupation, a part execution of the agreement, which was incapable of being rescinded.' And *Lawes* v *Purser* (1856) 6 E & B 930 proceeded on the same ground, that the defendant had derived benefit from the execution of the contract. But in the present case it cannot possibly be said that the plaintiff received any portion of what he had agreed to buy. It is true that a motor car was delivered to him, but the person who sold it to him had no right to sell it, and therefore he did not get what he paid for — namely, a car to which he would have title; and under those circumstances the user of the car by the purchaser seems to me quite immaterial for the purpose of considering whether the condition had been converted into a warranty. In my opinion the plaintiff was entitled to recover the whole of the purchase money, and was not limited to his remedy in damages as the judge below held.

The appeal must be allowed.

Scrutton and Atkin LJJ concurred.

7.3.1.2 Mistake of fact

LARNER v LONDON COUNTY COUNCIL [1949] 2 KB 683 (CA)

DENNING LJ: When the men went to the war, many local authorities made up to them the difference between their war service pay and their civil pay. Sometimes overpayments were made and the question is whether the men are bound to repay the excess.

The real question in this case arises on the counterclaim: Are the council entitled to recover from Mr Larner the sums which they overpaid him? Overpay him they certainly did. That is admitted. And the overpayment was due to a mistake of fact. That is also admitted. They were mistaken as to the amount of his service pay. But it is said that they were voluntary payments, which were not made in discharge of any legal liability, and cannot therefore be recovered back. For this proposition reliance was placed on the dictum of Bramwell B in *Aiken v Short* (1856) 1 H&N 210; but that dictum, as Scott LJ pointed out in *Morgan v Ashcroft* [1958] 1 KB 49 cannot be regarded as an exhaustive statement of the law. Take this case. The London County Council, by their resolution, for good reasons of national policy, made a promise to the men which they were in honour bound to fulfil. The payments made under that promise were not mere gratuities. They were made as a matter of duty: see *National Association of Local Government Officers v Bolton Corporation* [1943] AC 166. Indeed that is how both sides regarded them. They spoke of them as sums 'due' to the men, that is, as sums the men were entitled to under the promise contained in the resolution. If then, owing to a mistake of fact, the council paid one of the men more than he was entitled to under the promise, why should he not repay the excess, at any rate if he has not changed his position for the worse? It is not necessary to inquire whether there was any consideration for the promise so as to enable it to be enforced in a court of law. It may be that, because the men were legally bound to go to the war, there was in strictness no consideration for the promise. But that does not matter. It is not a question here of enforcing the promise by action. It is a question of recovering overpayments made in the belief that they were due under the promise, but in fact not due. They were sums which the council never promised Mr Larner and which they would never have paid him had they known the true facts. They were paid under a mistake of fact, and he is bound to repay them unless he has changed his position for the worse because of them.

It is next said, however, that Mr Larner did change his position for the worse before the council asked for the money. He spent the money on living expenses — or his wife spent it for him — and he spent it in a way which he would not otherwise have done. This defence of estoppel, as it is called — or more accurately, change of circumstances — must, however, not be extended beyond its proper bounds. Speaking generally, the fact that the recipient has spent the money beyond recall is no defence unless there was some fault, as, for instance, breach of duty — on the part of the paymaster and none on the part of the recipient. In both *Skyring v Greenwood and Cox* (1825) B&C 281 and *Holt v Markham* [1923] 1 KB 504 there was a breach of duty by the paymaster and none by the recipient. See *Jones (R. E.) Ld v Waring and Gillow Ld* [1926] AC 670, per Lord Sumner.

But if the recipient was himself at fault and the paymaster was not — as, for instance, if the mistake was due to an innocent misrepresentation or a breach of duty by the recipient — he clearly cannot escape liability by saying that he has spent the money. That is the position here. On the judge's findings, the London County Council was not at fault at all, but Mr Larner was. He did not keep them accurately informed of the various changes in his service pay. It does not lie in his mouth to say that, if he had done so, it would have made no difference. It might well have put them on inquiry and the mistake might not have been made at all. It would be strange, indeed, if those who neglected their duty were to be allowed to keep their gain.

This view of the case makes it unnecessary to discuss the question of ultra vires.

The one remaining question is whether the London County Council were entitled to recoup themselves, after Mr Larner's return, by deductions from his wages. In point of law they were not entitled as of right to make deductions from his wages except by agreement with him and we do not think that the resolution is such an agreement. It is, however, of no practical consequence in this action because the amounts due on claim and counterclaim must clearly be set off one against the other. The judge below has given judgment for the balance and that is the correct way of doing it. This appeal must be dismissed.

Lord Goddard CJ and Birkett J concurred.

7.3.1.3   Discharge under compulsion, of the defendant's liability to a third party

EXALL v PARTRIDGE (1799) 8 Term R 308 (KB)

The plaintiff had paid off the defendant's rent arrears in order to recover some of his property which had been seized by the landlord from the defendant's premises.

LORD KENYON CJ: Some propositions have been stated, on the part of the plaintiff, to which I cannot assent. It has been said, that where one person is benefited by the payment of money by another, the law raises an assumpsit against the former; but that I deny: if that were so, and I owed a sum of money to a friend, and an enemy chose to pay that debt, the latter might convert himself into my debtor, nolens volens. Another proposition was, that the assignment from two of the defendants to the third, was not evidence against the plaintiff, because he was no party to it; that also I deny: it surely was evidence to shew in what relation the parties stood to this estate. I admit that where one person is surety for another, and compellable to pay the whole debt, and he is called upon to pay, it is money paid to the use of the principal debtor, and may be recovered in an action against him for money paid, even though the surety did not pay the debt by the desire of the principal: but none of those points affect the present question. As the plaintiff put his goods on the premises, knowing the interests of the defendants, and thereby placed himself in a situation where he was liable to pay this money, without the concurrence of two of the defendants, I thought at the trial that it was money paid to the use of the other defendants only; but on that point I have since doubted; and I rather think that the opinion I gave at the trial was not well founded.

Grose, Lawrence and Le Blanc JJ concurred.

7.3.2   CLAIMS ON A QUANTUM MERUIT BASIS FOR BENEFITS CONFERRED

CRAVEN-ELLIS v CANONS LTD [1936] 2 KB 403 (CA)

GREER LJ: In the year 1927 Sir Arthur du Cros and his son Phillip became interested in the development of a building estate known as Canons Estate. They desired to have the benefit of the plaintiff's skill and experience as an estate agent in the development of the estate. For a time the estate was vested in a company called the Park Estates, Ld. On November 11, 1927, the plaintiff wrote to Mr Phillip du Cros, and on November 29 to Sir Arthur du Cros, stating the terms on which he would be willing to give them the benefit of his skill and experience. On November 30 the plaintiff wrote to Sir Arthur du Cros stating revised terms on which his firm would act as managers of the Canons Park Estate. Subject to some modification to which the plaintiff agreed, Sir Arthur du Cros agreed to these terms on behalf of the Park Estates, Ld, the engagement to be for three years. On August 15, 1928, Canons Ld was formed to purchase from the Park Estates, Ld, the Canons Park Estate. It then became impossible for the plaintiff to go on working for the Park Estates, Ld, as that company had sold the property, but the plaintiff continued to do the same work for the new company. This company for the time being did not make any contract to employ the plaintiff or his firm on the terms formerly arranged, but without any express agreement they received and accepted the services he was rendering. The signatories to the memorandum and articles, being entitled to elect the first directors, nominated Mr Phillip du Cros, the plaintiff, and Mr A. W. Wheeler as the first directors on August 15, 1928, and on August 23 the directors co-opted Sir Arthur du Cros as a director. Under the articles these directors could act without qualification for two months, but after that time they became incapable of acting as directors as none of them had acquired the necessary qualification. The only issued shares of the company were in the two signatories to the memorandum, but there is little room for doubt that these gentlemen were nominees of the du Cros'. Be this as it may, it is clear that on the expiration of the two months, the directors having no qualification ceased to be directors, and were unable to bind the company except as de facto directors by agreements with outsiders or with shareholders. But all the directors must be taken to have known the facts. They became liable to penalties for acting as directors under the provisions of s. 73 of the Companies Act, 1908, then in force. On April 14, 1931, an agreement was executed under the seal of the company, purporting to be between the company and the plaintiff, stating the terms on which he was to act as managing director of the company. The seal was so affixed by resolution of the unqualified directors. The plaintiff in this action sought to recover from the defendant company the remuneration set out in the agreement, and as an alternative sought to recover for his services on a quantum meruit. Until the company purported to put an end to his engagement he continued to perform all the services mentioned in the agreement.

The company, having had the full benefit of these services, decline to pay either under the agreement or on the basis of a quantum meruit. Their defence to the action is a purely technical defence, and if it succeeds the Messrs du Cros as the principal shareholders in the company, and the company, would be in the position of having received and accepted valuable services and refusing, for purely technical reasons, to pay for them.

As regards the services rendered between December 31, 1930, and April 14, 1931, there is, in my judgment, no defence to the claim. These services were rendered by the plaintiff not as managing director or as a director, but as an estate agent, and there was no contract in existence which could present any obstacle to a claim based on a quantum meruit for services rendered and accepted.

As regards the plaintiff's services after the date of the contract, I think the plaintiff is also entitled to succeed. The contract, having been made by directors who had no authority to make it with one of themselves who had notice of their want of authority, was not binding on either party. It was, in fact, a nullity, and presents no obstacle to the implied promise to pay on a quantum meruit basis which arises from the performance of the services and the implied acceptance of the same by the company.

Greene LJ and Talbot J concurred.

BRITISH STEEL CORPORATION v CLEVELAND BRIDGE & ENGINEERING CO. LTD
[1948] 1 All ER 504 (QB)

BSC sought payment on a quantum meruit basis for the supply of 137 steel nodes. CBE alleged that there was a contract, which would entitle them to a substantial set-off against the payment because of late delivery.

ROBERT GOFF J: . . . Now the question whether in a case such as the present any contract has come into existence must depend on a true construction of the relevant communications which have passed between the parties and the effect (if any) of their actions pursuant to those communications. There can be no hard and fast answer to the question whether a letter of intent will give rise to a binding agreement: everything must depend on the circumstances of the particular case. In most cases, where work is done pursuant to a request contained in a letter of intent, it will not matter whether a contract did or did not come into existence, because, if the party who has acted on the request is simply claiming payment, his claim will usually be based on a quantum meruit, and it will make no difference whether that claim is contractual or quasi-contractual. Of course, a quantum meruit claim (like the old actions for money had and received and for money paid) straddles the boundaries of what we now call contract and restitution, so the mere framing of a claim as a quantum meruit claim, or a claim for a reasonable sum, does not assist in classifying the claim as contractual or quasi contractual. But where, as here, one party is seeking to claim damages for breach of contract, the question whether any contract came into existence is of crucial importance.

As a matter of analysis the contract (if any) which may come into existence following a letter of intent may take one of two forms: either there may be an ordinary executory contract, under which each party assumes reciprocal obligations to the other; or there may be what is sometimes called an 'if' contract, ie a contract under which A requests B to carry out a certain performance and promises B that, if he does so, he will receive a certain performance in return, usually remuneration for his performance. The latter transaction is really no more than a standing offer which, if acted on before it lapses or is lawfully withdrawn, will result in a binding contract.

The former type of contract was held to exist by Mr Edgar Fay QC, the official Referee, in *Turriff Construction Ltd* v *Regalia Knitting Mills Ltd* (1971) 202 EG 169; and it is the type of contract for which counsel for CBE contended in the present case. Of course, as I have already said, everything must depend on the facts of the particular case; but certainly, on the facts of the present case (and, as I imagine, on the facts of most cases), this must be a very difficult submission to maintain. It is only necessary to look at the terms of CBE's letter of intent in the present case to appreciate the difficulties. In that letter, the request to BSC to proceed immediately with the work was stated to be 'pending the preparation and issuing to you of the official form of sub-contract', being a sub-contract which was plainly in a state of negotiation, not least on the issues of price, delivery dates, and the applicable terms and conditions. In these circumstances, it is very difficult to see how BSC, by starting work, bound themselves to any contractual performance. No doubt it was envisaged by CBE at the time they sent the letter that negotiations had reached an advanced stage, and that a formal contract would soon be signed: but, since the parties were still in a state of negotiation, it is impossible to say with any degree of certainty what the material terms of that contract would be . . . my conclusion in the present case is that the parties never entered into any contract at all.

In the course of his argument counsel for BSC submitted that, in a contract of this kind, the price is always an essential term in the sense that, if it is not agreed, no contract can come into existence. In support of his contention counsel relied on a dictum of Lord Denning MR in *Courtney & Fairbairn Ltd* v *Tolaini Bros (Hotels) Ltd* [1975] 1 All ER 716 at 719, [1975] 1 WLR 297 at 301 to the effect that the price in a building contract is of fundamental importance. I do not however read Lord Denning MR's dictum as stating that in every building contract the price is invariably an essential term, particularly as he expressly referred to the substantial size of the contract then before the court. No doubt in the vast majority of business transactions, particularly those of substantial size, the price will indeed be an essential term, but in the final analysis it must be a question of construction of the particular transaction whether it is so. This is plain from the familiar trilogy of cases which show that no hard and fast rule can be laid down but that the question in each case is whether, on a true construction of the relevant transaction, it was consistent with the intention of the parties that even though no price had been agreed a reasonable price should be paid (*May & Butcher Ltd* v *R* (1929) [1934] 2 KB 17, [1929] All ER Rep 679, *W N Hillas & Co. Ltd* v *Arcos Ltd* (1932) 147 LT 503, [1932] All ER Rep 494 and *Foley* v *Classique Coaches Ltd* [1934] 2 KB 1, [1934] All ER Rep 88). In the present case, however, I have no doubt whatsoever that, consistently with the view expressed by Lord Denning MR in *Courtney & Fairbairn Ltd* v *Tolaini Bros (Hotels) Ltd*, the price was indeed an essential term, on which (among other essential terms) no final agreement was ever reached.

It follows that BSC are entitled to succeed on their claim and that CBE's set off and counterclaim must fail.

TRENTHAM LTD v *ARCHITAL LUXFER* [1993] 1 Lloyd's Rep 25 (CA)

STEYN LJ: This is an appeal against a judgment on preliminary issues given by His Honour Judge Rich, QC, sitting as an Official Referee, on December 19, 1991. The Judge was asked to decide whether two contracts were concluded between the plaintiffs ('Trentham') and the defendants ('Archital'). The Judge ruled that Trentham had established that the two contracts were concluded. He also made rulings as to the terms of the contracts. There are no independent grounds of appeal challenging the rulings as to the terms of the contracts. The grounds of appeal are directed solely at the Judge's rulings that the conclusion of the two contracts was established. Leave to appeal on questions of fact was given under ord. 58, r. 4(b).

The way in which the dispute arose must now be sketched. Trentham were building and civil engineering contractors. Municipal Mutual Insurance Ltd ('Municipal Mutual') engaged Trentham as main contractors to design and build industrial units in two phases on land known as the Summit Centre, Southwood, Cove, Farnborough, Hampshire. An agreement dated February 2, 1984 ('the main contract') governed phase 1. An agreement dated December 18, 1984 ('the supplemental agreement') governed phase 2. The work for both phases included the design, supply and installation of aluminium window walling, doors, screens and windows. It will be convenient to refer to such work as 'window works'. Archital carried on business as manufacturers, suppliers and installers of aluminium window walling, doors, screens and windows. It is common ground that Archital in fact undertook for Trentham the window works in phase 1 and in phase 2, and that Trentham paid Archital for the carrying out of the window works. Trentham contends that two separate sub-contractors, one covering phase 1 window works and the other phase 2 window works, came into existence. Archital denies that the dealing between the parties ever resulted in the conclusion of binding sub-contracts.

A distinctive feature of the case is that the transaction between Trentham and Archital were fully executed. Archital performed the agreed work and Trentham made the agreed payments. That fact calls for an explanation of the relevance of the dispute about the formation of the two alleged sub-contracts. The answer is to be found in subsequent claims made by Municipal Mutual against Trentham under the main contracts. Those claims were for alleged delays and defects. The claims were put forward in arbitration. Two interim awards have been made against Trentham in the sums of £558,335 and £343,820. Trentham instituted proceedings against seven sub-contractors for an indemnity in respect of such sums as Trentham is liable to pay Mutual Insurance. One of these sub-contractors is Archital, the first defendant in the proceedings. Trentham alleges that there were defects in the window works in both phase 1 and phase 2. Trentham's claim against Archital is brought in contract. Archital by their amended defence deny or do not admit the alleged defects. But Archital also disputes that any sub-contracts ever came into existence. . . .

Before I turn to the facts it is important to consider briefly the approach to be adopted to the issue of contract formation in this case. It seems to me that four matters are of importance. The first is the fact that English law generally adopts an objective theory of contract formation. That means that in practice our law generally ignores the subjective expectations and the unexpressed mental reservations of the parties. Instead the governing criterion is the reasonable expectations of honest men. And in the present case that means that the yardstick is the reasonable expectations of sensible businessmen. Secondly, it is true that the coincidence of offer and acceptance will in the vast majority of cases represent the mechanism of contract formation. It is so in the case of a contract alleged to have been made by an exchange of correspondence. But is is not necessarily so in the case of a contract alleged to have come into existence during and as a result of performance. See, *Brogden* v *Metropolitan Railway* (1877) 2 AC 666; *New Zealand Shipping Co. Ltd* v *A. M. Satterthwaite & Co. Ltd* [1974] 1 Lloyd's Rep 534 at p. 539, col. 1; [1975] AC 154 at p. 167 D-E; *Gibson* v *Manchester City Council* [1979] 1 WLR 294. The third matter is the impact of the fact that the transaction is executed rather than executory. It is a consideration of the first importance on a number of levels. See *British Bank for Foreign Trade* v *Novinex* [1949] 1 KB 628, at p. 630. The fact that the transaction was performed on both sides will often make it unrealistic to argue that there was no intention to enter into legal relations. It will often make it difficult to submit that the contract is void for vagueness or uncertainty. Specifically, the fact that the transaction is executed makes it easier to imply a term resolving any uncertainty, or, alternatively, it may make it possible to treat a matter not finalised in negotiations as inessential. In this case fully executed transactions are under consideration. Clearly, similar considerations may sometimes be relevant in partly executed transactions. Fourthly, if a contract only comes into existence during and as a result of performance of the transaction it will frequently be possible to hold that the contract impliedly and retrospectively covers pre-contractual performance. See *Trollope & Colls Ltd* v *Atomic Power Construction Ltd* [1963] 1 WLR 333.

The story starts on January 12, 1984 when Archital submitted four alternative quotations for phase 1 window works to Trentham. Discussions followed. On January 24, 1984 Archital substituted a revised offer in respect of one of the earlier quotations at a revised price of the order of £140,000. The offer was conditional on the incorporation of Archital's standard conditions on the so-called blue form. Trentham was not prepared to accept this offer but made a counter-offer contained in Order No. 8285 dated January 30,

1984. This counter-offer stipulated the work and price described in Archital's revised offer but was conditional on the incorporation of Trentham's standard terms of sub-contract. Moreover, the order was expressed to be—

. . . subject to (a) Form of sub-contract being entered into . . . [and] (b) the signing and immediate return of the attached acknowledgment slip .

Neither of these formalities for acceptance was ever completed. The counter-offer was subject to measurement and/or adjustment on completion. By an addendum dated February 1, 1984 this last stipulation was deleted and it was made clear that it was a lump sum contract. That was the offer which was open for acceptance by Archital from February 1, 1984. On February 2, 1984 the main contract for phase 1 was concluded.

On February 10, 1984 Archital responded by letter to Trentham's counter-offer as revised on February 1, 1984. Archital confirmed that 'we have entered the contract into our Drawing Office Programme'. In the context, the Judge held, one should read 'contract' as meaning 'project'. Two obstacles remained. First Archital's letter stated that at the meeting which led to Trentham's counter-offer—

. . . it was confirmed that the sub-contracts would be in the Blue Form of sub-contract.

In other words, Archital thought that there had been agreement to use Archital's preferred standard terms and conditions. Secondly, Archital said that they would not be able to comply with a programme with a commencement date of May 14.

On February 17, 1984 Trentham's regional office at Rainham sent a reminder to Archital. It stated:

Our order is subject to the signing and immediate return of the Acknowledgment slip as stated in the order form.

Negotiations then continued between Mr Chapple, on behalf of Trentham, and Mr Hazell, on behalf of Archital.

On February 17 Trentham's site office wrote to Archital as follows:

We confirm our Contract period is very short and that it is essential that you make every effort to meet the dates agreed with your Mr Rogers. We also confirm that you have already commenced working drawings, that you have sufficient information to enable you to proceed with your drawings, and that further details will be forwarded to you to enable you to complete your drawings as soon as possible.

The Judge inferred that between February 10 and 17, 1984 Mr Chapple had agreed the programme with Mr Rogers, although in terms which were not proved before the Judge. The appellants submit that there was no evidence on which to base this finding, and that the letter referred to a discussion which took place before February 10. Having regard to the terms of the letters of February 10 and February 17 I regard it as more probable than not that the Judge's inference was right. It follows that one obstacle to the conclusion of a contract was removed.

That left the problem of Archital's request or the use of their preferred standard conditions. Mr Hazel reiterated this preference in a letter dated February 24, 1984. This letter reads as follows:

Thank you for your letter dated 16th February 1984, we note your comments but our query was in connection with the sub-contract document.

We wish the sub contract to be carried out under the terms and conditions of the Standard Blue Form of Sub Contract as agreed at the meeting attended by our Mr Rogers.

Please confirm that we are to return your own form and that the Blue Form will be forwarded to us.

In this letter, and in a letter of the same date from Archital to Trentham's Rainham office, Archital described their reaction as a 'query'. Archital thought that Trentham had accepted Archital's request. Contrary to the submission of the appellant's Counsel, I take the view that the Judge was entitled to conclude that the letter of February 24 was not a rejection of the counter-offer as revised on February 10. This construction is reinforced by the letter of March 9, 1984 from Archital to Trentham which shows that the issue as to the standard conditions had been resolved.

The Judge pointed out that there were now three matters to be considered: (i) payment procedure; (ii) insurance of unfixed goods: and (iii) disputes procedure. The Judge found as a fact that the payment procedure had been agreed by February 24 and that the letter merely confirmed the position. In any event, from this time regular stage payments were made 'on the basis of the timetable provided in the Grey Form'. These findings are not challenged. But it is important to note that by March 9 Archital had already commenced the work and that from about this time Trentham made regular stage payments.

The second matter relates to Archital's request that Trentham should pay the cost of insuring unfixed goods which remained the property of Archital. Trentham did not agree to bear these costs. But the Judge made the following findings of fact:

Archital nevertheless delivered such goods to the site at its own risk. In accepting such risk, they accepted that in this respect the provisions of PGT's main contract should apply to their relationship with PGT in performing work at Southwood.

This finding of fact is challenged on the ground that there was no evidence to support it. I disagree. By a letter of March 23, 1984 Trentham refused to accept these costs. Trentham described the risk as minimal. On April 2, 1984 Archital wrote to say that they were asking brokers for a quotation, and that they would write again. They failed to mention the matter again. Instead they continued to deliver goods to the site, to perform work and to receive stage payments. In these circumstances I am satisfied that there was sufficient evidence to support the Judge's finding of fact. This obstacle to the conclusion of a contract was removed in April, 1984.

The third matter to be considered is the lack of agreement on dispute resolution. The Judge held that agreement on dispute resolution was not essential to the conclusion of the contract: the parties were content to treat it as a matter for further agreement after the conclusion of the contract. It was plainly not an essential matter as far as Trentham was concerned. Archital described their point of view as based on company policy. Nevertheless the letter describes Archital's concern about the identity of the adjudicator and stakeholder as a 'query'. This supports the view that Archital was also content to treat a dispute resolution mechanism as a non-essential matter. This ruling is criticised on the basis that there is no evidence to support it. I disagree. The Judge's inference was reasonable and legitimate. In any event the parties subsequently agreed on the adjudicator and stakeholder. It is conceded that there was agreement on the stakeholder. By letter dated April 22, 1985 Archital said in respect of phase 2 that they took it that Trentham agreed to the same adjudicator and stakeholder 'as agreed for that contract' (i.e. phase 1). That is retrospectant evidence showing earlier agreement on the identity of both the adjudicator and stakeholder. It is true that Mr Steer, who testified on behalf of Trentham, was unaware of this agreement but he was not directly involved in the negotiations. It is also fair to add that the Judge could not identify the adjudicator. On behalf of Archital it is submitted that there was no evidence to support the Judge's finding of fact. That submission is wrong: there was strong evidence to support his finding.

The Judge also found that Trentham delivered to Archital four separate orders for additional work in phase 1 all '. . . subject to the conditions and terms of the original order'. These supplementary orders were accepted and executed by Archital, and Trentham made appropriate additional payments. Moreover, the Judge pointed out that in the context of exchanges about phase 2, Archital offered to perform the work on the basis that the terms and conditions would be 'as for the original contract'.

The Judge's conclusion was as follows:

I therefore conclude that Mr Chapple modified the terms of PGT's offer contained in their Order dated 30th January, in his telephone conversation with Mr Hazell on 9th March, and that those terms were accepted on behalf of Archital by the letter dated the same day. If such acceptance is to be construed as being subject to the resolution of the issues of insurance and of the disputes procedure, rather than, as I think, those 'queries' being left for subsequent agreement, those matters were, in fact, duly resolved in the following months. At least from that point, Archital accepted PGT's modified offer by their conduct in carrying out the sub-contract work, and applying for and accepting payment on the agreed terms.

Conclusions on phase 1

On behalf of Archital Counsel challenged specific findings of fact regarding successive stages of the dealings between the parties on the ground that there was no evidence to support the findings. I have held that the individual criticisms were not well-founded. But ultimately the only issue is whether there is sufficient evidence to support the Judge's central finding of fact that a binding contract on phase 1 came into existence. Even if, contrary to my view, a particular finding was not supported by evidence, it would not matter provided that there was sufficient evidence to support the ultimate finding of fact.

In a case where the transaction was fully performed the argument that there was no evidence upon which the Judge could find that a contract was proved is implausible. A contract can be concluded by conduct. Thus in *Brogden* v *Metropolitan Railway*, sup., decided in 1877, the House of Lords concluded in a case where the parties had acted in accordance with an unsigned draft agreement for the delivery of consignments of coal that there was a contract on the basis of the draft. That inference was drawn from the performance in accordance with the terms of the draft agreement. In 1992 we ought not to yield to Victorian times in realism about the practical application of rules of contract formation. The argument that there was insufficient evidence to support a finding that a contract was concluded is wrong. But, in deference to Counsel's submissions, I would go further.

One must not lose sight of the commercial character of the transaction. It involved the carrying out of work on one side in return for payment by the other side, the performance by both sides being subject to agreed qualifying stipulations. In the negotiations and during the performance of phase 1 of the work all obstacles to the formation of a contract were removed. It is not a case where there was a continuing stipulation that a contract would only come into existence if a written agreement was concluded. Plainly the parties intended to enter into binding contractual relations. The only question is whether they succeeded in doing so. The contemporary exchanges, and the carrying out of what was agreed in those exchanges support the view that there was a course of dealing which on Trentham's side created a right to performance of the work by Archital, and on Archital's side it created a right to be paid on an agreed basis. What the parties did in respect of phase 1 is only explicable on the basis of what they had agreed in respect of phase 1. The Judge analysed the matter in terms of offer and acceptance. I agree with his conclusion. But I am, in any event, satisfied that in this fully executed transaction a contract came into existence during performance even if it cannot be precisely analysed in terms of offer and acceptance. And it does not matter that a contract came into existence after part of the work had been carried out and paid for. The conclusion must be that when the contract came into existence it impliedly governed pre-contractual performance. I would therefore hold that a binding contract was concluded in respect of phase 1.

Neill and Ralph Gibson LJJ concurred.

7.3 End of Chapter Assessment Question

Cruisers Ltd, a business which hired out ocean yachts, ordered a new yacht for its fleet from Ted. The yacht was to be delivered on 1 May, ready for the beginning of the summer charter season. The contract provided for the payment of agreed damages of £5,000 per week for each week by which delivery was delayed.

The yacht was not ready for delivery until 1 July. As a result Cruisers Ltd lost charter fees of £3,000 per week for seven weeks, and a fee of £6,000 agreed with a television company, for the use of the yacht in the making of a television programme during the eighth week.

During the first four weeks of the delay Cruisers Ltd could have hired a similar yacht from another firm for a fee of £2,000 per week. Cruisers Ltd now claim damages.

Advise Ted.

7.4 End of Chapter Assessment Outline Answer

It is open for the parties to agree on the amount of damages to be paid in the event of a breach of contract. If the sum specified is a genuine pre-estimate of loss, i.e. liquidated damages, and not a penalty then that sum is payable whether or not the actual loss is greater or smaller than that sum. Guidelines facilitating the distinction between a liquidated damages clause and a penalty clause are to be found in *Dunlop Pneumatic Tyre Co. Ltd* v *New Garage and Motor Co. Ltd*. Two factors of particular importance are the amount specified in relation to the greatest loss which could flow from the breach, and whether the clause is a threat, *in terrorem*, to ensure performance.

Here, the 'agreed damages' specified amount to £5,000 per week. If at the time of making the contract the loss envisaged from breach was £3,000 (the normal charter fee presumably) then the clause may well be a penalty and therefore void. If, however, the loss envisaged was £6,000 (from the television contract) then the clause could be a liquidated damages clause and therefore enforceable as such. If the clause is void as a penalty, then damages must be assessed as unliquidated damages.

The rule on unliquidated damages was established in *Hadley* v *Baxendale*. A successful plaintiff can only recover damages subject to a 'remoteness' test, and will not necessarily be compensated for all the loss suffered. The damage which may be compensated is either 'normal loss', i.e. that which can be reasonably contemplated because it arises naturally, according to the usual course of things, or 'abnormal loss' which can be reasonably contemplated by the parties because of special circumstances made known at the time of the contract. In this case, the miller could not recover for his loss of profits caused by the carrier's delay because in the usual course of things he would have had a spare driveshaft, and the absence of such had not been made known to the carrier. Similarly, in *Victoria Laundry Ltd* v *Newman Industries Ltd*, the laundry could only recover the normal profits from the loss of the lucrative dyeing contracts because 'lucrative' profits do not arise in the usual course of things (even when dealing with a government department) and the true situation had not been made known at the time of the contract.

Cruisers Ltd has lost normal profits based on a charter fee of £3,000 per week for seven weeks and those would appear to be recoverable as loss which was reasonably contemplatable as arising in the usual course of things. The loss of profits based on a charter fee of £6,000 per week would not be recoverable unless the 'special circumstances' were known to Ted at the time of the contract.

Finally, a plaintiff cannot recover for loss which would not have been incurred if reasonable steps had been taken to mitigate the loss. Thus, in *Brace* v *Calder*, an employee whose employment was wrongfully terminated had failed to mitigate his loss by not accepting a new offer of employment and was therefore only entitled to nominal damages.

Cruisers Ltd could, quite reasonably, have hired another yacht and thus reduced its loss. It seems that it has failed to mitigate its loss, and so this would reduce its damages.